```
D1637420
```

Commentary
on the
Book of Mormon

Commentary on the Book of Mormon

By
GEORGE REYNOLDS

A Member of the First Council of the Seventy, 1890-1909
Author of
A COMPLETE CONCORDANCE OF THE BOOK OF MORMON
A DICTIONARY OF THE BOOK OF MORMON
THE MYTH OF THE MANUSCRIPT FOUND
THE STORY OF THE BOOK OF MORMON

and
JANNE M. SJODAHL

Editor and Associate-Editor of *Deseret News*, 1890-1913
Author of
AN INTRODUCTION TO THE STUDY OF THE BOOK OF MORMON
THE REIGN OF ANTI-CHRIST
Co-Author of
DOCTRINE AND COVENANTS COMMENTARY

VOLUME II — THE WORDS OF MORMON AND THE BOOK OF MOSIAH

Edited and arranged by PHILIP C. REYNOLDS
Published by DESERET BOOK COMPANY
Salt Lake City, Utah—1976

GEORGE REYNOLDS

In a note near the close of his great contribution to L.D.S. Church literature, *New Witnesses for God*, President B. H. Roberts penned this remarkable tribute to the labors of Elder George Reynolds:

"It is a pleasure to note the work of this my brother, and fellow President in the First Council of the Seventies, in this field of Book of Mormon labor. I feel myself much indebted to him because of his great achievements in this field of research.

"First, for his excellent *Book of Mormon Chronological Table*, published now for many years in connection with the late Elder F. D. Richards' *Compendium*.

"Second, for his *Myth of the Manuscript Found*.

"Third, for his *Story of the Book of Mormon*.

"Fourth, for his *Dictionary of the Book of Mormon*.

"Fifth, for a series of articles appearing in the *Contributor*, Vol. 5, on the *History of the Book of Mormon*.

"Sixth, for a second series of articles in the *Contributor*, Vol. 17, under the title, *Evidences of the Book of Mormon; Some External Proofs of its Divinity*.

"Seventh, and last, and greatest achievement of all, I thank him for his *Complete Concordance of the Book of Mormon*. The amount of patient, painstaking labor required for the production of this magnificent work will never be known to the general reader. Only the close student of the Nephite Scriptures will ever appreciate it. What Cruden and Young have done for Bible students, Elder Reynolds has more abundantly done for Book of Mormon students. The Elders of the Church through all generations to come will, I am sure, feel deeply grateful to Elder Reynolds for his great work which will stand as a monument to his painstaking habits of thorough application to a task; but what is better still, the work will stand as a monument of his love for the Book of Mormon."

JANNE M. SJODAHL

An editorial published in the *Deseret News*, June 25, 1939, will serve to acquaint those who know little of the life and labors of the co-author of this *Commentary*.

"Physically frail but mentally energetic; of serious manner, studious volition and sedentary habit; Janne Mattson Sjodahl lived simply and labored faithfully beyond the eighty-fifth anniversary of his birth. A native of Sweden, he was educated in Stockholm and London, becoming identified in early manhood with the Scandinavian Baptist Union having headquarters in Trondhjem, Norway.

"At the age of 33 he came to the United States and was converted to Mormonism after his arrival in Utah over a half century ago. His ability as a writer, his faculty for research, his skill as a translator brought him instant recognition and a life-time of labor.

"As a writer and as an editor he had been connected with the *Deseret News*, the *Improvement Era*, the *Millennial Star* and various foreign language publications once circulated by his Church. He served on various missions to Palestine, Switzerland, England, and Sweden. In the latter country he presented a special edition of the Book of Mormon to the king, who received the Utah delegation at the Royal Palace.

"Mr. Sjodahl was the author of many ecclesiastical works and a prolific writer of pamphlets and special articles relating to the organization of which he was a distinguished member. He devoted his whole time, energy, ability, and thought to religious issues and inquiries. Absorbed in meditation almost to a point of asceticism, subjecting his vigor and vitality to constant exertion, he lived many years longer than his acquaintances believed possible for a tireless soul that occupied a frame so fragile."

With the late Elder Hyrum M. Smith, of the Council of Twelve Apostles, Elder Sjodahl was the author of, and the compiler of the *Doctrine and Covenants Commentary*.

CHRONOLOGY — VOLUME II

The four dates marked ** are based upon the supposition that Zeniff re-occupied the Land of Lehi-Nephi 200 B.C. This may not be the exact year, but it is approximate.

The three dates marked * are based upon the idea that the "young man," Alma, was twenty-five years old when Abinadi was martyred.

The Book of Mormon appears to furnish no clue to the date of Lehi's colony landing in South America. It is supposed to have been about ten or twelve years after its departure from Jerusalem.

B.C. signifies before the birth of Christ.

N.A. signifies Nephite Annals, or years after the departure of Lehi from Jerusalem.

	B.C.	N.A.
Lehi and colony leave Jerusalem, and journey to the Valley of Lemuel by the Red Sea.	600	1
Lehi and colony reach the Land Bountiful, in Arabia, where they build a ship.	592	9
As near as can now be told, the record given on the *Smaller Plates of Nephi* ends; the abridged record of Mormon's begins with the account of King Benjamin and his reign; it being taken from the *Larger Plates of Nephi*.	200	400
**About this date Zeniff leaves Zarahemla to re-occupy the Land of Lehi-Nephi. He makes a treaty with King Laman, and obtains the Lands of Lehi-Nephi and Shemlon.	200	401
**The Lamanites make war upon the people of Zeniff, but are repulsed with a loss of 3,043 men. Alma, the Elder, born in the Land of Lehi-Nephi.	173	428
**King Laman, having died, his son, who succeeded him, attacks the people of Zeniff, but is driven back.	161	440
**Zeniff confers his kingdom upon his son Noah.	160	441
Mosiah II, born in the Land Zarahemla.	154	447
*The Prophet Abinadi appears in the Land of Lehi-Nephi, and reproves Noah and his subjects for their iniquities.	150	451
*Abinadi appears again, prophesies, and is martyred.	148	453
*Alma establishes a Christian Church at the Waters of Mormon, and afterwards, because of King Noah's persecutions, removes with his people in Helam.	147	454

	B.C.	N.A.
First Christian Church established in Zarahemla by King Benjamin, who also consecrates his son, Mosiah, king.	125	476
A company sent by King Limhi, son of King Noah, to find Zarahemla, wander far to the north country and discover numerous relics of the Jaredites.	123	478
King Benjamin dies. A company under Ammon start from Zarahemla to find their brethren in the Land of Lehi-Nephi. They succeed, help them to escape from the Lamanites, and bring them safely back to Zarahemla.	122	479
Moroni, commander of the Nephite armies, born.	99	502
Alma, the Elder, dies, age eighty-two. Mosiah II dies, age sixty-three. Alma, the Younger, elected Chief Judge of the newly founded *Nephite Republic*.	91	510

The year 510 of the Nephite Annals marks the first year of the *Reign of the Judges* over the people of Nephi, and closes the Reign of King Mosiah.

THE LABORS OF THE NEPHITE SERVANTS OF GOD IN THIS LAND

Amid the trials and the disappointments of life, the doubts and uncertainties that seem, at times, almost to overwhelm us, it is, indeed pleasant to lay aside, for a moment, the tasks of the day and turn to Him who said: "Come unto me, all ye that labor and are heavy laden, and I will give you rest." It is a gentle voice bidding us, "Come, refresh ourselves with the waters of life that abound in the wells of Salvation." "As the dew from heaven" it revives our drooping spirits, and as the "fresh'ning breeze and the clear blue skies" it imparts courage and strength to our tired frames, weary and worn with the toils of everyday life.

As we recall these gracious words of the Lord's, we remember other glorious promises that are to be fulfilled in our behalf. We remember the *voice* heard by the righteous Lamanites, "Yea, a pleasant voice, as if it were a whisper, saying, Peace, peace be with you, because of your faith in my well beloved, who was from the foundation of the world." (Helaman 5:47) We also remember God's promise to ancient Israel, "Peace, peace be to those that are far and to those that are near." It is good to pause in our struggle for the things of the world and search for that "which maketh us truly rich."

Many of the Saints residing in the Land of Lehi-Nephi had grown exceeding prosperous in prospecting for gold and for silver, which in the land wherein they lived, "did abound most plentifully." Lehi's son, Jacob, upon the death of his elder brother, Nephi, became their spiritual leader and admonished them, saying, "But before ye seek for riches, seek ye for the kingdom of God." (Jacob 2-18) In this generation the Lord said through the Prophet Joseph Smith, "Behold, he that hath eternal life is rich." (Doc. & Cov. 6:7) We can now understand, more fully, the words of those great throngs of good men and women who have already gone our way, "The rewards of righteousness are more to be desired than all the riches of the earth."

It is good to depart from all selfish pursuits and seek Eternal Life. It is good to forsake all sinful pleasures and learn to listen to that still small voice which cometh from the Father, to lead, and to direct, and to warn of things to come. It restores the soul and makes more bright and beautiful, the sunshine that is around us. Too often we neglect "That which is good and what the Lord doth require of us." (Micah 6:8) We become so engrossed in the world and the things thereof that we have little or no time or thought for anything but: "What shall we eat? or, What shall we drink? or, Wherewithal shall we be clothed?" (III Nephi 13:31)

When these questions present themselves, it is then we should remember, "Man shall not live by bread alone, but by every word that proceedeth out of the mouth of God." (Matthew 4:4) When we see and recognize this great truth, the words of His servants become as meat and drink to our souls. By them our thirst is slaked, and we hunger no more. They feed us with knowledge and understanding from above, "And where the dark clouds hide the shining, let in the bright sunlight of love."

All the bounties of God express His gracious words: the fair and fragrant flowers that blossom along our way, the ripened grains that overflow our bins, the fruit that gladdens the heart of the husbandman—all are like the comforting words of His holy prophets. They hedge our paths and guide our feet; they raise us when we are fallen; and, whether it be the voice of Abraham, of Isaac, of Jacob, or the prophet teachings of the Jews, the labors of the Nephite servants of God in this land, the Apostolic Message of the Twelve, "Jesus is the Son of God," or the fullness of the Gospel, proclaimed by Joseph, the Seer, their words reveal our Father's Plan of Salvation. Too, they have an eternal authority that is quickly recognized by everyone who desires to know the mind and will of God.

This volume, with its many imperfections, is concerned principally with the labors of the Nephite servants of God in this land. From them we learn more of God's great love and His mercy. We shall see that, "The word of the Lord was verified, which he spake unto" their "fathers, saying that, Inasmuch as ye will keep my commandments ye shall prosper in the land." We will hear them proclaim the great truths of the Gospel of Jesus Christ, and we shall know that,

"I am he who speaketh." (Ether 4:8)

As we heed their words and walk in the path to which they point, we will grow in grace and in the knowledge of the glory of Him who created all things. What is more, in the nurture and admonition of God we will increase in the fear of Him and the time will not be far distant until, with joy, we will begin to say, as did the prophet of old,

From now on, henceforth and forever, I will serve God and keep his commandments.

One cannot read the story of Alma, the Younger, his conversion and his missionary experiences, nor of Nephi, the son of Helaman, "one of the greatest prophets who ever trod the earth, or to whom the God of our salvation revealed His holy mind and will" without being more and more constrained to,

"Shout praises to the Holy One of Israel." (I Nephi 31:13)

We feel that we can do no better than to add here, the last three verses of our *Preface* to Volume I,

"In the ages that came and went between their times, many holy prophets of the Nephites added and recorded their prophecies and their wisdom upon the plates from which the BOOK OF MORMON was translated. We offer the following comments which is *our* understanding of, and *our* testimony to, the great truths they unfold.

"To Elders George Reynolds and Janne M. Sjodahl, who spent much of their time and ability in ferreting out the accumulated evidence herewith presented, we owe the credit for the comments and the biographical notes.

"In humility we offer them, praying our Heavenly Father, by His Spirit, to render them most for our good and greatest for His glory. With full purpose of heart, we dedicate them to all who desire to know the 'Mind and Will of God.'"

—Philip C. Reynolds.

In Righteous Behavior, There Is No Such Thing As Time

In the Book of Mormon, frequent mention is made of specific years and of exact times. These dates are given so that the reader may better comprehend the great truths that are being related. They aid the reader to measure the progress of this branch of the House of Israel, and to observe that whenever Israel's children were faithful and called upon the Lord in truth, He was always near them. The beautiful assurance, "Thou wilt not hide Thy face from any generation of Thy children that seek after Thee," is always present.

From the time that Lehi and his family left the land of their inheritance in search of a land which God had prepared for them, the Sacred Record shows that Lehi's posterity were prospered according to their faithfulness. When they were disobedient and unfaithful they were destroyed.

A short time after the death of the valiant servant, Lehi, a serious division took place amongst his children. Some were immovable in keeping the commandments of God while others grew negligent in observing the Law of Moses. To avoid further, and probably more serious misunderstandings between them, the two groups separated.

Those who were firm in serving the Lord, followed Nephi, the fourth son of the Patriarch. Those who were jealous, and envied Nephi's calling as the head of the little company, followed Laman, Lehi's eldest son. Ever after the two peoples were known as *Nephites* and as *Lamanites*. The history of both peoples is intertwined with the exortations of the righteous, and the rejection of these appeals by the wicked. The record shows there were righteous among both peoples. At times, the Lamanites grew to be more righteous than were the Nephites, and then again, the Nephites would listen more attentively to the voices of God's servants, when again, they would begin to prosper in every way.

In the many years covered by the Sacred Record, or from the time he left Jerusalem, the journey of Lehi's colony in the wilderness of Judea, their crossing of the "many waters," their landing in their *new home,* their growth as a nation, their development under the wise rule of the three great prophet-kings, Mosiah I, his son, Benjamin, and his grandson, Mosiah II, the reign of the Judges, the ministry of Christ, the period when peace filled the hearts of every Nephite and there were no Lamanites, to the great and last civil war in which the Nephites were destroyed, we can feel the presence and the power, and understand the purposes of God.

Anthropologists and historians, place all the peoples of antiquity in a column and give each of them a number. In this way their chronology is made to appear more important than their accomplishments. *When* they lived thus becomes weightier than *how* they lived.

Historians have divided time into past and present. Soothsayers attempt to divine that which is to come. But today, after ages have passed and most of what occurred in them forgotten, we feel closer to some who are long since gone, than to many who are now great and powerful. Death, of course, is not the end; "man's immortal spirit never dies but lives on to inspire us, and move us to noble deeds and righteous endeavors, and blessing us evermore." This benediction, though general, is pronounced particularly upon our heads by all the Lord's faithful who have ever lived on this land.

Many regard the facts of history as originating in fortuitous circumstances. Even the Creation, itself, they say, occurred by chance. They forget that, "He commanded and they were created." Lord Chesterfield once said, "I am now as old as Solomon, though not so wise as he; yet I can sympathize with him when he says, 'All is vanity,' for I've been behind the scenes and know that it is so." Chesterfield was a philosopher and a skeptic. Much of his time was spent in company with Voltaire, the great French infidel; it may be that many of his conclusions were influenced thereby. However, all is *not* vanity. In this Chesterfield was mistaken. The wise old Hebrew king showed that all the labors of man are vain, that they are unenduring, and that the world goes on, not because of what man does, but in spite of it.

The simple truth is, some men's works live longer than do others. The arts and architecture of ancient peoples, their writings, and their ideas of God—many of which have lasted down through the centuries and have moulded our thoughts—bind us closer to "those who are far," than the ages can undo. The pyramids of Egypt, the writings of Moses, the interpretations of the Law by Ezra, the Hebrew scholar and historian who led the Jews back to Jerusalem after the Babylonian captivity, the records of the Nephites, the architecture of Greece, the paintings and sculpture of both Greece and Rome, and the beauty and originality that mark the "Golden Age of the Maya" here in America are the remains of nations and peoples who appeared upon the horizon of civilization and who became great and dominant before they passed away, leaving behind that which they cherished most highly. From them mankind has learned many lessons. He is the heir of vast stores of knowledge and information that have accumulated from the beginning. He is the possessor of the lessons mankind has learned. These are ties that bind the present and the past and cannot be measured in the terms of an almanac.

There are things more important than time. As an illustration, consider the Jews. The belief in the "Only True and Living God" that characterized their religion, gathered together and has cemented the relations of vast hosts of men and women in every land that even the years cannot separate, nor the trials of life, overwhelm. They are an entity that testifies, in a rapidly changing world, that the bonds of thought and the association of ideas are ties that bind stronger than time or place. Today they stand as a monument, "full of iron," to their faith in "the God of their fathers" and, what is still more wonderful, after centuries of sorrow and tribulation, they, in their unshaken zeal, fulfill every word that has been spoken by their holy prophets, and their souls will, again, "be as a watered garden" and they will suffer no more. (See Jeremiah 31:12)

When we recall that two thousand years ago, the Savior, here in America, stooped to bless the little children, and at almost the same time repeated what is, perhaps, the most beautiful portion of sacred literature, "The Sermon on the Mount," we see no gap in the lives of men we do not bridge, and no time in which we may be separate. The past ages "live, and move, and have a being" in the countless things they have bequeathed to us.

Nations do not just come and go. In no annals is there such a thing as *chance;* history does not even recognize the word. The dictionary says, "*By chance* means, *by accident.*" But, it is also said, "The accidents of man are the inspirations of God, and the incidents of this life, are the leadings and the guidings of Him who made it." All about us are proofs that this thing is so, and they bear witness that even the sparrow, on the housetop, does not fall except our Father in heaven knows and, "provides for small as well as great."

This thought should imbue each of us in leading our footsteps in our search for truth; then we will walk in paths of beauty and holiness. In the Book of Mormon, we find much to guide our feet when our steps seem uncertain. Therefore, "Let us walk in the light of the Lord," remembering, always, the words of the "elders of the Jews" who lived in Jerusalem at the time of Lehi, "In thy light shall we see light."

Though "time marches on," the lessons we learn are lessons that are far more important; it is not *when* we lived nor *where* we lived but *how* we lived that counts.

It is good to know that six hundred years before the birth of our Lord, Lehi and his little company landed somewhere on the Pacific side of South America, but it is far more important to know that they prospered when they kept the commandments of God. It is good to know that four thousand years ago, Moses led the Children of Israel in search of the Promised Land, but it is far more significant for us to know the laws and ordinances that guided them safely there. It is good to know that two thousand years ago, the first *Noel* resounded amongst the hills and plains of Judea, but it is far more important to know what was taught by Jesus, who was born that night in Bethlehem.

For ages wise men and prophets had told the Jews that they were a chosen people, and that the Messiah would be born of them and in their midst. But, far more important than the age of prophecy, are the *words* of those who were there when they crucified our Lord, and still more important is the *joy* recorded of them who beheld the Risen Redeemer, and who heard Him say, "All power is given me in heaven and in earth, Go ye therefore, and teach all nations, baptizing them in the name of the Father, and of the Son, and of the Holy Ghost: Teaching them to observe all things whatsoever I have commanded you: and, lo, I am with you alway, even unto the end of the world." (Matthew 28:18-19)

Reference to Volume I

Volume I, of this COMMENTARY ON THE BOOK OF MORMON is devoted to a discussion of that which is written upon the *Smaller Plates of Nephi*. Its contents relate to the incidents attending the departure of Lehi and his family from Jerusalem, near the close of the Sixth Century, B.C., to about 400 years later when they had become a numerous people. Lehi left Jerusalem with his wife, Sariah, his sons, and, we may presume, his daughters. They were, before long, joined by Ishmael and members of his family, and a few others. All of them formed the little company that reached the Pacific shores of America, the Land of Zion, about ten years later.

It has been estimated that not more than sixty persons comprised the group, yet in the following generations, whose history is recorded upon the *Smaller Plates of Nephi*, they, through the laws of natural increase, became a proud nation, skilled in government and religion, the arts and architecture, farming and stockraising, and in all manner of useful occupations. Many of Lehi's descendants were deeply religious. They were strict in keeping the *Law of Moses* and committed few crimes; they were also industrious.

During this period, and particularly in its beginning, some of the most sublime truths ever vouchsafed to man were providentially made known to them through their divinely-inspired leaders. They had revelations from heaven to guide them; angels ministered unto them; they prospered in material things, and those who were zealous in keeping the Lord's commandments were benefited and blessed.

A short time after Lehi and his people disembarked from the ship they had made, to establish new homes in the Promised Land, and not a very long time after Lehi's death, they separated into two contending factions. Some stayed with Laman, while the others followed Nephi. From them arose great nations called *Lamanite* and *Nephite*.

We discussed the progress they made as distinct peoples, yet, we always kept in mind that they were both of the same Hebrew origin. We considered the revelations they received, and which they recorded upon the plates Nephi had made. We gave *our* understanding of them, and added *our* testimony to the truthfulness of the principles they make known. We ended the consideration of these people, as their history is outlined upon the *Smaller Plates of Nephi*, with Amaleki's statement that as he was childless, he would give the plates to King Benjamin.

THE WORDS OF MORMON

Before we continue our consideration of this grand and glorious revelation, the Book of Mormon, let us pause, here, and acquaint ourselves with the literary construction of the second part of the sacred record. At this point the history of Lehi's descendants, as it is written on the Smaller Plates of Nephi, ends, and Mormon's abridgment of the larger plates of Nephi begins. In both volumes of plates the great saving truths for Salvation are enunciated. One reads these pages of Nephite Scripture with astonishment. They speak boldly and plainly, and speak of Eternal Life in the Kingdom of God. They tell man how he may become eligible to inherit a place in that eternal home. The power and authority of God, the road man must take to enter that Celestial Abode are clearly pointed out.

In pondering the everlasting principles of Salvation, and analyzing each one of them carefully, the doctrines stated in the Smaller Plates of Nephi, become an overwhelming portion in the lives of the Book of Mormon prophets. The inspired historians who wrote upon those plates also recorded their joys and their sorrows, and the vicissitudes through which they passed. They wrote of the mold in which their days had been cast, using the personal pronoun, "I." In translating their words, the Prophet Joseph Smith adopted the same designation.

As we pursue our studies of the Nephite annals we now give ear to a "third party," the abridger, Mormon.

Mormon, after whom the Book of Mormon is named, tells in his own words the wonderful story of the ancient inhabitants of America, the *Nephites* and the *Lamanites*. He often enlarges upon the data he transmits with annotations compiled by himself, both historical and exegetical.

Nephi, on separate occasions, was commanded by the Lord to make a set of metal plates from the precious ore that his brother, Jacob, says, "did abound most plentifully" in the land wherein they lived. The purpose for which Nephi was commanded to prepare these plates, being, he declared, "That I might engraven upon them the record of my people." (1 Nephi 19:1) These plates were identified by him as the *Larger Plates of Nephi,* and the *Smaller Plates of Nephi.* They became known to Nephi's followers, and are today, known to us by these same terms. The first plates which Nephi made, the larger plates, were afterwards kept by the kings, or the other rulers, all of whom were placed in that high and holy office by their righteous predecessors. After making the *Larger Plates* as he was instructed, and before he relinquished them to another, Nephi engraved upon them, ". . . the record of my father; also our journeyings in the wilderness," and then he adds, "the prophecies of my father; and many of mine own. . . ." (Ibid. *See* also pp. 194 ff. Vol. I, COMMENTARY ON THE BOOK OF MORMON)

During the thousand years that the records of the Nephites were kept on the Larger Plates of Nephi, many plates were added to those originally made by Nephi. In fact, when Mormon obtained custody of all the plates that had been used for this purpose, and which had been kept together by Divine Providence,* there were far too many to attempt, wisely, the presentation of them to whom they had been written.

THE WORDS OF MORMON

1. Mormon's Abridgment of the Larger Plates of Nephi—2. The Relation of the Foregoing Part of the Book of Mormon to that which Follows—3. Concerning King Benjamin.

1. *Mormon's Abridgment and the Smaller Plates of Nephi.*

1. And now I, Mormon, being about to deliver up the record which I have been making into the hands of my son Moroni, behold I have witnessed almost all the destruction of my people, the Nephites.

VERSE 1. *I, Mormon.* Who was Mormon? Mormon was the last great prophet-general of the Nephite nation, but he is better known to us as the custodian and the compiler of the records of his people. He was the editor of the greater portion of the work named after him and known to us as the Book of Mormon. Mormon's father was a descendant of Nephi. He had the same name as his illustrious son, who was born on the northern continent in 311 A.D.

When the younger Mormon was eleven years of age, he went with his father to Zarahemla. A year before their departure south, he became acquainted with Ammaron, the keeper of the sacred records. Because of the iniquity of the people, Ammaron hid these records in a hill in the Land Antum. He informed young Mormon of what he had done, and placed Mormon, who was then only ten years old, in charge of the buried treasure. Ammaron instructed Mormon to go, when he was about twenty-four years of age, to the hill where he had hid them and take the Plates of Nephi, and record thereon, the things he had observed concerning the people. The remainder of the records, and other holy things which he had buried with the plates, Ammaron told Mormon to leave where they were. Mormon did as he was bid, but soon events occurred that altered his instructions.

Mormon was, as was Nephi in the beginning, commanded by the Lord to make a set of plates. Upon these plates, he was to condense into an abbreviated account what he found written upon the "Larger Plates of Nephi." Mormon, through the spirit of prophecy and of revelation, discovered many instructions which would be valuable and important to future generations to whom they might come. These teachings Mormon included in his abridgment.

2. And it is many hundred years after the coming of Christ that I deliver these records into the hands of my son; and it supposeth me that he will witness the entire destruction of my peo-

---

In his inspired preface, and written after he had finished his abridgment, Mormon wrote:

Wherefore, it is an abridgment of the record of the people of Nephi, and also of the Lamanites—Written to the Lamanites, who are a remnant of the house of Israel; . . . Written by way of commandment, and also by the spirit of prophecy and of revelation—

. . . and also to the convincing of the Jew and Gentile that Jesus is the Christ, the Eternal God, manifesting himself unto all nations. . . .

Nephi wrote concerning the second set of plates (the Smaller Plates) he made:

And I knew not at the time when I made them that I should be commanded of the Lord to make these plates; wherefore, the record of my father, and the genealogy of his fathers, and the more part of all our proceedings in the wilderness are engraven upon those plates of which I have spoken; wherefore, the things that transpired before I made these plates are, of a truth, more particularly made mention upon the first plates.

And after I had made these plates by way of commandment, I, Nephi, received a commandment that the ministry and the prophecies, the more plain and precious parts of them, should be written upon these plates; and that the things which were written should be kept for the instruction of my people, who should possess the land, and also for other wise purposes, which purposes are known to the Lord." (1 Nephi 19:2-3)

The Smaller Plates relate the story of the departure of Lehi and his family from Jerusalem, 600 B.C., to about 200 years before the birth of the Messiah in Judea.

When Nephi grew old, and was about to die, he gave the Smaller Plates to his younger brother, Jacob, who succeeded him as leader of the Saints whose chief city was in the Land of Lehi-Nephi. Of the Smaller Plates, Jacob says,

And he gave me, Jacob, a commandment that I should write upon these plates a few of the things which I considered to be most precious; that I should not touch, save it were lightly, concerning the history of this people which are called the people of Nephi.

For he said that the history of his people should be engraven upon his other plates, and that I should preserve these plates and hand them down unto my seed from generation to generation.

And if there were preaching which was sacred, or revelation which was great, or prophesying, that I should engraven the heads of them upon these plates, and touch upon them as much as it were possible, for Christ's sake, and for the sake of our people. (Jacob 1:2-4)

It should be noted, here, that, in addition to Nephi, who wrote the greater part of the Smaller Plates, Jacob, and seven of Jacob's descendants also engraved upon them.

That the Smaller Plates should be preserved for the benefit and blessing of future generations, is, we may be sure, the purpose for which Nephi was commanded to make them. We shall see in the pages that follow, the fulfillment of the prophetic words of Mormon; we shall see in them, the presence, and the power, and the purposes of God.

VERSE 2. *Many hundred years.* "And it is many hundred years after the coming of Christ that I deliver these records into the hands of my son." That we may get a better understanding of Mormon's words, let us follow the Nephite people

| ple. But may God grant that he may survive them, that he may write somewhat concerning them, | and somewhat concerning Christ, that perhaps some day it may profit them. |

through the events of their last one hundred years. They were a people who had apostatized from the Church of Christ, and who had fallen from the blessed heights of peace, to the bitter depths of unfathomable depravity. Only a short time previously these same people had attained a pinnacle of righteous living that had never before, or since, been reached. For 200 years after the Risen Redeemer ministered to their forefathers in the Land Bountiful, they were bound together by the loftiest ideals of their relationship one to another. They believed that all men were brothers, and that God was the Father of all men. Each sought to do the Savior's bidding, and all walked in the "strait and narrow path" which leads to Eternal Life. It is written in their sacred record that not one of them was lost. They were a happy, holy people; angels descended to minister to their wants, and revelations from heaven were their constant guide. Now, all was changed. The conditions under which they lived were completely reversed. The things they once hated, they now loved. What once they loved, they now despised. Instead of peace, there was war. Instead of brotherly love, there was hatred. Wickedness and abandonment to the meanest purposes of diseased and depraved hearts usurped the place of goodness and purity. Crime, degradation, and filth speeded the course of them who rushed headlong into destruction. Truly, we can see that the Lord, because of their wickedness, had forsaken them. They were left almost alone.

In the year A.D. 335, or in the 935th year of the Nephite annals, Mormon obtained the plates as Ammaron had directed. Forty years later he removed them all from the Hill Shim to prevent their destruction by marauding bands of Lamanites. Ten years later Mormon recorded:

". . . having been commanded of the Lord that I should not suffer the records which had been handed down by our fathers, which were sacred, to fall into the hands of the Lamanites, (for the Lamanites would destroy them) therefore I made this record out of the plates of Nephi, and hid up in the Hill Cumorah all the records which have been entrusted to me by the hand of the Lord, save it were these few plates which I give to my son Moroni. (Mormon 6:6)

The year A.D. 322, saw actual warfare break out between the Nephites and the Lamanites for the first time since the Risen Redeemer's appearing among them. A number of battles were fought in which the armies of the Nephites were victorious. These Nephite successes ended, for a while, the awful bloodshed that is incident to open warfare, but in four years the savage contest was renewed. In the interim, iniquity had greatly increased.

When the warring began again, the youthful Mormon, only fifteen years of age, was appointed to lead the Nephite armies. In the following two years, disaster after disaster followed the cause for which he led them, and by A.D. 329, rapine, revolution, and carnage, prevailed throughout all the land. For many years warfare continued; first the Nephites overwhelmed their enemy, and then the Lamanites were successful in routing the Nephites, until, at length, both armies were near exhaustion.

This resulted in a treaty of peace with the Nephites as one party, and the Lamanites and Gadianton Robbers as the other. The provisions of this treaty, which proved to be only a temporary cessation of hostilities, were that the Nephites possessed the country north of the Isthmus, and the Lamanites, the regions south. A peace of ten years followed this treaty. In A.D. 360, the Lamanites, through their king, again declared war. Again the land was the scene of widespread conflict. For

3. And now, I speak somewhat concerning that which I have written; for after I had made an abridgment from the plates of Nephi, down to the reign of this king Benjamin, of whom Amaleki spake, I searched among the records which had been delivered into my hands, and I found these plates, which contained this small account of the prophets, from Jacob down to the reign of this king Benjamin, and also many of the words of Nephi.

4. And the things which are upon these plates pleasing me, because of the prophecies of the coming of Christ; and my fathers knowing that many of them have been fulfilled; yea, and I also

---

more than twenty years, combat, contention, rapine, pillage, and all the horrors of corrupt and brutal passions filled the entire countryside, which seemed to be centered in the Land Desolation, until the Lamanites drove the Nephites far to the North. This state of things grew increasingly worse, until, at last, when every nerve had been strained for conquest, and every man who could be found was enlisted, the two vast hosts, with unquenchable hatred and unrelenting obstinacy, met at the Hill Cumorah to decide the destiny of half the world. It was the final struggle which was to end in the extermination of one, or both of the races that for nearly a thousand years had conjointly inhabited America. When the days of that final struggle were ended all but twenty-four of the Nephite army had been swept into untimely graves. A few Nephites fled to the land southward. Two of the twenty-four were Mormon, and his son, Moroni, who later tells us, (A.D. 400) that his father had been killed by the Lamanites who hunted and slew every member of the House of Nephi they could find.

Mormon was equally as great a religious teacher as he was a soldier. His annotations throughout his compilation of the Sacred Record show this, as do also his instructions and epistles to his son. Shortly before the great and final struggle near the Hill Cumorah, Mormon hid all the plates, or records, entrusted to his care there, save the abridged account of the Larger Plates of Nephi, which he gave to his son, Moroni. Mormon ends his statement regarding the horrors of the then continuing war with a prayer that his son may survive the ferocity of its carnage, and live to write the last chapter of his people's history, and, also to testify, therein, to them of Christ. We may understand, somewhat, Mormon's great character, and his stellar faith and integrity, by the power of his writings. Forgiveness of his apostate people's backsliding, and a desire to aid in their future welfare, was the prayer that filled his heart. He saw their fallen condition in the future, but his faith, upheld and sustained by his own righteousness, is expressed in the hope that what Moroni will write "some day it may profit them." Today, centuries later, we see, with ever-increasing clarity, the answer to Mormon's praying. The descendants of these same people are, today, beginning to obey the voice of Israel's Shepherd, and are coming into His fold. And we ask, "Why not?" when we remember that they, too, are of Israel.

Verses 3-6. *I speak somewhat concerning that which I have written.* When Mormon had finished or had nearly completed his Abridgment, he found upon examining the great number of plates in his possession, the Smaller Plates of Nephi. On searching them, he found that they contained a part of the history which was included on the Larger Plates of Nephi.* It is a duplicate account of Nephite history

---

*In the First Edition of the Book of Mormon there is a Preface written by the Prophet Joseph Smith. He states therein that in the 116 pages of manuscript which were lost by Martin Harris this part of the Sacred Record was called "The Book of Lehi."

know that as many things as have been prophesied concerning us down to this day have been fulfilled, and as many as go beyond this day must surely come to pass—

5. Wherefore, I chose these things, to finish my record upon them, which remainder of my record I shall take from the plates of Nephi; and I cannot write the hundreth part of the things of my people.

6. But behold, I shall take these plates, which contain these prophesyings and revelations, and put them with the remainder of my record, for they are choice unto me; and I know they will be choice unto my brethren.

7. And I do this for a wise purpose; for thus it whispereth me, according to the workings of the Spirit of the Lord which is in me. And now, I do not know all things; but the Lord knoweth all things which are to come; where-fore, he worketh in me to do according to his will.

---

up to the reign of King Benjamin, or up to about 200 B.C. However, there was this difference, the Smaller Plates had engraven on them "many of the words of Nephi," many of the revelations he had received for the guidance of his people, and certain prophecies concerning the "Coming of Christ." These choice portions of their Scriptures were not written upon the Larger Plates. Mormon read them, and re-read them. He was amazed. He hadn't seen the Smaller Plates before. They were so important to him, and, knowing that many of the events they prophesied had already come to pass, and that the remainder must surely do so, he put them with his own abridgment, for, he said, "They are choice to me; and I know they will be choice unto my brethren."

VERSE 7. *And I do this for a wise purpose.* The meaning of this verse is so obvious that it needs no comment. (By way of interpolation, let us note, that many passages of the Book of Mormon are so plain and easy to understand that if we do comment on them, we may be forced to comment on our own comments!) A statement of certain facts may be enlightening to the thoughtful student, when we consider, in conjunction with Mormon's declaration, a few experiences endured by the Prophet Joseph Smith in the translation of the Sacred Record. On April 12 or there about, 1828, Martin Harris, who had aided the Prophet on different occasions, began to write as the Prophet dictated the words of translation.

In a relatively short time, by June 14, or two months later, the Prophet had translated, and Harris had written, 116 pages of what is commonly known as *foolscap* paper. It appears that Martin Harris had considerable trouble at home with his wife. Spending so much of his time and money assisting in what she believed to be a hoax, only worsened conditions that were already difficult. In his desire to change her mind, and to prove to her and to others of his relatives and numerous of his friends that Joseph Smith had the "golden plates" which he claimed to possess, he, using undue pressure, persuaded the Prophet to let him show the manuscript they had finished to them. Martin Harris was so insistent that he even asked Joseph to seek the Lord, through the Urim and Thummim, for permission so to do. The Prophet did. After several refusals the request was at last granted. The result was that these pages were lost or were stolen from Harris who broke his solemn promise to the Prophet. The gift of translation was, because of this, temporarily taken from Joseph; the sacred records, too, were taken back by the heavenly keeper of them. We may imagine the torment of soul and the suffering that the Prophet experienced. In deep remorse for his sin, he repented his mistake, and the sacred plates and other implements were returned to him by the angel to whom Joseph had been required to surrender them.

Before the plates were forfeited by Joseph Smith to the Angel Moroni, the Prophet, through the use of the Urim and Thummim, received the following revelation,

The works, and the designs, and the purposes of God cannot be frustrated, neither can they come to naught, for God doth not walk in crooked paths; neither doth He turn to the right hand nor to the left; neither doth He vary from that which He hath said; therefore His paths are straight and His course is one eternal round.

Remember, remember, that it is not the work of God that is frustrated, but the work of men; for although a man may have many revelations, and have power to do many mighty works, yet, if he boasts in his own strength, and sets at naught the counsels of God, and follows after the dictates of his own will and carnal desires, he must fall and incur the vengeance of a just God upon him.

Behold, you have been entrusted with these things, but how strict were your commandments; and remember also, the promises which were made to you, if you did not transgress them; and behold, how oft you have transgressed the commandments and the laws of God, and have gone on in the persuasion of men; for behold, you should not have feared man more than God, although men set at naught the counsels of God, and despise His words, yet you should have been faithful, and He would have extended His arm, and supported you against all the fiery darts of the adversary, and He would have been with you in every time of trouble.

Behold thou art Joseph, and thou wast chosen to do the work of the Lord, but because of transgression, if thou are not aware thou wilt fall; but remember, God is merciful, therefore, repent of that which thou hast done, which is contrary to the commandment which I gave you, and thou art still chosen, and art again called to the work; except thou do this, thou shalt be delivered up and become as other men, and have no more gift.

And when thou deliverest up that which was sacred into the hands of a wicked man, who has set at naught the counsels of God, and has broken the most sacred promises which were made before God, and has depended upon his own judgment, and boasted in his own wisdom; and this is the reason that thou hast lost thy privilges for a season; for thou hast suffered the counsel of thy director to be trampled upon from the beginning. Nevertheless My work shall go forth; for inasmuch as the knowledge of a Savior has come into the world, through the testimony of the Jews, even so shall the knowledge of a Savior come unto My people, and to the Nephites, and the Jacobites, and the Josephites, and the Zoramites, through the testimony of their fathers; and this testimony shall come to the knowledge of the Lamanites, and the Lemuelites, and the Ishmaelites, who dwindled in unbelief because of the iniquity of their fathers, whom the Lord has suffered to destroy their brethren, the Nephites, because of their iniquities and their abominations; for this very purpose are these plates preserved which contain these records, that the promises of the Lord might be fulfilled, which He made to His people; and that they might know the promises of the Lord, and that they might believe the Gospel, and rely upon the merits of Jesus Christ, and be glorified through faith in His name; and that through their repentance they might be saved. Amen. (History of the Church, Vol. I, pp. 21-22)

Following Joseph's ordeal, and after the plates had been returned to him, he inquired of the Lord as to the work of the translation. He was granted the following revelation, which then alters the course of future translation.

Now, behold I say unto you, that because you delivered up those writings which you had power given unto you to translate by the means of the Urim and Thummim, into the hands of a wicked man, you have lost them;

And you also lost your gift at the same time, and your mind became darkened;

Nevertheless, it is now restored unto you again; therefore see that you are faithful and continue on unto the finishing of the remainder of the work of translation as you have begun.

Do not run faster or labor more than you have strength and means provided to enable you to translate, but be diligent unto the end:

Pray always that you may come off conqueror; yea, that you may conquer Satan, and that you may escape the hands of the servants of Satan that do uphold his work.

Behold, they have sought to destroy you; yea, even the man in whom you have trusted has sought to destroy you.

And for this cause I said he is a wicked man, for he has sought to take away the things wherewith you have been entrusted, and he has also sought to destroy your gift;

And because you have delivered the writings into his hands, behold, wicked men have taken them from you;

Therefore you have delivered them up, yea, that which was sacred, unto wickedness.

And, behold Satan hath put it into their hearts to alter the words which you have caused to be written, or which you have translated, which have gone out of your hands;

And, behold, I say unto you, that because they have altered the words, they read contrary from that which you translated and caused to be written,

And on this wise the devil has sought to lay a cunning plan that he may destroy this work; for he hath put it into their hearts to do this, that by lying they may say they have caught you in the words which you have pretended to translate.

Verily, I say unto you, that I will not suffer that Satan accomplish his evil design in this thing; . . .

Verily, verily, I say unto you, that Satan has a great hold upon their hearts; . . .

Verily, verily, I say unto you, wo be unto him that lieth to deceive, because he supposeth that another lieth to deceive, for such are not exempt from the justice of God.

Now, behold, they have altered these words, because Satan saith unto them, He hath deceived you—and thus he flattereth them away to do iniquity, to get thee to tempt the Lord thy God.

Behold, I say unto you that you shall not translate again those words which have gone forth out of your hands; for, behold, they shall not accomplish their evil designs in lying against those words. For, behold, if you should bring forth the same words they will say that you have lied, that you have pretended to translate, but that you have contradicted yourself;

And, behold, they will publish this, and Satan will harden the hearts of the people to stir them up to anger against you, that they will not believe my words.

Thus Satan thinketh to overpower your testimony in this generation:

But, behold, here is wisdom, and because I show unto you wisdom and give you commandments concerning these things, what you should do, show it not unto the world until you have accomplished the work of translation.

Marvel not that I said unto you, here is wisdom, show it not unto the world;
. . ."
                                         (*Doctrine and Covenants*, Sec. 10)

Instead of citing only the first paragraph on page xiv, Volume I, COMMENTARY ON THE BOOK OF MORMON, we publish it in full. It is summed up in a few words.

The wisdom and foreknowledge of the Lord was manifest in the early part of his latter-day work. Martin Harris, than whom, perhaps, there was none other more ready and willing to help the cause than he, in his anxiety to prove to his friends and his relatives that Joseph Smith had the plates, the possession of which he claimed and the work was of God, prevailed upon the Prophet to let him show the first 116 pages of the manuscript to them. These pages were lost. Were it not for the wisdom of him, "Who knoweth all things," an insurmountable difficulty may have arisen. The pages lost covered the same period of time as was covered by the Smaller Plates. In other words, a double record was had of these times. Can we imagine of anything more wise or more "foreknowing" than this?

2. The relation of the foregoing part of the Book of Mormon to that which follows.

8. And my prayer to God is concerning my brethren, that they may once again come to the knowledge of God, yea, the redemption of Christ; that they may once again be a delightsome people.

9. And now, I, Mormon, proceed to finish out my record, which I take from the plates of Nephi; and I make it according to the knowledge and the understanding which God has given me.

10. Wherefore, it came to pass that after Amaleki had delivered up these plates into the hands of king Benjamin, he took them and put them with the other plates, which contained records which had been handed down by the kings, from generation to generation until the days of king Benjamin.

VERSE 8. *See Comments verse 2.*

VERSE 9. *And now I, Mormon, proceed to finish out my record.* After Mormon's soliloquy, or speech to himself, in which he included a prayer to God, "concerning my brethren," that they may once again "be a delightsome people," he affirmed his intention of carrying on the work he had already started. Of his abridgment, he says, "I make it according to the knowledge and the understanding which God has given me." He thus testifies that the record he makes, and the knowledge he transmits, is the truth, and only the truth. How like the sacred oath, attesting our veracity, we affirm, today. The words of our oath, "So help me God," is another way of saying exactly what Mormon said in this verse. This is strong evidence that what he says is, in fact, true. It challenges man to recall if in his experience there ever was a failure when anyone said, "With the help of the Lord," I will do a certain thing. If the resolve comes from a contrite heart, and with full purpose of mind, "There never was a vain attempt, never a wasted effort." We may rely on the record of Mormon.

VERSE 10. *King Benjamin puts both the Larger and the Smaller Plates together.* Amaleki was the last to write upon the Smaller Plates. Finding that they were filled with the writings of others who had preceeded him, as well as his own short account, and being childless he gave them to King Benjamin.

King Benjamin was the second of the great and wise prophet-kings who reigned over the Nephites from Zarahemla, their capital city. His father was Mosiah I, who, being warned by the Lord to flee out of the Land of Lehi-Nephi, took those who would go with him, and led them northward where they found the people of Mulek. The two peoples joined, and chose Mosiah to be their king. In course of time, Mosiah died, and Benjamin, Amaleki recorded, "reigneth in his stead." Benjamin was a "just man before the Lord," says Amaleki, "I shall deliver up these plates unto him." (Omni 25)

In one of the many explanatory notes which Mormon inserts in the record he makes, he informs us that after Amaleki had placed the Smaller Plates of Nephi in the possession of King Benjamin, he, that is King Benjamin, put them with the other, or the Larger Plates. The Larger Plates contained what we have called, the *secular history* of the Nephite people. Thus, the two sets of plates, coming into the hands of one man, did what had not been done since Nephi had made them hundreds of years before. King Benjamin thus became the first to compile the full

11. And they were handed down from king Benjamin, from generation to generation until they have fallen into my hands. And I, Mormon, pray to God that they may be preserved from this time henceforth. And I know that they will be preserved; for there are great things written upon them, out of which my people and their brethren shall be judged at the great and last day, according to the word of God which is written.

---

history of the people upon one set of plates. In this, we see the purposes of God, for together, in them, we will observe that the profane and the religious history combined into one complete account, the development of the Nephite people as one great nation.

VERSE 11. *And they were handed down from King Benjamin, from generation to generation until they have fallen into my hands.* The Smaller Plates of Nephi containing the sacred annals of Nephi's people were not entirely filled with engravings until about 200 years before Christ. They were started by Nephi between 570-560 B.C. But the history they contain goes back to the time when Lehi left Jerusalem, or 600 B.C. So in reality they contain the history of God's dealings with that branch of the House of Israel for about four hundred years.

When Nephi died, he transferred these sacred records to the care of his brother, Jacob. From then until Moroni finally hid them in the Hill Cumorah, they continued in the hands of four families, who had charge of them as near as can be told from the abridgment. We may summarize as follows: Jacob and his descendants held them from 546 B.C. to about 200 B.C., when they were transferred to King Benjamin. He, with his son, Mosiah, held them until 91 B.C., at which time they were given into the care of Alma, the Chief Judge. Alma and his posterity retained them until 320 years after the advent of the Messiah. After these, Mormon and Moroni were the custodians until the close of the record in the year A.D. 420.

Here are the facts concerning the custodianship of the sacred plates from the foregoing statement of the Prophet Mormon. Beginning with Amaleki, he gave the plates to King Benjamin about 200 B.C. Of King Benjamin, we read ". . . that when King Benjamin had made an end of all these things, and had consecrated his son Mosiah to be a ruler and a king over his people, and he had given him all the charges concerning the kingdom . . ." (Mosiah 6:3) Which "charges" we may declare, was to be the keeper of the sacred things, including the plates. We read further in the account of Mosiah's reign, "He took the plates of brass, and all the things which he had kept, and conferred them upon Alma, who was the son of Alma; yea, all the records, . . ." (Mosiah 28:20) This was in 91 B.C.

Alma, about seventeen years later, entrusted the plates to his son, Helaman. It is recorded in the Book of Alma, 37:1-2, "And now, my son Helaman, I command you that ye take the records which have been entrusted with me; And I also command you that you keep a record of this people, according as I have done, upon the Plates of Nephi, and keep all these things sacred which I have kept, even as I have kept them; for it is for a wise purpose that they are kept."

In the year 544 of the Nephite Annals, or fifty-seven years before the birth of Christ, Helaman died, and Shiblon, his brother, we are told, ". . . took possession of these sacred things which had been delivered unto Helaman by Alma." (Alma 63:1)

Four years later, or 53 B.C., Shiblon died, and, "It became expedient for Shiblon to confer those sacred things, before his death, upon the son of Helaman, being called after the name of his father." (Alma 63:11)

In 39 B.C., "Helaman died, and his eldest son Nephi began to reign in his stead." (Helaman 3:37) Of him it is written:

And Nephi, the son of Helaman, had departed out of the land of Zarahemla, giving charge to his son Nephi, who was his eldest son, concerning the plates of brass, and all the records which had been kept, and all those things which had been kept sacred from the departure of Lehi out of Jerusalem. Then he departed out of the land, and whither he went, no man knoweth; and his son Nephi did keep the records in his stead, yea, the record of this people. (3 Nephi 1:2-3)

Nephi, the son of Nephi and the grandson of Helaman, thus, shortly before the birth of the Savior in Bethlehem of Judea, received the Sacred Records with instructions as to their care. This second Nephi was chosen by the Risen Redeemer to be a member of the Twelve whom He named. Nephi, the second, kept the plates in his possession until after the glorious appearing of the Savior, when he gave them into the care of his son, who was also named Nephi. He, presumably, was a young man at that time, for he kept them seventy-six years, or until A.D. 110, when a son, named Amos received them. "And he kept it eighty and four years," . . . "and he kept it upon the plates of Nephi also." (4 Nephi 20, 19)

And it came to pass that Amos died also (and it was an hundred and ninety and four years from the coming of Christ) and his son Amos kept the record in his stead; and he also kept the record upon the plates of Nephi; . . . (4 Nephi 21)

And it came to pass that after three hundred and five years had passed away, (and the people did still remain in wickedness) Amos died; and his brother, Ammaron, did keep the records in his stead. (4 Nephi 47)

Ammaron hid up all the plates in the Hill Shim. (4 Nephi 48-49)

Ammaron gave them to Mormon. (Mormon 1:2-3)

Mormon obtained the plates as Ammaron had directed. (Mormon 4:23)

Mormon hid all the records in the Hill Cumorah, save the abridged ones, which he gave to his son, Moroni. (Mormon 6:6)

Moroni said, "I am the son of Mormon. . . . And I am the same who hideth up this record unto the Lord; . . ." (Mormon 8:14) And I seal up these records, . . ." (Moroni 10:2)

The following are the names of the Nephite historians, with the times during which they held the plates. Where a blank space is noted, the information is not given in the Book of Mormon, and therefore can only be guessed at, which we choose not to do.

Nephi, from .... to 546 B.C.	Helaman, the Elder, from 73 to 57.
Jacob, from 546 to	Shiblon, from 57 to 53.
Enos, from .... to 422.	Helaman, the Younger, from 53 to 39.
Jarom, from 422 to 362.	Nephi, from 39 to 1.
Omni, from 362 to 318.	Nephi, the Disciple, from 1 to A.D. 34.
Amaron, from 318 to 280.	Nephi, the son of the Disciple, 34 to 110.
Chemish, from 280 to	Amos, from 110 to 194.
Abinadom, from .... to	Amos, the Younger, from 194 to 306.
Amaleki, from .... to 200 (circa).	Ammaron, from 306 to 320.
King Benjamin, from 200 to 125.	Mormon, from 320 to 385.
King Mosiah, from 125 to 91.	Moroni, from 385 to 420. Record closes.
Alma, the Younger, from 91 to 73.	

3. *Concerning King Benjamin.*

12. And now, concerning this king Benjamin—he had somewhat of contentions among his own people.

13. And it came to pass also that the armies of the Lamanites came down out of the land of Nephi, to battle against his people. But behold, king Benjamin gathered together his armies, and he did stand against them; and he did fight with the strength of his own arm, with the sword of Laban.

14. And in the strength of the Lord they did contend against their enemies, until they had slain many thousands of the Lamanites. And it came to pass that they did contend against the Lamanites until they had driven them out of all the lands of their inheritance.

15. And it came to pass that after there had been false Christs, and their mouths had been shut, and they punished according to their crimes;

16. And after there had been false prophets, and false preachers and teachers among the people, and all these having been punished according to their crimes; and after there having been much contention and many dissensions away unto the La-

---

VERSE 12. *Now, concerning this King Benjamin.* A mighty man in the midst of Israel, was Benjamin. Blessed were the people over whom he reigned, for he governed them in righteousness, and for their welfare; he indeed labored with all the might of his body and all the faculty of his soul. Holy and pure in his individual life, he was ministered to by angels, and was often the recipient of revelations from on high.

VERSES 13-14. *And in the strength of the Lord they did contend against the enemy.* The reign of King Benjamin was a long one when he died in Zarahemla at a very advanced age. Some time during his tenure upon the throne, the aggressive Lamanites, not content with occupying the Land of Nephi, actually followed the Nephites into the Land of Zarahemla, and invaded that also. The war that followed was a bloody one. King Benjamin led his forces, and with his own strong arm slew many of the enemy. He was armed with the historic Sword of Laban, which appears to have been handed down from monarch to monarch from the day that Nephi first wielded it. King Benjamin was ultimately successful in driving the invading Lamanites out of all the regions belonging to his people. Many thousands of the Lamanites were slain.

VERSES 15-18. *False Christs, and false teachers, quieted.* The reign of King Benjamin was also troubled with various religious impostors, false Christs, and pretended prophets, who, with an effervescent zeal, caused much dissension among the people, and, by their preachments, induced some to apostatize. This was a source of great sorrow to King Benjamin, who, himself, was like a father to them, and who also labored with his own hands to set a good example to those over whom he ruled.

However, with the aid of many of the righteous men who dwelt in Zarahemla, King Benjamin exposed to the understanding of his people, the false claims of the self-styled Messiahs, the untrue assertions of the pseudo-prophets, and the hollow teachings of them who attempted to belie the truth. In doing this, unity was

manites, behold, it came to pass that king Benjamin, with the assistance of the holy prophets who were among his people—

17. For behold, king Benjamin was a holy man, and he did reign over his people in righteousness; and there were many holy men in the land, and they did speak the word of God with power and with authority; and they did use much sharpness because of the stiff-neckedness of the people—

18. Wherefore, with the help of these, king Benjamin, by laboring with all the might of his body and the faculty of his whole soul, and also the prophets, did once more establish peace in the land.

---

restored throughout all the land, peace of mind was re-established, and the worship of the God of Israel, in its correct form, was practised by those who bowed only to the True and Living God. In the event that any of the impostors broke the Nephite law, they were tried, and if found guilty, were punished according to its demands. It must be remembered that freedom of conscience was absolutely protected among the Nephites, and even the civil law was administered with a showing of great mercy in the days of Benjamin, and of his father, Mosiah I, and of his son, Mosiah II.

It is not so stated, but we may presume, that, what we call a "revival in religion" entered the spiritual thinking of many of those lately-consolidated people. To many of them, only recently were the glories of God's Plan of Salvation made known. The coming of the Messiah to dwell among the children of men was, for them, an event that they anxiously looked forward to. Their hearts were filled with joyous hope. They looked beyond the horizon for that day to come. We may imagine that they, being in such a mental and spiritual condition, were readily susceptible to the deceptions of those who cried, "Lo, the Christ is come!" or, "Behold, a great prophet hath arisen." We may trace this peculiar form of spiritual activity to an increased desire on their part to learn, and it shows a keen interest in religion among them. To it, we may attribute the frequency with which false prophets troubled the reign of King Benjamin. But, says Mormon, "For behold, King Benjamin was a holy man," and, as we have said, that with the help of many righteous men who did support him, *he shut their mouths,* and did again "establish peace in the land."

NOTES

A Great Number of Plates. That which follows answers the question frequently asked, "What became of the Book of Mormon Plates?" President Brigham Young, at a special conference held at Farmington, Utah, June 17, 1877, on which occasion the Davis Stake of Zion was organized, said,

When Joseph got the Plates, the angel instructed him to carry them back to the Hill Cumorah, which he did. Oliver Cowdery says that when Joseph and he went there, the hill opened, and they walked into a cave, in which there was a large and spacious room. He says that he did not think, at the time, whether they had the light of the sun or artificial light, but it was as light as day. They laid the Plates on a table. It was a large table that stood in the middle of the room. Under this table there was a pile of plates as much as two feet high, and there were altogether in this room more plates than many wagon loads. They were piled up in the corners and along the walls. The first time they went there, the Sword of Laban hung upon the wall, but when they went again, it had been taken down and laid upon the table across the Gold Plates. It was unsheathed, and on it was written these words, "This Sword will never be sheathed again until the kingdoms of this world become the Kingdom of our God and His Christ." (*Journal of Discourses*, Vol. 19, p. 38)

President Young, in the same discourse, said that he had this from Oliver Cowdery, himself, and from others familiar with the incident related. "Don Carlos Smith," he says, "was a witness to these things."

THE BOOK OF MOSIAH

CHAPTER 1

1. King Benjamin's Exhortations to His Sons—2. Mosiah Chosen to Succeed His Father—3. Mosiah Receives the Records.

1. *King Benjamin's exhortations to his sons.*

1. And now there was no more contention in all the land of Zarahemla, among all the people who belonged to king Benjamin, so that king Benjamin had continual peace all the remainder of his days.

2. And it came to pass that he had three sons; and he called their names Mosiah, and Helorum, and Helaman. And he caused that they should be taught in all the language of his fathers, that thereby they might become men of understanding; and that they might know concerning the prophecies which had been spoken by the mouths of their fathers, which were delivered them by the hand of the Lord.

3. And he also taught them concerning the records which were engraven on the plates of brass, saying: My sons, I would that ye should remember that were it not for these plates, which contain these records and these commandments, we must have suffered in ignorance, even at this present time, not knowing the mysteries of God.

4. For it were not possible that our father, Lehi, could have remembered all these things, to have taught them to his children, except it were for the help of these plates; for he having been taught in the language of the Egyptians therefore he could read these engravings, and teach them to his

VERSE 1. *And now there was no more contention in all the Land of Zarahemla.* During the long reign of King Benjamin, there was considerable strife and contention between the Nephites and the Lamanites, (Words of Mormon 14) and also among his own people. (Ibid 16) At length, however, peace was established throughout the Land of Zarahemla. The most notable event of King Benjamin's extended and benevolent reign was a great spiritual revival when his entire people solemnly entered into a covenant to serve the Lord and keep His commandments.

VERSE 2. *Benjamin's three sons taught that thereby they might become men of understanding.* The names of the three were, Mosiah, who became king, Helorum, and Helaman. They were instructed, at the bidding of their father, in all the learning of their people, both sacred and secular, and in the history of the Nephites, with especial reference to God's dealings with, and His preserving care over them. This is the only mention in the Book of Mormon of Helorum and Helaman.

VERSES 3-5. *The records which were engraven on the Plates of Brass.* Here, between the lines, we read a remarkable testimony to the truth we find expressed

children, that thereby they could teach them to their children, and so fulfilling the commandments of God, even down to this present time.

5. I say unto you, my sons, were it not for these things, which have been kept and preserved by the hand of God, that we might read and understand of his mysteries, and have his commandments always before our eyes, that even our fathers would have dwindled in unbelief, and we should have been like unto our brethren, the Lamanites, who know nothing concerning these things, or even do not believe

---

in the history of the Mulekites. In their great hurry to escape from Jerusalem and the ravages of a conquering enemy who showed no pity, the forefathers of these people failed to take with them a copy of the Hebrew Scriptures as Lehi had done a short while before.

At the time Mosiah I found the descendants of the Jewish prince, Mulek, dwelling in their city, Zarahemla, which was situated on the west banks of the River Sidon, they were a very numerous, but an unenlightened people. Their principal business seems to have been warfare, and consequently many had fallen by the sword. Without the light of *God's Holy Word* to guide them, and bereft of the exhortations of His holy prophets, the Mulekites had continued to sink deeper and deeper into abysmal ignorance of the glories and the mysteries of God. Their language was corrupted because they had no records to preserve their mother tongue. Many even denied the existence of their Creator. However, Mormon tells us in his abridgment that they did exceedingly rejoice, and, that their King, Zarahemla, did also rejoice because the Lord had sent the people of Mosiah with the Plates of Brass "which contained the record of the Jews." We may imagine the joy of the Mulekites at this fresh expression of Divine love. Benjamin told his sons that it was because their Nephite forefathers brought these plates out of Jerusalem with them that they always had the commandments of God before their eyes. These plates, which are sometimes called the *Plates of Laban,* had engraved upon them, in Egyptian characters, the history of God's dealings with those from whom the Lehites had descended. Lehi, it must be remembered, was a scholar. In some way he had come into contact with the Egyptians; he could read their writings; he understood their language, and he was versed in the learning of their wise men.

It must also be remembered that Egypt was then the greatest and the first in nearly all the pursuits of life. In architecture, in astronomy, in commerce, and in government, its people excelled. Lehi could read what was engraven upon the Plates of Brass. He was not forced to leave to a sometimes faulty memory those things that had been written concerning the handiwork of God; nor, was he compelled to rely on hearsay. He conveyed to all his children, and thus to all the generations which followed him, the knowledge he had obtained, and those things he had learned through actual communion with the people of Egypt. His knowledge and understanding of the ways of the Lord was a mighty bastion in the defense of his faith, and proved to be a firm foundation in the instruction of his children. He read to them from these plates how God had always preserved His righteous children from the attacks of the adversary, and that, not by learning and not by might, but by wisdom in keeping the commandments of God, did man know Him.

Without the knowledge these plates contained, King Benjamin emphatically told his sons, they, too, would have become like the Lamanites who knew nothing of the glories of God, and who did not believe them even when they are taught them when they are taught them, because of the traditions of their fathers, which are not correct.

6. O my sons, I would that ye should remember that these sayings are true, and also that these records are true. And behold, also the plates of Nephi, which contain the records and the sayings of our fathers from the time they left Jerusalem until now, and they are true; and we can know of their surety because we have them before our eyes.

7. And now, my sons, I would that ye should remember to search them diligently, that ye may profit thereby; and I would that ye should keep the commandments of God, that ye may prosper in the land according to the promises which the Lord made unto our fathers.

8. And many more things did king Benjamin teach his sons, which are not written in this book.

2. *Mosiah chosen to succeed his father.*

9. And it came to pass that after king Benjamin had made an end of teaching his sons, that he waxed old, and he saw that he

---

them. This deplorable condition was because of the traditions of the Lamanite fathers who had neglected these sacred things.

In addition to the Book of Moses,* which these plates contained, they had engraved on them, the prophecies of Isaiah and a history of the Jews by Samuel and other Hebrew prophets down to the reign of Zedekiah. This included, presumably, the "Psalms of David" and the "Wisdom of Solomon." These represented the "Golden Age of Hebrew Literature."

We may understand, somewhat, of the beauty and the force of the teachings they found written thereon, when we read the wonderful words of the Prophet Samuel. It appears that Saul, the king of the Jews, offered many sacrifices in the hope he would mitigate the severity of any punishment for the disobedience of which he was guilty. Samuel said, "Hath the Lord as great delight in burnt offerings and sacrifices, as in obeying the voice of the Lord? Behold to obey is better than sacrifice, and to hearken than the fat of rams." (I Samuel 15:22) The wise King Solomon said, "Let us hear the conclusion of the whole matter: **Fear God and keep his commandments, for this is the whole duty of man.**" (Eccl. 12:13)

VERSES 6-8. *Behold, also the Plates of Nephi.* King Benjamin, besides exhorting his sons to keep the Lord's commandments, testified to them of the truthfulness of the things written on them, (the Plates of Brass) and he further confirmed the truth of that which is contained upon the Plates of Nephi. "They are true," he said, "and we may know of their surety because we have them before our eyes." In other words, "We can see them; we can handle them, and now I will see to it that you receive all the learning and understanding necessary to know that they tell the truth." "Search them diligently, that ye may profit thereby"; "Keep the commandments of God, that ye may prosper in the land according to the promises which the Lord made unto our fathers." (2 Nephi 1:20)

VERSE 9. *King Benjamin waxed old.* The education of King Benjamin's sons may have been, and probably was, over a period of several years, for we are told

---

*See COMMENTARY ON THE BOOK OF MORMON, Vol. I, p. 205, v. 23.

must very soon go the way of all the earth; therefore, he thought it expedient that he should confer the kingdom upon one of his sons.

10. Therefore, he had Mosiah brought before him; and these are the words which he spake unto him, saying: My son, I would that ye should make a proclamation throughout all this land among all this people, or the people of Zarahemla, and the people of Mosiah who dwell in the land, that thereby they may be gathered together; for on the morrow I shall proclaim unto this my people out of mine own mouth that thou art a king and a ruler over this people, whom the Lord our God hath given us.

11. And moreover, I shall give this people a name, that thereby they may be distinguished above all the people which the Lord God hath brought out of the land of Jerusalem; and this I do because they have been a diligent people in keeping the commandments of the Lord.

---

that when they had been taught "in all the language of his fathers, that thereby they might become men of understanding," King Benjamin saw that he must shortly die. The Sacred Record says, "He waxed old." *Waxed old*, means *grew old*, and although the word *wax* is seldom in modern-day favor, it is good English so to use it. Feeling the infirmities of great age, and realizing that each passing year added burdens to the weight he already carried, King Benjamin deemed it wise to appoint one of his sons to be ruler in his stead.

Verse 10. *King Benjamin had Mosiah brought before him.* King Benjamin knew that his son Mosiah was a just and an upright person. Through him, the king called a conference of all the Saints living in Zarahemla, and also the people over whom Mosiah presided under him. One purpose in having them gather together was, "On the morrow I shall proclaim unto this my people out of mine own mouth that thou art a king and a ruler over this people. . . ." On the morrow, does not necessarily mean *tomorrow*, but may mean *presently*, or *at an early date*.

"*On the Morrow.*" The observation has been made that Zarahemla must have been a small country, if all the people in it could have been notified one day to come to conference at the capital the next day. But that is a too hasty conclusion. For, while *on the morrow* certainly can mean the following twenty-four hours, it also, and very often or frequently, stands for *soon* or *shortly*. For instance, the Lord commanded Lehi to "take his journey" from the Valley of Lemuel "on the morrow." (1 Nephi 16:9) He obeyed by beginning his preparations, but these were not made in a day. (1 Nephi 16:9-12) The same observation is true of the departure of the travelers from the Land Bountiful in Arabia. (1 Nephi 18:5-6) A ship is not loaded and provisioned in one day. In 3 Nephi 1:13 we read that the Lord promised the Prophet Nephi, "On the morrow come I into the world." The people understood that. "They began to know that the Son of God must shortly appear." (Verse 17) Then again, when Jesus told His disciples: "Take therefore no thought for the morrow (3 Nephi 13:24) he did not mean for the next twenty-four hours, but for the future in general. The story in Mosiah shows that this is the meaning of the phrase there. The people heard the proclamation, and prepared to keep its obligations.

Verses 11-12. *I shall give this people a name.* Another purpose of King Benjamin in calling this conference of all the people over whom he reigned, was, that upon them he promised to confer a name, which because of their integrity and diligence

12. And I give unto them a name that never shall be blotted out, except it be through transgression.

13. Yea, and moreover I say unto you, that if this highly favored people of the Lord should fall into transgression, and become a wicked and an adulterous people, that the Lord will deliver them up, that thereby they become weak like unto their brethren; and he will no more preserve them by his matchless and marvelous power, as he has hitherto preserved our fathers.

14. For I say unto you, that if he had not extended his arm in the preservation of our fathers they must have fallen into the hands of the Lamanites, and become victims to their hatred.

3. Mosiah receives the records.

15. And it came to pass that after king Benjamin had made an end of these sayings to his son, that he gave him charge concerning all the affairs of the kingdom.

16. And moreover, he also gave him charge concerning the records which were engraven on the plates of brass; and also the plates of Nephi; and also, the sword of Laban, and the ball or director, which led our fathers through the wilderness, which was prepared by the hand of the Lord that thereby they might be

---

in serving the Lord, they had merited. This name would distinguish them from all other people; it would be a sign to the Lamanites, and the Zoramites, and every other "ite" that, here, the people of King Benjamin served the Lord, that here, they kept the commandments of God. It is of great interest to us to know that as long as they did not transgress the laws of God, that name would always remain with them. That name was yet to be given them.

VERSES 13-14. *If this . . . favored people . . . should fall into transgression . . . the Lord will deliver them up.* The prophet-king foretells the fate of any people, who, having known the Lord, His marvelous ways, and His might, apostatize therefrom, and, who, thus knowingly transgress His laws. "He will deliver them up." Without the strength of His sustaining arm to uphold them, they will become weak, like the Lamanites, who at that time were an idle and a degenerate people. The Lord will not preserve the followers of Laman in their condition of slothfulness, as He had protected the Nephites when they obeyed His laws. Otherwise, King Benjamin says, "They must have fallen into the hands of the Lamanites, and become the victims to their hatred."

King Benjamin recognized the fact that if their forefathers had not repented of evil ways and had not coupled with it a determination to do the Lord's will, they would have been left to their own devices, which at strongest were not very strong. He does not say, but, we know that when left alone, man's utmost strength is absolute weakness, and his wisdom but a mixture of foolishness and folly, when compared to the wisdom and the understanding of the Lord. Frequently the Nephite historians point to this truth expressed here in the words of King Benjamin!

VERSES 15-17. *He gave Mosiah charge of all the affairs of the kingdom.* The abdication of King Benjamin was made less unpleasant, and the assumption of the

led, every one according to the heed and diligence which they gave unto him.

17. Therefore, as they were unfaithful they did not prosper nor progress in their journey, but were driven back, and incurred the displeasure of God upon them; and therefore they were smitten with famine and sore afflictions, to stir them up in remembrance of their duty.

18. And now, it came to pass that Mosiah went and did as his father had commanded him, and proclaimed unto all the people who were in the land of Zarahemla that thereby they might gather themselves together, to go up to the temple to hear the words which his father should speak unto them.

kingly prerogatives by Mosiah made more impressive by the outgoing ruler's handing over to his son and successor, the Plates of Brass, the Plates of Nephi, the Sword of Laban, and the Liahona. Benjamin, here, relates to Mosiah the story of the Liahona; how it worked only by the faith of those of their fathers who gave heed to Him, and were diligent in serving the Lord. (For a discussion of the Liahona, *See* COMMENTARY ON THE BOOK OF MORMON, Vol. I, pp. 187, 188, 274.)

VERSE 18. *Mosiah did as his father commanded him.* Without any delay, Mosiah proceeded to do the things his father desired. He sent a proclamation throughout all the land for the people to meet on the morrow in conference at the temple that had been erected in Zarahemla, where with great joy, the king, as directed by the Lord, would appoint Mosiah to be his successor on the Nephite throne.

King Benjamin had much to declare to his subjects. A spirit of rejoicing spread throughout the land, and an anticipated spiritual feast, caused them, in vast numbers, to respond to the call of King Benjamin. What his message was, and the name he gave to his people, we, in this COMMENTARY, take great joy in relating.

BENJAMIN

The second of the three prophet-kings of the Nephites who reigned in the Land of Zarahemla. He was the son of Mosiah I, and the father of Mosiah II, and like them, was most probably a seer. He undoubtedly held the priesthood, as he received the ministrations of angels, was favored with revelations from the Lord, and organized the Church of Jesus Christ among his people. He was also the custodian of the Sacred Record, etc., having received them from Amaleki, who was childless. The time and place of his birth is not given in the holy writings, though it was probably in the Land of Nephi. He lived to a great age, and died full of peace and honor in Zarahemla, 122 B.C. He is illustrious for the justice and mercy with which he administered the law, for his great devotion to God, and for the love he had for his people. One of his most outstanding qualities was the frugality and simplicity of his personal life which he always maintained. Three of his sons are mentioned by name, Mosiah, Heloram, and Helaman, whom he caused to be educated in all the learning of his fathers, giving special attention to their religious training, and instruction in the history of God's dealings with their forefathers.

The reign of Benjamin was not one of uninterrupted peace. Sometimes during its continuance the aggressive Lamanites, not content with occupying the Land of Nephi, actually followed the Nephites into the Land of Zarahemla, and invaded that also. The war was a fierce one. King Benjamin led his forces, armed with the historic sword of Laban, and with it slew many of the enemy. Benjamin was ultimately successful in driving the invading hosts out of all the regions occupied by his people, with a loss to the Lamanites of many thousands of warriors slain.

The reign of King Benjamin was also troubled with various religious impostors, false Christs, pretended Messiahs and prophets, who caused apostasy and dissensions among the people, much to the sorrow of the good king. However, by the aid of some of the many righteous men who dwelt in his dominions, he exposed the heresies, made manifest the falsity of the claims of the self-styled messiahs and prophets, and restored unity, and faith, and worship, among his subjects, and in such cases where these innovators had broken the civil law, they were arraigned, tried, and punished by that law.

We may presume that the original inhabitants of Zarahemla, just awakening to a newness of religious life, were particularly subject to the influence brought by these impostors. They had but lately learned the mysteries of the Plan of Salvation, and of the coming of the Messiah to dwell among the sons of men. The glory and the beauty of this divine advent filled their new-born souls with joyous hope. Looking forward for the arrival of that happy day, with their first love undiminished and their zeal unslackened, they were especially open to the deceptions of those who cried, "Lo, the Christ is come!" or, "Behold, a great prophet hath arisen!"

There was another class, who, moved by the spirit of unrest, were a source of perplexity to the king. They were those who, having left the Land of Nephi with the righteous, still permitted their thoughts and affections to be drawn towards their former homes and old associations. The natural consequence was that they were constantly agitating the idea of organizing expeditions to visit their old homes. The first of these that actually started, of which we have an account, fought among themselves with such fury that all were slain except fifty men, who, in shame and sorrow, returned to Zarahemla to recount the miserable end of their expedition. Yet some remained unsatisfied and under the leadership of a man named Zeniff another company started on the ill-advised journey. Nothing was heard of them while Benjamin reigned.

When King Benjamin was well stricken with years, the Lord directed him to consecrate his son, Mosiah, to be his successor on the Nephite throne. Feeling that age was impairing his energies, he directed his son to gather the people together at the temple that had been erected in Zarahemla, and he would give them his parting instructions. (125 B.C.) Agreeable to this call the people gathered at the temple, but so numerous had they grown that it was too small to hold them. They also brought with them the firstlings of their flocks that they might offer sacrifices and burn offerings according to the Mosaic law. As the assembled thousands could not get inside the temple, they pitched their tents by families, every one with its door towards the building, and the king had a tower erected near the temple from which he spoke.

The teachings of King Benjamin at these meetings were some of the most divine and glorious ever uttered by man. He preached to his hearers the pure principles of the Gospel — the duty which man owed to his God, and to his fellows. He also told them how he had been visited by an angel, and what wonderful things the angel had shown him concerning the coming of the God of Israel to dwell with men in the flesh.

When King Benjamin had made an end of speaking the words which had been delivered to him by the angel, he observed that the power of his testimony had so worked upon the Nephites that they, in the deep sense of their own unworthiness, had fallen to the ground. Then and there, they cried out confessing their faith in the coming Messiah, and pleading that through his atoning blood they might receive the forgiveness of their sins, and that their hearts might be purified. After they had lifted their deep-felt cry to heaven, the Spirit of the Lord came down upon them, and because of their exceeding faith, they received a remission of their sins. When the king had finished his discourse he gave them a new name, because of the covenant they desired to make, which thing he greatly desired. The name they were to bear forever after was the name of Christ, which should never be blotted out except through transgression. Thus, was established the first Christian Church in Zarahemla (125 B.C.), for every soul who heard these teachings (except the little children who could not understand) entered into this sacred covenant with God, which most of them kept and faithfully observed to the end of their mortal lives.

King Benjamin's truly royal work was now done. He had lived to bring his people into communion with their Creator; his spirit was full of heavenly joy, but his body trembled under the weight of many years. So before he dismissed the multitude, he consecrated his son, Mosiah, to be their king, appointed priests to instruct the people in the ways of the Lord, and with his patriarchal blessing dismissed his subjects. Then, according to their respective families they all departed for their own homes.

Mosiah now reigned in his father's stead, while Benjamin, beloved and honored, remained yet another three years on the earth before he returned to the presence of his Father in Heaven.

MOSIAH II

The third king of the Nephites in the land of Zarahemla where he was born B.C. 154; he was consecrated king by his father *Benjamin* B. C. 124 and died in Zarahemla, B.C. 91, aged 63 years. He came to the throne under most happy circumstances: he had the full confidence of his subjects who were a righteous, God-fearing people, the Lamanites were at peace with the Nephites and internal development and prosperity characterized the condition of his kingdom. Individually he proved to be one of the greatest and best of kings; his whole energies were devoted to the good of his people, and they loved him with an intensity of affection scarcely equaled in the annals of any race. In the fourth year of his reign the expedition under *Ammon* started which resulted in the return to Zarahemla of nearly all the living descendants of the company that left under *Zeniff* to re-occupy the land of Lehi-Nephi. The leader of one of these companies was *Alma*, the elder, whom Mosiah called to take charge of the church in Zarahemla. Soon after the arrival of these fugitives from the land of Nephi, Mosiah gathered all the people together and had them made acquainted with the vicissitudes and sorrows through which the newcomers had passed since their fathers left Zarahemla. Also taking advantage of the presence of so many of his subjects he addressed them on such matters as he deemed necessary and desirable. At his request Alma also taught them. When assembled in large bodies Alma went from one multitude to another preaching repentance and faith in the Lord; afterwards, by Mosiah's direction, he went through the land organizing and establishing churches and ordaining priests and teachers over every church. Thus were seven churches established at this time in the land of Zarahemla.

In the course of years many of the rising generation gave no heed to the word of God. These were mostly such as were too young to enter into covenant with the Lord at the time that Benjamin anointed Mosiah to be his successor. Not only did they themselves reject the doctrines of the atonement, the resurrection and other Gospel principles but they led away many who were members of the Church and sorely persecuted those who remained faithful to God and his laws. Encouraged by the fact that four of Mosiah's sons and one of Alma's were leaders in this crusade they paid no attention to the national law which guaranteed freedom of conscience to all men alike. By divine interposition, through a holy angel, these young men were turned from the error of their way and afterwards became strong pillars in the church and messengers of salvation to both Nephites and Lamanites. The four sons of Mosiah (named *Aaron, Ammon, Omner and Himni*) not content with their zealous labors among their countrymen proposed to go and labor among the Lamanites. The good king, like many of his subjects, did not favorably regard this proposal. He feared for the lives of his sons but having inquired of the Lord and received assurances of heavenly protection he gladly let them go.

Mosiah now felt that it was time that the question of the succession of the throne should be settled. In his magnanimity he sent among the people to learn whom they would have for their king. The people chose his son Aaron but Aaron would not accept the royal power, his heart was set upon the conversion of his fellow-men to the knowledge of the Gospel. This refusal troubled the mind of Mosiah; he apprehended difficulties if Aaron at some future time should change his mind and demand his rights. Mosiah therefore issued another address in which he proposed to retain the kingdom during the remainder of his life after which the Nephites should be governed by judges elected by themselves. In other respects also Mosiah consented to newly arrange the affairs of the people and, if we may so express it, to codify the laws. This code became the constitution of the nation under the rule of the Judges which limited the powers of the officials and guaranteed the rights of the people. This compilation was acknowledged by the people whereupon the historian remarks "Therefore they were obliged to abide by the laws which he had made" and from that time they became supreme throughout the nation. It is stated in another place that this change was made by the direct command of Jehovah. But besides being a king Mosiah was also a seer. The gift of interpreting strange tongues and languages was his. By this gift he translated from the twenty-four plates of gold, found by the people of King Limhi, the record of the Jaredites. No wonder that a man possessed of such gifts, so just and merciful in the administration of the law, so perfect in his private life, should be esteemed more than any man by his subjects and that they waxed strong in their love towards him. As a king he was a father to them but as a prophet, seer and revelator he was the source from whence divine wisdom flowed unto them.

His sons having started on their missions to the Lamanites (B.C. 91) Mosiah gave the sacred plates and the associate holy things into the care of the younger Alma and the same year passed away to the rest of the Just.

CHAPTER 2

1. King Benjamin Builds a Tower from which He Addresses His People.

1. King Benjamin builds a tower from which he addresses his people.

1. And it came to pass that after Mosiah had done as his father had commanded him, and had made a proclamation throughout all the land, that the people gathered themselves together throughout all the land, that they might go up to the temple to hear the words which king Benjamin should speak unto them.

2. And there were a great number, even so many that they did not number them; for they had multiplied exceedingly and waxed great in the land.

3. And they also took of the firstlings of their flocks, that they might offer sacrifice and burnt offerings according to the law of Moses;

4. And also that they might give thanks to the Lord their God, who had brought them out of the land of Jerusalem, and who had delivered them out of the hands of their enemies, and had appointed just men to be their teachers, and also a just man to be their king, who had established peace in the land of Zarahemla, and who had taught them to keep the commandments of God, that they might rejoice and be filled with love towards God and all men.

VERSES 1-8. *Multitudes being so great, King Benjamin built a tower so all could hear his words.* The people heard the proclamation; then they began to gather in Zarahemla on the day appointed. They brought with them the firstlings of their flocks and their choicest young bullocks so that they might offer sacrifices and burnt offerings according to the Law of Moses, which they had been taught to observe. They came in such numbers that they were not to be counted. The king expected no such a multitude. Under the wise rule of King Benjamin, they had prospered greatly, both in numbers and in material.

We may surmise the great response to the call of Mosiah. The people loved King Benjamin who had been as a father to them. He had protected them when, from within and without, their enemies assailed them with false claims to proper conduct. He guided them aright. Now he was bowed down with the weight of many years and trembled under the responsibilities he carried, and would soon go to his God who had, in wisdom, appointed him to be their king. They welcomed the time when they could meet together and, as one, hear from his own lips, the words telling of God's wonderful ways. They hoped to be where they could hear his parting instructions. They gathered in Zarahemla with songs of joy and thanksgiving. All were imbued with the holy impulse, "I will rejoice in the Lord, I will joy in the God of my Salvation." "Thanks be to God," their historian wrote, "who had brought them out of Jerusalem, and who had delivered them out of the hands of their enemies, and had appointed just men to be their teachers, and also a just man to be their king."

They rejoiced that Benjamin was their king. By example and by precept he had taught them to keep the laws of God, that thereby they might take delight in

5. And it come to pass that when they came up to the temple, they pitched their tents round about, every man according to his family, consisting of his wife, and his sons, and his daughters, and their sons, and their daughters, from the eldest down to the youngest, every family being separate one from another.

6. And they pitched their tents round about the temple, every man having his tent with the door thereof towards the temple, that thereby they might remain in their tents and hear the words which king Benjamin should speak unto them;

7. For the multitude being so great that king Benjamin could not teach them all within the walls of the temple, therefore he caused a tower to be erected, that thereby his people might hear the words which he should speak unto them.

8. And it came to pass that he began to speak to his people from the tower; and they could not all hear his words because of the greatness of the multitude; therefore he caused that the words which he spake should be written and sent forth among those that were not under the sound of his voice, that they might also receive his words.

---

serving the Lord, "and be filled with love towards God and all men." Their hearts overflowed with gratitude to the Great Giver of all these things. "O magnify the Lord with me, and let us exalt His name together," (Psalm 34:3) was the righteous desire of their hearts, and in the end, the purpose of the conference they held in Zarahemla.

May we suggest the advice given to Moses by his father-in-law, Jethro, the priest of Midian, concerning the Children of Israel, which advice Moses accepted. Jethro said, "Thou shalt provide out of all the people able men, such as fear God, men of truth, hating covetousness; and place such over them, to be rulers. . . ." (Exodus 18:21) Such a man was Benjamin!

Agreeable to the call that was made, the people, as we have noted, gathered in Zarahemla. So many came that the temple could not hold them. The plan had been to hold the general assemblies within its walls. So that more of those attending the sessions could hear his instructions, King Benjamin had a tower, or platform, erected, from which he spoke. This proved not to be enough, although the many visitors there pitched their tents around the temple lot, each tent with its opening facing the sacred building so that the people there could remain within their tents and hear what might be said. Even this arrangement was not sufficient to accommodate everyone. To instruct them King Benjamin had his words written down and distributed among those who were not within "sound of his voice, that they might also receive his words."

The sermons preached by King Benjamin at these meetings were some of the most divine and glorious recorded in the sacred annals of any people. They show, in his own life, the development of the loftiest conception of man's relationship to God, that is, "The Fatherhood of God, and the brotherhood of man."

The realization of that great truth came to him through his service to others. He testified to them that God had kept and preserved him, to "serve you with all the might, mind and strength which the Lord hath granted unto me." The most menial of his subjects, he said, was like unto him in the sight of that God, before

9. And these are the words which he spake and caused to be written, saying: My brethren, all ye that have assembled yourselves together, you that can hear my words which I shall speak unto you this day; for I have not commanded you to come up hither to trifle with the words which I shall speak, but that you should hearken unto me, and open your ears that ye may hear, and your hearts that ye may understand, and your minds that the mysteries of God may be unfolded to your view.

10. I have not commanded you to come up hither that ye should fear me, or that ye should think that I of myself am more than a mortal man.

11. But I am like as yourselves, subject to all manner of infirmities in body and mind; yet I have been chosen by this people, and consecrated by my father, and was suffered by the hand of the Lord that I should be a ruler and a king over this people; and have been kept and preserved by his matchless power, to serve you with all the might, mind and strength which the Lord hath granted unto me.

12. I say unto you that as I have been suffered to spend my days in your service, even up to this time, and have not sought gold nor silver nor any manner of riches of you;

---

whom there is no inequality or rank. His sermons reveal to our senses, what *Prof. Henri Bergson** says, are conditions, "consistent with the satisfaction of our highest ideals." These conditions were, everywhere, to be met, and King Benjamin even went so far as to labor with his own hands in order to be an example, that his people should not be grieved with burdensome taxes and tasks that would end in their being slaves to the taskmaster, or victims of the tyrant's oppression.

VERSES 9-15. *And these are the words which he spake.* Saying, "My brethren," is a wonderful example of the humility and grace of King Benjamin's character. He thus approached them over whom he ruled, as "My brethren," and not like one who because of station, ascribes to himself, honor, and majesty. "Brethren" is the distinction he applied to those, who like himself, kept the Lord's commandments. There is nothing that equalizes men more than walking together in the paths of righteousness. In God's justice there is no inequality or inferiority among those who stand before Him, save as to them who do, and them who do not, obey His Laws. We remember the words of Micah: "He hath shewed thee, O man, what is good; and what doth the Lord require of thee, but to do justly, and to love mercy, and to walk humbly with thy God." (Micah 6:8) To walk humbly with God, makes the rough places, *smooth,* and the journey, *sweet.*

In perusing this sermon of King Benjamin's, we are impressed with the nobility of his teachings; he says, "that ye might understand." Operating with his words, and raising them to sublime heights one can feel the warmth of brotherly love and kindness which unites all men in the spirit of the Gospel of Jesus Christ. He preached to them of Christ's atoning Sacrifice. They looked forward to His coming, and they kept the Law of Moses because they saw in it the likeness of Him who would bring them Salvation. Looking forward to the Messiah was to them as

---

*Late Professor of Philosophy, University of Paris.

13. Neither have I suffered that ye should be confined in dungeons, nor that ye should make slaves one of another, nor that ye should murder, or plunder, or steal, or commit adultery; nor even have I suffered that ye should commit any manner of wickedness, and have taught you that ye should keep the commandments of the Lord, in all things which he hath commanded you—

14. And even I, myself, have labored with mine own hands that I might serve you, and that ye should not be laden with taxes, and that there should nothing come upon you which was grievous to be borne—and of all these things which I have spoken, ye yourselves are witnesses this day.

15. Yet, my brethren, I have not done these things that I might boast, neither do I tell these things that thereby I might accuse you; but I tell you these things that ye may know that I can answer a clear conscience before God this day.

---

effective as it is for us to look back. (Jarom 1:14) They were united in all good things.

For unity to be lasting and real, it must be upheld and sustained by righteousness. When men combine in evil, it is recognized as intrigue and conspiracy; when they unite with no fixed purpose, it is merely coalition. But the tie that bound together King Benjamin's people was not a plot, nor a scheme that would end with success or failure according to the strength or weakness of those involved. It was love — love of the Word of God, love of truth, and love for one another. This unity was innate in Benjamin and his followers. It recalls the words of the Psalmist, "How good and how pleasant it is for brethren to dwell together in unity."

To develop this unity of purpose, Benjamin did not use harsh, disciplinary measures. He was not tyrannical or arbitrary. He had not caused any man to be confined in dungeons, nor had he suffered any of them to be made slaves*. He labored with his own hands to provide the necessary things of life; he had sought neither gold nor silver from them by way of taxes, which to the poor among them might be grievous or oppressive. Through all this he taught them to keep the commandments of God. He did not boast these things, nor did he offer any apologies, pretexts, or excuses for his past; he entered calmly and even joyously on the prospects of answering before God for that which he had encouraged to be done.

The righteous behavior of the Nephites under King Benjamin, we may conclude, was the outgrowth of common principles, the reciprocity of mutual affections, "the inspiration of the heart, not the discipline of the rod." Jesus said, "Draw near unto me, and I will draw near unto you"; we should not forget that the nearer we are to God, the nearer we are to one another. This seems to have been the case with Benjamin's people. They were united in serving the Lord, and, together they were united as one big family of brethren in obeying and honoring His prophet. When we consider King Benjamin's salutation, "My Brethren," we recall the words of Jesus, our Redeemer, "Whosoever shall do the will of my Father which is in heaven the same is my . . . brother."

---

*From the words of King Benjamin, we learn that slavery was forbidden. The Nephites, being of the House of Israel, could not observe the Law of Moses and enslave their brethren.

16. Behold, I say unto you that because I said unto you that I had spent my days in your service, I do not desire to boast, for I have only been in the service of God.

17. And behold, I tell you these things that ye may learn wisdom; that ye may learn that when ye are in the service of your fellow beings ye are only in the service of your God.

18. Behold, ye have called me your king; and if I, whom ye call your king, do labor to serve you, then ought not ye to labor to serve one another?

VERSES 16-17. *I have only been in the service of God.* To serve God, means, among many other things, a daily sacrifice on our part of all selfish longings. To minister to the needs of His children is but a "thank-offering" to God for the blessings we receive from Him; in serving others we put to the highest use the things He has entrusted to our care. We thus become His servants; we do His will. In past ages of the world, God's servants did not oppress His children, nor were any considered more mighty than were others, save those who in *might* sought to do His will and yearned to be in His service. It is good to remember that none were ever overcome who put their trust in the Great Father of us all by ministering to His children, our fellows. The service we render to God is measured in the same terms, and by the same *rod* with which we serve one another. We should always keep in our minds, that to serve Him is perfect freedom, and to worship Him is life's greatest happiness and its true satisfaction. King Benjamin said, "In my days of service to you . . . I have only been in the service of God." In serving His children we may become poorer in the things of the world, but, we will be richer in heavenly treasures.

In King Benjamin's sermons, no lessons are more boldly proclaimed than is this lesson of service. The conclusion is not to be escaped that we serve God best by sharing with the needy the gifts we receive from His bounteous hands, by showing compassion for the distressed, by upholding the falling, by loosing the bound. Truly, we can ennoble our lives no more graciously than by serving God with deeds of loving-kindness to our fellow men.

VERSE 17. *I tell you . . . that you may learn wisdom.* In King Solomon's Book of the Proverbs we read, "The fear of the Lord, that is wisdom." That means *wisdom* is in doing His Will; it lies in serving God. Whether it is in the home, in the schoolroom, out in the open spaces, or elsewhere, our service to God, manifest in the aid we render to our fellows, adds to the total of wisdom with which we eventually will be crowned.

"Love one another," was the cardinal principle that permeated the entire mission of our Savior. "God so loved the world . . ." is the reason for man's redemption. King Benjamin was truly conscious that God is the loving Father of all men; he taught his people, "When you are in the service of your fellow beings ye are in the service of your God!" The Lord is the strength of all who serve Him, and the praise of them that love to do His will. Herein is wisdom. "Happy is the man that findeth wisdom, and the man that obtaineth understanding."

VERSE 18. *Then ought not ye to labor to serve one another?* Here, King Benjamin draws an astute comparison between his life of helpful devotion to his people, and the obligation they have to aid one another. He said, in effect, "I, whom ye call your king, have spent all my days ministering to your wants, in bringing you" succor, according to the hour and the power of your needs, and, for it, "I ask of you nothing, no recompense save that you serve God," "then ought not ye to labor to serve one another?"

19. And behold also, if I, whom ye call your king, who has spent his days in your service, and yet has been in the service of God, do merit any thanks from you, O how you ought to thank your heavenly King!

20. I say unto you, my brethren, that if you should render all the thanks and praise which your whole soul has power to possess, to that God who has created you, and has kept and preserved you, and has caused that ye should rejoice, and has granted that ye should live in peace one with another.

21. I say unto you that if ye should serve him who has created you from the beginning, and is preserving you from day to day, by lending you breath, that ye may live and move and do according to your own will, and even supporting you from one moment to another—I say, if ye should serve him with all your whole souls yet ye would be unprofitable servants.

22. And behold, all that he requires of you is to keep his commandments; and he has promised you that if ye would keep his commandments ye should prosper in the land; and he never doth vary from that which he hath said; therefore, if ye do keep his commandments he doth bless you and prosper you.

VERSE 19. *O how you ought to thank your heavenly King.* "If I, Benjamin, your earthly king, by serving you, merit any thanks," "O how you ought to thank your heavenly King" for the blessings He constantly bestows.

VERSES 20-21. *Ye would be unprofitable servants.* Benjamin, here, reminds his listeners of a great truth, we, ourselves, constantly lose sight of — that is the greatness of God, and the nothingness of man. He extols the might and power of God which is shown by Him bestowing His tender mercies upon them. Life itself, His watchful care over them, the food they eat, the clothes they wear, His sustaining arm, and above these things which He abundantly provides, He sends *Peace,* His most precious gift. Truly, King Benjamin's people drank deeply of the waters of peace which flowed down upon them in a river of righteousness.

But, King Benjamin says that no strength of their own, no power inherent in themselves, could render unto the Great Giver of all these things, praise and thanksgiving equal to the end thereof. If we, he said, should attempt to pay the Lord in full for the blessings He with unending grace supplies by serving Him to the utmost of our ability, we would still be "unprofitable servants."

VERSE 22. *And behold, all that he requires of you is to keep his commandments.* The words and phrases, *behold, and it came to pass, now I say unto you,* and some others, were commonly used by ancient Hebrew writers. This custom was carried on by the Nephites.

Now, let us put ourselves in the position of Benjamin's people, and ponder our inability to repay the Lord for his goodness. What would be our reaction to any demand for payment? We have already quoted the words of the prophet, "He hath shewed thee, O man, what is good; and what doth the Lord require of thee, but to do justly, and to love mercy, and to walk humbly with thy God." (Micah 6:8) But, we have noted, "to walk humbly with thy God," means to keep His commandments. This is what the Lord desires, King Benjamin, as well as many other holy men, emphasize. He expects no more, He will accept no less.

23. And now, in the first place, he hath created you, and granted unto you your lives, for which ye are indebted unto him.

24. And secondly, he doth require that ye should do as he hath commanded you; for which if ye do, he doth immediately bless you; and therefore he hath paid you. And ye are still indebted unto him, and are, and will be, forever and ever; therefore, of what have ye to boast?

25. And now I ask, can ye say aught of yourselves? I answer you, Nay. Ye cannot say that ye are even as much as the dust of the earth; yet ye were created of the dust of the earth; but behold, it belongeth to him who created you.

26. And I, even I, whom ye call your king, am no better than ye yourselves are; for I am also of the dust. And ye behold that I am old, and am about to yield up this mortal frame to its mother earth.

27. Therefore, as I said unto you that I had served you, walking with a clear conscience before God, even so I at this time have caused that ye should assemble yourselves together, that I might be found blameless, and that your blood should not come upon me,

---

Benjamin's statement to his people, "that ye may live and move and do according to your own will," (v. 21) reminds us of our *Free Agency*, being "free forever, knowing good from evil; to act for" ourselves "and not to be acted upon." (2 Nephi 2:26-27) But, we are also reminded, "That to serve Him is perfect freedom, and to worship Him, the soul's purest happiness."

VERSES 23-24. *He hath created you.* There are two things to begin with, Benjamin told his people, all of whom were members of God's Church, which you, if you labored forever, could not pay back. First, he said, *"He created you,"* and gave you life. Secondly, *He demands obedience* to His laws. (v. 22) Here is another lesson for us to learn. It does not matter to what heights we climb, or to the depths into which we descend, the riches of the earth we acquire, or the joys we entertain; in spite of what we are and the worldly goods we accumulate, we are only the custodians of them; He is the owner, and we are the keepers whether good or bad. We can boast of nothing.

VERSES 25-27. *Can ye say aught of yourselves?* King Benjamin reminded his people of a fact they knew well. It is contained in the Hebrew Scriptures, copies of which they had made from the Brass Plates of Laban. In them was the story of man's Creation. The Scriptures were the constant guides and the companions of the Nephites. A knowledge of them was a large portion of their learning, as it was to the Jews in Jerusalem. They knew they were created out of the dust of the earth, and sooner or later, would return thereto. They knew they lived only as *tenants* in a grand and glorious Creation. All they had, and even that of which they were made was borrowed from Him who is the Creator of all, and to whom everything belongs.

King Benjamin's people understood his words and realized their humble station in life. Again they reasoned among themselves — "The greatness of God, and the nothingness of men." (*See,* Mosiah 4:11)

Though Benjamin was a righteous leader whom they called their *king*, yet, he told them, he was like unto them, made of dust. He was getting old, he said, and

when I shall stand to be judged of God of the things whereof he hath commanded me concerning you.

28. I say unto you that I have caused that ye should assemble yourselves together that I might rid my garments of your blood, at this period of time when I am about to go down to my grave, that I might go down in peace, and my immortal spirit may join the choirs above in singing the praises of a just God.

in a few years would give back to its source, the body they then beheld, the body of Benjamin, their King. Notwithstanding his regal calling, his end on earth was like that of all men — a return to dust.

As one of them who was about to die, and whose spirit would then return to God who created it, Benjamin told his subjects that he had called them together to end his active service to them, which with a clear conscience before God he had diligently performed. He desired to again bear witness of God's goodness and mercy, and to testify to them once more of the Messiah who would Redeem mankind from the effects of Adam's great sin. He did not want any dereliction of his to be an excuse for one of them to urge *lack of knowledge*, let alone to commit sin. He would stand before God, on the Day of Judgment, knowing well that he had fulfilled every command of the Lord in instructing his people.

VERSE 28. *And my immortal spirit may join the choirs above.* Benjamin, here, expresses the desire to be fully prepared to "join the choirs above." Compare Mormon 7:7, where we are told that those who are found guiltless will have the privilege of dwelling in the presence of God, and singing "ceaseless praises with the choirs above."

Does it seem improbable that there are choirs in the realm inhabited by the redeemed? The ability to sing and to compose and play music is a divine gift. The very purpose of it is to enable man to praise the Lord and to glorify His name. There is no music so inspiring, so elevating, so refining, as sacred music, and it is a great question whether any other kind, especially martial music, is not best characterized as a poor, worthless imitation.

We know that John the Beloved, on several occasions in his Apocalyptic visions, became aware of singing and music of heavenly origin. (Rev. 5:9; 14:3; 15:3) We also know that at the time of the birth of our Lord, a heavenly host sang praises to God, audible to mortal ear. (Luke 2:13-14)

And here, let me,* in all humility, place on record that to my own personal knowledge, singing and music were heard in the Manti Temple at the time of its dedication. On two separate occasions I had the privilege of hearing the super-earthly harmonies. The first was just before the beginning of the services on the day I attended. It sounded as a very distant organ music, for a brief moment, as if a door had been opened and then almost immediately closed. The second occasion was a few days later, when I was preparing to perform some ordinance work for some of my friends on the other side. It sounded as the singing of male voices, also for a brief moment, and came as from a far distance. There were other manifestations during those days, never to be forgotten. During the service I noticed that some of the Twelve, notably Elder Heber J. Grant, the late President of the Church, and also John W. Taylor, were surrounded by rays of light, resembling the colors of the rainbow, only softer.

Yes, there are choirs on the other side, and bands, and John describes their performances as "the voice of many waters, and as the voice of a great thunder: . . . and the voice of harpers harping with their harps." (Rev. 14:2)

*Janne M. Sjodahl

29. And moreover, I say unto you that I have caused that ye should assemble yourselves together, that I might declare unto you that I can no longer be your teacher, nor your king;

30. For even at this time, my whole frame doth tremble exceedingly while attempting to speak unto you; but the Lord God doth support me, and hath suffered me that I should speak unto you, and hath commanded me that I should declare unto you this day, that my son Mosiah is a king and a ruler over you.

31. And now, my brethren, I would that ye should do as ye have hitherto done. As ye have kept my commandments, and also the commandments of my father, and have prospered, and have been kept from falling into the hands of your enemies, even so if ye shall keep the commandments of my son, or the commandments of God which shall be delivered unto you by him, ye shall prosper in the land, and your enemies shall have no power over you.

32. But, O my people, beware lest there shall arise contentions

---

VERSES 29-30. *I can no longer be your . . . king.* King Benjamin called this conference of all the Saints dwelling in his domain just three years before he died. The record does not say when he was born, nor where. We presume it was in the Land of Lehi-Nephi where his father, Mosiah, at the command of the Lord, gathered the righteous into one large group, and led them to Zarahemla where they found the People of Mulek. He passed away in that city 122 B.C., greatly mourned and much loved by his subjects. Benjamin lived for many years, and ruled his people in the fear of the Lord.

No people, ever, were ruled by a king more gracious than was Benjamin. He labored constantly for their well-being, and for their spiritual happiness; he continued nearly all the days of his life to be their untiring servant.

But, now his old and worn frame could no longer support his desire to carry on. He trembled as one having the palsy; his enfeebled body refused to stand alone. King Benjamin, dwelling in that poor, dilapidated, and decrepit, old house, the body of Benjamin the High Priest, solemnly bowed before "The Majesty on High" and before his devoted people he acknowledged the Lord's watchful care over him. At the same time Benjamin declared, "I can no longer be your teacher, or your king." He also said, in a manner appropriate to his exalted calling, "The Lord hath commanded me that I should declare unto you this day, that my son Mosiah is a king and a ruler over you."

VERSE 31. *Keep the commandments of God which shall be delivered to you by my son.* Among King Benjamin's parting instructions was an appeal to his devoted people that they follow their newly appointed King's advice and counsel. Just as they had observed his very own, and also as they had hearkened to the words of Mosiah I, who was Benjamin's father, they should attend to Mosiah's commandments which would come to them from God.

As in the past when their fathers kept the Lord's commandments they were benefited and blessed, Benjamin promised similar prosperity, and added the further assurance, "Your enemies shall have no power over you."

VERSES 32-33. *Beware . . . ye list to obey the evil spirit.* The word, *list*, as used here, is archaic, or antiquated. It is not used in ordinary conversation. Its

among you, and ye list to obey the evil spirit, which was spoken of by my father Mosiah.

33. For behold, there is a wo pronounced upon him who listeth to obey that spirit; for if he listeth to obey him, and remaineth and dieth in his sins, the same drinketh damnation to his own soul; for he receiveth for his wages an everlasting punishment, having transgressed the law of God contrary to his own knowledge.

34. I say unto you, that there are not any among you, except it be your little children that have not been taught concerning these things, but what knoweth that ye are eternally indebted to your heavenly Father, to render to him all that you have and are; and also have been taught concerning the records which contain the prophecies which have been spoken by the holy prophets, even down to the time our father, Lehi, left Jerusalem;

35. And also, all that has been spoken by our fathers until now. And behold, also, they spake that which was commanded them of the Lord; therefore, they are just and true.

---

meaning has, however, been preserved in Scriptural writings, in poetry, and sometimes in legal documents. Here, it means *hearken, heed,* or *attend to.*

In these verses King Benjamin warned his faithful people against heeding the suggestions offered by evil-doers who sought to stir up strife and angry passions among them. He made known to them the awful consequences of such folly. He decried contention, and we imagine he reminded them of their community of interests and the responsibilities they owed to one another. If any were beguiled into committing error, and persisted in sin, dying therein, and not having repented therefrom, he pronounced *wo.* That one cannot, Benjamin said, transgress God's Laws willfully and knowingly, without, at last, obtaining as wages for intentional disobedience "an everlasting punishment" which is sure to come.

The designs of Satan and his wicked servants is to rend asunder the just and benevolent purposes of Almighty God. They are servants of evil. They know that "In unity there is strength"; they also know that *dissension* is a prolific progenitress; and that one of her offspring is *doubt. Doubt,* itself, begets *sin.* It excuses evil-doers by refusing to recognize proper *authority;* and by denying and deriding the *good,* the *just,* and the *pure.*

Uncertainty in the minds of God's children, and dissension among them, no matter how little, will prolong the coming of that *Day* when the knowledge of the Lord shall fill the earth.

VERSES 34-35. *There are not any among you . . . that have not been taught concerning these things.* Continuing his discourse, Benjamin reminded his listeners that from their childhood days, when first they began to understand Gospel principles and saw them in the beauties of God's boundless glory, they had been taught to love and to fear Him. Endless proof of His goodness and mercy toward them fortified Benjamin's people in their resolve to render to God "all they have and are." In doing so, a payment was made on a debt they eternally owed to their Heavenly Father who had created them, and who, in His great love, gave them life.

Benjamin's people could not avoid the reasoned judgment that his words were true, because they had before them the records of the Jews which told them of

36. And now, I say unto you, my brethren, that after ye have known and have been taught all these things, if ye should transgress and go contrary to that which has been spoken, that ye do withdraw yourselves from the Spirit of the Lord, that it may have no place in you to guide you in wisdom's paths that ye may be blessed, prospered, and preserved—

37. I say unto you, that the man that doeth this, the same cometh out in open rebellion against God; therefore he listeth to obey the evil spirit, and becometh an enemy to all righteousness; therefore, the Lord has no place in him, for he dwelleth not in unholy temples.

38. Therefore if that man repenteth not, and remaineth and dieth an enemy to God, the demands of divine justice do awaken his immortal soul to a lively sense of his own guilt, which doth cause him to shrink from the presence of the Lord, and doth fill his breast with guilt, and pain, and anguish, which is like an unquenchable fire, whose flame ascendeth up forever and ever.

39. And now I say unto you, that mercy hath no claim on that man; therefore his final doom is to endure a never-ending torment.

40. O, all ye old men, and also

God's marvelous ways and His unending purpose. Even down to the reign of Zedekiah, the last of Judah's kings, the words of their holy prophets were written "with a pen of iron, and with the point of a diamond," (Jeremiah 17:1) upon the plates Lehi had brought from Jerusalem.

These plates, or copies of them, were available to all the Nephites, and of course, they became familiar with the promises of the Lord given by His Hebrew servants.

Besides these, the Nephites had in their possession, the records of their fathers, also engraven on metal plates. In them were written the things God had commanded His Nephite servants to proclaim. Their exhortations to the righteous, their rebukes of the wicked, and their many blessings, were all included in the chronicles upon these plates which had been handed down by each generation of their ancestors, and now were in the care of King Benjamin.

King Benjamin's people knew that what was written on these plates was true, and further, they also knew that the Lord who had directed the assemblage of them was "just and true" in all His ways.

VERSES 36-39. *After you have known all these things the man that doeth contrary is in open rebellion against God.* King Benjamin now summed up the many points he had made in the foregoing part of his inspiring and inspiriting address. He admonished his people, that now after you have received all this written testimony, and have been taught from your youth that it is true, the burden of carrying forth the work of the Lord rests upon the shoulders of each one of you.

He said to them, "do not withdraw yourselves from the Spirit of the Lord," that thereby you may be led in "wisdom's paths." Learn to listen to that still small voice which comes from the Father to lead, and to direct, and to warn of things to come. Undoubtedly King Benjamin remembered the words of the Psalmist which he had read on the brass plates of Laban: Create in me a clean heart, O God; and renew a steadfast spirit within me. Cast me not away from thy presence;

ye young men, and you little children who can understand my words, for I have spoken plainly unto you that ye might understand, I pray that ye should awake to a remembrance of the awful situation of those that have fallen into transgression.

41. And moreover, I would desire that ye should consider on the blessed and happy state of those that keep the commandments of God. For behold, they are blessed in all things, both temporal and spiritual; and if they hold out faithful to the end they are received into heaven, that thereby they may dwell with God in a state of never-ending happiness. O remember, remember that these things are true; for the Lord God hath spoken it.

---

and take not thy spirit from me. Restore unto me the joy of thy salvation, and let a willing spirit uphold me. (Psalm 51:10-12 Jewish Rendition). Then you will be preserved and prospered, and your prayers will be answered in blessings on your heads.

But if, he said, on the contrary, you reject the knowledge you have received, and refuse to obey God's commands, you become an enemy to Him. All thoughts of Him you reduce to excuses for your actions, and soon you will recall your words in His praise.

Little by little, such a man "listeth" to the *evil spirit;* he becomes dead to all righteousness, and hardened to the demands of justice. He, himself, forces God's Holy Spirit to leave his unworthy body, for "He dwelleth not in unholy temples." This man, unless he repents and turns to God, lives and dies His enemy. Conscience, that court of righteous and holy decisions which is folded up in the bosoms of all of us, awakens in him a "lively sense of his own guilt," thus removing from him the desire to mingle with those who serve the Lord and who seek to do His will. In other words, "He is the author of his own damnation." There is only one end to him, he receives a just reward for his sins, "which is like an unquenchable fire, whose flame ascendeth up forever and ever." That means just this: a sinner by his transgressions, loses certain privileges and blessings accruing to the righteous for their faithful performance of duty. The sinner may later repent and obtain the promised forgiveness of his trespasses, but he can never regain the place he lost when he was beguiled into by-and-forbidden paths. In the "strait and narrow way," he finds himself far behind those who have remained unwavering and true to God's commands. He cannot overtake them. Thus, forever, he lags behind them; behind those who were "firm and steadfast, and immovable in keeping the commandments of the Lord." (1 Nephi 2:10) In this way the opportunities he once parted with may be returned, but he, himself, is the one entirely responsible for any delay in their delivery. The sinner's punishment is that he can never escape the effects of his slothfulness, nor his willful disobedience. We, from this can understand how his pain and anguish are like a fire that cannot be quenched, "whose flame ascendeth up forever and ever."

When the transgressor, or the offender, whichever we choose to call him, sees before him, the multitudes of the righteous and thinks that he might have been among them had he also been upright in all his days, the thought dooms him to endure "a never ending torment," which in his breast is remorse.

VERSES 40-41. *O, all ye old men.* O, all ye old men upon whom has rested the burden of carrying forth, for so many years, knowledge of the matchless ways of the Lord, His marvelous works, and the Salvation He has prepared for His children; let not your years be a reason for slackening your zeal; let it be the reverse. If the light we call *life* is nearly extinguished, let us work harder ere it go out. To the young men and the children who can understand his "words," Benjamin alludes to the "awful situation of those that have fallen into transgression." He says in effect, "Let us not fan ourselves into that silly delusion, that someday, perhaps when our backs are bent with the weight of years, then we will serve the Lord, that then we will keep the commandments of God." To everyone he says, "Consider on the blessed and happy state of those who keep the commandments of God. For behold, they are blessed in all things, both temporal and spiritual." We know of no better expression to describe King Benjamin's words than the exhortation of Alma to his son, Shiblon, "And now, my son, I trust that I shall have great joy in you, because of your steadiness and your faithfulness unto God; for as you have commenced in your youth to look to the Lord your God, even so I hope that you will continue in keeping his commandments; for blessed is he that endureth to the end." (Alma 38:2)

CHAPTER 3

1. *King Benjamin's Address Continued*—2. *His Prophecy Concerning Christ.*—3. *The Atonement.*

1. *King Benjamin's address continued.*

1. And again my brethren, I would call your attention, for I have somewhat more to speak unto you; for behold, I have things to tell you concerning that which is to come.

2. And the things which I shall tell you are made known unto me by an angel from God. And he said unto me: Awake; and I awoke, and behold he stood before me.

3. And he said unto me; Awake, and hear the words which I shall tell thee; for behold, I am come to declare unto you the glad tidings of great joy.

4. For the Lord hath heard thy prayers, and hath judged of thy righteousness, and hath sent me to declare unto thee that thou mayest rejoice; and that thou mayest declare unto thy people, that they may also be filled with joy.

VERSES 1-4. *And he said unto me, Awake!* After the first session of the conference was over, allowing the aged King Benjamin to seek a much needed rest, he again began to instruct his God-fearing people. The spirit of prophecy was greatly with him, and they, by that same spirit, understood his words. With exceeding great joy he declared unto them many things that would yet come to pass.

Firmly, but with a heart filled with gladness, he proclaimed the coming of the Messiah, Jesus Christ, at a time not far distant when, with power, He would bring Salvation to everyone who believed on His name.

We may imagine the magnificent effect of his words when we remember that Benjamin was their High-Priest, as, also, he was their king.

The scene presented here was almost inspiring, certainly inspiriting. Bowed down with the weight of years, his white hair flowing with the breeze, his voice trembling and scarcely audible even to the multitude that had gathered to hear his parting instructions, King Benjamin solemnly raised his arms toward heaven and at the same time he told them of a visit by an angel to him, and of the wonderful things the angel had said.

He told them how he had been roused from a peaceful slumber by a voice that said, "Awake; and hear the words which I shall tell thee." This was the voice of one sent down from On High: "For behold, I am come to declare unto thee the glad tidings of great joy."

The heavenly messenger then imparted to Benjamin his divine commitment, saying that, because of thy righteousness and thy prayers, which the Lord hath heard, He "hath sent me to declare unto thee that thou mayest rejoice; and that thou mayest declare unto thy people, that they may also be filled with joy."

The remaining verses of Chapter 3, are a record of the things the angel said to King Benjamin. The angel ended his visit with the King and High-Priest with these words, "Thus hath the Lord commanded me. Amen."

King Benjamin proceeded to declare to his people, by way of prophecy, the "glad tidings" committed to him by the angel.

2. Prophecy Concerning Christ.

5. For behold, the time cometh, and is not far distant, that with power, the Lord Omnipotent who reigneth, who was, and is from all eternity to all eternity, shall come down from heaven among the children of men, and shall dwell in a tabernacle of clay, and shall go forth amongst men, working mighty miracles, such as healing the sick, raising the dead, causing the lame to walk, the blind to receive their sight, and the deaf to hear, and curing all manner of diseases.

6. And he shall cast out devils, or the evil spirits which dwell in the hearts of the children of men.

7. And lo, he shall suffer temptations, and pain of body, hunger, thirst, and fatigue, even more than man can suffer, except it be unto death; for behold, blood cometh from every pore, so great shall be his anguish for the wickedness and the abominations of his people.

VERSES 5-7. *The time cometh . . . that the Lord Omnipotent shall come down from heaven.* King Benjamin prophesied to his faithful people of the Messiah, "the Lord Omnipotent who reigneth, who was and is from all eternity to all eternity," and who, with great power, would come down from heaven to dwell among the children of mortality, and who would take upon Himself a body of flesh and blood. King Benjamin confirmed, by the spirit of prophecy which imbued both him and his people, many of the things which had been foretold by the prophets concerning the Messiah, the Redeemer of the world, Who was to come.

But, however, with words that were painful to their hearts and, no doubt, were perplexing to their minds, he spoke of the sufferings of our Lord; that He should endure the wrath of men; that He should be tempted, tried, and be afflicted; that His body should be racked with pain, and that His anguish, because of the wickedness and abominations of the world, should be so great that blood would exude from every pore. Benjamin also told them that the Messiah would perform many mighty miracles when He lived among men. He would heal the sick, raise the dead, cause the blind to see, and cure all manner of diseases.

It is worthy of note, that many of the miracles wrought by the Savior when he visited the Nephites were, when they are compared, found to be of the same character as the wondrous works He performed among the Jews. Frequently, too, they were more marvelous and more glorious in Bountiful on account of the greater faith of the Nephites. He healed the sick, cast out devils, raised the dead in Bountiful as He did in Judea and Galilee.

But there were other manifestations that were somewhat different that, so far as the record goes, were entirely dissimilar. In the Land of Jerusalem, Jesus miraculously fed five thousand by increasing the store of loaves and fishes that had been provided; in Bountiful He administered the Emblems of His Body and Blood when neither the Disciples nor the multitude had brought either bread or wine. Angels ministered to men during His labors among the Jews; they did so more abundantly during His visits to the Nephites. Again, though we are told in the Bible of the Holy Redeemer blessing little children, we nowhere read therein of the glorious manifestations, the outpouring of the Spirit, the ministry of the angels, the baptism of fire that took place when the Risen Redeemer blessed the little ones of the Nephites.

8. And he shall be called Jesus Christ, the Son of God, the Father of heaven and earth, the Creator | of all things from the beginning; and his mother shall be called Mary.

VERSE 8. *And He shall be called Jesus Christ, the Son of God.* One of the most noteworthy things connected with the ancient Nephite Church was the great plainness and the detail with which the incidents of the birth, life, and death of the Lord Jesus Christ were understood and prophesied by the Nephite servants of God who dwelt on the earth before He tabernacled in mortality.

Among others things it was declared of Him, that:

God, Himself, shall come down from heaven among the children of men and shall redeem His people. (Mosiah 15:1)

He shall take upon Him flesh and blood. (Mosiah 7:27)

He should be born in the Land of Jerusalem, the name given by the Nephites to the land of their forefathers, whence they came. (Alma 7:10) (*See* Chapter 13, 1 Nephi.)

His mother's name should be *Mary.* (Mosiah 3:8, Alma 7:10)

She should be a virgin of the City of Nazareth; very fair and beautiful, a precious and chosen vessel.[1] (1 Nephi 11:13; Alma 7:10)

She should be overshadowed and conceive by the power of the Holy Ghost. (Alma 7:10)

He should be called Jesus Christ, the Son of God.[2]

He should be baptized by John at Bethabara, beyond Jordan. (1 Nephi 10:9)

John should testify that he had baptized the Lamb of God, (1 Nephi 10:9) who should take away the sins of the world. (1 Nephi 10:10)

After His baptism the Holy Ghost should come down upon Him out of heaven, and abide upon him in the form of a dove. (1 Nephi 11:27; 2 Nephi 31:8)

We do not insert here the prophecies of Isaiah and other Jewish prophets that are recorded in the Bible concerning Him, and which are also included in the Book of Mormon. Neither do we include the prophecies made by His servants that appear beyond this book, (Mosiah) except those contained in Alma 7:10, which later and in their proper order we shall consider.

His mother shall be called Mary. Mary, the mother of Christ, is twice mentioned by name in the prophecies of the ancient Nephite worthies. Here, in the prophetic sermon of King Benjamin, and by Alma, the younger, in preaching to the people of Gideon (83 B.C.). Alma declared that Jesus should be born "of Mary . . . she being a virgin, a precious and chosen vessel, who shall be overshadowed, and conceive by the power of the Holy Ghost, and bring forth a son, yea, even the Son of God." (Alma 7:10) She was also shown to Nephi in a vision (600 B.C.) though he does not mention her by name. He records, "I beheld a virgin, and she was exceedingly fair and white." Of this virgin an angel told him, "The virgin whom thou seest is the mother of the Son of God, after the manner of the flesh." Further on, he states, "I looked and beheld the virgin again, bearing a child in her arms. And the angel said unto me, Behold the Lamb of God, yea, even the Son of the Eternal Father!" (1 Nephi 11:13-21)

She being a virgin. For a discussion of this term, *See* COMMENTARY ON THE BOOK OF MORMON, Vol. I, pp. 81-83.

---

[1]*See* Vol. I, pp. 81ff. COMMENTARY ON THE BOOK OF MORMON, also,
[2]*See* comments on Chapter 15, Book of Mosiah, this COMMENTARY.

3. The Atonement.

9. And lo, he cometh unto his own, that salvation might come unto the children of men even through faith on his name; and even after all this they shall consider him a man, and say that he hath a devil, and shall scourge him, and shall crucify him.

10. And he shall rise the third day from the dead; and behold, he standeth to judge the world; and behold, all these things are done that a righteous judgment might come upon the children of men.

VERSE 9. *And lo, He cometh unto His own, that Salvation might come unto the children of men.* King Benjamin continued his discourse by expounding the doctrines of Christ. The Atonement and the purpose of Christ's mission is herein made plain. Notwithstanding the many proofs of His Divinity, and the miracles wrought by Him among the Jews, showing forth the power and authority of God, the Jews would still consider Him only a man, and, too, a man who was possessed with an evil spirit. Without knowledge of His true being, and with malice, they would take Him and ruthlessly crucify Him. The point King Benjamin makes in this portion of his address is that Salvation comes by faith on His name, not only to those who would see and then would believe, but also, to them that through faith alone looked to Him for that life which is eternal.

VERSE 10. *And He shall rise the third day from the dead.* The Bible confirms the fulfillment of this part of King Benjamin's prophecy. Each of the four writers of the Gospels ends his account with the beautiful but amazing story of the Resurrection of Christ. May we draw attention to the Gospel according to Mark?

And when the sabbath was past, Mary Magdelene, and Mary the mother of James, and Salome, had bought sweet spices, that they might come and anoint him. And very early in the morning the first day of the week, they came unto the sepulchre at the rising of the sun. And they said among themselves, Who shall roll us away the stone from the door of the sepulchre? And when they looked, they saw that the stone was rolled away: for it was very great. And entering into the sepulchre, they saw a young man sitting on the right side, clothed in a long white garment; and they were affrighted. And he said unto them, Be not affrighted: Ye seek Jesus of Nazareth, which was crucified: he is risen; he is not here: behold the place where they laid him. But go your way, tell his disciples and Peter that he goeth before you into Galilee: there shall ye see him, as he said unto you. And they went out quickly, and fled from the sepulchre; for they trembled and were amazed: neither said they any thing to any man; for they were afraid. Now when Jesus was risen early the first day of the week, he appeared first to Mary Magdalene, out of whom he cast seven devils. And she went and told them that she had been with him, as they mourned and wept. And they, when they had heard that he was alive, and had been seen of her, believed not. After that he appeared in another form unto two of them, as they walked, and went into the country. And they went and told it unto the residue: neither believed they them. Afterward he appeared unto the eleven as they sat at meat, and upbraided them with their unbelief and hardness of heart, because they believed not them which had seen him after he was risen. And he said unto them, Go ye into all the world, and preach the gospel to every creature. He that believeth and is baptized shall be saved; but he that believeth not shall be damned. And these signs shall follow them that believe; In my name shall they cast out devils; they shall speak with new tongues; They shall take up serpents; and if they drink any deadly thing, it shall not hurt them; they shall lay hands on the sick, and they shall recover. So then after the Lord had spoken unto them, he was received up into heaven, and sat on the right hand of God. And they went forth, and preached

4. Concerning the Atonement.

11. For behold, and also his blood atoneth for the sins of those who have fallen by the transgression of Adam, who have died not knowing the will of God concerning them, or who have ignorantly sinned.

---

every where, the Lord working with them, and confirming the word with signs following. Amen.

Verses 11-13. *His blood atoneth.* King Benjamin's people increasingly rejoiced in his words, for they knew he declared unto them the things that were told him by the angel.

He expounded the *Atonement* of Christ, and the *Fall* of Adam. Benjamin gloried in the Messiah who was to come, and of Him, he said, "Jesus Christ, the Son of God, the Father of heaven and earth, the Creator of all things from the beginning," "shall come down from heaven among the children of men, and shall dwell in a tabernacle of clay, and shall go forth amongst men." "And lo, he cometh unto his own, that salvation might come unto the children of men even through faith on his name." In reading his sermons, we are prompted to call Benjamin, not *King,* but *Prophet;* for he left the sphere of earthly sovereignty and entered into a realm of glory, where only the *spirit of prophecy* reigns.

The thanksgiving and gladness that ruled in the hearts of Benjamin's people remind us of the words of the angel when he awakened Benjamin and introduced himself to the King, ". . . behold, I am come to declare unto thee the glad tidings of great joy . . . that thou mayest rejoice; and that thou mayest declare unto thy people, that they may also be filled with joy." While listening to the "glad tidings" bourne by their king, the people thought of Isaiah's words which were written upon the brass *Plates of Laban,* "Thou shalt rejoice in the Lord, and glory in the Holy One of Israel," (Isaiah 41:16) and Mosiah records of them, "They also took of the firstlings of their flocks, that they might offer sacrifice and burnt offerings according to the law of Moses," (Mosiah 2:4) and they did this "with rejoicing and with singing." (Chronicles 23:18) Their joy also reminds us of the time when the Jews dedicated the wall around their holy city; "And at the dedication of the wall of Jerusalem they sought the Levites out of all their places, to bring them to Jerusalem, to keep the dedication with gladness, both with thanksgiving, and with singing, with cymbals, psalteries, and with harps. . . . Also that day they offered great sacrifices, and rejoiced: *for God had made them rejoice with great joy. . . .*" (Nehemiah 12:27 and 43)

The angel told Benjamin, and the Prophet and King made it known to his people, that the justice and mercy of God — His loving-kindness — extends, not only to His righteous children, but also to those who through no fault of their own, died "not knowing the will of God concerning them, or who have ignorantly sinned." His blood atoneth for their sins.

Jacob, the son of Lehi and the brother of Nephi, exclaimed, "O how great the holiness of our God! For he knoweth all things, and there is not anything save he knows it." Jacob then goes on and explains this very doctrine:

And he cometh into the world that he may save all men if they will hearken unto his voice; for behold, he suffereth the pains of all men, yea, the pains of every living creature, both men, women, and children, who belong to the family of Adam.

And he suffereth this that the resurrection might pass upon all men, that all might stand before him at the great and judgment day.

12. But wo, wo unto him who knoweth that he rebelleth against God! For salvation cometh to none such except it be through repentance and faith on the Lord Jesus Christ.

And he commandeth all men that they must repent, and be baptized in his name, having perfect faith in the Holy One of Israel, or they cannot be saved in the kingdom of God.

And if they will not repent and believe in his name, and be baptized in his name, and endure to the end, they must be damned, for the Lord God, the Holy One of Israel, has spoken it.

Wherefore, he has given a law; and where there is no law given there is no punishment; and where there is no punishment there is no condemnation; and where there is no condemnation the mercies of the Holy One of Israel have claim upon them, because of the atonement; for they are delivered by the power of him.

For the atonement satisfieth the demands of his justice upon all those who have not the law given to them, that they are delivered from that awful monster, death and hell, and the devil, and the lake of fire and brimstone, which is endless torment; and they are restored to that God who gave them breath, which is the Holy One of Israel. (II Nephi 9:20-26)

The Prophet Abinadi adds testimony to this great truth:

And these are those who have part in the first resurrection; and these are they that have died before Christ came, in their ignorance, not having salvation declared unto them. And thus the Lord bringeth about the restoration of these; and they have a part in the first resurrection, or have eternal life, being redeemed by the Lord. (Mosiah 15:24)

This is a complete and satisfactory reply to that question we so often hear, "What will become of those who have never heard the Gospel message?" God is just! He is also merciful. His loving-kindness extends to all His children, and the Atonement is infinite. There is a *justice* which is *injustice*; sometimes *infinite mercy* is *perfect justice*.

VERSE 12. *But wo, wo unto him who knoweth that he rebelleth against God.* Again, we bring before you, the words of Abinadi, that in them, all might see the great knowledge the Nephite servants of God had of the Plan of Salvation.

But behold, and fear, and tremble before God, for ye ought to tremble; for the Lord redeemeth none such that rebel against him and die in their sins; yea, even all those that have perished in their sins ever since the world began, that have willfully rebelled against God, that have known the commandments of God, and would not keep them; there are they that have no part in the first resurrection.

Therefore ought ye not to tremble? For salvation cometh to none such; yea, neither can the Lord redeem such; for he cannot deny himself; for he cannot deny justice when it has its claims. (Mosiah 15:26-27)

A complete concordance of the *word*, WO.

Wo be unto—

1 Nephi	14:6	Therefore, w., be unto the Gentiles
2 Nephi	28:15	W. be unto them, saith the Lord God
	32	W. be unto the Gentiles, saith the Lord
Mosiah	4:23	W. be unto that man, for his substance
	11:20	W. be unto this people, for I have seen
	26	W. be unto you for perverting the ways

Helaman	13:15	W. be unto the city of Gideon
	16	Yea, and w. be unto all the cities
Ether	8:24	Or w. be unto it, because of the blood
Moroni	7:37	W. be unto the children of men
	10:25	And w. be unto the children of men

Wo be unto him—

2 Nephi	27:14	W. be unto him that rejecteth the word
	28:24	W. be unto him that is at ease in Zion
	25	W. be unto him that crieth, All is well
	29	W. be unto him that shall say, We have
3 Nephi	28:34	W. be unto him that will not hearken
Moroni	8:16	W. be unto him that shall pervert the way

Wo unto him—

2 Nephi	9:27	But w. unto him that has the law given
Mosiah	3:12	W. unto him who knoweth that he
Helaman	12:22	W. unto him to whom he shall say this
	13:11	But w. unto him that repenteth not
3 Nephi	18:33	For w. unto him whom the Father condemneth
	29:5	W. unto him that spurneth at the doings
	7	W. unto him that shall say at that day

Wo unto them—

2 Nephi	9:36	W. unto them who commit whoredoms
	15:8	W. unto them that join house to house
	11	W. unto them that rise up early in the
	18	W. unto them that draw iniquity with
	20	W. unto them that call evil good, and
	20:1	W. unto them that decree unrighteous decisions
	25:14	For w. unto them that fight against God
	27:27	W. unto them that seek deep to hide their counsel from the Lord
	28:16	W. unto them that turn aside the just
Helaman	15:2	And w. unto them that are with child
Moroni	10:26	W. unto them who shall do these things

Wo unto—

1 Nephi	1:13	He read, saying, w., w. unto Jerusalem
2 Nephi	9:30	W. unto the rich, that are rich as to the
	31	W. unto the deaf, that will not hear
	32	W. unto the blind, that will not see
	33	w. unto the uncircumcised of heart
	34	W. unto the liar, for he shall be thrust
	35	W. unto the murderer, who deliberately
	38	W. unto all those who die in their sins
	13:9	W. unto their souls! for they have reward
	11	W. unto the wicked! for they shall perish
	15:21	W. unto the wise in their own eyes
	22	W. unto the mighty to drink wine
	28:28	In fine, w. unto all those who tremble
Jacob	3:3	W., w., unto you that are not pure in
Alma	5:31	W. unto such an one, fo rhe is not prepared
	32	Even, w. unto all ye workers of iniquity

13. And the Lord God hath sent his holy prophets among all the children of men, to declare these things to every kindred, nation, and tongue, that thereby whosoever should believe that Christ should come, the same might receive remission of their sins, and rejoice with exceeding great joy, even as though he had already come among them.

3 Nephi	9:2	W., w., w. unto this people; w. unto
Mormon	8:31	But w. unto such, for they are in the
Moroni	8:21	W. unto such, for they are in danger
	9:15	Behold, my heart cries, W. unto this

Wo—

2 Nephi	1:13	Down to the eternal gulf of misery and w.!
	16:5	Then said I, w. is unto me! for I am
Mosiah	2:33	There is a w. pronounced upon him
Alma	9:11	W. unto such an one, for he is not prepared
	26:36	And my redemption from everlasting w.
	28:11	They are consigned to a state of endless w.
	33:22	If so, w. shall come upon you; but if
Helaman	5:12	Down to the gulf of misery and endless w.
	7:16	Down to everlasting misery and endless w.
	22	For this cause w. shall come unto you
3 Nephi	16:8	But w., saith the Father, unto the unbeliever
Mormon	2:19	And w, is me, because of their wicked

Yea, wo—

2 Nephi	9:37	Yea, w. unto those that worship idols
	28:26	Yea, w. unto him that hearkeneth
	27	Yea, w. be unto him that sayeth, We have
Mosiah	12:2	Yea, w. be unto this generation
Helaman	7:25	Yea, w. be unto you because of that great
	26	Yea, w. shall come unto you because
	27	Yea, w. be unto you because of your wicked
	13:12	Yea, w. unto this great city of Zarahemla
	12	Yea, w. unto this great city, for I perceive
	14	Yea, w. be unto this great city, because
	24	Yea, w. unto this people because of this
	15:3	Yea, w. unto this people who are called
3 Nephi	21:14	Yea, w. be unto the Gentiles, except they
	29:5	Yea, w. be unto him that shall deny the Christ
	6	Yea, w. unto him that shall deny the revelations

VERSE 13. *And the Lord God hath sent his holy prophets among all the children of men, to declare these things to every kindred, nation, and tongue.* The Prophet Nephi, early after his father, Lehi, left Jerusalem taking all his family into the wilderness with him, said:

And behold, it is wisdom in God that we should obtain these records, [the Plates of Laban] that we may preserve unto our children the language of our fathers;

And also that we may preserve unto them the words which have been spoken by the mouth of all the holy prophets, which have been delivered unto them by the Spirit and power of God, since the world began, even down unto this present time. (1 Nephi 3:19-20)

14. Yet the Lord God saw that his people were a stiffnecked people, and he appointed unto them a law, even the law of Moses.

15. And many signs, and wonders, and types, and shadows showed he unto them, concerning his coming; and also holy proph-

Over 500 years later, Alma, the High Priest of the *Church of Christ*, exhorted the people of Ammonihah to repent, and called the scriptures to verify his utterances:

. . . Behold, the scriptures are before you; if ye will wrest them it shall be to your own destruction.

And now it came to pass that when Alma had said these words unto them, he stretched forth his hand unto them and cried with a mighty voice, saying; Now is the time to repent, for the day of salvation draweth nigh;

Yea, and the voice of the Lord, by the mouth of angels, doth declare it unto all nations; yea, doth declare it, that they may have glad tidings of great joy; yea, and he doth sound these glad tidings among all his people, yea, even to them that are scattered abroad upon the face of the earth; wherever they have come unto us.

And they are made known unto us in plain terms, that we may understand, that we cannot err; and this because of our being wanderers in a strange land; therefore, we are thus highly favored, for we have these glad tidings declared unto us in all parts of our vineyard.

For behold, angels are declaring it unto many at this time in our land; and this is for the purpose of preparing the hearts of the children of men to receive his word at the time of his coming in his glory. (Alma 13:20-24)

(The word, *wrest*, used in Alma's quote, means (1) to *turn; twist;* especially, to *pull* or *force* away by violent wringing or twisting. (2) To twist from its natural *order* or proper *use* or *meaning* by violence; to *distort*. (*Webster's New Collegiate Dictionary*)

Yet another 500 years and Moroni declared:

And God also declared unto prophets, by his own mouth, that Christ should come. (Moroni 7:23)

Already come among them.

Wherefore, the prophets, and the priests, and the teachers, did labor diligently, exhorting with all long-suffering the people to diligence; teaching the law of Moses, and the intent for which it was given; persuading them to look forward unto the Messiah, and believe in him to come as though he already was. And after this manner did they teach them. (Jarom 1:11)

Elsewhere we say, that they looked forward to Christ even as we look back. Both visions of Him are equally efficacious.

In addition to the words of Nephi, Alma, and Moroni we have just quoted, the following passages from the Book of Mormon will enlighten us concerning the declaration and the promise made in this verse:

Mosiah	18:19	Been spoken by the mouth of the holy prophets
Alma	13:26	Unto just and holy men, by the mouth of angels
3 Nephi	1:13	Caused to be spoken by the mouth of my holy prophets
Ether	15:3	Spoken by the mouth of all the prophets

VERSE 14. *Yet the Lord God saw that his people were a stiffnecked people.* (See, Comments Chapter 13:29-30)

VERSE 15. *And many signs, and wonders, and types, and shadows showed he unto them.* (See, Comments Chapter 13:31-33)

ets spake unto them concerning his coming; and yet they hardened their hearts, and understood not that the law of Moses availeth nothing except it were through the atonement of his blood.

16. And even if it were possible that little children could sin they could not be saved; but I say unto you they are blessed; for behold, as in Adam, or by nature, they fall, even so the blood of Christ atoneth for their sins.

17. And moreover, I say unto you, that there shall be no other name given nor any other way nor means whereby salvation can come unto the children of men, only in and through the name of Christ, the Lord Omnipotent.

VERSE 16. *Little Children are blessed.* The promise of the Lord concerning little children, their salvation and the effect on them of His Atoning Sacrifice, is so clearly set forth in the Book of Mormon that we will only direct attention to the following passages of Book of Mormon scripture:

Mosiah	2:34	Except it be your little children
	40	You little children, who can understand
	3:16	Possible that little children could sin
	18	Humble yourselves and become as little children
	21	Blameless before God, except it be little children
	6:2	Not one soul, except it were little children
	15:25	Little children also have eternal life
	26:1	Being little children at the time he spake
Alma	32:23	Little children do have words given unto them . . . which confound the wise
3 Nephi	17:11	That their little children should be brought
	12	So they brought their little children and sat
	21	He took their little children, one by one
Moroni	8:5	Concerning the baptism of your little children
	8	Wherefore little children are whole
	9	Mockery . . . that ye should baptize little children
	10	Humble themselves as their little children
	10	Shall be saved with their little children
	11	Their little children need no repentance
	12	But little children are alive in Christ
	12	How many little children have died without baptism
	13	If little children could not be saved without baptism
	14	He that supposeth that little children need baptism
	17	Wherefore I love little children with a perfect love; and they are all alike and partakers of salvation
	19	Little children cannot repent; wherefore it is awful wickedness to deny the pure mercies of God unto them
	20	Saith, That little children need baptism denieth the mercies of Christ
	22	All little children are alive in Christ.

VERSE 17. *Christ, the only name whereby salvation can come unto the children of men.* Through Christ, and Him alone, is man redeemed from the effects of Adam's transgression. To a people who were taught to observe all the requirements of the Law of Moses, and were strict to conform their lives to its rules, Benjamin proclaimed that no matter how careful they were in its observance, it "availeth nothing" for their Salvation except "it were through the atonement of his blood."

There shall be no other name given by which salvation is brought about, and notwithstanding the many ordinances and signs which the Lord, in His loving-

18. For behold he judgeth, and his judgment is just; and the infant perisheth not that dieth in his infancy; but men drink damnation to their own souls except they humble themselves and be-

come as little children, and believe that salvation was, and is, and is to come, in and through the atoning blood of Christ, the Lord Omnipotent.

19. For the natural man is an

kindness gave to the Children of Israel, they were all a foreshadowing of Christ and pointed to His coming.

Christ

2 Nephi	10:3	It must needs be expedient that Christ
	7	Shall believe in me, that I am Christ
	11:6	Save Christ should come, all men must perish
	7	But there is a God, and he is Christ
	25:29	And Christ is the Holy One of Israel
	26:1	After Christ shall have risen from the dead
	12	That Jesus is the very Christ
	12	That Jesus is the Christ, the eternal God
	33:11	For Christ will show unto you, with power
Jacob	1:4	For Christ's sake, and for the sake of others
	6:8	All the words which have been spoken concerning Christ
	7:9	Deniest the Christ who shall come
	9	If there should Be a Christ, I would not
	11	They have spoken concerning this Christ
	14	And also, that Christ shall come
	17	Confessed the Christ, and the power of
	19	I have lied unto God: for I have denied the Christ
Words of M.	2	May write . . . somewhat concerning Christ
Mosiah	3:13	Whosoever should believe that Christ should
	5:15	Christ, the Lord Omnipotent, may seal
	7:27	That Christ was the God, the Father of
	15:24	That have died before Christ came
	16:6	If Christ had not come into the world
	7	If Christ had not risen from the dead

These references only to end of Book of Mosiah.

UNTO CHRIST—

2 Nephi	25:24	Look forward with steadfastness unto Christ
	26:8	Look forward unto Christ with steadfastness
	33:9	Except they shall be reconciled unto Christ*
Jacob	1:7	Persuade them to come unto Christ
Omni	1:26	I would that ye should come unto Christ
Moroni	10:30	That ye would come unto Christ
	32	Come unto Christ, and be perfected in him

THROUGH CHRIST—

Mosiah	15:23	Thus they have eternal life through Christ
	16:13	Only in and through Christ ye can be saved
	15	Redemption cometh through Christ the Lord
Alma	22:13	From the foundation of the world, through Christ
	38:9	Can be saved, only in and through Christ
Moroni	3:3	And remission of sins through Jesus Christ

Reconcile, (1) Is to cause to be *friendly again*; to bring back into *harmony*. (2) To *adjust; settle*; as, to adjust or reconcile differences. (3) To make *consistent* or *congruous*. (4) To bring to *acquiescence*, or *quiet submission*. (Webster's *New Collegiate Dictionary*)

enemy to God, and has been from the fall of Adam, and will be, forever and ever, unless he yields to the enticings of the Holy Spirit, and putteth off the natural man and becometh a saint through the atonement of Christ the Lord, and becometh as a child, submissive, meek, humble, patient, full \of love, willing to submit to all things which the Lord seeth fit to inflict upon him, even as a child doth submit to his father.

20. And moreover, I say unto you, that the time shall come when the knowledge of the Savior shall spread throughout every nation, kindred, tongue, and people.

21. And behold, when that time cometh, none shall be found blameless, before God, except it be little children, only through repentance and faith on the name of the Lord God Omnipotent.

22. And even at this time, when thou shalt have taught thy people the things which the Lord thy God hath commanded thee, even then are they found no more blameless in the sight of God, only according to the words which I have spoken unto thee.

Through Adam's Fall, sin came into the world. Sin is the enemy of all righteousness; he who commits sin is also an enemy. We reverently speak of God as the *Alrighteous Father;* in Him there is no sin. "Man is carnal, sensual, and devilish." (Alma 42:10) Because of iniquity man was cast out from God's presence. Sin cannot abide with Him. The Father is separated from His children.

The way must be found, a plan prepared, whereby the Father and His children may be re-united, else His purposes will fail, and all His promises to them go unfulfilled.

That *Way* has been found, a Plan for all His children to regain what once was theirs—an abode with God in the Celestial Home—has been made. Christ is the *Way,* and there is no other.

The Prophet Nephi, the son of Lehi, in a discourse to his brothers delivered to them after his glorious vision, said, "And now, behold, my beloved brethren, this is the way; and there is none other way nor name given under heaven whereby man can be saved in the kingdom of God. And now, behold, this is the doctrine of Christ, and the only and true doctrine of the Father, and of the Son, and of the Holy Ghost, which is one God, without end." (II Nephi 31:21)

Verse 19. *Becometh as a child.* (See, verse 16)

Verses 20-22. *I say unto you . . . the knowledge of the Savior shall spread throughout every nation . . .* The fulfillment of the words of the angel cannot be denied. King Benjamin repeated by way of prophecy what is now becoming an established fact—God's inspired teachers and evangelists are going among all nations declaring the Glad Tidings of Man's Redemption through the Lord, Jesus Christ. Salvation, they proclaim, cometh to all by repentance and faith on His name.

King Benjamin again admonished his people to learn God's commandments, and do them. By observing all the *rites* and *obligations* demanded by the Law of Moses, and further, only by looking forward to Christ and his Atoning Sacrifice, which the Law foreshadowed, can man be "found blameless in the sight of God." This, King Benjamin said, "Is according to the words which I have spoken unto

23. And now I have spoken the words which the Lord God hath commanded me.

24. And thus saith the Lord: They shall stand as a bright testimony against this people, at the judgment day; whereof they shall be judged, every man according to his works, whether they be good, or whether they be evil.

25. And if they be evil they are consigned to an awful view of their own guilt and abominations, which doth cause them to shrink from the presence of the Lord into a state of misery and endless torment, from whence they can no more return; therefore they have drunk damnation to their own souls.

26. Therefore, they have drunk out of the cup of the wrath of God, which justice could no more deny unto them than it could deny that Adam should fall because of his partaking of the forbidden fruit; therefore, mercy could have claim on them no more forever.

27. And their torment is as a lake of fire and brimstone, whose flames are unquenchable, and whose smoke ascendeth up forever and ever. Thus hath the Lord commanded me. Amen.

---

thee." He meant, no doubt, that he repeated, for emphasis, what he had already said. It is by repetition we learn.

VERSE 23. *I have spoken the words which the Lord God commanded me.* In concluding his great sermon, King Benjamin affirmed his first, or introductory words —that an angel from heaven, in the name of God, commanded him to declare these things to his people that they may "be filled with joy."

CHAPTER 4

1. *King Benjamin's Address Concluded—2. The Conditions of Salvation—3. Man's Dependence Upon God—4. Liberality, Wisdom and Diligence Enjoined.*

1. King Benjamin's address concluded.

1. And now, it came to pass that when king Benjamin had made an end of speaking the words which had been delivered unto him by the angel of the Lord, that he cast his eyes round about on the multitude, and behold they had fallen to the earth, for the fear of the Lord had come upon them.

2. And they had viewed themselves in their own carnal state, even less than the dust of the earth. And they all cried aloud with one voice, saying: O have mercy, and apply the atoning blood of Christ that we may receive forgiveness of our sins, and our hearts may be purified; for we believe in Jesus Christ, the Son of God, who created heaven and earth, and all things; who shall come down among the children of men.

3. And it came to pass that after they had spoken these words the Spirit of the Lord came upon them, and they were filled with

VERSE 1. *When King Benjamin had made an end of speaking . . . he cast his eyes round about on the multitude.* King Benjamin's powerful address, repeating the words which the angel had said to him, so prevailed upon his listeners that when he finished talking he observed that they had all fallen to the ground.

To fall to the earth is a recognition of the greatness of God, and of man's nothingness. It expresses the soul's deepest humility, or its state or quality of being humble in spirit. To prostrate oneself before "The Majesty on High," with one's face toward the ground, signifies *humble adoration.* With freedom from pride and arrogance, having a desire to do good, and with a great love for the coming Savior in their hearts, the people of King Benjamin fell down and worshipped the Lord.

Bowing the head and *closing the eyes* is but a simple, yet not unlike gesture in which we avow our fealty to God. Doing so, exhibits the same qualities as we have noted above.

VERSE 2. *For we believe in Jesus Christ, the Son of God.* The deep sense of their own unworthiness caused the multitude that had gathered together in the conference of the Saints in Zarahemla, to pray unanimously that the Lord would, in His loving-kindness, purify their hearts, and make them worthy of the blessings the Messiah would bring to those who served Him, and who have, as Benjamin said, "Faith on his name."

As if they were one, being of the same mind, they entreated the Great Giver of all good to accord to them the blessings brought about by Christ's Atoning Sacrifice, for, they testified before God and each other that they believed in Him who was the Creator of all things, "who shall come down among the children of men."

VERSE 3. *They were filled with joy.* The prayers offered by the assembled worshipers were quickly answered in blessings from above: the holy Spirit of the Lord came upon them; their sins were all forgiven; they were filled with joy even joy, having received a remission of their sins, and having peace of conscience, because of the exceeding faith which they had in Jesus Christ who should come, according to the words which king Benjamin had spoken unto them.

4. And king Benjamin again opened his mouth and began to speak unto them, saying: My friends and my brethren, my kindred and my people, I would again call your attention, that ye may hear and understand the remainder of my words which I shall speak unto you.

5. For behold, if the knowledge of the goodness of God at this time has awakened you to a sense of your nothingness, and your worthless and fallen state—

6. I say unto you, if ye have come to a knowledge of the goodness of God, and his matchless power, and his wisdom, and his patience, and his long-suffering towards the children of men; and also, the atonement which has been prepared from the foundation of the world, that thereby salvation might come to him that should put his trust in the Lord, and should be diligent in keeping his commandments, and continue in the faith even unto the end of his life, I mean the life of the mortal body—

7. I say, that this is the man who receiveth salvation, through the atonement which was prepared from the foundation of the world for all mankind, which ever were since the fall of Adam, or who are, or who ever shall be, even unto the end of the world.

2. The Conditions of Salvation.

8. And this is the means whereby salvation cometh. And there is none other salvation save this which hath been spoken of; neither are there any conditions whereby man can be saved except the conditions which I have told you.

---

as the angel had said to Benjamin; *Peace, God's most precious gift*" was allotted to them, "Because," the Sacred Record says, "of their exceeding faith which they had in Jesus Christ."

VERSE 4. *My friends and my brethren. See, p. 42.*

VERSES 5-7. *This is the man who receiveth salvation.* That if, said Benjamin, the knowledge of God's goodness had aroused in them a conviction of their fallen state, and further will cause them to be diligent in keeping the commandments of the Lord, "This is the man who receiveth salvation."

VERSE 8. *And this is the means whereby salvation cometh.* The doctrine of Adam's Fall is explicitly explained in the Book of Mormon. The orthodox view has been that although our first parents were created innocent and holy, they were deceived by the fallen angel, sinned and fell from the original state of moral perfection, and thereby brought death, sin, and endless misery upon their children and all creation.

Many modern theological writers have tried to eliminate the story of Adam's fall completely, explaining it away as a venerable myth. Evolutionists have seen in the story a proof of their theory of the descent of man from a brute ancestry, forgetting the apparent fact that there is not a *brute* animal that does not stand higher than the *moral* level of a great many depraved, debased human beings, thus furnishing no starting point there for a supposed upward evolution.

To the Book of Mormon prophets and writers, the Fall was a necessary part of the Great Plan. Adam and Eve were, in the beginning, immortal beings, and were not subject to death. But, "Subject to death they must become, however, if their posterity should inherit corruptible bodies. The Fall, then, was a deliberate use of law, by which act Adam and Eve became mortal, and could beget mortal children." (John A. Widtsoe, *Rational Theology*, p. 47) The story of the Fall is not a myth. It is a record, in poetic, highly-figurative language, of an actual occurrence. It is a record of the transition of man from a state of innocent, childlike purity, to that of a more mature age, when, the immediate divine tutelage having been completed, Adam and Eve were prepared to begin for themselves the struggle for existence and progress. And so, "Adam fell that man might be."

All the particulars of the story are not clear. That Adam and Eve were, literally, our ancestors, and that the "serpent" was Lucifer, the rebellious outcast from heaven, is certain. Just what facts are represented by the symbolism of the tree, the fruit, the eating thereof, is not obvious. The tree of life, which Lehi saw in his vision, the angel explains, was "a representation of the love of God," as manifested in the earthly mission of His Only Begotten Son. (I Nephi 11:20-33; 15:33)

We may be sure that the tree of knowledge and the tree of life, in the narrative of the Fall, represent important realities in the experience of our first ancestors.

The consequences of the partaking of the forbidden tree by our first parents were that they came in possession of knowledge of good and evil, but were "cut off both temporally and spiritually from the presence of the Lord." This ushered in *death*. And in this condition they became self-willed, "carnal, sensual and devilish." (Alma 42:3-10) That was a "fall" which called for a plan of salvation. God supplied that Plan, and therefore, and thereby, the fall became a "fall upward."

The Atonement which was prepared from the foundation of the World. A Plan of Salvation, as just noted, had already been prepared. On this subject the Book of Mormon is exceedingly clear. Were it not for the Atonement all mankind would perish. The Atonement was effected through the sufferings and death of the Son of God. He took upon Himself the transgressions of His people, and atoned for the sins of the world. His atonement is specially for those "who have fallen by the transgression of Adam, who have died not knowing the will of God concerning them, or who have ignorantly sinned." That includes all who have died outside the light of revelation. The Atonement satisfies the demands of justice. Mercy comes because of the Atonement, and it brings about the resurrection and makes it possible for the children of Adam to return to the presence of God.

The modern spirit of so-called enlightenment is entirely out of sympathy with the Christian doctrine of Atonement. It has placed man on a pedestal of independence, where he needs no divine Plan of Redemption or Salvation. But the fact remains: Outside this Plan the world is "dead." Through Christ alone can man regain "paradise lost."*

References: 2 Nephi 9:26; 25:16; Mosiah 3:11; 4:7; 13:28; Alma 33:22; 34:8-9; 36:17; 42:23.

*See Notes.

9. Believe in God; believe that he is, and that he created all things, both in heaven and in earth; believe that he has all wisdom, and all power, both in heaven and in earth; believe that man doth not comprehend all the things which the Lord can comprehend.

10. And again, believe that ye must repent of your sins and forsake them, and humble yourselves before God; and ask in sincerity of heart that he would forgive you; and now, if you believe all these things see that ye do them.

VERSES 9-10. *Believe in God; believe that he is.* The Book of Mormon and the Bible resemble each other in that they take for granted, "He lives!" Handbooks on theology generally begin by stating the philosophical arguments supposed to *prove* that there is a Supreme Being, but God's books do not argue the question. "In the beginning God created the heavens and the earth," is the sublime opening statement of the Bible. One of the first incidents told in the Book of Mormon is that of a vision of the Prophet Lehi, in which he saw "God sitting upon his throne, surrounded by numerous concourses of angels in the attitude of singing and praising their God." (I Nephi 1:8) There is no attempt at argument; no appeal to the reasoning faculty of man, only a plain statement of a sublime fact, in the simplest possible language: *God Is.*

And yet, when the inspired writer has occasion to rebuke atheism, he applies the cosmological argument with the greatest possible force. He says:

"If there be no God, we are not, for there could have been no creation." (2 Nephi 11:7)

That argument is unanswerable.

Philosophers have, indeed, asserted that God is not needed to account for the existence of worlds. Matter itself, they argue, possesses all the potency necessary to account for all established facts. In this conclusion, vast numbers of our superficial age concur and, at least pretend to, find satisfaction. Many are banded together, and with increasing numbers both among learned and unlearned, seek to spread their faith destroying opinions throughout every field of human endeavor. Their aims are freely stated: Do away with chaplains in Congress, legislatures, and in the army and navy. Recognize no religious festivals. Stop "bootlegging" Bible and religion in the schools. Use no Bibles to take an oath on. Do away with Christian morality. Take "In God We Trust" off the coins. The program they have adopted has been espoused by an ever-growing fraternity.

Against the ignorant, blasphemous, arrogant atheism which is fostered, the writers of the Book of Mormon stand up, as if it were from their graves, in righteous rebuke. They say, in substance: You atheists, you materialists, you monists, you do not go far enough in your negation. You deny the existence of God, but, in order to be consistent, you must also deny the existence of the land in which you live, and the mountains, the islands of the sea, the sun, the stars, and, above all, your own existence, and say that the whole Creation is only a figment of the imagination. To admit the reality of the Creation, and then deny the existence of the Creator thereof, is an inconsistency, a self-contradiction, impossible in the reasoning of any intelligent being.

The Book of Mormon testifies to the existence of God in this and other passages (2 Ne. 2:13-14; 11:7; Mor. 9:19) against all forms of atheism, and gives as complete a picture of the Godhead as we, in our mortal state, can perceive.

11. And again I say unto you as I have said before, that as ye have come to the knowledge of the glory of God, or if ye have known of his goodness and have tasted of his love, and have received a remission of your sins, which causeth such exceeding great joy in your souls, even so I would that ye should remember, and always retain in remembrance, the greatness of God, and your own nothingness, and his goodness and long-suffering towards you, unworthy creatures, and humble yourselves even in the depths of humility, calling on the name of the Lord daily, and standing steadfastly in the faith of that which is to come, which was spoken by the mouth of the angel.

12. And behold, I say unto you that if ye do this ye shall always rejoice, and be filled with the love of God, and always retain a remission of your sins; and ye shall grow in the knowledge of the glory of him that created you, or in the knowledge of that which is just and true.

13. And ye will not have a mind to injure one another, but to live peaceably, and to render to every man according to that which is his due.

14. And ye will not suffer your children that they go hungry, or naked; neither will ye suffer that they transgress the laws of God, and fight and quarrel one with another, and serve the devil, who is the master of sin, or who is the evil spirit which hath been spoken

---

VERSE 11. *And again I say unto you as I have said before.* King Benjamin repeated to his people the wonderful lessons they had learned, and the number of gifts vouchsafed to them by the Lord.

Among the blessings they had received, he counted many: They had come to a knowledge of the Lord; they had tasted of His love; their sins had been forgiven them, which, he said, "Causeth such great joy in your souls."

But, he also said, that in the trials and disappointments of life that are sure to follow, always remember the *greatness of God, His goodness and long-suffering* toward you, and in the depths of humility, call "on the name of the Lord daily." At all times, was his exhortation, remain "firm and steadfast, and immovable" in the faith which you have in the coming Savior of whom the angel spoke.

VERSE 12. *If ye do this.* In this verse King Benjamin reached one of the highest points in his address. The dignity of his words, the greatness of his spiritual understanding, the love he had for his people, prompted a benediction which came from his great heart. He promised them that "If ye do this" [the things outlined in verse 11] ye shall always rejoice; you will be filled with the love of God; your sins will be no longer counted against you; ye shall "grow in the knowledge of the glory of him that created you," which he likened to "the knowledge of that which is just and true."

This verse is so beautiful, Benjamin's promises so sure, that we, transported in our minds to the temple lot in Zarahemla, hear his words and resolve with his people to obey his voice. May we suggest that the entire verse be memorized.

VERSES 13-18. *Other promises.* In addition to the great self-inspiring promises Benjamin made to his faithful believers he pronounced other blessings which will attend the faithful performance of the angel's words. He promised them, that: Ye

of by our fathers, he being an enemy to all righteousness.

15. But ye will teach them to walk in the ways of truth and soberness; ye will teach them to love one another, and to serve one another.

16. And also, ye yourselves will succor those that stand in need of your succor; ye will administer of your substance unto him that standeth in need; and ye will not suffer that the beggar putteth up his petition to you in vain, and turn him out to perish.

17. Perhaps thou shalt say: The man has brought upon himself his misery; therefore I will stay my hand, and will not give unto him of my food, nor impart unto him of my substance that he may not suffer, for his punishments are just—

18. But I say unto you, O man, whosoever doeth this the same hath great cause to repent; and except he repenteth of that which he hath done he perisheth forever, and hath no interest in the kingdom of God.

3. Man's dependence upon God.

19. For behold, are we not all beggars? Do we not all depend upon the same Being, even God, for all the substance which we have, for both food and raiment, and for gold, and for silver, and for all the riches which we have of every kind?

20. And behold, even at this time, ye have been calling on his name, and begging for a remission of your sins. And has he

suffered that ye have begged in vain? Nay; he has poured out his Spirit upon you, and has caused that your hearts should be filled with joy, and has caused that your mouths should be stopped that ye could not find utterance, so exceeding great was your joy.

21. And now, if God, who has created you, on whom you are dependent for your lives and for all

---

will live peaceably one with the other; ye will not suffer your children to go hungry or naked, nor transgress the laws of God; ye will teach them the ways of truth and to love and serve one another.

These are all fruits that will be gathered by the faithful. Those who have an interest in God's Kingdom will divide their substance with the needy and those who have no helper but the Lord. Him, will the Lord remember in time of need. Whosoever refuses to feed the hungry and clothe the naked when he, himself, has abundance, "hath great cause to repent." "Ye," Benjamin continued, "will not suffer that the beggar putteth up his petition to you in vain, and turn him out to perish."

VERSES 19-26. *Are we not all beggars?* King Benjamin pointed to a truth which was clear to his people's vision and was, by them, easily understood. He compared their own *fallen* condition with that of a beggar. "Do we not all," he asked, "depend upon the same Being, even God, for all the substance which we have, for food and raiment . . . and for all the riches we have of every kind?"

Even during this Conference of Saints, your cries to Him increase. You never cease "begging for a remission of your sins." And now I ask you, "Have ye begged

that ye have and are, doth grant unto you whatsoever ye ask that is right, in faith, believing that ye shall receive, O then, how ye ought to impart of the substance that ye have one to another.

22. And if ye judge the man who putteth up his petition to you for your substance that he perish not, and condemn him, how much more just will be your condemnation for withholding your substance, which doth not belong to you but to God to whom also your life belongeth; and yet ye put up no petition, nor repent of the thing which thou hast done.

23. I say unto you, wo be unto that man, for his substance shall perish with him; and now, I say these things unto those who are rich as pertaining to the things of this world.

24. And again, I say unto the poor, ye who have not and yet have sufficient, that ye remain from day to day; I mean all you who deny the beggar, because ye have not; I would that ye say in your hearts that: I give not because I have not, but if I had I would give.

25. And now, if ye say this in your hearts ye remain guiltless, otherwise ye are condemned; and your condemnation is just for ye covet that which ye have not received.

26. And now, for the sake of these things which I have spoken unto you—that is, for the sake of retaining a remission of your sins from day to day, that ye

in vain?" King Benjamin answered his own question, "Nay." The Lord has abundantly blessed each one of you; He has poured out His Spirit upon you; He has filled your hearts with joy, far beyond your power to comprehend.

Now, if God, to whom you owe your very lives, grants you blessings even before they are asked, "O then, how ye ought to impart of the substance that ye have one to another." (*See,* Mosiah 2:16-19)

Condemn not the man who asks for your help, nor keep from him a just portion of your worldly goods. In doing so you may cause him to perish, and furthermore, you will deny that very God who giveth to all men liberally, and to Whom everything belongs. Benjamin drew the only logical conclusion from such a condition as he contemplated. He reasoned that such a man who refuses to share his substance with the needy when asked, justly deserves greater condemnation than another who gives not, but says, "I give not because I have not, but if I had I would give."

VERSE 23. *Wo be unto that man.* A complete commentary on Benjamin's words recorded in this verse is found in a sermon preached by Jacob, the brother of Nephi: "But wo unto the rich, who are rich as to the things of the world. For because they are rich they despise the poor, and they persecute the meek, and their hearts are upon their treasure; wherefore, their treasure is their God. And behold, their treasure shall perish with them also." (2 Nephi 9:30)

VERSE 26. *I would that ye should impart of your substance to the poor.* Sharing with others the many bounties we receive from God's hand, not only adds peace and comfort to our hearts, but it awakens within us a love for His children that increases with each passing day. We show by our actions that we are truly His children and that He is the Father of all.

may walk guiltless before God—I would that ye should impart of your substance to the poor, every man according to that which he hath, such as feeding the hungry, clothing the naked, visiting the sick and administering to their relief, both spiritually and temporally, according to their wants.

4. Liberality, wisdom and diligence enjoined.

27. And see that all these things are done in wisdom and order; for it is not requisite that a man should run faster than he has strength. And again, it is expedient that he should be diligent, that thereby he might win the prize; therefore, all things must be done in order.

28. And I would that ye should remember, that whosoever among you borroweth of his neighbor should return the thing that he borroweth, according as he doth agree, or else thou shalt commit sin; and perhaps thou shalt cause thy neighbor to commit sin also.

29. And finally, I cannot tell you all the things whereby ye may commit sin; for there are divers ways and means, even so many that I cannot number them.

30. But this much I can tell you, that if ye do not watch yourselves, and your thoughts, and your words, and your deeds, and observe the commandments of

It is indisputable that "feeding the hungry, clothing the naked, visiting the sick and administering to their relief, both spiritually and temporally," renders us more obedient to God's commandments and thereby creates in us a clean heart and renews a steadfast spirit within us. (See, Psalm 51-10) Doing so is a sacrifice of righteousness when, in offering it, we put our trust in the Lord. There is no surer way to remember the Lord, His goodness and mercy, than to serve His children who want and have not.

Blessings without number attend the giver of these things. Not only do we retain a remission of our sins, but it follows that also we may walk "guiltless before God," who is our loving parent.

VERSE 27. See that all these things are done in wisdom. It is not required of a man to give more than he is able, nor to impart such that will overcome him and make of him another who is in want. Be diligent, Benjamin implored, and do all things in proper order. That means just this: be constant in attending to those who are in need, and with meekness minister to their wants, but remember neither do them in excess nor with ceremony.

VERSE 28. He who borroweth of his neighbor. King Benjamin closed his sermon by giving some practical instructions. Among other things he told them were teachings in regard to those who borrow and fail to return that which they borrowed. He warned his people that in so doing they sinned, and not only did they transgress but by chance caused others to also commit sin.

VERSES 29-30. And now, O man, remember. In conclusion, and with a great appeal to all who heard him, King Benjamin warned that there were many ways open for man to transgress God's holy laws. Even their thoughts and words, he said, as well as their deeds, were counted for or against them. Continue steadfast all

God, and continue in the faith of | the end of your lives, ye must per-
what ye have heard concerning | ish. And now, O man, remember,
the coming of our Lord, even unto | and perish not.

---

your days in your faith in the words of the angel concerning the coming of our
Lord. Do not falter in your determination to serve Him, that thereby you may be
found blameless when you stand before Him. King Benjamin ended his mighty
address with a further appeal to all: "And now, O man, remember, and perish not."

COMPLETE CONCORDANCE

ADAM

1 Nephi	5-11	Also of A. and Eve, who were our
2 Nephi	2:19	After A. and Eve had partaken of the
	22	If A. had not transgressed, he
	25	A. fell that man might be;
	9:21	Who belong to the family of A.
Mosiah	3:11	Who have fallen by the transgression of A.
	16	As in A., or by nature they fall,
	19	And has been from the fall of A.
	26	Than it could deny that A. should
	4:7	Which ever were since the fall of A.
	28:17	Even from that time back until the creation of A.
Alma	12:22	A. did fall by the partaking of
	23	Possible for A. to have partaken of
	18:36	The creation of A., and told him all
	22:12	He began from the creation of A.
	13	The scriptures, from the creation of A.
	40:18	From the days of A., down to the
	42:5	If A. had put forth his hand im
Helaman	14:16	All mankind, by the fall of A.
Mormon	3:20	Every soul who belongs to the family of A.
	9:12	He created A., and by A. came the fall
Ether	1:3	The creation of the world, and also of A.
	4	Things which transpired from the days of A.
Moroni	8:8	The curse of A. is taken from them
	10:3	From the creation of A., even down

FALL OF ADAM

The Fall (of Adam)

2 Nephi	2:4	The way is prepared from the f. of
	25	Adam fell that men might be, and men
	26	Redeem the children of men from the f.
	26	That they are redeemed from the f.
	9:6	Needs com unto man by reason of the f.
	6	The f. came by reason of transgression
Mosiah	3:16	As in Adam, or by nature they f.
	19	And has been from the f. of Adam
	26	That is could deny that Adam should f.
	4:7	Which ever were since the f. of Adam
	16:3	Parents, which was the cause of their f.

Alma	12:22	Adam did f. by the partaking of the forbidden
	22	By his f., all mankind became a lost
	18:36	All the things concerning the f. of man
	22:13	Laying the f. of man before him
	42:9	The f. had brought upon all mankind
Helaman	14:16	All mankind, by the f. of Adam, bei
Mormon	9:12	And by Adam came the f. of an
	12	Because of the f. of man, came Jesus
Ether	3:2	Because of the f., our natures have
	13	Because thou knowest these things, ye are redeemed from the f

ATONE

Alma	33:22	He shall suffer and die to a. for their sins
	34:8	He shall a. for the sins of the world
	11	Which will a. for the sins of another
	36:17	A Son of God, to a. for the sins of the

ATONEMENT

Through the atonement—

Jacob	4:11	Unto him through the a. of Christ
Mosiah	3:15	Except it were through the a. of Christ
	19	A saint, through the a. of Christ
	4:7	Through the a. which was prepared
Alma	13:5	Through the a. of the only begotten Son
	34:9	Perish except it be through the a.
Moroni	7:14	Have hope through the a. of Christ

Atonement—

2 Nephi	2:10	To answer to the ends of the a.
	9:7	It must needs be an infinite a.
	7	Save it should be an infinite a.
	25	Have claim upon them, because of the a.
	26	The a. satisfieth the demands of his just
	10:25	Death by the power of the a.
	25:16	The a., which is infinite for all mankind
Jacob	4:12	For why not speak of the a. of Christ
	7:12	I know if there should be no a. made
Mosiah	4:6	The a. which has been prepared
	13:28	The a. which God himself shall make
Alma	21:9	Of Christ, and the a. of his blood
	24:13	Shall be shed for the a. of our sins
	30:17	Telling them that there could be no a.
	34:9	Expedient that an a. should be made
	9	There must be an a. made
	12	Nothing which is short of an infinite a.
	42:15	Except that an a. should be made
	23	Mercy cometh because of the a.
	23	The a. bringeth to pass the resurrection
Moroni	8:20	Setteth at naught the a. of him

Atoneth

Mosiah	3:11	His blood a. for the sins of those
	16	The blood of Christ a. for their sins
Alma	22:14	The death of Christ, a. for their sins
	42:15	Therefore God himself a. for the sins

Atoning

Mosiah	3:18	In and through the a. blood of Christ
	4:2	And apply the a. blood of Christ
Helaman	5:9	Only through the a. blood of Jesus

GENERAL NOTES

There are two widely divergent views concerning the existence of man on earth.

One of these has been called the scientific view, although it is scientific only in ascertaining a certain class of facts. Outside this preparatory work, it becomes un-scientific in the highest degree. Its conclusions are not scientific. In other words, it reminds one of a building of cardboards erected on a solid rock foundation. But such a structure would be no more lasting than one built on sand.

The other is Scriptural, and therefore, in fact, scientific both in foundation and superstructure.

In the so-called scientific view, man is the product of selection and heredity, surroundings and training. He is merely a wonderful and complicated machine. As such he delivers his products as a machine. He who knows the parts of a machine can calculate its motions and control its purposes. In the same way, the acts and even thoughts of man can be controlled by one who knows the human machinery. There can be no personal responsibility in a machine; nor in man, if he is but another machine. And even if a degree of responsibility is admitted, there can be no self-determination. The acts and thoughts are determined by the construction of the different parts. It is all mechanical.

The Scriptural view of the existence of man is different. In this view, man is the child of God. He has come, in accordance with an eternal, divine decree upon this earth, as a wonderful institute of learning, in order to get an experience necessary for eternal progress. His body, be the origin of it clearly understood or not, is the tabernacle in which the eternal and immortal spirit dwells during its existence in the material world; it is also the wonderful collection of tools by means of which that spirit is in contact with the material world, and thereby able to fulfill the purpose of its existence on the earth.

In this view, man is a personality, dwelling in flesh, with independence, volition, and responsibility. He has a peculiar place in the history of the universe as the bearer of the highest ideals, and as subject to moral responsibility. As the child of God, man has a unique place in the creation, which can be comprehended only in the light of divine revelation.

This is the Scriptural view of the existence of man on earth.

It is also the only scientific view.

And because he is the child of God, his place is in the Church of God, even on this earth. Jesus in the temple should be our pattern. His question, "Wist ye not that I must be about my Father's business?" means in a few words that the dwelling of God is where a child of God ought to be found; and that he ought to be occupied with the things that belong to God. It seems that it was in the Temple of God that the consciousness of the dignity of Jesus awakened to life. That is Scriptural proof enough to us that our place as human beings and the children of God is in

His Church and His Temple, and that our chief concern ought to be that which belongs to Him, our Eternal Father.

With from one to three million distinct species in the animal and vegetable world, not a single species has been traced to another. Until species in the animal and vegetable world can be linked together, why should we assume without proof that man is a blood relative of any lower form of life? Those who become obsessed with the idea that they have brute blood in their veins devote their time to searching for missing links in the hope of connecting man with life below him; why do they prefer jungle ancestry to creation by God Almighty for a purpose and according to a divine plan?"

(William Jennings Bryan)

CHAPTER 5

1. *Effect of King Benjamin's Address*—2. *The People Repent and enter into Covenant with Christ, and are Called by His Name.*

1. *Effect of King Benjamin's Address.*

1. And now, it came to pass that when king Benjamin had thus spoken to his people, he sent among them, desiring to know of his people, if they believed the words which he had spoken unto them.

2. And they all cried with one voice, saying: Yea, we believe all the words which thou hast spoken unto us; and also, we know of their surety and truth, because of the Spirit of the Lord Omnipotent, which has wrought a mighty change in us, or in our hearts, that we have no more disposition to do evil, but to do good continually.

3. And we, ourselves, also, through the infinite goodness of God, and the manifestations of his Spirit, have great views of that which is to come; and were it expedient, we could prophesy of all things.

4. And it is the faith which we have had on the things which our king has spoken unto us that has brought us to this great knowledge, whereby we do rejoice with such exceeding great joy.

2. *The People Repent and enter into Covenant with Christ, and are Called by His Name.*

5. And we are willing to enter into a covenant with our God to do his will, and to be obedient to his commandments in all

VERSE 1. *King Benjamin desired to know if his people believed his words.* Benjamin, their inspired ruler, continued his discourse. He enlarged therein on the truths of the Atonement and other soul-saving doctrines. When he was through with his sermon, he sent amongst his hearers to know whether, or nay, they believed and thereby accepted the heavenly truths he had taught them.

VERSES 2-4. *Yes, we believe all the words which thou hast spoken unto us.* Great was the joy of King Benjamin when he found that they not only believed his words but also because of the working of the Spirit of the Lord in their hearts, they knew of their truth. Still more, the Holy Spirit had wrought such a change within them that they had no more disposition to do evil but to do good continually. The visions of eternity were opened to their minds; their souls were filled with the spirit of prophecy, and they longed to serve the Lord with undivided hearts. Peace, joy, exceeding gladness, overflowed the confines of their beings. With knowledge and understanding they praised the great name of the Lord. They rehearsed, before Him, His marvelous works, and together they spoke of the glory of His Kingdom, and talked of His might. They exulted in the Lord Omnipotent and rejoiced in the God of their Salvation.

VERSES 5-8. *We are willing to enter into a covenant with our God to do His will.* All who heard King Benjamin were anxious to serve the Lord as long as they should

things that he shall command us, all the remainder of our days, that we may not bring upon ourselves a never-ending torment, as has been spoken by the angel, that we may not drink out of the cup of the wrath of God.

6. And now, these are the words which king Benjamin desired of them; and therefore he said unto them; Ye have spoken the words that I desired; and the covenant which ye have made is a righteous covenant.

7. And now, because of the covenant which ye have made ye shall be called the children of Christ, his sons, and his daugh-ters; for behold, this day he hath spiritually begotten you; for ye say that your hearts are changed through faith on his name; therefore, ye are born of him and have become his sons and his daughters.

8. And under this head ye are made free, and there is no other head whereby ye can be made free. There is no other name given whereby salvation cometh; therefore, I would that ye should take upon you the name of Christ, all you that have entered into the covenant with God that ye should be obedient unto the end of your lives.

---

live, and expressed a desire to enter such an obligation so to do. The first Christian Church in Zarahemla was then established. King Benjamin gave his people a new name because of the agreement they entreated should be made, which thing was the very thing that Benjamin wished them to do. Everyone, except the little children who could not understand, entered this binding covenant, and which, we might say, most of them kept faithfully. The name they were to bear ever afterward was the "children of Christ," by which they would be known as long as they hearkened to His voice and kept His commandments. In giving them this new name King Benjamin said, "Because of the covenant which ye have made ye shall be called the children of Christ, his sons, and his daughters." Perhaps this passage together with the one found in Mosiah 15:1-4, will help us understand why Jesus is called both the *Father* and the *Son*.

The word *children* is frequently used in a figurative sense in the Hebrew vocabulary. *Children* of Israel were all the descendants of the Patriarch, Jacob. The *children* of the world are selfish, materialistic persons, while the *children* of light love the truth and live accordingly. The *children* of the devil are doing his work, while the *children* of God love and obey Him. The *children* of Christ are His faithful followers. (See John 8:36-44)

VERSE 8. *And under this head ye are made free.* Elsewhere we remark, thus making Benjamin's words more emphatic to us, that to serve God is perfect freedom, and to worship Him in truth brings life's noblest compensation and satisfaction.

There is no other name given whereby salvation cometh. In this same sermon given by King Benjamin, we find a statement that confirms and makes more forceful the knowledge herein made plain:

"And moreover, I say unto you, that there shall be no other name given nor any other way nor means whereby salvation can come unto the children of men, only in and through the name of Christ, the Lord Omnipotent." (Mosiah 3:17)

Also the Prophet Nephi, who came out of Jerusalem, said to his brothers, some of whom were more than inclined to unbelief:

9. And it shall come to pass that whosoever doeth this shall be found at the right hand of God, for he shall know the name by which he is called; for he shall be called by the name of Christ.

10. And now it shall come to

"And now, behold, my beloved brethren, this is the way; and there is none other way nor name given under heaven whereby man can be saved in the kingdom of God. And now, behold, this is the doctrine of Christ, and the only and true doctrine of the Father, and of the Son, and of the Holy Ghost, which is one God, without end. Amen." (2 Nephi 31:21)

VERSES 9-13. *Whosoever taketh upon himself the name of Christ shall be found upon the right hand of God.* Whosoever assumes (takes upon himself) the name of Christ and thereupon covenants to serve Him and keep the Lord's commandments will be protected and supported by the power of God.

The word *hand* is sometimes used for power, as in I Samuel 5:6-7. This is especially the case where the expression *right hand* is used.

To pour water on any one's hand, meant to *serve* him, 2 Kings 3:11.

To wash one's hands, denoted that the person was *innocent* of crime, Deut. 21:6-7; Matthew 27:24.

To kiss one's hand is an act of *adoration,* Job 31:27.

To lift up one's hand was a *posture* used in *praying for a blessing,* Leviticus 9:22.

To lift up the hand against one, is to *rebel* against him, II Samuel 20:21.

To give one's hand, means to *swear friendship,* to promise *security,* to make *alliance,* II Kings 10:15.

The right hand denotes *power* or *strength.* The scripture generally imputes to God's *right hand* all the effects of his omnipotence, Exodus 15:6; Psalm 17:7; 20:6; 44:3.

Often, to be at one's right hand signifies to *defend,* to *protect,* to *support.* Psalm 16:8; 109:31.   (Cruden's *Concordance of the Bible*)

In the Book of Mormon the expression, *right hand,* is used with the same meaning as it has in the Bible. So that the reader may obtain a fuller understanding of the phrase, we render a complete list of its usage in the Sacred Record.

I Nephi	20:13	My r. h. hath spanned the heavens
II Nephi	19:20	And he shall snatch on his r. h.
Mosiah	5:9	Shall be found at the r. h. of
	26:23	Unto the end, a place at my r. h.
	24	Shall have a place eternally at my r. h.
Alma	5:58	Grant an inheritance at my r. h.
	24:23	Neither . . . turn aside to the r. h.
	28:12	Are raised to dwell at the r. h. of God
Helaman	3:30	Their immortal souls, at the r. h. of God
III Nephi	13:3	Thy left hand know what thy r. h. doeth
	22:3	Thou shalt break forth on the r. h.
	29:4	The sword of his justice is in his r. h.
	29:9	Turn the r. h. of the Lord unto
Ether	12:4	Even a place at the r. h. of God
	14:2	Kept the hilt of his sword . . . in his r. h.
Moroni	7:27	Hath set down on the r. h. of God
	9:26	Jesus Christ, who sitteth on the r. h. of his power

pass, that whosoever shall not take upon him the name of Christ must be called by some other name; therefore, he findeth himself on the left hand of God.

The name of Christ. The name by which all true believers in Christ are known. We also add here every mention in the Book of Mormon of the expression, *the name of Christ*.

II Nephi	31:13	Take upon you the name of C., by
	32:9	Ye shall pray unto the Father in the name of C.
	33:12	I pray the Father in the name of C.
Enos	1:15	Ye shall receive in the name of C.
Mosiah	3:17	Only in and through the name of C.
	5:8	Ye should take upon you the name of C.
	9	For he shall be called by the name of C.
	10	Whosoever shall not take upon them the name of C.
	6:2	Had taken upon them the name of C.
	25:23	Desirous to take upon them the name of C.
Alma	1:19	Had taken upon them the name of C.
	5:38	Which is the name of C.
	34:38	Take upon you the name of C.
	46:15	The name of C., or Christians
	18	We take upon us the name of C.
	21	Take upon them the name of C.
3 Nephi	27:5	Ye must take upon you the name of C.
Mormon	8:38	Ashamed to take upon you the name of C?
	9:21	Ask the Father in the name of C.
Moroni	3:2	Prayed unto the Father in the name of C.
	4:2	Pray to the Father in the name of C.
	6:3	They took upon them the name of C.
	10:4	Ask God, the Eternal Father, in the name of C.

VERSE 10. *Some other name*. All must have a name; some are called the *Children of Christ*, they having covenanted with Him to keep His commandments. Others are called by *some other name*, and are not known to Him as His own. They will find themselves on His left hand, and therefore will not be protected by His power, or sustained by His might. In fact, they will be left almost alone to bring about their own end.

Many years after Benjamin reigned over the Nephites in Zarahemla, the Risen Redeemer established His Church among the inhabitants of the Western Hemisphere. He chose Disciples here, as He had chosen Apostles in Jerusalem. He taught them the Gospel; He also empowered them to teach the people the same things He had showed to them.

One day the Disciples, as they journeyed about baptizing in the name of Jesus, met together in "mighty prayer and fasting." The question uppermost in their minds was one that, too, bothered many of the Saints. What name was the newly founded Church to bear? They pondered; some had offered one name, some another, still others favored something else. They disagreed among themselves for they did not understand the mighty works of the Lord. The Disciples, as they had been taught, earnestly sought the Lord for His answer to their dilemma.

While thus engaged in calling upon the Lord, He suddenly appeared among them and asked, "What will ye that I shall give unto you?"

11. And I would that ye should remember also, that this is the name that I said I should give unto you that never should be blotted out, except it be through transgression; therefore, take heed that ye do not transgress, that the name be not blotted out of your hearts.

12. I say unto you, I would that ye should remember to retain the name written always in your hearts, that ye are not found on the left hand of God, but that ye hear and know the voice by which ye shall be called, and also, the name by which he shall call you.

They, answering, replied, "Lord, we will that thou wouldst tell us the name whereby we shall call this church; for there are disputations among the people concerning this matter."

"And the Lord said unto them: Verily, verily, I say unto you, why is it that the people should murmur and dispute because of this thing?

"Have they not read the scriptures, which say ye must take upon you the name of Christ, which is my name? For by this name shall ye be called at the last day;

"And whoso taketh upon him my name, and endureth to the end, the same shall be saved at the last day.

"Therefore, whatsoever ye shall do, ye shall do it in my name; therefore ye shall call the church in my name; and ye shall call upon the Father in my name that he will bless the church for my sake.

"And how be it my church save it be called in my name? For if a church be called in Moses' name then it be Moses' church; or if it be called in the name of a man then it be the church of a man; but if it be called in my name then it is my church, if it so be that they are built upon my gospel."   (3 Nephi 27:1-8)

Verily is a word frequently used by the prophets the same as *behold* and *it came to pass.* It means *of a truth, certainly,* or *truly.*

We have here the very words of the Savior concerning the *name* by which His children shall be called, and He further brings to the attention of His Disciples the fact that the Scriptures add to His own words, the testimony of the prophets, "Ye must take upon you the name of Christ, which is my name."

Again, we draw the attention of the reader to the loss they sustain in the expurgation by Jewish editors of all mention of Christ in the Sacred Scriptures. Any reference to His Holy Name, Christ, has been deleted by them. His great name is objectionable to their present worship, and their pious greed has divested from their devotions any allusion to the *Greatest of their Prophets,* the Messiah for whom they have long waited, the poor *Galilean* whom their fathers so much despised.

The words of the Savior confirm those of King Benjamin, "And the Lord God hath sent his holy prophets among all the children of men, to declare these things to every kindred, nation, and tongue, that thereby whosoever should believe that Christ should come, the same might receive remission of their sins, and rejoice with exceeding great joy, even as though he had already come among them." (Mosiah 3:13)

VERSE 11. *This is the name I said I should give unto you.* See Mosiah 1:11-12. King Benjamin warned his people to always keep the Lord's commandments; do not transgress His laws, that you "may always have his spirit to be with" you, was the thought he wanted most to leave with them ere he departed.

VERSE 12. *Retain the name written always in your hearts.* The heart, then as now, was spoken of as the abiding place of love and the seat of our affections. If

13. For how knoweth a man the master whom he has not served, and who is a stranger unto him, and is far from the thoughts and intents of his heart?

14. And again, doth a man take an ass which belongeth to his neighbor, and keep him? I say unto you, Nay; he will not even suffer that he shall feed among his flocks, but will drive him away, and cast him out. I say unto you, that even so shall it be among you if ye know not the name by which ye are called.

15. Therefore, I would that ye

---

our love was for God, it came from the heart. If compassion for the sick and the needy filled our breasts, it came first from the heart. The heart is the symbol of fidelity and loving-kindness. It is in our hearts we remember the tender care of a mother, and her prayers for our welfare, also the untiring obligation a father felt to plant comfort, happiness and peace in our home.

It is also in the heart that we remember the things of God. We once heard a great speaker say, "I can prove Mormonism is true just like I can prove two times two is four." We were young then, but we knew our knowledge of the truthfulness of the Gospel was not a mental conclusion, but it stemmed from our hearts. We have seen the *lamp of truth* burn but dimly in the minds of the learned, however in the *hearts* of the humble and true it has proved to be a light which guided the wayfarer and found the *sheep* that had been lost.

I delight to do thy will, O my God: yea, thy law is within my *heart*. (Psalm 40:8)

And as they went on their way, they came unto a certain water: and the eunuch said, See, here is water; what doth hinder me to be baptized?

And Philip said, If thou believeth with all thine *heart*, thou mayest. And he answered and said, I believe that Jesus Christ is the Son of God. (Acts 8:36-37)

And this shall be my covenant that I will make with the house of Israel; After those days, saith the Lord: I will put my law in their inward parts, and write it in their *hearts;* and will be their God, and they shall be my people. (Jeremiah 31:33)

I perceive that they [the commandments of God] are not written in your hearts. (Mosiah 13:11)

That ye hear and remember the voice by which ye shall be called. The younger Alma, who became the Presiding High Priest of the Church, and of him we will later learn many things, offered this comment on a similar thought:

Behold, I say unto you, that the good shepherd doth call you; yea, and in his own name doth he call you, which is the name of Christ; and if ye will not hearken unto the voice of the good shepherd, to the name by which ye are called, behold, ye are not the sheep of the good shepherd. (Alma 5:38)

VERSES 13-14. *How knoweth a man the master whom he has not served.* We will gain great knowledge by associating these words with those of the Apostle Paul:

That if thou shalt confess with thy mouth the Lord Jesus, and shalt believe in thine heart that God hath raised him from the dead, thou shalt be saved.

For with the heart man believeth unto righteousness; and with the mouth confession is made unto salvation.

For the scripture saith, Whosoever believeth on him shall not be ashamed.

For there is no difference between the Jew and the Greek: for the same Lord over all is rich unto all that call upon him.

For whosoever shall call upon the name of the Lord shall be saved.

should be steadfast and immovable, always abounding in good works, that Christ, the Lord God Omnipotent, may seal you his, that you may be brought to heaven, that ye may have everlasting salvation and eternal life, through the wisdom, and power, and justice, and mercy of him who created all things, in heaven and in earth; who is God above all. Amen.

How then shall they call on him in whom they have not believed? And how shall they believe in him of whom they have not heard? and how shall they hear without a preacher?

And how shall they preach, except they be sent? . . . (Romans 10:9-15)

Paul teaches two great truths in these words; **First,** The authority by which men preach the Gospel of Christ—they must be sent. **Second,** that Salvation comes by serving Him, and to gain knowledge of Him is Eternal Life.

And again doth a man take an ass which belongeth to his neighbor, and keep him? To emphasize the point Benjamin has made, he compared the keeping of a strange ass, feeding it and caring for it, to looking after animals of one's own. He said, "He (meaning any man) will not even suffer that he (a strange ass) shall feed among the flocks, but will drive him away, and cast him out." It will be the same with the *sheep of Israel's fold,* and the *renegade* who scatters the flock. The Good Shepherd will not permit a wolf to enter in among His sheep. He will not leave them, but will make them "to lie down in green pastures, and will lead them "beside the still waters." They will follow Him, "for they know His voice," and from a stranger they will flee.

Again we remind you of the words of Alma which we quoted in verse twelve.

VERSE 15. *I would that ye should be steadfast and immovable.* King Benjamin ended his sermon, which ranks near the greatest recorded in the Book of Mormon, with an appeal to his people to be steadfast and true. He admonished them to let their good works abound in great plenty, that Christ, the Lord Omnipotent, through your faith in Him, "may seal you his."

In the name of Him who created all things in heaven and on earth, and in His wisdom, and power, and justice, King Benjamin invoked *Salvation and Eternal Life* upon all his people. His earnest prayer was that they "may be brought to heaven" through Christ, "who is God above all." Then in solemn ratification of all he had said, King Benjamin closed his earthly kingship by uttering the familiar word, *Amen* (may it be so). (*See* COMMENTARY ON THE BOOK OF MORMON, Vol. I, pp. 144 and 257)

NOTES

"The inference that the Church of Jesus Christ of Latter-day Saints is not a Christian organization is too absurd to require any extended comment. The foundation upon which the Church rests is faith in God the Eternal Father, His Son Jesus Christ, and the Holy Ghost, which constitute the Godhead. The Church teaches and its members testify that Jesus Christ is the Son of God, that by Him the worlds were created, and that through the redemption wrought out, because of the Atonement which He made, all mankind are redeemed from death, the penalty which was pronounced upon our father Adam because of transgression, and that through obedience to the doctrines which He taught we may be redeemed from personal sin.

"We bear witness to the world that there is no other name under heaven, nor is there any other means by which man can attain to glory, exaltation and Eternal Life except through the medium of Christ our Lord." (From a General Conference Address by Pres. Anthony W. Ivins, April 3, 1927)

CHAPTER 6

1. Names of People Recorded—2. Priests Appointed—3. Beginning of Mosiah's Reign—4. Death of King Benjamin.

1. Names of people recorded.

1. And now, king Benjamin thought it was expedient, after having finished speaking to the people, that he should take the names of all those who had entered into a covenant with God to keep his commandments.

2. And it came to pass that there was not one soul, except it were little children, but who had entered into the covenant and had taken upon them the name of Christ.

2. Priests appointed.

3. And again, it came to pass that when king Benjamin had made an end of all these things, and had consecrated his son Mosiah to be a ruler and a king over his people, and had given him all the charges concerning the kingdom, and also had appointed priests to teach the people, that thereby they might hear

---

VERSE 1. *All who had entered into a covenant with God.* Even as it is an obligation in these latter-days to record the names of those who have covenanted to serve the Lord, so also was it with the Nephites under the rule of King Benjamin. The custom to keep in touch with every Church member through the recording of every name was practised by all generations of the Nephites. Keeping a record of the membership is an important part of the Gospel Plan. Here it is written as plain as word can be:

And after they had been received unto baptism, and were wrought upon and cleansed by the power of the Holy Ghost, they were numbered among the people of the Church of Christ; and their names were taken, that they might be remembered and nourished by the good word of God, to keep them in the right way, to keep them continually watchful unto prayer, relying alone on the merits of Christ, who was the author and the finisher of their faith.   (Moroni 6:4)

VERSE 2. *Every soul . . . had taken upon them the name of Christ.* Mosiah, the historian of this part of the Sacred Record, says that every person, except the little children who could not understand, entered into that covenant, and hereby took upon themselves the "New Name" which King Benjamin gave them.

VERSE 3. *King Benjamin appointed priests to teach the people.* When King Benjamin had finished taking the census of his people, and had appointed his son, Mosiah, to be his successor on the Nephite throne, as the Lord had directed, and had also appointed priests to lead his people and thereby constantly remind them of the obligations they had entered into to serve the Lord, he dismissed those who had gathered in Zarahemla that they might return to their places of abode.

Here is recorded one of the finest periods of Nephite history. That so many, at one time, pledged their allegiance to the Kingdom of God, and, then and there, resolved to be "firm and steadfast, and immovable in keeping the commandments

and know the commandments of God, and to stir them up in remembrance of the oath which they had made, he dismissed the multitude, and they returned, every one, according to their families, to their own houses.

---

of the Lord," (Mosiah 5:15) has a counterpart when the Children of Israel stood before Mt. Sinai and made that solemn compact with the Lord, that they would be faithful to Him if He would be their God. (Exodus 19)

The covenant they made at the conference held in Zarahemla, raised the followers of Nephi to a glory and a prosperity that had not been surpassed in any of their bygone ages. What to them was once a duty, now became a pleasure, and serving the Lord was their delight. We need not wonder at this when we remember that the Nephites, themselves, were a deeply religious and a goodly people. A goodly people are a happy people, and, let us remember, also, "Happy is the people whose God is the Lord." (Hebrew saying)

Their conference now ended, we can conceive of the rejoicing that resounded in the tents of the Nephites, for, behold, in those never-to-be-forgotten days, when the glorious splendor of His Majesty illumined the understanding of all, they had heard the message of their Salvation through Jesus Christ, coming to them from the mouth of Benjamin.

And, now, before we close this account of the conference held by the Nephites in Zarahemla, 125 years before the Savior was born in Judea, may we offer this prayer:

"O Lord, our God: Thou Who art our Rock and our Redeemer; the delight of them that serve Thee, and the joy of all who do Thy will. We love and revere Thy holy name, may it be hallowed in all the earth, and amongst all people. Hear, Thou, our prayer. Bless every effort made to serve Thee and to advance Thy cause among men. Grant, our Heavenly Father, that Thou mayest be a light unto us in the darkness, and a lamp unto our feet. Teach us Thy ways, and we will surely walk in Thy paths. We recall, that in loving kindness, Thou didst bestow Thy bounties upon Thine ancient people of Zarahemla; we pray, that we, like unto them, may be worthy of Thy choicest blessings; that we, having the same Father as did they, may at all times see in them, our brothers; that we may profit by the lessons they shall teach us; that, as we grow in years, we may grow in grace and in the knowledge of Thy glory, or of that which is just and true. (See Mosiah 4:12)

"May the day come quickly, Father, when thy Will, done in heaven, shall be done upon the earth; when all Thine enemies shall be subdued; when goodness and purity shall dwell in every heart; then will the voice of Salvation be heard in every land, and thy Kingdom fill the earth. Then will the words of King Benjamin, Thine ancient servant, be fulfilled, 'Moreover, I say unto you, that the time shall come when the knowledge of the Savior shall spread throughout every nation, kindred, tongue, and people.' (Mosiah 3:20) Then, but not 'til then, shall Thy peace cover the earth, even as do the waters cover the mighty deep."

With feelings of joy, and with the Law of the Gospel of Jesus Christ in their hearts, the people of King Benjamin departed to their own homes, and carried thereto, the Glad Tidings of Man's Redemption through Christ, the Messiah who was yet to come.

The truths revealed by King Benjamin enlightened every mind, and illumined every path which led to the Eternal Home, and most of these Nephites faithfully walked therein the balance of their mortal lives.

4. And Mosiah began to reign in his father's stead. And he began to reign in the thirtieth year of his age, making in the whole, about four hundred and seventy-six years from the time that Lehi left Jerusalem.

5. And king Benjamin lived three years and he died.

6. And it came to pass that king Mosiah did walk in the ways of the Lord, and did observe his judgments and his statutes, and did keep his commandments in all things whatsoever he commanded him.

7. And king Mosiah did cause his people that they should till the earth. And he also, himself, did till the earth, that thereby he might not become burdensome to his people, that he might do according to that which his father had done in all things. And there was no contention among all his people for the space of three years.

One passage that may describe the joy that filled their hearts is: "Light is sown for the righteous, and gladness for the upright in heart." (Psalm 97:11) The seeds of righteousness sown by King Benjamin found fertile soil in every heart, and grew, as we shall presently see, into a bounteous harvest of them who loved the Lord and sought to do His Will.

VERSES 4-5. *Mosiah began to reign in his father's stead.* King Benjamin's royal work was now done. He had lived to bring his people into communion with their Creator. His spirit was full of heavenly joy, but his body was bent under the weight of many years. His hair was white, and his voice could scarcely be heard. However, before his subjects returned to their homes, Benjamin gave them, as was his privilege, his patriarchal blessing.

Mosiah now reigned in his father's stead, whilst Benjamin, beloved and honored, remained yet another three years on the earth before he returned to the presence of his Heavenly Father.

VERSES 6-7. *King Mosiah did walk in the ways of the Lord.* To recapitulate: Mosiah was born in the Land of Zarahemla 154 or 155 years before the coming of the Savior. He was instructed in all the learning of the Nephites, and trained up in his youth in the fear of the Lord. By the direction of the Almighty, he was consecrated by his father to succeed him on the throne. This ceremony was attended to at the time the entire nation gathered at the temple in Zarahemla to listen to the words of their aged and beloved ruler. At this same time each one of them covenanted with God to be His servant. There, in the presence of his future subjects, under the shadow of the holy temple, Mosiah was set apart to rule a people whose sins were forgiven through their abiding faith in the as yet unborn Redeemer. Could a king come to the throne under more auspicious circumstances? Profound peace ruled with all who were outside his dominions, and within its borders reigned union, contentment, prosperity, happiness, and what is more, righteousness.

Mosiah was thirty years old when he began to reign. This was 476 years after Lehi left Jerusalem. Mosiah followed in the footsteps of his father and taught his people to be industrious; he also set them a good example by tilling a portion of the earth to maintain himself and his dependents.

CHAPTER 7

1. Expedition to the Land of Lehi-Nephi—2. Ammon and King Limhi—3. People of Lehi-Nephi in Bondage to the Lamanites.

1. Expedition to the Land of Lehi-Nephi.

1. And now, it came to pass that after king Mosiah had had continual peace for the space of three years, he was desirous to know concerning the people who went up to dwell in the land of Lehi-Nephi, or in the city of Lehi-Nephi; for his people had heard nothing from them from the time they left the land of Zarahemla; therefore, they wearied him with their teasings.

2. And it came to pass that king Mosiah granted that sixteen of their strong men might go up to the land of Lehi-Nephi to inquire concerning their brethren.

3. And it came to pass that on the morrow they started to go up, having with them one Ammon, he being a strong and mighty man, and a descendant of Zarahemla; and he was also their leader.

4. And now, they knew not the

VERSE 1. *He was desirous to know concerning the people who went up to dwell in the Land of Lehi-Nephi.* Continued peace for a number of years in Mosiah's realm caused many of his subjects to wonder more and more about the fate of those who had returned to their old homes in the Land of Lehi-Nephi. The Sacred Record says, "They wearied him with their teasings," for they had heard nothing of them for many years, not since they had left to re-establish their homes in that land.

VERSE 2. *Sixteen strong men were chosen to go to Lehi-Nephi.* Under King Mosiah's direction, sixteen strong and presumably young men were provisioned and made ready to proceed to the Land of Lehi-Nephi, or to the City of Lehi-Nephi, to ascertain the fate of their brethren.

Meaning of the Name. We take the meaning of this name to be the Land of Nephi, or the *City* of Nephi in the *Land* of Lehi, to distinguish them from the land and city of the same name in Zarahemla, where there also was a land and a city largely occupied by Nephites. It is, as if one would say, the "Utah-Jordan," to distinguish that river from the famous "Palestine-Jordan." Helaman, the son of Helaman, later in the record informs us, "The land south was called Lehi, and the land north was called Mulek, which was after the son of Zedekiah; for the Lord did bring Mulek into the land north, and Lehi into the land south." (Helaman 6:10)*

VERSES 3-6. *Not knowing the course they should travel, they took forty days in their wanderings.* An expedition consisting of sixteen strong men, headed by Ammon, a descendant of King Zarahemla, needed forty days to reach a hill north in the

*Elder George Reynolds, in his The Story of the Book of Mormon says that the Mulekites landed in the southern portion of North America, and in after years moved southward to the place where they were discovered by Mosiah I. Accepting this as authentic, the editor of this Commentary ventures the suggestion that the guardians of the child Mulek escaped to Jaffa, where they found a "Tarshish"-ship that would take them to Spain, and possibly, across the Atlantic. Jonah, it will be remembered, on his flight, went to Jaffa, where he found a ship going to Tarshish, Spain, on which he took passage. (Jonah 1:3)

course they should travel in the wilderness to go up to the land of Lehi-Nephi; therefore they wandered many days in the wilderness, even forty days did they wander.

5. And when they had wandered forty days they came to a hill, which is north of the land of Shilom, and there they pitched their tents.

6. And Ammon took three of his brethren, and their names were Amaleki, Helem, and Hem, and they went down into the land of Nephi.

7. And behold, they met the king of the people who were in the land of Nephi, and in the land of Shilom; and they were surrounded by the king's guard, and were taken, and were bound, and were committed to prison.

2. Ammon and King Limhi.

8. And it came to pass when they had been in prison two days they were again brought before the king, and their hands were loosed; and they stood before the king, and were permitted, or rather commanded, that they should answer the questions which he should ask them.

9. And he said unto them: Behold, I am Limhi, the son of Noah, who was the son of Zeniff, who came up out of the land of Zarahemla to inherit this land, which was the land of their fathers, who was made a king by the voice of the people.

10. And now, I desire to know

Land of Shilom, a district contiguous to the Land of Lehi-Nephi. But they were lost in the wilderness for some days. The ruler of these expatriates from Zarahemla was Limhi, a grandson of Zeniff, who had led the malcontents to their former homes.

VERSE 7. In verse six we are told that Ammon made what he thought were the proper arrangements to fulfill his mission. He chose three of their number to accompany him, "and they went down into the Land of Nephi." Their names were Amaleki, Helem, and Hem. When Ammon and his companions reached Lehi-Nephi, King Limhi happened to be outside the confines of the city. King Limhi's guards, fancying that Ammon and those who were with him were spies, or perhaps some of the priests of Noah, put Ammon and his party in prison. This suspected Noah, before his death, was king of the land over which Limhi ruled.

VERSE 8. *They were brought before the king.* Ammon and his companions remained in prison two days. Then they were brought forth and made to stand before the king. The bands that held them tightly were released, or, at least, loosened and Ammon was commanded to answer any question the king might ask him.

VERSES 9-11. *And he said unto them: Behold, I am Limhi . . . Ye are permitted to speak.* King Limhi disclosed his identity to Ammon and his brethren, proving himself to be king, the son of Noah, and the grandson of Zeniff, who, himself, had been made king by the voice of the people. He asked Ammon why he had been so bold, so foolhardy, and so rash, as to approach the defended city when he knew it was the custom to slay anyone who, without apparent reason, happened to do so. Ammon's life and the lives of his companions were solely in the hands of the king.

the cause whereby ye were so bold as to come near the walls of the city, when I, myself, was with my guards without the gate?

11. And now, for this cause have I suffered that ye should be preserved, that I might inquire of you, or else I should have caused that my guards should have put you to death. Ye are permitted to speak.

12. And now, when Ammon saw that he was permitted to speak, he went forth and bowed himself before the king; and rising again he said: O king, I am very thankful before God this day that I am yet alive, and am permitted to speak; and I will endeavor to speak with boldness;

13. For I am assured that if ye had known me ye would not have suffered that I should have worn these bands. For I am Ammon, and am a descendant of Zarahemla, and have come up out of the land of Zarahemla to inquire concerning our brethren, whom Zeniff brought up out of that land.

14. And now, it came to pass that after Limhi had heard the words of Ammon, he was exceeding glad, and said. Now, I know of a surety that my brethren who were in the land of Zarahemla are yet alive. And now, I will rejoice; and on the morrow I will cause that my people shall rejoice also.

15. For behold, we are in bondage to the Lamanites, and are taxed with a tax which is grievous to be borne. And now, behold, our brethren will deliver us out of our bondage, or out of the hands of the Lamanites, and we will be their slaves; for it is better that we be slaves to the Nephites than to pay tribute to the king of the Lamanites.

16. And now, king Limhi commanded his guards that they should no more bind Ammon nor

---

VERSES 12-13. *I am Ammon, and am a descendant of Zarahemla.* With due regard for the courtesies due one of royal station, Ammon paid obeisance to his regal captor. He recounted, after praising God for the privilege of speaking, his own birth and how he had come from Zarahemla to bring succor if it were needed, and thereby learn of the circumstances surrounding the condition of their brethren whom Zeniff had "brought up out of the land." The mistake King Limhi had made, was now corrected, and an explanation of it was quickly realized by Ammon.

VERSES 14-16. *Better that we be slaves to the Nephites than to pay tribute to the king of the Lamanites.* The Nephites, who under King Limhi dwelt in the land of Lehi-Nephi, like their brethren in Zarahemla, had heard nothing of the others since they parted many years before. At one time they all lived in that great city which was their capital, but restive souls among them, urged many to unite and return to Lehi-Nephi where it was hoped they could re-establish homes in the land which under the Mosaic Law they believed was the land of their inheritance. Many who departed with Zeniff and also many who remained in Zarahemla felt bereft of the association of friends and loved ones from whom they hoped to hear.

The uncertainty of the fate of the others preyed heavily upon them. They wished to know what had become of one another. They grew insistent to the extent that King Mosiah, who lived in Zarahemla, ordered a party of strong men to go

his brethren, but caused that they should go to the hill which was north of Shilom, and bring their brethren into the city, that thereby they might eat, and drink, and rest themselves from the labors of their journey; for they had suffered many things; they had suffered hunger, thirst, and fatigue.

3. People of Lehi-Nephi in Bondage to Lamanites.

17. And now, it came to pass on the morrow that king Limhi sent a proclamation among all his people, that thereby they might gather themselves together to the temple to hear the words which he should speak unto them.

18. And it came to pass that when they had gathered themselves together that he spake unto them in this wise, saying: O ye, my people, lift up your heads and be comforted; for behold, the time is at hand, or is not far distant, when we shall no

---

search them out. After forty days they found their ill-fortuned brethren existing in a most grievous manner. Ammon learned that they were abused, spied upon, and were watched continually by the Lamanites who had imposed taxes which were beyond any measure of need. In fact they were in bondage.

King Limhi, though sorely burdened, rejoiced because now that their brethren in Zarahemla would soon know of their oppression, they would be delivered. In his hour of thankfulness, the king even expressed the willingness of his people to be slaves of their brethren if they so desired. But, however, this thing could not be done; the Law of Moses prohibited brethren from enslaving brethren. In any event, Limhi, the wretched overseer — for he was only nominally a king — determined that, if possible, his people would no longer pay tribute to the Lamanite king. "I will rejoice," he said, "and on the morrow I will cause that my people shall rejoice also."

King Limhi then bid his soldiers to release Ammon and his friends and to take such help to the others of Ammon's companions that he had left at the camping place near Shilom, for they were, doubtless, weary and worn with the toils of a long journey in which they had "suffered hunger, thirst, and fatigue."

VERSE 17. *King Limhi sent a proclamation to all his people.* It was the custom among the Nephites to meet at the call of their ruler at some sacred place where they could receive any message they had to deliver. Jacob had imparted the word of the Lord to the Nephites from the temple his brother, Nephi, had caused to be erected; King Benjamin sent heralds throughout all the land to proclaim a conference at the temple in Zarahemla; in similar manner King Limhi now ordered his people to present themselves at the temple in Lehi-Nephi where they "would hear the words he should speak to them."

VERSE 18. *O ye, my people, lift up your heads and be comforted.* The people gathered as King Limhi had commanded, and he spoke words of comfort and courage to them. He told them that the time was coming and "is not far distant," when with joy they would cease to be tyrannized by their enemies, that in spite of the many vain struggles that they had made to escape their oppressive bondsmen, they now would be delivered, and that they would be set free from being the slaves of the Lamanites.

longer be in subjection to our enemies, notwithstanding our many strugglings, which have been in vain; yet I trust there remaineth an effectual struggle to be made.

19. Therefore, lift up your heads, and rejoice, and put your trust in God, in that God who was the God of Abraham, and Isaac, and Jacob; and also, that God who brought the children of Israel out of the land of Egypt, and caused that they should walk through the Red Sea on dry ground, and fed them with manna that they might not perish in the wilderness; and many more things did he do for them.

20. And again, that same God has brought our fathers out of the land of Jerusalem, and has kept and preserved his people even until now; and behold, it is because of our iniquities and abominations that he has brought us into bondage.

21. And ye all are witnesses this day, that Zeniff, who was made king over this people, he being over-zealous to inherit the land of his fathers, therefore being deceived by the cunning and craftiness of king Laman, who having entered into a treaty with king Zeniff, and having yielded up into his hands the possessions of a part of the land, or even the city of Lehi-Nephi, and the city of Shilom; and the land round about—

VERSES 19-20. *Therefore, lift up your heads, and rejoice, and put your trust in God.* Unlike his father, King Noah, who had preceded him on the throne, Limhi was a courageous and a God-fearing man. He had seen the afflictions of his people increase with the examples his father had set, and, with them, he had suffered the burdensome tasks that were imposed by their Lamanite bondsmen.

No doubt, Limhi was a student of the Sacred Scriptures; in them he found where God had delivered the Children of Israel from Egyptian bondage and had caused that they should escape the perils of their long journey in the wilderness. He read where the Lord had brought them through the Red Sea on dry ground, and that He had fed them with manna from above. King Limhi also read where, in the dry Arabian Desert, water, by the power of God, was brought forth from the granite rock so that the Children of Israel could slake their thirst. Of these things, Limhi reminded his people, and from hearing them again they gained courage and hope.

Limhi then turned to their own experiences. This same God, he said, brought their fathers out of Jerusalem and thereby saved them from wicked bondage under unpitying enemies. God has preserved this people until now according to the promise He made to them when first Lehi's colony disembarked from the ship which under divine guidance they had prepared. The Lord promised them that as long as they were obedient and kept His commandments, they would be blessed and prospered in the land. King Limhi now declared that through no other faults than their own, they were in sore bondage to the Lamanites. He said it was the result of wickedness and the abominations of which they were guilty that the Lord "has brought us into bondage."

VERSES 21-23. *Zeniff was deceived by King Laman.* Limhi pointed to the trials which his people had undergone because of wickedness. He began his resume by citing the exploits of his grandfather, Zeniff. He told them that Zeniff was a man of redoubtable will; he was not easily discouraged but persevered so greatly in his

22. And all this he did, for the sole purpose of bringing this people into subjection or into bondage. And behold, we at this time do pay tribute to the king of the Lamanites, to the amount of one half of our corn, and our barley, and even all our grain of every kind, and one half of the increase of our flocks and our herds; and even one half of all we have or possess the king of the Lamanites doth exact of us, or our lives.

23. And now, is not this grievous to be borne? And is not this, our affliction, great? Now behold, how great reason we have to mourn.

24. Yea, I say unto you, great are the reasons which we have to mourn; for behold how many of our brethren have been slain, and their blood has been spilt in vain, and all because of iniquity.

25. For if this people had not fallen into transgression the Lord would not have suffered that this great evil should come upon them. But behold, they would not hearken unto his words; but there arose contentions among them, even so much that they did shed blood among themselves.

26. And a prophet of the Lord have they slain; yea, a chosen man of God, who told them of

---

scheme to re-colonize their old homes that he became "overzealous to inherit the land of his fathers."

Zeniff, Limhi reminded his people, made a treaty with the king of the Lamanites whereby he and his followers obtained much of the choicest land in the Lamanite kingdom. This treaty also gave them the cities of Lehi-Nephi and Shilom. Zeniff, by the voice of the people was then made king over all the Nephites who dwelt in that land.

King Laman had only one object in mind when he made that favorable treaty with Zeniff, Limhi declared. The well hidden purpose of the Lamanite king was to have settled in the midst of his indolent subjects a thrifty and industrious people as were the Nephites. When they became settled in their new homes, and the land given them began to yield an abundance of the field, the intention of King Laman was to extract as tribute from the hard-working Nephites a goodly portion of their income. In fulfillment of this plot Limhi declared that even then they were paying to the Lamanite king, one half of all the grain they produced, one half of the increase of their flocks and their herds, and even, he said, "one half of all we possess." We do this as he demands or we forfeit our lives.

Not to pity himself or his people, nor to offer any excuses for the past, King Limhi contrasted their awful condition with what it might have been had they served the Lord as was their portion. For them to see their almost hopeless state in their bitter remorse was sufficient cause for them to mourn.

VERSES 24-25. *Many of our brethren have been slain.* In addition to the bondage in which the Nephites were held, King Limhi recounted to them the several unsuccessful efforts they had made to gain liberty. In these vain attempts "many of our brethren have been slain," "and all because of iniquity," he said.

If we had not yielded to the blandishments of sin, and had not rejected the words of God's servants whom He sent to warn us, the Lord would not have suffered this great affliction to come upon us. King Limhi further reminded his people of the discord and the contentions among them that sometimes rose to such heights that they even shed the blood of their antagonists.

their wickedness and abominations, and prophesied of many things which are to come, yea, even the coming of Christ.

27. And because he said unto them that Christ was the God, the Father of all things, and said that he should take upon him the image of man, and it should be the image after which man was created in the beginning; or in other words, he said that man was created after the image of God, and that God should come down among the children of men, and take upon him flesh and blood, and go forth upon the face of the earth—

28. And now, because he said this, they did put him to death; and many more things did they

do which brought down the wrath of God upon them. Therefore, who wondereth that they are in bondage, and that they are smitten with sore afflictions?

29. For behold, the Lord hath said: I will not succor my people in the day of their transgression; but I will hedge up their ways that they prosper not; and their doings shall be as a stumbling block before them.

30. And again, he saith: If my people shall sow filthiness they shall reap the chaff thereof in the whirlwind; and the effect thereof is poison.

31. And again he saith: If my people shall sow filthiness they shall reap the east wind, which bringeth immediate destruction.

VERSES 26-28. *A prophet of the Lord have they slain.* King Limhi continued the indictment of his people. So recently had they connived in the Prophet Abinadi's death that the circumstances of it were fresh in everyone's mind. Because he spoke boldly of their sins and called upon them to forsake their wicked ways, they became angry with him and caused him to be burned at the stake.

To show them the enormity of their wickedness, King Limhi set forth in detail many of the things Abinadi prophesied, and for these, he said, you have taken him and "put him to death." To excuse your blameworthy conduct you betook yourselves all manner of evil doings. "Therefore," he asked them, "who wondereth that they [we] are in bondage, and that they [we] are smitten with sore afflictions?"

VERSE 29. *I will not succor my people in the day of their transgression.* Succor means *aid, help,* or *assist.*

VERSE 30. *If my people shall sow filthiness.* Like the passage quoted in verse twenty-nine, we do not find these words in the Hebrew Scriptures. However, a similar meaning is conveyed in Hosea 8:7:

For they [Israel] have sown the wind, and they shall reap the whirlwind: it hath no stalk: the bud shall yield no meal.

also,

Even as I have seen, they that plow iniquity, and sow wickedness, reap the same.   (Job 4:8)

VERSE 31. *If my people shall sow filthiness, they shall reap the east wind.* The reference to "the east wind" as an agent of destruction shows that the author of these texts was influenced by a mode of thinking that obtained in ancient Palestine. In

32. And now, behold, the promise of the Lord is fulfilled, and ye are smitten and afflicted.

33. But if ye will turn to the Lord with full purpose of heart, and put your trust in him, and serve him with all diligence of mind, if ye do this, he will, according to his own will and pleasure, deliver you out of bondage.

---

that country the east wind then as now is harmful to vegetation. In the winter it is dry and cold, and in the summer it is dry and hot. It carries off the moisture on the leaves rapidly causing them to wither and die. On the Mediterranean this east wind is known as a *levanter,* and is regarded as dangerous to sailors. It was in such a storm that Paul was shipwrecked, and, with all the crew and passengers, stranded on the island of Malta. (*See* Acts 27:14-44) The Prophet Habakkuk (Hab. 3:17) describes in a few words what may be expected when the east wind reaps its harvest of destruction: "Although the fig tree shall not blossom, neither shall fruit be in the vines; the labour of the olive shall fail, and the fields shall yield no meat; the flock shall be cut off from the fold, and there shall be no herd in the stalls: Yet I will rejoice in the LORD, I will joy in the God of my salvation." (*See* Mosiah 12:6)

VERSE 32. *The promise of the Lord is fulfilled.* This conclusion of King Limhi's was based on the words of the Prophet Abinadi, who, when the flames of the fire the wicked priests of King Noah had kindled began to sear his aching feet, cried out against them, saying:

Behold, even as ye have done unto me, so shall it come to pass that thy seed shall cause that many shall suffer even the pains of death by fire; and this because they believe in the salvation of the Lord their God.
And it will come to pass that ye shall be afflicted with all manner of diseases because of your iniquities.
Yea, and ye shall be smitten on every hand, and shall be driven and scattered to and fro, even as a wild flock is driven by wild and ferocious beasts.
And in that day ye shall be hunted, and ye shall be taken by the hand of your enemies, and then ye shall suffer, as I suffer, the pains of death by fire.
Thus God executeth vengeance upon those that destroy his people. O God, receive my soul.

VERSE 33. *If you will turn to the Lord.* The people knew that King Limhi spoke the truth; every word of Abinadi's had been fulfilled. They had been driven and hunted by the Lamanites who resisted every effort the Nephites made to escape the ravages of their taskmaster's hatred. Disease and pestilence had taken their toll. Insurrection from within, and invasion of their capital city, made them like a "wild flock . . . driven by wild and ferocious beasts." King Noah, like Abinadi, was burned to death. The people had only one recourse. King Limhi pointed to it. He, no doubt, remembered the words of the Psalmist, "I will lift up mine eyes unto the hills, from whence cometh my help. My help cometh from the Lord, which made heaven and\earth. . . . he shall preserve thee from all evil." (Psalm 121) Like being bourne aloft on an eagle's pinions, far above the rugged pursuits of life, the memory of these words raised King Limhi to heights of which he never before had dreamed. A prayer left his lips: "Almighty God, in all our trials we turn unto Thee, who art our ever-present help in time of trouble. Forsake us not nor abandon us. Make us feel that Thou art near unto all who call upon Thee, who call upon Thee in truth. Guide us by Thy counsel and lead us in Thy love. . . . (Jewish Prayer) May we find favor in Thy sight."

King Limhi rejoiced in the Lord; he bade his people also to rejoice and promised them that notwithstanding the errors of the past, if they would put their trust in the Lord and determine in their hearts to serve Him, at His own will and pleasure, He will "deliver you out of bondage." (Mosiah 17:15-19)

AMMON

A descendant of Zarahemla, (either his son or grandson) who led a party of sixteen picked men from Zarahemla to Lehi-Nephi in the reign of Mosiah II in the endeavor to discover what had become of the people of Zeniff. They were unacquainted with the road and wandered for forty days in the wilderness before they reached their destination. Ammon then chose three companions, Amaleki, Helem and Hem to go forward and reconnoiter. They were discovered by King Limhi and his guards when near the city and cast into prison, being mistaken for the apostate priests of King Noah. After two days they were again brought before the king, when mutual explanations ensued and Ammon to his joy found that he had reached those for whom he was in search. But Limhi's people were in great distress and in bondage to the Lamanites. The next day Limhi assembled his people at the temple that they might all hear of the prosperity of their brethren in Zarahemla, at the recital of which they greatly rejoiced. Limhi and his people also wished to make covenant with God by baptism but there was no one among them authorized to administer this ordinance and Ammon would not, considering himself an unworthy servant. Their next duty was to escape from their Lamanitish task-masters which they shortly afterwards effected with the aid of Ammon and Gideon; Ammon and his brethren guiding them through the wilderness to the land of Zarahemla (B.C. 112).

HELEM

A brother of Ammon, the leader of the party that went from Zarahemla to Lehi-Nephi to discover the people of Zeniff (B.C. 122). Helem accompanied his brethren on this expedition and was one of the four cast into prison by King Limhi, under the supposition that they were some of the priests of his father, Noah, who had carried off the daughters of the Lamanites. Helem is only mentioned by name in connection with this incident but it is evident that if he was a brother of Ammon, according to the flesh, he was a descendant of Zarahemla and doubtless was born in the land of that name and returned to it with the rest of the party when they led the people of Limhi out of the land of Lehi-Nephi.

LAMAN

A king of the Lamanites. His father's name is said to have been the same as his own. Presuming him to have been the son of the monarch who made the treaty with Zeniff, he came to the throne about B.C. 160 and immediately commenced war with the Nephites in the land of Lehi-Nephi. As long as Zeniff lived the Lamanites were unsuccessful and were driven back to their own possessions with great slaughter; but when the weak and corrupt Noah reigned in the place of his father they became more successful. Their first invasion in Noah's reign was, however, unsuccessful but after his people had slain the prophet Abinadi, the Lord used the Lamanites to scourge them for their iniquities. The hosts of this people came upon Lehi-Nephi from the borders of Shemlon. Noah ordered a precipitate retreat into the wilderness; but being incumbered with women and children, the Lamanites overtook them. The coward king commanded that the women and children should be left to the mercy of the invaders and that the men continue their flight. Some obeyed but many refused. Those who remained with their families caused their women to plead with the Lamanites for their lives. Then the latter, charmed with the beauty of the Nephite women, had compassion on them, spared their lives but held the Nephites in tribute—one-half of all they possessed was the amount of the Lamanite exaction. Laman set guards around the land of Nephi to prevent the escape of any of the Nephites; their tribute was too valuable to the indolent Lamanites to permit of its decease or stoppage. In this condition things remained for two years.

At this time there was a romantic spot in the land of Shemlon, where the Lamanitish maidens were in the habit of gathering on pleasure bent. Here they sang, danced and made merry with all the gaiety of youthful innocence and overflowing spirits. One day, when a few were thus gathered, they were suddenly surprised, and twenty-four of their number were carried off by strange men, who from their appearance, were unmistakably Nephites.

On learning of this act of treachery the Lamanites were stirred to uncontrollable anger and without seeking an explanation they made a sudden incursion into the territory held by King Limhi. This attack, however, was not successful, for their movements, though not understood, had been discovered and their intended victims poured forth to meet them.

With Limhi and his people it was a war for existence: to be defeated was to be annihilated; his warriors therefore fought with superhuman energy and desperation and eventually they succeeded in driving the Lamanites back. So speedy did the flight become, that in their confusion the Lamanites left their wounded king lying among the heaps of slain. There he was discovered by the victors. In the interview between him and Limhi that followed, mutual explanations ensued. The Lamanite king complained bitterly of the outrage committed on the daughters of his people, while Limhi protested that he and his subjects were innocent of the base act. Further investigation developed the fact that some of the iniquitous priests of King Noah, who had fled into the wilderness from the dreaded vengeance of their abused countrymen, at the time that monarch was killed, were the guilty parties. Being without wives and fearing to return home, they had adopted this plan to obtain them.

On hearing this explanation King Laman consented to make an effort to pacify his angry hosts. At the head of an unarmed body of Nephites he went forth and met his armies who were returning to the attack. He explained what he had learned and the Lamanites, possibly somewhat ashamed of their rashness, renewed the covenant of peace.

This peace, unfortunately, was of short duration. The Lamanites grew arrogant and grievously oppressive and under their exactions and cruelty the condition of Limhi's subjects grew continually worse until they were little better off than were their ancestors in Egypt before Moses, their deliverer, arose. Three times they broke out in ineffectual rebellion and just as often their task-masters grew more cruel and exacting, until their spirits were entirely broken; they cowered before their oppressors, and bowed "to the yoke of bondage, submitting themselves to be smitten and to be driven to and fro and burdened according to the desires of their enemies."

In process of time the Lord softened the hearts of the Lamanites so that they began to ease the burdens of their slaves but he did not deliver the Nephites out of bondage at once. They, however, gradually prospered and raised more grain, flocks and herds, so that they did not suffer with hunger. And in the Lord's due time they escaped from their Lamanite oppressors and in safety reached the land of Zarahemla.

Great was the excitement among the subjects of Laman when they found their Nephite vassals had disappeared. An army was immediately sent in pursuit. It followed the fugitives for some distance but did not overtake them and lost itself in the wilderness. In their wandering the Lamanite troops found the priests of Noah and their Lamanitish wives and later they came across the people of Alma in the land of Helam. The Lamanites extended their suzerainty over both these peoples and King Laman appointed Amulon, the leader of the priests of Noah, the local ruler.

LIMHI

The son of Noah, and third king over the colony which left Zarahemla and returned to Lehi-Nephi. His reign was little more than a nominal one, as his people were in bondage to the Lamanites to whom they paid one-half of all they possessed and one-half of the products of their yearly toil. Out of this were paid the guards who were set to watch that none of the Nephites escaped. Limhi's reign was marked by several disastrous wars, one brought on by the fugitive priests of King Noah (see Laman, Amulon), the others were the abortive attempts of the people of Limhi to throw off the oppressor's yoke but in every case the revolt ended in its suppression and the infliction of heavier burdens and more cruel indignities upon the unfortunate Nephites. All of this was in fulfillment of the words of the prophet Abinadi. Thus the years slowly and painfully wore away. The Lord, after a time, softened the hearts of the Lamanites so that they treated their captives with less cruelty. He also prospered them in their labors that they did not suffer any more from hunger.

In this sad condition of bondage and serfdom the people of Limhi had one hope. It was to communicate with their Nephite friends in the land of Zarahemla. To this end Limhi secretly fitted out an expedition consisting of a small number of men. This company became lost in the wilderness and traveled a long distance northward until they found a land covered with the dry bones of men who appeared to have fallen in battle. Limhi's people thought this must be the land of Zarahemla and that their Nephite brethren who dwelt there had been destroyed. But in this they were wrong for they found with the dead some records engraved on plates of gold, which, when afterwards translated by the power of God, showed that these bones were those of some of the Jaredites who had been slain in war. They evidently missed the land of Zarahemla, having traveled to the west of it and passed northward through the Isthmus of Panama.

Shortly after this a small company, numbering sixteen men, reached them from Zarahemla. Their leader's name was Ammon. He had been sent by King Mosiah to the land of Nephi, to find out what had become of the people who left with Zeniff, Limhi's grandfather. At first Ammon's men were taken for spies and cast into prison. The next day the mistake was discovered and Limhi and his people were overjoyed to hear from their friends. Soon plans were laid to effect the escape of the enslaved Nephites, which, under the guidance of Limhi, Ammon and Gideon were successfully accomplished. The Lamanite guards were made drowsy through a large present of wine which they freely drank. While in this condition the Nephites escaped through an unfrequented pass, crossed the wilderness and reached the land of Zarahemla in safety (B.C. 122). After the arrival of his people in Zarahemla we hear nothing more of Limhi, save that he and all who accompanied him from Lehi-Nephi were baptized by Alma, the elder, and became members of the church of God.

CHAPTER 8

1. *Ammon Learns of the Discovery of Twenty-four Gold Plates with Engravings*—2. *He Suggests their Submission to King Mosiah, Prophet and Seer.*

1. *Ammon learns of the discovery of twenty-four gold plates with engravings.*

1. And it came to pass that after king Limhi had made an end of speaking to his people, for he spake many things unto them and only a few of them have I written in this book, he told his people all the things concerning their brethren who were in the land of Zarahemla.

2. And he caused that Ammon should stand up before the multitude, and rehearse unto them all that had happened unto their brethren from the time that Zeniff went up out of the land even until the time that he himself came up out of the land.

3. And he also rehearsed unto them the last words which king Benjamin had taught them, and explained them to the people of king Limhi, so that they might understand all the words which he spake.

4. And it came to pass that after he had done all this, that king Limhi dismissed the multitude, and caused that they should return every one unto his own house.

VERSE 1. *Limhi told his people about their brethren in Zarahemla.* In the abridgment he made of the great number of plates in his possession, Mormon notes that after King Limhi had finished speaking to his distraught and greatly distressed people, he told them all the things Ammon had previously made known unto him concerning "their brethren in Zarahemla." By way of interpolation, Mormon also notes that only a few of the things King Limhi said in addressing his people were written by the abridger, himself, "in this book."

VERSES 2-4. *King Limhi caused that Ammon should also speak.* The second-hand account which King Limhi gave to his people concerning their brethren in Zarahemla was verified by Ammon, who stood before the multitude that had gathered there and rehearsed to them the many things that had happened in Zarahemla under the reign of King Benjamin, or from the time Zeniff and his followers left their capital city until "the time that he himself came up out of the land."

Ammon told the assembled throng of the peaceful reign of King Benjamin and of the growth of the people there in both numbers and materials. He told them of the righteous desires of Benjamin for his people, and of the examples he set for them to follow. He recounted how King Benjamin had "labored with his own hands" that his people should not be burdened with taxes which might become oppressive, and, also that Benjamin desired no recompense for his service to them, save that they serve God by ministering to each others' wants.

Many other of Benjamin's teachings were explained to Limhi's people by Ammon. How great, they thought, was the difference under which they, themselves, had been forced to live by wicked King Noah and the unselfish rule of Benjamin in Zarahemla. It is worthy of note to remember that for many years Limhi's people had not been taught Gospel principles. Noah's priests had explained none of them

5. And it came to pass that he caused that the plates which contained the record of his people from the time that they left the land of Zarahemla, should be brought before Ammon, that he might read them.

6. Now, as soon as Ammon had read the record, the king inquired of him to know if he could interpret languages, and Ammon told him that he could not.

7. And the king said unto him: Being grieved for the afflictions of my people, I caused that forty and three of my people should take a journey into the wilderness, that thereby they might find the land of Zarahemla, that we might appeal unto our brethren to deliver us out of bondage.

8. And they were lost in the wilderness for the space of many days, yet they were diligent, and found not the land of Zarahemla but returned to this land, having traveled in a land among many waters, having discovered a land which was covered with bones of men, and of beasts, and was also covered with ruins of buildings of every kind, having discovered a land which had been peopled with a people who were as numerous as the hosts of Israel.

9. And for a testimony that the things that they had said are true they have brought twenty-

---

to the people of Lehi-Nephi, but rather had led them into transgression. They were confused by Ammon's remarks concerning the angel's visit to Benjamin and the wonderful things the angel had said to him. Ammon, with great care, explained to them the coming of the Christ, His Atoning sacrifice and the Salvation prepared for the children of men. He pointed out, so that they might understand, the fulfillment of the Law of Moses in the coming of the Messiah which, he said, according to the words of Benjamin was "not far distant."

When Ammon had finished telling King Limhi's people the wonderful story about Benjamin and his people in Zarahemla, Limhi dismissed the eager throng that had listened to Ammon's recital. As they each went to their own homes, we may imagine the anguish that every memory of King Noah and his wicked priests produced in their aching hearts.

VERSES 5-6. *Limhi had the records of his people brought before Ammon to read.* The Nephites in Lehi-Nephi, notwithstanding their many faults, had kept a record of their doings from the time of Zeniff to when Ammon came among them. The plates upon which this record was kept were brought before him that Ammon might read them.

The ease with which Ammon read the record of Limhi's people astonished Limhi; his evident understanding of many obscure writings therein, and his knowledge of different races and nations of men, including the Jews and their contemporary peoples, prompted Limhi to inquire of Ammon, "if he could interpret languages." "Ammon told him that he could not." We presume that Ammon had become acquainted with Jewish history by intently reading the Hebrew Scriptures, which you remember were written upon the brass plates of Laban.

VERSES 7-11. *King Limhi sent an expedition to find Zarahemla.* In the hope that they would get help in their efforts to escape from Lamanite bondage, King Limhi told Ammon that, in dire distress, he had chosen forty-three of "my people" to go to Zarahemla and seek assistance to that end.

four plates which are filled with engravings, and they are of pure gold.

10. And behold, also, they have brought breastplates, which are large, and they are of brass and of copper, and are perfectly sound.

11. And again, they have brought swords, the hilts thereof have perished, and the blades thereof were cankered with rust; and there is no one in the land that is able to interpret the language or the engravings that are on the plates. Therefore I said unto thee: Canst thou translate?

12. And I say unto thee again: Knowest thou of any one that can translate? For I am desirous that these records should be translated into our language; for, perhaps, they will give us a knowledge of a remnant of the people who have been destroyed, from whence these records came; or, perhaps, they will give us a knowledge of this very people who have been destroyed; and I am desirous to know the cause of their destruction.

The men Limhi selected became lost in the surrounding wilderness; they did not know the proper way to travel, nor the distance between Lehi-Nephi and Zarahemla. They only knew it was far to the north and traveled for many days in that direction. At last they reached a land "of many waters."

In this land, they found the remains of a great people. There, they discovered the ruins of many buildings. Scattered among the broken arches and displaced columns of a strange architecture they came across the dry bones of great numbers of men who had evidently fallen in battle. The sacred record describes them as, "a people who were as numerous as the hosts of Israel."

To prove to Limhi that the discovery they had made was true, and that their supposition was correct in which they supposed that their brethren in Zarahemla were all destroyed in battle, they brought back with them many relics of these dead people.

Among the proofs of their *surmise* were many artifacts used by their supposed brethren. They carried back to King Limhi in Lehi-Nephi, copper breastplates which were undamaged by age and were yet sound; they also brought swords whose hilts were decayed and gone, and the blades thereof were corroded with rust.

But, by far, the most important of their *finds* was a set of twenty-four *gold plates*, which they brought with them on their return. These gold plates were filled with engravings written in a strange language which no one in King Limhi's domain could translate. Again and again, he sought their interpretation; he felt that in them was hidden a great mystery. The anxiety to learn what this mystery was, greatly induced Limhi to ask Ammon once more, "Canst thou translate?"

VERSE 12. *Knowest thou of any one that can translate?* King Limhi proceeded to question Ammon further concerning the translation of the plates that had fallen into his hands. He made no mention of their probable worth, they being made of gold, but talked to Ammon only of the great store of knowledge and understanding which he felt was hidden behind the faces of numberless, and to him, incomprehensible glyphs. Ammon listened to Limhi's words as the king intently explained to him the reasons why he desired that they be translated "into our language." Perhaps, he ventured, they may tell us of those people who were destroyed, and the causes therefore. Now I ask you again, "Knowest thou of any one that can translate?"

2. He Suggests their Submission to King Mosiah, Prophet and Seer.

13. Now Ammon said unto him: I can assuredly tell thee, O king, of a man that can translate the records; for he has wherewith that he can look, and translate all records that are of ancient date; and it is a gift from God. And the things are called interpreters, and no man can look in them except he be commanded, lest he should look for that he ought not and he should perish. And whosoever is commanded to look in them, the same is called seer.

14. And behold, the king of the people who are in the land of Zarahemla is the man that is commanded to do these things, and who has this high gift from God.

15. And the king said that a seer is greater than a prophet.

16. And Ammon said that a seer is a revelator and a prophet also; and a gift which is greater can no man have, except he should possess the power of God, which no man can; yet a man may have great power given him from God.

17. But a seer can know of things which are past, and also of things which are to come, and by them shall all things be revealed, or, rather, shall secret things be made manifest, and hidden things shall come to light, and things which are not known shall be made known by them, and also things shall be made known by them which otherwise could not be known.

18. Thus God has provided a means that man, through faith, might work mighty miracles; therefore he becometh a great benefit to his fellow beings.

VERSES 13-18. *I can assuredly tell thee, O king, of a man that can translate the records.* Ammon answered the king and said that there is a man in Zarahemla who has a gift from God, who can translate all records of ancient peoples. He has "wherewith that he can look" and by the power of God, can translate writings belonging to ages now long past dead. The *wherewith* of which Ammon spoke, he said "are called *interpreters*," and that no man could look in them and receive the blessings they imparted unless he was commanded by the Lord so to do. Whosoever the Lord commanded "to look in them," Ammon said, "is called *seer.*"

The Presiding High Priest in Zarahemla, who also is the king of that land, he continued, is he who is commanded by the Lord to "do these things, and who has this high gift from God."

King Limhi then observed that a "seer is greater than a prophet," to which Ammon explained to the king the many different gifts had by each. A seer, he said, is a revelator and a prophet, too, and no gift is greater than, by the power of God, to reveal the history of any nation in the undecipherable writings of their prophets and wise men.

Not only, Ammon went on to explain, does a *seer* know the history of peoples now long forgotten, but also of things to come. By them all things are made known; hidden things are brought to light, and secret things are made manifest. Things, "that otherwise could not be known" are made known by a seer. He is both *prophet* and *seer.*

19. And now, when Ammon had made an end of speaking these words the king rejoiced exceedingly, and gave thanks to God, saying: Doubtless a great mystery is contained within these plates, and these interpreters were doubtless prepared for the purpose of unfolding all such mysteries to the children of men.

20. O how marvelous are the works of the Lord, and how long doth he suffer with his people; yea, and how blind and impenetrable are the understandings of the children of men; for they will not seek wisdom, neither do they desire that she should rule over them!

21. Yea, they are as a wild flock which fleeth from the shepherd, and scattereth, and are driven, and are devoured by the beasts of the forest.

VERSE 18. *Thus God had provided a means.* Ever mindful of the needs of His children, the Lord, in His watchful care over them, has provided the *means* whereby they can obtain great knowledge and understanding; this *means*, also, through faith, is a lamp unto their feet and an unending source of spiritual help in time of need.

VERSES 19-21. *Limhi rejoiced exceedingly, and gave thanks to God.* Limhi was filled with joy as he heard Ammon discourse on the gift God had endowed King Mosiah with. His great hope regarding these twenty-four gold plates would now be fulfilled. For a moment, he forgot all plans to escape the bondage his people were in. With great reason he proclaimed the *majesty of God,* and thanked the Giver of all good for his mercy and kindness to his children. He was persuaded that a great mystery was contained in these plates, and from it, his own people would learn many lessons. It was but natural that Limhi, abounding in the new faith and hope Ammon's visit had inspired, interposed his heartfelt conclusion, "these interpreters were doubtless prepared for the purpose of unfolding all such mysteries to the children of men."

O how marvelous are the works of the Lord. King Limhi remembered the wickedness of his people under the profligate rule of his father, Noah. He began to realize that the Lord, not because of their waywardness but in spite of it, prepared ways for their preservation from folly and weakness the consequences of which they had brought upon themselves.

He took a retrospect of all his past life, and likened it unto the lives of his people. They had not sought for wisdom. Limhi remembered the words of Solomon, "I neither learned wisdom, nor have the knowledge of the holy." (Proverbs 30:3) Yet, in the future, we imagine he resolved that like unto Joshua he would serve God and keep His commandments.

Wisdom, implies, *spiritual insight.* His people had refused to be guided by its holy promptings.

GENERAL NOTES

Hundreds of years later than the events herein recorded, the last of the Nephite prophets, Moroni, in commenting on this particular subject which was included in the history of the Jaredites written on the twenty-four plates of gold, said,

And it came to pass that the Lord said unto the brother of Jared: Behold, thou shalt not suffer these things which ye have seen and heard to go forth unto the world, until the time cometh that I shall glorify my name in the flesh; wherefore, ye shall treasure up the things which ye have seen and heard, and show it to no man.

And behold, when ye shall come unto me, ye shall write them and shall seal them up, that no one can interpret them; for ye shall write them in a language that they cannot be read.

And behold, these two stones will I give unto thee, and ye shall seal them up also with the things which ye shall write.

For behold, the language which ye shall write I have confounded; wherefore I will cause in my own due time that these stones shall magnify to the eyes of men these things which ye shall write.

And when the Lord had said these words, he showed unto the brother of Jared all the inhabitants of the earth which had been, and also all that would be; and he withheld them not from his sight, even unto the ends of the earth.

For he had said unto him in times before, that if he would believe in him that he could show unto him all things—it should be shown unto him; therefore the Lord could not withhold anything from him, for he knew that the Lord could show him all things.

And the Lord said unto him: Write these things and seal them up; and I will show them in mine own due time unto the children of men.

And it came to pass that the Lord commanded him that he should seal up the two stones which he had received, and show them not, until the Lord should show them unto the children of men.   (Ether 3:21-28)

And the Lord commanded the brother of Jared to go down out of the mount from the presence of the Lord, and write the things which he had seen; and they were forbidden to come unto the children of men until after that he should be lifted up upon the cross; and for this cause did king Mosiah keep them, that they should not come unto the world until after Christ should show himself unto his people.

And after Christ truly had showed himself unto his people he commanded that they should be made manifest.

And now, after that, they have all dwindled in unbelief, and there is none save it be the Lamanites, and they have rejected the gospel of Christ; therefore I am commanded that I should hide them up again in the earth.

Behold, I have written upon these plates the very things which the brother of Jared saw; and there never were greater things made manifest than those which were made manifest unto the brother of Jared.

Wherefore the Lord hath commanded me to write them; and I have written them. And he commanded me that I should seal them up; and he also hath commanded that I should seal up the interpretation thereof; wherefore I have sealed up the interpreters, according to the commandment of the Lord.   (Ether 4:1-5)

For this cause did King Mosiah keep them. (Ether 4:1) This Mosiah, the son of King Benjamin, was the last of the kings of Zarahemla, preceding the judges. He was the translator of the contents of the twenty-four plates of gold, which were delivered to him by King Limhi. The translation was made by "the means of two stones which were fastened into the two rims of a bow." The stones, we read in the Book of Mosiah, were "prepared from the beginning, and were handed down from generation to generation, for the purpose of interpreting languages." (Mosiah 28:11-14) They were in all probability, the stones which were given to Moriancumr, and, later, to the Prophet Joseph by the resurrected prophet of the Nephites, Moroni.

How did King Mosiah get them? We turn to the Book of Omni. We read there that during the reign of the first Mosiah, the father of King Benjamin, a large stone with engravings thereon was brought to Zarahemla, to the king. He translated the text "by the gift and power of God," and found that it contained an "account of one Coriantumr and the slain of his people." The chronicler (Amaleki) adds the explanation that Coriantumr had been found by the people of Zarahemla—perhaps by hunters—and that he had lived in that country the last nine moons—months—of his life.

Coriantumr was the last king of the Jaredites of whom we have any historical record, as Ether was the last of their prophets. He fought his savage enemy, Shiz, at Ramah, until both their armies were annihilated. Then he ended the life of his antagonist. He, himself, lay on the battlefield, apparently lifeless. But he recovered, and began his pilgrimage which eventually ended in Zarahemla. As the head of the Jaredite government, or kingdom, Coriantumr may have had charge of the *Interpreters,* although they were useless to him, and brought them with with him to Zarahemla where they were later given into the custody of King Mosiah, the father of Benjamin.

If the conversation between Limhi and Ammon regarding the *Interpreters* refers to the Urim and Thummim, as it undoubtedly does, it is evident that the two stones were no part of Limhi's treasure. Limhi had the plates, there is no doubt about that, and King Mosiah had the *Interpreters* long before he received the plates to interpret.

All dwindled in unbelief. Moroni also informs us that the Nephites had dwindled in unbelief and the Lamanites had rejected the Gospel, therefore he had been commanded to hide the sacred relics in the earth to come forth again at some future time. These relics were the account of Moriancumer of his visions on the mount as he wrote it and sealed it up until the appearance of Christ on this continent. There were also the plates of brass, the plates of Nephi, the translation of the twenty-four plates, the plates themselves, and the Interpreters, all of which sacred objects had been used by the Church of Christ on this continent. (*Compare* Mosiah 28:11-13) All these the Prophet Moroni entrusted to the bosom of motherly earth, there to rest until the Gentiles would repent and exercise faith in the Lord. (Ether 4:7)

The Two Stones. These two stones, which are also known as the *Interpreters* (Ether 4:5; Mosiah 28:20) were, as we read here, entrusted to the care of Moriancumer before he descended from the ever memorable scene of his visions and revelations. They were delivered to him with the admonition that they be sealed up, together with the sacred records that were kept, and thus hidden from the eyes of the world until they, in the due time of the Lord, were to come forth. Their purpose is stated to be to "magnify," that is to say, to make clear, "the things which ye shall write." (Ether 4:7)

According to the Doctrine and Covenants (17:1) the sacred instrument that was deposited in the Hill Cumorah and delivered to the Prophet Joseph Smith, was the *Urim and Thummim** which was received by the Brother of Jared while on the mount. When the Prophet Joseph received the *stones,* Sept. 22, 1827, they were framed in silver bows and fastened to a *breastplate.* (Pearl of Great Price, Joseph Smith 2:35)

From the Doctrine and Covenants 130:8-9, where God is said to dwell on a globe which is a *Urim and Thummim,* the name by which we know the *Interpreters,* we learn that the earth is to be sanctified and made immortal—"made like a *crystal* and will be a *Urim and Thummim* to the inhabitants thereon." We conclude from that statement, that the *two stones* were *crystals.* The Prophet Joseph, further, adds to our information that the "white stone" mentioned in Revelation 2:17 "will become a *Urim and Thummim* to each who receives one, and that "a white stone" will be given to everyone who is privileged to come into the Celestial Kingdom. On the *stone* a new name will be written. By that means "things pertaining to a higher order of kingdoms, even all kingdoms, will be made known."

All the inhabitants of the earth. When Moriancumr had received the *Urim and Thummim,* the Lord opened his vision, possibly by means of these *stones,* and he was shown the human race, past and future, passing as if in panorama.

Enoch had a similar view of "many generations" upon Mt. Simeon (Pearl of Great Price, Moses 7:2-6, 22-69). Abraham, who received the *Urim and Thummim* while he was in Ur, of the Chaldees, (Abraham 3:1) had marvelous visions and

---

*Meaning, *Lights and perfections.*

revelations concerning the creation of the universe and the intelligences that were organized "before the world was." (Abraham 1:28 and Chapters 4 and 5) He was thus prepared for his mission to Egypt. (Abraham 3:15) Moses, too, who may have had in his possession the same *Urim and Thummim* that had been given to Abraham, had similar visions. (Moses 1:1ff) He "beheld the earth, yea, even all of it; and there was not a particle of it which he did not behold. . . . And he beheld also the inhabitants thereof, and there was not a soul which he beheld not; and he discerned them by the Spirit of God. . . . And he beheld many lands; and each land was called earth, and there were inhabitants on the face thereof." (Moses 1:27-29)

Twenty-four plates. These plates, which were found by the explorers of King Limhi, and from which Mosiah compiled the Book of Ether (Ether 1:2), were of "pure gold," or, as Mosiah explains (Mosiah 21:27) of "ore." The art of the goldsmith is very ancient. It was one of the crafts of the Jews who came out of Egypt under Moses. For we read in Exodus 39:3, that those who made the sacred robes of Aaron to wear in his temple duties or services, "beat gold into thin plates, and cut" these into fine wires which were twined into the blue, purple, scarlet and fine linen yarn of which the cloth was artfully woven.

THE RECORD OF ZENIFF

An account of his people, from the time they left the Land of Zarahemla until they were delivered out of the hands of the Lamanites.

Comprising chapters 9 to 22 inclusive.

CHAPTER 9

1. *Zeniff goes to possess the land of Lehi-Nephi*—2. *A spy among the Lamanites*—3. *The craftiness of King Laman.*

1. *Zeniff goes to possess the land of Lehi-Nephi.*

1. I, Zeniff, having been taught in all the language of the Nephites, and having had a knowledge of the land of Nephi, or of the land of our fathers' first inheritance, and having been sent as a spy among the Lamanites that I might spy out their forces, that our army might come upon them and destroy them — but when I saw that which was good among them I was desirous that they should not be destroyed.

2. Therefore, I contended with my brethren in the wilderness, for I would that our ruler should make a treaty with them; but he being an austere and a bloodthirsty man commanded that I should be slain; but I was rescued by the shedding of much blood; for father fought against father,

---

In addition to the frequency with which King Benjamin's reign was troubled with false prophets, there was another class, who, moved by the spirit of unrest, were also a source of perplexity to the king. They were those who left the Land of Lehi-Nephi with the righteous under Mosiah and still permitted their thoughts and affections to be drawn toward their former homes and old associations. Like Lot's wife they hankered for that which they had left behind. The natural consequence was that they were constantly agitating the idea of organizing expeditions to visit their old homes.

The first of these expeditions, of which there is a record, was led by an austere and bloodthirsty man totally unfit for leadership. He was slain in a battle that was fought between members of his own group. Those who were not killed returned to Zarahemla.

Leaving Zarahemla during the early years of Mosiah's reign, the next and perhaps the most successful of these migrations came to a bitter ending, when, under their king, the Nephites escaped from bondage which the Lamanites had fastened upon them.

VERSES 1-2. *Lamanites . . . I was desirous that they should not be destroyed.* Zeniff, a man who evidently was somewhat learned, had a personal knowledge of the Land of Lehi-Nephi, and also was acquainted with the language spoken by the Lamanites therein, was therefore appointed a spy to learn, if possible, the size and strength of the Lamanite armies. It must always be remembered that the Nephites regarded Lehi-Nephi as the land of their father's first inheritance. The idea of the leader of this first expedition was to overwhelm the Lamanite armies and take

and brother against brother, until the greater number of our army was destroyed in the wilderness; and we returned, those of us that were spared, to the land of Zarahemla, to relate that tale to their wives and their children.

3. And yet, I being over-zealous to inherit the land of our fathers, collected as many as were desirous to go up to possess the land, and started again on our journey into the wilderness to go up to the land; but we were smitten with famine and sore afflictions; for we were slow to remember the Lord our God.

4. Nevertheless, after many days' wandering in the wilderness we pitched our tents in the place where our brethren were slain, which was near to the land of our fathers.

2. *A spy among the Lamanites.*

5. And it came to pass that I went again with four of my men into the city, in unto the king, that I might know of the disposition of the king, and that I might know if I might go in with my people and possess the land in peace.

possession of the whole land. But, Zeniff, in making his report of the conditions he found among the Lamanites, told of so many good things which he saw that, he says, "I was desirous that they should not be destroyed."

Instead, Zeniff advocated that a treaty be arranged with the king of the Lamanites for his people to repossess their old homes. He argued with such ardor that a great contention arose between members of the expedition who favored this peaceful settlement of their purposes and those who preferred a war-like attack, and the leader of them ordered Zeniff to be slain. But in the attempt to carry out that order a riot ensued in which all but fifty of their number perished by violence. These survivors returned to their starting place to tell of the sad ending, the failure of their attempts.

VERSE 3. *And yet, I being over-zealous to inherit the land.* Zeniff now gathered around him everyone who was ready and willing to make a further try at regaining possession of their homes. Anyone who has sought to make a new home in a new land knows of some of the difficulties encountered.

These trials the Nephites remembered. In spite of many hardships that presented themselves, Zeniff, being "over-zealous to inherit the land," subdued them, and soon a rather large company started in a southerly direction through the wilderness "to go up to the land." However, the blessings of heaven were not with them to crown their efforts; they did not merit them because, "We were slow to remember the Lord our God."

VERSE 4. *We pitched our tents . . . near to the land of our fathers.* After many days in which they wandered in the wilderness, being smitten and afflicted with hunger and by pestilence, they rested at the same place where the members of the first expedition had slain one another.

VERSES 5-7. *I, with four of my men went in unto the king.* Zeniff, with four others of his men went into the city where he had several conversations with the king of Lehi-Nephi. Zeniff's purpose was made known to the king, and a peaceful

6. And I went in unto the king, and he covenanted with me that I might possess the land of Lehi-Nephi, and the land of Shilom.

7. And he also commanded that his people should depart out of the land, and I and my people went into the land that we might possess it.

8. And we began to build buildings, and to repair the walls of the city, yea, even the walls of the city of Lehi-Nephi, and the city of Shilom.

9. And we began to till the ground, yea, even with all manner of seeds, with seeds of corn, and of wheat, and of barley, and with neas, and with sheum, and with seeds of all manner of fruits; and we did begin to multiply and prosper in the land.

3. The craftiness of King Laman.

10. Now it was the cunning and the craftiness of king Laman, to bring my people into bondage, that he yielded up the land that we might possess it.

11. Therefore it came to pass, that after we had dwelt in the land for the space of twelve years that king Laman began to grow uneasy, lest by any means my people should wax strong in the land, and that they could not overpower them and bring them into bondage.

12. Now they were a lazy and an idolatrous people; therefore they were desirous to bring us into bondage, that they might glut themselves with the labors of our hands; yea, that they might feast themselves upon the flocks of our fields.

---

solution of Zeniff's request was finally arrived at. A treaty between Zeniff and the king was made in which the king covenanted with Zeniff that his people could possess the Land of Lehi-Nephi and also the Land of Shilom. The king further commanded his subjects to leave the land which he had covenanted with Zeniff that he should have. Zeniff and his followers then took possession of the covenanted land.

VERSES 8-9. *We began to build buildings and repair the walls of the city.* The followers of Zeniff immediately began to repair the buildings and fortifications of the cities of Lehi-Nephi and of Shimlon which had been allowed to go to disrepair under the careless rule of their Lamanite guardians. They also began to till the soil and to plant and to prepare all manner of seeds to insure a bounteous harvest which they would need. Corn and wheat and barley were planted, also, the historian says, "and with neas, and with sheum," and with all different kinds of fruit. *Neas* and *sheum* may have been kinds of grain; *sheum* is a name singularly like the Hebrew *shum,* meaning *garlic.* It is found in Numbers 11:5. Altogether, the beginning of Zeniff's occupancy of their traditional homeland presaged a very flourishing and fortunate future. Zeniff says, "We did begin to multiply and prosper in the land."

VERSES 10-12. *It was the cunning and the craftiness of King Laman.* In making the treaty we have just noted, and in permitting Zeniff and his followers to possess the choice land in and about the cities of Lehi-Nephi and Shilom, the king of the Lamanites was not as friendly as he had pretended. His objective was to get the

13. Therefore it came to pass that king Laman began to stir up his people that they should contend with my people; therefore there began to be wars and contentions in the land.

14. For, in the thirteenth year of my reign in the land of Nephi, away on the south of the land of Shilom, when my people were watering and feeding their flocks, and tilling their lands, a numerous host of Lamanites came upon them and began to slay them, and to take off their flocks, and the corn of their fields.

15. Yea, and it came to pass that they fled, all that were not overtaken, even into the city of Nephi, and did call upon me for protection.

16. And it came to pass that I did arm them with bows, and with arrows, with swords, and with cimeters, and with clubs, and with slings, and with all manner of weapons which we could

invent, and I and my people did go forth against the Lamanites to battle.

17. Yea, in the strength of the Lord did we go forth to battle against the Lamanites; for I and my people did cry mightily to the Lord that he would deliver us out of the hands of our enemies, for we were awakened to a remembrance of the deliverance of our fathers.

18. And God did hear our cries and did answer our prayers; and we did go forth in his might; yea, we did go forth against the Lamanites, and in one day and a night we did slay three thousand and forty-three; we did slay them even until we had driven them out of our land.

19. And I, myself, with mine own hands, did help to bury their dead. And behold, to our great sorrow and lamentation, two hundred and seventy-nine of our brethren were slain.

---

industrious Nephites to settle in the midst of his own people, and then by his superior numbers make the Nephites his slaves, for his people were a "lazy and an idolatrous people," an unprogressive race. In the course of twelve years the abundant harvests garnered by the people of Zeniff through their thrift and industry, began to make them strong and numerous. This caused King Laman to grow uneasy. He desired to bring them into bondage that his people might reap the benefits of the Nephites' labors. They were growing so fast that he thought that if he did not put a stop to their increase they would be the stronger of the two peoples.

VERSES 13-14. *King Laman began to stir up his people.* To prevent the development of the Nephites' strength, and also to stop their growth, King Laman began to stir up anger against them in the hearts of his own people. He was so successful that in the thirteenth year of Zeniff's reign as king of the Nephites in the Land of Lehi-Nephi, a numerous host of Lamanites suddenly fell upon his people while they were feeding and watering their flocks, and began to slay both the men and women. They also carried off some of their cattle, and the corn from their fields.

VERSES 15-19. *They did call on me for protection.* Those of the Nephites who were not slain or overtaken by the Lamanites fled to Zeniff for protection. As quickly as he could, he armed his people with bows and arrows, swords and cimeters, clubs and slings, and with every other kind of weapon they could invent. Thus armed, they went forth in the strength of the Lord to meet the enemy, for in their hour of peril they had cried mightily to Him, and He heard their cries and answered their prayers. From one day's sunup to that of the next they fought with a determination that was born of right and righteousness, but to their sorrow 279 of their own were slain, although the number of Lamanites slain was 3043. Only when all the Lamanites were driven "out of our land" did the carnage cease.

ZENIFF

The first of the three kings who reigned over the colony of Nephites who returned from Zarahemla and established themselves in the land of Lehi-Nephi, about B.C. 200.

Zeniff and his people, having left Zarahemla, traveled southward toward the land of Nephi. The blessings of the Lord were not greatly with them, for they did not seek him nor strive to do his will. In the wilderness they lost their way and suffered from famine and many afflictions; but after many days they reached the neighborhood of the city of Lehi-Nephi the former home of their race. Here Zeniff chose four of his company and accompanied by them went to the king of the Lamanites. This monarch, whose name was Laman, received them with the appearance of kindness. He made a treaty with them and gave them the lands of Lehi-Nephi and Shilom to dwell in. He also caused his own people to remove out of these cities and the surrounding country that Zeniff's people might have full possession. King Laman was in reality not so friendly as he pretended to be. His object was to get the industrious Nephites to settle in the midst of his people and then by his superior numbers to make them his slaves; for his own subjects were a lazy, unprogressive race.

As soon as Zeniff and his followers occupied their new possessions they went to work to build houses and to repair the walls of the city, for the idle Lamanites had suffered them to fall into decay. They also commenced to till the ground and to plant all manner of seeds of grain, vegetables and fruit therein. Soon, through their thrift and industry, they began to prosper and multiply. This caused King Laman to grow uneasy. He desired to bring them into bondage that his people might reap the benefits of the labors of the Nephites. But they were growing so rapidly that he feared that if he did not soon put a stop to their increase they would be the stronger of the two peoples. To prevent this he began to stir up the hearts of his people in anger against the Nephites. He succeeded so well that in the thirteenth year of Zeniff's reign in the land of Lehi-Nephi a numerous host of Lamanites suddenly fell upon his people while they were feeding and watering their flocks and began to slay them. They also carried off some of their flocks and the corn from their fields.

Those of the Nephites who were not slain or overtaken fled to Zeniff. As quickly as he could he armed his people with bows and arrows, swords and cimeters, clubs and slings and with such other weapons as they could invent. Thus armed they went forth in the strength of the Lord to meet the enemy, for in their hour of peril they had cried mightily unto him and he heard their cries and answered their prayers.

Thus strengthened they met their foes. The battle was an obstinate and a bloody one. It lasted all day and all night. At last the Lamanites were driven back with a loss of 3,043 warriors, while the people of Zeniff had to mourn the death of 279 of their brethren. After this there was peace in the land for many years.

During this time of peace Zeniff taught his people to be very industrious. He caused his men to till the ground and raise all kinds of fruit and grain. The women he had spin and make cloth for clothing, fine linen, etc. In this way, for twenty-two years, they prospered and had uninterrupted peace.

At this time the old King Laman died and his son succeeded him upon the throne. Like many young princes he desired to distinguish himself in war. So he gathered a numerous host of the Lamanites and having armed them in the same manner as the Nephites, he led them to the north of the land of Shemlon which lay near the land of Nephi-Lehi.

When Zeniff learned of the approach of young King Laman's armies he caused the women and children of his people to hide in the wilderness but every man, young or old who was unable to bear arms was placed in the ranks to go out against the foe. Zeniff himself was then an aged man but he still continued to command his forces and led them in person to battle. Strengthened by the faith Zeniff implanted in their hearts the Nephites gained a great victory and so numerous were the slain of the Lamanites that they were not counted. After this there was peace again in the land. Shortly after this Zeniff died and unfortunately for his kingdom chose for his successor an unworthy son, named Noah.

CHAPTER 10

1. *King Laman Dies—*2. *Zeniff and his People Prevail against their Oppressors.*

1. King Laman dies.

1. And it came to pass that we again began to establish the kingdom and we again began to possess the land in peace. And I caused that there should be weapons of war made of every kind, that thereby I might have weapons for my people against the time the Lamanites should come up again to war against my people.

2. And I set guards round about the land, that the Lamanites might not come upon us again unawares and destroy us; and thus I did guard my people and my flocks, and keep them from falling into the hands of our enemies.

3. And it came to pass that we did inherit the land of our fathers for many years, yea, for the space of twenty and two years.

4. And I did cause that the men should till the ground, and raise all manner of grain, and all manner of fruit of every kind.

5. And I did cause that the women should spin, and toil, and work, and work all manner of fine linen, yea, and cloth of every kind, that we might clothe our nakedness; and thus we did prosper in the land—thus we did have continual peace in the land for the space of twenty and two years.

6. And it came to pass that king Laman died, and his son began to reign in his stead. And he began to stir his people up in rebellion against my people; therefore they began to prepare for war, and to come up to battle against my people.

VERSES 1-5. *We again began to possess the land in peace.* After the days of warfare were over and the Lamanites were driven out of the land occupied by the Nephites, a peace of twenty-two years enabled the people of Zeniff to learn many of the arts that accompany days of tranquillity and calm. Zeniff taught his people to be industrious. He caused his men to till the ground and to raise all kinds of fruit and grain. He had the women spin and make cloth for clothing, and for fine linen. Although this was a period of peace, preparing for war was not neglected. Zeniff caused that weapons of warfare be accumulated in the eventuality the Lamanites should again come to battle against them. He set guards over them and also over their flocks so that they, thus protected, would not fall into the hands of their enemies.

VERSE 6. *King Laman died, and his son began to reign in his stead.* At this time the old king, Laman, died, and his son succeeded him upon the throne. Like many another young man, he desired to distinguish himself in war. So he gathered a numerous host of Lamanites, and, having armed them in the same manner as the Nephites, he led them to the north of the **Land of Shemlon**, which bordered the **Land of Lehi-Nephi.**

2. Zeniff and his people prepare —

7. But I had sent my spies out round about the land of Shemlon, that I might discover their preparations, that I might guard against them, that they might not come upon my people and destroy them.

8. And it came to pass that they came up upon the north of the land of Shilom, with their numerous hosts, men armed with bows, and with arrows, and with swords, and with cimeters, and with stones, and with slings; and they had their heads shaved that they were naked; and they were girded with a leathern girdle about their loins.

9. And it came to pass that I caused that the women and children of my people should be hid in the wilderness; and I also caused that all my old men that could bear arms, and also all my young men that were able to bear arms, should gather themselves together to go to battle against the Lamanites; and I did place them in their ranks, every man according to his age.

10. And it came to pass that we did go up to battle against the Lamanites; and I, even I, in my old age, did go up to battle against the Lamanites. And it came to pass that we did go up in the strength of the Lord to battle.

11. Now, the Lamanites knew nothing concerning the Lord, nor the strength of the Lord, therefore they depended upon their own strength. Yet they were a strong people, as to the strength of men.

VERSE 7. *I sent spies . . . that I might guard against them.* One of the favorite tactics of the Lamanites was to take their opponents by surprise. To obviate any chance of being taken by surprise, Zeniff sent into their camps men who were to discover what preparations the Lamanites were taking to carry out their designs. In this way he could prepare himself against the Lamanites' plans.

VERSE 8. *The soldiers of the Lamanites were almost naked.* An army of the Lamanites was a strange sight to look upon. Their heads were shaven, the only covering of their bodies being a leathern girdle about their loins. Their weapons were bows and arrows, slings, swords, and rocks.

VERSE 9. *I caused that the women and children should be hid.* When Zeniff learned of the approach of young King Laman's armies, he caused the women and children of his people to hide themselves in the wilderness, but every man, young or old, who was able to bear arms was placed in the ranks to go out against the foe.

VERSE 10. *We did go up to battle in the strength of the Lord.* Zeniff was now an old man, but he continued to lead his forces in person and to command them in battle.

VERSE 11. *The Lamanites knew nothing concerning the Lord.* From the very first, Laman and his followers conceived the idea that they were wronged, and that Nephi had usurped certain prerogatives that rightfully belonged to the elder male member of each family. They took no cognizance of the fact that obedience to the laws of God is a determining constituent of leadership. They reviled and mocked

12. They were a wild, and ferocious, and a blood-thirsty people, believing in the tradition of their fathers which is this—Believing that they were driven out of the land of Jerusalem because of the iniquities of their fathers, and that they were wronged in the wilderness by their brethren, and they were also wronged while crossing the sea;

13. And again, that they were wronged while in the land of their first inheritance, after they had crossed the sea, and all this because that Nephi was more faithful in keeping the commandments of the Lord—therefore he was favored of the Lord, for the Lord heard his prayers and answered them, and he took the lead of their journey in the wilderness.

14. And his brethren were wroth with him because they understood not the dealings of the Lord; they were also wroth with him upon the waters because they hardened their hearts against the Lord.

15. And again, they were wroth with him when they had arrived in the promised land, because they said that he had taken the ruling of the people out of their hands; and they sought to kill him.

Nephi's steadfastness in serving the Lord. They taught their children that they had been grossly sinned against, that God did not really exist, that they were the victims of oppression and not the instigators of the fiendish practices of which the Nephites accused them. After many years of such tradition the Lamanites believed nothing of the purposes of the Almighty, and they put their trust in the things of the world.

VERSE 12. *They were a wild, and ferocious . . . people.* The bitter passions that occupied the hearts of the Lamanites were constantly fanned into a malignant hatred for their brethren, the Nephites, in spite of every effort the Nephites made to counteract such folly. They even were taught that they had been driven out of Jerusalem because of their unrighteous parentage. They were allowed to suffer in the wilderness and on the sea, they believed, by their brethren.

VERSE 13. *The Lamanites believed they were wronged in the land of their first inheritance.* A prime excuse for one's own folly is to blame someone else for it. At this the Lamanites were masters. They justified their own faults by accusation. The mirror in which they saw themselves, distorted and confused the past. They forgot that the Lord favored Nephi because he was more diligent in keeping the commandments of the Lord.

VERSE 14. *They understood not the dealings of the Lord.* Man cannot put God out of his heart and then understand the ways of the Lord. Neither can he harden his heart against Him and enjoy the blessings of heaven. Nephi's brothers grew angry with him because he perceived the Lord's wishes and received an answer to his prayers.

VERSES 15-16. *They said he robbed them.* Laman and Lemuel, both, told their children, and thus it was passed on to every generation of their seed, that Nephi had unrighteously taken possession of leadership in the first place, and that to be the ruler of his people was not in his province. For usurping this leadership they had sought his life.

Again, the historian recounts that, when conditions within the little company

16. And again, they were wroth with him because he departed into the wilderness as the Lord had commanded him, and took the records which were engraven on the plates of brass, for they said that he robbed them.

17. And thus they have taught their children that they should hate them, and that they should murder them, and that they should rob and plunder them, and do all they could to destroy them; therefore they have an eternal hatred towards the children of Nephi.

18. For this very cause has king Laman, by his cunning, and lying craftiness, and his fair promises, deceived me, that I have brought this my people up into this land, that they may destroy them; yea, and we have suffered these many years in the land.

19. And now I, Zeniff, after having told all these things unto my people concerning the Lamanites, I did stimulate them to go to battle with their might, putting their trust in the Lord; therefore, we did contend with them, face to face.

20. And it came to pass that we did drive them again out of our land; and we slew them with a great slaughter, even so many that we did not number them.

21. And it came to pass that we returned again to our own land, and my people again began to tend their flocks, and to till their ground.

22. And now I, being old, did confer the kingdom upon one of my sons; therefore, I say no more. And may the Lord bless my people. Amen.

---

of refugees grew unbearable, and they separated into two factions, some following Laman and others Nephi, the followers of Nephi took with them the Plates of Brass and other sacred things. Those who followed Laman cried, "Robbery," and ever after asserted, vehemently, this lie, forgetting, too, that it was Nephi who had first obtained them.

VERSES 17-18. *All these things have they taught their children.* To teach their children to hate the Nephites, to rob them, and to plunder and destroy them was the aim of the misguided Lamanites. This was the reason King Laman, cunningly and craftily, agreed that Zeniff's people should occupy the land in his domain. He was quick to see an opportunity to enslave and thus destroy them as a nation. For many years they groaned under the yoke he put on them.

VERSES 19-22. *We did contend with them, face to face.* Zeniff's recital of the reasons for the Lamanites' hatred of all Nephites proved to be a rallying call. His followers no longer feared battle, nor did they shrink from it. In the strength of the Lord, with prayers for their deliverance, they "did contend with them, face to face."

Strengthened by the faith Zeniff inspired in their hearts, the Nephites won a great victory, and so many Lamanites were slain that they were not counted. After this battle there was peace again that continued throughout all the days of Zeniff. Before he died Zeniff chose, unfortunately, for his successor an unworthy son, Noah, who led the people into many sins and ruled with such folly and weakness that they fell an easy prey to the ever-watchful Lamanite foe that everywhere surrounded them.

CHAPTER 11

1. *The Wicked King Noah and his Priests*—2. *The Prophet Abinadi Denounces the Prevailing Wickedness*—3. *King Noah Seeks the Life of Abinadi.*

1. *The wicked King Noah and his priests.*

1. And now it came to pass that Zeniff conferred the kingdom upon Noah, one of his sons; therefore Noah began to reign in his stead; and he did not walk in the ways of his father.

2. For behold, he did not keep the commandments of God, but he did walk after the desires of his own heart. And he had many wives and concubines. And he did cause his people to commit sin, and do that which was abom- inable in the sight of the Lord. Yea, and they did commit whoredoms and all manner of wicked- ness.

3. And he laid a tax of one fifth part of all they possessed, a fifth part of their gold and of their silver, and a fifth part of their ziff, and of their copper, and of their brass and their iron; and a fifth part of their fatlings; and also a fifth part of all their grain.

4. And all this did he take to

VERSES 1-2. *Zeniff conferred the kingdom upon Noah.* In the closing paragraph of Chapter 10 we noted that when Zeniff died, he conferred the kingship upon his son, Noah. Noah reigned in his father's stead, but he was a dissolute fellow who proved to be a tyrant. Unlike his father, Zeniff, he did not guide his people according to God's commandments. He walked in darkness and sin, always pursuing that which satisfied his lusts or gratified the desires of a depraved heart. The history of his reign is a composite of crime and cruelty. It is one of the most perplexing sections of Nephite annals. As a people they had, more than once, been delivered by the Lord from the vengeance of Lamanite hatred and bloodthirstiness. They prospered when they kept the Laws of God; they grew in numbers, and the fat of the land sustained them. They were happy when they ate of the labor of their hands. They were a righteous people, and the Lord delivered them in the day of evil. Their paths were in the light when they heeded the voice of God's holy servants. The Church of God was established among them, and Zeniff had appointed priests to act in the ordinances of the Law of Moses, in which form of worship the Nephites were most zealous.

Human nature being as it is, the example set by wicked King Noah lured many of his people to forget the goodness of the Lord to their fathers and to follow him in evil practices. The king, who was also traditionally the spiritual leader of his subjects, replaced the good priests Zeniff had consecrated by others of his own ilk. He caused those with whom he associated to surround themselves, as he had done, with wives and concubines and encouraged his people to commit all "manner of wickedness."

VERSES 3-7. *And he laid a tax of one fifth part of all they possessed.* The wanton living of Noah and his favored courtiers needed much of the wealth accumulated by his industrious people to pay the expenses of a capricious court. Like most tyrants, he burdened his people with heavy taxes. Luxuries and prodigal living called for more and more of the wealth of his kingdom. It was not long before the wickedness and profligate abandonment of King Noah reached its

support himself, and his wives and his concubines; and also his priests, and their wives and their concubines; thus he had changed the affairs of the kingdom.

5. For he put down all the priests that had been consecrated by his father, and consecrated new ones in their stead, such as were lifted up in the pride of their hearts.

6. Yea, and thus they were supported in their laziness, and in their idolatry, and in their whoredoms, by the taxes which king Noah had put upon his people; thus did the people labor exceedingly to support iniquity.

7. Yea, and they also became idolatrous, because they were deceived by the vain and flattering words of the king and priests; for they did speak flattering things unto them.

8. And it came to pass that king Noah built many elegant and spacious buildings; and he ornamented them with fine work of wood, and of all manner of precious things, of gold, and of silver, and of iron, and of brass, and of ziff, and of copper;

9. And he also built him a spacious palace, and a throne in the midst thereof, all of which was of fine wood and was ornamented with gold and silver and with precious things.

10. And he also caused that his workmen should work all manner of fine work within the walls of the temple, of fine wood, and of copper, and of brass.

11. And the seats which were

---

zenith. He levied taxes upon his people that were unendurable. One-fifth of all they possessed was then confiscated by a law he enacted. The record says that one-fifth part of their gold and silver, a like part of their ziff* and their copper, iron and brass, also one-fifth part of their fatlings and of the fruit and grain of their fields, was taken from them by way of tribute which he called a tax. From the spoils of this ill-gotten levy, King Noah sustained his corrupt court in autocratic splendor. When we recall that, at about this same time, the righteous King Benjamin labored in Zarahemla with his own hands to save his people from being taxed to support his wants, we see the difference between a God-fearing ruler and one who, urged on by selfish motives, surrendered himself to the meanest purposes mankind can devise or evil power achieve. Thus, in this manner, King Noah "changed the affairs of the kingdom." And thus, he also, by flattering his people, and by speaking fine but meaningless words to them, lured many into idolatrous ways so that they labored excessively to furnish his court with excessive means for ribaldry. In doing this, the historian wrote, "Thus did the people labor exceedingly to support iniquity."

VERSES 8-15. *King Noah built many elegant and spacious buildings.* Although King Noah was a vicious and debauched creature who cared nothing for that which was just and right, he built a very grand palace for himself in Lehi-Nephi. And, for his own comfort and conceit, ornamented it with gold and silver, **and in the midst thereof he erected a throne made of fine wood.** He also caused that the temple be embellished and that many fine buildings be erected in the Land of Shilom.

---

*Ziff, a metal now unknown. The word ziff, in Hebrew, means *brightness*, metallic brightness. The word is used in Daniel 2:31, and in Isaiah 30:22, where it means "overlaying metal."

set apart for the high priests, which were above all the other seats, he did ornament with pure gold; and he caused a breastwork to be built before them, that they might rest their bodies and their arms upon while they should speak lying and vain words to his people.

12. And it came to pass that he built a tower near the temple; yea, a very high tower, even so high that he could stand upon the top thereof and overlook the land of Shilom, and also the land of Shemlon, which was possessed by the Lamanites; and he could even look over all the land round about.

13. And it came to pass that he caused many buildings to be built in the land Shilom; and he caused a great tower to be built on the hill north of the land Shilom, which had been a resort for the children of Nephi at the time they fled out of the land; and thus he did do with the riches which he obtained by the taxation of his people.

14. And it came to pass that he placed his heart upon his riches, and he spent his time in riotous living with his wives and his concubines; and so did also his priests spend their time with harlots.

15. And it came to pass that he planted vineyards round about in the land; and he built wine-presses, and made wine in abundance; and therefore he became a wine-bibber, and also his people.

16. And it came to pass that the Lamanites began to come in upon his people, upon small numbers, and to slay them in their fields, and while they were tending their flocks.

He built watchtowers so high that all the surrounding country could be seen from their tops. Furthermore, he planted many vineyards and made presses. From the wine he made, he became a "wine-bibber,"* and following his example, his people, also, became drunkards. All this he did from the riches he obtained by grinding down his tax-oppressed people.

VERSES 16-19. *The Lamanites began to come in upon his people.* Again the Lamanites attacked the Nephites while they were engaged in their labors and killed some of the Nephites and drove off their flocks. King Noah set guards around the land but in such small numbers that they, too, were destroyed. He finally sent his armies and drove the Lamanites away. This victory made him and his people

---

*He became a wine-bibber. King Noah planted vineyards throughout his kingdom, made wine from the fruit therefrom, and became a drunkard, corrupting the people by his contaminating example. The story in this part of the Sacred Record shows vividly that wine drinking became the beginning of the downfall of the nation. Drunkenness bred other vices, neglect of religious duties, crimes, such as the murder of the servants of the Lord; and, finally, when the measure of their iniquity was full, the people, through drunkenness, lost their independence and their prosperity, with the departure of the people of Limhi. (See Mosiah 22:11-16)

According to an Associated Press dispatch, dated New Haven, Conn., March 6, 1938, it has been found by recent investigation that some of the aborigines of America were fond of intoxicants. They made, it is claimed, many kinds of wine and beer from various plants. Intoxicants were used, it seems, in religious ceremonies, dances, and socials. They were also used as medicine and as an offering when rain was desired.

17. And king Noah sent guards round about the land to keep them off; but he did not send a sufficient number, and the Lamanites came upon them and killed them, and drove many of their flocks out of the land; thus the Lamanites began to destroy them, and to exercise their hatred upon them.

18. And it came to pass that king Noah sent his armies against them, and they were driven back, or they drove them back for a time; therefore, they returned rejoicing in their spoil.

19. And now, because of this great victory they were lifted up in the pride of their hearts; they did boast in their own strength, saying that their fifty could stand against thousands of the Lamanites; and thus they did boast, and did delight in blood, and the shedding of the blood of their brethren, and this because of the wickedness of their king and priests.

2. The Prophet Abinadi Denounces the Prevailing Wickedness.

20. And it came to pass that there was a man among them whose name was Abinadi; and he went forth among them, and began to prophesy, saying: Behold, thus saith the Lord, and thus hath he commanded me, saying, Go forth, and say unto this people, thus saith the Lord—Wo be unto this people, for I have seen their abominations, and their wickedness, and their whoredoms; and except they repent I will visit them in mine anger.

21. And except they repent and turn to the Lord their God, behold, I will deliver them into the hands of their enemies; yea, and they shall be brought into bondage; and they shall be afflicted by the hand of their enemies.

22. And it shall come to pass that they shall know that I am the Lord their God, and am a jealous God, visiting the iniquities of my people.

23. And it shall come to pass that except this people repent and turn unto the Lord their God, they shall be brought into bondage; and none shall deliver them, except it be the Lord the Almighty God.

24. Yea, and it shall come to pass that when they shall cry

conceited and boastful, and developed the desire to shed the blood of the Lamanites, who were their brethren. We can see the gradual decay of the moral and spiritual fibre of King Noah's people, and therein we can see, also, the polluting and defiling influences of godless leadership. We shall see, too, that, "A king is not saved by the multitude of a host."

Verses 20-25. *Wo be unto this people, for I have seen their wickedness.* At this time the Prophet Abinadi, appeared among the people of King Noah's domain. He announced that the Lord had commanded him to warn them of the dire consequences of their wickedness, and that the Lord would visit them in anger if they did not repent. Bondage to the Lamanites for them and their children was predicted

unto me I will be slow to hear their cries; yea, and I will suffer them that they be smitten by their enemies.

25. And except they repent in sackcloth and ashes, and cry mightily to the Lord their God, I will not hear their prayers, neither will I deliver them out of their afflictions; and thus saith the Lord, and thus hath he commanded me.

3. King Noah Seeks the Life of Abinadi.

26. Now it came to pass that when Abinadi had spoken these words unto them they were wroth with him, and sought to take away his life; but the Lord delivered him out of their hands.

27. Now when king Noah had heard of the words which Abinadi had spoken unto the people, he was also wroth; and he said: Who is Abinadi, that I and my people should be judged of him, or who is the Lord, that shall bring upon my people such great affliction?

28. I command you to bring Abinadi hither, that I may slay him, for he has said these things that he might stir up my people to anger one with another, and to raise contentions among my people; therefore I will slay him.

29. Now the eyes of the people were blinded; therefore they hardened their hearts against the words of Abinadi, and they sought from that time forward to take him. And king Noah hardened his heart against the word of the Lord, and he did not repent of his evil doings.

---

by this holy man of God. He prophesied boldly, and without fear, of their coming fate; he told them that unless they abandoned the idolatry into which they had been led by Noah and his priests, and turned unto the Lord who had been merciful unto their fathers, they would be brought down and made slaves by their enemies. Bondage of the sorest kind would be their lot, and none but the Almighty God could deliver them. They would be smitten and afflicted, and, "The Lord will not hear their prayers" and "will be slow to hear their cries," he said the Lord had commanded him to say.

VERSES 26-29. King Noah was wroth; and he said: Who is Abinadi? Bring him hither, that I may slay him. King Noah, like many despots before and after him, listened to the flattery of his craven priests, and gave no heed to the warning cries of the would-be benefactor of his people. He did not repent, nor did he admonish his subjects to. He was dead as to the counsel of God's servant. His conscience, dulled by prolonged debauchery, was insensible to the demands of justice, to right and to wrong. "Who is this Abinadi, that he should judge my people?" he cried. "Who is the Lord," that He should be so vengeful? "Bring Abinadi hither, that I may slay him," for he seeks only to stir up my people to anger one with another. These were the words of one stupefied by habitual drinking. The people, now blinded by the promises and the flattery of King Noah, were ready to follow him in whatever action he wished to take. They sought Abinadi and, with the cowardly priests of Noah, would have put him to death if they could have found him. However, Abinadi was saved by the power of the Almighty; he was to come again to warn these people of Lehi-Nephi of the punishment to be meted out to them unless they abandoned their wicked ways, and cried to the Lord their God for deliverance.

ABINADI

A Nephite prophet whom the Lord raised up in the land of Lehi-Nephi to reprove the wicked people of King Noah for their sins. As near as we can tell he delivered his prophecies about 150 B.C. At his first appearance he announced as the word of the Lord that if the people did not repent of their iniquities they should be brought into bondage and none should deliver them except the Lord and He would be slow to hear their prayers in the days of their tribulations. The people did not repent but sought the life of Abinadi and his words were fulfilled in the days of Noah's son, Limhi. Two years later he reappeared in disguise, so that the people knew him not, and pronounced yet greater woes upon the unrepentant Noah and his subjects. Slavery of the most oppressive kind, famine, pestilence and death were to be their lot and but a few years passed before Abinadi's prophecies were fulfilled. For his bold denunciations of their abominations he was taken by the priests of the king, with whom he had a long controversy on the principle of the atonement and other laws of God, which ended in his being condemned to death. In accordance with this sentence he was burned at the stake in the City of Lehi-Nephi. One man only, Alma the elder, of whom we have record, pleaded with Noah in behalf of Abinadi and this so incensed the sin-degraded king that he sought to take Alma's life. Alma, however, escaped and in his place of retreat made a record of the teachings and acts of Abinadi and to that record we are indebted for some of the most precious gospel teachings in the Book of Mormon.

NOAH

The son of Zeniff and second king over the Nephite colony which returned from Zarahemla to the Land of Lehi-Nephi. Unlike his father he was not a righteous man but gave way to drunkenness and harlotry, and as is often the case with monarchs of his disposition grievously oppressed his people. He surrounded himself with creatures after his own heart, and placed the Holy Priesthood in the hands of men who were as corrupt as himself. He greatly beautified the temple in the City of Lehi-Nephi which he befouled with his debaucheries; while the cost of the rich adornment with which he lavishly ornamented it was wrung from his unwilling subjects in a tax of one-fifth of all they possessed. Not only did he greatly beautify the temple but he built himself a magnificent palace and erected many other costly buildings in the city of Lehi-Nephi and in the neighboring Valley of Shilom. He also built two very high watch towers, one of which stood near the temple and the other on the hill to the north of the Land of Shilom. Later he planted many vineyards and made an abundance of wine which resulted in him and his people becoming drunkards.

Noah had not been long on the throne before small marauding bands of Lamanites began to harass the Nephites and drive off their flocks. The king set guards around his possessions to keep the Lamanites off but he did not post them in sufficient numbers and they were slain or driven away. He finally sent his armies and drove the Lamanites back. This victory made him and his people conceited and boastful, and developed a delight in them to shed the blood of the Lamanites.

At this time (about B.C. 150) a prophet named Abinadi appeared among them and predicted that they would be brought into bondage to their enemies unless they repented of their wickedness. The king and the people were very angry with Abinadi and sought to take his life. Two years later he came among them in disguise. This time he uttered, in the name of the Lord, very terrible prophecies against Noah and his people, all of which were fulfilled in a very few years. But the people would not heed Abinadi and the more he exposed their iniquities the more furious raged their anger against him. They finally took him, bound him and hurried him with railing accusations before the king. There the priests began to cross-question him that they might confuse him and cause him to say something that would give them a pretext for slaying him. This conduct gave Abinadi the chance in turn to question his accusers, by which he exposed their deceit and iniquity; and it also enabled him to explain many of the principles of the Gospel of life and salvation. His teachings were, however, exactly what Noah's infidel priests did not want. They charged Abinadi with having reviled the king and on this charge obtained Noah's consent for his execution. And finally, Abinadi was cruelly tortured and burned to death by his fellow citizens in the sin-stained City of Lehi-Nephi.

Abinadi's cruel death was, in the providences of the Lord, made the means of establishing the Church of Christ among Noah's subjects. One of the young priests, named Alma, was converted by the prophet's teachings; he wrote them down and taught them to others. A Church was organized on the outskirts of the city but in a little while, the movement reached the ears of the king and he sent his soldiers to capture the believers. Being warned of the Lord the latter fled and escaped their pursuers.

Soon after the return of Noah's army from their unsuccessful attempt to capture Alma and his people a great division grew up among that monarch's subjects. They were heartily tired of his tyranny and his debaucheries. One of those most dissatisfied was an officer of the king's army named Gideon. In the disturbance that now arose between Noah and his people Gideon sought to slay the king. But Noah fled to the tower near the temple. From its top he beheld an advancing host of Lamanites. Pleading with Gideon for his life he ordered his people to flee. They did so but being encumbered with their families the Lamanites soon overtook them and began to slay them. The craven-hearted king then commanded his men to leave the women and children to the mercy of their savage foes and flee into the wilderness. Some obeyed while others refused. Those who followed Noah soon grew ashamed of their cowardice and desired to return to meet the Lamanites to avenge the slaughter of their wives and little ones or perish as they had done. King Noah objected and his unworthy priests sustained him. At this the soldiers grew exceedingly angry, all love for him as a man was crushed out, all respect for him as a monarch was lost; they took him and burned him to death as he had done Abinadi, and would have sacrificed the priests in the same way had they not fled from them. They turned their faces towards Lehi-Nephi and were overjoyed to meet some messengers who bore the welcome tidings that the Lamanites had spared the lives of those who had been left behind, though they held them in bondage. Noah was succeeded by his son Limhi.

CHAPTER 12

1. *Abinadi, for Denouncing Evil-doers, Is Cast into Prison—2. The False Priests Sit in Judgment upon Him—3. They Are Confounded.*

1. *Abinadi, for Denouncing Evil-doers Is Cast into Prison.*

1. And it came to pass that after the space of two years that Abinadi came among them in disguise, that they knew him not, and began to prophesy among them saying: Thus has the Lord commanded me, saying—Abinadi, go and prophesy unto this my people, for they have hardened their hearts against my words; they have repented not of their evil doings; therefore, I will visit them in my anger, yea, in my fierce anger will I visit them in their iniquities and abominations.

2. Yea, wo be unto this generation! And the Lord said unto me: Stretch forth thy hand and prophesy saying: Thus saith the Lord, it shall come to pass that this generation, because of their iniquities, shall be brought into bondage, and shall be smitten on the cheek; yea, and shall be driven by men, and shall be slain; and the vultures of the air, and the dogs, yea, and the wild beasts, shall devour their flesh.

3. And it shall come to pass that the life of king Noah shall be valued even as a garment in a hot furnace; for he shall know that I am the Lord.

4. And it shall come to pass that I will smite this my people with sore afflictions, yea, with famine and with pestilence; and I will cause that they shall howl all the day long.

5. Yea, and I will cause that they shall have burdens lashed upon their backs; and they shall be driven before like a dumb ass.

6. And it shall come to pass that I will send forth hail among them, and it shall smite them; and they shall also be smitten with the east wind; and insects shall pester their land also, and devour their grain.

7. And they shall be smitten with a great pestilence—and all

VERSE 1. *After a space of two years, Abinadi again comes among them in disguise.* Hunted by the iniquitous priests of King Noah, who were assisted by many of the king's subjects, Adinadi awaited in hiding for two years before he appeared again, in disguise, to warn of impending disaster. The Lord, once more, commanded Abinadi to prophesy to the people of Lehi-Nephi concerning that which was to come unless they repented of their sins and began to do His will. This time Abinadi uttered, in the name of the Lord, terrible prophecies against Noah and his people.

VERSES 2-8. *Except they repent I will utterly destroy them.* Abinadi, at God's command, stretched forth his hand and, in the name of the Lord, told them that they, not some future people, should be brought into bondage, that they should be smitten like dumb beasts and slain, that vultures and dogs should devour their carcasses, that famine and pestilence should come upon them, and that hail and

this will I do because of their iniquities and abominations.

8. And it shall come to pass that except they repent I will utterly destroy them from off the face of the earth; yet they shall leave a record behind them, and I will preserve them for other nations which shall possess the land; yea, even this will I do that I may discover the abominations of this people to other nations. And many things did Abinadi prophesy against this people.

9. And it came to pass that they were angry with him; and they took him and carried him bound before the king, and said unto the king: Behold, we have brought a man before thee who has prophesied evil concerning thy people, and saith that God will destroy them.

10. And he also prophesieth evil concerning thy life, and saith that thy life shall be as a garment in a furnace of fire.

11. And again, he saith that thou shalt be as a stalk, even as a dry stalk of the field, which is run over by the beasts and trodden under foot.

12. And again, he saith thou shalt be as the blossoms of a thistle, which, when it is fully ripe, if the wind bloweth, it is driven forth upon the face of the land. And he pretendeth the Lord hath spoken it. And he saith all this shall come upon thee except thou repent, and this because of thine iniquities.

13. And now, O king, what great evil hast thou done, or what great sins have thy people committed, that we should be condemned of God or judged of this man?

14. And now, O king, behold,

---

insects should destroy their crops. They were warned that if they did not repent, they should be utterly destroyed. He also, warned King Noah that his life would be like a garment in a hot fire. This was evidently a foreshadowing of his death by fire, which later took place when King Noah was burned at the stake by his own people. Everything that Abinadi prophesied was fulfilled in only a few years. It must not be overlooked that Abinadi told of a record, one that the Lord would preserve, which would tell how the generation of King Noah was smitten and afflicted because it refused to obey the voice of God's holy servant. The Lord, in speaking of these records, said, "I will preserve them for other nations which shall possess the land." It is this "Record of Zeniff" we are now considering. The Lord has preserved it to become an integral part of what is now The Book of Mormon.

VERSES 9-16. *They were angry with Abinadi.* Abinadi was one of the greatest of prophets; he was filled with the Holy Ghost, but the people would not listen to his warnings. The more he exposed their iniquities, the more furious raged their anger against him. Neither did they believe his words. In their own opinion they were everything that was good; they were mighty in their own strength, and unapproachably wise in their own conceit. Never, if you could believe them, had a better, more valiant, more innocent people lived. Filled with this spirit of self-conceit, they took Abinadi, bound him, and hurried him with railing accusations, before King Noah. "Here is the man, we deliver him into thy hands; thou mayest

we are guiltless, and thou O, king hast not sinned; therefore, this man has lied concerning you, and he has prophesied in vain.

15. And behold, we are strong, we shall not come into bondage, or be taken captive by our enemies; yea, and thou hast prospered in the land, and thou shalt also prosper.

16. Behold, here is the man, we deliver him into thy hands; thou mayest do with him as seemeth thee good.

2. The False Priests Sit in Judgment Upon Him.

17. And it came to pass that king Noah caused that Abinadi should be cast into prison; and he commanded that the priests should gather themselves together that he might hold a council with them what he should do with him.

18. And it came to pass that they said unto the king: Bring him hither that we may question him; and the king commanded that he should be brought before them.

19. And they began to question him, that they might cross him, that thereby they might have wherewith to accuse him; but he answered them boldly, and withstood all their questions, yea, to their astonishment; for he did withstand them in all their questions, and did confound them in all their words.

---

do with him as seemeth thee good." As has been pointed out before, the king was the head, the ruler, and the ultimate appeal of all.

VERSE 17. *King Noah caused that Abinadi should be cast into prison.* The cringing, craven King Noah, not willing to assume the responsibility of his royal prerogatives, called his false priests to advise him as to what he should do with Abinadi.

VERSE 18. *Bring him hither that we may question him.* The priests of King Noah, stiffnecked and conceited, demanded that Abinadi should be brought before them, and, then and there, answer any questions or any charges they might make against him. Their purpose was not to get knowledge, or to obtain understanding, but to subject him to their gibes and taunting accusations. Their spite was keen and unlimited; their hard hearts were like granite; they were destitute of grace. Instead of seeking truth, they hoped to ensnare Abinadi by placing in his way, the fouler's net. They loved vanity and sought for falsehood.

VERSE 19. *And they began to question him.* The arrogance and vanity of the priests were quickly turned into consternation as Abinadi, in defiance of the privileges given them by King Noah, reiterated to them the warnings he had previously made. He told them that the Lord was displeased with the wickedness abounding among them. Firmly he declared that the judgments of the Lord Omnipotent would be sorely visited upon them unless they repented without delay and turned to God who in times past had delivered their fathers. In their cross-examination of Abinadi they found no words of his that might condemn him. He uttered the truth, and he knew whereof he spoke. The sacred record says, "He did withstand them in all their questions, and did confound them in all their words."

20. And it came to pass that one of them said unto him: What meaneth the words which are written, and which have been taught by our fathers, saying: 21. How beautiful upon the

---

VERSE 20. *What meaneth the words which are written?* One of the priests of King Noah who had gathered to hear Abinadi's defense asked him to explain the meaning of that passage of scripture in which Isaiah proclaims the approach of a messenger whose feet upon the distant mountains are beautiful to behold. (Isaiah 52:7-10) This prophecy was known to all the Nephites — the words of Isaiah being recorded upon the brass plates that their fathers had brought out of Jerusalem over 400 years before. Isaiah had envisioned a forerunner of good tidings, a precursor of peace and salvation.

These words of Isaiah's are beautiful, and form one of the most meaningful of his inspired predictions. It has, however, caused many divergent interpretations by commentators of the Bible. They appear confused as to whom it refers, and the message it bears. One writer says one thing; another, something else. To many the passage portrays a messenger from the field of battle heralding the good tidings of victory. To others, it means the return of the captive Jews from their long exile. Still others see in it the coming back to Jerusalem of the king who had left his sacred city to battle the common enemy, and, who, in regal splendor returns and jubilantly proclaims peace through victory, and salvation from woe. The people of Jerusalem had, many times in their history, awaited anxiously and almost impatiently for the watchmen on its ruined walls to proclaim, with almost exultant voices, the sounding of such good tidings. (*See* II Samuel 18:25-26) In spite of the great learning evinced by some of these scholars, and the piety that guides them in their research, we say, definitely, Their conclusions are wrong! The one spoken of is the Lord, the Mighty King of heaven and earth. The salvation He proclaims is the salvation of the human soul, not the cessation of tribulation for which the Jews, for many years, had hoped. The Lord publishes "Peace, good will toward men," or as some interpret it, "Peace to men of good will." The majesty of His coming, the glory of His approach, is not understood by those who see in it only the advent of an earthly potentate who sometime before departed to conquer and vanquish the foes of Jerusalem.

At first reading, the passage may not seem important, but it is. The priests had a knowledge of the writings of Isaiah as can be noted in verses 19ff, when a question was asked Abinadi with words quoted from Isaiah. It appears that the followers of Nephi made many copies of the writings they found engraven upon the Plates of Brass, and that such a copy was in the possession of the people of King Noah. They probably retained it from the time Zeniff brought it from Zarahemla when he led his unsteady followers to the old homes of their fathers in the Land of Lehi-Nephi.

One of the priests. The sacred record is silent as to whom the priest was that questioned Abinadi, but on reading, time and time again, the continuing account of these people, and giving much consideration to the matter of his identity, we conclude, "It was Alma." We are told that Alma followed the counsel of Abinadi and did repent. Alma wrote down all the words he had heard the Prophet speak. When Abinadi was condemned to suffer death, Alma became his defender, and, thereafter, championed his cause. He went to King Noah and plead for Abinadi's life, that it be spared. We may assume that Alma, from this time forth, kept, or caused them to be kept, the records of the Nephites in the Land of Lehi-Nephi; also that he, in like manner, kept the record of the "people of the Lord, who were driven into the wilderness by the people of King Noah."

mountains are the feet of him that bringeth good tidings; that publisheth peace; that bringeth good tidings of good; that publisheth salvation; that saith unto Zion, Thy God reigneth;

Dwelling in Zarahemla where the persecuted but faithful outcasts, mentioned above, fled for refuge, King Mosiah caused their records to be read in the presence of both those whose history they preserved and of his own subjects. After the reading of their records was completed by King Mosiah, he desired that Alma speak to the assembled multitude which Alma did. But their number was so great that they were divided into groups so everyone could hear. Then Alma went from one assembly to another preaching repentance and faith in the Lord. (See Chapter 25)

The request made, we presume by Alma, gave Abinadi the opportunity to declare to the assembled throng of both priests and people, the good tidings of Salvation which was to be made, and the resurrection of Jesus, and its subsequent victory over death. In the accounts of His servants proclaiming His words, we see that the evil intents of men in seeking to destroy and bring to naught His divine purposes, are often turned to the glory of God. Were it not for the wicked designs of Noah's priests in summoning Abinadi into their presence, and there subjecting him to all manner of questioning, there, undoubtedly, would have been many who never would have heard the glorious message he bore. Again, we are reminded of the words of the poet, "Out of evil, still educing good."

An incident with which many of us are familiar will serve to show the truth of that oft repeated saying. A few years ago some photographs of the sacred confines of the Salt Lake Temple were surreptitiously obtained by a questionable character. They were offered to several different magazines for a price. The General Authorities of the Church became aware of their proposed publication. They saw in it a wonderful way to preach the Gospel of Jesus Christ, and thereby tell of the temple ordinances and holy ceremonies performed therein. They sent, gratis, to every magazine that so wished it, much better pictures of the interior of the sacred edifice than those that had been offered them for money. Each picture was accompanied by a proper description, telling the purpose for which each object portrayed was used in the Plan of Salvation. Thus, was a great and an effective missionary labor undertaken, and, thereby, thousands who never would have had the Gospel principles presented to them, now had them explained in a simple and persuasive manner. In this we can see the marvelous ways of the Lord in bringing to serve His honor and glory, the wicked designs of men.

VERSE 21. *How beautiful upon the mountains are the feet of him that bringeth good tidings.* The magnificent and stately language used by Isaiah in proclaiming this great event of prophecy, sets it apart, making more bright and beautiful, the exalted and majestic picture he here presents. "How beautiful upon the mountains" expresses his jubilation as Isaiah proclaims the coming of Him, who is King. Not any king, but the *King* of kings. The term *mountains*, or *mountain* is used throughout the Scriptures, and usually means, when not referring to a particular mountain, the *glory*, or the *power*, or the *Temple of God*. The whole earth is God's Temple; its Holy of Holies is in our hearts. It is that place where we bring our prayers, and our praise, and our offerings of homage to Him. It is a temple, not made with hands. It is a "mighty fortress of our God," whose parapets shine with the burnished armour of His servants.

"Who shall ascend into the *mountain* of the Lord and who shall stand in His holy place? He that hath clean hands, and a pure heart; who hath not taken My name in vain, and hath not sworn deceitfully. He shall receive a blessing from the Lord, and righteousness from the God of his salvation. Such is the generation of

22. Thy watchmen shall lift up the voice; with the voice together shall they sing; for they shall see eye to eye when the Lord shall bring again Zion;

---

them that seek Thee; that seek Thy presence, O God of Jacob." (Psalm 24; Hebrew translation)

"And many nations shall come, and say, Come, and let us go up to the *mountain* of the Lord, and to the God of Jacob; and he will teach us of his ways, and we will walk in his paths: for the law shall go forth of Zion, and the word of the Lord from Jerusalem." (Micah 4:2; Isaiah 2:2-3)

The words of the Psalmist find fulfillment here: "Honor and majesty are before him: strength and beauty are in his sanctuary." (Psalm 96:6)

As Jerusalem was centered with mountains round about, the Jews, conscious of the mighty defense these mountains afforded their beloved city, making it a citadel, understood the words of the prophet. The imagery created by Isaiah's lofty comparison appealed to the subtle and discerning minds of those who had waited the coming of Him of whom the prophets had long foretold. He was their King, and to them, a Messenger of Salvation, their Rock and their Redeemer. He, they had been told for ages, would lead them into battle and would bring them peace through victory over their enemies. Jerusalem would be enthroned above all the nations of the earth. Their praise of Him was bounded only by their hopes in Him, and by the vision of His glorious appearing which Isaiah announced anew.

Thy God reigneth. This is the grand and final message their King proclaims. All the others are subordinated. Peace, good tidings of man's Redemption are published by Him whom they see approaching on the distant mountains. They watch Him as He draws nearer; His feet are like stars; His raiment, new, like the dawn of day; His voice is like thunder, the reverberations of which shake the earth. He declares His message, "Thy God reigneth." Not, "Thy God will reign," or "He will be King," but "He is King," now and forever. Yesterday, today, and tomorrow, He is the same; our King, our Deliverer, our All. They see the King, they hear His voice. "Peace, God's most precious gift to man," is now declared to be his portion. The Jews remembered the words of the Psalmist, "The Lord will give strength unto His people; the Lord will bless His people with peace." (Psalm 29:11)

VERSE 22. *Thy watchmen shall lift up the voice.* This verse refers not to the watchmen who are set about Jerusalem in its towers to warn of approaching enemies, but to all the holy prophets who in times past have raised their voices to declare His coming, and, like watchmen, notify the people of Jerusalem of evil purposes when they first become known. Who, we may ask, were the first to see the King? The prophets whom Isaiah calls *watchmen.* The King had sent them as His emissaries to warn the city and to prepare it for things that were to come. They never slept. The words of King David were ever with them, "Except the Lord keep the city, the watchmen waketh in vain." When they behold His glorious appearance and hear His triumphant shout, they unite themselves in His joyful march, at the same time they bid everyone to join in the exultant cry, "Behold, the King! Our God reigneth!" They see eye to eye with Him; their united purpose is the Redemption of Zion. Their joy is serving the King; their gladness is praising Him. But, we may ask by way of interpolation, "How can we praise Him unless we do His will?"

Watchmen. The inspired teachers of God's children, the watchmen set out at night, are like keepers of sheep. They work for only one Master. They lead His flock to pleasant places; they guide them along the right paths to where the Good

23. Break forth into joy; sing together ye waste places of Jerusalem; for the Lord hath comforted his people, he hath redeemed Jerusalem;

24. The Lord hath made bare his holy arm in the eyes of all the nations, and all the ends of the earth shall see the salvation of our God?

Shepherd awaits their coming. He knows them all, and calls them by name. He loves each one. Some have fallen by the way; some are lost; some are hunted by the wolf; others are hungry, helpless, and cold. All need His care. "Therefore, O ye shepherds, hear the word of the Lord; . . . Behold I, even I, will both search My sheep, and seek them out. . . . I will strengthen the sick, and will bind up that which was broken. . . . I will feed them in a good pasture, and upon the high mountains of Israel shall their fold be. . . . I will feed my flock. . . ." (See Ezekiel Chapter 34) Great comfort to ancient Judah was the promise of His coming. I will "seek them out," are the words of the Lord. We will rejoice with them because we are assured "He will find them, and will take them in His arms, and will carry them to His fold," and will rejoice with them, for, "Together they shall sing . . . when the Lord shall bring again Zion." (Isaiah 52 v. 8) (The *Targum* renders it, "When He shall bring back His Shekinah (Spirit) to Zion." The Dead Sea Scroll ends the last line by adding, "in mercy.")

VERSE 23. *He hath redeemed Jerusalem.* Redeem means, (1) To buy again something that has been sold, by paying back the price that bought it. (Lev. 25:25; 27:20) (2) To deliver and bring out of bondage those who were kept prisoners by their enemies. (Deut. 7:5; 32:6) *Cruden's Concordance of the Bible.* Jerusalem had been sold, figuratively speaking, by the apostate Jews. They had perverted the ways of the Lord, and, too, they had abandoned the covenant their fathers had made with the Lord at Mount Sinai. The land of Jerusalem was the land of their inheritance. The Mosaic Law provided that land which had been sold, among other things, could be redeemed. However, a price was demanded for its redemption. What was the price? Jerusalem had not been bartered away for gold or for silver, nor was it sold as common merchandise. There was only One who could meet the prescribed terms. That One was their King! Isaiah said, "He hath redeemed Jerusalem"; not with money or with the might of a great army, but He hath Redeemed it with the blood that was shed on Mount Calvary; the Redemption brought about by Jesus of Nazareth, the King of the Jews.

VERSE 24. *The Lord hath made bare His holy arm.* The power and authority of God, often referred to as *His holy arm,* is, in the Redemption of Jerusalem, made manifest to all nations. When Isaiah says, "Jerusalem," we may interpret it as meaning the entire *earth* and all *mankind.* "The earth is the Lord's and the fulness thereof; the world, and they that dwell therein." (Psalm 24:1) The Salvation of His children is the great purpose to which all God's providences are consecrated, and in them, all the people of the earth will behold His Redemption.

Break forth into joy. The glorious appearance of the King and His royal entourage brought forth shouts of joy that swelled into a mighty "Hosanna." Isaiah now bids all, "Break forth into joy." (Lit. "Break forth, sing together.") All ye who have grown weary waiting for the King to come, also, ye who are become withered like an unwatered garden, ye, too, that love the Law of the Lord, "who wait for Him more than the watchmen wait for the morning." "Sing together." The Lord has not forgotten His people, neither will He see them perish. He hath redeemed Zion. Great is our King! Who is our King, but the Lord? And, who is the Lord, save He is God! "Let the heavens be glad, and the earth rejoice; let

the fields exult, and all that is therein!" (Jewish Adage. See I Chronicles 16:31-32)
The Lord hath comforted His people. Sing aloud! Isaiah knew the strength of song.

Singing was an important part of Israel's worship. Music was heard throughout
the land. Songs of praise to God lifted the most menial of tasks to His service. The
vine, the fruitful field, the harvest, the flocks, doves, lilies, sorrow, delight, and
victory — all were remembered in songs of memorial to His goodness. Israel
sought comfort in song. "When my cares are many within me, songs in Thy praise
delight my soul." (Hebrew proverb) "For the Lord will comfort Zion: He will
comfort all her waste places and will make her wilderness like Eden, and her
desert like the garden of the Lord; joy and gladness shall be found therein, thanksgiving, and the voice of melody." (Isaiah 51:3) In weakness, as in strength; in
failure, as in success, they sang songs of joy and thanksgiving. In them, they
expressed their innermost thoughts. "O sing unto the Lord, a new song: sing unto
the Lord, all the earth. Sing unto the Lord; bless His name; proclaim His salvation from day to day." (Psalm 96:1-2. Jewish rendition)

A good conception of the influence singing the songs of Zion had upon ancient
Judah may be obtained by reading the first four verses of the 137th Psalm. Words of
poetry memorializing this sorrowful experience in Israel's history are, today, sung
by both Jews and their Christian brethren. These words are found in the Hymn
Book of the Church of Jesus Christ of Latter-day Saints. They not only express
Judah's sorrow in her Babylonian captivity, but also, as is pointed out in the King
James Translation of the Bible, her "constancy under captivity."

> Down by the river's verdant side,
>   Low by the solitary tide,
> There, while the peaceful waters slept,
>   We pensively sat down and wept,
> And on the bending willows hung
>   Our silent harps through grief unstrung.
>
> For they who wasted Zion's bowers
>   And laid in dust her ruined towers
> In scorn their weary slaves desire
>   To strike the chords of Israel's lyre,
> And in their impious ears to sing
>   The sacred songs to Zion's King.
>
> How shall we tune those lofty strains
>   On Babylon's polluted plains,
> When low in ruin on the earth
>   Remains the place that gave us birth,
> And stern destruction's iron hand
>   Still sways our desolated land.
>
> O never shall our harps awake,
>   Laid in the dust for Zion's sake,
> For ever on the willows hung,
>   Their music hushed; their chords un-strung;
> Lost Zion! city of our God,
>   While groaning 'neath the tyrant's rod.
>
> Still mold'ring lie thy leveled walls
>   And ruin stalks along thy halls.
> And brooding o'er thy ruined towers
>   Such desolation sternly lowers,
> That when we muse upon thy woe,
>   The gushing tears of sorrow flow!

25. And now Abinadi said unto them: Are you priests, and pretend to teach this people, and to understand the spirit of prophesying, and yet desire to know of me what these things mean?

26. I say unto you, wo be unto you for perverting the ways of the Lord! For if ye understand these things ye have not taught them;

therefore, ye have perverted the ways of the Lord.

27. Ye have not applied your hearts to understanding; therefore, ye have not been wise. Therefore, what teach ye this people?

28. And they said: We teach the law of Moses.

And while we toil through wretched life
And drink the bitter cup of strife,
Until we yield our weary breath,
And sleep released from woe in death,
Will Zion in our memory stand—
Our lost, our ruined native land.

VERSE 25. *And now Abinadi said unto them.* Abinadi did not immediately answer the priest's question. He turned from being the one questioned, to the questioner. From the prosecuted, he became the prosecutor. His indictment of the priests was serious. He charged that they were hypocrites and frauds. They had long pretended to understand the Scriptures, and by the spirit of prophecy to teach the people what was meant therein. Now they asked him the meaning of Isaiah's words.

VERSE 26. *If ye understand these things, ye have not taught them.* Ye have perverted the ways of the Lord, is his solemn accusation. *Pervert* means "to turn." (1) To cause to turn from what is considered right, natural, or true; misdirect; lead astray; corrupt. (2) To turn to an improper use, misuse. (3) To change or misapply the meaning of; misinterpret; distort; twist. (4) To bring into a worse condition; debase. (*Webster's New World Dictionary.*) Any one of these definitions, or all of them would fit the depraved purposes of the priests.

VERSE 27. *What teach ye this people?* Wisdom and understanding lie in knowing the meaning of the prophet's words. Abinadi accused the priests: You have not sought to discern evil, but through the prophecies seek to excuse your wicked ways. Only through the precepts of the Lord will come understanding, and with it, wisdom. You seek neither. Without them, "What teach ye this people?"

VERSE 28. *We teach the Law of Moses.* The Nephites were of Israel. All Israelites of ancient times were taught to accept the Law as their guide. It was emblematic of things to come. It pointed out the way to Christ, the Messiah, whose coming they awaited. By their faith they saw these things as though they had already happened. The Law thus promised Salvation to everyone who looked to Christ for Redemption. Faith in that which is to come is not unusual, nor is it strange. There is no doubt, faith imposes burdens, but its rewards are sure. The plowman plants his seed because he is assured a time of harvest will come; the merchant buys his goods because he believes he will get a profit in their sale; the mariner has confidence he will reach a distant strand, one which, perhaps, he has never seen, by following a course marked out for him. So he starts out on his voyage; the plowman plants his seed; the herdsman cares for his flock, and the merchant buys his goods. All things are done by the power of faith. Israel, in the days of Moses, as now, walked by faith. Ancient Israel looked forward to His coming; we look back. Both visions are equally effective.

29. And again he said unto them: If ye teach the law of Moses why do ye not keep it? Why do ye set your hearts upon riches? Why do ye commit whoredoms and spend your strength with harlots, yea, and cause this people to commit sin, that the Lord has cause to send me to prophesy against this people, yea, even a great evil against this people?

30. Know ye not that I speak the truth? Yea, ye know that I speak the truth; and you ought to tremble before God.

31. And it shall come to pass that ye shall be smitten for your iniquities, for ye have said that ye teach the law of Moses. And what know ye concerning the law of Moses? Doth salvation come by the law of Moses? What say ye?

32. And they answered and said that salvation did come by the law of Moses.

33. But now Abinadi said unto them: I know if ye keep the commandments of God ye shall

---

VERSE 29. *If ye teach the Law of Moses why do ye not keep it?* If one teaches the principles of moral conduct then to demonstrate their worth, he must observe them. To set an example to the learner is the proper way to teach any truth. Ill-begotten wealth, immorality, wrongful influence are the results of lives spent in unbridled pretense of justice. By their actions, these priests led King Noah's people to commit all manner of sin and grow in wickedness. To warn them of the punishment that was in store for them if they did not repent, the Lord sent Abinadi.

VERSE 30. *Know ye not that I speak the Truth?* The spirit of prophecy that was with Abinadi gave him power of speech to declare to the iniquitous priests the folly of their ways. This spirit led him to see their secret paths, which, they thought, were known only to them. The spirit of prophecy is always the spirit of truth. Jacob, the brother of Nephi and the son of the Prophet Lehi, in speaking of prophesying, once said, "It speaketh of things as they really are, and of things as they really will be." (Jacob 4:13) Evil and error quake in its presence, the wicked fear and tremble.

VERSE 31. *Doth salvation come by the Law of Moses?* Abinadi again pronounces evil against the wrongdoers, and warns them that to say the Law of Moses is given as a guide, and then not to teach its observance, is only compounding iniquity. If man refuses to walk in the way of his guide, no matter who he is, for him to advise others is wicked foolishness. They may do as he does. "All the paths of the Lord are mercy and truth unto such as keep His covenant and His testimonies." (Psalm 25:10) The Lord gave the Law of Moses to guide the humble in justice and to teach them His way. But Abinadi says that only by obedience to all its requirements, its statutes and judgments, can their salvation come. "What say ye?"

VERSE 32. *They said salvation did come by the Law of Moses.* In answer to the question asked by Abinadi, the priests of King Noah said that salvation did come by the Law of Moses.

VERSE 33. *I know if ye keep the commandments of God ye shall be saved.* Again, Abinadi used the knowledge that was imparted to the priests by the Hebrew Scriptures, a copy of which was in their possession. Abinadi quoted passages to them from the *Book of Moses* which has now been divided into five parts. (*See* p.

be saved; yea, if ye keep the com- | livered unto Moses in the mount
mandments which the Lord de- | of Sinai, saying:

205, v. 23, also p. 450, Vol. I, COMMENTARY ON THE BOOK OF MORMON) These five parts, or books, are known as the *Pentateuch. Deuteronomy* is the last book of the Pentateuch, or the fifth of the Bible. With what is now called Genesis, Exodus, Leviticus, and Numbers, it was included on the brass plates of Laban. It means "the repetition of," or "the second time the Law is given."

Principally, Deuteronomy contains three sermons preached by Moses to all Israel at the end of their long sojourn in the wilderness. Israel was then encamped on the Plains of Moab, eastwardly of the Dead Sea. This was at the time just prior to their crossing of the Jordan River and the subsequent march of the armies of Israel, under Joshua, into the Promised Land.

In his sermons, Moses told Israel of God's love for those who served Him diligently, and reminded them of God's watchful care over them during their forty year exodus. He reviewed the experience of their wanderings and renewed to them the commandments and ordinances God had given them at Mount Sinai.

During their years of bondage, many of the Children of Israel had forgotten the "God of their fathers" and had adopted the customs and habits of the Egyptians. They toiled, as did their taskmasters, on the day the Lord had set apart as their day of rest and one on which to think of Him. They took great oaths, as did also the Egyptians, and they made for themselves gods of wood and gods of stone and of precious metals. To these they bowed down and worshiped. Moses then gave them, what the Master called, "The first and great commandment." (Matthew 22:38) Moses said, "Hear, O Israel: the Lord our God is one Lord. And thou shalt love the Lord thy God with all thine heart, and with all thy soul, and with all thy might. And these words, which I command thee this day, shall be in thine heart: And thou shalt teach them diligently unto thy children. . . ." (Deut. 6:4-7) (*See* p. 483, Vol. I, Verse 2, COMMENTARY ON THE BOOK OF MORMON.)

A short time previous to giving the "first and great command," "Moses called all Israel, and said unto them, Hear, O Israel, the statutes, and judgments which I speak in your ears this day, that ye may learn them, and keep, and do them." (Deut. 5:1)

"Hear O Israel; hear and heed, hear and remember, hear, that you may learn, and keep, and do; else your learning is to no purpose. When we hear the word of God we must set ourselves to learn it, that we may have it ready to use on all occasions, and what we have learned we must put in practice, for that is the end of hearing and learning; not to fill our heads with notions, or our mouths with talk, but to rectify and direct our affections and conversations." (Matthew Henry)

In the words of an inspired prayer, Moroni said, ". . . and witness unto thee, O God the Eternal Father, that they are willing to take upon them the name of thy Son, and always remember him, *and keep his commandments which he hath given them,* that they may always have his Spirit to be with them." Moroni 4:3)

This is the prayer of all the Saints who have dwelt in this land. (*See* Mormon 9:36-37)

"Now these are the commandments, the statutes, and the judgments, which the Lord your God commanded to teach you, that ye might do them in the land whither ye go to possess it: That thou mightest fear the Lord your God, to keep all his statutes and his commandments, which I command thee, thou, and thy son, and thy son's son, all the days of thy life; . . . Hear therefore, O Israel, and observe to do it. . . ." (Deut. 6:1-3)

34. I am the Lord thy God, who hath brought thee out of the land of Egypt, out of the house of bondage.

35. Thou shalt have no other God before me.

36. Thou shalt not make unto thee any graven image, or any likeness of any thing in heaven above, or things which are in the earth beneath.

37. Now Abinadi said unto them, Have ye done all this? I say unto you, Nay, ye have not. And have ye taught this people that they should do all these things? I say unto you, Nay, ye have not.

THE FIRST COMMANDMENT

VERSES 34-36. *Thou shalt have no other God before me.* In enumerating to the Children of Israel the requirements of the "Law," great emphasis, by way of constant repetition, is placed upon this commandment, number one of the Ten Words, or Ten Commandments. Moses further warned his people, ". . . Beware lest thou forget the Lord, which brought thee forth out of the land of Egypt, from the house of bondage. Thou shalt fear the Lord thy God, and serve him, and shalt swear by his name. Ye shall not go after other gods. . . ." (Deut. 6:12-13)

Abinadi, like the great Law Giver, Moses, made the fact important that God, the Lord Omnipotent, is the mighty Ruler of all, that He is the Giver of all good, who must be obeyed. Abinadi also showed that by God's power, their fathers were brought out from Egyptian bondage and were led, by His watchful care, to a land where His purposes would find fulfillment.

"Great and marvelous are the works of the Lord," hence, "Thou shalt have no other God before me." The commandment given does not only mean lesser gods, but all other gods who, in some hearts, may rival the pre-eminence of the True and Living God. But the commandment is that thou shalt have no God save Yahweh, the Creator and the Maker of all. Of Yahweh they knew; He it was who went before them out of Egypt in a pillar of cloud by day, and in a pillar of fire by night; He cared for them through tribulation, and He provided for their wants. There was no other God, real or unreal, to whom they owed obeisance. "Who is like unto Thee, Almighty God?" "The Lord, our God, is not many gods, but one Lord." Therefore, Moses taught that ye shall bow down and worship Him, the only "True and Living God." In his teaching this commandment, Abinadi was filled with the spirit of prophecy.

The priests of King Noah grew in laziness. In their desire to please the people, the priests spent their days in idle praise and in placing before the king's subjects the vain hope that the gods they made of wood, and stone, and metals, which they could both see and touch, would bring them joy and happiness far beyond any promised by the "God of their fathers" whom they had never seen. The flattering words of Noah's priests caused his people to pay, willingly, the burdensome taxes that he put upon them. "Thus did the people labor exceedingly to support their iniquity," and thus did the laziness of the priests and the wickedness to which it gave birth lead the people to become worshipers of idols and gods they fashioned after the things they imagined controlled every turn of life.

Thou shalt not make unto thee any graven image. (*See* Mosiah Chapter 13:12.)

VERSE 37. *Have ye done all this? Have ye taught this people that they should do all these things?* (*See* Mosiah Chapter 13)

GENERAL NOTES

The Day of the Lord Foretold by Isaiah and all the Holy Prophets.

In the beauty of holiness, in power and authority, surrounded by an unnumbered concourse of angels singing praises to His name, the Lord Omnipotent, He who was, and is from all eternity to all eternity, the mighty Prince of Peace, shall come down from heaven to reign in great glory upon the earth.

No language, however sublime, can declare the majesty of His coming; no words can tell the glorious splendor of His habitation, when He shall, again, abide in His Holy Mountain. From Mount Zion shall go forth the Law and the Word of the Lord. "How beautiful," says the prophet, "upon the mountains are the feet of Him that bringeth good tidings; that publisheth peace; that bringeth good tidings of good; that publisheth salvation; that sayeth unto Zion, Thy God reigneth."

Surely, He is our King, our Lord and our God, our Light and our Salvation. Good tidings of man's redemption through Him shall resound from one end of the earth to the other. Christ's millennial reign shall be inaugurated. Peace shall fill the earth. Not the peace that is purchased on the field of battle, not the peace that is woven into treaties in the far-away capitals of the world, not the peace of political accord, but peace that is founded upon truth, upheld and sustained by the righteousness of God's children everywhere. Any peace not preserved by righteousness is "Peace, peace, when there is no peace!" It is the work of righteousness, ever, to establish peace. Peace, the Lord's peace, is our portion; it is the source whence springs our fullness of joy, and our gladness; our happiness and content; our love for God's Law. "Great peace have they which love Thy law." (Psalm 119:165)

Let us remember, too, "The law of the Lord is perfect, converting the soul; the testimony of the Lord is sure, making wise the simple. . . ." (Psalm 19:7-10) The Lord is our God, and, "beside Him there is none other."

When that peaceful day, the day of the Lord, shall come; when all men shall invoke His holy name, when evil and error are no more, when hatred shall disappear, when His name shall be worshiped in all the earth, then shall our children be taught of the Lord, and great shall be their peace. (*See* 3 Nephi 22:13)

In that day, the lamb, unafraid, shall lie down at the side of the lion; "the olive and the palm will grow in the soil that is now beaten hard by the tramp of the soldier's feet." The understanding of God's Law shall fill the earth, and men shall observe it with their whole hearts. The voice of the Almighty One heard by the righteous people of Lehi-Nephi, yea a pleasant voice as if it were a whisper, shall swell into a mighty anthem, ceaselessly rendered, and universally heard, "Peace, peace be unto you, because of your faith in my Well Beloved, who was from the foundation of the world." (Helaman 5:47) Then all Israel shall see Him, and shall hear His voice, and they shall know that "I am He that doth speak." (3 Nephi 20:39) "Thy God reigneth."

In that day, and in our midst; in the midst of those whom He loved so well, but who nailed Him to a cross, Jesus of Nazareth the King of the Jews, shall be enthroned above all and shall be crowned King of kings and Lord of lords. Then will the hosts of heaven unite with the people of the earth in, not saying, but shouting, "Glory! Honor! Might! Majesty! and Dominion! be unto Him, for He has been crowned our King, and He shall reign for ever and for ever."

CHAPTER 13

1. *Abinadi, the Prophet, Protected by Divine Power. He Withstands the Priests and Cites the Law and the Gospel.*

1. *Abinadi, the Prophet, Protected by Divine Power.*

1. And now when the king had heard these words, he said unto his priests: Away with this fellow, and slay him; for what have we to do with him, for he is mad.

2. And they stood forth and attempted to lay their hands on him; but he withstood them, and said unto them:

3. Touch me not, for God shall smite you if ye lay your hands upon me, for I have not delivered the message which the Lord sent me to deliver; neither have I told you that which ye requested that I should tell; therefore, God will not suffer that I shall be destroyed at this time.

4. But I must fulfil the commandments wherewith God has commanded me; and because I have told you the truth ye are angry with me. And again, because I have spoken the word of God ye have judged me that I am mad.

VERSE 1. *Away with this fellow, and slay him.* Now, Abinadi had turned into a forum, the proceedings brought against him by the iniquitous priests of King Noah. This provided the means by which Abinadi further proclaimed the wonderful message he was to deliver. With strong arguments he refuted the claims of the priests that they used righteous efforts in declaring God's holy word. Also, he propounded to them many questions that if answered would plainly show the wicked neglect of which they were guilty.

The words of Abinadi proved unwelcome testimony that, although the priests asserted they taught the Law of Moses, they utterly failed to impress upon the minds of their charges the necessity of obedience to its commandments. In effect he said, "You have not taught this people that they should observe all the statutes and requirements of the sacred Law, neither have you done them yourselves." The accusation made by Abinadi enraged Noah; Abinadi was deranged, "He is mad," Noah declared. "Away with him, and slay him," he said.

VERSES 2-9. *Touch me not . . . because I have told you the truth ye are angry with me.* At the King's command, the unfriendly throng that had gathered in Noah's counsel chamber, including among them his wanton priests, attempted to seize Abinadi to carry out the dread decision of the wasted king. Protected by divine power he "withstood them"; they were unable to overcome the strength Abinadi received from On High.

Do me no harm; do not even "touch me," was his defiant challenge to them. "God shall smite you if ye lay your hands upon me."

Emboldened by the knowledge he had of the wondrous ways of the Lord, and further strengthened by his inspired calling to proclaim them, Abinadi warned the priests and their cohorts, who had become a disorderly crowd, that, as yet, he had not delivered to them, the message the Lord had given him, and, besides, he had not answered the request made to him by the priests to explain certain words spoken by the Prophet Isaiah. Until this was done, Abinadi declared that the Lord would not "suffer him to be destroyed."

I will do the things the Lord has commanded me to do. (See COMMENTARY ON THE BOOK OF MORMON, Vol. I, p. 31) The faith and integrity of Abinadi knew no bounds. He said, "I must fulfil the commandments wherewith God has commanded me"; moreover, he charged the priests, "You hate the truth, you are dismayed by the things I say of your wickedness; you, therefore, are angry with me and hope to completely destroy me that your sins may be blotted out amongst men and remembered, by them, no more."

God permitted Noah and his priests to reach "that goal, beyond which, the last effort of human wickedness cannot pass."

Noah imagined that by doing away with Abinadi, his own sins would be known to none but himself. This, too, was the idea of his companions. Today, it is the conclusion of many who think their vices, as well as their virtues, are unknown to God above. There is a God in heaven who knoweth all things.

Men, sometimes, seek to pervert His ways to abet their own wicked plans. They excuse themselves in doing that which is most to be eschewed; at the same time they point to a merciful Father who neither wishes to punish nor to inflict sorrow upon His wayward children.

God is slow to anger, but, if ever the thought presents itself to you that your actions are not known to Him, remember the words of King David, "Understand, . . . he that planted the ear, shall he not hear? He that formed the eye, shall he not see? He that teacheth man knowledge, shall not he know? (Psalm 94:8-10) All our ways are known to the Lord.

Cognizant of the enmity of King Noah and his priests, their designs against him and the conspiracy into which they had entered to destroy him, Abinadi was, nevertheless, determined to fulfill his divine commission though it may cost his life.

How like the faith of the Prophet Lehi was the unquestioning belief of Abinadi, this heroic servant of God. How like the firmness of purpose shown by Nephi in doing the will of the Lord was the resolute quality of his mind. Abinadi knew but one course to pursue, "I will do the things the Lord has commanded me to do."

We may learn, here, a lesson in *Obedience.* Read, if you will, the story told in the Bible, that dear and precious book, of Esther and Mordecai. The story of Abinadi found in the Book of Mormon is equally impressive, also the story of Lehi and Nephi.

In terms of years, about eighty had passed since he and his family left their homeland in Judea to seek a land which God had prepared for them, the same fidelity and devotion shown by Lehi in obeying the voice of the Lord, was manifest by Esther in her loyalty to her fathers, and by Mordecai, her cousin, whose determination to worship, only the True and Living God, thwarted the evil designs of Haman to destroy God's chosen people.

In remembrance of their faithfulness, the Jews, in humble supplication to the Giver of all Good, offer a prayer in which we will do well to unite. Let us borrow a portion of its words and add the names of Lehi and Nephi, not forgetting those of Esther and Mordecai, and beseech that same Mighty Ruler —

"Imbue us, O God, with the faith of former generations of Israel. Give us courage and steadfastness that," like Lehi, Thy servant of old, we may learn to listen to the promptings of that *Still Small Voice* which cometh from Thee to lead, and to direct, and to warn of things to come. "Uphold us," that like Nephi, "we may walk undaunted in the path of duty and loyalty even though it cost all we hold dear."

As is often the case when evil men are confronted with the truth concerning their wicked practices, when the good in them is smothered by depraved yearnings, and the darkness about them, like a beast, seeks to devour the pure and the noble; they no longer hate the bad, despise the lewd, and shrink from error, but, instead,

5. Now it came to pass after Abinadi had spoken these words that the people of king Noah durst not lay their hands on him, for the Spirit of the Lord was upon him; and his face shone with exceeding luster, even as Moses' did while in the mount of Sinai, while speaking with the Lord.

---

they treat with wrath and derision the person to whom their guilt is known. They condemn the wise, and scorn the just. King Noah refused to turn from his wicked ways as the prophet of the Lord called him to do, but in the place of repentance, he added anger to the crimes he had already committed, and judged his accuser to be insane because Abinadi declared the Word of God.

VERSE 5. *The people of King Noah durst not lay their hands on him.* Abinadi the prophet of the Lord, was only one against the many who sought his life, yet he showed no fear. His anxiety was for those who persecuted him. Humbly, his thoughts were like those of David's, when, in exultation, the Jewish king cried, "The Lord is my light and my salvation; whom shall I fear? The Lord is the strength of my life; of whom shall I be afraid? Though an host should encamp against me, my heart shall not fear." (Psalm 27:1-3) In their rendition of this heroic poem, the Jews add to the last line, "For thou art with me."

The assembled throng dared not interfere with Abinadi, nor did they molest him, for they saw in his countenance, the Spirit of God, making it bright like "Rays of Living Light." His face shone with exceeding luster, the Sacred Record says, even as Moses' did while in the mount of Sinai, while speaking with the Lord. (Exodus 34:29-30; 35)

Moses spent forty days and forty nights in the Mount of Sinai in close communion with God, conversing with the Lord. Amid thunders and lightnings, and fire that did not burn, he received from Yahweh "the words of the covenant, the ten commandments," written by the finger of God upon tables of stone.

At the end of this period of divine instruction he came down from the mount, and, "Moses wist not that the skin of his face shone while he talked" with the Lord. He came down "greatly enriched and miraculously adorned." Enriched because he had in his possession the two tables of the law which God had given him, and adorned by the glory of Him with whom he had sojourned, and with Him who imparted to Israel, the sacred promise, "I will be thy God."

Let us now turn to the record in the Book of Mormon of the sons of Helaman, Nephi and Lehi. (Helaman 5) Here we will read of these servants of the Lord who were sustained by His power, and who by diligence in serving Him, turned the wicked purposes of men to the glory of God, and to His honor. Their faces, too, shone as did Abinadi's.

Anxious in the service of God, and zealous in their mission to preach the Word of the Lord to the Lamanites, Nephi and Lehi went far south into the Land of Lehi-Nephi, where they were thrust into prison by the guards of the king of that land.

In prison, Nephi and Lehi were outraged by all the indignities the cruelness of their captors could suggest, or evil power achieve. Their clothes were taken from them; for many days they were without food; they were fastened to their cell with chains of iron.

The walls of the prison rocked beneath the surges of an earthquake. Those who had gathered there to revile the servants of God became afraid, as if a "solemn fear came upon them." They could not move, they could not flee, a sudden darkness enshrouded them about. In the tumult which followed, scenes they had never before witnessed, contrasts so striking, through the darkness that encircled the Laman-

6. And he spake with power and authority from God; and he continued his words, saying:

7. Ye see that ye have not power to slay me, therefore I finish my message. Yea, and I perceive that it cuts you to your hearts because I tell you the truth concerning your iniquities.

8. Yea, and my words fill you with wonder and amazement, and with anger.

9. But I finish my message; and then it matters not whither I go, if it so be that I am saved.

10. But this much I tell you, what you do with me, after this, shall be as a type and a shadow of things which are to come.

11. And now I read unto you the remainder of the commandments of God, for I perceive that they are not written in your hearts; I perceive that ye have studied and taught iniquity the most part of your lives.

---

ites, they saw Nephi and Lehi in the attitude of prayer, singing praises to God. Their faces "did shine exceedingly, even as the faces of the angels."

VERSES 6-8. *He spake with power and authority from God.* Abinadi was direct in his manner of speech. He offered no apologies, no pretexts, or excuses. His condemnation of King Noah's wickedness was not diluted with meaningless words, nor was it a polemical discussion of what is right, or what is wrong. Abinadi did not argue that. The priests said they taught the Law of Moses; they knew the good, and recognized evil. They willfully sinned against God. Abinadi's words were convincing to those who desired to know the truth. With power and authority from God, he rebuked the priests; he reproved the error of their ways, and called for them to abandon the course they then pursued.

This account of the words of Abinadi is strangely like the record presented in the Bible, when, after a sermon preached by Jesus, the greatest Teacher of them all, Matthew says, ". . . the people were astonished at his doctrine: *For he taught them as one having authority, and not as the scribes.*" (Matthew 7:29)

Also, we read in that sacred book, "Then he called his twelve disciples together, and gave them *power and authority* . . . and he sent them to preach the kingdom of God." (St. Luke 9:1)

VERSES 9-10. *But I finish my message.* Abinadi saw that the priests could not then harm him, for the protecting might of the Lord was over him. In reading the account of Nephi and Lehi, to which we have referred, (Helaman 5) verse twenty-five is a complete comment on this part of the story of Abinadi.

To Abinadi, it mattered not as to the things of the world, or, upon death, where he would go, just as long as he delivered his divine message, and was saved in the Kingdom of God. But he warned them, that, whatever they did to him, after he had finished the work the Lord had given him to do, it would be but a type, a foreshadowing "of things which are to come."

In all events, Abinadi said, "I finish my message."

VERSE 11. *And now I read unto you the remainder of the commandments of God.* Previously, Abinadi had read unto the priests of King Noah the First and Second of the Ten Commandments given to the Children of Israel when on Mount Sinai the Lord entered into a covenant with them that, if they would be faithful to Him, He would be their God. (See Chapter 12:35-36) Moses stood as the intermediary between Yahweh (Jehovah) and Israel when this Covenant was made, and near the end of their long sojourn in the wilderness he reminded them that, "The Lord made

12. And now, ye remember that I said unto you: Thou shalt not make unto thee any graven image, or any likeness of things which are in heaven above, or which are in the earth beneath, or which are in the water under the earth.

13. And again: Thou shalt not bow down thyself unto them, nor serve them; for I the Lord thy God am a jealous God, visiting the iniquities of the fathers upon the children, unto the third and fourth generations of them that hate me;

14. And showing mercy unto thousands of them that love me and keep my commandments.

---

not this covenant with our fathers, but with us, even us, who are all of us here alive this day." (Deut. 5:3)

THE SECOND COMMANDMENT

VERSES 12-14. *Thou shalt not make unto thee any graven image.* In Exodus 20:4-6, this commandment is rendered,

Thou shalt not make unto thee any graven image, or any likeness of any thing that is in heaven above, or that is in the earth beneath, or that is in the water under the earth.

Thou shalt not bow down thyself to them, or serve them: for I the Lord thy God am a jealous God, visiting the iniquity of the fathers upon the children, unto the third and fourth generation of them that hate me.

And shewing mercy unto thousands of them that love me and keep my commandments.

Except for a few changes in wording, the translations of the Ten Commandments found in the Bible and the Book of Mormon agree. The main difference is found in the 5th verse, where the Book of Mormon has the word *iniquity*, translated into the plural, *iniquities*. To recognize this difference is important to the thoughtful student because it warns all mankind that suffering is the lot of those who break any of God's commands. Not only does this commandment denounce and forbid any form of idolatry, but it threatens by some outward sign or expression, the children of them who willfully choose to do evil when good is placed before them. Sacred history is replete with such examples. The Book of Mormon reader need go no further than the account of the Lamanites. At first they were a "white and delightsome people," but their fathers refused to worship God in the manner in which they had been taught. Slothfulness and iniquities of every nature turned their children into dark-skinned haters of God. We cannot deny that the Lord visited the children of Laman with the outward sign of, not an inward grace, but, His displeasure. He caused a dark skin to mark them and their children for many generations, but with this promise that they will again become a "white and delightsome people."

Visiting the iniquities of the fathers upon the children. If the children continue to walk in the steps of their fathers, and here idolatry is particularly intended, they will be visited with the judgments of the Lord. We take this to mean "national judgments."

Thou shalt not make unto thee any graven image, is the command given by the Lord. The Hebrew word *pasal* denotes to *hew, carve,* or *grave.* The word used here, *pesel,* may therefore signify all images upon which the graving tool, or the chisel, or axe have been used, whether it is of metal, wood, or stone.

The Children of Israel had been servants in Egypt for generations. They had adopted many of the habits and customs of their bondsmen, and had allowed the Egyptian form of worship to dominate the homage and reverence they owed to the God of their fathers. In the great number of deities adored and worshiped in that land, Jacob's descendants were gradually weaned from the memory of the Lord their God. The Egyptians were idolators in the extreme; it has been said of them that at this time a god was easier to find than it was, a man.

Or any likeness of things which are in heaven above. That means any *winged fowl.* Among the objects of Egyptian idolatry were the ibis (stork), crane, and hawk.

Or which are in the earth beneath. The ox was the particular object of Egyptian reverence and idolatry; the heifer, too. The ox was worshiped and even adored by some because they believed that Osiris, their supreme god, had taken up his abode in one of them, and that upon its death he entered into the body of another. The name of this famous ox-god was *Apis* and *Mnevis.* Even the most casual student of Egyptology knows that *Osiris* and his wife *Isis* were not exceeded in power or authority by any other of their many gods. Take ye therefore good heed unto yourselves . . . lest ye corrupt yourselves, and make you a graven image, the similitude of any figure, the likeness of *male* or *female."* (Deut. 4:15-16) In the second verse following those just quoted, Moses included in this command, "The likeness of anything that creepeth on the ground." The crocodile, serpents, and beetles, (scarabeus) were objects of Egyptian adoration.

Or which are in the water under the earth. "All fish were esteemed sacred animals among the Egyptians, and were subject to their adoration." (Dr. Adam Clarke) The ancients believed that the sea extended under the land and therefore this commandment referred also to the fish of the ocean.

In short, *oxen, heifers, sheep, goats, lions, dogs,* and *cats;* the *ibis,* the *crane,* and the *hawk;* the *crocodile, serpents, frogs, flies,* and the *beetle,* or *scarabeus;* the *Nile* and its *fish;* the *sun, moon, planets,* and *stars; fire, light, air, darkness,* and *night,* were all objects of Egyptian idolatry, and all included in this very circumstantial prohibition as detailed in Deuteronomy (4), and very forcibly in the general terms of the text: *Thou shalt not make unto thee any graven image, or any likeness of any thing that is in the* HEAVENS *above, or that is in the* EARTH *beneath, or that is in the* WATER *under the earth.* And the reason for the command becomes self-evident, when the various objects of Egyptian idolatry are considered. (Dr. Adam Clarke, *Commentary on the Old Testament,* Vol. I, p. 401)

To countenance its *image worship,* the *Roman Catholic* Church has left the whole of this second commandment out of the decalogue, and thus lost one whole commandment out of the *ten;* but to keep up the *number* they have divided the *tenth* into two . . . The verse is found in every MS. of the *Hebrew Pentateuch* that has ever yet been discovered. It is in all the ancient versions, *Samaritan, Chaldee, Syriac, Septuagint, Vulgate, Coptic,* and *Arabic;* also in the *Persian,* and in all *modern versions.* There is not one word of the whole verse wanting in the many hundreds of MSS. collected by *Kennicott* and *De Rossi.* (Ibid.)

Showing mercy unto thousands. As love for God is the incentive which causes men to obey His command, there can be no obedience thereto without love. In return, God loves the obedient child; he said of Israel, "Yea, I have loved thee with an everlasting love." (Jeremiah 31:3) Although the Children of Israel have not always been as firm in keeping God's commands as His blessings to them have been constant, yet, through them has come all our knowledge of Him. We remember the exhortation of Moses to Israel: "Know therefore this day, and consider in thine heart, that the Lord he is God in heaven above, and upon the earth beneath: there is none else." (Deut. 4:39)

15. Thou shalt not take the name of the Lord thy God in vain; for the Lord will not hold him guiltless that taketh his name in vain.

16. Remember the Sabbath day, to keep it holy.

17. Six days shalt thou labor and do all thy work;

18. But the seventh day, the sabbath of the Lord thy God, thou shalt not do any work, thou, nor thy son, nor thy daughter, thy man-servant, nor thy maid-ser-

---

The Lord, Himself, comments upon these words of the Covenant: And the Lord passed by before Him [Moses], and proclaimed, The LORD, the LORD GOD, merciful and gracious, longsuffering, and abundant in goodness and truth, Keeping mercy for thousands, forgiving iniquity and transgression and sin . . . visiting the iniquity of the fathers upon the children, and upon the children's children, unto the third and fourth generation. (Exodus 34:6-7)

Mercy means *compassion;* pity for the undeserving and the guilty. In the Revised Versions of the Bible the *word* is frequently rendered *lovingkindness.*

I the Lord thy God am a jealous God. The love God had for the Children of Israel may be compared, but in a very imperfect way, to the love a tender husband has for the wife of his bosom. He exacts exclusive devotion, and is intolerant concerning her fidelity, because in her faithfulness he sees their happiness. Idolatry has aptly been termed *spiritual adultery.* "For thou shalt worship no other god: for the Lord, whose name is Jealous, is a jealous God." (Exodus 34:14) "But the Lord is good, a stronghold in the day of trouble; and he knoweth them that trust in him." (Nahum 1:7)

THE THIRD COMMANDMENT

VERSE 15. *Thou shalt not take the name of the Lord thy God in vain.* The Egyptians were in the habit of taking great oaths. They, piously or not, expressed their impulses by making a solemn appeal to one of their many gods. Through intimate association with them this custom grew to be a habit among the Children of Israel, who also swore by Egypt's gods.

It became necessary to impress upon the minds of Moses' people that the name of God (Jehovah or Yahweh) was a sacred thing, not to be used lightly nor uselessly.

There are many who, while speaking, punctuate their conversation with the names of Deity. How revolting is the habit to man's finer nature, and how repulsive it sounds even to the hardened of heart! God will punish them who use His name carelessly or wantonly.

THE FOURTH COMMANDMENT

VERSES 16-19. *Remember the sabbath day, to keep it holy.* From reading the text we must conclude that the sabbath was instituted before the time this commandment was given, and that the knowledge of it was part of ancient understanding. In Genesis we read, And God blessed the seventh day, and sanctified it: because that in it he had rested from all his work which God created and made. (Genesis 2:3)

Remember the sabbath day, was the commandment. *Remember* suggests that the observance of it was lost in the confusion attending the servitude of Israel in Egypt. It also intimates that heeding the custom was prohibited by their taskmasters; or that Jacob's children had undergone a progressive degeneration from the

vant, nor thy cattle, nor thy stranger that is within thy gates; 19. For in six days the Lord made heaven and earth, and the sea, and all that in them is; wherefore the Lord blessed the sabbath day, and hallowed it.

---

spiritual heights they attained under the Shepherd Kings to the forlorn depths of religious indifference where despair and utter distress took possession of them. At any rate they were reminded that its observance was indeed necessary.

The Sabbath is a day of rest, and one in which to think of the Lord, our God. The Commandment is, Not to do that which should have been done during the six days preceding the Sabbath, or seventh day, and let remain undone, those things that can wait 'til the day following the Sabbath. Any labor not necessary is forbidden on the Sabbath. Observance of this "Word" was enjoined upon Israel, and complying with it, the people were continually blessed with precepts imparted from above.

The Hebrew word *Shabbath,* means rest or *cessation* from *labor.* The statement found in Genesis 2:2, is that God rested on, and hallowed the seventh day. By the Jewish law given at Sinai the seventh day was to be a day of rest, in which no secular work was to be done, and which was to be kept holy to God.

At a later period the simple Jewish law of early days was added to by the traditions of the elders, until the Sabbath rules became burdensome, and, in some cases, foolish. It was against this, and not against God's Law of the Sabbath that Jesus set himself in his teaching and healing.

The Sabbath, one day out of each week, was kept by the Jews on the day now called Saturday. How early this was taken to be the seventh day is not known. After the Ascension of Jesus the Disciples met on the first day of each week for prayer and praise. The Jewish Christians for a long time kept both the first and seventh; but as Gentile Christians, having never kept any such day before, celebrated only the first day of the week as the Lord's day. The celebration of the seventh day by Christians was finally abandoned.   (*Cruden's Concordance of the Bible*)

Throughout the ages the Jews have accepted the Sabbath as Israel's heritage, and declare that they who take pleasure in the Sabbath shall find peace and joy. "They who take delight therein, to restrain their feet from following their usual paths on God's holy day, shall tread upon the high places of happiness and shall enjoy the heritage of the House of Israel." They, too, offer this prayerful thought:

Our God and God of our fathers, grant that our rest on this Sabbath be acceptable to Thee. May we, sanctified through Thy commandments, become sharers in the blessings of Thy word. Teach us to be satisfied with the gifts of Thy goodness and gratefully to rejoice in all Thy mercies. Purify our hearts that we may serve Thee in truth. O help us to preserve the Sabbath as Israel's heritage from generation to generation, that it may ever bring rest and joy, peace and comfort to the dwellings of our brethren, and through it Thy name be hallowed in all the earth.

Praised be Thou, O Lord, who sanctifieth the Sabbath.

(Jewish Union Prayer Book)

May we say this in conclusion, that, as "on the seventh day God ended his work which he had made; and he rested on the seventh day from all his work which he had made" (Genesis 2:2), let us serve and honor Him daily, but dedicate one day a week to His praise and to His honor and glory. In doing this we render unto the Maker of a grand and glorious Creation the feeble thanks of a grateful people.

20. Honor thy father and thy mother, that thy days may be long upon the land which the Lord thy God giveth thee.	22. Thou shalt not commit adultery. Thou shalt not steal.
21. Thou shalt not kill.	23. Thou shalt not bear false witness against thy neighbor.

THE FIFTH COMMANDMENT

VERSE 20. *Honor thy father and thy mother.* The rightful place in the home is for parents to act, as it were, in the place of God. The father and mother direct and guide their youthful offspring, often suffering themselves for the wounds of their children. A child is not rebellious, it looks to its source for counsel; but, however, when one of them refuses to accept the lawful commandments of its parents it has been likened to rebellion against God.

This precept therefore prohibits, not only all injurious acts, irreverent and unkind speeches to parents, but enjoins all necessary acts of kindness, filial respect, and obedience. God requires the children to provide for their parents, as He required the parents to feed, nourish, support, instruct, and defend the children when they were in the lowest state of helpless infancy.   (Dr. Adam Clarke)

That thy days may be long. Dr. Clarke also notes, as did the Apostle Paul, (Eph. 6:2) that this is the first of the commandments to which God has annexed a promise; and "therefore we may learn in some measure how important the duty is in the sight of God. In Deut. 5:16 it is said, *And that it may go well with thee.*

We may therefore conclude that it will go ill with the disobedient. As children are bound to succor their parents, so parents are bound to educate and instruct their children in all useful and necessary knowledge, and not bring them up in ignorance or idleness. They should teach their children the fear and knowledge of the Lord, for how can they expect affection or dutiful respect from those who have not the fear of God before their eyes?"

THE SIXTH COMMANDMENT

VERSE 21. *Thou shalt not kill.* This forbids malice and hatred, *for he that hateth his brother is a murderer.* (See 1 John 3:15; also, Matthew 5:22)

THE SEVENTH COMMANDMENT

VERSE 22. *Thou shalt not commit adultery.* This commandment forbids all forms of unchastity, including fornication, and all mental or sensual uncleanness. The Lord said, "You have heard that it was said by them of old time, Thou shalt not commit adultery; But I say unto you, That whosoever looketh on a woman to lust after her hath committed adultery with her already in his heart." (Matthew 5:28)

THE EIGHTH COMMANDMENT

VERSE 22. *Thou shalt not steal.* This means the acquiring of anything unlawfully or clandestinely. It also means that to not return that which is borrowed, or not to pay any debt that can be paid, any rents or wages that are due, is stealing.

THE NINTH COMMANDMENT

VERSE 23. *Thou shalt not bear false witness.* Neighbor is any other human being, whether he is an enemy or friend. This commandment prohibits not only false oaths and wrongful testimony being uttered, but it enjoins that truth and ve-

24. Thou shalt not covet thy
neighbor's house, thou shalt not
covet thy neighbor's wife, nor his
man-servant, nor his maid-ser-
vant, nor his ox, nor his ass, nor
anything that is thy neighbor's.
25. And it came to pass that
after Abinadi had made an end
of these sayings that he said unto

them: Have ye taught this people
that they should observe to do all
these things for to keep these
commandments?
26. I say unto you, Nay; for
if ye had, the Lord would not
have caused me to come forth and
to prophesy evil concerning this
people.

---

racity be spoken at all times. Slander, tale-bearing, and evil speaking of anybody
come under the infringement of this law. Suppressing of a truth when it is known,
or deposing as true, a falsehood that may injure the person or property of another, is
also a violation of the Ninth Commandment.

THE TENTH COMMANDMENT

VERSE 24. *Thou shalt not covet.* Covet means *to desire, to long for,* especially
for something belonging to another person. A *covetous* person is one who is in-
ordinately desirous to obtain for his own use the property of someone else. This applies to all the possessions of another, his lands, his cattle, his wife, or his servants,
or "anything that is thy neighbor's." The man who attempts to deprive another of
his legal rights by clandestine or unjustifiable means cannot excuse his actions when
this law is considered. "Thou shalt not," is the bold assertion of the Great Law
Giver, because He knows that *crime* and *folly* often emerge from an uncontrolled desire to obtain, or the longing for that which is forbidden.

VERSES 25-26. *Have you taught the people to keep these commandments?* Abinadi, after he had read the Ten Commandments from the Hebrew Scriptures, a copy
of which presumably had been made of the writings found on the brass plates of
Laban, asked the priests to tell him whether or not they taught their people to observe them.

As priests to a people who claimed fellowship with their Nephite brethren in
Zarahemla all of whom were taught to observe the Law of Moses, did they fulfill unto
their own believers this obligation of the Priesthood?

They had been appointed priests by wicked King Noah, but how different was
their course than that taken by the priests ordained by Benjamin, the King in
Zarahemla.

Three years before he died, and at the time he gave authority to his son, Mosiah,
to reign in his stead, King Benjamin "appointed priests to teach the people, that
therefore they might hear and know the commandments of God." (Mosiah 6:3)

No doubt Abinadi read to the priests the instructions Moses gave unto the Children of Israel long after the marvelous showing of God's power on Mount Sinai.
Moses said, "Now therefore hearken, O Israel, unto the statutes and unto the judgments, which I teach you, for to do them. . . . Ye shall not add unto the word which
I command you, neither shall ye diminish ought from it, that ye may keep the commandments of the Lord your God. . . ." (Deut. 4:1-2)

Also, "And thou shalt love the Lord thy God with all thine heart, and with all
thy soul, and with all thy might. And these words which I command thee this day,
shall be in thine heart: And thou shalt teach them diligently unto thy children, and
thou shalt talk of them when thou sitteth in thine house, and when thou walkest by
the way, and when thou liest down, and when thou riseth up. And thou shalt bind

27. And now ye have said that salvation cometh by the law of Moses. I say unto you that it is expedient that ye should keep the law of Moses as yet; but I say unto you, that the time shall come when it shall no more be expedient to keep the law of Moses.

28. And moreover, I say unto you, that salvation doth not come by the law alone; and were it not for the atonement, which God himself shall make for the sins and iniquities of his people, that they must unavoidably perish, notwithstanding the law of Moses.

29. And now I say unto you that it was expedient that there should be a law given to the children of Israel, yea, even a very strict law; for they were a stiffnecked people, quick to do iniquity, and slow to remember the Lord their God;

30. Therefore there was a law

---

them for a sign upon thine hand, and they shall be as frontlets between thine eyes. And thou shalt write them upon the posts of thy house, and on thy gates." (Deut. 6:5-9)

Moses, in the instructions just cited, said, "And these words which I command thee this day, shall be in thine heart . . ." "Why?" "To what end?" We imagine Abinadi asked. Noah's priests knew the answer, yet they opened not their mouths. We presume Abinadi then read to them the reply of the Lord, himself: To the end "that ye may remember, and do all my commandments: and be holy unto your God . . . I am the Lord your God." (Numbers 15:39-42)

Abinadi said to the priests, "The commandments of God . . . are not written in your hearts."

Abinadi also said that the commandments of God are not part of your lives; you have spent your days in the study of deceit and folly. The law, according to you, was made to break, and not to keep. Abinadi was wrathful in denouncing Noah's priests.

When we think of the utter neglect of the priests in teaching God's commandments to the people, we think, too, of the prayer offered by King David, with which the priests were undoubtedly familiar, "Show me thy ways, O Lord; teach me thy paths. Lead me in thy truth, and teach me: for thou art the God of my salvation; on thee do I wait all the day." (Psalm 25:4-5)

VERSES 27-28. *Ye have said that salvation cometh by the law of Moses. Expedient,* as used here, means *suitable to the end in view, advantageous,* or *wise.* Abinadi took this favorable opportunity to declare his divinely inspired message, for he knew the sound of it would be heard throughout Noah's Kingdom. He said he knew that it was suitable to the end in view, and even necessary at that time to "keep the law of Moses," but, also, he uttered in prophetic tones "the time shall come when it shall no more be" necessary, or suitable, or required of you, to do so.

Abinadi had waited long for this time to come. He no longer felt restrained, but inspired to proclaim the Salvation of the Lord. "The Atonement of God for the sins of the world" was his message. The words he uttered were not new, but to the priests they were strangers. The prophets before him had all told of the great *Sacrifice* which was to be made, now Abinadi published it anew. And without it, he said, "they must unavoidably perish, notwithstanding the law of Moses."

VERSES 29-30. *It was expedient that a very strict law be given to the Children of Israel.* From the very first, Israel was an obstinate and a stubborn and a stiffneck-

given them, yea, a law of per- | strictly from day to day, to keep
formances and of ordinances, a | them in remembrance of God and
law which they were to observe | their duty towards him.

---

ed people. Often they refused to walk in the Lord's paths which had been shown to them, but chose different ways that led them along the road to sorrow and degradation. This is especially true of the Jews of whose history we have a more or less complete account. (*See Commentary on the Book of Mormon*, Vol. I, pp. 470-471)

One may conclude Israel's moral and mental, yea, its spiritual habits, by reading the words of the prophets describing the workings of the minds of its people. They reveal a gradual and a persistent falling away from the place they occupied as the Lord's people to the utter despair and anguish of bondage to a Gentile nation.

In referring the reader to the inspired teachings of those servants of God, we do not wish to imply that Israel was always the ungracious recipient of providential care. There were periods of peace and righteous endeavor when they chose to keep God's commandments, not taking from them or adding thereto, but joyously serving the Lord.

For they were a stiffnecked people.

And the Lord said unto Moses, Depart, and go up hence, thou and the people which thou hast brought up out of the land of Egypt, unto the land which I sware unto Abraham, to Isaac, and to Jacob, saying, Unto thy seed will I give it.

And I will send an angel before thee; . . .

Unto a land flowing with milk and honey: for I will not go up in the midst of thee; for thou art a stiffnecked people: lest I consume [destroy] thee in the way.
(Exodus 33:1-3)

And be not like your fathers, and like your brethren, which trespassed against the Lord God of their fathers, who therefore gave them up to desolation, as ye see.

Now be ye not stiffnecked, as your fathers were, but yield yourselves unto the Lord, and enter into his sanctuary, which he hath sanctified for ever: and serve the Lord your God, that the fierceness of his wrath may turn away from you.
(II Chron. 30:7-8)

Ye stiffnecked and uncircumcised of heart and ears, ye do always resist the Holy Ghost: as your father did, so do ye.   (The Acts 7:51)

The Nephites were also of the House of Israel, and also had frequent periods of apostasy. In the Book of Mormon, we read:

But behold, the Jews were a stiffnecked people; and they despised the words of plainness, and killed the prophets, and sought for things that they could not understand. Wherefore, because of their blindness, which blindness came by looking beyond the mark, they must needs fall; for God hath taken away his plainness from them, and delivered unto them many things which they cannot understand, because they desired it. And because they desired it God hath done it, that they might stumble.   (Jacob 4:14)

And how merciful is our God unto us, for he remembereth the house of Israel, both roots and branches; and he stretches forth his hands unto them all the day long; and they are a stiffnecked and a gainsaying people; but as many as will not harden their hearts shall be saved in the kingdom of God.   (Jacob 6:4)

And there were exceeding many prophets among us. And the people were a stiffnecked people, hard to understand.   (Enos 22)

Yet the Lord saw that his people were a stiffnecked people, and he appointed unto them a law, even the law of Moses.   (Mosiah 3:14)

O ye wicked and ye perverse generation; ye hardened and ye stiffnecked people, how long will ye suppose that the Lord will suffer you? Yea, how long will ye suffer yourselves to be led by foolish and blind guides? Yea, how long will ye choose darkness rather than light?   (Helaman 13:29)

The Savior said to the Nephites,

This much did the Father command me, that I should tell unto them [the Jews at Jerusalem].

That other sheep I have which are not of this fold; them also must I bring, and they shall hear my voice; and there shall be one fold, and one shepherd.

And now, because of stiffneckedness and unbelief they understood not my word; therefore I was commanded to say no more of my Father concerning this thing unto them.   (3 Nephi 15:16-18)

There are many more passages in both the Bible and the Book of Mormon which give an understanding of the word *stiffnecked,* and which show us the mental condition with which it is associated. We herewith note every reference to it made in the Book of Mormon:

Stiff

| 2 Nephi | 28:14 | They wear s. necks |
| Jacob | 2:13 | And wear s. necks |

Stiffen

| 2 Nephi | 10:5 | They at Jerusalem will s. their |

Stiffened

| 2 Nephi | 6:10 | Hardened their hearts and s. |

Stiffnecked

2 Nephi	25:28	My people, ye are a s. people
Jacob	4:14	The Jews were a s. people
	6:4	They were a s. and a gainsaying
Enos	1:22	The people were a s. people
Jarom	1:4	For they are not all s.
	4	And as many as are not s.
Omni	1:28	Their leader being a s. man
Mosiah	3:14	Saw that his people were a s.
	13:29	For they were a s. people
Alma	9:5	Were a hardhearted and a s.
	31	Were a hardhearted and a s.
	15:15	Remained a hardhearted and a s.
	20:30	More hardhearted and a more s.
	26:24	As s. a people as they are
	37:10	Many thousands of our s. brethren
Helaman	4:21	Saw that they had been a s. people
	5:3	Was not all; they were a s. people
	9:21	Ye s. people, do ye know how
	13:29	Ye hardened and ye s. people
Mormon	8:33	O ye wicked . . . and s. people

Stiffneckedness

1 Nephi	2:11	Because of the s. of L. and L.
2 Nephi	32:7	Ignorance, and the s. of men
Words of Mormon	17	Because of the s. of the people
3 Nephi	15:18	And now because of s. and unbelief

31. But behold, I say unto you, that all these things were types of things to come.
32. And now, did they understand the law? I say unto you, Nay, they did not all understand the law; and this because of the hardness of their hearts; for they understood not that there could not any man be saved except it were through the redemption of God.

33. For behold, did not Moses prophesy unto them concerning the coming of the Messiah, and that God should redeem his people? Yea, and even all the prophets who have prophesied ever since the world began—have they not spoken more or less concerning these things?
34. Have they not said that God himself should come down among the children of men, and

Stiffness			
2 Nephi	25:12	And the s. of their necks
Jarom	3	And the s. of their necks

From the foregoing passages of Scripture we can form the final judgment that the Children of Israel were often disobedient to God's commands, that they were obstinate and stubborn, that they were prone to set up other gods and worship them. The Ten Commandments given them disclose not only they were inclined to follow after false gods of whom they made images to worship, but they were also breakers of the Sabbath. They took oaths to the Egyptian gods carelessly, and with little meaning, and thought little or nothing of committing the several vices forbidden in the last of the commandments.

In short, the Book of Mormon, itself, gives in a very few words, the sum and substance of Israel's faults and its failings, and also that it was because of these transgressions that God gave unto them the Law of Moses to guide them, and to which He demanded obedience. It says of the Children of Israel, "For they were a stiffnecked people, quick to do iniquity, and slow to remember the Lord their God."

VERSES 31-33. *All these things were types of things to come.* The Law of Moses was, we may say, prophetic. It commanded *sacrifice,* which was indicative of the great Sacrifice that was to be made. Its performances and ordinances were visible signs of the Messiah whose coming they foretold. We place on record here as the best comment, the testimony of King Benjamin:

And the Lord God hath sent his holy prophets among all the children of men, to declare these things to every kindred, nation, and tongue, that thereby whosoever should believe that Christ should come, the same might receive remission of their sins, and rejoice with exceeding great joy, even as though he had already come among them.

Yet the Lord saw that his people were a stiffnecked people, and he appointed unto them a law, even the law of Moses.

And many signs, and wonders, and types, and shadows showed he unto them, concerning his coming; and also holy prophets spake unto them concerning his coming; and yet they hardened their hearts, and understood not that the law of Moses availeth nothing, except it were through the atonement of his blood.

(Mosiah 3:13-15)

VERSES 34-35. *Have they not said.* We are reminded by Abinadi's statement in these verses of the loss of the many books that formerly were part of Hebrew Scripture. Jewish editors, it is charged, have taken whole writings which pertained

take upon him the form of man, and go forth in mighty power upon the face of the earth? 35. Yea, and have they not said also that he should bring to pass the resurrection of the dead, and that he, himself, should be oppressed and afflicted?

---

to Christ and expurgated them from what is now claimed by them to be their Scriptures.

In this way believers in Yahweh (Jehovah) as the only true and living God are deprived of many prophecies concerning the coming of Christ, His atonement, and His resurrection.

VERSE 34. *See* comments Chapter 15:1.

VERSE 35. *See* comments Chapter 16:7-8.

GENERAL NOTES—THE TEN COMMANDMENTS

The laws given on Mount Sinai have been variously named. In Deut. 4:13, they are called *asereth haddebarim*, the TEN WORDS. In Exodus Chapter Nineteen, verse 5, God calls them *eth berithi*, my COVENANT, i.e., the agreement he entered into with the people of Israel to take them for his peculiar people, if they took him for their God and portion. *"If ye will obey my voice indeed*, and KEEP MY COVENANT, THEN *shall ye be a peculiar treasure unto me."* And the word *covenant* here evidently refers to the *laws* given in this chapter, as is evident from Deut. 4:13: *"And he declared unto you his* COVENANT, which he commanded you to perform, even TEN COMMANDMENTS."

They have also been termed the *moral law*, because they contain and lay down rules for the regulation of the *manners* and *conduct* of men. Sometimes they have been termed *the* LAW, *hattorah*, by way of eminence, as containing the grand system of spiritual instruction, direction, guidance, &c. (*See* Exodus 12:49)

DECALOGUE, is a literal translation into Greek of the *asereth haddebarim*, or TEN WORDS of Moses.

Students of Scripture have generally divided the TEN WORDS into two parts, the first and the second tables. The FIRST *table* containing the *first, second, third,* and *fourth* commandments, and comprehending the whole system of *theology,* the true notions we should form of the Divine nature, the reverence we owe, and the religious service we should render to Him. The SECOND, containing the *six* last commandments, and comprehending a complete system of *ethics,* or *moral duties* which man owes to his fellows, and on the due performance of which the order, peace, and happiness of society depend.

By this division, the FIRST table contains our *duty* to God; the SECOND our duty to our NEIGHBOR. This division, which is natural enough, refers us to the grand principle, love to God and love to man, through them both tables are observed. 1. Thou shalt love the Lord thy God with all thy heart, soul, mind, and strength. 2. Thou shalt love thy neighbor as thyself. On these two hang all the law and the prophets. (Matt. 22:37-40) (Dr. Adam Clarke.)

It should be noted that the laws comprising the *Ten,* which are included in the Covenant God made with Israel on Mount Sinai, were not original at that time. There are some who think that they were new to Moses' people, but that is not the case. Adam understood them, Noah and the prophets who preceded him, proclaimed them. They had been given to man from the very beginning, only sin had effaced them in their hearts and so defaced the writing of them before their eyes that the fearsome display of God's power on Mount Sinai was necessary to revive the knowledge of them.

CHAPTER 14

Abinadi quotes Isaiah to the priests of king Noah—Compare Isaiah 53.

For behold, Isaiah spake many things which
were hard for many of my people to understand;
for they know not concerning the manner of
prophesying among the Jews. . . .

Wherefore, hearken, O my people, which are
of the house of Israel, and give ear unto my words;
for because the words of Isaiah are not plain unto
you, nevertheless they are plain unto all those
that are filled with the spirit of prophecy. . . .

Yea, and my soul delighteth in the words
of Isaiah, for I came out from Jerusalem, and mine
eyes hath beheld the things of the Jews, and I
know that the Jews do understand the things of
the prophets, and there is none other people that
understand the things which were spoken unto the
Jews like unto them, save it be that they are taught
after the manner of the things of the Jews.

(II Nephi 25:1-4-5)

This is one of the celebrated *Servant Poems*, or Songs, written by the Prophet
Isaiah. It is a glorious paean in praise of Him who is the Servant of all. It is
not a *lament*, but a song of rejoicing. Israel's strength is often expressed in its
powerful songs. "And the ransomed of the Lord shall return, and come to Zion
with *songs* and everlasting joy upon their heads; they shall obtain joy and gladness,
and sorrow and sighing shall flee away." (Isaiah 35:10) Today, with the same
exultant voices, the faithful sing songs of joy in God's Salvation. Singing the songs
of Zion will uphold the willing heart, and, in the end, quicken one that is dead
in trespass and in sin.

"Come, come, ye Saints, no toil nor labor fear," are the beginning words of
a song sung by modern Israel. It imparts courage to the faint and hope from
above, and though it mentions sorrow, yet it is a hymn of joy and thanksgiving.
It indicates that grief may be the portion of the righteous, yet it heralds God's
blessings.

Singing songs of praise to God strengthens the weakest of Saints; it also comforts those who mourn. Isaiah knew the strength of song. The same spirit—the spirit of
prophecy—that enlightened Isaiah was with William Clayton when he wrote his
immortal poem. A strong parallel is found when both are compared. The Saints
of each period of time needed spiritual help and comfort.

Commentators of the Old Testament are not united in fixing the identity of
the *Servant*. Many expose themselves to the idea that Judah, itself, is that one.
They point to the history of the Jews as fulfilling every requirement concerning
the *Servant* that the lofty poem even suggests. The Jews, they say, were despised
and hated by all; to recognize them as friends was, by their neighbors, thought to
be an ill omen.

In spite of the traditions that had grown up around them, and their religion that, for ages, had bound them together, the Jews became obdurate, and proud in the thought that they were God's chosen people. Their pride and stubbornness weakened them, and they became the prey of their ambitious neighbors. Time and time again, hordes of warriors from Babylon, Chaldea, and Egypt came upon them. The Jews, themselves, were not without blame. Within and without the Kingdom of Judah, hatred, envy, strife, and angry passions ruled their relations with each other. This is not all; the worship of the True and Living God, which had been bequeathed to them through their fathers, became a shelter for those who interpreted the Law to serve their own devious ends. They grew arrogant, avaricious, and unkind, even to their own fellows. It is said of them, "They were an unattractive people," little esteemed by their neighbors, and were afflicted by enemies who could pierce them, and humiliate them in degrading bondage.

But, the *Servant* of Isaiah is not a nation, neither is He a number of nations joined as one. The *Servant* is an individual. His sufferings may be likened to the travail and oppression to which the Jews were subjected, however, there the likeness ends. The Jews were servants, but He is the Servant of servants. It is said, "He who is greatest in the Kingdom of God, let Him be the servant of all."

In Chapter 53. Two great things which the Spirit of Christ in the Old Testament prophets testified beforehand were the sufferings of Christ and the glory that should follow. (I Peter 1:11) And that which Christ himself, when he expounded Moses and all the prophets, showed to be the scope of them was that He ought to suffer and then enter into his glory. (Luke 24:26-27) But nowhere in the Old Testament are these two things so plainly and fully prophesied as here in this chapter, out of which many passages are quoted with application to Christ in the New Testament. This chapter is so replenished with the unsearchable riches of Christ that it may be called the *gospel* of the "evangelist" Isaiah rather than the *prophecy* of the "prophet" Isaiah.

We may observe here:

1. The reproach of Christ's sufferings—the humbleness of his appearance, the greatness of his grief, and the prejudices which many conceived in consequence against his doctrine. (v. 1-3)

2. The rolling away of his reproach, and the stamping of immortal honor upon his sufferings, notwithstanding the disgrace and ignominy of them by four considerations:

    1. That therein he did his Father's will. (Vs. 4, 6, 10.)

    2. That thereby he made atonement for the sin of man, vs. 4-6, 8, 11, 12 for it was not for any sin of his own that he suffered. (V. 9.)

    3. That he bore his sufferings with an invincible and exemplary patience. (V. 7.)

    4. That he should prosper in his undertaking, and his sufferings should end in his immortal honour. (Vs. 10-12.)

By mixing faith with the prophecy of this chapter we may improve our acquaintance with Jesus Christ and him crucified, with Jesus Christ and him glorified, dying for our sins and rising for our justification. (Matthew Henry, *Commentary on the Bible*, Vol. IV, p. 300, Fleming H. Revell Company.)

This chapter foretells the sufferings of the Messiah, the end for which he was to die, and the advantages resulting to mankind from that illustrious event. It begins with a complaint of the infidelity of the Jews, 1; the offense they took at his mean and humble appearance, 2; and the contempt with which they treated him, 3. The prophet then shows that the Messiah was to suffer for sins not his own; but that our iniquities were laid on him, and the punishment of them exacted of him, which is the meritorious cause of our obtaining pardon and salvation, 4-6.

He shows the meekness and placid submission with which he suffered a violent and unjust death, with the circumstances of his dying with the wicked, and being buried with the great, 7-9; and that, in consequence of his atonement, death, resurrection, and intercession, he should procure pardon and salvation to the multitudes, insure increasing prosperity to his Church, and ultimately triumph over all his foes, 10-11. This chapter contains a beautiful summary of the most peculiar and distinguishing doctrines of Christianity.

That this chapter speaks of none but Jesus must be evident to every unprejudiced reader who has ever heard the history of his sufferings and death. The Jews have endeavoured to apply it to their sufferings in captivity; but, alas for their cause, they can make nothing out in this way. Allowing that it belongs to our blessed Lord, (and the best men and the best scholars agree in this) then who can read verses 4, 5, 6, 8, 10, without being convinced that his death was a vicarious sacrifice for the sins of mankind? (Dr. Adam Clarke, *Commentary on the Old Testament*, Vol. IV, p. 205, Edition of G. Lane & P. P. Sanford, 1843)

1. *Abinadi quotes Isaiah to the Priests of King Noah.*

1. Yea, even doth not Isaiah say: Who hath believed our report, and to whom is the arm of the Lord revealed?

VERSE 1. *Who hath believed our report? and to whom is the arm of the Lord revealed?* We prefer to render this passage of scripture: "Who hath believed our words of Him *in* whom the power and authority of God is made known?," or, "Who hath believed our words of Him *in* whom is the arm of the Lord revealed?" (*See* Mosiah 12:24) In the translation of the manuscripts used by the eminent scholars who prepared the King James Version of the Holy Bible, the question asked by the Prophet Isaiah appears to be two queries. But it is not; it is one! The translators failed to understand the purport of the prophet's words. They render the last part of his question, "*To* whom is the arm of the Lord revealed?" This is incorrect. The *Servant* is the central figure of the poem, not someone else. He is the Lord, Jesus Christ. The whole poem is written concerning Him; His growth as a child, His ministry, death, and resurrection, and the manner of the reception to be accorded Him by the Jewish nation, which then was apostate.

We eliminate the conjunction *and*. In the place of *to*, we substitute the preposition *in*. Doing so makes the entire poem appear more to our understanding. Many of the commentators on Isaiah either neglect or deliberately overlook the fact that he was a great advocate of the coming of the Lord, the Messiah, Jesus Christ, who in this lyrical song, he calls the *Servant*. Isaiah, and it may be said of all the Hebrew prophets, understood the mission of the Messiah whose coming he foretold. He talked of Christ; he rejoiced in Christ; he preached of Christ; he prophesied of Christ, and he wrote according to the prophecies. (*See* 2 Nephi 25:26)

Every translator is, indeed, a commentator. The words he chooses to use are limited to his own understanding; thus he gives color, and shape, and sometimes improper form to much he does not comprehend. (*See* COMMENTARY ON THE BOOK OF MORMON, Vol. I, p. 67, Notes)

Before any objections are considered to the changes made by us in the rendering of the first verse of Isaiah 53, it is well to remember that the division of the books of the Bible into chapters and verses and even sentences, is not a part of the original arrangement of the sacred book.

"The present divison of the Scriptures into chapters and verses . . . are not of divine origin, nor are they of great antiquity. The Vulgate was the first version

2. For he shall grow up before him as a tender plant, and as a root out of dry ground; he hath no form nor comeliness; and when we shall see him there is no beauty that we should desire him.

---

divided into chapters: a work undertaken by Cardinal Hugo, in the 13th Century, or as Jahn thinks, by Langton, archbishop of Canterbury, 1227. He introduced the division into chapters only. The Hebrew Scriptures were similarly divided by Mordecai Nathan, in 1445, and in 1661 Athias added in his printed text, the division into verses. The New Testament was divided in the same way by Robert Stephens, who is said to have completed it in the year 1551, during a journey (*inter equitandum*), from Paris to Lyons.

"As might be expected, these divisions are very imperfect, and even when not inaccurate, they tend to break the sense and to obscure the meaning." (*Bible Handbook*, by Dr. Joseph Angus, p. 60.)

Let us remember, too, that the ancient Hebrew scribes did not write the vowels; they used few, if any, conjunctions or prepositions. They did not punctuate, and they wrote their words using a long, single scroll which formed, as it were, a continuous block of writing.

When they, the translators of Isaiah, render the second part of his question "*to* whom," they do so capriciously, and with little understanding of the text. We choose to say, "*in* whom," because it magnifies the service rendered by the *Servant*, and it acknowledges Him to be the particular *Servant of God*.

The question stated, is asked by Isaiah for himself and all the holy prophets, "Who hath believed our words," and the implied answer is, "No one." None, or few, recognized the divine message they bore, or saw in it the working of God's power in His Servant, Jesus Christ.

A thought that may have merit, is expressed by some of the most learned students, including Dr. Adam Clarke, who have made a study of Old Testament prophecy and religion. They refer to a portion of the second part of Isaiah's question in which "the arm of the Lord" is made mention. They contend the translation of the word *arm* is wrong, "the connexion broken, and the sense obscured." The Hebrew word, *zeroa*, is translated *arm*, from the root, *zara*, which, contrary to the interpretation given it by the translators, means, to *sow*, or *plant*; also, it means *seed*. If, they argue, we translate the word *zeroa* in the sense that it means *seed*, the true meaning of the text would then be given.

The same word, *zeroa*, meaning *seed*, can be found in Genesis 3:15; 22:17; 26:4, and in Genesis 28:14. Isaiah, in effect, calls the offspring of the Patriarch Abraham, "The seed (children) of the Lord." *Zara*, then in this place, should be understood to mean not only "the seed of herbs," but also children, offspring, or posterity." Thus, *zara* should be understood to mean Jesus Christ. Jesus Christ, by the power and authority of God, is the one who is made known. If we agree with this as being the right interpretation of the word, *zeroa*, or its root-word, *zara*, the passage with our correction would read, "Who hath believed our words of Him, in whom the seed of the Lord (i.e. the Child is born, and a Son is given, or as John says, 'the Son of God, the only Begotten of the Father') is revealed."

VERSE 2. *For he shall grow up before him as a tender plant.* For many ages their wise men and poets had told the Jews that their Lord and their Redeemer,

---

The word *zara* is the Peruvian for "corn" or "maize." But it seems to have its roots in the Hebrew word of the same spelling and the same meaning, especially in the sense of offspring. Hemla is probably the Hebrew, *hamulah*, meaning *abundance*. The Mulekite name, *Zarahemla*, would then mean, when applied to a country, "a place where there is an abundance of seed." Applied to a person, it would mean "one who has a numerous offspring."

the Messiah for whom they waited, would come among them exhibiting great power. As a conquering hero, He would lead them into battle which in every case would be victorious, and would thus subdue all Judah's foes. When that long-awaited day should come, Jerusalem, the beloved city of the Jews, would be the capital of the world, and they would rule the nations of the earth in regal splendor.

The Messiah would be their king, and they would be His loyal subjects. He was to be of noble parentage, a "Son" of King David; of a family whose great name was "like unto the name of the great men that are in the earth." (II Samuel 7:9) His emissaries, they were told, would be princes and nobles.

But, when Christ was born in Bethlehem, He came of a family whose home was with the despised inhabitants of the Roman Province of Galilee. His father was a carpenter, and most of His relations were fishermen. He was born in a manger, the only lodging obtainable in the city where Joseph, His father, went to pay taxes. Jesus' birth, however, brought to pass a prophecy uttered many hundred years before, "But, thou, Bethlehem, Ephratah, though thou be little among the thousands of Judah, yet out of thee shall he come forth unto me that is to be ruler in Israel; whose goings forth have been from of old, from everlasting." (Micah 5:2)

The humble birth of Jesus was not what the Jews expected of the Messiah. And Nazareth by the blue waters of Galilee, where, as a child, He played, grew to manhood, and studied, was of such little repute that when Philip told Nathaniel, "We have found him, of whom Moses in the law, and the prophets, did write, Jesus of Nazareth, the son of Joseph," Nathaniel replied, "Can there any good thing come out of Nazareth?" (John 1:45-46)

Truly, Christ's fathers were of the kingly and illustrious "House of David," but when He came, its glory had long since departed, and its splendor was remembered only in song.

As a root out of dry ground. "And there shall come forth a rod out of the stem of Jesse, and a Branch shall grow out of his roots." (Isaiah 11:1) Jesse was the father of King David, but when the "fruit of his loins," (Acts 2:30) Christ, was raised up to sit on David's throne, the age of prophecy had passed. The Jews had rejected any new *Word* coming from God; many of His servants were slain, and the laws given by Him, through Moses, had been changed to meet the ambitious purposes of priests and kings.

As a nation, the Jews were apostate. There appeared to be a famine in the land. ". . . not a famine of bread, nor a thirst for water, but of hearing the words of the Lord." (Amos 8:11) When the Psalmist wrote of "green pastures" and "still waters," he had in mind, *hearing the word of God.* Hearing it, restores the soul; by it, He leads one in the paths of righteousness. (*See* Psalm 23)

The voice of God's holy prophets had been stilled. The Jews roamed in the twilight of a brilliant past. As a "watered garden" when prophets and patriarchs ministered to them, now, desert and stones were in the place where formerly were fields of grain and fountains of water. Out of "dry ground" means out of "spiritual dearth," a starving spiritual environment.

He hath no form nor comeliness. "He hath no form, nor any beauty, that we should regard him; nor is his countenance such that we should desire him." (Symmachus, an ancient historian and translator who reduced the Old Testament into idiomatic Greek, and who it seems, many scholars have noted, has interpreted this passage "rightly.")

He shall grow up as a tender plant. He shall grow up under the watchful care of God, and not before men; in the nurture of a tender and loving Father, the Servant, who is Christ, our Lord, will go from strength to strength, from infancy to manhood, always waxing greater in knowledge and wisdom.

3. He is despised and rejected | hid as it were our face from him; of men; a man of sorrows, and | he was despised, and we esteemed acquainted with grief; and we | him not.

As a tender plant, whose beauty is often seen in a desert place and sometimes growing out of the rocky soil, His Father, the great *Multi-florist* of the universe, will hedge it about, will water it, and will protect it. He will preserve it at all times.

VERSE 3. *A man of sorrows, and acquainted with grief.* Some MSS. say, "Familiar with grief," others, "and knowing grief."

And we hid as it were our faces from him. We looked the other way when we saw Him. His sorrows begat no compassion within our hearts. This recalls the parable of the Good Samaritan (Luke 10:30-37); "A certain man," the Savior said, "went down from Jerusalem to Jericho, and fell among thieves, which stripped him of his raiment, and wounded him, and departed, leaving him half dead. And by chance there came down a certain priest that way: and when he saw him, he passed by on the other side. And likewise a Levite, when he was at the same place, came and looked at him, and passed by on the other side," etc. Although this story was told to teach a different lesson, that of the *good neighbor,* we may draw from it a clear conception of the way the Jews received Jesus Christ. They passed Him by, and pretended not to see Him.

He was despised and rejected, rejected by men, a man of sorrows, and acquainted with grief. He gave His back to the smiters, and His cheeks to them that plucked off the hair, He hid not His face from shame and spitting. (Handel, *The Messiah.* Text by Charles Jennens)

He was despised . . . and we esteemed him not. Many commentators, familiar with the Hebrew text, prefer to say,

"He was despised . . . and we held him of no account."

In the coming of the Messiah, the disappointment evinced by the Jews, culminating in their denial of Him, is made to appear all the more bitter when we read the beautiful words written in commemoration of that great event. These words are found in the *Hymn Book* of the Church of Jesus Christ of Latter-day Saints.

> A poor wayfaring Man of grief
>   Hath often crossed me on my way,
> Who sued so humbly for relief
>   That I could never answer, Nay.
> I had not power to ask his name,
> Whereto he went, or whence he came;
> Yet there was something in his eye
> That won my love; I knew not why.
>
> Once, when my scanty meal was spread,
>   He entered, not a word he spake;
> Just perishing for want of bread,
>   I gave him all; he blessed it, brake,
> And ate, but gave me part again;
> Mine was an angel's portion then,
> For while I fed with eager haste,
> The crust was manna to my taste.
>
> I spied him where a fountain burst
>   Clear from the rock; his strength was gone;

4. Surely he has borne our griefs, and carried our sorrows; | **yet we did esteem him stricken, smitten of God, and afflicted.**

The heedless water mocked his thirst;
He heard it, saw it, hurrying on.
I ran and raised the sufferer up;
Thrice from the stream he drained my cup,
Dipped and returned it running o'er;
I drank and never thirsted more.

Twas night; the floods were out; it blew
A winter hurricane aloof;
I heard his voice abroad and flew
To bid him welcome to my roof.
I warmed and clothed and cheered my guest
And laid him on my couch to rest,
Then made the earth my bed, and seemed
In Eden's garden while I dreamed.

Stript, wounded, beaten nigh to death,
I found him by the highway side;
I roused his pulse, brought back his breath,
Revived his spirit, and supplied
Wine, oil, refreshment, he was healed;
I had myself a wound concealed,
But from that hour forgot the smart,
And peace bound up my broken heart.

In prison I saw him next, condemned
To meet a traitor's doom at morn;
The tide of lying tongues I stemmed,
And honored him 'mid shame and scorn—
My friendship's utmost zeal to try,
He asked if I for him would die;
The flesh was weak; my blood ran chill;
But the free spirit cried, "I will!"

Then in a moment to my view
The stranger started from disguise;
The tokens in his hands I knew;
The Savior stood before mine eyes.
He spake, and my poor name he named,
"Of me thou hast not been ashamed;
These deeds shall thy memorial be,
Fear not, thou didst them unto me."

VERSE 4. *Surely he hath borne our griefs, and carried our sorrows.* Some Mss. have it, "Surely our afflictions he hath borne, and our sorrows he carrieth them." (Seventeen MSS., two being ancient, belonging to Dr. Kennicott's collection, and two of De Rossi's, have the word, hu, "he" before sebalam, "carrieth them," in the text. (Dr. Adam Clarke, *Commentary on the Old Testament*, Vol. IV, p. 206, published by G. Lane & P. P. Sanford, New York City, 1843) Dr. Clarke observes, "This adds force to the sense, and elegance to the construction."

In spite of the service the Servant rendered, and all else He did, we judge that God had stricken Him, inflicting upon Him the appearance of that which was considered impure, or unnatural. We withdrew from His presence as though we heard a voice crying, "Unclean, unclean!"

5. But he was wounded for our transgressions, he was bruised for our iniquities; the chastisement of our peace was upon him; and with his stripes we are healed.

The victims of dread leprosy were, in ancient times, thought to be grievously afflicted by Providence because of some transgression known only to the one stricken. Some commentators believe that Isaiah had this in mind, when he likened the Servant's appearance to one whose aspect was pitiable to behold.

VERSE 5. *The chastisement of our peace was upon him.* The word, *chastisement,* is a noun, and while its meaning here is obscure, we may understand it to be, *burden,* or the *burden of establishing.* We prefer the latter. *Our peace,* is the peace which comes to one who serves the Lord. It is founded upon truth, upheld and sustained by righteousness. Any peace that is not founded on righteousness is, "Peace, peace, when there is no peace." (Jeremiah 6:14) "And the work of righteousness shall be peace; and the effect of righteousness, quietness and assurance for ever." (Isaiah 32:17)

When the Children of Israel were wanderers in the Wilderness of Arabia, and early in the period of their famous exodus from Egyptian bondage, the Lord said, "I will bless them." At that same time He commanded Moses to instruct Aaron and his sons to also bless them and say to His people, "The Lord bless thee, and keep thee: The Lord make his face shine upon thee, and be gracious unto thee: The Lord lift up his countenance upon thee, and give thee peace." (Numbers 6:24-27; See 3 Nephi 19:25)

The Jews always remembered this remarkable blessing commanded by the Lord. It was a benediction pronounced upon all Israel by the great Giver of All Good. "Peace, God's most precious gift to man" is declared to be "Israel's portion."

But in time the different tribes of Israel apostatized from the inspired teachings of the prophets, and began all manner of false worship. Some even offered human sacrifice. They forgot the God of their fathers, the Only True and Living God. For many centuries they quarreled among themselves, and also with their neighbors. Battles were fought and cities destroyed. Cruel bondage awaited the vanquished. Hatred, envy, and malice towards each other leavened the meal that sustained their lives. They ate the bread of sorrow and drank from the cup of bitterness.

"Thou feedest them with the bread of tears; and giveth them tears to drink in great measure." (Psalm 80:5)

Nor, is that all; oriental rant and rancor stirred the bitter passions of many, and thereby all thoughts of God were crowded from their hearts. Bickering took the place of rejoicing; turmoil, instead of peace with healing in its wings, begat grief and sorrow.

It was only a short path that lead from the confusion surrounding the Jews to where they offered pretexts and excuses. Many were beguiled to follow this way and that. They sought to justify slothfulness by making sin a pleasure, and they hoped to vindicate the wicked by interpreting the Law to feed the hunger of infatuation and greed. The history of the Jews at this time reminds us of the words of the Lord to Cain, the brother of Abel, "If thou doest well, shalt thou not be accepted? and if thou doest not well, sin lieth at the door." (Genesis 4:7) Surely, sin was at the door of Judah.

"There is no peace, saith my God, to the wicked." (Isaiah 57:31)

Now, Isaiah proclaims that the burden is upon the Servant to re-establish the peace they once had, to bring back to them "a state of peace and favor with God" which they once enjoyed. The Servant, by accepting punishment for sins He did not commit, shifted the weight of transgression from the backs of the transgressor

6. All we, like sheep, have gone astray; we have turned every one to his own way; and the Lord hath laid on him the iniquities of us all.

7. He was oppressed, and he was afflicted, yet he opened not his mouth; he is brought as a lamb to the slaughter, and as a sheep before her shearers is

to Himself. Thus, the Prophet says, "And with his stripes we are healed." He meant by that, that by the sufferings He, the Servant, endured, our peace is restored, our favor with God is re-established, and we are become as we formerly were, *whole*.

Again, we are reminded of the words of the Psalmist, "Give ear, O Shepherd of Israel, thou that leadest Joseph like a flock; . . . stir up thy strength, and come and save us. Turn us again, O God, and cause thy face to shine; and we shall be saved." (Psalm 80)

VERSE 6. *And the Lord hath laid on him the iniquity of us all.* Isaiah begins the sentiment he here expresses with the unhappy conclusion, "All we like sheep have gone astray; we have turned every one to his own way." In other words, he says, we have sought for that which would please the fancy, or satisfy our whims. We care little, or nothing for the welfare of Zion, the fold of Israel's sheep. "The sheep of Israel's fold," has been the favorite comparison of God's holy prophets when they speak of His children. The Savior often likened His disciples to a flock of sheep, He being the "Good Shepherd." "I will feed my flock," is the promise of the Lord through the prophet. (Ezekiel 34:15)

Yet, in spite of the tender appeal God made to be vigilant and "follow me," when He likened His disciples to a flock of sheep over whom He ceaselessly watched, we have gone, some here and some there, all to places we deemed more pleasant, and where the pastures, we thought, were greener.

O ye workers of iniquity; ye that are puffed up in the vain things of the world, ye that have professed to have known the ways of righteousness nevertheless have gone astray, as sheep having no shepherd, notwithstanding a shepherd hath called after you and is still calling after you, but ye will not hearken unto his voice!

Behold, I say unto you, that the good shepherd doth call you; yea, and in his own name he doth call you, which is the name of Christ; and if ye will not hearken unto the voice of the good shepherd, to the name by which ye are called, behold, ye are not the sheep of the good shepherd. (Alma 5:37-38)

But, God is long suffering, slow to anger, always ready to forgive the repentant sinner, and has provided ways and means whereby he can be saved. All God's purposes are eternal. The Salvation of His children is the purpose to which His glory is consecrated. "For the eternal purposes of the Lord shall roll on, until all his promises shall be fulfilled." (Mormon 8:22)

God promised Salvation to every one of His children, but they cannot be saved in their sins. A Savior, whom Isaiah calls "the servant," has been provided, and upon Him the Lord hath laid the iniquity of us all.

He substituted himself in the room of sinners, as a sacrifice. He made his soul an offering for sin; he himself explains this (Matthew 20:28), that he came to give his life a ransom for many. . . . Thus he shall bear the iniquities of the many that he designed to justify (v. 11) and shall take away the sin of the world by taking it upon himself. (John 1:29) . . . Whenever we think of the sufferings of Christ, we must see him in them bearing our sin.

(*Commentary on the Bible,* Matthew Henry)

VERSES 7-8. *He was oppressed, and he was afflicted, yet he openeth not his mouth. And who shall declare his generation?* Here, the Prophet continued the

dumb so he opened not his mouth.

8. He was taken from prison and from judgment; and who shall declare his generation? For he was cut off out of the land of the living; for the transgressions of my people was he stricken.

---

description of the reception accorded the Servant by the Jews. He was despised by them, and as their long-awaited Messiah, he was rejected. He was of sorrowful mien, and, plainly, One who carried many burdens. He came from Galilee, of a poor, contemptible family. They said that He was of no account, a law-breaker, one who broke the Sabbath.

Isaiah says, "He was oppressed." We may understand from these words that He was trampled down by abuse of power and authority vested in the Jewish Hierarchy. Seventy-one of its elders and wise men formed a council known as the *Sanhedrin* which, under their Roman conquerors, had complete jurisdiction over the religious, civil, and criminal affairs of the people. They sought to crush Him, and scatter His followers.

He was afflicted. This same *Sanhedrin* which oppressed Him, not only permitted Him to be abused, (—their duty was to protect Him—) but also, its members joined in the cries against Him, and suffered Him to be wounded. They heaped sorrows (pains) upon Him that amounted to physical calumny.

Yet, he openeth not his mouth. Notwithstanding the harsh treatment afforded Him by the Jews, and in spite of the many false accusations His enemies made against Him, He offered no excuses, no apologies, no pretexts, to extenuate His course or make it more pleasing to them, but calmly, and even joyously He went about teaching His Gospel of Salvation.

Notwithstanding the many attempts of Jewish scholars to mitigate and explain the actions of the *Sanhedrin* in the part it took in the trial and condemnation of Jesus, the legal benefits of the Jewish law of which He was deprived stand out more and more clearly as their arguments to free it from the consequences of its guilt are made known. The more they explain, the weaker becomes their position. They declare themselves to be, not the defenders of truth, the advocates of more light, but the purveyors of falsehood, the sowers of bad seed.

Dr. Adam Clarke in his *Commentary on the Old Testament* previously cited, gives one example of the many customs to which Jesus had an appeal, but of it He had not benefit. Dr. Clarke says:

A learned friend has communicated to me the following passages from the *Mishna*,* and the Gemara of Babylon, as leading to a satisfactory explication of this difficult place. It is said in the former, that before anyone was punished for a capital crime, proclamation was made before the prisoner by the public crier, in these words: *col mi shioda lo zachoth yabo vayilmad alaiv*, "Whosoever knows any thing of this man's innocence, let him come and declare it." *Tract. Sanhedrim. Surenhus.* Part iv, p. 233. On which passage the Gemara of Babylon** adds, that "before the death of Jesus this proclamation was made for forty days; but no defence could be found." On which words Lardner observes: "It is truly surprising to see such falsities, contrary to well-known facts." *Testimonies*, Vol. 1, p. 198. The report is

---

*Mishna, *Mishnah;* pl. *Mishnayoth* Heb. mishnah, i.e., instructions, oral law, fr. Heb. *shannah* to repeat, in post-Biblical Heb. to teach, learn. A, The traditional doctrine of the Jews as developed chiefly in the decisions of the rabbis before the 3rd century A.D. B, A single tenent; a view of a rabbi. C, Any collection of such tenents. D, The collection of Halakoth, which is the basis of the Talmud.   (Webster's *New Collegiate Dictionary*)

**Gemara. Jewish Lit. The commentary of the *Talmud.*

Talmud. Heb. *talmudh* instruction, fr. *lamadh* to learn. The body of Jewish civil and canonical law, consisting of the combined *Mishna*, or text, and *Gemara*, or commentary; also, restrictedly, the *Gemara* alone.   (*Ibid.*)

9. And he made his grave with the wicked, and with the rich in his death; because he had done | no evil, neither was any deceit in his mouth.

---

certainly false; but this false report is founded on the supposition that there was such a custom, and so far confirms the account given from the *Mishna.* The *Mishna* was composed in the middle of the second century according to Prideaux; Lardner ascribes it to the year of Christ 180.

Casaubon has a quotation from Maimonides which farther confirms this account: —*Exercitat.* in *Baronii Annales,* Art. lxxvi, Ann. 34. Num. 119: "It was customary when sentence of death was passed upon a criminal, and he was led out from the seat of judgment to the place of punishment, a crier went before, and spoke as follows:— 'This man is going to suffer death by .... because he has transgressed by .... such a transgression, in such a place, in such a time; and the witnesses against him are .... He who may know any thing relative to his innocence, let him come and speak in his behalf.'

Now it is plain from the history of the Four Evangelists, that in the trial and condemnation of Jesus no such rule was observed; though, according to the account of the Mishna, it must have been in practice at that time, no proclamation was made for any person to bear witness to the innocence and character of Jesus; nor did any one voluntarily step forth to give his attestation to it. And our Savior seems to refer to such a custom, and to claim the benefit of it, by his answer to the high priest, when he asked him of his disciples and of his doctrine: "I spoke openly to the world; I ever taught in the synagogue and in the temple, whither the Jews always resort; and in secret have I said nothing. Why asketh me? ask them who heard me, what I have said unto them, behold, they know what I said." (John 18:20-21) This, therefore; was one remarkable instance of hardship and injustice, among others predicted by the prophet, which our Savior underwent in his trial and sufferings.

He was stricken. Ancient translators add to these words and render them, "He was smitten to death." (The Septuagint reads *lemaveth,* which, in the Greek into which the Old Testament was translated, means "to death.") The *Coptic* and *Saidic* versions of the Old Testament also include these words; however it may be that they are had from the Septuagint,* which is the older.

And who shall declare his generation? This has been interpreted, "And his manner of life who would declare?" Although we quote concerning the meaning stated of the question that is asked, we prefer to believe that it refers to the growth of the numbers of Christ's followers. "Of the increase of his government and peace there shall be no end. (Isaiah 9:7) "And he shall reign over the house of Jacob for ever; and of his kingdom there shall be no end." (Luke 1:33)

Some, by *His generation* understand "His spiritual seed." Who can count the vast numbers of converts that shall, by the Gospel, be begotten to Him, like the dew of the morning?

> When thus exalted he shall live to see
> A numberless believing progeny
> Of His adopted sons; the godlike race
> Exceed the stars that heav'n's high arches grace.
>
> Sir R. Blackmore.
> (Quoted by Matthew Henry, *Commentary on the Bible*)

VERSE 9. *And he made his grave with the wicked, and with the rich in his death.* Some commentators have thought that the words, *kibro,* "His grave," and *bemothaiv,*

Septuagint, L. septuaginta seventy. The pre-Christian Greek version of the Old Testament still in use in the Eastern Church; so called from the legend that the translation was made by seventy emissaries from Jerusalem for Ptolemy II. About B.C. 270.

(*Webster's New Collegiate Dictionary*)

10. Yet it pleased the Lord to bruise him; he hath put him to grief; when thou shalt make his soul an offering for sin he shall see his seed, he shall prolong his days, and the pleasure of the Lord shall prosper in his hand.

11. He shall see the travail of his soul, and shall be satisfied; by his knowledge shall my right-eous servant justify many; for he shall bear their iniquities.

12. Therefore will I divide him a portion with the great, and he shall divide the spoil with the strong; because he hath poured out his soul unto death; and he was numbered with the trans-gressors; and he bore the sins of many, and made intercession for the transgressors.

"in His death," have been transposed by editors or secretaries who copied the words of the prophet. They suggest that a better translation of them would be:

> Yea, His death was appointed among the wicked;
> And with a rich man, His tomb.

If we agree that such a transposition was actually made, the text is more agree-able to our understanding.

VERSE 10. *And the pleasure of the Lord shall prosper in his hand.* That the purposes of the Lord shall be brought about, and all His words be fulfilled wherein He promised Eternal Life to mankind, the Lord permitted His righteous Servant to suffer and make His life an offering for sin. That we may be pardoned of our sins and receive Salvation in His Kingdom was the end for which the Servant, Jesus Christ, suffered and died; "He was smitten to death."

The exact completion of this prophecy by Isaiah will be fully shown by adding here the several circumstances of the burial of Jesus. All are collected from the accounts of the evangelists:

There was a rich man from Arimathea, named Joseph, a member of the San-hedrin, and of a respectable character, who had not consented to their counsel and act. He went to Pilate and begged the body of Jesus. He laid it in his own new tomb, which had been hewed out of the rock, near the place where Jesus was crucified; having first wound it in fine linen with spices, as the manner of the Jews was to bury the rich and great."

(Dr. Adam Clarke, *Commentary on the Old Testament*)

CHAPTER 15

1. Abinadi's Prophecy—2. Why Jesus Christ is Called the Father and the Son.

1. Abinadi's prophecy.

1. And now Abinadi said unto them: I would that ye should understand that God himself shall come down among the children of men, and shall redeem his people.

Verse 1. *God himself shall come down among the children of men.* Along the many pleasant paths the thoughtful reader of the Book of Mormon will walk in his perusal of the Sacred Record, none will be more vividly seen, nor longer remembered, than when, in his journey, he encounters the Nephite servants of God declaring His holy word. In their own beautiful, but sometimes unhappy words, they proclaim the wonderful purposes of the Lord. The simplicity of their language, the straightness of the path to which they point, the sureness of the way, the oneness of the Gospel Plan, together, are a lamp to our feet, and a light in the darkness if, perchance, night overtakes us and we find ourselves "far from home."

There is a custom, presently formidable among a group of Bible commentators, to hide a truth beneath a canopy of apologies, pretexts, and excuses; there like a flower buried under a growth of rank grass, it may lie unnoticed, seen by only a few, and destined to delight still fewer.

God's truths thrive in the light.

A truth spoken in plainness is best understood. Whether the knowledge of it comes to us by experience, or through the voice of prophecy, words do not enhance its value; truth does not lose its force by a paucity of adverbs or adjectives; they often confuse its meaning. Around the most plain and precious truths man has built a wall of meaningless words, and like a theme he has borrowed from an old melody, he plays it, and replays it, improvising throughout. To the untrained ear it sounds like the original. But it is not. It is different. The difference is the distance between right and wrong, true and false, the real and the imitation.

Nearly four hundred years before the time of Abinadi, which was about the 450th year in the Nephite annals, Jacob, the son of Lehi, became the Presiding High Priest among the Saints who dwelt in the Land of Lehi-Nephi. He was a mighty teacher and preacher of righteousness. In the records kept by his brother, Nephi, upon the *Smaller Plates,* many of Jacob's teachings are included. Later, upon the death of Nephi, Jacob was raised to the holy office of Chief among the priests. He strongly called for moderation and self-restraint in the manner in which his people expressed the workings of the spirit of prophecy in their hearts. The spirit of prophecy is a sign that follows all true believers in Christ, and in this gift the Nephites of old were immeasurably blessed. Jacob said, "Behold, my brethren, he that prophesieth, let him prophesy to the understanding of men; for the Spirit speaketh the truth and lieth not. Wherefore, it speaketh of things as they really are, and of things as they really will be; wherefore, these things are manifested unto us plainly, for the salvation of our souls." (Jacob 4:13) Nephi said, "Wherefore, I shall speak unto you plainly, according to the plainness of my prophesying. For my soul delighteth in plainness; for after this manner doth the Lord God work among the children of men. For the Lord God giveth light unto the understanding; for he speaketh unto men according to their language, unto their understanding." (2 Nephi 31:2-3) He also said, "I glory in plainness; I glory in truth." (2 Nephi 33:6) (*See* Commentary on the Book of Mormon, Vol. I, p. 470, *Ibid,* p. 446)

2. Why Jesus Christ is Called the Father and the Son.

2. And because he dwelleth in flesh he shall be called the Son of God, and having subjected the flesh to the will of the Father, being the Father and the Son—
3. The Father, because he was conceived by the power of God; and the Son, because of the flesh; thus becoming the Father and Son—
4. And they are one God, yea, the very Eternal Father of heaven and of earth.
5. And thus the flesh becoming

To Abinadi we owe a debt of gratitude for stating in a few words some of the most marvelous truths contained in the doctrinal part of the Book of Mormon. His statements need no advocate to explain them, no interpreters to declare what they mean. They are quickly understood by all who have the spirit of prophecy.

The Prophet Abinadi said, "God himself. . . ." Not an emissary sent down from the Courts of Glory with a divine commission to perform; not His ambassador to act in His stead. But God, *himself*, the Mighty King of Heaven, "shall come down among the children of men, and shall redeem* his people."

VERSES 2-5. *The Father because he was conceived by the power of God; and the Son, because of the flesh.* Jesus Christ is both the Father and the Son. He is the Father because He subjected himself to the will of God; He placed Himself in the position of sinners and offered His life for their redemption from transgression. He is the *Author,* or the *Father* of our Salvation. Jesus Christ proposed the *Plan,* He marked the *Way* by which we are saved. His Sacrifice was the expression of His love for God's children, as also it was the price which was asked for their redemption. In the Great Council in heaven Jesus Christ presented His Plan for its acceptance or rejection. Paul the Apostle, thoroughly understood why Christ is called *The Father,* when he said, "Though he were a Son, yet learned he obedience by the things which he suffered; And being made perfect, he became the *author* of eternal salvation unto all them that obey him." (Hebrews 5:8-9)

It is more than interesting to note the words of Isaiah as they are translated in the *Septuagint*:**

"For a little Child is born unto us; and a Son is given unto us, whose dominion is on his shoulder; and his name shall be called:—

> *Messenger* of the Great Council,
> Wonderful Counselor,
> Strong Mighty One, [in authority]
> Ruler of Peace,
> *Father* of the Coming Age."   (Isaiah 9:6)

Jesus Christ was actually the "Messenger of the Great Council . . ." and the "Father of the Coming Age." The prophets understood the part He took in the Great Council, and why, therefore, He is called "The Father."

Abinadi explained that Jesus Christ is also the Son, because He "dwelleth in the flesh." He was conceived by the power of God, and took upon Himself a body of flesh and blood, "thus becoming the Father and Son."

VERSE 4. *And they are one God.* According to the Book of Mormon, as well as the Bible, there are three glorious, exalted, sovereign persons in the Godhead: The

---

*See *Complete Concordance* of the word, *Redeem,* at end of Chapter 16; *also, Comments* Chapter 12:23.
**See, *Septuagint, Comments* Mosiah 14:7-8.

subject to the Spirit, or the Son to the Father, being one God, suffereth temptation, and yieldeth not to the temptation, but suffereth himself to be mocked, and scourged, and cast out, and disowned by his people.

Father, the Son and the Holy Ghost. (See COMMENTARY ON THE BOOK OF MORMON, Vol. I, p. 93)

Originally the term *God* included the entire plurality of divine personages, and even archangels and angels. The divine name, *Elohim* (the plural form) proves the plurality, but gradually that form of the word became the name of the supreme Ruler of the universe. He is the Elohim, the mighty One, also called the Father, and the plural form of the name is retained to denote the greatness of His majesty, power, and glory. Generally, when the name is used without any qualification, it stands for the first Person in the Godhead. (See COMMENTARY ON THE BOOK OF MORMON, Vol. I, p. 199)

The Father. Christ taught the doctrine of the Fatherhood of God, and the brotherhood of man. That is the conception of the relationship between God and man in which we find comfort. It is as old as mankind. Christ revived it. His disciples proclaimed it, and endeavored to put it into practice. It was almost lost sight of, as it was beforetime to the Jews, until the Reformation when it was brought to the attention of those who yearned for human liberty, and it contributed greatly to the success of the world struggles which culminated in the form of government upon which our republic rests. For this government recognizes human rights as between man and man, rulers and ruled, and it has become clear that God, Himself, who raised up men to institute this government, surely respects the rights and privileges He had given His children, which are the very foundation of their responsibility as free agents.

With the attention thus turned to the doctrine of the Fatherhood of God, the life of Christ has been studied more closely than ever, since it is in Christ, that God, the Father, is most clearly revealed.

In the *Book of Mormon*, God is revealed as the Eternal Father, the Creator, Omnipotent, Infinite in Perfection, in wisdom, goodness, in love and mercy, as well as justice. He reigns supreme and He proclaims His Son to the children of men: "Behold my Beloved Son, in whom I am well pleased, in whom I have glorified my name—hear ye him." (3 Nephi 11:7)*

It is perfectly clear that God, in the *Book of Mormon,* is revealed as a sovereign, but who rules as a wise, good, loving and just Father in the midst of His family; not as an Eastern despot in the midst of slaves and sycophants. He is the supreme Ruler of beings to whom He has given free agency, and He rules under the Celestial Law of Equality, or equal rights to all. In His sovereignty He controls even that which seems accidental. Even seemingly trifling means, and sometimes the wicked, serve, unknown to themselves, His purposes. He forgives the repentant sinner. He hears and answers prayer, and He takes care of those who put their trust in Him, as loving, obedient children.**

The Son. There is a tendency among modern professors of Christianity to accept the doctrine of the Divinity of Jesus, on the slippery ground that every human is divine. This, they argue, follows from the fact that all nature is permeated by

---

*References: 1 Nephi 11:21; 17:36; 1:14; 16:35; 22:26; 13:40; 2 Nephi 1:10; 1:15; 4:21; 9:17; 26; 46; 2:24; Jacob 3:2; 4:9; Mosiah 3:5; 4:11; 3:38; 12:21; 13:14; 15:4; 3 Nephi 11:3-7; 12:48.

**References: 1 Nephi 16:20; Jacob 7:22; Mosiah 27:14; Alma 19:36; 26:37; 29-8; 33:4-6; 3 Nephi 17:15-21.

the divine, supreme essence. In one sense, they say, all men are divine, and Christ is no more divine than we all are, or that all existing creatures are, for that matter. The only difference between Him and us, in their view, is this, that He realized that He was Divine, while we hope to be able to realize our divinity—some day.

It is not denied that there is some truth in the conception of a universal divinity. We are all God's children. But Christ is much more than a child among children. He is the Creator, our Savior, our Redeemer, the Captain of our Salvation, the Mediator between the Father and the rest of God's children. And that is a great difference.

The Book of Mormon is a mighty witness for the divine character and mission of our Lord. (*See* COMMENTARY ON THE BOOK OF MORMON, Vol. I, p. 93)

The Sacred Record states expressly that He is God: "There is a God, and He is Christ."

He is the "Eternal God," (*Inspired Preface to Book of Mormon* by Mormon) and "Lord God Omnipotent." (Mosiah 3:21) He who died for us is the "Creator," the "Father of heaven and earth, the Creator of all things." (Mosiah 3:8) He is "the Father," "Eternal Father,"

the *"Beginning* and the *End,* the *First* and the *Last."*

He is so intimately associated with God, the Father, that, in His relation to the children of men, He is both the Father and the Son. He stands in God's stead. God has delegated to Him all power in heaven and on earth; He is One Member of the great, divine, presiding, and governing Council of Three, the Father, the Son, and the Holy Ghost, to whose communion, baptism in His name and by His authority admits the redeemed child of God. He is, furthermore, "without beginning of days or end of years."*

But although He is, in this sense, God, the Father; God, clothed in majesty and power and glory, He is also the Son of God. He is the "Beloved Son,"

in whom the Father has glorified His name; He is the "Only Begotten Son," and also the "Redeemer" and the "Lamb of God," and the only "Savior" of mankind.**

It may be seen from these references that in the Book of Mormon, Christ is, as already stated, revealed as "being the Father and the Son." This is explained thus: "Because he dwelleth in the flesh, he shall be called the Son of God," and the Father "because he was conceived by the power of God," thus becoming the Father and the Son.

The Holy Ghost. The third person in the great, divine Council of Three is the Holy Ghost, also called the Holy Spirit, and the Spirit of the Lord. (*See* COMMENTARY ON THE BOOK OF MORMON, Vol. I, p. 93) In 1 Nephi 11:11, if we read the passage correctly, Nephi in his prophetic vision sees the Holy Ghost as a personage of spirit, in the form of a man. He sees him coming down out of heaven at the baptism of our Lord. He represents him as the exalted person who confers divine authority on the servants of God; as one who sanctifies those that, through faith and repentance, enter the High Priesthood; one who imparts knowledge, faith, the gift to speak, power to ordain to the Priesthood, and "many" other gifts of God, enumerated in Moroni 10:9-19.***

---

*References: 2 Nephi 9:5; 11:7; 26:12; 5:15; 15:2; Alma 11:38; Helaman 14:12; 3 Nephi 11:27; Ether 3:14.
**References: 1 Nephi 10:17; 11:17; Jacob 4:5-11; Mosiah 15:1-4; 16:13; Alma 12:13-16; 12:33-34; 34:7-14; 38:9; Helaman 5:12; 3:28; 3 Nephi 9:15; 11:7; Moroni 3:3; Ether 3:14.
***References: 1 Nephi 10:22 11:27; 2 Nephi 26:13; 31:8; 32:3; 33:1; Jacob 7:12; Alma 13:12; 3 Nephi 16:4; Ether 12:33; Moroni 3:4; 10:8-19; 19:7.

It is the Holy Ghost that "bears record," or testifies, of the Father and the Son. He manifests, or expounds, the word of God. It is, therefore, a great sin to deny him, or to contend against him.*

The Three are *One*, but not one individual person. They are Three Persons, in one great Divine Council.

"The Godhead is a type of unity in the attributes, powers, and purposes of its members. Jesus, while on earth, and in manifesting Himself to His Nephite servants, repeatedly testified of the unity existing between Himself and the Father, and between Them both and the Holy Ghost. This cannot rationally be construed to mean that the Father, the Son, and the Holy Ghost are one in person, nor that the names represent the same individual under different aspects. . . . Immediately before His betrayal, Christ prayed for His disciples, the Twelve, and other converts, that they should be preserved in unity, 'that they all may be one' as the Father and the Son are one. We cannot assume that Christ prayed that His followers lose their individuality and become one person, even if a change so directly opposed to nature were possible." (Dr. James E. Talmage, *Articles of Faith*, p. 40.)

The doctrine of some modern philosophers that the Father, the Son, and the Spirit are merely terms expressing three modes in which the all-permeating divine essence relates itself to the experience of man, finds no support in the *Book of Mormon*. Nor does this Book teach that in the Father we see "the Absolute in its original oneness"; in the Son, its "self objectification," and in the Spirit "the reunion of the two," a set of phrases, the uselessness of which is their most conspicuous feature. On the contrary, the *Book of Mormon*, as the *Bible*, teaches, we repeat, that there are three distinct persons, perfectly united in their divine council, in their plans and purposes; united into one in the same sense, as *Dr. Talmage* reminds us, that Jesus, our Lord, was, and is, one with the Twelve.

The doctrine is exceedingly clear in the *Book of Mormon*:

"And now, behold, this is the doctrine of Christ, and the only and true doctrine of the Father, and of the Son, and of the Holy Ghost, which is one God without end." (2 Nephi 31:21)

Again:

"Christ the Son, and God the Father, and the Holy Spirit, which is one Eternal God." (Alma 11:44)

The Holy Spirit. But, according to the Book of Mormon, as well as other Scripture, there is also a Holy Spirit, sometimes called the Holy Ghost, which is not a person, but rather a divine essence, a force, or fluid—for want of a better term— which permeates all that exists. It is the medium through which God communicates with the world, and especially with His children. It is through the presence of this holy, divine spirit that order is preserved in the universe. Were this mighty force withdrawn, the world would return to chaos. The planets would stop revolving in their wonted courses. The fountains of the great deep would again break its fetters and overflow; and even human society would fall into ruins. It is that Spirit, in whom "we live, and move, and have our being." It is through His Spirit that Christ gives light to all things. It "proceedeth forth from the presence of God to fill the immensity of space; it is the light which is in all things; which giveth life to all things; which is the law by which all things are governed; even the power of God who sitteth upon his throne, who is in the bosom of eternity, who is in the midst of all things." (*Doc. and Cov.* 88:4-13) It is through this Spirit that God "is above all things, and in all things, and is through all things, and is round about all things." (*Doc. and Cov.* 88:41)

---

*References: 1 Nephi 10:11; 2 Nephi 28:4; Alma 34:38; 39:5-6; Ether 11:36; Moroni 8:9.

It is this Spirit that is imparted to the repentant believer who receives baptism and the laying on of hands by an authorized servant of the Lord. And it is through this Spirit that the spiritual gifts are distributed.*

The Spirit of the Lord. "For I spake unto him as a man speaketh; for I beheld that he was in the form of a man; yet, nevertheless, I knew that it was the Spirit of the Lord." (1 Nephi 11:11) How can the Spirit of the Lord be in the form of a man and yet be imparted by the laying on of hands? The late *President Joseph F. Smith* says:

"The terms The Holy Ghost and The Spirit of God are frequently used synonymously. We often say The Spirit of God when we mean The Holy Ghost; we likewise say The Holy Ghost when we mean The Spirit of God. The Holy Ghost is a personage in the Godhead, and is not that which lighteth every man that comes into the world." (*Doctrine and Covenants Commentary*, Vol. 1, p. 240)

It is not the third person of the Godhead that is imparted by the laying on of hands, but the Spirit that fills the universe. Speaking of The Holy Ghost, the divine person, President Heber C. Kimball says:

"Let me tell you, The Holy Ghost is a man; he is one of the sons of the Father and our God; and he is that man that stood next to Jesus Christ, just as I stand by Brother Brigham." (*Jour. of Dis.*, Vol. 5, p. 179; also compare Alma 7:10 and 9:44)

It is necessary to have clearly before our minds the difference between the Holy Ghost as a divine person, one with the Father and the Son, and the Holy Ghost or Spirit, which is the medium of communication between God and His creation, His children, as previously explained. The Prophet Joseph says, "There is a difference between the Holy Ghost and the gift of the Holy Ghost. Cornelius received the Holy Ghost before he was baptized which was the convincing power of God unto him of the truth of the Gospel; but he could not receive the gift of the Holy Ghost until after he was baptized. Had he not taken this sign, or ordinance, upon him, the Holy Ghost, which convinced him of the truth of God, would have left him." (*History of the Church*, Vol. IV, p. 555)

The Holy Ghost opened personally, as it were, the door of the Gospel to the Gentile world, by pouring out upon those in the house of Cornelius the power and influence which enabled them to accept truth, speak with tongues, and magnify God. But the full measure of this divine gift came after baptism and the laying on of hands; otherwise, baptism in water would have been superfluous, as many in our day regard it. Until Cornelius observed the ordinances and received the gift of the Holy Ghost by the laying on of hands, he could not have healed the sick or commanded an evil spirit in the name of the Lord. The distinction has been made between the Holy Ghost as a person and a divine element: "The term *Holy Ghost* and its common synonyms, *Spirit of God, Spirit of the Lord,* or simply *Spirit, Comforter,* and *Spirit of Truth,* occur in the *Scriptures* with plainly different meanings, referring in some cases to the *person* of God, the *Holy Ghost,* and in other instances to the *power* or *authority* of this great being." (*Dr. James E. Talmage*)

In the *Book of Mormon* the distinction as we have seen, is made between the Holy Ghost, the person, and "*Fire and the Holy Ghost,*" the divine element or essence. This is a significant distinction.

Human language is but imperfect, and it is doubtful whether there is a word fully expressive of the true nature of this divine person and the medium through which God operates. In the *Doctrine and Covenants*, the divine element is called

---

*References: 1 Nephi 3:20; 13:12; Alma 5:47; Helaman 5:45; 3 Nephi 19:9-23; Moroni 10:8-9.

6. And after all this, after working many mighty miracles among the children of men, he shall be led, yea, even as Isaiah said, as a sheep before the shearer is dumb, so he opened not his mouth.

7. Yea, even so he shall be led, crucified, and slain, the flesh becoming subject even unto death, the will of the Son being swallowed up in the will of the Father.

"the light which now shineth." (Sec. 88:11-33) *Orson Pratt* calls it a "substance." We may, with *Dr. Talmage* refer to it as a "power," or an influence, or couple it with the term "fire." And it is all that. But it is more. It is "Holy Spirit,"—a substance, an influence, a power, a light, a fire that proceeds from the Father and the Son and permeates everything. It is the Glory of God, the manifestation of the divine presence; the fire and smoke, which made Sinai tremble; the glory which rested on the Mercy Seat in the tabernacle and the temple; the wind which filled the house on the Day of Pentecost. It is divine intelligence, since *"the glory of God is intelligence."* It is the force before which mountains flee and worlds perish, for "the presence of the Lord shall be as a fire that burneth, and as a fire which causes water to boil." (*Doctrine and Covenants* 133:41)

VERSE 5. *And thus the flesh becoming subject to the Spirit.* Jesus Christ, having taken upon Himself a body of flesh and blood, thereby, became subject to all the pains and temptations that mortals endure. How could He know our grief unless He partook of them; and how could He measure our temptations unless He withstood them, Himself? Our Father in Heaven knew this, and the Son knowing it, suffered pain and anguish, allowing temptation to test His marvelous powers. Yet, said the Prophet Abinadi, He "Yieldeth not to the temptation, but suffered himself to be mocked, and scourged, and cast out, and disowned by his people." (See Mosiah 14:2-5)

VERSE 6. *After working many mighty miracles.* After showing forth the power and authority of God, in healing the sick, raising the dead, making the blind to see and the lame to walk, and many other wonderful works, Jesus was considered by the Jews to be only a man, and a man, too, who was of little or no account. He was led before His accusers as a sheep is led before the shearers, yet, "he opened not his mouth." (See Mosiah 14:7; *also*, Matthew 26:63; Acts 8:32.) He offered no excuses, no defense of what He had done. They accused Him of sacrilege, saying, "He desecrated the Sabbath," and also, they said, "He is a law-breaker."

VERSE 7. *Yea, even so he shall be led, crucified, and slain.* After all the wondrous works performed by the Son, and the mighty miracles wrought by Him, going forth among men and doing good continually, He shall be led, crucified, and slain.

The Mighty Jehovah, who created all things both in heaven and on earth, was taken by wicked men and slain. Not only did He suffer pain and sorrow as do all mortals, but, He, like they, was subject "even unto death." He "took upon him the form of a servant, and was made in the likeness of men: And being found in fashion as a man, he humbled himself, and became obedient unto death, even the death of the cross." (Philippians 2:7-8)

Wicked and subversive men took the Lord Jesus and put Him to an ignominious death, not because of what He did, but in spite of it.

We may understand the latter part of this verse better by reading the words of the Savior when He was criticised by the Jews for curing a crippled man in Bethesda on the Sabbath. He replied to their censure: "I can of mine own self do

8. And thus God breaketh the bands of death, having gained the victory over death; giving the Son power to make intercession for the children of men—

9. Having ascended into heav-

---

nothing: as I hear, I judge: and my judgment is just; because I seek not mine own will, but the will of the Father which hath sent me." (John 5:30) Later, when after He had celebrated the Passover with His disciples, and had administered to them the Bread and Wine, explaining its meaning, Jesus, followed by them, went to the Mount of Olives to pray. There the Savior left them and went away about a stone's throw, where He, being alone, sought comfort and strength from the Almighty Father. Knowing that the hour of His passion had come, and that He would be crucified for sins He did not commit, Jesus prayed. His anguish was so great that drops of blood came from every pore. An angel came and ministered to Him so great was His agony. The flesh, being weaker than the Spirit, caused Him to cry in humble supplication, "Father, if thou be willing, remove this cup from me: nevertheless not my will, but thine, be done." (Luke 22:42)

In humble submission to the will of God, but with mighty power and strength, Jesus, the Holy One of Israel, bowed before *The Majesty On High* and paid the *price* of man's Redemption, thereby breaking the bands of death. Christ's spiritual triumph over the demands of the flesh reminds one of Isaiah's words: "Trust ye in the Lord for ever: for in the Lord JEHOVAH is everlasting strength." (Isaiah 26:4)

Death, having come into the world by transgression, held fast in its clutches the inevitable decree: "Thou shalt surely die." (Genesis 2:17) Man was helpless; of himself, he could do nothing. He was cast out of God's presence, "For they are carnal and devilish, and the devil has power over them," (Mosiah 16:3) said Abinadi. Evil, in no form, can dwell with God. A way must be found, a plan prepared, whereby His children can regain the place they once had — a home with Him in the Celestial Abode. Unless and until that is done, all of God's promises to them will go unfulfilled.

But the *Way* has been found, a *Plan* prepared; that *Plan* is the Gospel of Jesus Christ. His great Sacrifice on Calvary paved the way for man's return to glory. The Resurrection of Christ from the dead broke the shackles that held man in its inexorable grasp. Through His Atonement we shall live again, and because of His resurrection we will be raised to Immortality and Eternal Life, never to die again. "He is the light and the life of the world; yea, a light that is endless, that can never be darkened; yea, and also a life which is endless, that there can be no more death." (Mosiah 16:9)

Thanks be to God, "For as the Father hath life in himself; so hath he given to the Son to have life in himself." (John 5:26)

Wherefore, beloved brethren, be reconciled unto him through the antonement of Christ, his Only Begotten Son, and ye may obtain a resurrection, according to the power of the resurrection which is in Christ, and be presented as the first-fruits of Christ unto God, having faith, and obtained a good hope of glory in him before he manifesteth himself in the flesh.   (Jacob 4:11)

The word *reconcile* means, (1) To cause to be *friendly* again. (2) to *adjust; settle;* as, to *settle* or *reconcile* differences. (3) To make *consistent* or *congruous.* (4) To bring back to *harmony.* (*Webster's Collegiate Dictionary*)

VERSES 8-9. *And thus God breaketh the bands of death.* The great Sacrifice and Resurrection of the Son broke, by God's power and mercy, the bands of death that otherwise would have held men forever in their fallen state. Christ's triumphant

en, having the bowels of mercy; being filled with compassion towards the children of men; standing betwixt them and justice; having broken the bands of death, taken upon himself their iniquity and their transgressions, having redeemed them, and satisfied the demands of justice.

10. And now I say unto you, who shall declare his generation? Behold, I say unto you, that when his soul has been made an offering for sin he shall see his seed. And now what say ye? And who shall be his seed?

11. Behold I say unto you, that whosoever has heard the words of the prophets, yea, all the holy prophets who have prophesied concerning the coming of the

Lord—I say unto you, that all those who have hearkened unto their words, and believed that the Lord would redeem his people, and have looked forward to that day for a remission of their sins, I say unto you, that these are his seed, or they are the heirs of the kingdom of God.

12. For these are they whose sins he has borne; these are they for whom he has died, to redeem them from their transgressions. And now, are they not his seed?

13. Yea, and are not the prophets, every one that has opened his mouth to prophesy, that has not fallen into transgression, I mean all the holy prophets ever since the world began? I say unto you that they are his seed.

Resurrection gave Him power to intercede for us; thus through Him all men will be resurrected and placed beyond the power of hell and the grave.

Abinadi extolled the loving-kindness in which Christ suffered and died for men, Christ's patience in serving them, and His compassion for their helpless condition. Christ stood between men and their just punishment. He took "upon himself their iniquities and their transgressions." "Surely our afflictions he hath borne, and our sorrows he carrieth them." (*See* Mosiah 14:4)

Having redeemed them. (*See* Mosiah 12:23)

Satisfied the demands of justice. The idea stated herein by Abinadi is commented upon by the late President John Taylor:

Is justice dishonored? No; it is satisfied, the debt is paid. Is righteousness departed from? No; this is a righteous act. All requirements are met. Is judgment violated? No; its demands are fulfilled. Is mercy triumphant? No; she simply claims her own. Justice, judgment, mercy and truth all harmonize as the attributes of Deity. "Justice and truth have met together, righteousness and peace have kissed each other." Justice and judgment triumph as well as mercy and peace; all the attributes of Deity harmonize in this great, grand, momentous, just, equitable, merciful and meritorious act.   (*Mediation and Atonement*)

VERSES 10-13. *Who shall declare his generation? And who shall be his seed?* Abinadi now answers the question asked by Isaiah, and recorded in Mosiah 14:8, "Who shall declare his generation?"

Christ, the Immortal Son of God, the Father of Salvation, the Mighty Prince, who brought peace to men's troubled souls, although He died a sacrifice for sin and suffered almost alone, He shall see the numberless hosts of them that, in holiness, worship Him and have taken upon them, His name.

14. And these are they who have published peace, who have brought good tidings of good, who have published salvation; and said unto Zion: Thy God reigneth!

15. And O how beautiful upon the mountains were their feet!

16. And again, how beautiful upon the mountains are the feet of those that are still publishing peace!

17. And again, how beautiful upon the mountains are the feet of those who shall hereafter publish peace, yea, from this time henceforth and forever!

18. And behold, I say unto you, this is not all. For O how beautiful upon the mountains are the feet of him that bringeth good tidings, that is the founder of peace, yea, even the Lord, who has redeemed his people; yea, him who has granted salvation unto his people;

19. For were it not for the redemption which he hath made for his people, which was prepared from the foundation of the world, I say unto you, were it not for this, all mankind must have perished.

20. But behold, the bands of death shall be broken, and the Son reigneth, and hath power over the dead; therefore, he bringeth to pass the resurrection of the dead.

21. And there cometh a resurrection, even a first resurrection; yea, even a resurrection of those that have been, and who are, and who shall be, even until the resurrection of Christ—for so shall he be called.

22. And now, the resurrection of all the prophets, and all those that have believed in their words, or all those that have kept the commandments of God, shall come forth in the first resurrec-

---

Who shall be his seed? Every one who has heard and believed the words of the prophets concerning Christ are His seed. Also, all the holy prophets themselves. The inspired Abinadi was filled with joy as he proclaimed their Salvation, for he said, "These are his seed, or they are the heirs of the kingdom of God." (*See Comments, Who shall declare his generation?* Mosiah 14:8)

Verses 14-20. *O how beautiful upon the mountains were their feet.* Abinadi now answers the question that was asked by one of King Noah's priests. (Mosiah 12:20-24. *See Comments*)

Thy God reigneth. (*See Comments* Mosiah 12:21)

Verses 21-24. *And there cometh a resurrection, even a first resurrection.* Although all men will be resurrected before the final Judgment Day of the Lord, some will be raised from the grave unto immortal life sooner than will others.

The late Elder James E. Talmage says of the Resurrection:

"Two general resurrections are mentioned in the scriptures, and these may be specified as first and final, or as the resurrection of the just and the resurrection of the unjust. The first was inaugurated by the resurrection of Jesus Christ; immediately following which many of the saints came forth from their graves. A continuation of this, the resurrection of the just, has been in operation since, and will be greatly extended, or brought to pass in a general way, in connection with the coming of

tion; therefore, they are the first resurrection.

23. They are raised to dwell with God who has redeemed them; thus they have eternal life through Christ, who has broken the bands of death.

24. And these are those who have part in the first resurrec-tion; and these are they that have died before Christ came, in their ignorance, not having salvation declared unto them. And thus the Lord bringeth about the res-toration of these; and they have a part in the first resurrection, or have eternal life, being redeemed by the Lord.

Christ in His glory. The final resurrection will be deferred until the end of the thousand years of peace, and will be in connection with the last judgment."

We refer the reader to the following Book of Mormon scripture:

And I said unto them that our father also saw that the justice of God did also divide the wicked from the righteous; and the brightness thereof was like unto the brightness of a flaming fire, which ascendeth up unto God forever and ever, and hath no end.

And they said unto me: Doth this thing mean the torment of the body in the days of probation, or doth it mean the final state of the soul after the death of the temporal body, or doth it speak of the things which are temporal?

And it came to pass that I said unto them that it was a representation of things both temporal and spiritual; for the day should come that they must be judged of their works, yea, even the works which were done by the temporal body in their days of probation.

Wherefore, if they should die in their wickedness they must be cast off also, as to the things which are spiritual, which are pertaining to righteousness; wherefore, they must be brought to stand before God, to be judged of their works; and if their works have been filthiness they must needs be filthy; and if they be filthy it must needs be that they cannot dwell in the kingdom of God; if so, the kingdom of God must be filthy also.

But behold, I say unto you, the kingdom of God is not filthy, and there cannot any unclean thing enter into the kingdom of God; wherefore there must needs be a place of filthiness prepared for that which is filthy.

And there is a place prepared, yea, even that awful hell of which I have spoken, and the devil is the foundation of it; wherefore the final state of the souls of men is to dwell in the kingdom of God, or to be cast out because of that justice of which I have spoken.

Wherefore, the wicked are rejected from the righteous, and also from that tree of life, whose fruit is most precious and most desirable above all other fruits; yea, and it is the greatest of all gifts of God. And thus I spake unto my brethren. Amen.
(1 Nephi 15:30-36)

Now this is the state of the souls of the wicked, yea, in darkness, and a state of awful, fearful looking for the fiery indignation of the wrath of God upon them; thus they remain in this state, as well as the righteous in paradise, until the time of their resurrection.

Now, there are some that have understood that this state of happiness and this state of misery of the soul, before the resurrection, was a first resurrection. Yea, I admit it may be termed a resurrection, the raising of the spirit or the soul and their consignation to happiness or misery, according to the words which have been spoken.

And behold, again it hath been spoken, that there is a first resurrection, a resurrection of all those who have been, or who are, or who shall be, down to the resurrection of Christ from the dead.

Now, we do not suppose that this first resurrection, which is spoken of in this manner, can be the resurrection of the souls and their consignation to happiness or misery. Ye cannot suppose that this is what it meaneth.

25. And little children also have eternal life.

26. But behold, and fear, and tremble before God, for ye ought to tremble; for the Lord redeemeth none such that rebel against him and die in their sins; yea, even all those that have perished in their sins ever since the world began, that have wilfully rebelled against God, that have known the commandments of God, and would not keep them; these are they that have no part in the first resurrection.

27. Therefore ought ye not to tremble? For salvation cometh to none such; for the Lord hath redeemed none such; yea, neither can the Lord redeem such; for he cannot deny himself; for he cannot deny justice when it has its claim.

28. And now I say unto you that the time shall come that the salvation of the Lord shall be declared to every nation, kindred, tongue, and people.

29. Yea, Lord, thy watchmen

Behold, I say unto you, Nay; but it meaneth the reuniting of the soul with the body, of those from the days of Adam down to the resurrection of Christ.

Now, whether the souls and the bodies of those of whom has been spoken shall all be reunited at once, the wicked as well as the righteous, I do not say; let it suffice, that I say that they all come forth; or in other words, their resurrection cometh to pass before the resurrection of those who die after the resurrection of Christ.

Now, my son, I do not say that their resurrection cometh at the resurrection of Christ; but behold, I give it as my opinion, that the souls and the bodies are reunited, of the righteous, at the resurrection of Christ, and his ascension into heaven.

But whether it be at his resurrection or after, I do not say; but this much I say, that there is a space between death and the resurrection of the body, and a state of the soul in happiness or in misery until the time which is appointed of God that the dead shall come forth, and be reunited, both soul and body, and be brought to stand before God, and be judged according to their works.

Yea, this bringeth about the restoration of those things of which has been spoken by the mouths of the prophets.

The soul shall be restored to the body, and the body to the soul; yea, and every limb and joint shall be restored to its body; yea, even a hair of the head shall not be lost; but all things shall be restored to their proper and perfect frame.

And now, my son, this is the restoration of which has been spoken by the mouths of the prophets—

And then shall the righteous shine forth in the kingdom of God.

But behold, an awful death cometh upon the wicked; for they die as to things pertaining to things of righteousness; for they are unclean, and no unclean thing can inherit the kingdom of God; but they are cast out, and consigned to partake of the fruits of their labors or their works, which have been evil; and they drinks the dregs of a bitter cup.   (Alma 40:14-26)

VERSE 25. *Little children also have eternal life.* See Mosiah 3:16-21.

VERSES 26-27. *The Lord redeemeth none such . . . that die in their sins.* Those who have not repented and die knowing that their sins created in them no desire to obey God's commandments, but on the other hand induced them to openly and wilfully rebel against His wishes, or to declare no reliance upon Him, "the Lord redeemeth none such."

VERSE 28. *The salvation of the Lord shall be declared.* See Mosiah 16:1.

shall lift up their voice; with the voice together shall they sing; for they shall see eye to eye, when the Lord shall bring again Zion.

30. Break forth into joy, sing together, ye waste places of Jerusalem; for the Lord hath comforted his people, he hath redeemed Jerusalem.

31. The Lord hath made bare his holy arm in the eyes of all the nations; and all the ends of the earth shall see the salvation of our God.

VERSE 29. *Thy watchmen shall lift up their voice.* See Mosiah 12:22. In the King James Translation of the Bible this is translated, Thy watchmen shall lift up *the* voice.

VERSE 30. *Break forth into joy.* See Mosiah 12:23-24.

VERSE 31. *The Lord hath made bare his holy arm.* See Mosiah 12:23-24.

CHAPTER 16

1. Abinadi Continues His Prophecy—2. Christ the Only Redeemer—3. Resurrection and Judgment.

1. *Abinadi continues his prophecy.*

1. And now, it came to pass that after Abinadi had spoken these words he stretched forth his hand and said: The time shall come when all shall see the salvation of the Lord; when every nation, kindred, tongue, and people shall see eye to eye and shall confess before God that his judgments are just.

VERSE 1. *The time shall come when all shall see the salvation of the Lord.* Recorded in Mosiah 15:28 is Abinadi's prophecy concerning the preaching of the Lord's Salvation to all peoples. He makes it plain that it shall be so declared. In this verse he foretells the solemn truth that when the Lord's Salvation is thus proclaimed all nations, kindreds, tongues, and peoples "shall see eye to eye and shall confess before God that his judgments are just."

The expression *eye to eye* is figurative, and here it means that all people, as one, will understand and discern that the judgments of the Lord are just. Their minds will apprehend His justice and unitedly they will sing His praises. (*See* Mosiah 12:22; *also* 3 Nephi 16:18; 20:32)

Alma, the younger, in giving to his son, Helaman, a father's blessing said,

Yea, and now behold, O my son, the Lord doth give me exceeding great joy in the fruit of my labors;

For because of the word which he has imparted unto me, behold, many have been born of God, and have tasted as I have tasted, and have seen *eye to eye* as I have seen; therefore they do know of these things of which I have spoken, as I do know; and the knowledge which I have is of God.   (Alma 36:25-26)

Passages in the Book of Mormon which may give us a better understanding of the words, *eye to eye*, are listed here:

2 Nephi	9:44	He view me with his all-searching e.
Jacob	2:10	The glance of the piercing e. of the Almighty
	15	With one glance of his e., he can smite
Mosiah	12:22	For they shall see e. to e. when the Lord
	15:29	For they shall see e. to e. when the Lord
	16:1	When every nation . . . shall see e. to e.
	18:21	They should look forward with one e.
	27:31	Beneath the glance of his all-searching e.
Alma	5:15	Do you look forward with an e. of faith
	32:40	Looking forward with an e. of faith
	36:26	And have seen e. to e., as I have seen
3 Nephi	7:15	Having seen angels, and being e. witnesses
	15	Also being e. witness to their quick return
	12:38	Behold, it is written, an e. for an e.
	13:22	The light of the body is the e.
	22	If therefore thine e. be single, thy whole body
	3	But if thine e. be evil, thy whole body
	14:3	The mote that is in thy brother's e.
	23	Considerest not the beam that is in thine own e.

2. And then shall the wicked be cast out, and they shall have cause to howl, and weep, and wail, and gnash their teeth; and this because they would not hearken unto the voice of the Lord; therefore the Lord redeemeth them not.

3. For they are carnal and devilish, and the devil has power over them; yea, even that old serpent that did beguile our first parents, which was the cause of their fall; which was the cause of all mankind becoming carnal, sensual, devilish, knowing evil from good, subjecting themselves to the devil.

4. Thus all mankind were lost; and behold, they would have been endlessly lost were it not that God redeemed his people from their lost and fallen state.

5. But remember that he that persists in his own carnal nature, and goes on in the ways of sin and rebellion against God, remaineth in his fallen state and the devil hath all power over him. Therefore, he is as though there was no redemption made, being an enemy to God; and also is the devil an enemy to God.

6. And now if Christ had not come into the world, speaking of things to come as though they had already come, there could have been no redemption.

7. And if Christ had not risen from the dead, or have broken the bands of death that the grave should have no victory, and that death should have no sting, there could have been no resurrection.

	4	Let me pull the mote out of thine e.
	4	—and behold, a beam is in thine own e.?
	5	First cast the beam out of thine own e.
	5	To cast the mote out of thy brother's e.
	16:18	For they shall see e. to e. when the Lord
	17:16	They bear record; the e. hath never
	20:32	Sing: for they shall see e. to e.
	28:8	Be changed in the twinkling of an e.
Mormon	8:15	Shall be done with an e. single to his glory
Ether	12:19	Which they had beheld with an e. of faith

VERSES 2-8. *And then shall the wicked be cast out.* The wicked among the nations who rejected the Lord and the words of His servants shall no longer dwell with the righteous, but will be cast out of their presence where the Lord presides. They once refused to listen to His holy words; they would not hearken unto the voice by which God's children are called, and therefore they were not prepared to receive the blessings that the atoning blood of Christ had made available to them.

They will be resurrected beings, but Abinadi said of them, that they are carnal and devilish, doing the will of the devil and thus being subject to him.

We also include at this point the words of Alma to another of his sons, Corianton, which explains and makes clear the prophecy of Abinadi found in the verses under discussion:

But behold, it was appointed unto man to die—therefore, as they were cut off from the tree of life they should be cut off from the face of the earth—and man became lost forever, yea they became fallen man.

2. Christize the Only Redeemer.

8. But there is a resurrection, therefore the grave hath no victory, and the sting of death is swallowed up in Christ.
9. He is the light and the life of the world; yea, a light that is endless, that can never be darkened; yea, and also a life which is endless, that there can be no more death.

And now, ye see by this that our first parents were cut off both temporally and spiritually from the presence of the Lord; and thus we see they became subjects to follow after their own will.

Now behold, it was not expedient that man should be reclaimed from this temporal death, for that would destroy the great plan of happiness.

Therefore, as the soul could never die, and the fall had brought upon all mankind a spiritual death as well as a temporal, that is, they were cut off from the presence of the Lord, it was expedient that mankind should be reclaimed from this spiritual death.

Therefore, as they had become carnal, sensual, and devilish, by nature, this probationary state became a state for them to prepare; it became a preparatory state.

And now remember, my son, if it were not for the plan of redemption, (laying it aside) as soon as they were dead their souls were miserable, being cut off from the presence of the Lord.

And now, there was no means to reclaim men from this fallen state, which man had brought upon himself because of his own disobedience;

Therefore, according to justice, the plan of redemption could not be brought about, only on conditions of repentance of men in this probationary state, yea, this preparatory state; for except it were for these conditions, mercy could not take effect except it should destroy the work of justice. Now the work of justice could not be destroyed; if so, God would cease to be God.

And thus we see that all mankind were fallen, and they were in the grasp of justice; yea, the justice of God, which consigned them forever to be cut off from his presence.

And now, the plan of mercy could not be brought about except an atonement should be made; therefore God himself atoneth for the sins of the world, to bring about the plan of mercy, to appease the demands of justice, that God might be a perfect, just God, and a merciful God also.   (Alma 42:6-15)

VERSES 7-8. *The grave should have no victory, and death should have no sting.* The preaching of the Prophet Abinadi to King Noah and his priests reminds one of the Apostle Paul when he proclaimed the resurrection of the dead to the Corinthians. Paul was a very little man, he was lame and personally unimpressive, as he, himself, declared in one of his epistles.

Clothed in a body of such mean proportions, and plagued by weaknesses of the flesh gnawing at his side, the Apostle, feeling his infirmities but realizing his victory over death, solemnly laid his hands upon his breast and we imagine he said, "You may wonder at it, ye sophists of Greece and you incredulous of Rome, but this poor, miserable, decrepit body you see, with all these certain traces of death shall be swallowed up in everlasting and glorious victory." "O death," he said, "where is thy sting? O grave, where is thy victory?" And then, in a most triumphant voice he cried, "Thanks be to God, which giveth us the victory through our LORD Jesus Christ." (I Corinthians 15:55-57)

VERSE 9. *He is the light and the life of the world.* The whole Book of Mosiah is replete with words spoken by kings and prophets which signify to us the lofty heights that were attained by the Nephites of old. This verse contains some of them. When we consider the wonderful sentiments that are expressed therein, and

3. Resurrection and Judgment.

10. Even this mortal shall put on immortality, and this corruption shall put on incorruption, and shall be brought to stand before the bar of God, to be judged of him according to their works whether they be good or whether they be evil—

---

the depth of spiritual philosophy they make plain to our understanding, we become amazed at the knowledge these ancient people of the Americas had for their guidance and inspiration.

VERSES 10-13. *This mortal shall put on immortality.* It is remarkable that many of the same thoughts inspired the Nephite servants of God as later they did His servants in and about Jerusalem. Often the same words were spoken concerning the same doctrine. We need not wonder at this, because, when we remember the same God, or His Spirit, directed the utterances of His inspired teachers and evangelists we must, necessarily, expect to find the same phraseology, more or less. Then, again, His teachings are perfect; they cannot be improved upon.

Here is what the Apostle Paul said, also to the Corinthians:

Now this I say, brethren, that flesh and blood cannot inherit the kingdom of God; neither doth corruption inherit incorruption.

Behold, I shew you a mystery; We shall not all sleep, but we shall all be changed.

In a moment, in the twinkling of an eye, at the last trump: for the trumpet shall sound, and the dead shall be raised incorruptible, and we shall be changed.

For this corruptible must put on incorruption, and this mortal must put on immortality.

So when this corruptible shall have put on incorruption, and this mortal shall have put on immortality, then shall be brought to pass the saying that is written, Death is swallowed up in victory.

Shall be brought before the bar of God, to be judged of him according to their works. See the following references:

2 Nephi	28:23	And be judged according to their works
	29:11	Every man according to their w.
Mosiah	16:10	To be judged of him according to their w.
Alma	3:26	Read their rewards, according to their w.
	11:41	And be judged according to their w.
	44	To be judged according to their w.
	12:8	To be judged according to their w.?
	33:22	To be judged . . . according to their w.
	40:21	And be judged according to their w.
	41:3	Should be judged according to their w.
	42:23	To be judged according to their w.
Helaman	12:24	For grace, according to their w.
3 Nephi	27:15	May be judged according to their w.

Of their works—

1 Nephi	15:32	They must be judged of their w.
	33	Before God, to be judged of their w.
2 Nephi	9:44	When all men shall be judged of their w.
Alma	9:28	All men shall reap a reward of their w.
	40:26	The fruits of their labors or their w.
3 Nephi	26:4	Before God, to be judged of their w.

11. If they be good, to the resurrection of endless life and happiness; and if they be evil, to the resurrection of endless damnation being delivered up to the devil, who hath subjected them, which is damnation—

12. Having gone according to their own carnal wills and desires; having never called upon the Lord while the arms of mercy were extended towards them; for the arms of mercy were extended towards them, and they would not; they being warned of their iniquities and yet they would not depart from them; and they were commanded to repent and yet they would not repent.

13. And now, ought ye not to tremble and repent of your sins, and remember that only in and through Christ ye can be saved?

| 27:12 | For it is because of their w. that they are hewn down |
| 14 | Stand before me to be judged of their w. |

Judgment day or day of judgment—

2 Nephi	9:22	Before him at the great and judgment day
	46	Even the d. of judgment, that ye may
Mosiah	3:24	Testimony against this people, at the judgment d.
Alma	9:15	More tolerable for them in the d. of judgment
	33:22	To be judged at the last and judgment d.
Helaman	8:25	Heaping . . . wrath against the d. of judgment
3 Nephi	28:32	Wrought by them, before that judgment
	40	To remain until the judgment d. of
Mormon	7:7	Found guiltless before him at the judgment d.
	10	Shall be well with you in the d. of judgment

VERSE 11. *If they be good, to the resurrection of endless life and happiness.* As we have noted all men will be brought forth from the grave, and will be judged "according to their works." The following passages from the Book of Mormon will further enlighten us regarding the Resurrection and the Day of Judgment:

And I said unto them that our father also saw that the justice of God did also divide the wicked from the righteous; and the brightness thereof was like unto the brightness of a flaming fire, which ascendeth up unto God forever and ever, and hath no end.

And they said unto me: Doth this thing mean the torment of the body in the days of probation, or doth it mean the final state of the soul after the death of the temporal body, or doth it speak of the things which are temporal?

And it came to pass that I said unto them that it was a representation of things both temporal and spiritual; for the day should come that they must be judged of their works, yea, even the works which were done by the temporal body in their days of probation.

Wherefore, if they should die in their wickedness they must be cast off also, as to the things which are spiritual, which are pertaining to righteousness; wherefore, they must be brought to stand before God, to be judged of their works; and if their works have been filthiness they must needs be filthy; and if they be filthy it must needs be that they cannot dwell in the kingdom of God; if so, the kingdom of God must be filthy also.

But behold, I say unto you, the kingdom of God is not filthy, and there cannot

14. Therefore, if ye teach the law of Moses, also teach that it is a shadow of those things which are to come—

15. Teach them that redemption cometh through Christ the Lord, who is the very Eternal Father. Amen.

---

any unclean thing enter into the kingdom of God; wherefore there must needs be a place of filthiness prepared for that which is filthy.

And there is a place prepared, yea, even that awful hell of which I have spoken, and the devil is the foundation of it; wherefore the final state of the souls of men is to dwell in the kingdom of God, or to be cast out because of that justice of which I have spoken.

Wherefore, the wicked are rejected from the righteous, and also from that tree of life, whose fruit is most precious and most desirable above all other fruits; yea, and it is the greatest of all the gifts of God. And thus I spake unto my brethren. Amen.   (1 Nephi 15:30-36)

And he doth not dwell in unholy temples; neither can filthiness or anything which is unclean be received into the kingdom of God; therefore I say unto you the time shall come, yea, and it shall be at the last day, that he who is filthy shall remain in his filthiness.   (Alma 7:21)

And because of the redemption of man, which came by Jesus Christ, they are brought back into the presence of the Lord; yea, this is wherein all men are redeemed, because the death of Christ bringeth to pass the resurrection, which bringeth to pass a redemption from an endless sleep, from which sleep all men shall be awakened by the power of God when the trump shall sound; and they shall come forth, both small and great, and all shall stand before his bar, being redeemed and loosed from this eternal band of death, which death is temporal death.

And then cometh the judgment of the Holy One upon them; and then cometh the time that he that is filthy shall be filthy still; and he that is righteous shall be righteous still; he that is happy shall be happy still; and he that is unhappy shall be unhappy still.   (Mormon 7:13-14)

VERSES 14-15. *Therefore, if ye teach the law of Moses.* Abinadi brought his great sermon to an end with the conclusion that the Law of Moses is but a foreshadowing of the Atoning Sacrifice of Christ. He warned the priests of King Noah to teach "it is a shadow of those things which are to come." "Teach them that redemption cometh through Christ the Lord, who is the very Eternal Father. Amen."

When we read the prophetic sermon by Abinadi, we think of the 23rd Psalm of King David. "Yea, though I walk through the valley in* the shadow of death, I will fear no evil: for thou art with me; thy rod and thy staff they comfort me." *Thy rod and thy staff* is *the Word of God.* The Bible and the Book of Mormon bring comfort to every heart. They strengthen the weak, and uphold the falling; they give courage and hope from above.

In this beautiful poem the Psalmist sings of man's journey through life which he calls *a valley.* Always, he says that we are *overshadowed* by death. *Life* is a *valley,* and *death* casts a *shadow.* But it has been said, "There can be no *shadow* unless there is *sunshine.*" And that *sunshine* is the *Word of the Lord;* the word of *Him* who is the *Son of Righteousness,* the *Light of the World.*

Thy rod and thy staff they comfort me. There are many roads that traverse this valley. Some are pleasant, others are rough. But always, when at last we

---

*We have changed the preposition *OF* to *IN.* We think it is the better interpretation. *The valley of the shadow of death* is just a name; *In the shadow of death,* gives meaning to what is otherwise only a beautiful expression.

realize our day's pilgrimage on earth is nearly ended, and the shadows of night
begin to gather about us, the *Word of the Lord* spreads over us a canopy of peace
and fills our hearts with a joyous hope of life everlasting.

We no longer fear that of which we had been most afraid, and death, itself,
instead of being a dark and gloomy chasm through which we must pass and where
despair and anguish take possession of our souls, has now become illumined with
God's glory, because as we enter that land "where all have gone and all must go,"
we see emblazoned upon the very portals of Eternal Life the words of our Lord and
Savior, Jesus of Nazareth, "I am the resurrection, and the life: he that believeth in
me, though he were dead, yet shall he live: And whosoever liveth and believeth
in me shall never die."

Dear Reader, these are teachings of the Book of Mormon in the language of
the Bible.

REDEEM

2 Nephi	2:26	May r. the children of men from the fall
	4:31	O Lord, wilt thou r. my soul?
	7:2	My hand shortened at all that it cannot r.
Mosiah	15:12	To r. them from their transgressions
	27	Neither can the Lord r. such
Alma	9:27	He cometh to r. those who will be baptized
	19:13	He shall r. all mankind who believe on
	21:7	The Son of God shall come to r. mankind
Helaman	5:9	Remember that He cometh to r. the world
	10	Should not come to r. them in their sins
	10	But to r. them from their sins
	11	He hath power ... to r. them from their
	13:19	None shall r. it because of the curse
	14:2	Then cometh the Son of God to r. all
Ether	3:14	Foundation of the world to r. my people
	8:8	A plan whereby she could r. the kingdom

Redeem His people—

Mosiah	13:33	And that God should r. His people
	15:1	Children of men, and shall r. His people
	11	Believed that the Lord would r. His
Alma	5:21	Who should come to r. His people
	27	Christ, who will come to r. His people
	6:8	Who should come to r. His people
	11:40	Come into the world to r. His people
	33:22	That He will come to r. His people
Helaman	5:10	The Lord surely should come to r. His people

Redeemed—

1 Nephi	20:20	The Lord hath r. His servant Jacob
2 Nephi	1:15	The Lord hath r. my soul from hell
	2:3	Wherefore, I know that thou art r.
	26	Because that they are r. from the fall
	8:11	The r. of the Lord shall return
	27:33	Saith the Lord, who r. Abraham
	33:6	For He hath r. my soul from hell
Mosiah	12:23	Having r. them, and satisfied the demands
	15:9	He hath r. Jerusalem

	18	Even the Lord, who has r. His people
	23	To dwell with God who has r. them
	24	Eternal life, being r. by the Lord
	27	For the Lord hath r. none such
	30	He hath r. Jerusalem
	16:4	Were it not that God r. His people
	18:9	That ye may be r. of God
	20	The Lord, who had r. His people
	26:26	But they would not be r.
	27:24	And have been r. of the Lord
	25	Being r. of God, becoming His sons
	29	My soul hath been r. from the gall
Alma	1:4	Created all men, and had also r. all
	12:18	For they cannot be r. according to God's
	41:7	These are they that are r. of the Lord
	46:39	Firmly believing that their souls were r.
	58:41	God, who has r. us and made us free
Helaman	8:23	That they were r. by Him
3 Nephi	16:19	Comforted His people, He hath r. Jerusalem
	20:13	The Lord their God, who hath r. them
	24	He hath r. Jerusalem
	38	And ye shall be r. without money
Moroni	9:13	Yea, this is wherein all men are r.
	13	R. and loosed from this eternal band
Ether	3:13	Because thou knowest these things, ye are r.

REDEEMER

Of their Redeemer—

1 Nephi	15:14	Also to the knowledge of the Gospel of their R.
	14	They shall come to the knowledge of their R.
2 Nephi	6:11	Shall come to the knowledge of their R.
	10:2	Give them the true knowledge of their R.
Mosiah	18:10	Came to the knowledge of their R.
	27:36	Yea, to the knowledge of their R.
Alma	37:10	To the knowledge of their R.
Helaman	15:13	Which is the knowledge of their R.

Their Redeemer—

1 Nephi	10:14	The true Messiah, their Lord and their R.
	17:30	Their R., going before them
	19:18	They would remember the Lord their R.
	23	Persuade them to believe in the Lord their R.
	22:12	And their R., the Mighty One of Israel
2 Nephi	1:10	Their R. and their God
Mosiah	26:26	That I am their R.; but they would not
Alma	37:9	To rejoice in Jesus Christ their R.
3 Nephi	5:26	Then shall they know their R.
	10:10	Unto the Lord Jesus Christ, their R.
	16:4	Brought to a knowledge of me, their R.

Redeemer—

1 Nephi	10:5	Or this R. of the world
	6	Save they should rely on this R. of the world

	11:27	I looked and beheld the R. of the world
	20:17	Thus saith the Lord, thy R.
	21:7	Thus saith the Lord, the R. of Israel
	26	And thy R., the Mighty One of Jacob
2 Nephi	2:3	Because of the righteousness of thy R.
	6:18	And thy R., the Mighty One of Jacob
	11:2	He verily saw my R., even as I have seen
	28:5	The R. hath done His work
	31:17	That your Lord and your R. should do
Enos	1:27	My rest, which is with my R.
Alma	7:7	The R. liveth and cometh among His people
	19:13	As thou liveth . . . I have seen my R.
	28:8	The R. of all men, bless their souls for
	61:14	In the cause of our R. and our God
Helaman	5:11	Which bringeth unto the power of the R.
	12	It is upon the rock of our R.
3 Nephi	22:5	And thy R. the Holy One of Israel
	8	Mercy on thee, saith the Lord thy R.
Moroni	8:8	Listen to the words of Christ, your R.

Redeemeth—

Mosiah	15:26	For the Lord r. none such
	16:2	Therefore the Lord r. them not
Helaman	14:16	R. all mankind from the first death
	17	The resurrection of Christ r. mankind

Redeeming—

Alma	5:9	And they did sing r. love
	26	Felt to sing the song of r. love
	26:13	They are brought to sing r. love

REDEMPTION

Plan of Redemption—

Jacob	6:8	To make a mock of the great plan of r.?
Alma	12:25	If it had not been for the plan of r.
	25	But there was a plan of r. laid
	26	The plan of r. would have been frustrated
	30	And made known unto them the plan of r.
	32	Having made known unto them the plan of r.
	32	For on such the plan of r. could have
	33	(This being the plan of r. which was laid
	17:16	Bring them to know the plan of r.
	18:39	Expounded unto them the plan of r.
	22:13	Their carnal state and also the plan of r.
	29:2	Repentance, and the plan of r.
	34:16	About the great and eternal plan of r.
	31	The great plan of r. be brought about
	39:18	Necessary that the plan of r. should be
	42:11	If it were not for the plan of r.
	13	The plan of r. could not be brought

Redemption—

1 Nephi	1:19	And also the r. of the world
2 Nephi	2:6	R. cometh in and through the Holy Messiah
Jacob	6:9	That the power of the r. and the resurrection
Omni	1:26	Salvation, and the power of his r.
Wd. of Mormon	8	Yea, the r. of Christ
Mosiah	13:32	Except it were through the r. of God
	15:19	Were it not for the r. which he hath
	16:5	As though there was no r. made
	6	There could have been no r.
	15	R. cometh through Christ the Lord
	18:2	And the r. of the people
	7	Preach unto them repentance and r.
	13	Life, through the r. of Christ
Alma	5:15	Do ye exercise faith in the r.?
	11:41	As though there had been no r. made
	12:18	As though there had been no r. made
	13:2	To look forward to his Son for r.
	3	A preparatory r. for such
	15:8	If thou believest in the r. of Christ
	21:9	There could be no r. for mankind
	26:36	And my r. from everlasting wo
	34:7	R. cometh through the Son of God
	42.26	Thus cometh the r. of men
Helaman	8:18	That even r. should come unto them
3 Nephi	6:20	Testifying unto them concerning the r.
	9:17	By me r. cometh, and in me is the law
	21	To bring r. unto the world
Mormon	7:7	Brought to pass the r. of the world
	9:12	Because of Jesus Christ came the r.
	13	Because of the r. of man, which came
	13	Bringeth . . . a r. from an endless sleep
Moroni	7:38	As though there had been no r. made
	8:20	Atonement of him and the power of his r.
	22	For the power of r. cometh on all

RESURRECTION—

Mosiah	15:21	Even until the r. of Christ
Alma	40:16	Down to the r. of Christ
	18	From the days of Adam, down to the r. of Christ
	19	Who die after the r. of Christ
	20	Cometh at the r. of Christ
	20	The r. of Christ, and his ascension
	41:2	The power and r. of Christ
Helaman	14:17	The r. of Christ redeemeth mankind
3 Nephi	6:20	Or in other words, the r. of Christ

Resurrection of the dead—

2 Nephi	2:8	Bring to pass the r. of the dead
Mosiah	13:35	Bring to pass the r. of the dead
	15:20	He bringeth to pass the r. of the dead
	18:2	Concerning the r. of the dead

	26:2	Concerning the r. of the dead
Alma	4:14	Because of the r. of the dead
	12:8	Concerning the r. of the dead
	24	Is after the r. of the dead
	25	Could have been no r. of the dead
	25	Bring to pass the r. of the dead
	16:19	And also the r. of the dead
	21:9	Concerning the r. of the dead
	40:1	Worried concerning the r. of the dead
	3	Bringeth to pass the r. of the dead
	3	That is concerning the r.
	42:23	Bringeth to pass the r. of the dead
	23	And the r. of the dead bringeth back man into the presence
Helaman	14:15	He dieth, to bring to pass the r. of
Mormon	7:6	He bringeth to pass the r. of the dead
Alma	11:45	Concerning the r. of the mortal body

First resurrection—

Mosiah	15:21	Cometh a r., even a first r.
	22	Shall come forth in the first r.
	22	Therefore, they are the first r.
	24	Are those who have a part in the first r.
	24	And they have a part in the first r.
	26	That have no part in the first r.
	18:9	Numbered with those of the first r.
Alma	40:15	Before the r., was a first r.
	16	There is a first r.; a r. of all those
	17	We do not suppose that this first r.

Of the resurrection—

2 Nephi	9:12	It is by the power of the r. of the Holy One
	10:25	From death by the power of the r.
Jacob	4:11	According to the power of the r.
Alma	4:14	Joy, because of the r. of the dead

Resurrection—

2 Nephi	9:6	Must needs be a power of r.
	6	And the r. must needs come unto man by reason of the fall
	22	That the r. might pass upon all
	26:3	Birth, and also of his death and r.
Jacob	4:11	That ye may obtain a r.
	12	To attain to a knowledge of a r.?
	6:9	And the r. which is in Christ
Mosiah	15:21	And there cometh a r.
	21	Even a r. of those that have been
	22	The r. of all the prophets, and all
	16:7	There could have been no r.
	8	But there is a r., therefore the grave
	11	If they be good, to a r. of endless
	11	If they be evil, to a r. of endless

CHAPTER 17

1. *Martyrdom of Abinadi—2. While Suffering Death by Fire He Predicts Retribution upon His Murderers—3. Conversion of Alma.*

1. Martyrdom of Abinadi.

1. And now it came to pass that when Abinadi had finished these sayings, that the king commanded that the priests should take him and cause that he should be put to death.

2. But there was one among them whose name was Alma, he also being a descendant of Nephi. And he was a young man, and he believed the words which Abinadi had spoken, for he knew concerning the iniquity which Abinadi has testified against them; therefore he began to plead with the king that he would not be angry with Abinadi, but suffer that he might depart in peace.

3. But the king was more wroth, and caused that Alma should be cast out from among them, and sent his servants after him that they might slay him.

4. But he fled from before them and hid himself that they found him not. And he being concealed for many days did write all the words which Abinadi had spoken.

5. And it came to pass that the king caused that his guards should surround Abinadi and take

---

VERSE 1. *King Noah commanded that Abinadi be put to death, and is defended by Alma.* The teachings of Abinadi were exactly what the infidel priests of King Noah did not want to hear. The wickedness that had blackened King Noah's hard heart lay hold of him and carried him down to depths where a righteous appeal could not be heard. His intemperance had led him from the paths of duty and loyalty that his contemporary, King Benjamin, in Zarahemla, walked. King Noah had no discernment; he did not understand, and, therefore, he could not fulfill the words of Abinadi; he was callous and wine had made him dull. The demands of justice, of right and wrong, were imperceptible to his senses. He ordered his priests to seize and slay Abinadi.

VERSES 2-3. *Alma believed the words Abinadi had spoken.* However, all the people did not, in their hearts, consent to Abinadi's death. One among them, especially, whose name was Alma "believed the words Abinadi had spoken." He knew that the grave charges that the prophet made were true. Alma was a young man, one of Noah's priests, and when the clamor was highest for Abinadi's death, he went to King Noah and pleaded in Abinadi's behalf. This so angered Noah that he had Alma cast out of his presence, and then sent his servants after the young priest to slay him also.

VERSE 4. *In concealment, Alma "did write all the words which Abinadi had spoken."* Alma hid from his pursuers, and during the many days that his presence was unknown to the guards of King Noah, he wrote down all the words he had heard Abinadi speak. The words of this holy prophet, as they are recorded by Alma, form one of the most important parts of the doctrinal portions of the Book of Mormon. They testify of the Messiah, Christ, the only Redeemer; of His Resurrection, and the Day of Judgment.

him; and they bound him and cast him into prison.

6. And after three days, having counseled with his priests, he caused that he should again be brought before him.

7. And he said unto him: Abinadi, we have found an accusation against thee, and thou art worthy of death.

8. For thou hast said that God himself should come down among the children of men; and now, for this cause thou shalt be put to death unless thou wilt recall all the words which thou hast spoken evil concerning me and my people.

9. Now Abinadi said unto him:

I say unto you, I will not recall the words which I have spoken unto you concerning this people, for they are true; and that ye may know of their surety I have suffered myself that I have fallen into your hands.

10. Yea, and I will suffer even until death, and I will not recall my words, and they shall stand as a testimony against you. And if ye slay me ye will shed innocent blood, and this shall also stand as a testimony against you at the last day.

11. And now king Noah was about to release him, for he feared his word; for he feared that the judgments of God would come upon him.

VERSES 5-8. *Abinadi is accused and "thou art worthy of death."* Abinadi was cast into prison by the guards of King Noah, who, having counseled with the king's priests, decided to give Abinadi a chance to repudiate his words. This Abinadi refused to do although he was threatened with death for failing to comply.

The exact crime for which Abinadi was accused was, "Thou hast said that God himself should come down among the children of men." This accusation was only an excuse, a pretext for them to slay righteous Abinadi. King Noah and his priests smarted most because they knew Abinadi spoke truthfully of their wicked ways. Therefore, they wished to be rid of the reproach by doing away with their accuser. This vindictive mode of thinking is always a common way of escape with those who believe they can do no wrong, and also to those who seek an excuse. They writhe under indictment.

King Noah let it be known to the Prophet Abinadi, that if he would recall the words "which thou hast spoken evil concerning me and my people," then he would not be put to death.

VERSES 9-11. *Abinadi said, "I will not recall the words which I have spoken . . . for they are true."* One of the most common devices to which mankind often resorts, is to contrive an excuse which one may impose upon another's back, all responsibility for one's own misdeeds. Abinadi had accused Noah of great wrongdoing. Noah stood guilty in the eyes of his people. The prophet was vehement in the charges he made. With an increasing fury, Abinadi recalled the wickedness of King Noah. He had been everything but what the name *King* implied, a *Father*.

To prove to his people that Abinadi was wrong, King Noah contrived a stratagem. He thought if he offered Abinadi an excuse or a pretext whereby Abinadi could escape punishment for the crime of which the prophet had been declared guilty, and if he made it so tempting that Abinadi would accept it, he would then be

2. *While suffering death by fire Abinadi predicts retribution upon his murderers.*

12. But the priests lifted up their voices against him, and began to accuse him, saying: He has reviled the king. Therefore the king was stirred up in anger against him, and he delivered him up that he might be slain.

13. And it came to pass that they took him and bound him, and scourged his skin with faggots, yea, even unto death.

14. And now when the flames began to scorch him, he cried unto them, saying:

15. Behold, even as ye have done unto me, so shall it come to pass that thy seed shall cause that many shall suffer even the pains of death by fire; and this because they believe in the salvation of the Lord their God.

16. And it will come to pass that ye shall be afflicted with all manner of diseases because of your iniquities.

17. Yea, and ye shall be smitten on every hand, and shall be

---

relieved of all liability as to Abinadi's death. "Recant what you have said, or die." The choice was left to the prophet.

"I will not recall the words which I have spoken . . . for they are true, and if ye slay me ye will shed innocent blood, and this shall stand against you at the last day."

The king became faint. He had been eager to accept a trumped-up apology from Abinadi, which did not come. At length King Noah grew worried. He was about to release Abinadi "for he feared his word" and also, he feared "the judgments of God would come upon him."

VERSES 12-13. *But the priests lifted up their voices against him.* The priests grew more intolerant of Abinadi's words as the prophet refused to recant what he had said. They twisted and turned the meaning of his warnings so that the king became exceeding angry. Noah's anger flared fiercely as they accused Abinadi of using abusive and insulting speech toward him. The priests said, "He has reviled the king." This ribald accusation stirred up Noah's pride and arrogance to a point where he could no longer resist their evil clamor, "and he delivered him up that he might be slain."

VERSES 14-19. *When the flames began to scorch him, he cried unto them, saying.* The Prophet Abinadi, pronounced guilty by the loathsome King Noah and sentenced by him to die, calmly looked about the king's chambers and expressed no regrets. He offered no excuses, nor did he plead for mercy or for clemency. What mattered most to him, "*he had proclaimed the message God sent him to deliver!*"

In spite of the scorn King Noah's people had for Abinadi's words, and the contempt they showed in refusing to obey them, Abinadi was true to the promise he had made, "I finish my message." (Mosiah 13:9)

Led forth by Noah's wicked priests and by the clamoring throng that in carnival spirit had gathered to mock him, the prophet was hastened to his place of death and neither flinched nor feared his coming doom.

As the flames of the martyr's pyre began to scorch his weary frame, Abinadi cried unto them, saying many terrible things that would happen unto them: That because many Lamanites should "believe in the salvation of the Lord their God," their seed driven and scattered to and fro, even as a wild flock is driven by wild and ferocious beasts.

18. And in that day ye shall be hunted, and ye shall be taken by the hand of your enemies, and then ye shall suffer, as I suffer, the pains of death by fire.

19. Thus God executeth vengeance upon those that destroy his people. O God, receive my soul.

---

would cause them to "suffer the pains of death by fire," even as "ye have done unto me." Also, because of iniquity among them, pestilence and disease would be sowed broadcast. In addition to that, he said, "Yea, and ye shall be smitten on every hand, and shall be driven and scattered to and fro, even as a wild flock is driven by wild and ferocious beasts."

Abinadi continued his prophecy, and in a few years all his words were fulfilled: King Noah suffered death by fire even by the same hands and in the same manner that Abinadi had been put to death. The Lamanites invaded the lands of the Nephites, and they stole many of their flocks and herds and much of the grain they had stored. They were driven from their homes and were hunted as the hunter follows his game. Sickness and disease made them an easy prey to their unpitying enemies. Indeed, they became a pitiful lot.

One can easily recall Alma's account concerning the fulfillment of Abinadi's prophetic denouncement:

And behold, now it came to pass that those Lamanites were more angry because they had slain their brethren; therefore they swore vengeance upon the Nephites; and they did no more attempt to slay the people of Anti-Nephi-Lehi at that time.

But they took their armies and went over into the borders of the land of Zarahemla, and fell upon the people who were in the land of Ammonihah, and destroyed them.

And after that, they had many battles with the Nephites, in the which they were driven and slain.

And among the Lamanites who were slain were almost all the seed of Amulon and his brethren, who were the priests of Noah, and they were slain by the hands of the Nephites;

And the remainder, having fled into the east wilderness, and having usurped the power and authority over the Lamanites, caused that many of the Lamanites should perish by fire because of their belief—

For many of them, after having suffered much loss and so many afflictions, began to be stirred up in remembrance of the words which Aaron and his brethren had preached to them in their land; therefore they began to disbelieve the traditions of their fathers, and to believe in the Lord, and that he gave great power unto the Nephites; and thus there were many of them converted in the wilderness.

And it came to pass that those rulers who were the remnant of the children of Amulon caused that they should be put to death, yea, all those that believed in these things.

Now this martyrdom caused that many of their brethren should be stirred up to anger; and there began to be contention in the wilderness; and the Lamanites began to hunt the seed of Amulon and his brethren and began to slay them; and they fled into the east wilderness.

And behold they are hunted at this day by the Lamanites. Thus the words of Abinadi were brought to pass, which he said concerning the seed of the priests who caused that he should suffer death by fire.

For he said unto them: What ye shall do unto me shall be a type of things to come.

And now Abinadi was the first that suffered death by fire because of his belief in God; now this is what he meant, that many should suffer death by fire, according as he had suffered.

20. And now, when Abinadi had said these words, he fell, having suffered death by fire; yea, having been put to death because he would not deny the commandments of God, having sealed the truth of his words by his death.

And he said unto the priests of Noah that their seed should cause many to be put to death in the like manner as he was, and that they should be scattered abroad and slain, even as sheep having no shepherd is driven and slain by wild beasts; and now behold, these words were verified, for they were driven by the Lamanites, and they were hunted, and they were smitten. (Alma 25:1-12)

The events of the next few years following the martyrdom of Abinadi are a complete commentary on the fulfillment of his dying words: "Thus God executeth vengeance upon those that destroy his people," and with saying that, he cried aloud, "O God receive my soul."

VERSE 20. *And now, when Abinadi had said these words, he fell, having suffered death by fire.* For his testimony of Jesus among the people of Lehi-Nephi, Abinadi was consigned to the flames by wicked King Noah. Some of the disciples of our Lord were cast into furnaces of fire, although they were miraculously rescued, as had been the Three Hebrew Children in Babylon. (4 Nephi 32)

From these examples it appears that the peoples of the Book of Mormon were in the habit of committing captives to the flames.

Burning of prisoners was extensively practised by natives at the time of the arrival of the Spanish explorers. The Apaches used to put prisoners to death by fire.[1] In Tezcuco, the punishment for certain unnatural crimes was torture and burning at the stake.[2] At the festival in honor of Xiuhtecutli, the god of fire, the people raised a "May pole," elaborately decorated. At the appointed time, the officiating priests hurled a number of prisoners, stripped of clothing and bound hand and foot, upon a great heap of smoldering coals, where they suffered untold agony, until raked out and slaughtered on the altar, whereupon the people enjoyed themselves singing and dancing around the pole.[3] At the termination of an age—a cycle of fifty-two years was so called—the sacred fires were permitted to go out, and a new fire was kindled by friction of sticks placed on the breast of a wounded prisoner provided for that purpose. The flame was soon communicated to a funeral pyre on which the victim was consumed.[4] Surely there is historical connection between the flames of persecution recorded in the Book of Mormon and the cruelties practised, sometimes in behalf of "justice" and sometimes as religion, by the later occupants of American soil.

That the Jews in Palestine burned human victims in honor of Moloch is clear from Isaiah 30:33 and Ezekiel 20:26, and other passages.

---

[1]Bancroft, *Native Races*, Vol. 1, p. 498.
[2]*Ibid.*, Vol. 2, p. 467.
[3]*Ibid.*, Vol. 2, p. 329.
[4]Prescott, *Conquest of Mexico*, Vol. 3, p. 129.

CHAPTER 18

1. *The Waters of Mormon*—2. *Alma Baptizes Helam and Others*—3. *The Church of Christ Organized*—4. *King Noah Sends an Army to Destroy Alma and His Followers.*

1. *The Waters of Mormon.*

1. And now, it came to pass that Alma, who had fled from the servants of king Noah, repented of his sins and iniquities, and went about privately among the people, and began to teach the words of Abinadi—

2. Yea, concerning that which was to come, and also concerning the resurrection of the dead, and the redemption of the people, which was to be brought to pass through the power, and sufferings, and death of Christ, and his resurrection and ascension into heaven.

3. And as many as would hear his word he did teach. And he taught them privately, that it might not come to the knowledge of the king. And many did believe his words.

4. And it came to pass that as many as did believe him did go

---

VERSES 1-2. *Alma went about privately among the people, and began to teach them the words of Abinadi.* Mindful of his own safety, yet anxious in the cause of the Lord, Alma, from the seclusion of his hiding place, taught to everyone who would listen, the same great saving truths that he, as one of King Noah's priests, had heard Abinadi proclaim.

These teachings had sunk deeply into Alma's heart; he not only realized their truth, but also he comprehended their saving value. The first lesson they impressed upon his mind was the necessity of his own complete repentance. This he did, sincerely, and then he began to teach others the same lesson. Fearing the king, he did not teach openly, but secretly as the opportunities permitted. Alma had written down the words of Abinadi. We may presume, that they, who listened to him, had copies of the Hebrew Scriptures transcribed from the Plates of Brass. From them Alma was able to explain and expound the doctrines of the *Resurrection of the Dead,* the *Redemption of Mankind, Christ's Atoning Sacrifice, His Resurrection,* and *His Ascension into Heaven.* All of these doctrines, foreshadowed in the Law of Moses, the righteous Nephites thoroughly understood.

VERSES 3-7. *Those who believed in Alma's words went to a place which was called Mormon.* Alma's preaching of God's holy word was successful. Many accepted the truth with joy. Then they gathered to a place that was convenient, a spot on the borders of the wilderness not far from their city. This place was known as *Mormon,* having had that name given it by the king. It was admirably suited for a hiding place. It had formerly been infested by ravenous wild beasts, and was dreaded and avoided by the people. Near by was a thicket, or forest of small trees. Here the Gospel believers could hide should they be pursued by the king's servants; here also was a fountain of pure water, excellently adapted for the purposes of baptism. Here, Alma, with others of those who had shown a sincere repentance of their sins, organized the *Church of Christ,* and here, in the solitude of this primeval forest, the sacred rite of *baptism* was first administered to them that they, too, might obtain a remission of their sins.

forth to a place which was called Mormon, having received its name from the king, being in the borders of the land having been infested, by times or at seasons, by wild beasts.

5. Now, there was in Mormon a fountain of pure water, and Alma resorted thither, there being near the water a thicket of small trees, where he did hide himself in the daytime from the searches of the king.

6. And it came to pass that as many as believed him went thither to hear his words.

7. And it came to pass after many days there were a goodly number gathered together at the place of Mormon, to hear the words of Alma. Yea, all were gathered that believed on his word, to hear him. And he did teach them, and did preach unto them repentance, and redemption, and faith on the Lord.

2. Alma baptizes Helam and others.

8. And it came to pass that he said unto them: Behold, here are the waters of Mormon (for thus were they called) and now, as ye are desirous to come into the fold of God, and to be called his people, and are willing to bear one another's burdens, that they may be light;

9. Yea, and are willing to mourn with those that mourn; yea, and comfort those that stand in need of comfort, and to stand as witnesses of God at all times and in all things, and in all places

that ye may be in, even until death, that ye may be redeemed of God, and be numbered with those of the first resurrection, that ye may have eternal life—

10. Now I say unto you, if this be the desire of your hearts, what have you against being baptized in the name of the Lord, as a witness before him that ye have entered into a covenant with him, that ye will serve him and keep his commandments, that he may pour out his Spirit more abundantly upon you?

VERSES 8-9. *Behold, here are the waters of Mormon.* Alma was anxious to establish the Church of God in this land, as, no doubt, it had existed in the days when Nephi stood as its earthly head. Alma recognized that his brethren wanted to enter into the fold of Christ, and he also realized that they, too, desired to be called God's people, and wished to serve Him in deeds of loving-kindness to one another, and also that they might ease each other's burdens. Alma called on his converts to comfort the aching hearts of those who mourned, and also to bear witness of God at all times, not only by word of mouth, but also by keeping all His commandments, "that ye may have eternal life."

VERSES 10-16. *If this be the desire of your hearts, what have you against being baptized in the name of the Lord?* If, they, being willing to assume the obligations enumerated, and if they desiring to be redeemed of God, and longing to be numbered with those of the First Resurrection, he then asked, "What have you against being baptized in the name of the Lord?"

He explained to them, that as individuals, they would do this as a witness before

11. And now when the people had heard these words, they clapped their hands for joy, and exclaimed: This is the desire of our hearts.

12. And now it came to pass that Alma took Helam, he being one of the first, and went and stood forth in the water, and cried, saying: O Lord, pour out thy Spirit upon thy servant, that he may do this work with holiness of heart.

13. And when he had said these words, the Spirit of the Lord was upon him, and he said: Helam, I baptize thee, having authority from the Almighty God, as a testimony that ye have entered into a covenant to serve him until you are dead as to the mortal body; and may the Spirit of the Lord be poured out upon you; and may he grant unto you eternal life, through the redemption of Christ, whom he has prepared from the foundation of the world.

14. And after Alma had said these words, both Alma and Helam were buried in the water; and they arose and came forth out of the water rejoicing, being filled with the Spirit.

15. And again, Alma took another, and went forth a second time into the water, and baptized him according to the first, only he did not bury himself again in the water.

16. And after this manner he did baptize every one that went forth to the place of Mormon; and they were in number about two hundred and four souls; yea, and they were baptized in the waters of Mormon, and were filled with the grace of God.

God that they entered into a covenant with Him to do His will, and to keep His commandments. The blessings of the Lord would then be poured out upon them more abundantly.

VERSE 11. *This is the desire of our hearts.* The Sacred Record says that a goodly number heard this appeal made by Alma. Then, "They clapped their hands for joy, and exclaimed: This is the desire of our hearts." They evidently showed in some manner that they approved what Alma had said. A demonstration of this kind is little different than our exclamation, *Amen,* or the outcry of others when they shout, "*Hear, Hear,*" or "*Please Lord.*"

VERSES 12-16. *Alma took Helam, and went and stood forth in the water.* The first to go down into the waters of Mormon for baptism were Alma and a fellow believer named Helam. When they entered the water Alma lifted his voice in prayer, and besought the Lord for His Holy Spirit. This blessing having been bestowed, Alma proceeded with the sacred ordinance. The words of the ordinance which were later given by the Risen Redeemer to His servants in the Land Bountiful are different from those delivered by Alma on this occasion. Alma included a prayer for, we surmise, the benefit of Helam and also to impress on him and the others who waited for this glorious ministration, the importance of the covenant they made at that time. Alma then baptized Helam, immersing himself simultaneously.

Others, even unto the number of 204 souls, followed Helam into the waters of baptism, but in all these cases Alma did not again bury himself beneath the wave, but only the repentant sinners, or those who evidenced their determination to serve

17. And they were called the church of God, or the church of Christ, from that time forward. And it came to pass that whosoever was baptized by the power and authority of God was added to his church.

18. And it came to pass that Alma, having authority from God, ordained priests; even one priest to every fifty of their number did he ordain to preach unto them, and to teach them concerning the things pertaining to the kingdom of God.

19. And he commanded them that they should teach nothing save it were the things which he had taught, and which had been spoken by the mouth of the holy prophets.

20. Yea, even he commanded them that they should preach nothing save it were repentance and faith on the Lord, who had redeemed his people.

God. From this time we may date the organization of the Church of Jesus Christ in that land, and henceforth its members assembled for worship and testimony once a week.

VERSE 17. *And they were called the church of God, or the church of Christ.* See Concordance of the word *Church* at end of this chapter (18).

VERSES 18-23. *Alma . . . ordained priests.* Alma, having baptized all those who desired it and who showed by their works that they fully deserved to have the sacred ordinance performed, went a step further in the organization of the new Church. Holding the Holy Priesthood himself, he ordained other priests to teach the members of the Church "concerning the things pertaining to the kingdom of God." Alma appointed one priest to every fifty members of the Church who was to preach to them and lead them as he should direct.

Alma's instructions to the priests he had appointed were definite. He saw many pitfalls in the paths they had recently trod under the leadership of Noah's priests. Things that had been taught by these priests were unworthy of God's children, and, besides, many of their teachings were downright wicked. Therefore, Alma commanded those over whom he presided to teach nothing save they already had heard him declare it to be true.

Teach and preach nothing save it be "repentance and faith on the Lord, who had redeemed his people."

If we, in preaching the Gospel, would abide Alma's instructions, how many differences of opinion would we avoid. Repentance from wicked ways is necessary, and then baptism is enjoined upon us. These doctrines are undisputable among us, but when we venture outside what is divinely made known we enter a realm of imagination where "houses of cards" are built. Sooner or later, when opposition arises, they will fall as will a house built upon sand. Then we will find that we have been false interpreters of a grand and glorious *Plan* which in the end will save all men through faith in the Lord Jesus Christ.

In this verse Alma speaks of the Lord as having already redeemed His people. Many of the ancient prophets spoke of Him in this tense. It is called, *prophetic past.*

Alma cautioned the newly ordained priests against contention among themselves. He said that they were not to tolerate any personal opinions, but to unitedly pro-

---

On page 199ff, of this COMMENTARY, a few choice passages from these Nephite Scriptures have been added to supplement our knowledge of this sacred ordinance, baptism. Also, *See* Vol. 1, p. 431 ff, COMMENTARY ON THE BOOK OF MORMON.

21. And he commanded them that there should be no contention one with another, but that they should look forward with one eye, having one faith and one baptism, having their hearts knit together in unity and in love one towards another.

22. And thus he commanded them to preach. And thus they became the children of God.

23. And he commanded them that they should observe the sabbath day, and keep it holy, and also every day they should give thanks to the Lord their God.

24. And he also commanded them that the priests whom he had ordained should labor with their own hands for their support.

25. And there was one day in every week that was set apart that they should gather themselves together to teach the people, and to worship the Lord their God, and also, as often as it was in their power, to assemble themselves together.

26. And the priests were not to depend upon the people for their support; but for their labor they were to receive the grace of God, that they might wax strong in the Spirit, having the knowledge of God, that they might teach with power and authority from God.

---

claim "one faith and one baptism, having their hearts knit together in unity and in love towards another." (*See* Ephesians 4:4-5)

VERSE 23. *Alma commanded the priests to observe the sabbath day.* This commandment repeated by Alma leads us to believe the people of Lehi-Nephi had been negligent in obeying the Fifth of the Ten Commandments given by the Lord to all Israel. (*See* Chapter 13:16-19)

VERSES 24-26. *The priests . . . should labor with their own hands.* When the Nephite Kingdom was first established the people were so few that they could not possibly sustain the expenses incidental to royalty. This, also, was true of those who held the priesthood, and spent a goodly portion of time in the work of the ministry. It became the rule for the kings to supply themselves with the necessary things of life, and to maintain the dignity of the office they held.

Alma commanded that this same excellent custom should be adopted by the priests he had appointed, and this same course of action was continued by the Nephites as long as they were ruled by kings, and even throughout the times when their nation had grown rich and numerous.

References:

Mosiah	2:14	Have labored with mine o. h.
	18:24	Should labor with their o. h.
	27:4	Laboring with their o. h. for their
	5	Should labor with their o. h. for
Alma	30:32	I have labored . . . with mine o. h.
	32:5	Labored . . . to build with our o. h.

Alma sensed the responsibility of the priests in teaching the word of the Lord to the people; he also knew that if the burden of providing for their wants was put on the shoulders other than their own, they might become slothful and indolent. His

27. And again Alma commanded that the people of the church should impart of their substance, every one according to that which he had; if he have more abundantly he should impart more abundantly; and of him that had but little; but little should be required; and to him that had not should be given.

28. And thus they should impart of their substance of their own free will and good desires towards God, and to those priests that stood in need, yea, and to every needy, naked soul.

29. And this he said unto them, having been commanded of God; and they did walk uprightly before God, imparting to one another both temporally and spiritually according to their needs and their wants.

30. And now it came to pass that all this was done in Mormon, yea, by the waters of Mormon, in the forest that was near the waters of Mormon; yea, the

---

thought was that if the priests were forced to rely on the abundant strength the Lord had given them, that then they would increase in grace and in the knowledge of His glory. We must not forget that *knowledge is* power, and in that *knowledge* they would teach "with power and authority from God." They would grow in the *favor* of God.

VERSES 27-29. *Alma commanded that every one should impart of his substance.* It is not strange to us that the same ideals which inspired the early followers of Christ, also the Saints of this dispensation as well as those wherever His Church is organized, are alike.

One of the Prophet Joseph Smith's first teachings was concerning the poor and the needy. He wanted no poor among us; from those who were rich as to the things of the world, he demanded a considerable portion. He gave to the needy, and to the sick and afflicted he provided for their wants; he kept little for his own.

In Acts of the Apostles, Second Chapter, verses 41-47, it tells when the great experiment of rendering equal all members of the Church was made a reality:

"And all that believed were together, and had all things common;

"And sold their possessions and goods, and parted them to all men, as every man had need."

One of the first Church fathers, who was born in the year A.D. 104, truthfully said to the Emperor at Rome:

"Those of us who before delighted in impunities now rejoice in sobriety; those who practiced the magical arts now have devoted themselves to the benevolent and eternal Father; those who sought to acquire wealth, above all things, now have their possessions in common, and give to him that needeth; those who hated and slaughtered each other, and being of different tribes had no intercourse after the appearance of Christ, living in the same communion, pray for enemies and endeavor to convert those that unjustly hate us." Justin Martyr.

VERSES 30-35. *They took their tents and their families and departed into the wilderness.* "and these things were done in the borders of the land, that they might not come to the knowledge of the king." (v. 31) Notwithstanding the care and secrecy with which the members of the Church acted, Noah soon discovered that there was some hidden movement among his subjects, and by the help of his spies he discovered what was taking place at Mormon. Making the tyrants' usual excuse, that the

place of Mormon, the waters of Mormon, the forest of Mormon, how beautiful are they to the eyes of them who there came to the knowledge of their Redeemer; yea, and how blessed are they, for they shall sing to his praise forever.

31. And these things were done in the borders of the land, that they might not come to the knowledge of the king.

32. But behold, it came to pass that the king, having discovered a movement among the people, sent his servants to watch them. Therefore on the day that they were assembling themselves to-gether to hear the word of the Lord they were discovered unto the king.

33. And now the king said that Alma was stirring up the people to rebellion against him; therefore he sent his army to destroy them.

34. And it came to pass that Alma and the people of the Lord were apprised of the coming of the king's army; therefore they took their tents and their families and departed into the wilderness.

35. And they were in number about four hundred and fifty souls.

Christians were in rebellion against him, he sent his armies to capture and destroy them. But a greater than he stretched forth His arm to preserve His people. The Lord warned Alma of the king's intentions, and by divine direction he assembled his people, some 450 souls, gathered their flocks and herds, loaded up their grain, provisions and other supplies, and departed into the wilderness.

BAPTISM

When Lehi was only a few miles away from Jerusalem, whence the Lord had commanded him to depart, he saw in a vision many of the great and important things that pertained to his descendants. The Prophet told his children about the things he saw, and Nephi, his son, wrote down many of them. Later, Nephi recorded them on metal plates which the Lord had instructed him to prepare.

Great and marvelous were the things Lehi spake concerning what he had seen.

And he spake also concerning a prophet who should come before the Messiah, to prepare the way of the Lord—

Yea, even he should go forth and cry in the wilderness: Prepare ye the way of the Lord, and make his paths straight; for there standeth one among you whom ye know not: and he is mightier than I, whose shoe's latchet I am not worthy to unloose. And much spake my father concerning this thing.

And my father said he should baptize in Bethabara, beyond Jordan; and he also said he should baptize the Messiah with water.

And after he had baptized the Messiah with water, he should behold and bear record that he had baptized the Lamb of God, who should take away the sins of the world. (1 Nephi 10:7-10)

Nephi, believing his father, was also desirous of seeing and hearing the same things that had been shown to him. One day while meditating upon these things, he was caught up by the Spirit of the Lord and was carried into an exceeding high mountain, where he saw in vision, among other things, the life and ministry of the Messiah, who was yet to come.

In the vision, an angel of the Lord acted as Nephi's guide, and explained to him the different scenes that were presented. The angel said, "Look," and Nephi later wrote:

And I looked and beheld the Redeemer of the world, of whom my father had spoken; and I also beheld the prophet who should prepare the way before him. And the Lamb of God went forth and was baptized of him; and after he was baptized, I beheld the heavens open, and the Holy Ghost come down out of heaven and abide upon him in the form of a dove. (1 Nephi 11:27)

The great truths Nephi learned, here, were taught to his brothers and were, also, engraved by him upon the plates he had made. He cautioned his brothers, saying,

Wherefore, I would that ye should remember that I have spoken unto you concerning that prophet which the Lord showed unto me, that should baptize the Lamb of God, which should take away the sins of the world.

And now, if the Lamb of God, he being holy, should have need to be baptized by water, to fulfil all righteousness, O then, how much more need have we, being unholy, to be baptized, yea, even by water!

And now, I would ask of you, my beloved brethren, wherein the Lamb of God did fulfil all righteousness in being baptized by water?

Know ye not that he was holy? But notwithstanding he being holy, he showeth unto the children of men that, according to the flesh he humbleth himself before the Father, and witnesseth unto the Father that he would be obedient unto him in keeping his commandments.

Wherefore, after he was baptized with water the Holy Ghost descended upon him in the form of a dove.

And again, it showeth unto the children of men the straightness of the path, and the narrowness of the gate, by which they should enter, he having set the example before them.

And he said unto the children of men: Follow thou me. Wherefore, my beloved brethren, can we follow Jesus save we shall be willing to keep the commandments of the Father?

And the Father said: Repent ye, repent ye, and be baptized in the name of my Beloved Son.

And also, the voice of the Son came unto me, saying: He that is baptized in my name, to him will the Father give the Holy Ghost, like unto me; wherefore, follow me, and do the things which ye have seen me do.

Wherefore, my beloved brethren, I know that if ye shall follow the Son, with full purpose of heart, acting no hypocrisy and no deception before God, but with real intent, repenting of your sins, witnessing unto the Father that ye are willing to take upon you the name of Christ, by baptism—yea, by following your Lord and your Savior down into the water, according to his word, behold, then shall ye receive the Holy Ghost; yea, then cometh the baptism of fire and of the Holy Ghost; and then can ye speak with the tongue of angels, and shout praises unto the Holy One of Israel.

But, behold, my beloved brethren, thus came the voice of the Son unto me, saying: After ye have repented of your sins, and witnessed unto the Father that ye are willing to keep my commandments, by the baptism of water, and have received the baptism of fire and of the Holy Ghost, and can speak with a new tongue, yea, even with the tongue of angels, and after this should deny me, it would have been better for you that ye had not known me.

And I heard a voice from the Father, saying: Yea, the words of my Beloved are true and faithful. He that endureth to the end, the same shall be saved.

And now, my beloved brethren, I know by this that unless a man shall endure to the end, in following the example of the Son of the living God, he cannot be saved.

Wherefore, do the things which I have told you I have seen that your Lord and your Redeemer should do; for, for this cause have they been shown unto me, that ye might know the gate by which ye should enter. For the gate by which ye should enter is repentance and baptism by water; and then cometh a remission of your sins by fire and by the Holy Ghost.

And then are ye in this straight and narrow path which leads to eternal life; yea, ye have entered in by the gate; ye have done according to the commandments of the Father and the Son; and ye have received the Holy Ghost, which witnesses of the Father and the Son, unto the fulfiling of the promise which he hath made, that if ye entered in by the way ye should receive.

And now my beloved brethren, after ye have gotten into this straight and narrow path, I would ask if all is done? Behold, I say unto you, Nay; for ye have not come thus far save it were by the word of Christ with unshaken faith in him, relying wholly upon the merits of him who is mighty to save.

Wherefore, ye must press forward with a steadfastness in Christ, having a perfect brightness of hope, and a love of God and of all men. Wherefore, if ye shall press forward, feasting upon the word of Christ, and endure to the end, behold, thus saith the Father: Ye shall have eternal life.   (2 Nephi 31:4-20)

For many centuries after Lehi and his family left the Land of Jerusalem, the inspired teachers among the Nephites, promulgated the same doctrines and requirements that both Lehi and his son, Nephi, had proclaimed. About 147 years before the Savior was born in Judea, Alma, a righteous leader who grew up among a wayward people, uttered these words concerning *baptism* which were engraved upon the records of that people, who were descendants of one Zeniff. These words are part of the abridgment of the *Larger Plates of Nephi,* made by Mormon hundreds of years later:

Now I say unto you, if this be the desire of your hearts, what have you against being baptized in the name of the Lord, as a witness before him that ye have entered into a covenant with him, that ye will serve him and keep his commandments, that he may pour out his Spirit more abundantly upon you?

And now when the people had heard these words, they clapped their hands for joy, and exclaimed: This is the desire of our hearts.

And now it came to pass that Alma took Helam, he being one of the first, and went and stood forth in the water, and cried, saying: O Lord, pour out thy Spirit upon thy servant, that he may do this work with holiness of heart.

And when he had said these words, the Spirit of the Lord was upon him, and he said: Helam, I baptize thee, having authority from the Almighty God, as a testimony that ye have entered into a covenant to serve him until you are dead as to the mortal body; and may the Spirit of the Lord be poured out upon you; and may he grant unto you eternal life, through the redemption of Christ, whom he has prepared from the foundation of the world.

And after Alma had said these words, both Alma and Helam were buried in the water; and they arose and came forth out of the water rejoicing, being filled with the Spirit.

And again, Alma took another, and went forth a second time into the water, and baptized him according to the first, only he did not bury himself again in the water.

And after this manner he did baptize every one that went forth to the place of

Mormon; and they were in number about two hundred and four souls; yea, and they were baptized in the waters of Mormon, and were filled with the grace of God.

And they were called the church of God, or the church of Christ, from that time forward. And it came to pass that whosoever was baptized by the power and authority of God was added to his church. (Mosiah 18:10-17)

And now it came to pass that when Mosiah had made an end of speaking and reading to the people, he desired that Alma should also speak to the people.

And Alma did speak unto them, when they were assembled together in large bodies, and he went from one body to another, preaching unto the people repentance and faith on the Lord.

And he did exhort the people of Limhi and his brethren, all those that had been delivered out of bondage, that they should remember that it was the Lord that did deliver them.

And it came to pass that after Alma had taught the people many things, and had made an end of speaking to them, that king Limhi was desirous that he might be baptized; and all his people were desirous that they might be baptized also.

Therefore, Alma did go forth into the water and did baptize them; yea, he did baptize them after the manner he did his brethren in the waters of Mormon; yea, and as many as he did baptize did belong to the church of God; and this because of their belief on the words of Alma. (Mosiah 25:14-18)

The Lord instructed Alma, saying:

And he that will hear my voice shall be my sheep; and him shall ye receive into the church, and him will I also receive.

For behold, this is my church; whosoever is baptized shall be baptized unto repentance. And whomsoever ye receive shall believe in my name; and him will I freely forgive. (Mosiah 26:21-22)

Previously, Alma said,

And again, believe that ye must repent of your sins and forsake them, and humble yourselves before God; and ask in sincerity of heart that he would forgive you; and now, if you believe all these things see that ye do them." (Mosiah 4:10)

And it came to pass that whosoever did not belong to the church who repented of their sins were baptized unto repentance, and were received into the church. (Alma 6:2)

And it came to pass that the people came to him throughout all the borders of the land which was by the wilderness side. And they were baptized throughout all the land. (Alma 8:5)

And now I, Alma, do command you in the language of him who hath commanded me, that ye observe to do the words which I have spoken unto you.

I speak by way of command unto you that belong to the church; and unto those who do not belong to the church I speak by way of invitation, saying, Come and be baptized unto repentance, that ye also may be partakers of the fruit of the tree of life. (Alma 5:61-62)

When the Risen Redeemer visited the Nephites shortly after His resurrection, it is recorded in Third Nephi:

And when they had all gone forth and had witnessed for themselves, they did cry out with one accord, saying:

Hosanna! Blessed be the name of the Most High God! And they did fall down at the feet of Jesus, and did worship him.

And it came to pass that he spake unto Nephi (for Nephi was among the multitude) and he commanded him that he should come forth.

And Nephi arose and went forth, and bowed himself before the Lord and did kiss his feet.

And the Lord commanded him that he should arise. And he arose and stood before him.

And the Lord said unto him: I give unto you power that ye shall baptize this people when I am again ascended into heaven.

And again the Lord called others, and said unto them likewise; and he gave unto them power to baptize. And he said unto them: On this wise shall ye baptize; and there shall be no disputations among you.

Verily I say unto you, that whoso repenteth of his sins through your words and desireth to be baptized in my name, on this wise shall ye baptize them—Behold, ye shall go down and stand in the water, and in my name shall ye baptize them.

And now behold, these are the words which ye shall say, calling them by name, saying:

Having authority given me of Jesus Christ, I baptize you in the name of the Father, and of the Son, and of the Holy Ghost. Amen.

And then shall ye immerse them in the water, and come forth again out of the water.

And after this manner shall ye baptize in my name; for behold, verily I say unto you, that the Father, and the Son, and the Holy Ghost are one; and I am in the Father, and the Father in me, and the Father and I are one.

And according as I have commanded you thus shall ye baptize. And there shall be no disputations among you, as there have hitherto been; neither shall there be disputations among you concerning the points of my doctrine, as there have hitherto been. (3 Nephi 11:16-28)

Behold, this is not my doctrine, to stir up the hearts of men with anger, one against another; but this is my doctrine, that such things should be done away.

Behold, verily, verily, I say unto you, I will declare unto you my doctrine.

And this is my doctrine, and it is the doctrine which the Father hath given unto me; and I bear record of the Father, and the Father beareth record of me, and the Holy Ghost beareth record of the Father and me; and I bear record that the Father commandeth all men, everywhere, to repent and believe in me.

And whoso believeth in me, and is baptized, the same shall be saved; and they are they who shall inherit the kingdom of God.

And whoso believeth not in me, and is not baptized, shall be damned.

Verily, verily, I say unto you, that this is my doctrine, and I bear record of it from the Father, and whoso believeth in me believeth in the Father also; and unto him will the Father bear record of me, for he will visit him with fire and with the Holy Ghost.

And thus will the Father bear record of me, and the Holy Ghost will bear record unto him of the Father and me; for the Father, and I, and the Holy Ghost are one.

And again I say unto you, ye must repent, and become as a little child, and be baptized in my name, or ye can in nowise receive these things.

And again I say unto you, ye must repent and be baptized in my name, and become as a little child, or ye can in nowise inherit the kingdom of God.

Verily, verily, I say unto you, that this is my doctrine, and whoso buildeth upon this buildeth upon my rock, and the gates of hell shall not prevail against them.

And whoso shall declare more or less than this, and establish it for my doctrine, the same cometh of evil, and is not built upon my rock; but he buildeth upon a sandy foundation, and the gates of hell stand open to receive such when the floods come and the winds beat upon them.

Therefore, go forth unto this people, and declare the words which I have spoken, unto the ends of the earth. (3 Nephi 11:30-41)

Now this is the commandment: Repent, all ye ends of the earth, and come unto me and be baptized in my name, that ye may be sanctified by the reception of the Holy Ghost, that ye may stand spotless before me at the last day.

Verily, verily, I say unto you, this is my gospel; and ye know the things that ye must do in my church; for the works which ye have seen me do that shall ye also do; for that which ye have seen me do even that shall ye do;

(3 Nephi 27:20-21)

Therefore, repent all ye ends of the earth, and come unto me, and believe in my gospel, and be baptized in my name; for he that believeth and is baptized shall be saved; but he that believeth not shall be damned; and signs shall follow them that believe in my name.   (Ether 4:18)

And after they had been received unto baptism, and were wrought upon and cleansed by the power of the Holy Ghost, they were numbered among the people of the church of Christ; and their names were taken, that they might be remembered and nourished by the good word of God, to keep them in the right way, to keep them continually watchful unto prayer, relying alone upon the merits of Christ, who was the author and the finisher of their faith.   (Moroni 6:4)

Now, there are many who suppose that Salvation comes by moral precept alone. They say they believe that everyone who is good and pure will receive that priceless gift, Eternal Life in the Kingdom of God. This is not true. A life of goodness and purity may mark a just and an upright person; the desire to do good may be the first showing of a contrite heart. But neither goodness nor moral excellence will prepare one to receive exaltation in the Kingdom of God.

One passage of Scripture often quoted by those who believe that morals, alone, can save, is found in the teachings of Micah: "He hath showed thee, O man, what is good, and what doth the Lord require of thee, but to do justly, and to love mercy, and to walk humbly with thy God." (Micah 6-7) It must be remembered, however, that "to walk humbly with thy God" means to go where He goes, and to do the things which He has commanded.

The notion that there is "saving grace" in goodness and piety alone, is wrong. Who is good, and who is pure? Who of us can say; we do not know. Jesus said that "It is high to be a judge." Those who entertain such beliefs, probably believe that there are many roads that lead to heaven, every one choosing the path he will take. One might as well say that, "All roads lead to London." They do not, and neither do all roads lead to the "Holy City." It must not be forgotten, however, that good moral precepts strengthen faith in Jesus Christ. (See Alma 25:16)

There are also those who have the idea that only a few will receive a remission of their sins, and be saved in the Kingdom of our Father. This belief, too, is not true. They think that it matters not what one does, or what one does not do, if one is to be saved, it is fate so to be. They believe that one is predestined to be saved, or predestined to be damned. This conception of God's love and His grace is not compatible with the teachings of Him before whom there is no inequality nor preference. All men must walk the same path if they are to enter the "Celestial Abode."

Centuries before the time of the Savior's earthly ministry, the Prophet Nephi, in exhorting his brothers to follow the way that had been marked for them, said, "Behold, hath the Lord commanded any that they should not partake of his goodness? Behold I say unto you, Nay; but all men are privileged the one like unto the other, and none are forbidden." (2 Nephi 26:28)

Nephi also said to his brothers: "Wherefore, do the things which I have told you I have seen that your Lord and your Savior should do; for, for this cause have they been shown unto me, that ye might know the gate by which ye should enter." And that gate, he said, "Is repentance and baptism by water." (2 Nephi 31:17)

Eternal Life is the reward of the faithful. It is the heritage of them who keep the Lord's commandments, and of them who endure to the end. Jesus said, "And whoso believeth in me, and is baptized, the same shall be saved; and they are they who shall inherit the kingdom of God." (3 Nephi 11:33) At almost the same time He said, "And again I say unto you, ye must repent, and become as a little child, and be baptized in my name, or ye can in nowise receive these things." (3 Nephi 11:37)

Why childlike? Because a little child is willing to learn. He is content with the arrangements of his father and mother, his teachers, his lawful governors, to whom he is bound by love, admiration, and respect. Because of this disposition he fits perfectly in his place in the family, the school, or in society. It is also true with those who have experienced repentance, been born anew, or "born again," and have become as a little child in their willingness to serve the Lord. They can have a place in the Kingdom. They are never rebellious. They are as a stone laid in its proper place in the structure reared on the "Eternal Rock." (See 3 Nephi 11:39)

And now I speak concerning baptism. Behold, elders, priests, and teachers were baptized; and they were not baptized save they brought forth fruit meet that they were worthy of it.

Neither did they receive any unto baptism save they came forth with a broken heart and a contrite spirit, and witnessed unto the church that they truly repented of all their sins.

And none were received unto baptism save they took upon them the name of Christ, having a determination to serve him to the end. (Moroni 6:1-3)

But as oft as they repented and sought forgiveness, with real intent, they were forgiven. (Moroni 6:8)

And the office of their ministry is to call men unto repentance, and to fulfill and to do the work of the covenants of the Father, which he hath made unto the children of men, to prepare the way among the children of men, by declaring the word of Christ unto the chosen vessels of the Lord, that they may bear testimony of him. (Moroni 7:31)

And the first fruits of repentance is baptism; and baptism cometh by faith unto the fulfilling the commandments; and the fulfilling the commandments bringeth remission of sins. (Moroni 8:25)

Listen to the words of Christ, your Redeemer, your Lord and your God. Behold, I came into the world not to call the righteous but sinners to repentance; the whole need no physician, but they that are sick; wherefore, little children are whole, for they are not capable of committing sin; wherefore the curse of Adam is taken from them in me, that it hath no power over them; and the law of circumcision is done away in me. (Moroni 8:8)

And after this manner did the Holy Ghost manifest the word of God unto me; wherefore, my beloved son, I know that it is solemn mockery before God, that ye should baptize little children.

Behold I say unto you that this thing shall ye teach—repentance and baptism unto those who are accountable and capable of committing sin; yea, teach parents that they must repent and be baptized, and humble themselves as their little children, and they shall all be saved with their little children.

And their little children need no repentance, neither baptism. Behold, baptism is unto repentance to the fulfilling the commandments unto the remission of sins.

But little children are alive in Christ, even from the foundation of the world; if not so, God is a partial God, and also a changeable God, and a respecter to persons; for how many little children have died without baptism!

Wherefore, if little children could not be saved without baptism, these must have gone to an endless hell.

Behold I say unto you, that he that supposeth that little children need baptism is in the gall of bitterness and in the bonds of iniquity, for he hath neither faith, hope, nor charity; wherefore, should he be cut off while in the thought, he must go down to hell.

For awful is the wickedness to suppose that God saveth one child because of baptism, and the other must perish because he hath no baptism.

Wo be unto them that shall pervert the ways of the Lord after this manner, for they shall perish except they repent. Behold, I speak with boldness, having authority from God; and I fear not what man can do; for perfect love casteth out all fear.

And I am filled with charity, which is everlasting love; wherefore, all children are alike unto me; wherefore, I love little children with a perfect love; and they are all alike and partakers of salvation.

For I know that God is not a partial God, neither a changeable God, neither a changeable being; but he is unchangeable from all eternity to all eternity.

Little children cannot repent; wherefore, it is awful wickedness to deny the pure mercies of God unto them, for they are all alive in him because of his mercy.

And he that saith that little children need baptism denieth the mercies of Christ, and setteth at naught the atonement of him and the power of his redemption. Wo unto such, for they are in danger of death, hell, and an endless torment. I speak it boldly; God hath commanded me. Listen unto them and give heed, or they stand against you at the judgment-seat of Christ.

For behold that all little children are alive in Christ, and also all they that are without the law. For the power of redemption cometh on all them that have no law; wherefore, he that is not condemned, or he that is under no condemnation, cannot repent; and unto such baptism availeth nothing—

But it is mockery before God, denying the mercies of Christ, and the power of his Holy Spirit, and putting trust in dead works. (Moroni 8:9-23)

When Nephi received his glorious vision, showing him the life and the mission of the Messiah which was to come, Nephi heard the voice of the Father say,

Repent ye, repent ye, and be baptized in the name of my Beloved Son,

And also, the voice of the Son came unto me, saying: He that is baptized in my name, to him will the Father give the Holy Ghost, like unto me; wherefore, follow me, and do the things which ye see me do. (2 Nephi 31:11-12)

At the time Christ preached His Gospel to the Nephites in the Land Bountiful, He said,

Now this is the commandment: Repent, all ye ends of the earth, and come unto me and be baptized in my name, that ye may be sanctified by the reception of the Holy Ghost, that ye may stand spotless before me at the last day.

Verily, verily, I say unto you, this is my gospel; and ye know the things that ye must do in my church; for the works which ye have seen me do that shall ye also do; for that which ye have seen me do even that shall ye do.   (3 Nephi 27:20-21)

And moreover, I say unto you, that there shall be no other name given nor any other way nor means whereby salvation can come unto the children of men, only in and through the name of Christ, the Lord Omnipotent.   (Mosiah 3:17)

And now, behold, my beloved brethren, this is the way; and there is none other way nor name given under heaven whereby man can be saved in the kingdom of God. And now, behold, this is the doctrine of Christ, and the only and true doctrine of the Father, and of the Son, and of the Holy Ghost, which is one God, without end. Amen.   (2 Nephi 31:21)

CONCORDANCE

Following is a complete Book of Mormon concordance of the words,

BAPTISM AND CHURCH

Baptism—

2 Nephi	31:13	Take upon you the name of Christ, by b.
	13	Then cometh the b. of fire
	14	To keep my commandments, by the b.
	14	Have received the b. of fire and of the
	17	Is repentance, and b. by water
Mosiah	18:21	Having one faith and one b.
	21:35	An account of their b. shall be given
Alma	7:15	By going into the waters of b.
Moroni	6:1	And now I speak concerning b.
	2	Neither did they receive any unto b., save
	3	None were received unto b., save they
	4	After they had been received unto b.
	8:5	Concerning the b. of your little children
	10	Teach ... b. unto those who are accountable
	11	Little children need no repentance, neither b.
	11	B. is unto repentance to the fulfilling
	12	How many little children have died without b.
	13	If little children could not be saved without b.
	14	He that supposeth that little children need b.
	15	That God saveth one child because of b.
	15	The other must perish because he hath no b.
	20	He that sayeth, That little children need b.
	22	And unto such b. availaeth nothing
	25	The first fruits of repentance is b.
	25	B. cometh by faith unto the fulfilling

Baptize—

1 Nephi	10:9	He should b. in Bethabary
	9	He should b. with water
	9	He should b. the Messiah with water

2 Nephi	31:4	That should b. the Lamb of God
Mosiah	18:13	He said, Helam, I b. thee
	16	After this manner he did b. every one
	25:18	Alma did go forth . . . and did b. them
	18	He did b. them after this manner
	18	As many as he did b. did belong
Alma	5:3	Did b. his brethren in the waters of Mormon
	8:10	That he might b. them unto repentance
	15:13	Consecrated priests . . . to b. unto the Lord
	48:19	They did b. unto repentance all men
3 Nephi	9:20	Him will I b. with fire
	11:21	Power that ye shall b. this people
	22	He gave unto them power to b.
	22	On this wise shall ye b.
	23	On this wise shall ye b. them
	23	In my name shall ye b. them
	25	I b. you in the name of the Father
	27	After this manner shall ye b.
	28	Thus shall ye b.
	12:1	Authority to b., were twelve
	1	That they may b. you with water
	1	I will b. you with fire
	19:12	Out of the water and began to b.
	26:17	Began from that time forth to b.
Moroni	8:9	That ye should b. little children

BAPTIZED

To be baptized—

2 Nephi	31:5	He, being holy, should have need to be b.
	5	Need have we, being unholy, to be b.
Mosiah	21:33	His people were desirous to be b.
	35	They were desirous to be b.
Alma	15:13	Whosoever were desirous to be b.
	62:45	And to be b. unto the Lord their God
Helaman	16:3	Went away unto Nephi to be b.
	5	Went forth unto him to be b.
3 Nephi	11:23	Desireth to be b. in my name

Be baptized—

2 Nephi	9:23	Must repent and be b. in his name
	24	Believe in his name, and be b. in his name
	31:11	Repent ye, and be b. in the name
Mosiah	25:17	Limhi was desirous that he might be b.
	17	Were desirous that they might be b.
	26:4	They would not be b.
	22	Shall be b. unto repentance
Alma	5:62	Come and be b. unto repentance
	7:14	Come and be b. unto repentance
	9:27	Those who will be b. unto repentance
Helaman	16:1	Desiring that they might be b.
3 Nephi	7:25	Should be b. with water
	11:37	Be b. in my name
	38	Be b. in my name

	12:1	Believe in me, and be b.
	2	Depths of humility and be b.
	18:5	Who shall believe and be b.
	21:6	Come unto me, and be b.
	27:20	Come unto me and be b.
	30:2	Come unto me, and be b.
Mormon	7:8	Be b. in the name of Jesus
Ether	4:18	Believe in my Gospel, and be b. in my name
Moroni	7:34	Come unto me, and be b. in my name
	8:10	They must repent and be b.

Is baptized—

2 Nephi	31:12	Saying, He that is b. in my name
Mosiah	26:22	This is my church: whosoever is b.
Alma	32:16	Is b. without stubbornness of heart
3 Nephi	11:33	Whoso believeth in me, and is b.
	18:30	He that repenteth, and is b.
	23:5	Repenteth, and is b., the same shall
	27:16	Repenteth and is b. in my name
Mormon	9:23	Believeth and is b., shall be saved
Ether	4:18	He that believeth, and is b., shall be

Was baptized—

1 Nephi	11:27	The Lamb of God went forth and was b.
	27	And after he was b. I beheld
2 Nephi	31:8	After he was b. with water
Mosiah	18:17	Whosoever was b. by the power
3 Nephi	19:11	Into the water, and was b.

Were baptized—

Mosiah	18:16	They were b. in the waters of Mormon
	26:15	Who were b. in the waters of Mormon
Alma	4:4	And many were b. in the waters of Sidon
	4:4	They were b. by the hand of Alma
	5	About 3500 souls . . . and were b.
	6:2	Were b. unto repentance
	8:5	They were b. throughout all the land
	15:14	Round about Sidom, and were b.
	19:35	As many as did believe, were b.
Helaman	3:24	Were b. unto repentance
	5:17	Were b. unto repentance
	19	Were . . . b. unto repentance
3 Nephi	7:26	That were b. unto repentance
	9:20	Were b. with fire and with the Holy Ghost
	26:17	As many as were b.
	21	Were b. in the name of Jesus
	28:18	As many as were b.
4 Nephi	1:1	Were b. in the name of Jesus
Ether	12:14	Upon the L., that they were b. with fire
Moroni	6:1	Elders, Priests, and Teachers were b.

Baptized—

1 Nephi	10:10	After he had b. the Messiah
	10	That he had b. the Lamb of God
2 Nephi	31:6	Did fulfill all righteousness in being b. by water?

Mosiah	18:10	What have you against being b.
	15	Into the water, and b. him
Alma	15:12	Alma b. Zeezrom unto the Lord
	49:30	Being b. unto repentance, and sent for
3 Nephi	7:24	Who were not b. with water
	11:34	Is not b., shall be damned
	12:1	After that ye are b. with water
	18:11	Those who repent and are b.
	16	Who do repent and are b.
	19:12	B. all those whom Jesus had chosen
	13	When they were all b.
Mormon	3:2	Come unto me, and be ye b.
	7:10	Are b., first with water, then with fire
	9:29	See that ye are not b. unworthily
Moroni	6:1	They were not b. save they brought forth

Baptizing

Mosiah	26:37	Receiving many, and b. many
Helaman	3:26	B. and uniting to the church
	16:4	N. was b., and prophesying
3 Nephi	1:23	N. went forth . . . b. unto repentance
	27:1	Were b. in the name of Jesus
	28:18	In their preaching; b. them

CHURCH

Church of Christ—

Mosiah	18:17	The church of God, or the C. of Christ
Alma	4:4	Were joined to the c. of God
3 Nephi	26:21	Were baptized . . . were called the C. of C.
	28:23	Were united unto the C. of Christ
4 Nephi	1:1	The disciples of Jesus had formed a C. of C.
	26	They began to deny the true C. of C.
	29	They did persecute the true C. of C.
Moroni	**6:4**	Numbered among the people of the C. of C.

Belong to the Church—

Mosiah	25:18	He did baptize did belong to the c.
	26:38	Who did not belong to the c. of God
Alma	1:19	Whosoever did not belong to the c.
	19	Persecute those that did belong to the c.
	21	Persecute those that did not belong to the c.
	4:9	Pride of those that did not belong to the c.
	10	To those who did not belong to the c.
	5:62	Command unto you that belong to the c.
	62	Unto those who do not belong to the c.
	6:2	Whosoever did not belong to the c.
	3	That whosoever did belong to the c.
	46:14	By those who did not belong to the c.
	15	Those who did belong to the c. were
Helaman	3:33	Who professed to belong to the c.
	4:11	Who professed to belong to the c.
	11:21	Both the N. and the L., did belong to the c.
3 Nephi	28:19	By them who did not belong to the c.

To the Church—

Mosiah	27:33	Impart much consolation to the c.
	35	Injuries which they had done to the c.
Alma	1:21	Not any man belonging to the c., arise
	23	A cause of much affliction to the c.
3 Nephi	28:18	Uniting as many to the c. as would believe

Great and abominable church—

1 Nephi	13:6	I beheld this great and abominable c.
	8	The desires of this great and abominable c.
	26	The foundation of a great and abominable c.
	28	The hands of the great and abominable c.
	14:3	Digged . . . by that great and abominable c.
	9	And behold that great and abominable c.
	15	Poured out upon the great and abominable c.
	17	Harlots, which is the great and abominable c.
	22:13	The blood of that great and abominable c.
	14	Great and abominable c. shall tumble
2 Nephi	6:12	Unite themselves to that great and abominable c.
	28:18	That great and abominable c., the whore

In the church—

Mosiah	26:6	Did deceive many . . . who were in the c.
	6	Committed sin that were in the c.
	10	Not any such thing happened before in the c.
Alma	1:30	Whether out of the church, or in the c.
	5:2	Which he spake to the people in the c.
	30:33	Labors which I have performed in the c.
	34	What doth it profit us to labor in the c.
	34	Do not receive anything for our labors in the c.
	31:6	Himni he did leave in the c. in Zarahemla
	45:19	And the saying went abroad in the c.
	46:7	There were many in the c. who believed
	38	Did also maintain order in the c.
	38	Much peace and rejoicing in the c.
	49:30	Exceeding great prosperity in the c.
	62:44	A regulation should be made again in the c.
Helaman	3:1	Save it were a little pride . . . in the c.
	24	There was exceeding great prosperity in the c.
	4:1	There were many dissensions in the c.

Of the church—

1 Nephi	4:26	That I spake to the brethren of the c.
Mosiah	26:37	Alma did regulate all the affairs of the c.
	37	Prosper exceedingly in the affairs of . . . c.
	29:42	Charge concerning all the affairs of the c.
Alma	1:28	They did establish all the affairs of . . . c.
	29	Because of the steadiness of the c.
	30	Male or female, whether out of the c.
	2:4	Their rights and privileges of the c.
	4:11	Alma saw the wickedness of the c.
	11	He saw also that the example of the c.
	16	Who was among the elders of the c.
	6:4	To establish the order of the c.

	8:1	Having established the order of the c.
	16:15	Establishment of the c. became general
	31:10	Observe the performances of the c.
Helaman	3:25	So great was the prosperity of the c.
Moroni	7:3	I would speak unto you that are of the c.

Over the church—

Mosiah	26:8	Mosiah had given Alma the authority over the c.
	38	Fellow laborers do who were over the c.
Alma	1 HD.	And also the High Priest over the c.
	4:7	Consecrated . . . priests and elders over the c.
	18	The office of being high priest over the c.
	5:3	Alma, to be a high priest over the c. of
	6:1	To preside and watch over the c.
	8:11	That thou art high priest over the c.
	23	Alma, and am the high priest over the c.
	16:5	Knowing that Alma was high priest over the c.
	45:23	Appointed priests and teachers over the churches
	46:6	Their exceeding great care over the c.
	6	For they were high priests over the c.

The people of the church—

Mosiah	18:27	Alma commanded that the people of the c.
	26:35	Did number among the people of the c.
	36	Not numbered among the people of the c.
Alma	1:7	He might lead away the people of the c.
	10	Man who slew him was taken by the people of the c.
	21	There was a strict law among the people of the c.
	2:3	Was alarming to the people of the c.
	4:4	The high priest over the people of the c.
	6	The people of the c. began to wax proud
	8	The people of the c. began to be lifted up
	9	Contentions among the people of the c.
	6:1	End of speaking unto the people of the c.
Helaman	6:3	The people of the c. did have great joy
Moroni	6:4	Numbered among the people of the c.

His church—

2 Nephi	25:14	Fight against God and the people of his c.
Mosiah	18:17	Whosoever was baptized . . . was added to his c.
Alma	26:18	With mighty threatenings to destroy his c.
	29:11	And by this did establish his c.
	13	That same God did establish his c.
Moroni	7:39	Numbered among the people of his c.

My church—

Mosiah	26:22	For behold, this is my c.
	28	The same shall ye not receive into my c.
	27:13	The Lord hath said, This is my c.
3 Nephi	18:5	Bless it, and give it unto the people of my c.
	16	Even so shall ye pray in my c.
	21:22	I will establish my c. among them
	27:8	How be it my c., save it be called in
	8	Be called in my name, then it is my c.

	21	Know the things that ye must do in my c.
Mormon	3:2	Be ye baptized, and build up again my c.

Their church—

Mosiah	23:16	Alma . . . he being the founder of their c.
	29:47	Alma, who was the founder of their c.
Alma	1:31	Those who did not belong to their c.
	32	Those who did not belong to their c.
	43:30	Their lands, and their liberty and their c.
	45	For their rights of worship and their c.
	48:24	Had dissented from their c.
3 Nephi	2:12	To maintain . . . the privileges of their c.

Church—

1 Nephi	13:4	Among . . . the Gentiles the foundation of a great c.
	5	Said unto me: Behold the foundation of a c.
	32	Have been kept back by that abominable c.
	34	Have been kept back by that abominable c.
	14:10	One is the c. of the Lamb of God
	10	And the other is the c. of the devil
	10	Whoso belongeth not to the c. of the Lamb
	10	Belongeth to that great c. which is the
	12	I beheld the c. of the Lamb of God
	12	I beheld that the c. of the Lamb, who
	14	Upon the saints of the c. of the Lamb
2 Nephi	9:2	That shall be restored to the true c.
Mosiah	21:34	They did not . . . form themselves into a c.
	25:19	Ordain priests and teachers over every c.
	21	Every c. having their priests
	22	They were all one c.
	26:4	Neither would they join the c.
	6	Should be admonished by the c.
	17	Hast established a c. among this people
	21	Him shall you receive into the c.
	33	That he might judge the people of that c.
	27:1	Persecutions which were inflicted on the c.
	1	So great, that the c. began to murmur
	10	Sons of Mosiah, seeking to destroy the c.
	16	Seek to destroy the c. no more
Alma	1:3	Bearing down against the c.; declaring
	6	Even began to establish a c.
	23	Was the cause of much trial with the c.
	4:4	Began to establish the c. more fully
	10	The wickedness of the c. was a great
	10	Thus the c. began to fail in its progress
	5:3	He began to establish a c. in the land
	6	Brethren, you that belong to this c.
	14	Ask of you, my brethren of the c. have
	54	Wherewith they have been brought into this c.
	6:2	Repentance, and were received into the c.
	7	The c. which was in the city of Zarahemla
	8	To declare the word of God unto the c.
	8:11	We are not of thy c., and we do not believe

	12	Know that because we are not of thy c.
	15:13	Alma established a c. in the land of Sidom
	17	After Alma having established the c. at S
	16:21	After the c. having been established
	19:35	They did establish a c. among them
	20:1	They had established a c. in that land
	44:5	By our c., and by the sacred support
	45:17	Alma had said these words, he blessed the c.
	21	A regulation should be made throughout the c.
	22	Went forth to establish the c. again
	46:7	Therefore they dissented even from the c.
	61:14	May rejoice in the great privilege of our c.
Helaman	3:24	Who did join themselves unto the c.
	33	Pride which began to enter into the c.
	4:23	The c. had begun to dwindle
	11:21	The c. did spread through ... all the land
	21	The N. and L., did belong to the c.
3 Nephi	5:12	The land in which Alma did establish the c.
	12	The first c. which was established among
	6:14	Insomuch that the c. began to be broken
	14	In the 30th year the c. was broken up
	27:3	The name whereby ye shall call this c.
	7	Wherefore ye shall call the c. in my name
	7	That he will bless the c. for my sake
	8	For if a c. be called in Moses' name
	8	Then it be Moses' c.; or if it be called
	8	Then it be the c. of a man; but if it
	9	For the c., if it be in my name
	10	If it so be that the c. is built
4 Nephi	1:20	The people who had revolted from the c.
	28	And this c. did multiply exceedingly
	29	There was another c. which denied
Moroni	3:1	Disciples, who are called the elders of the c.
	4:1	The flesh and blood of Christ unto the c.
	2	And they did kneel down with the c.
	6:2	Witnessed unto the c. that they truly
	5	And the c. did meet together oft, to fast
	7	Three witnesses of the c. did condemn
	9	Their meetings were conducted by the c.

Churches—

1 Nephi	13:5	Most abominable above all other c.
	26	Most abominable above all other c.
	14:10	Behold there are save two c. only
	22:23	All c. which are built up to get gain
2 Nephi	26:20	That they have built up many c.
	21	There are many c. built up which cause
	28:3	That the c. which are built up
	3	Shall every one say that hath built up c.
	12	Their c. have become corrupted
	12	And their c. are lifted up
Mosiah	25:19	Granted unto Alma, that he might establish c.

	21	Together in different bodies, being called c.
	22	Notwithstanding there being many c.
	22	There was nothing preached in all the c.
	23	There were seven c. in the land of Zarahemla
	23	They did join the c. of God
	27:3	A strict command throughout all the c.
Alma	23:4	Establishing c., and consecrating priests
	45:22	Throughout all the land, over all the c.
	23	Appointed priests and teachers over the c.
4 Nephi	1:26	They began to build up c. unto themselves
	27	There were many c. in the land
	27	There were many c. which professed to know the
	34	False prophets to build up many c.
	41	They did still continue to build up c.
Mormon	8:28	And c. became defiled and be lifted up
	28	Even in a day when leaders of c.
	28	Envying of them who belong to their c.
	32	When there shall be c. built up
	33	Why have ye built up c. unto yourselves
	36	Your c. . . . have become polluted
	37	Ye do love . . . the adorning of your c. more than ye love the poor and the needy, the sick and the afflicted

GENERAL NOTES

In the discussion of the doctrine, *Baptism,* it is singularly important to combine the plain truths enunciated by the Nephite servants of God with those of His holy prophets who have dwelt among the children of men since the world began. Their teachings agree.

Moses wrote in "words as plain as words can be," the manner in which Adam was taught the necessity of obeying the Gospel Plan, which Plan had been taught him from the beginning of things.

And as Enoch spake forth the words of God, the people trembled, and could not stand in his presence.

And he said unto them: Because that Adam fell, we are; and by his fall came death; and we are made partakers of misery and woe.

Behold Satan hath come among the children of men, and tempteth them to worship him; and men have become carnal, sensual, and devilish, and are shut out from the presence of God.

But God hath made known unto our fathers that all men must repent.

And he called upon our father Adam by his own voice, saying: I am God; I made the world, and men before they were in the flesh.

And he also said unto him: If thou wilt turn unto me, and hearken unto my voice, and believe, and repent of all thy transgressions, and be baptized, even in water, in the name of mine Only Begotten Son, who is full of grace and truth, which is Jesus Christ, the only name which shall be given under heaven, whereby salvation shall come unto the children of men, ye shall receive the gift of the Holy Ghost, asking all things in his name, and whatsoever ye shall ask, it shall be given you.

And our father Adam spake unto the Lord, and said: Why is it that men must repent and be baptized in water? And the Lord said unto Adam: Behold I have forgiven thee thy transgression in the Garden of Eden.

Hence came the saying abroad among the people, That the Son of God hath atoned for original guilt, wherein the sins of the parents cannot be answered upon the heads of the children, for they are whole from the foundation of the world.

And the Lord spake unto Adam, saying: Inasmuch as thy children are conceived in sin, even so when they begin to grow up, sin conceiveth in their hearts, and they taste the bitter, that they may know to prize the good.

And it is given unto them to know good from evil; wherefore they are agents unto themselves, and I have given unto you another law and commandment.

Wherefore teach it unto your children, that all men, everywhere, must repent, or they can in nowise inherit the kingdom of God, for no unclean thing can dwell there, or dwell in his presence; for, in the language of Adam, Man of Holiness is his name, and the name of his Only Begotten is the Son of Man, even Jesus Christ, a righteous Judge, who shall come in the meridian of time.

Therefore I give unto you a commandment, to teach these things freely unto your children. . . .   (*Pearl of Great Price*, Moses 6:47-58)

ALMA, THE ELDER

Alma, The Elder was an Israelite of the Tribe of Manasseh, a direct descendant of Nephi the son of Lehi. He was born in the land of Lehi-Nephi, or a region contiguous, 173 years before the advent of the Redeemer, when Zeniff was king in that portion of the South American continent. He is first introduced to the readers of the Book of Mormon shortly before the martyrdom of the prophet Abinadi as a young man associated with the apostate and iniquitous priesthood of king Noah, the son of Zeniff. Unlike his soul-seared associates his heart was pricked by the warnings and teachings of Abinadi for he knew that his denunciations of the prevailing wickedness were true. Inspired with this knowledge he very courageously went to the tyrant Noah and pleaded for the prophet's life. His appeal in behalf of the devoted servant of the Lord was ineffectual; the infuriated and besotted king would not hearken to Alma's appeal for justice and mercy but on the contrary he ordered the young priest to be cast out from the midst of the people and when Alma fled from his anger he sent his servants to slay him. Alma, however, successfully hid from his pursuers and during his concealment wrote the words he had heard Abinadi speak, which teachings now form one of the most important of the doctrinal portions of the Book of Mormon.

The power, the importance, the efficiency of Abinadi's teachings had sunk deep in the heart of Alma; he not only realized their truth but he comprehended their saving value. The first lesson they impressed upon his mind was the necessity of his immediate and thorough repentance, combined with unfaltering faith in the Savior who was to come to redeem mankind. In much tribulation he sought the Lord with all his powers and the Great Father vouchsafed to him an abundant soul-satisfying answer. From this time Alma began to preach privately to the people the words of Gospel truth. To do this he received power from On High. We have no account of the time of his ordination, whether when a lad he had received the holy priesthood under the hands of some one of God's servants, before the days that Noah led his people into iniquity and corrupted the priesthood, or whether at this time he was ministered to by messengers from heaven. Perhaps both; but the time and place is but a secondary consideration, the important fact remains that he was commissioned by God to officiate in His name, which commission he ever after magnified to the salvation of his fellow-men. Alma's preaching of God's holy word was not without fruit. Many received the truth with joy. These gathered to a convenient spot on the borders of the wilderness but not far from their city. This place was called Mormon. It was admirably suited for a hiding place, having formerly been infested by ravenous beasts and was dreaded and avoided by the people. Near by was a thicket of small trees in which the Gospel believers could hide should they be pursued by the king's servants; here also was a fountain of pure water most excellently adapted for the purpose of baptism. Here in the midst of the luxuriance of tropical vegetation and by the side of the inviting stream did Alma proclaim the principles of everlasting life; here the people entered into covenant to serve the Great Father of all; here were the repentant believers baptized unto Christ for the remission of sins and here was the Church of God organized, the Holy Priesthood conferred and the work of God founded in power.

Alma and another servant of the Lord, named Helam, were the first to enter the water and when there Alma lifted his voice in prayer and besought the Lord for his Holy Spirit. This blessing having been bestowed he proceeded with the sacred ordinance. Addressing his companion he said, "Helam, I baptize thee, having authority from the Almighty God, as a testimony that ye have entered into a covenant to serve him until you are dead as to the mortal body; and may the Spirit of the Lord be poured out upon you; and may he grant unto you eternal life, through the redemption of Christ whom he has prepared from the foundation of the world." Alma having said these words both he and Helam were buried in the water whence they came forth rejoicing, being filled with the Holy Spirit. Others to the number of two hundred and four souls followed Helam into the waters of baptism but in all these cases Alma did not again bury himself beneath the liquid wave but only the repentant believers. From this time we may date the organization of the Church of Jesus Christ in that land and henceforth its members assembled for worship and testimony once a week.

Notwithstanding the care and circumspection with which the members of the Church acted, Noah soon discovered that there was some secret movement among his subjects and by the help of his spies he discovered what was taking place at Mormon. Making the tyrant's usual excuse, that the Christians were in rebellion against him, he sent his armies to capture and destroy them. But a greater than he stretched forth His arm to preserve His people. The Lord warned Alma of the king's intentions and in obedience to divine direction he assembled his people, some 450 souls, gathered his flocks and herds, loaded up his grain, provisions and other supplies and departed into the untrodden wilderness.

Being strengthened by the Lord, notwithstanding that they were impeded by their flocks and families, the pilgrims traveled with sufficient rapidity to escape the pursuing forces of King Noah, who were reluctantly compelled to return to the Land of Nephi without having accomplished the object of the expedition. At the end of eight days Alma's company ceased their flight and settled in a very beautiful and pleasant land where there was an abundant supply of pure water. We have no direct information with regard to the course taken by this colony but it is evident from the details of their later history that the new settlement lay somewhere between the Lands of Nephi and Zarahemla, though possibly somewhat aside from the most direct route. We think it far from improbable that it was situated at the head waters of some one of the numerous tributaries to the Amazon that take their rise on the eastern slopes of the Andes.

The colonists, whose industry is especially referred to by the inspired historian, immediately set to work to till the soil and build a city. The city, with the surrounding territory, they named the City and Land of Helam. Now that they were established as a separate people, independent of both Lamanite and Nephite princes, they desired a form of temporal government with Alma as their king. This honor he declined. He rehearsed to them the history of their fathers; he pictured to them the infamies of King Noah's reign; he showed them how a wicked ruler could lead his subjects into all manner of evil and how such things led to bondage; and on the other hand how much better it was to have the Lord as their King and Ruler and to be guided by His servants under His inspiration. This counsel the people wisely accepted. Alma, though not bearing the title of king, acted as their leader, as their High Priest and Prophet and as the mouthpiece of God to them whenever His holy word was graciously given them. In this happy state the people of Helam continued for some years, the Lord greatly prospering them and crowning their labors with abundant increase.

How long these blissful days lasted is not defined in the sacred record of the Book of Mormon; but as the Lord chastens those whom He loves, so, after a time, He permitted the Lamanites to discover their secluded and happy home and to bring them into bondage.

It so happened that a Lamanite army corps (that had been pursuing a body of fugitive Nephites under Limhi, the son of Noah, who had broken away from their bondage in the land of Nephi,) lost themselves in the wilderness. While traveling hither and thither, not knowing which way to go, they came across a body of men who had once been the priests of King Noah but who had fled from the face of their fellows to escape the just indignation their continued iniquities had aroused. These priests, at the instigation of Amulon, their leader, joined the Lamanite troops and unitedly endeavored to get back to the land of Nephi. While thus engaged they wandered near the city of Helam.

When the people of Alma first perceived the approach of ths body of men they were occupied in tilling the soil around their city, into which they immediately fled in great fear. In this perilous hour the faith and courage of Alma was conspicuous. He gathered his people around him, called upon them to cast aside their unsaintly fears and to remember the God who had delivered those who trusted in him. The words of their leader had the desired effect; the people silenced their fears and called mightily upon the Lord to soften the hearts of the Lamanites that they might spare their lives and those of their wives and little ones. Then, with the assurance in their hearts that God would hearken uno their prayers, Alma and his brethren went forth out of their city and delivered themselves up to their former foes.

The Lamanites were in a dilemma, therefore they were profuse in promises. They were willing to grant the people of Helam their lives and liberty if they would show them the way to the land of Nephi. Having obtained this information and reached home in safety they broke their promises and made Amulon king over a wide district of country, including the land of Helam.

Alma and Amulon had known each other in the days when they both belonged to King Noah's priesthood and with the venom so often conspicuous in apostates, the latter soon commenced to persecute those who were faithful to the Lord. He placed task-masters over them, he imposed inhuman burdens upon them and otherwise afflicted them grievously.

In their affliction the people of Alma cried unremittingly to heaven for deliverance but even their prayers were an annoyance to their task-masters and they were forbidden to lift up their voices in supplication to the Lord. But the tyrants could not prevent them from pouring out their hearts to Him who knoweth the inmost thoughts of all men. He answered in His own way; He did not bring them immediate deliverance but He strengthened their backs to bear the heavy burdens placed upon them, and, strong in the faith of their ultimate release from this bondage they toiled on with cheerfulness and patience.

In His due time the Lord delivered them. Having revealed His intentions to Alma, that the people might make ready, He caused a deep sleep to come upon the Lamanite guards and task-masters. The hour to strike for liberty had arrived but it was obtained at a heavy cost, that of their homes and possessions. Under the guidance of Alma they departed into the wilderness. At eventide they rested in a beautiful valley which they called Alma but they did not tarry there. The next day they pushed farther into the wilderness and continued their journey until they arrived at the land of Zarahemla, which they reached in twelve days' travel from the valley of Alma. Their arrival amongst their Nephite kindred was the occasion of great joy both to them and to the people of King Mosiah, which joy was intensified by the fact that Limhi and his subjects had also arrived in safety at the home of their forefathers a short time previously, thus uniting all the Nephite people (except the few apostates with Amulon) in one land and under one king.

Alma and his people must have dwelt in the land of Helam quite a number of years as he is called a young man at the time of Abinadi's martyrdom and at the time he led his people into the land of Zarahemla he was fifty years old, possibly several years older.

On the arrival of Alma in the land of Zarahemla King Mosiah gave him charge of the spiritual concerns of the Nephites. He became the High Priest to the whole nation. In this capacity he gathered the people together and in words of power and plainness he reminded them of their duties to heaven. Nor had he unwilling hearers; numbers hearkened to his words, renewed their covenants with God, went down into the waters of baptism and recommenced a life of godliness and faith. From place to place Alma bent his way, preaching, counseling, reproving, comforting, instructing, as the Holy Spirit led. Through these labors seven Churches, or rather seven branches of the Church, were established in Zarahemla, while great prosperity attended the faithful. As years rolled by the hearts of those who loved the Lord were pained by the unbelief and wickedness of the rising generation. Many of these not only rejected the truth but persecuted and reviled those who were righteous. This unholy crusade received great strength and assumed great effrontery owing to the fact that the four sons of King Mosiah and the son of the High Priest Alma were their ringleaders. Vain were the exhortations of these holy men to their wayward sons; they rebelled against their father's admonitions, and set their authority at defiance. Great was Alma's grief. The Lord of Hosts was his only recourse. In much sorrow, but with much faith, he earnestly and unceasingly prayed for his loved but rebellious son. The Lord heard his faithful servant's petitions, sent His angel to stay the young man's mad career and bring him to a knowledge of the truth. There, overpowered by the presence and message of the angel, he was struck dumb and paralyzed. When the news of this visitation reached his father he greatly rejoiced for he knew it was the power of God. He gathered his people to witness the miracle and assembled the priests that they might join him in prayer and fasting for his son's perfect restoration. Their prayers were heard; not only were the natural powers of the body restored but Alma became a changed man and from thenceforth was a valiant soldier of the Cross—a help, a comfort and a joy to his father who was now beginning to feel the effects of advancing years.

Before his death, Alma who had ordained his son a High Priest, gave the latter charge concerning all the affairs of the Church and then, full of years and honor, he departed this life. His death took place (B.C. 91) when he was eighty-two years old, five hundred and nine years having passed from the time Lehi and his family left Jerusalem.

HELAM

A Nephite of the land of Lehi-Nephi, in the days of King Noah. He accepted the teachings of Alma, the elder and was the first man baptized by him in the waters of Mormon. One thing remarkable about his baptism is that both he and Alma were together buried in the water and they arose and came forth out of the water rejoicing, being filled with the Spirit of God. We have no further mention of Helam but from the fact that the land (eight days' journey from Mormon) to which Alma and the Saints soon fled, received the name Helam from him, it is highly probable that Helam was one of the leading officers of the Church established by Alma, and was greatly respected by the people.

CHAPTER 19

1. *A Futile Search*—2. *Gideon's Insurrection*—3. *A Lamanite Invasion*—
4. *King Noah Suffers Death by Fire*—5. *His Son, Limhi, a Tributary Monarch.*

1. *A futile search.*

1. And it came to pass that the army of the king returned, having searched in vain for the people of the Lord.

2. And now behold, the forces of the king were small, having been reduced, and there began to be a division among the remainder of the people.

3. And the lesser part began to breathe out threatenings against the king, and there began to be a great contention among them.

2. *Gideon's insurrection.*

4. And now there was a man among them whose name was Gideon, and he being a strong man and an enemy to the king, therefore he drew his sword, and swore in his wrath that he would slay the king.

5. And it came to pass that he fought with the king; and when the king saw that he was about to overpower him, he fled and ran and got upon the tower which was near the temple.

6. And Gideon pursued after him and was about to get upon the tower to slay the king, and the king cast his eyes round about towards the land of Shemlon, and behold, the army of the Lamanites were within the borders of the land.

VERSES 1-3. *And it came to pass that the army of the king returned.* After the unsuccessful attempt to capture Alma and his people, the remnants of King Noah's army straggled back to the City of Lehi-Nephi. They were no longer a formidable group, who, by their greater numbers, could force the king's whims upon misguided subjects. Death and deflection had nearly exhausted the strength which formerly had been able to restrict the people's liberties and dictate their wants. The army's weakness now gave those who had grown weary of Noah's debaucheries the courage to rebel, and also to threaten his assumption of evil powers. A great contention arose, and murmurings against Noah were heard on every hand. Some offered violence toward him, and others prepared to seek elsewhere for more peaceable homes. It seemed that everyone was tired of King Noah's tyranny.

VERSES 4-9. *And now there was a man among them whose name was Gideon.* One of the most dissatisfied among the people was Gideon, an officer of the king's army. There is no reason to suspect that he was a wicked man, although he held an office under King Noah. Later he proved that he possessed all the virtues of a good, pure, and wise man. In the revolution that now arose between King Noah and his people, Gideon sought to slay the king. But Noah escaped to the tower he had constructed near the site of the temple. There Gideon, sword in hand, quickly followed him. The king mounted to the top of the tower, where he accidentally caught sight of an invading army of Lamanites in the Land of Shemlon, which lay

7. And now the king cried out in the anguish of his soul, saying: Gideon, spare me, for the Lamanites are upon us, and they will destroy us; yea, they will destroy my people.

8. And now the king was not so much concerned about his people as he was about his own life;

nevertheless, Gideon did spare his life.

9. And the king commanded the people that they should flee before the Lamanites, and he himself did go before them, and they did flee into the wilderness, with their women and their children.

3. A Lamanite invasion.

10. And it came to pass that the Lamanites did pursue them, and did overtake them, and began to slay them.

11. Now it came to pass that the king commanded them that all the men should leave their wives and their children, and flee before the Lamanites.

12. Now there were many that would not leave them, but had rather stay and perish with them. And the rest left their wives and their children and fled.

13. And it came to pass that those who tarried with their wives and their children caused

that their fair daughters should stand forth and plead with the Lamanites that they would not slay them.

14. And it came to pass that the Lamanites had compassion on them, for they were charmed with the beauty of their women.

15. Therefore the Lamanites did spare their lives, and took them captives and carried them back to the land of Nephi, and granted unto them that they might possess the land, under the conditions that they would deliver up king Noah into the hands of the Lamanites, and deliver up

near by. In the terror caused by this unexpected sight, he appealed to the patriotism of Gideon, and besought him to spare his life, so that he, as their king, could lead his people into battle and to safety. Noah made this plausible excuse, not that he cared for his people, but that he might preserve his life. Gideon consented to spare Noah's life, and the king, in mortal terror, ordered his people to flee into the wilderness so as to escape the advancing hosts of Lamanites.

VERSES 10-19. *The Lamanites did pursue them.* The people obeyed King Noah's command and fled into the wilderness. But the forces of the Lamanites, unencumbered with women and children, soon overtook them. Then the coward king commanded the men to continue their flight and leave their wives and children to the mercy of the enemy. Some obeyed and fled further into the uninhabited regions where they would not be found. Others preferred to stay and, if necessary, perish with those to whom they were the natural protectors. Those who stayed, in the agony induced in them when the Lamanites drew near, sent their fairest daughters to plead with their enemies for their lives. This act saved them. For the dark warriors of King Laman were so charmed with the beauty of the Nephite women that they spared all their lives. Yet, notwithstanding this, they took the Nephites captives, and carried their property, even one half of all they possessed, one half of their gold, and their silver, and all their precious things, and thus they should pay tribute to the king of the Lamanites from year to year.

16. And now there was one of the sons of the king among those that were taken captive, whose name was Limhi.

17. And now Limhi was desirous that his father should not be destroyed; nevertheless, Limhi was not ignorant of the iniquities of his father, he himself being a just man.

18. And it came to pass that Gideon sent men into the wilderness secretly, to search for the king and those that were with him. And it came to pass that they met the people in the wilderness, all save the king and his priests.

19. Now they had sworn in their hearts that they would return to the land of Nephi, and if their wives and their children were slain, and also those that had tarried with them, that they would seek revenge, and also perish with them.

4. King Noah suffers death by fire.

20. And the king commanded them that they should not return; and they were angry with the king, and caused that he should suffer, even unto death by fire.

21. And they were about to take the priests also and put them to death, and they fled before them.

22. And it came to pass that they were about to return to the

---

them back to Lehi-Nephi where they gave the Nephites permission to retain their homes and lands, but under very demanding conditions.

There were two conditions imposed by the Lamanite captors. First, they should surrender King Noah into the hands of the Lamanites. Second, they were to deliver up to the Lamanites one-half of every thing they possessed, and continue paying this tribute of one-half of their gains year after year.

King Noah's son, Limhi, who was a righteous man and who was among the captured Nephites, was not desirous that his father should be delivered to the Lamanites for he knew that they would destroy him, yet he also knew of his father's many sins. Being a just man, Limhi did not interfere with the demands of the Lamanites wherein his own people were spared their lives.

Gideon now sent men to search for King Noah so that he might be turned over to the Lamanites. They found the deserters — all except Noah and his priests. They also found that these men were ashamed of their cowardly flight, that they swore in their hearts that if their wives and children and the men who had remained with them had been killed, they would have revenge, and, if it so be, perish in like manner. To this end they resolved to return to Lehi-Nephi.

VERSES 20-24. *King Noah commanded them that they should not return.* The king commanded that they should not return, but they grew so angry with him, that they burned him to death, even as he had martyred Abinadi. Noah's priests were saved from a similar fate by flight further into the wilderness.

land of Nephi, and they met the men of Gideon. And the men of Gideon told them of all that had happened to their wives and their children; and that the Lamanites had granted unto them that they might possess the land by paying a tribute to the Lamanites of one half of all they possessed.

23. And the people told the men of Gideon that they had slain the king, and his priests had fled from them farther into the wilderness.

24. And it came to pass that after they had ended the ceremony, that they returned to the land of Nephi, rejoicing, because their wives and their children

5. Limhi, Noah's son, a tributary monarch.

were not slain; and they told Gideon what they had done to the king.

25. And it came to pass that the king of the Lamanites made an oath unto them, that his people should not slay them.

26. And also Limhi, being the son of the king, having the kingdom conferred upon him by the people, made oath unto the king of the Lamanites that his people should pay tribute unto him, even one half of all they possessed.

27. And it came to pass that Limhi began to establish the kingdom and to establish peace among his people.

28. And the king of the Lamanites set guards round about the land, that he might keep the people of Limhi in the land, that they might not depart into the wilderness; and he did support his guards out of the tribute which he did receive from the Nephites.

29. And now king Limhi did have continual peace in his kingdom for the space of two years, that the Lamanites did not molest them nor seek to destroy them.

When the men who had put Noah to death were about to return to the Land of Lehi-Nephi, they met Gideon's party, and informed them of Noah's end and of the escape of the priests. They also rejoiced in the news Gideon brought because they learned that their wives and children had been spared by the Lamanites.

VERSES 25-29. *And it came to pass that King Limhi did establish peace among his people.* Noah, now being dead, his son Limhi, was made king. It was almost an empty honor, for his people were in bondage to the Lamanites. Still he made a treaty with the king of the Lamanites, and, because he could bargain no better, he agreed for his Nephites to pay a yearly tribute of one-half of their increase.

To prevent the escape of the Nephites, guards were set all around the land. The Lamanites were anxious that the Nephites should not be freed for in their industry the Lamanites anticipated a vast income.

The Nephites were to all intents and purposes bond-servants, and the Lamanites obtained all the advantages of their labor without any of the responsibilities that generally fall upon slave owners. Out of the tribute, the guards who held the

Nephites in bondage were paid. This condition continued without an outbreak of war, or the Nephites being molested by the Lamanites for two years.

GIDEON

A Nephite patriot, slain by Nehor in B.C. 91. Gideon was evidently born in the land of Lehi-Nephi and in the rebellion that occurred in that land against the iniquitous king Noah, Gideon, being a strong and zealous man, took a leading part. We judge from the course he then pursued and the whole tenor of his after life that he had no hand in the martyrdom of Abinadi, or in Noah's other crimes. When the minority of the people revolted, Gideon, being exceedingly angry, drew his sword and sought to kill the king. Noah, realizing he was about to be over-powered, fled to the tower near the temple. Thither Gideon quickly followed. The king mounted to the top and there his eye accidentally caught sight of an army of Lamanites in the land of Shemlon. In the terror raised by this unexpected sight he appealed to Gideon's patriotism and besought him to spare him. Gideon consented and Noah, in mortal terror, ordered his people to flee into the wilderness from before the advancing hosts of the Lamanites.

The people obeyed their king's command and with their wives and children fled into the wilderness. But the forces of the Lamanites, unemcumbered with women and children, soon overtook them. Then the coward king commanded the men to continue their flight and leave their wives and children to the mercy of the enemy. Some obeyed and fled; others would not but preferred to stay and perish with those of whom they were the natural protectors. Gideon was among the latter. Those who stayed, in their terror, when the Lamanites drew near, sent their fair daughters to plead with their enemies for their lives. This act saved them. For the dark warriors of Laman were so charmed with the beauty of the women that they spared all their lives. Yet they took them captives, carried them back to Lehi-Nephi and gave them permission to retain that land but under the conditions that they should surrender King Noah and deliver up one-half of everything they possessed and continue this tribute of one-half of their property year by year.

Gideon now sent men to search for Noah that he might be delivered up to the Lamanites. They found that the men who were with Noah, being ashamed of their cowardly flight, swore that they would return and if their wives and children and the men who remained with them had been killed they would have revenge. The king commanded that they should not return at which they became very angry with him and burned him to death, as he had done Abinadi. When the men who put Noah to death were about to return to the land of Nephi they met Gideon and his party and informed him of the end of Noah and the escape of the priests and when they heard the news that Gideon brought they also rejoiced much that their wives and children had been spared by the Lamanites.

Noah was succeeded by his son Limhi. Gideon appears in his day to have been an officer of high standing in the Nephite forces and a man of much wisdom and intelligence. In the war that resulted from the seizure of a number of Lamanite maidens by the Priests of Noah, Gideon took a prominent part in bringing about a cessation of hostilities. It was he who suggested who the men really were that committed this vile act. (See Amulon.) In later years, when the people of Limhi escaped from the Lamanites and returned to Zarahemla under the guidance of Ammon, Gideon took a leading part, by his advice and example, in effecting their deliverance and directing that march. We next read of Gideon when he had become exceedingly old. He was still actively engaged in the service of the Lord. He was a teacher in the church, yet we cannot help thinking that, like many in these days, though acting as a teacher, he held a higher office in the priesthood. One day he met, in the streets of the city of Zarahemla, an apostate named Nehor, who had grown very popular and with his popularity, very conceited, headstrong and ambitious, he having built up a church composed of persons who accepted his pernicious doctrines. On this occasion Gideon plead with him to desist from his evil ways and strongly remonstrated against the course he was taking. Nehor, ill-used to such opposition, drew his sword and slew the aged teacher. For this crime he was arrested, tried, convicted and executed (B.C. 91). Gideon's memory was held in great respect among the Nephites and one of their most important cities was named after him.

CHAPTER 20

1. *Priests of King Noah Carry Off Daughters of the Lamanites*—2. *Lamanites Seek Revenge upon King Limhi and his People*—3. *They are Repulsed and Satisfied.*

1. *Priests of King Noah carry off daughters of the Lamanites.*

1. Now there was a place in Shemlon where the daughters of the Lamanites did gather themselves together to sing, and to dance, and to make themselves merry.

2. And it came to pass that there was one day a small number of them gathered together to sing and to dance.

3. And now the priests of king Noah, being ashamed to return to the city of Nephi, yea, and also fearing that the people would slay them, therefore they durst not return to their wives and their children.

4. And having tarried in the wilderness, and having discovered the daughters of the Lamanites, they laid and watched them;

5. And when there were but few of them gathered together to dance, they came forth out of their secret places and took them and carried them into the wilderness; yea, twenty and four of the daughters of the Lamanites they carried into the wilderness.

2. *Lamanites seek revenge upon King Limhi and his people.*

6. And it came to pass that when the Lamanites found that their daughters had been missing, they were angry with the people of Limhi, for they thought it was the people of Limhi.

7. Therefore they sent their armies forth; yea, even the king himself went before his people; and they went up to the land of Nephi to destroy the people of Limhi.

VERSES 1-5. *Now there was a place in Shemlon.* In those times there was a romantic spot in the Land of Shemlon, on the Nephite borders, where the Lamanitish maidens were in the habit of gathering to "sing, and to dance, and to make themselves merry." All the gaiety of innocence was theirs, and the overflowing spirit of youth abounded among them.

One day, unknown to the maidens, the fugitive priests of Noah discovered them. The priests hid themselves, and from their secret places, watched them play their games, and otherwise disport themselves. The priests laid in wait, and then when there were only a few gathered suddenly surprised them and carried twenty-four of them away. We may conjecture that there were some Lamanite girls who escaped the priests' grasp and they, undoubtedly, reported the strange men, unmistakably Nephites, as kidnappers.

VERSES 6-12. *They thought it was the people of Limhi.* On learning of this act of treachery, the Lamanites were stirred to uncontrollable anger, and without demanding an explanation they made a sudden incursion into the territory held by King

8. And now Limhi had discovered them from the tower, even all their preparations for war did he discover; therefore he gathered his people together, and laid wait for them in the fields and in the forests.

9. And it came to pass that when the Lamanites had come up, that the people of Limhi began to fall upon them from their waiting places, and began to slay them.

10. And it came to pass that the battle became exceeding sore, for they fought like lions for their prey.

3. They are repulsed and satisfied.

11. And it came to pass that the people of Limhi began to drive the Lamanites before them; yet they were not half so numerous as the Lamanites. But they fought for their lives, and for their wives, and for their children; therefore they exerted themselves and like dragons did they fight.

12. And it came to pass that they found the king of the Lamanites among the number of their dead; yet he was not dead, having been wounded and left upon the ground, so speedy was the flight of his people.

13. And they took him and bound up his wounds, and brought him before Limhi, and said: Behold, here is the king of the Lamanites; he having received a wound has fallen among their dead, and they have left him; and behold, we have brought him before you; and now let us slay him.

14. But Limhi said unto them: Ye shall not slay him, but bring him hither that I may see him. And they brought him. And Limhi said unto him: What cause have ye to come up to war against my people? Behold, my people

---

imhi. This attack, however, was not successful, for the movements of the Lamanites, though not understood, had been discovered, and their intended victims were ready for them.

VERSES 11-26. *They began to drive the Lamanites before them.* With King Limhi and his people it was a war for their very existence; to be defeated was to be annihilated. Consequently, his warriors fought with almost superhuman energy and desperation. They eventually succeeded in driving the Lamanites from their domain.

VERSE 12. *They found the Lamanite King among the dead.* So hasty was the flight of the Lamanites to escape the fury of the Nephite attack that in their hurry to leave the scene of combat, the Lamanites left their wounded king among the dead, thinking that he, too, had been slain. He was discovered by the victorious Nephites, who took him, bound up his wounds and carried him before King Limhi. They wanted to slay him.

VERSE 14. *Bring him hither that I may see him.* In the interview that followed between the two kings, the Lamanite king complained bitterly of the outrage committed on the daughters of his people. King Limhi protested that he and his subjects

have not broken the oath that I made unto you; therefore, why should ye break the oath which ye made unto my people?

15. And now the king said: I have broken the oath because thy people did carry away the daughters of my people; therefore, in my anger I did cause my people to come up to war against thy people.

16. And now Limhi had heard nothing concerning this matter; therefore he said: I will search among my people and whosoever has done this thing shall perish. Therefore he caused a search to be made among his people.

17. Now when Gideon had heard these things, he being the king's captain, he went forth and said unto the king: I pray thee forbear, and do not search this people, and lay not this thing to their charge.

18. For do ye not remember the priests of thy father, whom this people sought to destroy? And are they not in the wilderness? And are not they the ones who have stolen the daughters of the Lamanites?

19. And now, behold, and tell the king of these things, that he may tell his people that they may be pacified towards us; for behold they are already preparing to come against us; and behold also there are but few of us.

20. And behold, they come with their numerous hosts; and except the king doth pacify them towards us we must perish.

21. For are not the words of Abinadi fulfilled, which he prophesied against us—and all this because we would not hearken unto the words of the Lord, and turn from our iniquities?

22. And now let us pacify the king, and we fulfill the oath which we have made unto him; for it is better that we should be in bondage than that we should lose our lives; therefore, let us put a stop to the shedding of so much blood.

23. And now Limhi told the king all the things concerning his father, and the priests that had fled into the wilderness, and attributed the carrying away of their daughters to them.

24. And it came to pass that the king was pacified towards his people; and he said unto them:

---

were completely innocent of perpetrating the base act. Further investigation disclosed the fact that some of the iniquitous priests of King Noah, who had fled into the wilderness from the dreaded vengeance of their abused countrymen, were the guilty ones. Being without wives, and fearing to return home, they had adopted this plan to obtain them.

VERSE 23. *And now Limhi told the king all the things concerning his father, and the priests that had fled into the wilderness.* Limhi knew that the priests who had accompanied his father in the flight into the wilderness to escape the wrath of the invading Lamanites, had been alone, living without comforts of homes and wives. To this fact he put the responsibility upon the priests of "the carrying away of their daughters."

VERSES 24-26. *And it came to pass that the king was pacified.* On hearing this

Let us go forth to meet my people, without arms; and I swear unto you with an oath that my people shall not slay thy people.

25. And it came to pass that they followed the king, and went forth without arms to meet the Lamanites. And it came to pass that they did meet the Lamanites; and the king of the Lamanites did bow himself down before them, and did plead in behalf of the people of Limhi.

26. And when the Lamanites saw the people of Limhi, that they were without arms, they had compassion on them and were pacified towards them, and returned with their king in peace to their own land.

---

explanation, King Laman consented to make an effort to pacify his own angry armies who were already preparing further incursions into Nephite territory.

At the head of an unarmed body of Nephites, the king of the Lamanites went forth and met his armies as they were returning to attack. He explained to them what he had learned, and the Lamanites, possibly somewhat ashamed of their rash act in making war upon a peaceful people, renewed the covenant of peace which they formerly had entered into with the Nephites.

CHAPTER 21

1. *Abinadi's Prophecies Further Fulfilled*—2. *Nephites in Bondage Suffer Great Afflictions*—3. *The Lord Softens the Hearts of their Enemies*—4. *Concerning the Twenty-four Plates.*

1. *Abinadi's prophecies further fulfilled.*

1. And it came to pass that Limhi and his people returned to the city of Nephi, and began to dwell in the land again in peace.

2. And it came to pass that after many days the Lamanites began again to be stirred up in anger against the Nephites, and they began to come into the borders of the land round about.

3. Now they durst not slay them, because of the oath which their king had made unto Limhi; but they would smite them on their cheeks, and exercise authority over them; and began to put heavy burdens upon their backs, and drive them as they would a dumb ass—

4. Yea, all this was done that the word of the Lord might be fulfilled.

2. *Nephites in bondage suffer great afflictions.*

5. And now the afflictions of the Nephites were great, and there was no way that they could deliver themselves out of their hands, for the Lamanites had surrounded them on every side.

6. And it came to pass that the people began to murmur with

Verses 1-3. *Limhi and his people return to the City of Lehi-Nephi.* The industrious Nephites now returned, unmolested by the Lamanites, to the City of Lehi-Nephi and to their homes. They quickly began to care for their crops. One of the fruits of their labors was peace; and greatly blessed were they because prosperity and riches go together in that land where peace abides.

This peace, unfortunately, was not long to endure. The Lamanites grew arrogant and grievously oppressed the Nephites. Under their exactions and cruelty the condition of King Limhi's subjects grew continually worse, until, at last, they were little better off than were their ancestors in Egypt before Moses arose and delivered them.

Verse 4. *Yea, all this was done that the word of the Lord might be fulfilled.* Many afflictions and sorrows came upon the Nephites in fulfillment of the prophecies of Abinadi.

Verse 5. *And now the afflictions of the Nephites were great.* Not only did the Lamanites deal harshly with the Nephites, who had now become slaves to their taskmasters, but also the Lamanites constantly encroached upon the lands given to the Nephites. Gradually, and stealthily the Lamanites obtained possession of the rights and property of the Nephites. These rights had been assured the Nephites in the treaties made by their respective kings. On every side, until they were completely surrounded, the Nephites suffered loss, through theft, of crops and of cattle. The Lamanites hemmed them in and in every way conceivable harassed the peaceable Nephites.

Verse 6. *The people began to murmur to the king.* At last, the Nephites could

the king because of their afflictions; and they began to be desirous to go against them to battle. And they did afflict the king sorely with their complaints; therefore he granted unto them that they should do according to their desires.

7. And they gathered themselves together again, and put on their armor, and went forth against the Lamanites to drive them out of their land.

8. And it came to pass that the Lamanites did beat them, and drove them back, and slew many of them.

9. And now there was a great mourning and lamentation among the people of Limhi, the widow mourning for her husband, the son and the daughter mourning for their father, and the brothers for their brethren.

10. Now there were a great many widows in the land, and they did cry mightily from day to day, for a great fear of the Lamanites had come upon them.

11. And it came to pass that their continual cries did stir up the remainder of the people of Limhi to anger against the Lamanites; and they went again to battle, but they were driven back again, suffering much loss.

12. Yea, they went again even the third time, and suffered in the like manner; and those that were not slain returned again to the city of Nephi.

13. And they did humble themselves even to the dust, subjecting themselves to the yoke of bondage, submitting themselves to be smitten, and to be driven to and fro, and burdened, according to the desires of their enemies.

---

stand no more. They complained of their hardships to King Limhi. So incessant and bitter became their accusations against the Lamanites, and so unyielding their demands for revenge, that the king consented to their wishes, and permitted them to "do according to their desires" and drive the Lamanites "out of their land."

VERSES 7-8. *And they put on their armor and went forth against the Lamanites.* The sad comment on this is that the Lamanites "did beat them, and drove them back, and slew many of them."

VERSES 9-12. *There was great mourning and lamentation among the people of Limhi.* Because of the loss inflicted upon them, the people of Limhi were caused to mourn and weep, but not until later, when their cause seemed hopeless, did they turn from their iniquities to God who rewards all repentant sinners according to their needs and desires.

In the meantime, the cries of the fatherless and the widows continued to stir up the people. There was no respite to their pleadings for help. There seemed to be only one source whence help would come. That was some kind of warlike action. The Nephites became increasingly angry with the Lamanites. Three times they broke out in ineffectual rebellion, and just as often their taskmasters grew more cruel and exacting. At last their spirits were entirely broken. They cowered before their oppressors and bowed "to the yoke of bondage, submitting themselves to be smitten, and to be driven to and fro, and burdened, according to the desires of their enemies."

14. And they did humble themselves even in the depths of humility; and they did cry mightily to God; yea, even all the day long did they cry unto their God that he would deliver them out of their afflictions.

3. The Lord softens the hearts of their enemies.

15. And now the Lord was slow to hear their cry because of of their iniquities; nevertheless the Lord did hear their cries and began to soften the hearts of the Lamanites that they began to ease their burdens; yet the Lord did not see fit to deliver them out of bondage.

16. And it came to pass that

VERSE 14. *They did humble themselves and did cry mightily to God.* At last, when they were about to despair, the counsel of the righteous among them began to prevail. They remembered how in times past the Lord had delivered the Children of Israel from similar oppression. They read the words of Job (they possessed a copy of the Prophet's words) and remembered also his sufferings. They read of Job's reply to the reproof of his friends, of God's almighty power, and that nothing can stand against Him.

And Job answered and said, . . . I am as one mocked of his neighbor, who calleth upon God, and he answereth:

The Hebrew Scriptures told King Limhi's people that Job asked his tormentors if, ever they denied that his condition was the will, or the purpose of God. The Nephites were not slow in believing that this conclusion was true, neither was it lost in the maze of their transgressions. If they doubted that the anger of the Lord was shown in their tribulations, they were also told by this same prophet,

Ask now the beasts, and they shall teach thee; and the fowls of the air, and they shall tell thee:
Or speak to the earth, and it shall teach thee; and the fishes of the sea shall declare unto thee.
Who knoweth not in all these that the hand of the Lord hath wrought this? [their sufferings]
In whose hand is the soul of every living thing, and the breath of all mankind,

They were further told,

With him is strength and wisdom:
He looseth the bond of kings.
He poureth contempt upon princes, and weakeneth the strength of the mighty.
He increaseth the nations, and destroyeth them.
He taketh away the heart of the chief of the people of the earth, and causeth them to wander where there is no way.
Lo, mine eye hath seen all this, mine ear hath heard and understood.
(See Job 12)

They also remembered the Prophet Abinadi and the words he had spoken against them.

The Nephites repented of their sins, and besought the Lord to deliver them "out of their afflictions." All day long, and even when night came, they did not cease to cry unto Him for forgiveness.

VERSES 15-16. *Now the Lord was slow to hear their cries.* The Sacred Record says, "The Lord was slow to hear their cries because of their iniquities." Nevertheless, they began to prosper by degrees in the land, and began to raise grain more abundantly, and flocks, and herds, that they did not suffer with hunger.

17. Now there was a great number of women, more than there was of men; therefore king Limhi commanded that every man should impart to the support of the widows and their children, that they might not perish with hunger; and this they did because of the greatness of their number that had been slain.

18. Now the people of Limhi kept together in a body as much as it was possible, and secured their grain and their flocks;

19. And the king himself did not trust his person without the walls of the city, unless he took his guards with him, fearing that he might by some means fall into the hands of the Lamanites.

20. And he caused that his people should watch the land round about, that by some means they might take those priests that fled into the wilderness, who had stolen the daughters of the Lamanites, and that had caused such a great destruction to come upon them.

21. For they were desirous to take them that they might punish them; for they had come into the land of Nephi by night, and carried off their grain and many of their precious things; therefore they laid wait for them.

---

after a time the Lord softened the hearts of the Lamanites so that the burdens they placed upon the backs of the Nephites were not so heavy to bear, but he did not deliver them out of bondage at once. They, however, gradually prospered and raised more grain, flocks, and herds, so that they did not suffer the pangs of hunger.

VERSE 17. *King Limhi commanded that every man should impart to the support of the widows and their children.* Because so many men had been slain in their recent wars, there was a greater number of women than there were men. These, without help from those who were spared to live, became a heavy burden upon the king, so he, therefore, commanded that they should be taken care of by the men who remained, that they should not "perish with hunger."

VERSES 18-19. *The people of Limhi kept together.* The people of King Limhi kept together as much as possible for protection. Even the king did not trust himself outside the walls of the city without his guards, lest he might fall into the hands of the Lamanites.

VERSES 20-21. *He caused his people that they should watch the land round about for the priests who had fled into the wilderness.* Not only to prove their contention that the wicked priests who had fled into the wilderness were the abductors of the daughters of the Lamanites, but also to punish them for the misery and destruction which they had caused to come upon his people, King Limhi commanded his people to capture the priests so that they could be tried and punished.

Another cause for which the people of Limhi wanted to seize the priests was that they had come into the lands of the Nephites by night and had stolen much grain and many other precious things. To the end that they might capture them, the Nephites "laid wait for them."

22. And it came to pass that there was no more disturbance between the Lamanites and the people of Limhi, even until the time that Ammon and his brethren came into the land.

23. And the king having been without the gates of the city with his guard, discovered Ammon and his brethren; and supposing them to be priests of Noah therefore he caused that they should be taken, and bound, and cast into prison. And had they been the priests of Noah he would have caused that they should be put to death.

24. But when he found that they were not, but that they were his brethren, and had come from the land of Zarahemla, he was filled with exceeding great joy.

4. Concerning the twenty-four plates.

25. Now king Limhi had sent, previous to the coming of Ammon, a small number of men to search for the land of Zarahemla; but they could not find it, and they were lost in the wilderness.

26. Nevertheless, they did find a land which had been peopled; yea, a land which was covered with dry bones; yea, a land which had been peopled and which had been destroyed; and they, having supposed it to be the land of Zarahemla, returned to the land of Nephi, having arrived in the borders of the land not many days before the coming of Ammon.

27. And they brought a record with them, even a record of the people whose bones they had found; and it was engraven on plates of ore.

28. And now Limhi was again filled with joy in learning from the mouth of Ammon that king Mosiah had a gift from God, whereby he could interpret such engravings; yea, and Ammon also did rejoice.

VERSE 22. *There was no more disturbance between the Lamanites and the people of Limhi even until Ammon and his brethren came into the land.* (See Mosiah 7)

VERSES 23-24. (*See* Mosiah 7)

VERSES 25-28. *King Limhi had sent a small number of men in search for the land of Zarahemla.* In the sad condition of bondage and serfdom that the people of Limhi found themselves, they had one hope. It was to communicate with their brethren in the Land of Zarahemla. To this end Limhi secretly fitted out a small number of men, but the expedition became lost in the wilderness, and failed to find the object of their journeyings. In seeking for the City of Zarahemla they traveled far to the north until they found a land covered with the dry bones of men who appeared to have fallen in battle. Limhi's people thought this must be the Land of Zarahemla, and that their Nephite brethren who had dwelt there had been destroyed. (See Mosiah 8) But in this, their supposition was wrong. With the dead they found some records engraven upon *plates of ore.* They were later presented to King Mosiah in Zarahemla who had a *gift from God* and by it he translated them, and found thereon a record of the *Jaredites.* The bones they found were those of some of these people who had been killed in battle.

29. Yet Ammon and his brethren were filled with sorrow because so many of their brethren had been slain;

30. And also that king Noah and his priests had caused the people to commit so many sins and iniquities against God; and they also did mourn for the death of Abinadi; and also for the departure of Alma and the people that went with him, who had formed a church of God through the strength and power of God, and faith on the words which had been spoken by Abinadi.

31. Yea, they did mourn for their departure, for they knew not whither they had fled. Now they would have gladly joined with them, for they themselves had entered into a covenant with God to serve him and keep his commandments.

32. And now since the coming of Ammon, king Limhi had also entered into a covenant with God, and also many of his people, to serve him and keep his commandments.

33. And it came to pass that king Limhi and many of his people were desirous to be baptized; but there was none in the land that had authority from God. And Ammon declined doing this thing, considering himself an unworthy servant.

This expedition of Limhi's missed the Land of Zarahemla, having probably traveled too far west of it and passed northward through the Isthmus of Panama.

VERSES 29-31. *Yet Ammon and his brethren were filled with sorrow.* On learning that a great number of their brethren had been slain, that Noah and his priests had led the people into committing so many sins, and also of the death of Abinadi, Ammon and his brethren were filled with sorrow, for they knew the many afflictions the people of King Limhi had endured.

They related to Ammon the story of Alma and the people who departed into the wilderness with him. They told him how Alma, being wrought upon by the "strength and power of God," and through "faith on the words which had been spoken by Abinadi," organized a Church of Christ at a place called *Mormon,* and also how King Noah had accused Alma of rebellion against him, and how the king's armies had sought to destroy him and his followers. They explained to their visitors from Zarahemla how Alma escaped the evil designs of the king.

These wretched people also told Ammon and his companions that they did not know where Alma had led his people, or the fate that awaited them at the end of their journey. Ammon, learning of Alma's determination to serve the Lord, and in spite of the lack of any knowledge concerning his whereabouts or the conditions under which his people lived, he would have gladly joined with him, because he, too, had covenanted "with God to serve him and keep his commandments."

VERSE 32-35. *King Limhi and many of his people were desirous to be baptized.* The coming of Ammon's party from Zarahemla and the account of Mosiah's peaceful reign there, awakened the latent hopes in the breasts of Limhi and his people so that they saw in retrospect the errors they had committed, and resolved not to do them again.

Truly repentant and determined to serve the Lord and keep His commandments, King Limhi and many of his people desired to be baptized. However, there was no one in the Land of Lehi-Nephi who had the "authority from God" to perform the

34. Therefore they did not at that time form themselves into a church, waiting upon the Spirit of the Lord. Now they were desirous to become even as Alma and his brethren, who had fled into the wilderness.

35. They were desirous to be baptized as a witness and a testimony that they were willing to serve God with all their hearts; nevertheless they did prolong the time; and an account of their baptism shall be given hereafter.

36. And now all the study of Ammon and his people, and king

---

sacred rite. King Limhi's father, King Noah, had replaced the real priests Zeniff had appointed with others who not only were a fraud and a sham, but also who were indeed a wicked lot. Succession in the priesthood among Limhi's subjects was broken when Alma and his people, at the time of King Noah, departed out of Lehi-Nephi.* Ammon refused to act in this ordinance because he considered himself unworthy so to do.

VERSES 34-35. *Therefore they did not at that time form themselves into a church.* They recognized the *Priesthood of God,* and being without the authority it bears—for they knew that without it any observance of its commands was meaningless—they waited for the Spirit of the Lord to open the way that they might avail themselves of the blessings Church membership bestows.

With the new-found faith Ammon's visit had planted in their repentant hearts, Alma's departure into the wilderness, where he and his people could worship God according to their own beliefs, became the ruling incentive of their lives, overpowering all selfish motives. They desired to become even as Alma's people. They thought of little else.

Baptism is not only the *gate* through which all must pass to enter the Celestial Kingdom, but also, it is a witness to our fellows that we are willing to serve the Lord and keep His commandments. King Limhi and his people were anxious to enter that covenant, and it was not long until the Lord, in His wisdom and loving kindness, made it possible for them to take upon themselves His name. With the Saints in Zarahemla they rejoiced that He did not suffer them to be destroyed.

King Limhi's wish to be baptized soon became a reality for we read:

And he [Alma] did exhort the people of Limhi and his brethren, all those that had been delivered out of bondage, that they should remember that it was the Lord that did deliver them.

And it came to pass that after Alma had taught the people many things, and had made an end of speaking to them, that King Limhi was desirous that he might be baptized; and all his people were desirous that they might be baptized also.

Therefore, Alma did go forth into the water and did baptize them; yea, he did baptize them after the manner he did his brethren in the waters of Mormon; yea, and as many as he did baptize did belong to the church of God; and this because of their belief on the words of Alma. (Mosiah 25:16-18)

VERSE 36. *Now all the study of Ammon . . . and Limhi . . . was to deliver themselves from bondage.* When Limhi reached that awful conclusion that he and

---

*From the time Alma began to teach privately, the words of Gospel truth, he received help from On High. The Sacred Record gives no account of the time of his ordination to the Holy Priesthood. Whether when a lad he received it under the hands of one of God's servants —before the days that Noah led his people into iniquity and corrupted the priesthood—or whether at the time that he organized the Church of God at Mormon he was ministered to by messengers from heaven, we do not know. Perhaps he was blessed with both.

Limhi and his people, was to de- | of the Lamanites and from bond-
liver themselves out of the hands | age.

his people could not be baptized, a thing for which they greatly desired, their
thoughts turned to ways and means whereby they could be released from Lamanite
bondage. With Ammon they discussed many plans; they weighed this proposal, then
that. They sought the guidance of their Heavenly Father. Finally, the method of
their escape was decided.

CHAPTER 22

1. Plan to Throw off Lamanite Yoke—2. Gideon's Proposal—3. Lamanites made Drunk—4. The Entire People Escape and Return to Zarahemla—5. End of Zeniff's Record.

1. Plan to throw off Lamanite yoke.

1. And now it came to pass that Ammon and king Limhi began to consult with the people how they should deliver themselves out of bondage; and even they did cause that all the people should gather themselves together; and this they did that they might have the voice of the people concerning the matter.

2. And it came to pass that they could find no way to deliver themselves out of bondage, except it were to take their women and children, and their flocks, and their herds, and their tents, and depart into the wilderness; for the Lamanites being so numerous, it was impossible for the people of Limhi to contend with them, thinking to deliver themselves out of bondage by the sword.

2. Gideon's proposal.

3. Now it came to pass that Gideon went forth and stood before the king, and said unto him: Now O king, thou hast hitherto hearkened unto my words many times when we have been contending with our brethren, the Lamanites.

4. And now O king, if thou hast not found me to be an unprofitable servant, or if thou hast hitherto listened to my words in

---

VERSES 1-2. *Ammon and king Limhi began to consult with the people how they should deliver themselves out of bondage.* The arrival of Ammon and his sixteen brethren from Zarahemla, together with the report of King Mosiah's just reign there, only whetted the desire of the people of Lehi-Nephi to escape from their Lamanite bondage.

Both Ammon and King Limhi sought among the people for a way to free themselves which might be successful. So that everyone might be heard, they called a meeting to which every man and woman was bidden so they could "have a voice . . . concerning the matter."

No plan was devised, no way was seen that might lead to the freedom of the downtrodden people. It was suggested that a bold withdrawal of "their women and children, and their flocks, and their herds," together with their tents, be made, and all then would depart into the wilderness. This idea was not favorably received; the memory of recent clashes with their more numerous adversaries was fresh in their minds. Such a plan would mean war, and any attempt to deliver themselves "by the sword" was doomed to failure because of the greater number of the Lamanites who would rush to prevent the strategem.

VERSES 3-8. *Gideon went forth and stood before the king.* Gideon, formerly an officer in King Noah's army, presented himself before King Limhi, and reminded

any degree, and they have been of service to thee, even so I desire that thou wouldst listen to my words at this time, and I will be thy servant and deliver this people out of bondage.

5. And the king granted unto him that he might speak. And Gideon said unto him:

6. Behold the back pass, through the back wall, on the back side of the city. The Lamanites, or the guards of the Lamanites, by night are drunken; therefore let us send a proclamation among all this people that they gather together their flocks and herds, that they may drive them into the wilderness by night.

7. And I will go according to thy command and pay the last tribute of wine to the Lamanites, and they will be drunken; and we will pass through the secret pass on the left of the camp when they are drunken and asleep.

8. Thus we will depart with our women and our children, our flocks, and our herds into the wilderness; and we will travel around the land of Shilom.

3. *Lamanites made drunk.*

9. And it came to pass that the king hearkened unto the words of Gideon.

10. And king Limhi caused that his people should gather their flocks together; and he sent the tribute of wine to the Lamanites; and he also sent more wine, as a present unto them; and they did drink freely of the wine which king Limhi did send unto them.

---

him that many times in the past the king had hearkened to his advice when the king was contending with the Lamanites.

Gideon also said that if the king had found his former opinions worthy, and if they proved to have had merit, then he begged the king to listen to "my words at this time, and I will be thy servant and deliver this people out of bondage."

King Limhi granted Gideon the opportunity to speak.

Gideon reminded the king of certain features in the city's defenses. In the wall that surrounded the city there was a pass, and through it was a means of escape. The Lamanite guards that were placed there "by night are drunken." The plan was to notify all the people to gather their flocks and herds, "that they may drive them into the wilderness by night." Then Gideon would go according to the king's command and give the guards a tribute of wine. Then when they were in a drunken stupor, the Nephites would make good their escape through the pass that lies to the left of the Lamanites' camp. Later they would unite and take their course into the wilderness going around the Land of Shilom, and from there would go to Zarahemla.

VERSES 9-10. *It came to pass that the king hearkened unto the words of Gideon.* King Limhi listened to the things Gideon said, and agreed with them. It may be presumed that Ammon and his brethren agreed, as also did all the people.

The king caused that his people should make the necessary preparations. In the meantime he sent a present of strong wine to the Lamanite guards. He sent them a double portion, enough for them to drink freely. The more they drank, the more they wanted; soon they were drunk and fell asleep.

4. The entire people escape to Zarahemla.

11. And it came to pass that the people of king Limhi did depart by night into the wilderness with their flocks and their herds, and they went round about the land of Shilom in the wilderness, and bent their course towards the land of Zarahemla, being led by Ammon and his brethren.

12. And they had taken all their gold, and silver, and their precious things, which they could carry, and also their provisions with them, into the wilderness; and they pursued their journey.

13. And after being many days in the wilderness they arrived in the land of Zarahemla, and joined Mosiah's people, and became his subjects.

5. End of Zeniff's record.

14. And it came to pass that Mosiah received them with joy; and he also received their records, and also the records which had been found by the people of Limhi.

15. And now it came to pass when the Lamanites had found that the people of Limhi had departed out of the land by night, that they sent an army into the wilderness to pursue them;

16. And after they had pursued them two days, they could no longer follow their tracks; therefore they were lost in the wilderness.

Verses 11-13. *Ammon and his brethren led the people of Limhi to the Land of Zarahemla.* Taking with them their flocks and herds, their gold and silver and many precious things, including provisions, the people of Lehi-Nephi after many wearisome days in the wilderness, arrived in Zarahemla. They were led in their journey by Ammon and his brethren whom we may suppose were inspired in answer to the prayers and supplications of the now truly repentant Nephites.

When they arrived in Zarahemla, King Limhi and his people joined Mosiah's people, and became his subjects.

Verses 14-16. *Mosiah received them with joy.* It was with great joy that King Mosiah and the people of Zarahemla received their brethren from Lehi-Nephi. They had thought that Zeniff and their friends and relatives who had accompanied him to the old homes of their fathers had been slain. They had heard nothing from them, and presumed that all of them had been destroyed. Now that they had become united and once again could dwell in peace, "songs of delight filled each grateful heart." We may imagine the deep sense of thankfulness that arose from their lips as their leaders proclaimed the goodness of God in delivering them from Lamanite bondage.

Another cause of rejoicing in Mosiah's heart was that the people from Lehi-Nephi had preserved their records. They also had in their possession the Gold Plates which had been found by the men King Limhi had sent to find Zarahemla. Altogether, and notwithstanding that their trials and afflictions had been great, they rejoiced that they were numbered among those who loved the Lord and sought to do His will.

When the Lamanites found, to their surprise, that their bond servants had escaped, they sent an army to pursue them. At the end of the second day this corps of armed men could no longer follow the Nephites' tracks, and they, themselves, became lost in the wilderness. They could not tell which way to go, or whence they came.

We now leave both the Nephites who were rescued by Ammon, and the Lamanites who dwelt in Lehi-Nephi, and return to the "account of Alma, and the people of the Lord, who were driven into the wilderness by the people of King Noah."

An account of Alma and the people of the Lord, who were driven into the wilderness by the people of King Noah,

Comprising chapters 23 and 24.

CHAPTER 23

1. *Alma Refuses to be King.*—2. *Land of Helam Captured by Lamanites*—3. *Amulon, Leader of King Noah's Wicked Priests, Rules Subject to the Lamanite Monarch.*

1. Alma refuses to be king.

1. Now Alma, having been warned of the Lord that the armies of king Noah would come upon them, and having made it known to his people, therefore they gathered together their flocks, and took of their grain, and departed into the wilderness before the armies of king Noah.

2. And the Lord did strengthen them, that the people of king Noah could not overtake them to destroy them.

3. And they fled eight days' journey into the wilderness.

4. And they came to a land, yea, even a very beautiful and pleasant land, a land of pure water.

5. And they pitched their tents, and began to till the ground, and began to build buildings; yea, they were industrious, and did labor exceedingly.

VERSES 1-24. *The people were desirous that Alma should be their king.* In Mosiah 18:33-35, King Noah said, "Alma was stirring up the people to rebellion against him." Therefore, he sent his army to destroy him. There were about 450 persons who congregated around Alma, and who, too, believed in the words of Abinadi.

Alma had friends among the officers and men in the king's army; we may presume that one was Gideon, and that Alma was appraised of the king's intent. In verse 1, we are informed that the Lord warned Alma of the danger which was imminent. Whether it was made known to Alma by the direct interposition of God's power, or His operating through Alma's friends, the record does not state, nor does it matter; "God moves in a mysterious way." It was made known to Alma, and he in turn advised his followers. They, therefore, took their belongings, their flocks and herds, and grain, and "departed into the wilderness before the armies of king Noah."

VERSE 2. *The Lord did strengthen them.* The Lord rewarded their efforts to serve Him by giving them strength and the physical power to resist fatigue, as well as unbounded determination.

VERSE 3. *They fled eight days' journey into the wilderness.* The time consumed in this first hegira should be remembered, for we shall learn of another flight to be made by Alma and his people in their journey to Zarahemla. The two combined indicate the distance between Lehi-Nephi and the City of Zarahemla.

VERSES 4-5. *And they came to a beautiful and pleasant land.* At the end of eight days' journey in the wilderness, Alma and his followers came to a beautiful

6. And the people were desirous that Alma should be their king, for he was beloved by his people.

7. But he said unto them: Behold, it is not expedient that we should have a king; for thus saith the Lord: Ye shall not esteem one flesh above another, or one man shall not think himself above another; therefore I say unto you it is not expedient that ye should have a king.

8. Nevertheless, if it were possible that ye could always have just men to be your kings it would be well for you to have a king.

9. But remember the iniquity of king Noah and his priests; and I myself was caught in a snare, and did many things which were abominable in the sight of the Lord, which caused me sore repentance;

10. Nevertheless, after much

valley. There was an abundance of pure water there, and with its fertile fields and green low-lands, it was a suitable haven for them to make their homes.

The great strength given them by the Lord when they first commenced their journey from Lehi-Nephi now showed itself in the energy with which Alma and his people began to till the soil. They built houses and in many other ways provided for each other's needs. "They did labor exceedingly," are the words the Sacred Record uses to describe their activities. Undoubtedly, they were happy in the lot their lives were now cast.

VERSE 6. *The people desired that Alma should be their king.* Alma was beloved by all his people. His gentle ways, his self abnegation, and above all, his firm resolve to serve God, made him a ruler and a judge who stood above all the others. Consequently, the people wanted him to assume the title of *king,* the duties of such office he had already so disinterestedly fulfilled.

VERSE 7. *It is not expedient that we should have a king.* Alma, when the demands of his followers became more insistent that he be their king, told them that it was not the mind and will of the Lord that they should have a king to rule over them. The Lord was their King, and before Him all men are equal. The Lord recognized but one condition through which any man may be regarded to be above another; only one way he is justified in thinking himself better than his neighbor. That way is by obedience to God's commands. All other ways lead to destruction. Alma reminded his people of the words of Abinadi, "I must fulfil the commandments wherewith God hath commanded me." (Mosiah 13:4) Until this, we may be sure he said, was done, who could say which one is the greater? Therefore, "It is not expedient ye should have a king."

Expedient means (1) Apt and suitable to the end in view. (2) Conducive to special advantage rather than to what is universally right. (3) Advisable means dictated by practical wisdom. (*Webster's New Collegiate Dictionary*) The experience of Alma's followers under the reign of King Noah bore out the truth of his declaration to them.

VERSES 8-11. *If it were possible that ye could always have just men to be your kings it would be well for you to have a king.* The iniquitous rule of King Noah rankled in Alma's bosom. It had produced a festering and inflamed effect in his mind. The memory of it stirred up a strong revulsion in him to the rule of kings. He desired to draw away from any course that might thereafter lead to its repetition.

tribulation, the Lord did hear my cries, and did answer my prayers, and has made me an instrument in his hands in bringing so many of you to a knowledge of his truth.

11. Nevertheless, in this I do not glory, for I am unworthy to glory of myself.

12. And now I say unto you, ye have been oppressed by king Noah, and have been in bondage to him and his priests, and have been brought into iniquity by them; therefore ye were bound with the bands of iniquity.

13. And now as ye have been delivered by the power of God out of these bonds; yea, even out of the hands of king Noah and his people, and also from the bonds of iniquity, even so I desire that ye should stand fast in this liberty wherewith ye have been made free, and that ye trust no man to be a king over you.

In ancient times the right of kingship went from father to son. This seems to have been the custom among the Nephites who undoubtedly followed the established practice of the Jews from among whom their fathers came.

Zeniff, the first king of the people of Lehi-Nephi, was a righteous man, although a somewhat careless but a determined one. Noah, his son who succeeded him as heir, spent his time in prodigal living and in abusing the powers that pertained to the office he held. What a gap between them! Alma remembered the sufferings King Noah brought upon his subjects, and also the reproach the Lord heaped upon them. Alma believed the words of Abinadi, and through him saw the wicked ways which were so much despised by the Lord.

Although Alma was one of King Noah's priests, and in many ways had followed him in evil practices, yet when Abinadi warned them against their wicked actions, he believed all the Prophet said, and escaped the sorrowful consequences thereof by "sore repentance."

One way in which Alma showed his complete repentance was in prayer to God. He sought the Lord with all the humility of a penitent sinner who now saw the error of his ways and would amend them. In sorrow he lifted his voice to God and entreated Him to open the way so that, as an instrument in His hands, he might bring "many of you to a knowledge of the truth." The Lord, after much silence, answered Alma's prayer, and caused that those who heard Alma's voice should also repent. Thus through Alma's prayers, was established the *Church of Christ* in the Land of Lehi-Nephi.

Verse 11. *I am unworthy to glory of myself.* The humility of Alma is shown in this one sentence. He knew the Lord was with him yet he gloried not in himself. He testified to his people that he was "unworthy" of the Lord's confidence in making him to proclaim His Salvation. They, themselves, he implied, should glory in the blessings of the Lord, for He had armed them "with righteousness and with the power of God in great glory." (1 Nephi 14:14) Alma took no credit unto himself for the "plentiful harvest" that the Lord had garnered, but in thanksgiving to the Great Giver of all good, he praised his Maker, and offered homage to His holy name.

Verses 12-13. *Ye were bound with the bands of iniquity.* Alma reminded his people of the oppression of King Noah, and that along with the wickedness of Noah's priests they had been brought into the *bondage of iniquity*, which, in itself, is worse than being a slave. And now, Alma says, "Ye have been delivered by the power of

14. And also trust no one to be your teacher nor your minister, except he be a man of God, walking in his ways and keeping his commandments.
15. Thus did Alma teach his people, that every man should love his neighbor as himself, that there should be no contention among them.
16. And now, Alma was their high priest, he being the founder of their church.

17. And it came to pass that none received authority to preach or to teach except it were by him from God. Therefore he consecrated all their priests and all their teachers; and none were consecrated except they were just men.
18. Therefore they did watch over their people, and did nourish them with things pertaining to righteousness.
19. And it came to pass that

God out of these bonds," meaning the bonds that once held them in physical servitude and the bonds of iniquity and sin. He also told them to remain "firm and steadfast" in the freedom that comes to those who keep God's commandments. They were counseled to remember, "He whose law we obey is indeed the God of all goodness, the Father of all men, that to serve Him is perfect freedom and to worship Him the soul's purest happiness." Alma also adds this thought, see that "Ye trust no man to be a king over you."

VERSES 14-18. *Trust no man to be your teacher unless he be a man of God.* This advice is trustworthy. It is as pertinent today, as it was to Alma's people. From it we may learn how to escape the pitfalls into which they fell. Noah's priests were not men of God; they did not teach His commandments. How different they were from the young Ammonites of whom we later will learn.

Yea, they were men of truth and soberness, for they had been taught to keep the commandments of God and to walk uprightly before him.   (Alma 53:21)

Another passage from the Book of Mormon will be instructive here:

And all thy children shall be taught of the Lord; and great shall be the peace of thy children.
In righteousness shalt thou be established; thou shalt be far from oppression for thou shalt not fear, and from terror, for it shall not come near thee.
(3 Nephi 22:13-14)

VERSE 15. *Thus did Alma teach his people.* Alma knew that contention among his people would negate every effort to solidify them and make his people as one. Therefore, he warned against strife and contention. He wanted no quarreling or angry disputes to mar their peaceful way of life. Let "every man love his neighbor as himself."

Alma was, under God, the founder of His Church in Lehi-Nephi and was the High Priest to the people. He was not jealous of his office but instead exacted a full measure of devotion to God; he tolerated no rivalry in the worship of Him. Only those who were given authority to preach and to teach were permitted so to do. That authority came from God through Alma, and through him because he was the High Priest.

VERSES 19-20. *And they called the land Helam.* Under the righteous leadership of Alma and those whom he consecrated to be teachers and priests, the people they began to prosper exceedingly in the land; and they called the land Helam.

20. And it came to pass that they did multiply and prosper exceedingly in the land of Helam; and they built a city, which they called the city of Helam.

21. Nevertheless the Lord seeth fit to chasten his people; yea, he trieth their patience and their faith.

22. Nevertheless — whosoever putteth his trust in him the same shall be lifted up at the last day. Yea, and thus it was with this people.

23. For behold, I will show unto you that they were brought into bondage, and none could deliver them but the Lord their God, yea, even the God of Abraham and Isaac and of Jacob.

24. And it came to pass that he did deliver them, and he did show forth his mighty power unto them, and great were their rejoicings.

---

prospered greatly and increased in numbers. They gradually built a city which was in the land they called, *Helam*. They, too, called the city, *Helam*.

City of Helam. The city built by the people of Alma the Elder, in the Land of Helam. It was eight days' journey from the Waters of Mormon, in the direction of Zarahemla, when that people fled from the murderous persecution of King Noah. After a few years of peaceful occupancy, it was discovered and taken possession of by the Lamanites and placed by their king under the rule of Amulon, one of the former priests of King Noah. By him and his associates the righteous people of Helam were outrageously abused until the Lord, in His mercy, opened up the way for their escape. These events took place, as near as can be told, between the years 147 and 122 B.C. Nothing is recorded of the history of this city after it was deserted by the people of Alma.

Land of Helam. The country immediately surrounding the City of Helam lay somewhere between the Cities of Lehi-Nephi and Zarahemla. It was an eight days' journey, for immigrants, from the former city and fourteen from the latter. It is only mentioned in the Book of Mormon in connection with its occupancy for a few years by the persecuted people of Alma. After they left, it fell into the hands of the Lamanites and became a subdivision of the Land of Nephi.

Verses 21-24. *The Lord seeth fit to chasten his people.* One of the great purposes of this earthly life is that we may become strong in our love for righteous principles and thereby do the things the Lord requires of us. We overcome the world and the things of the world, not by making them part of our lives, nor by condoning them.

A life of comfort and ease usually begets indifference to righteousness. Almost unfailingly it drives all thoughts of God from one's heart. We take a deep plunge into the pseudo joys and follies of the world all the while forgetting the real purpose of life. To remind us that we owe to God a full measure of devotion to Him, and that He will surely require it, "He doth *chasten*" us, sometimes with sickness, hunger, pestilence, and many other trials and tribulations. *Chasten*, means (1) To correct by punishment or by subjection to suffering, trial, etc. (2) To purify and refine, by freeing from faults, especially with a lash, rod, or the like. (*Webster's New Collegiate Dictionary*)

A few passages from the Book of Mormon, and the Holy Bible, explain the meaning of, and the reason why, "the Lord doth chasten" His people:

And thus we see that except the Lord doth chasten his people with many afflictions, yea, except he doth visit them with death and with terror, and with famine and with all manner of pestilence, they will not remember him.   (Helaman 12:3)

Yea, wo unto this people who are called the people of Nephi except they shall repent, when they shall see all these signs and wonders which shall be showed them; for behold, they have been a chosen people of the Lord; yea, the people of Nephi hath he loved, and also hath he chastened them; yea, in the days of their iniquities hath he chastened them because he loveth them.   (Helaman 15:3)

And from the Bible:

Thou shalt also consider in thine heart, that, as a man chasteneth his son, so the Lord thy God chasteneth thee.   (Deut. 8:5)

He that spareth his rod hateth his son: but he that loveth him chasteneth him betimes.   (Proverbs 13:24)

For whom the Lord loveth he chasteneth, and scourgeth every son whom he receiveth.   (Hebrews 12:6)

As many as I love, I rebuke and chasten: be zealous therefore, and repent.   (Rev. 3:19)

Therefore, the sacred historian says of the people of Helam, "He trieth their patience and their faith." Nevertheless, he also says, "Whosoever putteth his trust in him the same shall be lifted up at the last day."

Be lifted up at the last day. From statements made by the Nephite prophets we can easily understand what these words imply.

And blessed are they who shall seek to bring forth my Zion at that day, for they shall have the gift and the power of the Holy Ghost; and if they endure unto the end *they shall be lifted up at the last day,* and shall be saved in the everlasting kingdom of the Lamb; and whoso shall publish peace, yea, tidings of great joy, how beautiful upon the mountains shall they be.   (1 Nephi 13:37)

And it came to pass that I said unto them that I knew that I had spoken hard things against the wicked, according to the truth; and the righteous have I justified, and testified that they *should be lifted up at the last day;* wherefore, the guilty taketh the truth to be hard, for it cutteth them to the very center.   (1 Nephi 16:2)

Having faith on the Lord; having a hope that ye shall receive eternal life; having the love of God always in your hearts, that ye may be *lifted up at the last day* and enter into his rest.   (Alma 13:29)

And now, O my son Helaman, behold, thou art in thy youth, and therefore, I beseech of thee that thou wilt hear my words and learn of me; for I do know that whosoever shall put their trust in God shall be supported in their trials, and their troubles, and their afflictions, and *shall be lifted up at the last day.*   (Alma 36:3)

Counsel with the Lord in all thy doings, and he will direct thee for good: yea, when thou liest down at night lie down unto the Lord, that he may watch over you in your sleep; and when thou risest in the morning let thy heart be full of thanks unto God; and if ye do these things, ye shall be *lifted up at the last day.*   (Alma 37:37)

And now my son, Shiblon, I would that ye should remember, that as much as ye shall put your trust in God even so much ye shall be delivered out of your trials, and your troubles, and your afflictions, and ye shall be *lifted up at the last day.*   (Alma 38:5)

Jesus Christ, the Risen Redeemer, said to the Nephites,

Verily, verily, I say unto you, this is my gospel; and ye know the things that ye must do in my church; for the works which ye have seen me do that shall ye also do; for that which ye have seen me do even that shall ye do.

Therefore, if ye do these things blessed are ye, for ye shall be *lifted up at the last day*. (3 Nephi 27:21-22)

Oftentimes, we are afflicted with trials. Why, we do not know; we are sorely vexed far beyond our seeming powers of endurance. We think our sufferings come upon us penally and punishing. When the great billows of adversity roll over us and we are almost overwhelmed, we begin to say, "My Lord hath forsaken me, and my Lord hath forgotten me." But, in the words of the Prophet Isaiah, which are also repeated in the Book of Mormon, the Lord says, "Yet I will not forget you." (Isaiah 49:14) (1 Nephi 21:15)

The trials and experiences of one generation often form the basis upon which lies the future of a whole people. Enjoyments experienced and sufferings endured leave impressions that are bequeathed by one generation to the next. Many of the conclusions of a people are inherited from their fathers, and their thoughts are generally influenced by what their predecessors believed to be true.

The quoted words of Isaiah's, were spoken to all Israel, but they carry a special message to each one of us. To the down-trodden and oppressed they say, "You shall be delivered," and to the slave, "You shall be set free." They bring comfort to the aching heart of the humble and pure. They say, "He loveth him that followeth after righteousness."

Alma's people took great comfort in Isaiah's words. They had a copy of them, made from the Brass Plates of Laban, which they read and discussed one with the other. They were in sore bondage, yet they knew they would be set free; they were oppressed, and yet these words told them that deliverance was nigh. They had been taught that the Lord does not forsake His people, neither will He permit them to perish. He strengthens the weak and the pure in heart wherever they may be. They knew that He preserves those who love Him.

The historian in the Sacred Record — we may presume it was Alma — who was quoted by Mormon in his abridgment of the *Larger Plates of Nephi*, says, "Yea, and thus it was with this people." (Whether Alma, himself, wrote the account of his people, or whether it was done under his supervision does not alter the fact, "It was Alma's account.")

VERSE 23. *I will show unto you that they were brought into bondage, and none could deliver them but the Lord their God*. Alma now promised to show how, in spite of their righteousness, his people were brought into the cruel and wicked servitude of even more cruel and wicked men.

The Lord had a purpose in permitting Alma's people to be made the slaves of their enemies. The beautiful surroundings of their new homes, the ease with which the earth was made to bring forth its many bounties, the peace which, contrasted with the unrest they had suffered in Noah's kingdom, caused some of them to become neglectful of God's commandments. Others, we may think, became indolent and careless in observing the Law of Moses. Then, too, farther to the north was the main body of the Nephites, who then were a peaceful and God-fearing people and who were ruled by a wise and just monarch, one appointed king at God's command.

From the events, which, we may say cast their shadows before them, one can understand the purposes of the Lord in thus preparing the way for the union of the two peoples under one ruler.

Sore were their afflictions, and many were the burdens put on Alma's people by their bondsmen, yet in marvelous ways did the Lord sustain them. Strength continued to come to them from On High, and succor also came according to their need. The Lord showed them His mighty power, and in countless ways, He delivered them from the snares of the crafty Lamanites. Great were their rejoicings when, at last

2. *Amulon, leader of King Noah's wicked priests, rules subject to the Lamanite monarch.*

25. For behold, it came to pass that while they were in the land of Helam, yea, in the city of Helam, while tilling the land round about, behold an army of the Lamanites was in the borders of the land.

26. Now it came to pass that the brethren of Alma fled from their fields, and gathered themselves together in the city of Helam; and they were much frightened because of the appearance of the Lamanites.

27. But Alma went forth and stood among them, and exhorted them that they should not be frightened, but that they should remember the Lord their God and he would deliver them.

28. Therefore they hushed their fears, and began to cry unto the Lord that he would soften the hearts of the Lamanites, that they would spare them, and their wives, and their children.

29. And it came to pass that the Lord did soften the hearts of the Lamanites. And Alma and his brethren went forth and deliv-ered themselves up unto their hands; and the Lamanites took possession of the land of Helam.

30. Now the armies of the Lamanites, which had followed after the people of king Limhi, had been lost in the wilderness for many days.

31. And behold, they had found those priests of king Noah, in a place which they called Amulon; and they had begun to possess the land of Amulon and had begun to till the ground.

32. Now the name of the leader of those priests was Amulon.

33. And it came to pass that Amulon did plead with the Lamanites; and he also sent forth their wives, who were the daughters of the Lamanites, to plead with their brethren, that they should not destroy their husbands.

34. And the Lamanites had compassion on Amulon and his brethren, and did not destroy them, because of their wives.

35. And Amulon and his brethren did join the Lamanites, and

---

and when all was ready, the Lord answered their prayers and delivered them from bondage. The Sacred Record says that only God could deliver them.

VERSES 25-39. *An army of the Lamanites was in the borders of the land.* The Lamanite army that pursued the people of King Limhi failed to overtake them, and they themselves, became lost in the wilderness. (Mosiah 22:15-16) They knew not where their city lay, nor which way would bring them there. While wandering hither and yon, not knowing where to go, they came across the priests of King Noah who had fled from their fellows to escape the just indignation their continued iniquities had aroused. These priests, at the suggestion of Amulon, their leader, joined the Lamanites, and unitedly endeavored to get back to the Land of Lehi-Nephi. While they were thus engaged they happened to come near the City of Helam.

When the people of Alma first perceived the approach of this body of Lamanite they were traveling in the wilderness in search of the land of Nephi when they discovered the land of Helam, which was possessed by Alma and his brethren. 36. And it came to pass that the Lamanites promised unto Alma and his brethren, that if they would show them the way which led to the land of Nephi that they would grant unto them their lives and their liberty. 37. But after Alma had shown them the way that led to the land of Nephi the Lamanites would not keep their promise; but they set guards round about the land of Helam, over Alma and his brethren. 38. And the remainder of them went to the land of Nephi; and a part of them returned to the land of Helam, and also brought with them the wives and the children of the guards who had been left in the land. 39. And the king of the Lamanites had granted unto Amulon that he should be a king and a ruler over his people, who were in the land of Helam; nevertheless he should have no power to do anything contrary to the will of the king of the Lamanites.

warriors, they were engaged tilling the soil around their city. In their great fear, occasioned by the appearance of this large body of men, they immediately fled to the City of Helam.

Alma's faith and courage were conspicuous as he gathered his people around him, and called them to cast aside their thoughtless ways and to remember God who had always delivered those who trusted in Him.

The words of Alma had the desired effect; the people silenced their fears and called mightily upon the Lord to soften the hearts of the Lamanites that they might spare their lives and those of their wives and little ones. Then, with the assurance in their hearts that the Lord would hearken to their prayers, Alma and his brethren went forth out of their city and delivered themselves up to their former foes. The Lamanites thereupon took possession of the Land of Helam, and posted guards over Alma and his people.

VERSES 36-39. *The Lamanites promised to grant Alma's people their lives and their liberty.* The Lamanites were in a dilemma and, therefore, were full of promises. They were willing to grant the people of Helam their lives and liberty if they would show them the way to the City of Lehi-Nephi. Alma then showed them the way they should take to return to their homes. He, however was deceived by them. "The counsels of the wicked are deceit." (Proverbs 12:5)

Having obtained the information they sought, and having reached their homes in safety, the Lamanites broke their promises to Alma, and made Amulon the king over the entire Land of Helam. Amulon, nevertheless, was a vassal monarch. He vowed homage and fealty to King Laman was was the ruler of all the Lamanites. Also, the historian wrote, Amulon should have no power, of himself, to do "anything contrary to the will of the king of the Lamanites."

AMULON

One of the most prominent of the degraded priests of King Noah. He undoubtedly took an active part in the martyrdom of the Prophet Abinadi though not mentioned by name (about B.C. 150). When King Noah was burned to death by his enraged subjects they would have killed his priests also, but the latter fled before them into the depths of the wilderness. Here the priests hid for a lengthened period, both afraid and ashamed to return to their families. In this dilemma, being without wives, they surprised and carried off a number of Lamanite maidens who had gathered to a much-frequented spot in the land of Shemlon on mirth and pleasure intent. This act led to a war between the Lamanites and Nephites in the land of Lehi-Nephi which was soon put to an end when the trouble was understood. Amulon and his associates with their Lamanite wives settled in and commenced to cultivate the land of Amulon. There they were discovered by the Lamanite soldiery who were searching for the people of Limhi, but as they plead most abjectly for mercy, in which petitions they were joined by their Lamanite companions, the Lamanites had compassion on them and did not destroy them because of their wives (B.C. 121). Amulon and his brethren then joined the Lamanites and soon after the king made Amulon the ruler, under his supreme authority, of the lands of Amulon and Helam. By this appointment Amulon and his associates became the overseers of the people of Alma and right brutally did they use their authority in oppressing the people of God until the day that the Lord delivered them. Amulon and his brethren were also made teachers and educators of the Lamanites by King Laman. These ex-priests instructed the people in the learning of the Nephites but they taught them nothing concerning the Lord or the law of Moses. Of Amulon's death we have no record.

CHAPTER 24

1. *Amulon Persecutes Alma and his Followers, The Lord Makes their Burdens Light and Delivers them from Bondage—2. They Journey to Zarahemla.*

1. *Amulon persecutes Alma and his followers.*

1. And it came to pass that Amulon did gain favor in the eyes of the king of the Lamanites; therefore, the king of the Lamanites granted unto him and his brethren that they should be appointed teachers over his people, yea, even over the people who were in the land of Shemlon, and in the land of Shilom, and in the land of Amulon.

2. For the Lamanites had taken possession of all these lands; therefore, the king of the Lamanites had appointed kings over all these lands.

3. And now the name of the king of the Lamanites was Laman, being called after the name of his father; and therefore he was called king Laman. And he was king over a numerous people.

4. And he appointed teachers of the brethren of Amulon in every land which was possessed by his people; and thus the language of Nephi began to be taught among all the people of the Lamanites.

5. And they were a people friendly one with another; nevertheless they knew not God; neither did the brethren of Amulon teach them anything concerning the Lord their God, neither the law of Moses; nor did they teach them the words of Abinadi.

6. But they taught them that they should keep their record, and that they might write one to another.

VERSES 1-3. *Amulon did gain favor in the eyes of the king.* Amulon and the former priests of Noah, possibly because of their Lamanitish wives, soon gained great favor with King Laman, and were made teachers to his people. Laman, who was king over a large area in the Land of Lehi, had the same name as did his father, and ruled a numerous people. In his domain were the Lands of Shemlon and Shilom, which were near the City of Lehi-Nephi. The Sacred Record also mentions the Land of Amulon, apparently the place where the priests had formerly made their homes. King Laman appointed subservient kings, or chiefs, over each of these divisions.

VERSES 4-6. *King Laman appointed Amulon's brethren to be teachers.* Here the student may obtain a fuller insight into King Laman's character when he understands that in his newly acquired subjects, Laman saw the chance to better his people's conditions by increasing their opportunity to learn the things of the more-enlightened Nephites. He therefore appointed Amulon's brethren, who were formerly the priests of King Noah, to positions of trust as teachers throughout the land where his people dwelt.

The Lamanites were not slothful in availing for themselves the opportunity to improve their lives. No doubt, King Laman and his followers were a bloodthirsty people. No doubt that they envied the more prosperous Nephites, and sometimes,

7. And thus the Lamanites began to increase in riches, and began to trade one with another and wax great, and began to be a cunning and a wise people, as to the wisdom of the world, yea, a very cunning people, delighting in all manner of wickedness and plunder, except it were among their own brethren.

8. And now it came to pass that Amulon began to exercise authority over Alma and his brethren, and began to persecute him, and cause that his children should persecute their children.

9. For Amulon knew Alma, that he had been one of the king's priests, and that it was he that believed the words of Abinadi and was driven out before the king, and therefore he was wroth with him; for he was subject to king Laman, yet he exercised authority over them, and put tasks upon them, and put task-masters over them.

10. And it came to pass that so great were their afflictions that they began to cry mightily to God.

11. And Amulon commanded

---

even by making war upon them, sought to gain the fruits of their labors by overpowering them.

Educated in the language of the Nephites, the priests began to instruct the Lamanites. They taught them nothing of the religion of the priests' fathers, or the Law of Moses, but they did instruct them how to keep their records, and to write one to another.

The Lamanites, among themselves, were friendly, but the hatred they had for the Nephites, and the false traditions handed down to them by their forefathers, precluded a belief by them in the Nephite God. They knew nothing of Him. The priests never explained to them the wonderful words—or the prophecies—of the Prophet Abinadi. How the Lord would come down from heaven and would dwell among men. How, through His ministrations, men would see that they were brothers, and would thereafter live in peace.

The bitter resentment that filled the hearts of the priests, together with their malignant dread of the truth, prevented much good they might have done, and prostituted what they did do to the meanest purposes of crime, idolatry, and unbelief. However, the coming of the priests of former King Noah among the Lamanites gave rise to a different, if not a more enlightened civilization. As a result, the Lamanites increased in wealth, and trade and commerce extended between them. In their dealings one with the other, they became cunning and wise. They waxed strong. In worldly goods they grew in power, yet they still were given to robbery, and to plundering their neighbor's households and farms. However, it is said of them that they never molested a member of their own clan.

VERSES 8-9. *Amulon knew Alma.* Alma and Amulon had known each other in the days of King Noah, when each was a priest under him. With the venom so often conspicuous in apostates, Amulon soon commenced to persecute those who were faithful to the Lord. He placed taskmasters over them, he imposed inhuman burdens upon them, and otherwise afflicted them grievously.

VERSES 10-15. *Because of their afflictions they cried mightily to the Lord.* In the agony of their hearts, Alma's people called continually upon the Lord for deliverance. Their prayers annoyed their cruel masters, and they were forbidden to pray aloud;

them that they should stop their cries; and he put guards over them to watch them, that whosoever should be found calling upon God should be put to death.

12. And Alma and his people did not raise their voices to the Lord their God, but did pour out their hearts to him; and he did know the thoughts of their hearts.

13. And it came to pass that the voice of the Lord came to them in their afflictions, saying: Lift up your heads and be of good comfort, for I know of the covenant which ye have made unto me; and I will covenant with my people and deliver them out of bondage.

14. And I will also ease the burdens which are put upon your shoulders, that even you cannot feel them upon your backs, even while you are in bondage; and this will I do that ye may stand as witnesses for me hereafter, and that ye may know of a surety that I, the Lord God, do visit my people in their afflictions.

15. And now it came to pass that the burdens which were laid upon Alma and his brethren were made light; yea, the Lord did strengthen them that they could bear up their burdens with ease, and they did submit cheerfully and with patience to all the will of the Lord.

16. And it came to pass that so great was their faith and their patience that the voice of the Lord came unto them again, saying: Be of good comfort, for on the morrow I will deliver you out of bondage.

17. And he said unto Alma: Thou shalt go before this people, and I will go with thee and deliver this people out of bondage.

18. Now it came to pass that Alma and his people in the nighttime gathered their flocks together, and also of their grain; yea, even all the night-time were they gathering their flocks together.

19. And in the morning the Lord caused a deep sleep to come upon the Lamanites, yea, and all their task-masters were in a profound sleep.

20. And Alma and his people departed into the wilderness; and when they had traveled all day they pitched their tents in a valley, and they called the valley Alma, because he led their way in the wilderness.

21. Yea, and in the valley of Alma they poured out their thanks to God because he had been merciful unto them, and

but no tyrants, however powerful and cruel, could prevent them praying in their hearts. This, the people of Alma continued to do fervently, and in due time, although not immediately, deliverance came.

In the meantime the Lord comforted and strengthened them in their afflictions so that their burdens were more easily borne.

VERSES 16-22. *I will deliver you out of bondage.* The time of their deliverance though it seemed to them to be long delayed, finally came. On a certain day the Lord promised them that on the morrow, "I will deliver you out of bondage." That eased their burdens, and had delivered them out of bondage; for they were in bondage, and none could deliver them except it were the Lord their God.

22. And they gave thanks to God, yea, all their men and all their women and all their children that could speak lifted their voices in the praises of their God.

2. They journey to Zarahemla.

23. And now the Lord said unto Alma: Haste thee and get thou and this people out of this land, for the Lamanites have awakened and do pursue thee; therefore get thee out of this land, and I will stop the Lamanites in this valley that they come no further in pursuit of this people.

24. And it came to pass that they departed out of the valley, and took their journey into the wilderness.

25. And after they had been in the wilderness twelve days they arrived in the land of Zarahemla, and king Mosiah did also receive them with joy.

---

night they were occupied in getting their flocks and provisions together, and preparing for the contemplated journey.

In the morning, when their Lamanite guards and taskmasters were in a deep sleep which the Lord caused to come over them, Alma and his people set out on their journey in the wilderness. After traveling all day, they pitched their tents in a valley which they called by the name of their leader, *Alma*. In the joy their newly-found freedom imparted, even the children as well as their fathers and mothers joined in praising the Lord for His goodness in bringing them from under the oppressor's heel. They knew that "none could deliver them except it were the Lord their God."

VERSES 23-35. *The Lamanites pursue Alma.* The Lord warned Alma to hasten out of this country because the Lamanites had wakened from their sleep and were pursuing them. However, the Lord said He would stop their pursuit when they came to the valley where Alma was then encamped. Alma and his company of faithful followers, traveled yet another twelve days, at the end of which time they arrived in Zarahemla where Mosiah reigned over a God-fearing and peace-loving people who greatly rejoiced in Alma's deliverance.

CHAPTER 25

1. Zarahemla, a Descendant of Mulek—2. The Record of Zeniff and the Account of Alma read to the People—3. Alma Authorized to Establish the Church of Christ Throughout the Land.

1. Zarahemla, a descendant of Mulek.

1. And now king Mosiah caused that all the people should be gathered together.

2. Now there were not so many of the children of Nephi, or so many of those who were descendants of Nephi, as there were of the people of Zarahemla, who was a descendent of Mulek, and those who came with him into the wilderness.

3. And there were not so many of the people of Nephi and of the people of Zarahemla as there were of the Lamanites; yea, they were not half so numerous.

4. And now all the people of Nephi were assembled together, and also all the people of Zarahemla, and they were gathered together in two bodies.

Verses 1-4. *King Mosiah did cause that all the people should gather together.* All the inhabitants of Zarahemla at this time were considered Nephites, although the descendants of Mulek were the most numerous. Mosiah II, who reigned in the capital city, also ruled those whose homes were in the surrounding area which also was called Zarahemla. His subjects were a consolidation of two races.

Though Mulek's people were the most in numbers, the Nephites were the governing race, and the kingship was only conferred upon those who were the descendants of Nephi, the son of Lehi. The Nephites ruled by right of their higher civilization and their possession of the records, both those that their fathers had brought from Jerusalem, and their own. The fact that the ruler of the Mulekites, Zarahemla, who was a descendant of the original Mulek, together with his followers, recognized that the Nephites had the Holy Priesthood with them also gave the Nephites the right to rule.

The recent advent of Limhi's people from Lehi-Nephi, as also the arrival of Alma and his brethren at almost the same time, were the causes of great rejoicing among the Nephites at Zarahemla.

There is another important fact which the historian of the Sacred Record draws to our attention: The inhabitants of South America were preponderantly Lamanites. They were twice as numerous as the combined people of Lehi-Nephi and Zarahemla. This was due, perhaps, to the fact that when any defection occurred among the Nephites, the dissatisfied portions of the community generally went over to the Lamanites and were eventually absorbed in that race.

Mosiah now caused that all the people should be gathered into one place. He then divided them into two groups. The first, were Nephites, who included the people of Limhi and the followers of Alma, together with all those over whom his father, King Benjamin, had appointed him to be ruler. The second group were the descendants of Mulek, the Jewish prince who, as an infant, had escaped the wrath of Nebuchadnezzar with his entourage, when that famous king carried his father, King Zedekiah, into Babylonian captivity. Mulek had founded the City of Zarahemla.

2. The Record of Zeniff and the account of Alma read to the people.

5. And it came to pass that Mosiah did read, and caused to be read, the records of Zeniff to his people; yea, he read the records of the people of Zeniff, from the time they left the land of Zarahemla until they returned again.

6. And he also read the account of Alma and his brethren, and all their afflictions, from the time they left the land of Zarahemla until the time they returned again.

7. And now, when Mosiah had made an end of reading the rec-

Mosiah's purpose in calling this conference was so that his people might know how the Lord had blessed both Limhi's and Alma's followers, and that the Lord is always with those who trust in Him.

VERSE 5. *Mosiah did read the records of Zeniff to his people.* Mosiah read the complete history of Zeniff's people as it was contained in the records which had been kept by them. He read how Zeniff, a determined but not a very wise man, gathered his followers in Zarahemla about him, and led them to the old homes of their fathers in Lehi-Nephi. He read how Zeniff made a treaty with Laman, who was king of the Lamanites in that land, and how Zeniff's people began to repair and recover the homes of their immediate ancestors which had been allowed to go into disrepair by Lamanite squatters.

Mosiah also read that Zeniff's people had prospered when they kept the commandments of the Lord; that they were a goodly people, and that they strictly observed the Law of Moses. The records of Zeniff showed that among them were men who held God's Holy Priesthood.

Then he read of Zeniff's death, and of the evil reign of Noah, Zeniff's son who succeeded him. He repeated the words of the Prophet Abinadi. He read of the Prophet's cruel martyrdom, and the rebuke of the Lord, pronounced by Abinadi, to King Noah, calling him to repent.

Mosiah read to the multitude about the wicked ways into which their brethren had been led by the priests of King Noah, and that vicious and degrading bondage was the result of their iniquities.

Finally, he read that the Nephites repented and in great sorrow sought the Lord to deliver them from their sore oppression. He also read, as many who were gathered there testified, that the repentant Nephites under King Limhi escaped the horrible persecutions of the Lamanites, and were at last led to their loved ones in Zarahemla by the Lord.

VERSE 6. *He also read the account of Alma and his brethren.* Continuing, Mosiah also read how Alma, who now stood among them, led those who had taken the name of God upon them at the Waters of Mormon into the wilderness before an army of King Noah that sought to destroy them.

He read of their afflictions and how, while under the servitude of wicked men, the Lord had eased their tasks, and their burdens became light to bear because of their prayers to Him. Mosiah read to them how, in a miraculous manner, the Lord guided Alma and his brethren to Zarahemla where with the main body of Nephites, they raised their voices in thanksgiving, praising God.

VERSES 7-11. *Mosiah's people were struck with wonder.* When Mosiah's people beheld Alma and those of whom the records spoke standing before them, and that Alma's group had come through the ravages of war and bondage, they were amazed.

ords, his people who tarried in the land were struck with wonder and amazement.

8. For they knew not what to think; for when they beheld those that had been delivered out of bondage they were filled with exceeding great joy.

9. And again, when they thought of their brethren who had been slain by the Lamanites they were filled with sorrow, and even shed many tears of sorrow.

10. And again, when they thought of the immediate goodness of God, and his power in delivering Alma and his brethren out of the hands of the Lamanites and of bondage, they did raise their voices and give thanks to God.

11. And again, when they thought upon the Lamanites, who were their brethren, of their sinful and polluted state, they were filled with pain and anguish for the welfare of their souls.

12. And it came to pass that those who were the children of Amulon and his brethren, who had taken to wife the daughters of the Lamanites, were displeased with the conduct of their fathers, and they would no longer be called by the names of their fathers, therefore they took upon themselves the name of Nephi, that they might be called the children of Nephi and be numbered among those who were called Nephites.

13. And now all the people of Zarahemla were numbered with the Nephites, and this because the kingdom had been conferred upon none but those who were descendants of Nephi.

14. And now it came to pass

But their wonder and amazement were turned into sadness when they thought of their brethren who had been slain by the inhuman Lamanites, and they shed many tears over their kindred dead.

Again, when they listened to the marvelous deliverances wrought by heaven in behalf of Alma and his faithful few, the assembled thousands raised their voices to God and gave thanks and renewed their pledges of fidelity to Him.

Still another shade of feeling came across their sympathetic hearts, even of pain and anguish for the sinful and polluted state of their Lamanite brethren, when their condition was explained to them.

VERSE 12. *The children of Amulon and the priests became displeased with the conduct of their fathers.* By way of interpolation, the historian of the Sacred Record informs us that the "children of Amulon and his brethren, who had taken to wife the daughters of the Lamanites, were displeased with the conduct of their fathers."

Evidently those Nephites who later became Lamanites continued to pursue the wicked ways they had walked as priests of Noah. Their children were ashamed to be called by the names of their fathers, and therefore chose to be called Nephites, and they took upon themselves the name of Nephi. Afterwards they were numbered among the Nephites.

VERSE 13. *All the people of Zarahemla were numbered with the Nephites.* See verses 1-4.

VERSES 14-16. *When Mosiah had finished speaking, he desired that Alma should also speak to the people.* When Mosiah had finished speaking to the people, he

that when Mosiah had made an end of speaking and reading to the people, he desired that Alma should also speak to the people.

15. And Alma did speak unto them, when they were assembled together in large bodies, and he went from one body to another, preaching unto the people repentance and faith on the Lord.

16. And he did exhort the people of Limhi and his brethren, all those that had been delivered out of bondage, that they should remember that it was the Lord that did deliver them.

17. And it came to pass that after Alma had taught the people many things, and had made an end of speaking to them, that king Limhi was desirous that he might be baptized; and all his people were desirous that they might be baptized also.

18. Therefore, Alma did go forth into the water and did baptize them; yea, he did baptize them after the manner he did his brethren in the waters of Mormon; yea, and as many as he did baptize did belong to the church of God; and this because of their belief on the words of Alma.

---

requested Alma to speak also. Together they addressed the large number of Mosiah's subjects on such subjects as they deemed necessary. Alma went from one multitude to another, preaching faith and repentance in the Lord.

Especially did Alma exhort Limhi and his people to remember that by the power of God, alone, were they delivered from the yoke of bondage which the Lamanites had fastened upon them. He reminded them that much of their own strength had been lost in their repeated but unsuccessful rebellions in which the Lamanites had slain many of their brethren. He told them that freedom from woe and affliction was not to be gained by any force, they, themselves, brought to bear, nor was it to be attained by the cunning of their wise men, but it was to be obtained only through the direct interposition of the Lord, the Mighty One who dwells On High.

Verses 17-18. *Limhi and all his people request baptism.* After hearing the teachings of Alma, Limhi and all his people requested that they be baptized. They were so struck with the truth of Alma's words and exhortations—that they should remember always the goodness and loving kindness of God in freeing them from the slavery of the Lamanites—that they cried unanimously that they desired to walk obediently before God, and circumspectly with their brethren in doing those things the Lord required.

Alma, we presume, after conferring with Mosiah, granted their request for baptism and thereupon went forth into the water. As he had baptized their brethren when still they dwelt in Lehi-Nephi, Alma now baptized them in the waters that were provided for this very purpose. (See Chapter 18)

It should be noted that the same ritual observed by Alma in performing this sacred ordinance is the same as the practice celebrated today by the Church of Jesus Christ of Latter-day Saints. (See Vol. I, p. 431, Commentary on the Book of Mormon)

Baptism is a commandment that must be complied with by everyone who desires membership in the Church of God. And everyone who is willing, and is baptized, becomes a member of His Church and is counted with the Saints of God. Even

3. Alma authorized to establish the Church of Christ throughout the land.

19. And it came to pass that king Mosiah granted unto Alma that he might establish churches throughout all the land of Zarahemla; and gave him power to ordain priests and teachers over every church.

20. Now this was done because there were so many people that they could not all be governed by one teacher; neither could they all hear the word of God in one assembly.

21. Therefore they did assemble themselves together in different bodies, being called churches; every church having their priests and their teachers, and every priest preaching the word according as it was delivered to him by the mouth of Alma.

22. And thus, notwithstanding there being many churches they were all one church, yea, even the church of God; for there was nothing preached in all the churches except it were repentance and faith in God.

23. And now there were seven churches in the land of Zarahemla. And it came to pass that whosoever were desirous to take upon them the name of Christ, or of God, they did join the churches of God;

24. And they were called the people of God. And the Lord did pour out his Spirit upon them, and they were blessed, and prospered in the land.

---

as it is today, this was the order of admittance into the *Church and Kingdom of God* in Mosiah's time.

VERSES 19-24. *King Mosiah granted unto Alma that he might establish churches throughout all the land of Zarahemla.* Alma, under the direction of King Mosiah, now went throughout all the land organizing branches of the Church. It was, of course, impossible for the priests and teachers of one congregation to care for the needs of all the Saints. It was for this reason that Alma established seven different branches of the Church in the Land of Zarahemla.

Every branch had its own priests and teachers who taught only what Alma taught them. To prevent any speculation and any private opinion from influencing their teachings, nothing was taught by them except it were "repentance and faith in God."

Thus did Alma enlarge the number of, may we say, the stakes and wards in Zion, and thus he provided many persons an opportunity to serve who, otherwise, may have been forgotten.

And then, the Sacred Record says, "It came to pass that whosoever were desirous to take upon them the name of Christ, or of God, they did join the churches of God; And they were called the people of God. And the Lord did pour out his Spirit upon them, and they were blessed, and prospered in the land."

CHAPTER 26

1. *Concerning Unbelievers and Evil Doers—2. The Lord Instructs Alma How to Deal with them.*

1. *Concerning unbelievers and evil doers.*

1. Now it came to pass that there were many of the rising generation that could not understand the words of king Benjamin, being little children at the time he spake unto his people; and they did not believe the tradition of their fathers.

2. They did not believe what had been said concerning the resurrection of the dead, neither did they believe concerning the coming of Christ.

3. And now because of their unbelief they could not understand the word of God; and their hearts were hardened.

4. And they would not be baptized; neither would they join the church. And they were a separate people as to their faith, and remained so ever after, even in their carnal and sinful state; for they would not call upon the Lord their God.

5. And now in the reign of Mosiah they were not half so numerous as the people of God; but because of the dissensions among the brethren they became more numerous.

6. For it came to pass that they did deceive many with their flattering words, who were in the church, and did cause them to commit many sins; therefore it became expedient that those who committed sin, that were in the church, should be admonished by the church.

VERSES 1-13. *There were many of the rising generation who did not believe the tradition of their fathers.* In the passing of years many of the rising generation gave no heed to the Word of God. These were mostly those who were too young to enter into a covenant with the Lord at the time that King Benjamin anointed Mosiah to be his successor.

Not only did they, themselves, reject the doctrines of the Atonement, the Resurrection, and other Gospel principles, but also they led away many of the members of the Church into darkness and iniquity. They abused, reviled, and persecuted those who remained faithful to the cause of Christ.

As is so often the practice with those who deride and deny the truth when it is presented to them, the unbelief of many of these youthful apostates in Zarahemla precluded any understanding by them of the marvelous ways of the Lord and their hearts became hardened.

They would not adjust themselves with God's people, nor would they join His Church. They separated, each one of them, spiritually, from the companionship of good and upright men and women, and, therefore, they sank deeper and deeper "into their carnal and sinful state." In the darkness that blinded them, they refused to call upon the Lord for a *lamp* to guide their feet.

During the latter part of King Mosiah's reign over the Nephites in Zarahemla, the number of these youthful offenders became so great as to awaken fear in the hearts of their brethren. By their shameless deeds they caused much dissension

7. And it came to pass that they were brought before the priests, and delivered up unto the priests by the teachers; and the priests brought them before Alma, who was the high priest.

8. Now king Mosiah had given Alma the authority over the church.

9. And it came to pass that Alma did not know concerning them; but there were many witnesses against them; yea, the people stood and testified of their iniquity in abundance.

10. Now there had not any such thing happened before in the church; therefore Alma was troubled in his spirit, and he caused that they should be brought before the king.

11. And he said unto the king: Behold, here are many whom we have brought before thee, who are

even among those who professed undying faithfulness to God and His commandments. Their number increased until more fraternized with the wicked than there were those who remained true and righteous.

Now, many left the Church, not by wilful apostasy, thus declaring their intent, but by their abandonment of those truths they had formerly and voluntarily professed. For many of them it was nearly a complete desertion of their principles and faith. Iniquity abounded among them, yet, some of them retained fellowship with the people of God. Soon it became necessary to admonish the sinful. This was done both in kindness and in severely reprimanding the transgressors by the priests and teachers who labored unceasingly that the work of the Lord should proceed onward.

VERSE 7. *They were brought before the priests.* The procedure in handling the wayward is herein outlined. The offender was brought before the priests by the teachers, who, in turn, gathered all the evidence, both for and against the accused, and together they went before the High Priest, who in this case was Alma.

VERSE 8. *King Mosiah had given Alma the authority over the Church.* Alma had been made the "court of highest appeal" in all church matters, he having the final decision.

VERSE 9. *The people stood and testified of iniquity.* Alma, only recently having joined the Saints in Zarahemla, was not acquainted with all the conditions to be found among them. He was alarmed at the sudden disclosure to him of the wickedness abounding there, and was depressed by its terrible forebodings. He, however, did not lose heart although a great number of witnesses made solemn declarations of its existence.

VERSE 10. *Alma caused that the wicked should be brought before him.* What he was to do concerning this evil was the thought uppermost in Alma's mind. There had been nothing like it that ever happened in the Church before, no precedence to guide him in his troubled deliberations. What should he do? Alma wanted to be just, yet he knew a stern policy toward the wicked was necessary. Prudence and wisdom, tempered by grace, was, he soon found, a stepping-stone to the solution of the problem that now faced him. In this dilemma, Alma sought the counsel of King Mosiah.

VERSE 11. *Alma said to the king, Here are many who have been taken in divers iniquities. They do not repent.* There were some, we imagine, who did repent and were forgiven. Others who transgressed were haughty and unashamed. They would not promise to give up their evil ways as they were exhorted to do.

accused of their brethren; yea, and they have been taken in divers iniquities. And they do not repent of their iniquities; therefore we have brought them before thee, that thou mayest judge them according to their crimes.

12. But king Mosiah said unto Alma: Behold, I judge them not; therefore I deliver them into thy hands to be judged.

13. And now the spirit of Alma was again troubled; and he went and inquired of the Lord what he should do concerning this matter, for he feared that he should do wrong in the sight of God.

14. And it came to pass that after he had poured out his whole soul to God, the voice of the Lord came to him, saying:

15. Blessed art thou, Alma, and blessed are they who were baptized in the waters of Mormon. Thou art blessed because of thy exceeding faith in the words alone of my servant Abinadi.

16. And blessed are they because of their exceeding faith in the words alone which thou hast spoken unto them.

17. And blessed art thou because thou hast established a church among this people; and they shall be my people.

18. Yea, blessed is this people who are willing to bear my name; for in my name shall they be called; and they are mine.

Alma then placed them at the mercy of the king, and asked that he pass sentence upon the guilty.

It appears that their government then was a theocracy, or a government which received its immediate direction of God, through His servants. Of this, we are about to learn. But neither the fear of the civil law, nor the divine one, restrained the wrongdoers from the wicked paths they pursued.

VERSE 12. *King Mosiah said, "Behold, I judge them not."* King Mosiah refused to enter that branch of government which he, in wisdom, had delegated to Alma. He, therefore, instructed Alma to be their judge.

VERSE 13. *The spirit of Alma was again troubled.* Once again, Alma was left without an appeal except to that great Judge who presides in the Courts Above. In fervent prayer he called unto Him for aid.

VERSES 14-16. *Blessed art thou, Alma.* Almost immediately after Alma had ceased to pray, the Lord called unto him saying that, because of his exceeding faith in the words of Abinadi, he was blessed. Not only was he alone blessed, but also all those who were baptized by him in the Waters of Mormon. The Lord further stated that they believed, having no additional witness to guide them save it were Alma's own words.

VERSES 17-18. *Thou hast established a church among this people.* The Lord continued his blessings upon Alma, for He said, "Thou hast established a church among this people." The Lord promised Alma that He would establish them in righteousness, and because they were willing to "bear my name," by that name shall they be called; "and they are mine."

Establish, means to *settle,* or *make firm.* To *confirm;* to *make good.*

Other usages of the word, *establish*, in the Book of Mormon are found in the following passages:

ESTABLISH

1 Nephi	13:40	Gentiles, shall e. the truth of the first
	21:8	Covenant of the people, to e. the earth
2 Nephi	11:3	God hath said, I will e. my word
	19:7	To e. it with judgment and with justice
	27:14	Deemeth him good, will he e. his word
Mosiah	10:1	We again began to e. the kingdom
	19:27	Limhi began to e. the kingdom
	25:19	E. churches throughout all the land
	27:13	This is my church, and I will e. it
	29:13	Kings, who would e. the laws of God
Alma	1:6	And even began to e. a church
	28	Thus did they e. the affairs of the church
	2:2	To e. Amlici to be a king over
	4:4	They began to e. the church more fully
	5:3	He began to e. a church in the land
	5	We began to e. the church of God
	6:4	They began to e. the order of the church
	12:1	And to e. the words of Amulek
	17:11	Go forth among the Lamanites ... and e. my work
	19:35	They did e. a church among them
	29:11	Bondage, and by this did e. his church
	13	That same God did e. his church
	43:29	Might e. a kingdom unto themselves
	45:22	Went forth to e. the church again
	46:5	And e. him to be their king
	34	To e. and to exercise authority over them
	51:5	And to e. a king over the land
	62:46	They did e. again the church of God
3 Nephi	5:12	In the which Alma did e. the church
	6:30	And to e. a king over the land
	7:1	They did not e. a king over the land
	11	It were their leaders did e. their laws
	14	But they did e. very strict laws
	11:40	And e. it for my doctrine, the same
	20:21	I will e. my people, O house of Israel
	22	This people will I e. in this land
	21:1	And shall e. again among them my Zion
	22	I will e. my church among them
Ether	10:9	Did e. himself king over all the land

Established—

1 Nephi	13:41	Words which will be e. by the mouth
	41	They both shall be e. in one
	21:13	Who are in the east shall be e.
	22:22	Which kingdom is e. among them
2 Nephi	9:2	And shall be e. in all their lands
	12:2	Mountain of the Lord's house shall be e.
	17:9	Not believe, surely ye shall not be e.

19. And because thou hast in- | 20. Thou are my servant; and
quired of me concerning the | I covenant with thee that thou
transgressor, thou art blessed. | shalt have eternal life; and thou

Mosiah	26:17	Because thou hast e. a church
	17	They shall be e., and they shall be
Alma	1:1	Nevertheless he e. laws, and they
	2:3	Must be e. by the voice of the people
Alma	5:2	The church which was e. in ... Zarahemla
	6:1	Which was e. in the city of Zarahemla
	8	Which was e. in the valley of Gideon
	7:4	Knowing that they are e. again
	8:1	Having e. the order of the church
	11	Over the church which thou hast e.
	11:4	They having been e. by ... Mosiah
	15:13	Alma e. a church in ... Sidom
	17	Alma having e. the church at Sidom
	16:21	The church having been e. throughout
	20:1	When they had e. a church in that
	27:9	The law ... which was e. by my father
	28:1	After the people of Ammon were e.
	1	And a church also e. in ... Jershon
	30:1	After the people of Ammon were e.
	52:15	Moroni, who had e. armies to protect
	62:42	Peace e. among the people of Nephi
Helaman	3:23	There was continual peace e.
	23	Combinations which Gadianton ... had e.
	5:2	Their governments were e. by the voice
	6:3	The church of God, which had been e.
	7:25	Secret band which was e. by Gadianton
3 Nephi	5:12	The first church which was e. among them
	7:14	They were e. according to the minds
	21:4	They should be e. in this land
	22:14	In righteousness shalt thou be e.
Ether	5:4	Mouth of three witnesses shall these things be e.
	10:10	After that he had e. himself king

Establishing—
2 Nephi	3:12	E. peace among the fruit of thy loins
Alma	23:4	E. churches, and consecrating priests

Establishment—
Alma	16:15	The e. of the church became general

VERSES 19-20. *Thou art blessed because thou hast inquired of me concerning the transgressor.* The Lord knew that Alma wanted to judge righteously the sinner, and also that he wanted to make no mistake in dealing with the transgressors. Alma's humility in this sorrowful experience brought forth the blessings of heaven, because from this time on he knew that the Lord was pleased with his integrity and devotion.

Too often we judge the sinner quickly, and without knowing the truth concerning his errors. Many things exist that influence man's actions and over them he has little or no control. A higher Judge than you or I has said that it is high to be a

shalt serve me and go forth in my name, and shalt gather together my sheep.

21. And he that will hear my voice shall be my sheep; and him shall ye receive into the church, and him will I also receive.

22. For behold, this is my church; whosoever is baptized shall be baptized unto repentance.

---

judge. Christ also said, "Judge not according to the appearance, but judge righteous judgment." (John 7:24) Alma felt incompetent, with no help, to judge his fellowmen. The thought that he, alone, should judge them weighed heavily upon his mind. The words spoken by the Savior over a hundred years later expressed the sentiments Alma desired would uphold him. Therefore Alma's prayer.

"Thou art my servant"; the Lord told Alma, "And I covenant with thee that thou shalt have eternal life." In addition the Lord said to him, "Thou shalt serve me and go forth in my name, and shalt gather together my sheep." No greater privilege could Alma ask, no greater blessing could he enjoy, than to hear from the Lord's own lips the wonderful assurance that the Master of all wanted him to labor by His side.

VERSE 21. *He that will hear my voice shall be my sheep.* My voice means *My commands,* or *the words My servants speak.* To *hear* is to *obey.* The Lord often likens His people to a flock, and one who is obedient and therefore willing to follow Him, a sheep of His fold. Such a one the Lord commands, "Thou shalt receive him into the church," and He gives the added words of comfort, "Him will I also receive."

A few years later than when this took place, Alma, who was the son of this Alma who then was the High Priest, said:

Yea, even wo unto all ye workers of iniquity; repent, repent, for the Lord God hath spoken it!

Behold, he sendeth an invitation unto all men, for the arms of mercy are extended towards them, and he saith: Repent, and I will receive you.

Yea, he saith: Come unto me and ye shall partake of the fruit of the tree of life; yea, ye shall eat and drink of the bread and the waters of life freely;

Yea, come unto me and bring forth works of righteousness, and ye shall not be hewn down and cast into the fire—

For behold, the time is at hand that whosoever bringeth forth not good fruit, or whosoever doeth not the works of righteousness, the same have cause to wail and mourn.

O ye workers of iniquity; ye that are puffed up in the vain things of the world, ye that have professed to have known the ways of righteousness nevertheless have gone astray, as sheep having no shepherd, notwithstanding a shepherd hath called after you and is still calling after you, but ye will not hearken unto his voice!

Behold, I say unto you, that the good shepherd doth call you; yea, and in his own name he doth call you, which is the name of Christ; and if ye will not hearken unto the voice of the good shepherd, to the name by which ye are called, behold, ye are not the sheep of the good shepherd.

And now if ye are not the sheep of the good shepherd, of what fold are ye? Behold, I say unto you, that the devil is your shepherd, and ye are of his fold; and now, who can deny this? Behold, I say unto you, whosoever denieth this is a liar and a child of the devil.

For I say unto you that whatsoever is good cometh from God, and whatsoever is evil cometh from the devil. (Alma 5:32-40)

VERSE 22. *For behold, this is my church.* It being the *Church of God,* or the *Church of the Creator,* (verse 23) the Lord set forth the conditions necessary for membership therein. We may ask, "Who is God, save He be the Lord?" And, "Who

And whomsoever ye receive shall believe in my name; and him will I freely forgive.

23. For it is I that taketh upon me the sins of the world; for it is I that hath created them; and it is I that granteth unto him that believeth unto the end a place at my right hand.

24. For behold, in my name are they called; and if they know me they shall come forth, and shall have a place eternally at my right hand.

25. And it shall come to pass that when the second trump shall sound then shall they that never knew me come forth and shall stand before me.

26. And then shall they know that I am the Lord their God, that I am their Redeemer; but they would not be redeemed.

---

is the Lord, but the Great Creator?" It is His Church; it is just and equitable that He receives all who abide His requirements. Baptism is the "gate" by which we may enter His fold, and that gate is open to them who in sorrow for their past sins, resolve to do them no more.

Alma received further word from the Lord who instructed him that whosoever is baptized shall believe "in my name." By taking upon themselves His name, through baptism, they shall be called by His name, (verse 18) and them, He said, "Will I freely forgive" their trespasses.

VERSES 23-24. *It is I that taketh upon me the sins of the world.* The Lord now confirmed to Alma what the prophets have always testified: that He is the Maker of all and the Creator of man. To save His wonderful works from the powers of evil who constantly sought their destruction, the Lord paid any claim sin imposed upon mortal man. He paid the price demanded. That price was the shedding of His blood, and thus He redeemed all mankind from the effects of sin, and the penalty of death.

Those who are faithful and believe in Him to the end, that is, all who keep His commandments throughout their whole lives, shall be granted "a place eternally at my right hand."

The expression, *right hand,* is used throughout the Bible and the Book of Mormon, and means the *power of God,* (See I Samuel 5:6-7) or the place reserved for the righteous. Other passages found in the Book of Mormon in which these words are used, are found on page 80 of this COMMENTARY.

We are reminded of the parable of Jesus which John records:

Verily, verily, I say unto you, He that entereth not by the door into the sheepfold, but climbeth up some other way, the same is a thief and a robber.

But he that entereth in by the door is the shepherd of the sheep.

To him the porter openeth; and the sheep hear his voice; and he calleth his sheep by name, and leadeth them out.

And when he putteth forth his own sheep, he goeth before them, and the sheep follow him: for they know his voice.

And a stranger will they not follow, but will flee from him: for they know not the voice of strangers.   (John 10:1-5)

VERSES 25-28. *Second trump shall sound.* Means *heralding the second resurrection.* Then will those who never heard His voice and knew not His name by which the faithful are called shall come forth. They will stand before Him and be judged by Him. Then will they know that He is the Lord their God, their Redeemer whom

27. And then I will confess unto them that I never knew them; and they shall depart into everlasting fire prepared for the devil and his angels.

28. Therefore I say unto you, that he that will not hear my voice, the same shall ye not receive into my church, for him I will not receive at the last day.

2. The Lord instructs Alma how to deal with them.

29. Therefore I say unto you, Go; and whosoever transgresseth against me, him shall ye judge according to the sins which he has committed; and if he confess his sins before thee and me, and repenteth in the sincerity of his heart, him shall ye forgive, and I will forgive him also.

30. Yea, and as often as my people repent will I forgive them their trespasses against me.

31. And ye shall also forgive one another your trespasses; for

they rejected. They once failed or refused to follow the Good Shepherd as their leader, and followed another who led them along the paths of sin and death.

The words of Alma, the younger, spell out the meaning of his father's thought, when later he said:

Therefore, if a man bringeth forth good works he hearkeneth unto the voice of the good shepherd, and doth follow him; but whosoever bringeth forth evil works, the same becometh a child of the devil, for he hearkeneth unto his voice, and doth follow him. (Alma 5:41)

VERSES 29-30. *Him shall ye forgive, and I will forgive him also.* After the Lord had instructed Alma concerning those who were worthy to be received into the Church of God, He further commanded Alma to go his way and judge the transgressor "according to the sins which he had committed." As we have noted, Alma greatly desired to judge righteously, and we may imagine that he being so disposed resolved to regulate, or adjust and settle peaceably all departures from Church regulations. No doubt Alma determined not to judge him guilty who is only supposed to be in error; neither, we presume, would he condemn any who were the victims of lying tongues, nor those who were helpless and had no helper. The rich in the things of the world and the poor were to be equal when they stood before him as their judge.

But one condition served to ameliorate any punishment Alma might pronounce: if the one taken in sin "confess his sins before thee and me, and repenteth in the sincerity of his heart, him shall ye forgive, and I will forgive him also."

One of Satan's most cunning ways to lead men on in wrongdoing is craftily to make them believe in the uselessness of repentance. "I have gone too far to repent; there is no forgiveness for me." That is not true. "Yea," the Lord said to Alma, "And as often as my people repent will I forgive them their trespasses against me." Of course there is forgiveness for everyone, if it were not so, God's great purposes would fail and this we do not believe. The poor sheep may be lost in the wood, hungry and helpless and cold, hunted by the wolf, falling over the precipice. "But the Good Shepherd is on His way and is looking for it, and will find it. And will take it into His arms and will carry it to the fold" and will rejoice that the lost is found and the dead is again alive.

VERSE 31. *And ye shall also forgive one another your trespasses.* What is perhaps

verily I say unto you, he that forgiveth not his neighbor's trespasses when he says that he repents, the same hath brought himself under condemnation.

32. Now I say unto you, Go; and whosoever will not repent of his sins the same shall not be numbered among my people; and this shall be observed from this time forward.

33. And it came to pass when Alma had heard these words he wrote them down that he might have them, and that he might judge the people of that church according to the commandments of God.

34. And it came to pass that Alma went and judged those that had been taken in iniquity, according to the word of the Lord.

35. And whosoever repented of their sins and did confess them, them he did number among the people of the church;

---

the best comment on this verse is for us to read a parable given by the Lord to His disciples, teaching them how often to forgive.

Then came Peter to him, and said, Lord, how oft shall my brother sin against me, and I forgive him? till seven times?

Jesus saith unto him, I say not unto thee, Until seven times: but, Until seventy times seven.

Therefore is the kingdom of heaven likened unto a certain king, which would take account of his servants.

And when he had begun to reckon, one was brought unto him, which owed him ten thousand talents.

But forasmuch as he had not to pay, his lord commanded him to be sold, and his wife and children, and all that he had, and payment to be made.

The servant therefore fell down, and worshipped him, saying, have patience with me, and I will pay thee all.

Then the lord of that servant was moved with compassion, and loosed him, and forgave him the debt.

But the same servant went out, and found one of his fellowservants, which owed him an hundred pence: and he laid his hands on him, and took *him* by the throat, saying, Pay me that thou owest.

And his fellowservant fell down at his feet, and besought him, saying, Have patience with me, and I will pay thee all.

And he would not: but went and cast him into prison, till he should pay the debt.

So when his fellowservants saw what was done, they were very sorry, and came and told unto their lord all that was done.

Then his lord, after that he had called him, said unto him, O thou wicked servant, I forgave thee all that debt, because thou desiredst me:

Shouldest not thou also have had compassion on thy fellowservant, even as I had pity on thee?

And his lord was wroth, and delivered him to the tormentors, till he should pay all that was due unto him.

So likewise shall my heavenly Father do also unto you, if ye from your hearts forgive not every one his brother their trespasses. (Matthew 18:21-35)

VERSE 32. *Whosoever will not repent of his sins.* From this time forth the non-repentant sinner will not be counted among those who have taken upon themselves the name of the Lord.

VERSES 33-36. *Alma wrote down the words of the Lord.* So that he would have always before him the Lord's own words concerning the proper way to handle the transgressors, Alma wrote down the words of instruction he had received. He was

36. And those that would not confess their sins and repent of their iniquity, the same were not numbered among the people of the church, and their names were blotted out.

37. And it came to pass that Alma did regulate all the affairs of the church; and they began again to have peace and to prosper exceedingly in the affairs of the church, walking circumspectly before God, receiving many, and baptizing many.

38. And now all these things did Alma and his fellow laborers do who were over the church, walking in all diligence, teaching the word of God in all things, suffering all manner of afflictions, being persecuted by all those who did not belong to the church of God.

39. And they did admonish their brethren; and they were also admonished, every one by the word of God, according to his sins, or to the sins which he had committed, being commanded of God to pray without ceasing, and to give thanks in all things.

---

strengthened thereby, and now felt worthy to judge the members of the Church who had fallen into sinful practices. There was only one course for him to follow and the Lord had pointed that way. Alma was loyal to God and his fellow men and in that fidelity which increased in him as he ministered to their needs as well as their shortcomings he began to reap a plentiful harvest to them that brought peace and prosperity to the Church, and who walked "circumspectly before God receiving many, and baptizing many."

VERSES 38-39. *Being commanded of God to pray without ceasing.* Alma and his associate brethren in the Priesthood labored diligently teaching and exhorting the members of the Church to walk uprightly before God, as they, themselves, did. This brought persecution upon Church members, and, with it, "all manner of afflictions," but their strength increased so that they withstood the wicked designs of their tormentors.

Those holding the Holy Priesthood admonished their brethren in kindness reproving the erring one humbly, and the sinful one with much love. They were directed in all things by the *Word* they received from the Almighty Father, and whether it came to them by the ministry of angels or through the Seers who had preceded them, they always adhered to the instructions they thus received.

Alma taught all to pray "without ceasing," and to give thanks to God for the blessings they enjoyed.

CHURCH DISCIPLINE

A Review

As in other practices, the methods adopted by the Nephite Church in their treatment of those who turned from righteousness were identical with the methods pursued in similar cases in the Church of God in other lands and in other ages. The erring ones were first labored with by the officers of the Church in the spirit of kindness and reconciliation; they were visited by the priests and teachers. If they repented of their transgressions, they were continued in the fellowship of the Saints. If they were obdurate and impertinent, they were severed from the communion of the Church. This method of handling the unrepentant sinner was followed throughout the history of the Nephites from the days of Alma, the elder, to those of Moroni.

In the Land of Zarahemla, when Mosiah was king and Alma was the Presiding High Priest of the Church, there was much hard-heartedness and evil-doing in the midst of the Nephites. It was at this time that the sons of King Mosiah and the younger Alma were leaders among those opposing the Church and persecuting its members. The iniquity that existed with those who had made covenant with God, or those who were their children, caused Alma the elder much pain and anxiety. The priests and teachers labored frequently in vain, and the presiding priesthood officers were sometimes in doubt with regard to the best course to pursue. They had no precedents to guide them, for such a state of things had never before existed among the Nephites.

Alma, the elder, applied to the king, but Mosiah refused to judge the offenders. He would not interfere in matters of Church discipline that he had assigned to Alma.

In this predicament, Alma saw but one course he, himself, could pursue. He appealed with all the fervor of his righteous being to the Lord who "knoweth the hearts of all men." In humble prayer, he inquired of Him what to do, for he was most desirous to do right in the sight of heaven. Then the voice of the Lord came to him directing him to follow the course pointed out in this Chapter, verses 15-32.

In this revelation we have the word of the Lord to guide the Nephite Church throughout all its dispensations.

The same spirit is manifested in the instructions the Risen Redeemer gave to the Nephites when He was with them in the Land Bountiful. They were full of love, mercy, and patience. On the other hand, they show that the Church of God must not be defiled by countenancing iniquity or otherwise permitting that which is holy to be handled by the unworthy.

Nearly four hundred years later, Moroni, speaking on Church government, said,

And they were strict to observe that there should be no iniquity among them; and whoso was found to commit iniquity, and three witnesses of the church did condemn them before the elders, and if they repented not, and confessed not, their names were blotted out, and they were not numbered among the people of Christ.

But as oft as they repented and sought forgiveness, with real intent, they were forgiven.

(Moroni 6:7-8)

From this quotation we perceive that the spirit of the ancient Church upon this continent, with regard to offenses and offenders, was uniform in all its dispensations, and identical in its methods with those of the latter-days.

CHAPTER 27

1. Persecution Forbidden and Equality Enjoined—2. Alma, the Younger, and the Four Sons of Mosiah, Among the Unbelievers—3. Their Miraculous Conversion—4. They Become Preachers of Righteousness.

1. *Persecution forbidden and equality enjoined.*

1. And now it came to pass that the persecutions which were inflicted on the church by the unbelievers became so great that the church began to murmur, and complain to their leaders concerning the matter; and they did complain to Alma. And Alma laid the case before their king, Mosiah. And Mosiah consulted with his priests.

2. And it came to pass that king Mosiah sent a proclamation throughout the land round about that there should not any unbeliever persecute any of those who belonged to the church of God.

3. And there was a strict command throughout all the churches that there should be no persecution among them, that there should be an equality among all men;

4. That they should let no pride nor haughtiness disturb their peace; that every man should esteem his neighbor as himself, laboring with their own hands for their support.

5. Yea, and all their priests and teachers should labor with their own hands for their support, in all cases save it were in sickness, or in much want; and

VERSE 1. *Alma and Mosiah conferred with the priests.* With increasing seriousness the persecution of members of the Church became almost unbearable. They began to murmur among themselves, and they complained to Alma of the unrestrained manner in which they were treated by their ungodly neighbors. The injuries inflicted upon them and the harassment of their leaders called forth serious consultation. Alma sought the advice of King Mosiah, and he besought the counsel of his priests.

VERSES 2-3. *Mosiah sent out a proclamation to all the people.* After great deliberation, King Mosiah issued a proclamation of equality to all his people, forbidding his subjects to persecute, vex, or otherwise abuse their fellows because of their faith or religion. In his edict, he also announced that in matters of conscience all men were equal before the law, and all were entitled to his protection.

VERSES 4-5. *Every man should labor with his own hands.* Mosiah took this favorable opportunity to warn his subjects not to let pride and haughtiness enter their manner of life. He advised them not to permit these evils to threaten, or even endanger, the peace that had, for so many years, guided them to undreamed of heights of prosperity and brotherly love.

Furthermore, Mosiah declared that every able-bodied man should labor with his own hands to support himself. This injunction included the priests and teachers who were capable so to do. There were to be no exceptions to this rule. In conforming themselves to these requirements, the people were blessed by the Lord, and soon they "did abound in the grace of God." We understand *grace* to mean, *favor, kindness, or mercy.*

doing these things, they did abound in the grace of God.

6. And there began to be much peace again in the land; and the people began to be very numerous, and began to scatter abroad upon the face of the earth, yea, on the north and on the south, on the east and on the west, building large cities and villages in all quarters of the land.

7. And the Lord did visit them and prosper them, and they became a large and wealthy people.

2. Alma, the Younger, and the four sons of Mosiah, among the unbelievers.

8. Now the sons of Mosiah were numbered among the unbelievers; and also one of the sons of Alma was numbered among them, he being called Alma, after his father; nevertheless, he became a very wicked and an idolatrous man. And he was a man of many words, and did speak much flattery to the people; therefore he led many of the people to do after the manner of his iniquities.

9. And he became a great hinderment to the prosperity of the church of God; stealing away the hearts of the people; causing much dissension among the people; giving a chance for the enemy of God to exercise his power over them.

VERSES 6-7. *There began to be much peace in the land.* The favor of the Lord in whose grace the people of Zarahemla were copiously blessed, was made evident in their growth and development as a great nation. Not only did they increase in numbers but also in power and riches. Colonists from their great city made their homes in every direction, and soon communities, both large and small, even large cities and villages, sprang up in "all quarters of the land." Their territorial expansion was from the north far to the south, and from, we imagine, the Atlantic Ocean on the East even to the Pacific on the West.

We are intrigued by the statement made in verse 7, "And the Lord did visit them and prosper them, and they became a large and wealthy people."

Up to this time no other city except Zarahemla is mentioned in the Book of Mormon as being in that land, but we may reasonably suppose that such cities as are mentioned in the annals of the next twenty years were built during that period. We have in mind such cities as, Aaron, Ammonihah, Gideon, Manti, Melek, and many others.

VERSES 8-9. *The sons of King Mosiah and a son of Alma, whose name was also Alma, were among the unbelievers.* Let us return to the account of the unbelievers. Many of them turned from their wicked ways, and were blessed and prospered of the Lord. They set about to obey Mosiah's proclamation. Still it required a greater power than an earthly king's to bring to naught the evil intents of the unbelievers. They had been greatly encouraged in their misdeeds by the fact that the king's four sons and one of Alma's own sons were their leaders.

Frequent and fervent were the prayers offered by Mosiah and the elder Alma in behalf of their rebellious sons, and these prayers prevailed with Him who sits on heaven's Eternal Throne.

Notwithstanding the fact of Alma's, the Elder's, devotion to God's laws, and the

3. Their miraculous conversion.

10. And now it came to pass that while he was going about to destroy the church of God, for he did go about secretly with the sons of Mosiah seeking to destroy the church, and to lead astray the people of the Lord, contrary to the commandments of God, or even the king—

11. And as I said unto you, as they were going about rebelling against God, behold, the angel of the Lord appeared unto them; and he descended as it were in a cloud; and he spake as it were with a voice of thunder, which caused the earth to shake upon which they stood;

12. And so great was their astonishment, that they fell to the earth, and understood not the words which he spake unto them.

13. Nevertheless he cried again, saying: Alma, arise and stand forth, for why persecutest thou the church of God? For the Lord hath said: This is my church, and I will establish it; and nothing shall overthrow it, save it is the transgression of my people.

14. And again, the angel said: Behold, the Lord hath heard the prayers of his people, and also the prayers of his servant, Alma, who is thy father; for he has prayed with much faith concerning thee that thou mightest be brought to the knowledge of the truth; therefore, for this purpose have I come to convince thee of the power and authority of God, that the prayers of his servants might be answered according to their faith.

15. And now behold, can ye dispute the power of God? For behold, doth not my voice shake the earth? And can ye not also behold me before you? And I am sent from God.

---

responsibilities he carried as the High Priest of the whole Church, his son Alma became a very "wicked and an idolatrous man!" Because Alma, the Younger, was a fine speaker, he flattered the people, and by it lead many to do the things he chose to do. Because of his relationship to the High Priest, Alma was looked upon as an example, one whom to follow. "And he became a great hinderment to the prosperity of the whole church."

VERSES 10-31. *Alma and the sons of Mosiah go about secretly to destroy the Church of God.* One day as Alma and his company were going about persecuting the members of the Church, an holy angel descended in a cloud and stopped them in the way. When the angel spoke, his voice was as thunder that caused the earth under their feet to tremble. Naturally, this manifestation of God's power spread terror and dismay in the hearts of those who witnessed it. They fell to the ground, and so confused and terrified were they that they failed to understand the words of the holy messenger.

"Alma, arise and stand forth," he cried. And when Alma arose, his eyes were opened to see who stood before him. It was an angel sent down from heaven. He had a divine mission to perform — to rebuke Alma and his companions.

The earth continued to shake as the angel spoke to them; the ground around them seemed ready to come apart. Again, they fell to the ground. We can understand

16. Now I say unto thee: Go, and remember the captivity of thy fathers in the land of Helam, and in the land of Nephi; and remember how great things he has done for them; for they were in bondage, and he has delivered them. And now I say unto thee, Alma, go thy way, and seek to destroy the church no more, that their prayers may be answered, and this even if thou wilt of thyself be cast off.

17. And now it came to pass that these were the last words which the angel spake unto Alma, and he departed.

18. And now Alma and those that were with him fell again to the earth, for great was their astonishment; for with their own eyes they had beheld an angel of the Lord; and his voice was as thunder, which shook the earth; and they knew that there was nothing save the power of God

---

their thoughts more forcibly if the words of the Psalmist are remembered, "Fearfulness and trembling are come upon me, and horror hath overwhelmed me." (Psalm 55:5)

"Why persecutest thou the church of God?," the angel asked of Alma. Knowest thou not, "that the Lord hath said, This is my church, and I will establish it." Further the Lord sayeth, "Nothing shall overthrow it, save it is the transgression of my people."

Besides these things, the angel spoke to Alma of his father's prayers in his behalf, and that because of these prayers he, the angel, was sent to convince Alma of the power of God.

He also recounted to Alma the captivity of his forefathers in the Lands of Lehi-Nephi and Helam, and of their miraculous deliverance. But Alma heard nothing of these latter sayings for the terrors of the first salutation had overpowered him.

VERSE 16. *Even if thou wilt of thyself be cast off.* This doubtlessly means: "Even if thou *will not* of thyself be destroyed."

When the angel departed, Alma was overcome and dismayed; soul stricken, he sank to the ground. When his companions gathered around him, they found he could not move, neither could he speak. Outwardly, he was dead to the world. The torments of the damned had taken hold of his soul, and, in the most bitter pain and mental anguish, he lay racked with the remembrance of all his past sins. The thought of standing before the *Bar of God* to be judged for his iniquities overwhelmed him with dread. He desired to become extinct, both body and spirit, so that he could not be brought before his Creator. Thus for three days and three nights he suffered the pains of hell. (See Alma 36:16. According to the author of the Book of Mosiah it was for a period of *two* days and *two* nights.) We prefer to accept the former as being correct because it is Alma's own statement. Whichever it may have been, in his racked conscience, it must have seemed an eternity.

VERSES 18-22. *Alma became dumb, and his companions carried him to his father.* When his companions found that Alma could neither speak nor move his limbs, they carried him to his father and related to him all that had happened. Strange as it must have seemed to them, the elder Alma's heart was filled with joy, and he praised God when he saw the apparently dead body of his much-loved son, for he realized it was the Lord's power that had wrought this manifestation, and that his long continued prayers had now been answered.

In his joy, Alma's father gathered the people together so that they also might

that could shake the earth and cause it to tremble as though it would part asunder.

19. And now the astonishment of Alma was so great that he became dumb, that he could not open his mouth; yea, and he became weak, even that he could not move his hands; therefore he was taken by those that were with him, and carried helpless, even until he was laid before his father.

20. And they rehearsed unto his father all that had happened unto them; and his father rejoiced, for he knew that it was the power of God.

21. And he caused that a multitude should be gathered together that they might witness what the Lord had done for his son, and also for those that were with him.

22. And he caused that the priests should assemble themselves together; and they began to fast, and to pray to the Lord their God that he would open the mouth of Alma, that he might speak, and also that his limbs might receive their strength — that the eyes of the people might be opened to see and know of the goodness and glory of God.

---

witness this great showing of the goodness and the power of God. He assembled the priests, sought their cooperation, and unitedly they fasted and prayed for the stricken youth.

If we recall the parable of Jesus' concerning *another son* who chose to do evil and thereby brought misery to his devoted father, we can understand, somewhat more fully, the joy that flowed from the elder Alma's heart when he beheld his own son lying unconscious before him.

Jesus told of a father who had two sons, the younger of whom asked that he be given his portion of his father's estate. When he had gathered it all together, he went to a distant land and "there wasted his substance in riotous living. And when he had spent all, there arose a mighty famine in that land; and he began to be in want. And he went and joined himself to a citizen of that country; and he sent him into his fields to feed swine," a labor thought by the Jews to be contemptible.

The son grew hungry and no one "gave unto him," whereupon he was glad to eat the food prepared for the swine.

One day as he meditated his lot, he thought of the home of his father. He remembered the fine clothes he wore and the abundance of good food there. Even his father's servants had more to eat than what they needed, "and I perish with hunger," he said.

The poor *Prodigal* was afar off, serving a strange master in a strange land, feeding on husks.

"I will arise and go to my father, and will say unto him, Father, I have sinned against heaven, and before thee!"

His father, in the meantime had all along expected his son to return, and when he saw him, he was yet a long way off. However, the father called to his friends to prepare with him, the ring for his son's withered finger, the robe for his naked body, the shoes for his sore feet, and the fatted calf which always he had in readiness for this time when it should come, and together with them he rejoiced, for he said, "For this my son was dead, and is alive again; he was lost, and is found. And they began to be merry." (Luke 15:11-24)

23. And it came to pass after they had fasted and prayed for the space of two days and two nights, the limbs of Alma received their strength, and he stood up and began to speak unto them, bidding them to be of good comfort:

24. For, said he, I have repented of my sins, and have been redeemed of the Lord; behold I am born of the Spirit.

25. And the Lord said unto me: Marvel not that all mankind, yea, men and women, all nations, kindreds, tongues and people, must be born again; yea, born of God, changed from their carnal and fallen state, to a state of righteousness, being redeemed of God, becoming his sons and daughters;

26. And thus they become new creatures; and unless they do this, they can in nowise inherit the kingdom of God.

27. I say unto you, unless this be the case, they must be cast off; and this I know, because I was like to be cast off.

28. Nevertheless, after wandering through much tribulation, repenting nigh unto death, the Lord in mercy hath seen fit to

---

Also, let us hear the Prophet Habakkuk. The East Wind had sowed destruction broadcast throughout the land; the fig tree did not blossom, there was no fruit on the vines, the labor of the olive failed, the flock was cut off from the fold, and there was no herd in the stalls. "Yet," said the prophet, "I will rejoice in the Lord, I will joy in the God of my salvation." (Habakkuk 3:17)

This same exultant cry left the heart of the elder Alma as he beheld his son, for he "knew it was the power of God."

For two days they continued their supplications to heaven. At the end of three days Alma, the younger, stood upon his feet and spoke. In his own account of the time he was unconscious, he stated, as we have noted, three days. The apparent discrepancy between the times mentioned may not be actual. Let us realize it may have been some distance that the young men had to travel in bringing the body of Alma to his father. It may have consumed a full day.

What Alma said when he had recovered sufficiently from his ordeal, were words of comfort to his father and to those gathered about him. We think the words, as divinely translated through the Prophet Joseph Smith, cannot be bettered. Here are the words that Alma, many years later related to his son, Helaman, in explaining the details of his conversion:

For I went about with the sons of Mosiah, seeking to destroy the church of God; but behold, God sent his holy angel to stop us by the way.

And behold, he spake unto us, as it were the voice of thunder, and the whole earth did tremble beneath our feet, for the fear of the Lord came upon us.

But behold, the voice said unto me: Arise. And I arose and stood up, and beheld the angel.

And he said unto me: If thou wilt of thyself be destroyed, seek no more to destroy the church of God.

And it came to pass that I fell to the earth; and it was for the space of three days and three nights that I could not open my mouth, neither had I the use of my limbs.

And the angel spake more things unto me, which were heard by my brethren, but I did not hear them; for when I heard the words—If thou wilt be destroyed of

snatch me out of an everlasting burning, and I am born of God.

29. My soul hath been redeemed from the gall of bitterness and bonds of iniquity. I was in the darkest abyss; but now I behold the marvelous light of God. My soul was racked with eternal torment; but I am snatched, and my soul is pained no more.

30. I rejected my Redeemer, and denied that which had been spoken of by our fathers; but now that they may foresee that he will come, and that he remembereth every creature of his creating, he will make himself manifest unto all.

31. Yea, every knee shall bow, and every tongue confess before him. Yea, even at the last day, when all men shall stand to be judged of him, then shall they confess that he is God; then shall they confess, who live without God in the world, that the judgment of an everlasting punishment is just upon them; and they shall quake, and tremble, and shrink beneath the glance of his all-searching eye.

---

thyself, seek no more to destroy the church of God—I was struck with such great fear and amazement lest perhaps I should be destroyed, that I fell to the earth and I did hear no more.

But I was racked with eternal torment, for my soul was harrowed up to the greatest degree and racked with all my sins.

Yea, I did remember all my sins and iniquities with the pains of hell; yea, I saw that I had rebelled against my God, and that I had not kept his holy commandments.

Yea, and I had murdered many of his children, or rather led them away unto destruction; yea, and in fine so great had been my iniquities, that the very thought of coming into the presence of my God did rack my soul with inexpressible horror.

Oh, thought I, that I could be banished and become extinct both soul and body, that I might not be brought to stand in the presence of my God, to be judged of my deeds.

And now, for three days and for three nights was I racked, even with the pains of a damned soul.

And it came to pass that as I was thus racked with torment, while I was harrowed up by the memory of my many sins, behold, I remembered also to have heard my father prophesy unto the people concerning the coming of one Jesus Christ, a Son of God, to atone for the sins of the world.

Now, as my mind caught hold upon this thought, I cried within my heart: O Jesus, thou Son of God, have mercy on me, who am in the gall of bitterness, and am encircled about by the everlasting chains of death.

And now, behold, when I thought this, I could remember my pains no more; yea, I was harrowed up by the memory of my sins no more.

And oh, what joy, and what marvelous light I did behold; yea, my soul was filled with joy as exceeding as was my pain!

Yea, I say unto you, my son, that there could be nothing so exquisite and so bitter as were my pains. Yea, and again I say unto you, my son, that on the other hand, there can be nothing so exquisite and sweet as was my joy.

Yea, methought I saw, even as our father Lehi saw, God sitting upon his throne, surrounded with numberless concourses of angels, in the attitude of singing and praising their God; yea, and my soul did long to be there.

4. They became preachers of righteousness.

32. And now it came to pass that Alma began from this time forward to teach the people, and those who were with Alma at the time the angel appeared unto them, traveling round about through all the land, publishing to all the people the things which they had heard and seen, and preaching the word of God in much tribulation, being greatly persecuted by those who were unbelievers, being smitten by many of them.

33. But notwithstanding all this, they did impart much consolation to the church, confirming their faith, and exhorting them with long-suffering and much travail to keep the commandments of God.

34. And four of them were the sons of Mosiah; and their names were Ammon, and Aaron, and Omner, and Himni; these were the names of the sons of Mosiah.

35. And they traveled throughout all the land of Zarahemla, and among all the people who were under the reign of king Mosiah, zealously striving to repair all the injuries which they had done to the church, confessing all their sins, and publishing all the things which they had seen, and explaining the prophecies and the scriptures to all who desired to hear them.

36. And thus they were instruments in the hands of God in bringing many to the knowledge of the truth, yea, to the knowledge of their Redeemer.

37. And how blessed are they! For they did publish peace; they did publish good tidings of good; and they did declare unto the people that the Lord reigneth.

But behold, my limbs did receive strength again, and I stood upon my feet, and did manifest unto the people that I had been born of God.

Yea, and from that time even until now, I have labored without ceasing, that I might bring souls unto repentance; that I might bring them to taste of the exceeding joy of which I did taste; that they might also be born of God, and be filled with the Holy Ghost.

Yea, and now behold, O my son, the Lord doth give me exceeding great joy in the fruit of my labors;

For because of the word which he has imparted unto me, behold, many have been born of God, and have tasted as I have tasted, and have seen eye to eye as I have seen; therefore they do know of these things of which I have spoken, as I do know; and the knowledge which I have is of God. (Alma 36:6-26)

VERSES 32-37. *Alma began from this time forward to teach the people.* From then on, to the end of his mortal career, Alma labored without ceasing to bring souls to Christ, and to guide his fellow men in the paths of Salvation.

What effect did this heavenly visit have upon the sons of Mosiah?

A very great one! From that moment on they were changed men. When the voice of the angel reached their astonished ears, the understanding of divinity entered their souls. They knew, they felt, they realized there was a God, and that they had been fighting against him. The sense of their own unworthiness filled their hearts; remorse and anguish reigned supreme therein, and they condemned themselves as the vilest of sinners.

Finally, the bitterness of their remorse was swallowed up in their faith in the coming of Christ, and they determined that, with the help of the Lord, they would undo the evil that their previous course had wrought. These resolutions they faithfully carried out. If they had been energetic in their wrongdoings, they were now doubly active in their works of restitution. They journeyed from city to city, from land to land, and everywhere bore triumphant testimony of their miraculous conversion. And in no equivocal tones they proclaimed the glorious Gospel of Christ, the love of God, and the Salvation of mankind.

CHAPTER 28

1. Mosiah Permits his Sons to Preach to the Lamanites—2. The Twenty-four Plates Translated—3. Alma, the Younger, made Custodian of the Records.

1. Mosiah permits his sons to preach to the Lamanites.

1. Now it came to pass that after the sons of Mosiah had done all these things, they took a small number with them and returned to their father, the king, and desired of him that he would grant unto them that they might, with these whom they had selected, go up to the land of Nephi that they might preach the things which they had heard, and that they might impart the word of God to their brethren, the Lamanites—

2. That perhaps they might bring them to the knowledge of the Lord their God, and convince them of the iniquity of their fathers; and that perhaps they might cure them of their hatred towards the Nephites, that they might also be brought to rejoice in the Lord their God, that they might become friendly to one another, and that there should be no more contentions in all the land which the Lord their God had given them.

3. Now they were desirous that salvation should be declared to every creature, for they could not bear that any human soul should perish; yea, even the very thoughts that any soul should endure endless torment did cause them to quake and tremble.

4. And thus did the Spirit of the Lord work upon them, for they were the very vilest of sinners. And the Lord saw fit in his infinite mercy to spare them; nevertheless they suffered much anguish of soul because of their iniquities, suffering much and fearing that they should be cast off forever.

5. And it came to pass that they did plead with their father many days that they might go up to the land of Nephi.

VERSE 1-9. *The sons of Mosiah desire to preach the Word of God to the Lamanites.* Notwithstanding the great good the sons of Mosiah were doing for the Nephites in their own land, they were not content to confine their labors to the dwellers in Zarahemla only.

The names of these brothers were Aaron, Ammon, Omner, and Himni. These names are given according to the apparent age of each, beginning with the eldest.

They longed to carry the message of Salvation to the benighted Lamanites. Ignoring the dangers and scorning the pains which such a mission would likely inflict, they pled for many days with their father to give his permission for them to go to the Land of Lehi-Nephi.

They envisioned the hope that they could dispel the old traditions of the Lamanites that had caused so much hatred and bloodshed between them and the Nephites. The thoughts of these young men lifted them to realms of godly love for their fellowmen from which they saw the great responsibility put upon them

6. And king Mosiah went and inquired of the Lord if he should let his sons go up among the Lamanites to preach the word.

7. And the Lord said unto Mosiah: Let them go up, for many shall believe on their words, and they shall have eternal life; and I will deliver thy sons out of the hands of the Lamanites.

8. And it came to pass that Mosiah granted that they might go and do according to their request.

9. And they took their journey into the wilderness to go up to preach the word among the Lamanites; and I shall give an account of their proceedings hereafter.

2. The Twenty-four Plates translated.

10. Now king Mosiah had no one to confer the kingdom upon, for there was not any of his sons who would accept of the kingdom.

11. Therefore he took the rec-

---

by their own marvelous conversion. They desired to take to their dark-skinned brethren "the knowledge of the Lord their God." They also saw in their labors the end to contention and warfare which for centuries had despoiled the beauties and the bounties of the land which the Lord had given them for an inheritance.

The thought that some of their brethren, the Lamanites, would be lost through not having been given the chance to hear the glorious message of Salvation, and that, therefore, the Lamanites "should endure endless torment did cause them to quake and tremble."

Notwithstanding that in the past the actions of these brothers put upon them the mark of vile and ruthless sinners, he who chronicled their times noted that the Lord in infinite mercy, saw fit to preserve them.

VERSE 6. *Mosiah inquired of the Lord.* The bloodthirsty, revengeful character of the Lamanites was too well known to the king for him to think of his sons going into their midst without causing him feelings of dread and apprehension. He had no desire to quench their holy zeal towards doing the work of God, or the love they had for their unfortunate fellows. He saw that in doing so, he might deny thousands the opportunity of hearing the everlasting truths of the Gospel.

Mosiah, therefore, inquired of the Lord.

VERSE 7. *Let them go up.* The Lord quickly answered Mosiah's supplications. The answer came, "Let them go up." The Lord quieted Mosiah's fears for the safety of his sons, saying, "I will deliver thy sons out of the hands of the Lamanites." He further gave Mosiah the blessed assurance that many of the Lamanites would believe the testimony offered by his sons and that they should have Eternal Life.

VERSE 8. *Mosiah granted that his sons might go.* Now with the divine promise that his sons would be spared from the treachery of the benighted Lamanites, Mosiah consented to their departure to the Land of Lehi-Nephi, the home of the Lamanite king. Shortly after receiving their father's permission, these four valiant God-fearing youths, with a few others they had chosen, started on their perilous mission.

VERSE 10. *Now King Mosiah had no one upon whom to confer the kingdom.* See Chapter 29:1-3.

ords which were engraven on the plates of brass, and also the plates of Nephi, and all the things which he had kept and preserved according to the commandments of God, after having translated and caused to be written the records which were on the plates of gold which had been found by the people of Limhi, which were delivered to him by the hand of Limhi;

12. And this he did because of the great anxiety of his people; for they were desirous beyond measure to know concerning those people who had been destroyed.

13. And now he translated them by the means of those two stones which were fastened into the two rims of a bow.

14. Now these things were prepared from the beginning, and were handed down from generation to generation, for the purpose of interpreting languages;

15. And they have been kept and preserved by the hand of the Lord, that he should discover to every creature who should possess the land the iniquities and abominations of his people;

16. And whosoever has these things is called seer, after the manner of old times.

Verses 11-20. *Mosiah translates the records which were on the "plates of gold."* The plates from which the Book of Ether was translated is first brought to our attention in a report of an interview between Limhi, the king over a Nephite colony in the country of Lehi-Nephi, and Ammon, a messenger from Zarahemla. (Mosiah 8:9) The king related a remarkable bit of history. He had, he said, at one time, sent an embassy with an important mission to Zarahemla. The delegates, being without a competent guide, lost their way in the wilderness and missed their destination. Instead of finishing their journey in Zarahemla, they came to a country where there were many ancient ruins and other evidence of terrible devastation. In corroboration of their strange report, they brought back with them twenty-four plates of gold with unknown engravings upon them, besides other remarkable antiques. King Limhi now desired to know whether Ammon could interpret such writings.

The visitor from Zarahemla replied frankly that he could not, but he hastened to add that the king over the people in his homeland had that gift, because he had in his possession certain miraculous interpreters. (Mosiah 8:14)

In due time King Limhi and his people broke away from their servitude under the Lamanites and found refuge in Zarahemla. King Mosiah, the son of Benjamin, received them with joy and took care of their valuable records. (Mosiah 22:14) Afterwards the royal prophet, Mosiah, translated the twenty-four plates.

Not an accidental discovery. The twenty-four plates were called *The Book of Ether* after its author. (Ether 1:2) Their discovery was not an accident. For, when Ether had finished his record, "He hid them in a manner that the people of Limhi did find them." (Ether 15:33)

The Visions of the Brother of Jared. Before the Jaredites left Moriancumer, their camp in the Old Country, the Brother of Jared was given indescribable visions on Mount Shelem. The Lord instructed him not to make them public during his lifetime, but to place them on record before his death, in the language commonly spoken before the building of the Tower of Babel but no longer known by later generations. This record was to be sealed. He also received two stones, prepared so as to *magnify*,

17. Now after Mosiah had finished translating these records, behold, it gave an account of the people who were destroyed, from the time that they were destroyed back to the building of the great tower, at the time the Lord confounded the language of the people and they were scattered abroad upon the face of all the earth, yea, and even from that time back until the creation of Adam.

18. Now this account did cause the people of Mosiah to mourn exceedingly, yea, they were filled with sorrow; nevertheless it gave them much knowledge, in the which they did rejoice.

19. And this account shall be written hereafter; for behold, it is expedient that all people should know the things which are written in this account.

or make clear, "the things which ye shall write." These were also to be sealed. (Ether 3:21-24, 27, 28)

From the information given by Moroni, we know that King Mosiah, the son of Benjamin, had the writings of the Brother of Jared, and that he kept them in case the time for their publication should come. We also know that those writings, together with "the interpretation thereof"—the translation by Mosiah—had come into his (Moroni's) possession, as also the interpreters. (Ether 4:1-5)

There is, then, no doubt that Mosiah, the son of Benjamin, was the custodian in his day of the Jaredite records and the stones of interpretation. (Mosiah 28:11-16)

The Jaredite record was part of the twenty-four plates of Ether which came providentially, into the hands of Mosiah through the expedition of Limhi. In all probability he received the interpreters from his father, Benjamin, who may have received them from Mosiah the First, his father.

Amaleki, the son of Abinadom, gives, in the Book of Omni, what is, perhaps, the correct clue to the question, how the stones of interpretation, originally given to the Brother of Jared, came into the hands of the kings in Zarahemla. He says that a large stone, possibly a monumental pillar or stele, was brought to King Mosiah the First, who interpreted the engravings by the "gift and power of God." We may, perhaps, infer that this means that he had the interpreters. By this power it was found that the stone contained an account of Coriantumr and the slain of his people. (Omni 20:22) Undoubtedly, Coriantumr had brought this information to Zarahemla. May he not have carried with him the interpreters also? It must be remembered that this survivor after the battle of Ramah had usurped the highest ecclesiastical as well as the political offices, and that he, therefore, may have had the sacred instrument in his possession, although it was useless to him. Ether prophesied that he would not fall in war, but that he would live, to be buried by another people. The influence is not far-fetched that he was spared for the very purpose of bringing to the Nephites the story of the dealings of God with the Jaredites.

Mosiah disposes of the sacred objects. King Mosiah, the son of Benjamin, was the custodian of the twenty-four plates, his own translation of the contents, the interpreters, the Plates of Brass, and other records. (Mosiah 1:16) Towards the end of his career, he delivered everything to Alma, the son of Alma, his being a high priest and the first Chief Judge of the country. (Mosiah 29:42) When transferring the responsibility of custody to Alma, Mosiah commanded him to keep and preserve the valuable artifacts, and to cause them to be handed down from one generation to another. (Mosiah 28:11-20)

The records preserved. At the proper time, Alma gave his son, Helaman, charge of the sacred treasures entrustd to him by Mosiah. (Alma 37:1-4) By such transfers they were preserved from generation to generation. About the year, 320 of our era, Ammaron, having received them from his brother Amos, prompted by the Spirit, did "hide them unto the Lord, that they might come again unto the remnant of the House of Jacob." (4 Nephi 48-49; *Comp.* Words of Mormon 10:11; Alma 37:4)

Mormon instructed concerning the records. The great Nephite commander and leader, Mormon, relates that, when he was about ten years old, Ammaron charged him to go to the Hill Shim, in the Land of Antum, when he should reach the age of about twenty-four years. The sacred writings had been deposited there, Ammon said. He instructed Mormon to take the Plates of Nephi and complete the records from his own observations. The other plates and articles were to be left in the hill. (Mormon 1:14; 2:17, 18)

Cumorah, the final place of safety. Mormon carried out his instructions. Later, he again went to the hill and "did take up all the records which Ammaron had hid up unto the Lord." (Mormon 4:23) He, finally, hid them in the Hill Cumorah, having first furnished his son, Moroni, with the entire story of the Plates of Nephi, in a greatly abridged form. (Mormon 6:6)

Moroni finished the tragic chapter of the final battle of Cumorah and then hid "up the records in the earth." (Mormon 8:4) presumably in the Hill Cumorah. But he also predicted that they would be found and come to light at some future day, (Mormon 8:14-16) a prophecy fulfilled through the instrumentality of the Prophet Joseph Smith.

Moroni gives one final reference to the miraculous interpreters, when he says: "But the Lord knoweth . . . that none other people knoweth our language; therefore he hath prepared *means* for the interpretation thereof." (Mormon 9:34) This *means* was the very crystals prepared for, and presented to the Brother of Jared on the mount. (D. & C. 17:1)

Only two Miraculous Interpreters. History knows of only two sacred instruments of this kind, also known as the Urim and Thummim, meaning *"lights and perfections."* One was given to Abraham in the City of Ur of the Chaldees. (Pearl of Great Price, Abraham 3:1). This was, probably, handed over by Moses to Aaron, the High Priest, who carried it in his "breastplate of judgment," an important part of his ecclesiastical equipment. (Exodus 28:30) It was finally lost sight of.

The other was given to the Brother of Jared. It was this that the Prophet Joseph had in his possession for some time.

"Urim and Thummim: According to the Hebrew, Exodus 28:30, the literal signification of these two words is *lights and perfections,* or *the shining and the perfect.* According to St. Jerome, *doctrine and judgment.* According to the Septuagint, *declaration* or *manifestation and truth.* They were worn in or attached to the breastplate of the high priest when inquiring of God." (Cruden's *Concordance of the Bible*)

Exodus	28:30	Breastplate of judgment, the U. and T.
Numbers	27:21	Counsel after the judgment of U.
Leviticus	8:8	Put in the breastplate the U. and T.
Deuteronomy	33:8	Let thy T. and U. be with thy holy
Ezra	2:63	Stood up priest with U. and T.
Nehemiah	7:65	Stood up priest with U. and T.
I Samuel	28:6	The Lord answered him not, neither by dreams, nor by U.

During the Millennial reign of the Son of God, when the great temples shall adorn the Old and New Jerusalem, they may again be needed for new revelations; for then "Out of Zion shall go forth the law, and the word of the Lord from Jerusalem." (Isaiah 2:30)

3. Alma, the Younger, made Custodian of the Records.

20. And now, as I said unto you, that after king Mosiah had done these things, he took the plates of brass, and all the things which he had kept, and conferred them upon Alma, who was the son of Alma; yea, all the records, and also the interpreters, and conferred them upon him, and commanded him that he should keep and preserve them, and also keep a record of the people, handing them down from one generation to another, even as they had been handed down from the time that Lehi left Jerusalem.

VERSE 20. *After King Mosiah had completed the translation of the gold plates, he took the plates of brass and other sacred things which had been left in his care, and conferred them upon Alma, the son of Alma.* When Mosiah had at length finished the work of translating the plates King Limhi had given into his keeping, he took all the sacred articles that had been given into his care and gave them into the custody of Alma, the younger. He also instructed Alma as to the manner that they were to be preserved by him.

Mosiah made it a special obligation on Alma's part, to hand them to whosoever was appointed to be his successor, and thereby continue the custom begun by Nephi when his father, together with Lehi's family, departed out of Jerusalem. (See Words of Mormon, v. 11.)

CHAPTER 29

1. *King Mosiah Discourses upon Kingcraft*—2. *Recommends Representative form of Government*—3. *Death of Alma, the Elder and Mosiah's Death end the Reign of the Nephite Kings.*

1. *King Mosiah discourses upon kingcraft.*

1. Now when Mosiah had done this he sent out throughout all the land, among all the people, desiring to know their will concerning who should be their king.

2. And it came to pass that the voice of the people came, saying: We are desirous that Aaron thy son should be our king and our ruler.

3. Now Aaron had gone up to the land of Nephi, therefore the king could not confer the kingdom upon him; neither would Aaron take upon him the kingdom; neither were any of the sons of Mosiah willing to take upon them the kingdom.

4. Therefore king Mosiah sent again among the people; yea, even a written word sent he among the people. And these were the words that were written, saying:

5. Behold, O ye my people, or my brethren, for I esteem you as such, I desire that ye should consider the cause which ye are called to consider—for ye are desirous to have a king.

6. Now I declare unto you that he to whom the kingdom doth rightly belong has declined, and will not take upon him the kingdom.

7. And now if there should be another appointed in his stead, behold I fear there would rise contentions among you. And who knoweth but what my son, to whom the kingdom doth belong, should turn to be angry and draw away a part of this people after him, which would cause wars and contentions among you, which would be the cause of shedding much blood and perverting the way of the Lord, yea, and destroy the souls of many people.

VERSES 1-10. *Mosiah desires to know who should be king.* Mosiah now felt that it was time that the question of the succession to the Nephite throne should be settled. In his magnanimity he sent among his people to learn whom they would have for their king.

They chose Mosiah's son, Aaron, but Aaron would not accept the royal powers; his heart was set upon converting his fellow men to the Gospel.

Aaron's refusal troubled the mind of Mosiah. He apprehended difficulties if Aaron, at some future date should change his decision and would demand his rights to the sovereignty.

Mosiah, therefore, issued another address to his much loved subjects. As usual, it was full of widsom and affection. In it, after recounting the peculiarities of the troubled situation, he said, "Let us be wise and consider these things, for we have no right to destroy my son, neither should we have any right to destroy another, if he should be appointed in his stead."

8. Now I say unto you let us be wise and consider these things, for we have no right to destroy my son, neither should we have any right to destroy another if he should be appointed in his stead.

9. And if my son should turn again to his pride and vain things he would recall the things which he had said, and claim his right to the kingdom, which would cause him and also this people to commit much sin.

10. And now let us be wise and look forward to these things, and do that which will make for the peace of this people.

11. Therefore I will be your king the remainder of my days; nevertheless, let us appoint judges, to judge this people according to our law; and we will newly arrange the affairs of this people, for we will appoint wise men to be judges, that will judge this people according to the commandments of God.

12. Now it is better that a man should be judged of God than of man, for the judgments of God are always just, but the judgments of man are not always just.

13. Therefore, if it were possible that you could have just men to be your kings, who would establish the laws of God, and judge this people according to his commandments, yea, if ye could have men for your kings who would do even as my father Benjamin did for this people—I say unto you, if this could always be the case then it would be expedient that ye should always have kings to rule over you.

14. And even I myself have labored with all the power and faculties which I have possessed, to teach you the commandments of God, and to establish peace throughout the land, that there should be no wars nor contentions, no stealing, nor plundering, nor murdering, nor any manner of iniquity;

15. And whosoever has committed iniquity, him have I punished according to the law which

VERSES 9-10. *If my son should turn again to his pride.* Aaron, by right of his birth—his being the eldest of King Mosiah's sons—had already rejected the kingship to which he was heir. He chose, rather to spend his time in missionary work. His father feared the prospect that Aaron might return to his evil ways.

Mosiah saw far enough into the future to see that if Aaron should ever recall the decision he had made to serve the Lord many would support his contentions, and this would divide the people.

"Let us be wise," said Mosiah. Now is the time to obviate any conditions that may otherwise arise from such an exigency. Look forward to this possibility, and dispose of it with understanding. Thereby we will preserve the peace that has brought so many blessings to this favored people.

VERSES 11-23. *Therefore I will be your king the remainder of my days.* King Mosiah, always seeking the righteous course to direct his people, warned them of the iniquity which follows the reign of a wicked monarch. He reminded them of King Noah and his profligate priests—how through unrestrained debauchery and lewdness Noah had led his people into committing sins which in turn brought them into

has been given to us by our fathers.

16. Now I say unto you, that because all men are not just it is not expedient that ye should have a king or kings to rule over you.

17. For behold, how much iniquity doth one wicked king cause to be committed, yea, and what great destruction!

18. Yea, remember king Noah, his wickedness and his abominations, and also the wickedness and abominations of his people. Behold what great destruction did come upon them; and also because of their iniquities they were brought into bondage.

19. And were it not for the interposition of their all-wise Creator, and this because of their sincere repentance, they must unavoidably remain in bondage until now.

20. But behold, he did deliver them because they did humble themselves before him; and because they cried mightily unto him he did deliver them out of bondage; and thus doth the Lord work with his power in all cases among the children of men, extending the arm of mercy towards them that put their trust in him.

21. And behold, now I say unto you, ye cannot dethrone an iniquitous king save it be through much contention, and the shedding of much blood.

22. For behold, he has his friends in iniquity, and he keepeth his guards about him; and he teareth up the laws of those who have reigned in righteousness before him; and he trampleth under his feet the commandments of God;

23. And he enacteth laws, and sendeth them forth among his people, yea, laws after the manner of his own wickedness; and whosoever doth not obey his laws he causeth to be destroyed; and whosoever doth rebel against him he will send his armies against them to war, and if he can he will destroy them; and thus an unrighteous king doth pervert the ways of all righteousness.

---

bondage. "And were it not for the interposition of their all-wise Creator, and this because of their sincere repentance, they must unavoidably remain in bondage until now."

Mosiah paid great tribute to his father, King Benjamin, saying that if kings like unto him could be had that ruled in righteousness, "then it would be expedient that ye should always have kings to rule over you." He also drew to the attention of his people, a fact which they well knew, because that with their own eyes they had seen it—Mosiah had brought *peace* to his people, they had greatly prospered; no wars nor contentions marred their happiness. He had labored with his whole heart and soul to teach them the commandments of God. Few crimes were committed among them, and, besides, he had not arbitrarily punished any man but had meted out just judgments according to the "law which had been given to us by our fathers." In justice, he had administered the laws of the land, which in most cases were the laws of God.

But, King Mosiah explained many other reasons why kings are sometimes not desirable rulers, therefore, he suggested a different form of government be set up

2. *Recommends representative government.*

24. And now behold I say unto you, it is not expedient that such abominations should come upon you.

25. Therefore, choose you by the voice of this people, judges, that ye may be judged according to the laws which have been given you by your fathers, which are correct, and which were given them by the hand of the Lord.

26. Now it is not common that the voice of the people desireth anything contrary to that which is right; but it is common for the lesser part of the people to desire that which is not right; therefore this shall ye observe and make it your law—to do your business by the voice of the people.

27. And if the time comes that the voice of the people doth choose iniquity, then is the time that the judgments of God will come upon you; yea, then is the time he will visit you with great destruction even as he has hitherto visited this land.

28. And now if ye have judges, and they do not judge you according to the law which has been given, ye can cause that they may be judged of a higher judge.

29. If your higher judges do not judge righteous judgments, ye shall cause that a small number of your lower judges should be gathered together, and they shall judge your higher judges, according to the voice of the people.

30. And I command you to do these things in the fear of the Lord; and I command you to do these things, and that ye have no king; that if these people commit sins and iniquities they shall be answered upon their own heads.

31. For behold I say unto you, the sins of many people have been caused by the iniquities of their kings; therefore their iniquities are answered upon the heads of their kings.

32. And now I desire that this inequality should be no more in this land, especially among this my people; but I desire that this land be a land of liberty, and every man may enjoy his rights and privileges alike, so long as the Lord sees fit that we may live and inherit the land, yea, even as long as any of our posterity remains upon the face of the land.

33. And many more things did

to guide the people aright and also to protect them in the new *liberty* he proposed should be theirs.

Verses 24-36. *Choose you by the voice of this people, judges.* Inspired and directed by the Lord, the king further advised many changes of the law, so that all things might be done by the voice of the whole people. These changes were gladly accepted by the people as they gave them greater liberty and a voice in all important national affairs.

As a law maker, Mosiah may be regarded among the most eminent this world has produced. We regard him in some respects as the Moses, in others the Alfred

king Mosiah write unto them, unfolding unto them all the trials and troubles of a righteous king, yea, all the travails of soul for their people, and also all the murmurings of the people to their king; and he explained it all unto them.

34. And he told them that these things ought not to be; but that the burden should come upon all the people, that every man might bear his part.

35. And he also unfolded unto them all the disadvantages they labored under, by having an unrighteous king to rule over them;

36. Yea, all his iniquities and abominations, and all the wars, and contentions, and bloodshed, and the stealing, and the plundering, and the committing of whoredoms, and all manner of iniquities which cannot be enumerated—telling them that these things ought not to be, that they were expressly repugnant to the commandments of God.

3. *Death of Alma, the elder, and the death of King Mosiah.*

37. And now it came to pass, after king Mosiah had sent these things forth among the people they were convinced of the truth of his words.

38. Therefore they relinquished their desires for a king, and became exceedingly anxious that every man should have an equal chance throughout all the land; yea, and every man expressed a willingness to answer for his own sins.

39. Therefore, it came to pass that they assembled themselves together in bodies throughout the land, to cast in their voices concerning who should be their judges, to judge them according to the law which had been given them; and they were exceedingly rejoiced because of the liberty which had been granted unto them.

40. And they did wax strong in love towards Mosiah; yea, they

the Great, of his age and his nation. But besides him being a king, he was also a seer. The gift of interpreting strange tongues and languages was his. By this gift he translated from the twenty-four plates of gold, found by the people of King Limhi, the records of the Jaredites.

No wonder that a man possessed of such gifts, so just and merciful in the administration of the law, so perfect in his private life, should be esteemed more than any man by his subjects, and that they waxed strong in their love towards him. As a king, he was a father to them, but as a prophet, seer, and revelator, he was the source from whence divine wisdom flowed unto them. We must go back to the days of the antediluvian patriarchs to find the peers of these three kings (the two Mosiahs and Benjamin), when monarchs ruled by right divine, and men were prophets, priests, and kings by virtue of heaven's gifts and God's will.

The sons of Mosiah having started on their mission to the Lamanites, he chose Alma, the younger, and gave the sacred plates and the other associate holy things into his care. The elder Alma made this same son of his the presiding High Priest of the Church, and the people chose him for their first Chief Judge. The Church, the

did esteem him more than any other man; for they did not look upon him as a tyrant who was seeking for gain, yea, for that lucre which doth corrupt the soul; for he had not exacted riches of them, neither had he delighted in the shedding of blood; but he had established peace in the land, and he had granted unto his people that they should be delivered from all manner of bondage; therefore they did esteem him, yea, exceedingly, beyond measure.

41. And it came to pass that they did appoint judges to rule over them, or to judge them according to the law; and this they did throughout all the land.

42. And it came to pass that Alma was appointed to be the first chief judge, he being also the high priest, his father having conferred the office upon him, and having given him the charge concerning all the affairs of the church.

43. And now it came to pass that Alma did walk in the ways of the Lord, and he did keep his commandments, and he did judge righteous judgments; and there was continual peace through the land.

44. And thus commenced the reign of the judges throughout all the land of Zarahemla, among all the people who were called the Nephites; and Alma was the first and chief judge.

45. And now it came to pass that his father died, being eighty and two years old, having lived to fulfil the commandments of God.

46. And it came to pass that Mosiah died also, in the thirty and third year of his reign, being sixty and three years old; making in the whole, five hundred and nine years from the time Lehi left Jerusalem.

47. And thus ended the reign of the kings over the people of Nephi; and thus ended the days of Alma, who was the founder of their church.

---

records, the nation, all being thus provided for, King Mosiah passed away to the joys of eternity. He was sixty-three years old, and he had ruled his people in righteousness for thirty-three years. When he passed away no fierce convulsions wrecked the ship of state, the political atmosphere was calm, the people joyfully assumed their new responsibilities, and the first of the judges succeeded the last of the kings without causing one disturbing wave on the placid waters of the national life.

THE LAW OF THE NEPHITES UNDER THE KINGS

The Laws of the Nephites—The Roman and Nephite Civilizations—The Laws under the kings—Position of the Priesthood—Slavery—Criminal Offenses.

If the existence of wise, just and liberal laws, administered in righteousness, be the rule by which we can judge of the true greatness of a nation and of the happiness and prosperity of its citizens, then the Nephites were a far happier and more prosperous people

THE BOOK OF MOSIAH

than were their contemporaries on the eastern continent. If this be not so, then we have not read history aright.

The Nephite nation was co-existent with the great Roman power that for so long triumphed over and crushed the surrounding people in Europe, Asia and Africa. True, Rome was founded more than a century before Lehi left Jerusalem,* but at the time of his exodus its growing power had scarcely begun to be felt outside of Italy. At the time that Moroni's record closed, the Nephites, as a nation, had become extinct, and the glory of the mistress of the world was rapidly fading away. Rome had been sacked by barbarians, the empire had been divided into two governments, the legs of Nebuchadnezzar's great image were forming; people and nations were rebelling and throwing off the iron yoke, and the idea of universal empire had become a thing of the past.† But how different the theory and genius of the two nations! The Nephite rulers governed by the power of just laws, the Romans by the might of the unsheathed sword. Among the former, every man was a free man, with his rights as a citizen guaranteed and protected by just laws. Among the latter, few could assert, as did the Apostle Paul, *Civis Romanus Sum*—I am a Roman citizen. The vast majority of the millions who formed its people were either abject allies, vanquished enemies or degraded slaves.‡ Neither of these had many rights that the Roman citizen felt himself called upon to respect. We are apt to be awed by the grand military exploits of the Roman generals, and to be dazzled with the magnificence of Rome in art and architecture, but we must recollect that the history of that city is the history of tyranny. Its power, during the greater portion of its continuance, was in the hands of the few, who used it for the interest of their class. The masses of the population were the subjects of oppression and violence.

No language could so well describe the spirit of Roman aggrandizement as that used by the prophet Daniel when interpreting to the Babylonish king the import of the terrible image he had seen in his dream. These are his words: And the fourth kingdom shall be strong as iron: forasmuch as iron breaketh in pieces and subdueth all things: and as iron that breaketh all these, shall it break in pieces and bruise. (Daniel 2:40.) And thus did Rome rule the eastern world as with a rod of iron. We need not refer to the other nations that existed on the eastern continent, for the people that Rome neither conquered nor destroyed were barbarians, who, during

---

*The generally accepted date for the foundation of Rome is 53 B.C.

†The eastern and western empires were divided A.D. 395. Alaric, the Goth, sacked Rome A.D. 410. Britain broke away from the empire A.D. 418. Gaul, Spain and Africa were soon afterwards lost.

‡In Sicily alone; goaded by ill treatment, the slaves rebelled. Their army numbered 200,000 (B.C. 134-132).

the existence of the Nephites, filled but a small page in the world's history.

These facts are presented as worthy of the consideration of all who study the social and political condition of the great and highly-favored people who flourished on this continent for so many centuries; and we imagine the student cannot fail to be impressed with the thought that they were at least a thousand years in advance of their fellow men in the science of true government; and in their polity find a type of the most advanced and most liberal forms of government of the present age. That this should be so, will not surprise us when we consider that they were a branch of the house of Israel, a people who enjoyed more political liberty (until their own follies had cut them off therefrom) than any of the other nations of antiquity, and that to the law of Moses they had added the divine teachings of the everlasting gospel, which in themselves are a perfect law of liberty. Further, it is a noteworthy fact which stares us in the face from the beginning to the end of the Book of Mormon, that when the people departed from gospel principles, it was then and then only that they fell into bondage, of whatever nature that bondage might be.

The political history of the Nephites may be consistently divided into five epochs:

First.—When they were governed by kings.

Second.—The republic, when they were ruled by judges and governors.

Third.—A short period of anarchy when they were divided into numerous independent tribes.

Fourth.—The Messianic dispensation, when they were controlled entirely by the higher law of the holy priesthood.

Fifth.—The chaotic state of internecine war which preceded their final extinction as a nation and as a race.

The first portion of the history of the Nephites when they were governed by kings, covers almost exactly one half of their national existence, or from the time of the landing of the colony on the coast of Chili to 509 years after the departure of Lehi from Jerusalem. Of the laws by which the people were governed during this period, which, however, we are told were exceedingly strict, we have few details, for the reason that the plates from which the greater portion of the Book of Mormon relates to this period was taken contain the records of their prophets rather than the annals of their kings. With regard to these kings, they of whose lives we have any particulars, viz: Nephi, the first king, and Mosiah I, Benjamin and Mosiah II, the three last, were eminently virtuous, just and merciful men,

who reigned as all monarchs should, but few do—with an eye single
to the good of their subjects. Of their kings in general the prophet
Jarom, about 400 years before Christ, remarks: Our kings and our
leaders were mighty men in the faith of the Lord: and they taught
the people the ways of the Lord. Indeed, we recollect no intimation,
in any place in the sacred record, of tyranny on the part of those
who reigned over the main body of the nation. The government
may, we think, be justly considered to approximate nearest to a
limited monarchy, in which, as in ancient Israel, the prophet often
exercised more power than the king. Though this is true of the
central government, it unfortunately cannot be so stated of the
colony which returned to the land of Nephi in the days of King
Benjamin; that people suffered beyond description from the tyranny
and wickedness, and the consequences resulting therefrom, of their
second king, Noah, the murderer of the servants of the true and
living God.

Of the life and character of the first king of the Nephites, the
father of his people, Nephi, the son of Lehi, we need say nothing
here. History affords no better model of the true prince. So thought
his people, and they, to retain in remembrance his name, and to
perpetuate the recollection of his virtues, called his successors, second
Nephi, third Nephi, etc., no matter what their original name might
have been.

The right of choosing his successor appears to have been vested
in the reigning sovereign. When Nephi became old, and saw that
he must soon die, he anointed a man to be a king and a ruler over
his people. King Benjamin chose his son Mosiah to reign in his
stead, and then gathered the people to receive his last charge and
ratify his selection. Mosiah gave the people yet greater liberty, and
instead of nominating his successor directed them to make their
own choice. The people highly appreciated this act of grace on the
part of their beloved king, and selected Aaron his son. Aaron, whose
heart was set upon the salvation of the Lamanites, declined the
kingly authority, when Mosiah very wisely advised his subjects not
to select another to fill the throne, lest it give rise, in the future, to
bloodshed and contention, but to elect judges to be their rulers,
instead of kings, which proposition they accepted with great joy.

With regard to the Nephite laws in the days of the kings, and
the manner of their execution, we can learn most from the parting
addresses of kings Benjamin and Mosiah II to their subjects. We
are frequently told by the sacred writers, from Nephi, the founder,
to Nephi, the disciple, that the people observed the law of Moses,
modified, we judge, in some of its details to suit the altered circumstances of the Nephites from those of their brethren in the land of

Palestine. As an instance we draw attention to the fact that, as there were none of the tribe of Levi in the colony that accompanied Lehi from Judea, the priestly office must necessarily have been filled and the required sacrifices and burnt offerings offered by some of the members of the tribes who were with them. Nephi (doubtless by the direction of the Lord) appointed his brothers Jacob and Joseph to be the priests for the people, they being of the tribe of Manasseh, and the care of the sacred records remained with the descendants of the first named for several generations. The members of the various orders of the priesthood, when not actually engaged in the work of the ministry, in the duties of the temple, or the service of the sanctuary, were required to labor for their own support, that they might not prove burdensome to the people. A merciful provision was, however, made for the sustenance of members of the priesthood in cases of sickness or when in much want.

Though the laws were strict, they were mercifully and equitably administered, which gave much greater stability to the government and respect for the law than if they had been adjudged loosely, and with partiality towards classes or persons. It has been wisely observed that it is not the severity of the law but the sureness of the punishment that deters the evil doer, and in this respect the Nephite nation had cause for thankfulness. All men were alike before the law, there were no privileged classes as in Rome, or in feudal Europe in later years. Mosiah says, Whosoever has committed iniquity, him have I punished according to the law which has been given to us by our fathers.

From the charge of king Benjamin to his son Mosiah we learn that slavery was forbidden. All the inhabitants of the continent being of the house of Israel, they could not observe the law of Moses and enslave their brethren.

Murder, robbery, theft, adultery and other sexual abominations were punished by law, as also was lying or bearing false witness.

Mormon states that in king Benjamin's days the false Christs, etc., were punished according to their crimes; but we are not informed if those crimes consisted in false personation, etc., or in fomenting, aiding and abetting treason and rebellion, as was almost universally the habit of those who apostatized from the gospel and sought to establish false religions in its place. King Benjamin also states that he had not permitted the people to be confined in dungeons; but we are uncertain whether to infer from this remark that the king intended his hearers to understand that he had not done this, as so many tyrants do, without cause and without trial, or that some other more effectual means had been found of punishing those transgressors not deemed worthy of death. We incline to the former opinion.

When the Nephite kingdom was first established the people were so few that they could not possibly sustain the expenses incidental to royalty. Thus it became the rule for the kings to sustain themselves. This unique, though most excellent custom continued as long as the monarchy lasted, even when the nation had grown rich and numerous. King Benjamin reminds his subjects that he had labored with his own hands that they might not be laden with taxes. Of Mosiah, his successor, it is written that he had not exacted riches of the people and that he had granted unto his people that they should be delivered from all manner of bondage.

We must not forget that, in connection with the civil law, the law of the gospel was almost unceasingly proclaimed during the whole period of the monarchy. Various false Christs and false prophets had arisen at different times, but the power of the priesthood had remained, ministering in holy things, rebuking iniquity and aiding in the suppression of vice. The kings of the Nephites, as we before observed, were, as a rule, men of God, holding the priesthood, and were often prophets and seers as well as temporal rulers. To this happy circumstance we must attribute greatly the peace and good order that so generally prevailed; the respect for the law that was so widespread; the large amount of liberty accorded to the people and the few abuses they made of that freedom. To use the idea of the Prophet Joseph Smith, for long years, they were taught correct principles, and they (to a great extent) governed themselves.

In the course of the centuries, as the people increased and spread far and wide over the land, they appear to have introduced local customs to suit their differing circumstances, or in some cases their whims and notions. Thus, until king Mosiah II established uniformity by law, nearly every generation and each section of the country had its own moneys, weights, measures, etc., which were altered from time to time according to the minds and circumstances of the people. This custom naturally caused confusion, annoyance and distrust, and to obviate these, and possibly greater evils, Mosiah consented to newly arrange the affairs of the people; and, if we may so express it, to codify the law. This code became the constitution of the nation under the rule of the Judges, which limited the powers of the officials and guaranteed the rights of the people. This compilation was acknowledged by the people, whereupon the historian remarks, Therefore they were obliged to abide by the laws which he had made. And from that time they became supreme throughout the nation. It is stated in another place that this change was made by the direct command of Jehovah.

ALMA, THE YOUNGER

Alma, the Younger, was born either in the land of Mormon, when his devout and intrepid father was there organizing the Church of Christ, or after the little colony of Christians had removed to the land of Helam. From a casual observation made in one of his discourses we are inclined to think it was in the latter place.

With his father, he came to the land of Zarahemla, and there, as the son of the Presiding High Priest of the entire Church, he became the associate and companion of the sons of the king. Their course was one too often pursued by the children of the great. They took pleasure in evil-doing; they had no faith in the revelations of God, while they ridiculed, mocked, and persecuted those who had.

We can well understand the anxiety, the distress, the sorrow this course caused their God-fearing parents; we can realize how frequent and how fervent were the prayers offered by the king, the high priest, and the people for those misguided youths. And their prayers did prevail before God.

As Alma and the sons of King Mosiah were trying to destroy the Church and to lead the people of the Lord astray, an angel descended in a cloud and stopped them on their way. When he spoke, his voice was as thunder and caused the earth to tremble beneath their feet. Naturally, this manifestation of the power of God spread terror and dismay in the hearts of those who witnessed it; simultaneously they fell to the ground. So confused and terrified were they, that they failed to understand the words of the holy messenger, "Arise, Alma and stand forth." When Alma arose his eyes were open to see who stood before him.

"Why persecutest thou the Church of God?" he was asked, "for the Lord hath said, This is my Church, and I will establish it; and nothing shall overthrow it, save it is the transgression of my people."

He further said, "If thou wilt of thyself be destroyed seek no more to destroy the Church of God."

In addition, the angel spoke of Alma's father's fervent prayers in his behalf and that because of those prayers of faith he, the angel, was sent to convince him of the power of God. He also recounted to Alma the captivity of his fathers in the lands of Helam and Nephi and of their miraculous deliverance. But Alma heard none of this, for the terrors of the first salutation had overpowered him.

Alma, bereft of the presence of the angel, dismayed and soul-stricken, sank to the ground. When his companions gathered around him, they found he could not move, neither could he speak; outwardly he was dead. The torments of the damned had taken hold of his soul, and in the most bitter pain and mental anguish he lay racked with the remembrance of all his past sins. The thought of standing before the bar of God to be judged for his iniquities overwhelmed him with horror; he would have rejoiced in annihilation; he desired to become extinct, both body and soul, without being brought before his abused Creator. Thus he continued for three days and three nights to suffer the pains of hell which, to his tortured conscience, must have seemed an eternity.

When his companions found that he could neither speak nor move, they carried him to his father and related to him what had happened. Strange as it must have seemed to them, the elder Alma's heart was filled with joy and praise when he looked upon the body of his much-loved son for he realized it was God's power that had wrought all this and that his long-continued prayers had been answered. In his joy he gathered the people to witness this mighty manifestation of the goodness and might of Jehovah. He assembled the priests, and sought their cooperation. Unitedly, in God's own way, they prayed and fasted for the stricken youth. For two days they continued their supplications, at the end of which time Alma stood upon his feet and spoke. He comforted them by declaring, "I have repented of my sins and have been redeemed of the Lord; behold I am born of the Spirit."

In later years Alma, in relating to his son, Helaman, the details of his conversion, described the causes that led him to bear this testimony.

Behold, I remembered also to have heard my father prophesy unto the people concerning the coming of one Jesus Christ, a Son of God, to atone for the sins of the world. Now, as my mind caught hold upon this thought, I cried within my heart: O Jesus, thou Son of God, have mercy on me, who am in the gall of bitterness, and am encircled about by the everlasting chains of death. And now, behold, when I thought this, I could remember my pains no more; yea, I was harrowed up by the memory of my sins no more. And oh, what joy, and what marvelous light I did behold; yea, my soul was filled with joy as exceeding as was my pain! Yea, I say unto you, my son, that there could be nothing so exquisite and so bitter as were my pains. Yea, and again I say unto you, my son, that on the other hand, there can be nothing so exquisite and sweet as was my joy. Yea, methought I saw, even as our father Lehi saw, God sitting upon his throne, surrounded with numberless concourses of angels, in the attitude of singing and praising their God; yea, and my soul did long to be there.

From that time to the end of his life, Alma labored without ceasing to bring souls to Christ and to guide his fellowmen in the paths of salvation.

Alma was the foremost man of his age and nation, the presiding high priest and chief judge of a mighty people, a great prophet filled with the spirit of his calling, an unceasing missionary, an undaunted soldier, a lucid expounder of the principles of the Everlasting Gospel, a proficient organizer of men, a distinguished warrior, and a triumphant general. There is a parallel in his conversion, extended missionary journeyings, and elaborate discourses on saving truths with Saul of Tarsus. We are also reminded of the recollections of Joshua, the son of Nun, as the great leader and prophet of his people and the victorious commander-in-chief of their armies.

The change in the life of Alma brought down upon him the persecutions of the wicked. They now treated him as he had previously treated the Saints. But in none of these things was he daunted or dismayed, for he had joy in preaching the word and in the conversion of many from their ungodliness.

So conspicuous as a champion of the cause of God did he become that Mosiah considered him the proper person to whom to confide the custody of the sacred plates and to act as the recorder of the nation's affairs and progress. In addition, when Aaron, the son of Mosiah, declined to succeed his father on the Nephite throne and it was wisely determined by the people that they would be ruled by judges for the future, Alma was chosen by the united voice of his countrymen to be their first chief judge. He was also their presiding high priest, his having been consecrated to this exalted position by his father, who shortly before his death, gave him charge of the affairs of the church throughout all the land (91 B.C.).

Five hundred and nine years had now passed away since Lehi left Jerusalem during which time the Nephites had been ruled by kings, the successors of the first Nephi. A wonderful but bloodless revolution now took place. The monarchy was merged into a republic, but so wise had been the steps taken by Mosiah, so equitably had he arranged the laws, that the change was made without tumult or disorder in the affairs of state. Indeed, the change was hailed with unbounded satisfaction by the people who greatly rejoiced in the more extended liberties now guaranteed to them.

In Alma, as their first chief judge, they had a man admirably adapted for the situation. He had the confidence of the people inasmuch as he was the Lord's mouthpiece to them; his worth and abilities claimed their trust and respect. He was a man of great talent, courage, faith, and energy, an unwearied worker for good, and as a judge he judged righteously. Still his position was not one of unmixed delights—apostates from the Church, pride and unbelief in its members, assaults and invasions from the national enemies, all combined to require his undiminished energies and undaunted faith. But above and beyond all, as compensation for these trials and annoyances, he had the right to receive the word of the Lord which was given to him as he needed or his people required.

The first year of Alma's judgeship was troubled by the apostasy of Nehor, a man of many personal attractions and great persuasiveness of manner. Nehor went about among the people preaching a kind of universalism—that all men would be saved. He also established priestcraft, making a lucrative business of spreading his pernicious ideas. His success in turning the hearts of the people was unfortunately extensive and the cause for many of the troubles that afterwards afflicted the Nephites. The individual career of Nehor, however, was short; he met an aged servant of the Lord named Gideon, and because the latter would not accept his dogmas but withstood him with the words of God, Nehor drew his sword and slew the venerable disciple. For this offense he was brought before Alma, tried by the law, found guilty, and condemned to death.

Notwithstanding the development of those follies and departures from the strictness of Gospel law, there was continued peace in the land until the fifth year of Alma's judgeship when a great division took place among the people. The corrupt portion wished to restore the monarchy and make a man after their own heart, named Amlici, king. The movement grew to so much importance that it was referred to the decision of all the people who gathered in large groups throughout the land and expressed their wishes for or against Amlici's elevation to the throne in the way prescribed by the law. The result was that Amlici's ambitious schemes were defeated by the voice of the majority, and the liberties of the republic were preserved.

This should have ended the matter, but it did not; the turbulent minority, incited by Amlici, would not accept this constitutional decision. They assembled and crowned their favorite as king of the Nephites and he at once began to prepare for war so that he might force the rest of the people to assent to his government.

Nor was Alma idle; he also made ready for the impending contest. He gathered his people and armed them with all the weapons known to Nephite warfare.

The two armies met near a hill, Amnihu, on the east bank of the River Sidon. There a bloody battle followed in which Amlici's forces were disastrously defeated with a loss of 12,532 men, while the victors had to mourn the loss of 6,562 warriors slain. After pursuing the defeated monarchists as far as he was able, Alma rested his troops in the Valley of Gideon. There he took the precaution to send out four officers with their companies to watch the movements and learn the intentions of the retreating foe. These officers were Zeram, Amnor, Manti, and Limher. The next day these scouts returned in great haste and reported that the Amlicites had joined a vast host of Lamanites in the land of Minon, where unitedly they were slaying the Nephite population and ravaging their possessions, and at the same time they were pushing rapidly towards the Nephite capital with the intent of capturing it before Alma's army could return.

Alma at once started his troops for Zarahemla and with all haste marched towards it. He reached the crossing of the Sidon without meeting the enemy, but while attempting to pass to the western bank, he was confronted by the allied armies. A terrible battle ensued. The Nephites were taken somewhat at a disadvantage, but being men of faith, they fervently sought heaven's aid and in the increased fervor this faith inspired, they advanced to the combat. With Alma at their head, the advance guard forded the river and broke up the enemy who stood awaiting them. By the fury of their charge they drove into the ranks of the enemy. As they pushed onward, they cleared the ground by throwing the bodies of their fallen foes into the Sidon, thus making an opening for the main body to obtain a foothold.

In this charge Alma met Amlici face to face, and they fought desperately. In the midst of this hand-to-hand combat, Alma prayed for renewed strength that he might not be overpowered but live to continue to do good for his people. His prayers were answered, and thereby he gained new vigor to battle with and eventually to slay Amlici. With Amlici slain, Alma now led the attack to the place where the king of the Lamanites fought. But that monarch retired before the impetuous valor of the high priest and commanded his guards to close in upon his assailant. The order was promptly obeyed, but it did not succeed.

Alma and his guards bore down upon them with such fury that the few of the monarch's warriors who escaped made a hasty retreat. Pushing steadily on Alma kept driving the allies before him until his whole army had crossed the Sidon. There the enemy, no longer able to meet his well-ordered advance, broke in all directions and retreated into the wilderness that lay to the north and west. They were hotly pursued by the Nephites as long as the latter's strength permitted and were met on all quarters by patriots rallying to the call of the commonwealth who slew them by thousands. A remnant eventually reached that part of the wilderness known as Hermounts. There many died of their wounds and were devoured by the wild beasts and vultures with which that region abounded.

To the Nephites was left the sad task of burying the unnumbered dead, many of whom were women and children who had become victims to the ravages of the foe.

A few days after this decisive battle, another invading Lamanite army was reported. This one advanced along the east bank of the Sidon. It appears to have been the plan of their military commanders to invade the Nephite territory with two separate armies, both traveling northward toward the city of Zarahemla but on opposite sides of the Sidon. That advancing on the west side moved the most rapidly and was met, conquered, and dispersed by Alma. Later the other army met the same fate at the hands of one of Alma's lieutenants, because he was too seriously wounded in one of the preceding battles to lead his troops in person.

The great loss sustained by the Nephites in war, not only of warriors but also of women and children, together with the vast amount of property destroyed, had the effect of humbling them and softening their wayward hearts, so that many thousands during the next few years were added to the church by baptism. But the recollection of their former disasters was quickly worn away by prosperity. Only three years later there was great inequality in the Church. Some were poor and some were rich, and the more powerful abused and oppressed their weaker brethren. This course proved a great stumbling-block to those who were not numbered with the church, as well as being the cause of much sorrow and ill-feeling among its members. Finding that no man could properly attend to the duties of his many offices, Alma determined to resign the chief judgeship and devote his entire time to his duties as the earthly head of the Church. Preparatory to his resignation, he selected one of the leading elders, Nephihah, to be his successor as chief judge. This choice was confirmed by the people (83 B.C.).

The cares of the state having thus been removed from his shoulders, Alma commenced his ministerial labors at Zarahemla the chief city of the nation and then proceeded throughout the land. As often happens in other nations, the capital was the center of pride, vanity, envy, hypocrisy, and class distinctions. These evils Alma severely rebuked. At the same time, he guided the minds of the people to the contemplation and understanding of the beauties and saving powers of redemption's wondrous plan. He also exhorted everyone to become members of Christ's holy church. His call was heeded by many; the church was set in order; the unworthy were disfellowshiped; elders, priests, and other officers were ordained to preside and watch over the Saints.

After this was accomplished, Alma took his journey eastward, crossed the River Sidon to the city of Gideon, where he happily found the church in a prosperous condition. Alma's teachings to this people were full of prophecies concerning the coming of the Messiah, which show how clearly he and his faithful fellow servants understood the details of the advent and life of the promised Redeemer. Having made firm the Church in Gideon, Alma returned to Zarahemla to rest and recruit for a short time before visiting other portions of the land.

At the commencement of the next year (82 B.C.) Alma turned his face eastward. He first visited the land of Melek where his labors were crowned with abundant blessings. Having satisfied himself with the good that he had accomplished, he "traveled three days' journey on the north of the land of Melek," to a great and corrupt city named Ammonihah. Here he found a godless people, filled with the falsehoods of Nehor and living in the committal of all manner of abominations without repentance, because they cherished the flattering lie as the foundation of their creed, that all men would be exalted.

The city was in the hands of a corrupt clique of judges and lawyers who stirred up sedition, tumult, and rioting, that they might make money out of the suits that followed such disturbances. Further than this, they were sercretly plotting to overthrow the government and rob the people of their highly-prized liberties. Among such a people Alma labored in vain, but no one would listen, and no one would obey. No one offered Alma rest or food. Instead, scorn and mockery were his reward, and he was spat upon, maltreated, and cast out of the city for his pains.

Weary in body and sick at heart because of the iniquity of the people after his many fruitless efforts, fervent prayers, and long fastings, Alma left the city to seek some other people more worthy of salvation's priceless gifts. He bent his way towards the city of Aaron; but as he journeyed an angel of the Lord (that same angel that had been the agent in his conversion to God) stood before him and blessed him. He told Alma to lift up his heart and rejoice for, because of his faithfulness, he had great cause to do so. The angel then directed Alma to return to the sin-cursed city he had just left and proclaim unto its godless citizens the awful message, "Except they repent the Lord will destroy them."

Speedily the prophet obeyed the angel's words. By another road he drew near the doomed city which he entered by its south gate. As he passed in he was an hungered and asked a man whom he met, "Will you give an humble servant of God something to eat?" With joy the man took him to his home and fed, clothed, and lodged him. Furthermore, Amulek, for this was his name, told Alma that he also had received a visit from an angel who had informed him of the high priest's coming and directed him to receive him into his house. Alma blessed Amulek and all his household and tarried and recruited under the generous hospitality which his home afforded. But his rest was not to be a lengthened one; the people waxed stronger in sin; the cup of their iniquity was nearly full. "Go," came the word of the Lord, "Go forth, and take with thee my servant Amulek and prophesy unto this people, saying, Repent ye for thus saith the Lord, except ye repent I will visit this people in mine anger; yea, I will not turn my fierce anger away."

Filled with the Holy Ghost, these servants of Israel's God went forth and valiantly delivered their terrible message. From place to place they went raising their Jonah-like cry. The heathen Ninevehites hearkened and repented; the sin-stained Israelites of Ammonihah laughed, scorned, mocked, and turned contemptuously away. A few, indeed, received the word but that only increased the anger of the majority, who, led and urged on by their still more depraved rulers and teachers, persecuted the prophets and martyred the believers.

The account given of the teachings of Alma and Amulek, their disputations with Zeezrom and other lawyers and rulers in Ammonihah, is given at length in the Book of Mormon and in consequence thereof, we have had handed down to us some of the plainest and profoundest teachings on the atonement, the resurrection, and the powers of the priesthood that are to be had. We cannot follow them here through all the varied incidents that led to the final catastrophe.

Faithfully the prophets warned Ammonihah of its approaching desolation; scornfully and incredulously the hardened people hurled back their words of warning with defiance. The few that believed, of which the crafty, hair-splitting Zeezrom was the most notable example, were cast out of the city, while Alma and Amulek were bound with strong cords and under false accusations of having reviled the laws, were cast into prison.

Having consigned Alma and his companion to a prison cell, the infuriated people hunted up the wives and the little ones of the believers whom they had cast out, with such others as had accepted the truth who still remained in the city, and gathering all of them in a body, they burned them in one great martyr's fire. Into the flames they also cast the records that contained the Holy Scriptures, as though they imagined in their blind fury that they could thereby destroy the truths that were so odious to them. In the refinement of their devilish cruelty they brought Alma and Amulek to the place of martyrdom, that they might be witnesses of the agonies of the suffering innocents and listen to the crackling and the roaring of the flames. With jeers, with mouthing, and derisive gestures they called upon the prophets to rescue their dying converts. Amulek's noble heart was pained beyond endurance; he besought Alma to exercise the power of God that was in them and to save the victims from the consuming flames. But Alma replied that the, ". . . Spirit constraineth me that I must not stretch forth mine hand, for behold the Lord receiveth them up unto himself in glory and he doth suffer that they may do this thing unto them, according to the hardness of their hearts, that the judgments which he shall exercise upon them in his wrath may be just and the blood of the innocent shall stand as a witness against them the last day." Then Amulek said, "Perhaps they will burn us also." To which Alma responded, "Be it according to the will of the Lord. But, behold, our work is not finished; therefore they burn us not."

When the fire had burned low, and the precious fuel of human bodies and sacred records were consumed, the chief judge of the city came to the two prophets as they stood bound and mocked them. He smote them on the cheek and sneeringly asked them if they would preach again that his people should be cast into a lake of fire and brimstone. But neither answered him a word. Seeing that they had no power to save those who had been burned, neither had God exercised his power in their behalf, he then smote them again and remanded them to prison.

After they had been confined three days, they were visited by many judges and lawyers, priests, and teachers after the order of Nehor who came to exult in the misery of their prisoners. They cross-questioned and badgered them, but neither would reply. They came again the next day and went through the same performance. They mocked, they smote, they spat upon the two disciples. They tantalized them with outrageous and blasphemous questions, such as, "How shall we look when we are damned?"

Patiently and silently all this was borne; day after day it was repeated; harder and harder grew the hearts of the Ammonihahites towards their prisoners; fiercer and stronger grew their hatred. They stripped Alma and Amulek of their clothes and when naked, bound them with strong ropes. They withheld food and drink from them and in various ways they tortured their bodies and sought to aggravate, tantalize, and harrow up their minds.

On the twelfth day of the tenth month of the tenth year of the Judges (82 B.C.) the chief judge and his followers again went to the prison. According to his usual custom he smote the brethren, saying as he did so, "If ye have the power of God deliver yourselves from these bands and then we will believe that the Lord will destroy this people according to your words." This impious challenge the crowd one by one repeated as they passed by the prophets and smote them in imitation of their leader. Thus each individual assumed the responsibility of the defiance cast at the Almighty and virtually said, "Our blood be upon our own heads."

The hour of God's power had now come—the challenge had been accepted. The prophets in the majesty of their calling rose to their feet; they were endowed with the strength of Jehovah; like burned thread the cords that bound them were snapped asunder and they stood free and unshackled before the terror-stricken mob. To rush from the prison was the first impulse of the God-defying followers of Nehor; in their fear all else was forgotten, some fell to the earth, others, impelled by the mob behind, stumbled and fell over their prostrate bodies until they became one confused, inextricable mass, blocking each other's way, struggling, yelling, cursing, pleading, fighting; frantically, but vainly, endeavoring to reach the outer gate.

At this moment of supreme horror an earthquake rent the prison walls; they trembled, then tottered, then fell on the struggling mass of humanity below, burying in one vast, unconsecrated grave, rulers and judges, lawyers and officers, priests and teachers. Not one was left of all the impious mob, who a few moments before defied heaven and challenged Jehovah's might. Alma and Amulek stood in the midst of the ruins unhurt. Straight way they left the scene of desolation and went into the city. Here the horrified people fled from them as a herd of goats flee from before two young lions.

Alma and Amulek, being so commanded, left the doomed city and passed over to the land of Sidom. Here they found the Saints who had been cast out of Ammonihah. To them they told the sad though glorious story of their martyred kin. With many words of wisdom and consolation they encouraged them to lives of devotion to Christ. Here, also, they found Zeezrom, the lawyer, racked in spirit with the recollection of his former infamies and tortured in body by the heat of a burning fever. At Zeezrom's request the two servants of the Most High visited him. They found he had repented in much tribulation for the past and that faith had developed in his heart.

Alma then exercised the power of his calling. Appealing to heaven, he cried, "O Lord, our God, have mercy on this man, and heal him according to his faith, which is in Christ." Zeezrom thereupon leaped upon his feet; his fever had left; he was made whole by the grace of God, while the people wondered and were astonished at this manifestation of God's goodness. Zeezrom was then baptized by Alma and became a zealous and faithful advocate of divine law.

The more complete organization of the Church in Sidom was the next work accomplished by Alma, which, having been satisfactorily attended to and the proper officers of the priesthood having been ordained and appointed, Alma, accompanied by his faithful friend, Amulek, returned to his home in Zarahemla.

The following year Ammonihah was destroyed. Less than four months had elapsed since the two inspired disciples had left it to its fate, when the Lamanites fell upon it like a whirlwind in its suddenness and as an avalanche in its utter destruction. For one day the fierce flames consumed the walls and towers of Ammonihah. The great city was no more; the word of the Lord had been fully accomplished; not one of its children remained. A desolation and a desert remained where dogs, vultures, and wild beasts struggled for the carcasses of the slain. Having resigned the office of chief judge, Alma no longer led the armies of Nephi. A righteous man named Zoram was their commander. Without delay he gathered his forces and prepared to meet the invading Lamanites. Knowing that Alma was the mouthpiece of God, he and his two sons went to the high priest and inquired how the campaign should be conducted. The word was given, its instructions were carried out, victory perched upon the Nephite banners. The Lamanites, utterly routed, retreated to their own lands. Then there was continued peace throughout the continent for three years.

During this period of peace Alma and his fellow priesthood members preached God's holy word in the power and demonstration of the Spirit and with much success. Great prosperity came to the Church throughout all the lands of the Nephites. At this happy time "there was no inequality among them, the Lord did pour out His Spirit on all the face of the land," as Alma supposed, to prepare the hearts of his people for the coming of Christ. With this object full in view he labored and rejoiced, preached, blessed, and prophesied, never tiring in his energies and feeling sorrowful only because of the hard-heartedness and spiritual blindness of some of the people.

In one most glorious event he had unspeakable joy. The companions of his youth, the sons of King Mosiah, returned from a fourteen years' mission among the Lamanites, during which time, after many sore trials and great tribulation, they, by the grace of their Father, had brought many thousands of that benighted race to a knowledge of the principles of the Everlasting Gospel.

Alma was traveling south on one of his missionary journeys from the land of Zarahemla to the land of Manti when he met Ammon and his brethren coming from the land of Nephi. On hearing the story of their mission, he at once returned home with them to Zarahemla. Here the condition of affairs among the Lamanites was rehearsed to the chief judge who laid the whole subject before the people so that whatever was done in relation to the Christian Lamanites might be done by common consent. The Nephites decided to give the land of Jershon, which lay south of the land of Bountiful, to these people for an inheritance. With this cheering news, Ammon, accompanied by Alma, returned into the southern wilderness, to the place where his people were awaiting the decision of the Nephites. Here they were ministered to and comforted by Alma and others after which they resumed their march to the land designated for their future abode.

We pass over the next few years of Alma's life, during which period he was laboring with his usual zest and devotion, to the latter portion of the seventeenth year of the Judges (75 B.C.). It was then that Korihor, the anti-Christ, appeared. His pernicious doctrines savor much of certain classes of modern religious delusion, but his principal arguments were directed against the advent and atonement of the Redeemer. From land to land he journeyed among the Nephites, spreading his false theories and notions. But as he claimed that as he taught so he believed, the law could not touch him for it was strictly forbidden in the Nephite constitution that any one should be punished on account of his belief; freedom of conscience was guaranteed to all. At last, not knowing what to do with him and as he was fomenting dissension and endangering the peace of the community, the local officers sent him to Alma and the chief judge for them to decide in the matter.

When he was brought before these officers, he continued, with great swelling words of blasphemy, to ridicule the holy principles of the Gospel and to revile the servants of God, falsely accusing them, among other things, of glutting themselves out of the labors of the people.

In Alma's answer to this charge we have a pleasing insight into his private life. He said, "Thou knowest that we do not glut ourselves upon the labors of this people, for behold, I have labored, even from the commencement of the reign of the judges until now, with mine own hands for my support, notwithstanding my many travels around about the land to declare the word of God unto my people; and notwithstanding the many labors I have performed in the church, I have not so much as received even one senine for my labor; either has any of my brethren, save it were in the judgment seat and then we have received only according to law for our time."

Korihor continued to withstand the prophet until in compliance with his impious importunities a sign was given him—an unwelcome and unexpected sign to him— he was struck dumb by the power of God. He was cast out from the face of society, a wanderer and a vagabond, begging from door to door for bread to sustain life. While thus dragging out a miserable existence, he was run over and trodden to death in the city of the Zoramites.

The Zoramites were a dangerous body of dissenters who also taught that there should be no Christ. They deluded themselves with the idea that they were the peculiar objects of heaven's favor, born to be saved, predestined to eternal glory while the rest of the world were the rejected, the foreordained damned. This consoling creed, to the corrupt and crime-stained, was rapidly growing and gaining influence at the time of Korihor's death and became the next object of Alma's ever-watchful care.

Accompanied by Amulek, Zeezrom, three of the sons of King Mosiah and two of his own sons, Alma went over to the regions inhabited by these apostates. This mission was one of the most important of his life and, like that to Ammonihah, was partially successful. As soon as Alma discovered the gross iniquity of this people and the peculiarities of their forms of worship, he held a council meeting with his fellow-missionaries, and having prayed fervently to the Lord, "he clapped his hands upon all who were with him. And behold, as he clapped his hands upon them they were filled with the Holy Ghost. After that they did separate themselves one from another; taking no thought for themselves what they should eat, or what they should drink, or what they should put on." And in all these things the Lord provided for them.

The missionaries labored diligently, they visited the people in their homes, they preached in their synagogues, they proclaimed the truth in their streets but the flattering errors of their false faith had so thoroughly taken possession of them that they rejected the truth and persecuted and even attempted to slay some of Alma's companions. However, this rejection was not universal. A number of the poorer and more humble Zoramites accepted the divine message in consequence of which they were soon driven from their homes and out of their country by their more numerous, more influential, and also more corrupt fellow-citizens.

When Alma and his associates had done all the good that seemed to them practicable, they retired to the land of Jershon where the Ammonites dwelt; there the believing Zoramites followed when they were expatriated by their fellow countrymen. In Jershon they were kindly received by its inhabitants and welcomed as brethren. Here Alma again ministered to them. Having done this, he and most of his co-laborers returned to Zarahemla.

Alma was now growing old. Notwithstanding his unceasing efforts and fervent prayers, the Nephites were again backsliding into iniquity. To every Nephite city and to every Nephite land he went, or sent, to revive the Gospel fires in the souls of the inhabitants. But many became offended because of the strictness of the Gospel's laws which forbade not only sin itself but also the very appearance of sin. As this feeling grew, Alma's heart became exceedingly sorrowful and he mourned the depravity of his people. Like many of the ancient patriarchs, when they felt that their mortal career was drawing to a close, he called his sons to him and gave them his last charge and blessing; speaking to each as the spirit of instruction and prophecy inspired. To Helaman, his eldest, he transferred the custody of the sacred plates with many words of warning and caution. With hearts strengthened and renewed by the inspiration of his fervent admonitions, his sons went forth among the people; nor could Alma himself rest while there was a soul to save or a wrong to make right. He also went forth once again in the spirit of his holy calling and raised his voice in advocacy of the principles of the everlasting gospel.

Another bloody war now commenced, one that before its close drew out the whole strength of both Nephites and Lamanites. The youthful but brilliant and God-fearing Moroni took charge of the armies of Nephi. He, not willing to trust to his own powers, sent to Alma for the divine word to direct his movements. As was his wont, the high priest was favored with the revelation of heaven's will which, being conveyed to Moroni, was in faith implicitly followed. We need not enter into the details of the terrible battle that ensued; victory crowned the inspired general's efforts. With the account of this battle, the record of Alma closes.

It was in the nineteenth year of the Judges (73 B.C.) that Alma took his beloved son, Helaman, and after having discovered through divers questions, the strength and integrity of his faith, he prophesied to Helaman of many important events which should transpire in the distant future, especially with regard to the destruction of the Nephites. This prophecy he commanded Helaman to record on the plates but not to reveal to any one. Alma then blessed Helaman and also his other sons. Indeed, he blessed all who should stand firm in the truth of Christ from that time forth. Shortly after this he departed out of the land of Zarahemla, as if to go to the land of Melek and was never heard of again. Of his death and burial no men were witnesses. Then the saying went abroad throughout the Church that the Lord had taken him, as he beforetime had taken Moses. This event occurred exactly one hundred years from the time of the elder Alma's birth.

CONCERNING THE PLATES OF THE
BOOK OF MORMON

There are, as far as we know, no data from which to calculate, with accuracy, the number of plates in, or the weight of, the original volume from which the Book of Mormon was translated. And yet, such questions have been discussed by unfriendly critics of the book.

The Reverend Mr. M. T. Lamb's Objections. The Reverend Mr. M. T. Lamb, for instance, who, in 1886 or 1887, favored the Saints in Utah, with a series of lectures against the sacred volume, and was courteously tendered the use of ward houses for that purpose, told us that the 563 pages of the Liverpool text, would have required at least an equal number of plates. Consequently, he said there were, on the most liberal estimate possible, enough plates only for from one-third to one-eighth of the text as printed in the edition then in common use. He arrived at this conclusion by accepting the dimensions of the plates as 7 x 8 inches, and the thickness of the volume as four inches. But the Prophet, he said, did not translate more than one-third of the two hundred which he allowed for the plates at fifty per inch; that is to say, sixty-six or sixty-seven plates, and Joseph Smith could not have obtained the entire book as we have it from such a small number of plates.[1]

Others have asserted that if the Prophet Joseph Smith had a sufficient number of gold plates to contain the entire text of the Book of Mormon, they would have been too heavy to handle as a book. They would have weighed 500 pounds or more.

By such statements the critics have hoped to break the "Mormon" pitcher at the threshold, as the Greek saying is. If they could make it appear that the Prophet could not have had a sufficient number of plates; or, if he had, that he could not have lifted them, they felt thereby they could remove the entire foundation of the Church, and have nothing more to discuss. It is, therefore, interesting to consider just what data is available, and what conclusions may be drawn from them.[2]

---

[1] M. T. Lamb, *The Golden Bible*, pp. 245-250.

[2] *The Prophet Joseph's Own Account.* The Prophet writes: "These records were engraven on plates which had the appearance of gold; each plate was six inches wide and eight inches long and not quite as thick as common tin. They were filled with engravings, in Egyptian characters, and bound together in a volume as the leaves of a book with three rings running through the whole. The volume was something near six inches in thickness, part of which was sealed. The characters on the unsealed part were small, and beautifully engraved. The whole book exhibited many marks of antiquity in its construction, and much skill in the art of engraving. With the records was found a curious instrument, which the ancients called 'urim and thummim,' which consisted of two transparent stones set in the rim of

No Definite Data now at Hand. It should be noted, however, that the Prophet Joseph does not enlighten us on the number or weight of the plates, any more than Moses does on the size and avoirdupois of the tables on which the Lord engraved the Law. It should also be remembered that the particulars furnished by eye witnesses were given many years after they had seen the plates, in answer to questions pressed upon them in the course of what amounted almost to cross examination. They gave, therefore, their individual estimates and nothing more.

Suppose, for the sake of illustration, that two or more men should be examined on the dimensions of a book—say *Webster's Dictionary*—twenty years after they had seen it. What would their answers be, provided there was no collusion between them? They would call up from the depths of their minds the images produced there many years ago and then each would give his own estimate, as best he could.

We remember an occasion on which some students were together, and the question of estimating dimensions came up. "A "stovepipe hat" was placed in the middle of the floor, where there was no object close to it to compare it with, and the question was asked, "What is the height of the hat?" The estimates, quickly made, varied and ranged all the way from four to ten inches. The actual height, we believe, was five-and-a-half inches. We dare say a carpenter, or any other mechanic, would have come closer to the right figure, when the object was before him, but what would be his estimate many years afterward? Probably it would have been more or less than the actual figure, but that would not effect his credibility as a witness to the fact that he had actually seen and handled the object in question.

Size of the Plates. The Prophet Joseph Smith gave the size as six-by-eight inches.

David Whitmer, in an interview in the *Kansas City Journal,* said of the plates, shortly before his death: "They appeared to be of gold, about six by nine inches in size, about as thick as parchment, a great many in number and bound together like the leaves of a book by massive rings passing through the edges."

Martin Harris, according to *Myth of the Manuscript Found,*[3] estimated the plates at eight-by-seven inches and the thickness of a volume of four inches, each plate being as thick as thick tin.

Orson Pratt had not seen the plates, himself, but his intimacy with the Prophet and the eye witnesses lend some weight to his words.

a bow fastened to a breastplate. Through the medium of the Urim and Thummim I translated the record by the gift and power of God." Joseph Smith, in a letter to John Wentworth, editor of the *Chicago Democrat,* March 1, 1842. *History of the Church,* Vol. 4, p. 535.

[3]An excellent little book by George Reynolds.

He tells us that the plates were eight-by-seven inches, while each plate was about as thick as common tin, and also that the entire volume was about six inches thick. Orson Pratt also said that two-thirds of the volume was sealed.

Such are the statements made on the dimensions of the plates and all show really slight variations. David Whitmer's estimate of the size amounts to fifty-four square inches, but he says nothing of the thickness of the volume. Martin Harris gives us fifty-six square inches as the size of the plates and four inches as the thickness of the volume. Orson Pratt accepts the first figure of Martin Harris but gives six inches as the thickness, as does the Prophet Joseph Smith. According to the latter, each plate had a surface of forty-eight square inches.

The real question is: "Could one-third (two-thirds being sealed) of a volume of metal plates (leaves) 6x8x6 (the Prophet Joseph), or 8x7x4 (Martin Harris), or 8x7x6 (Orson Pratt), contain a sufficient number of plates, each as thick as parchment or tin, to yield the necessary space for the entire text of the Book of Mormon? If so, what about their immense weight?

Two Remarkable Illustrations. The accompanying illustrations answer these questions.

The first is a facsimile of a sheet of paper, eight x seven inches, upon which a Hebrew translation of fourteen pages of the American text of the Book of Mormon have been written in the modern, square Hebrew letters in common use. The translation was made by our friend, Mr. Henry Miller, a Hebrew by birth, thoroughly versed in the Hebrew language, and a member of the Church. On this sheet it is demonstrated that the entire text of the Book of Mormon could have been written in Hebrew on 40-3/7 pages— twenty-one plates in all.

If it is thought that these characters are too small to be read with alacrity, it may be said that the illustrations, as Mr. Miller wrote them, were quite legible. But turn to the second illustration. This is a reproduction of a translation into Hebrew, also by Mr. Miller, and written in the old Phoenician or Israelitic characters which were known to Lehi and his contemporaries. It contains seven pages of the American text of the Book of Mormon. It proves that even if these larger characters are used, the entire book could be written or engraved on 80-6/7 pages—forty-one plates in all. Illustration No. 2 is also on seven x eight inch paper.

Hebrew translation of II Nephi, Chapters 5:20 to 11:3 inclusive,
(about 14 and ¾ pages of the English version.)

In the Old World the ancient Semitic Alphabet was, in due time, superceded by the Aramean. This system of writing was adopted by the Hebrews after the Babylonian captivity, chiefly, as Jewish tradition avers, through the influence of Ezra. The square Hebrew letters now in use are the modern offspring of the Aramean ancestors.

In Egypt the Hieroglyphic letters gradually receded into oblivion, and the Demotic or Enchorian script became popular. At the time of Herodotus, about 450 B.C., only the Hieratic and the Demotic characters were known outside the small circle of scholars.[4] It appears, therefore, that Nephi, in this part of the world, took the same course as regards the reformation of the alphabet as that followed

[4]E. A. Wallis Budge, *A History of Egypt,* Vol. 6, p. 198. *Scribner's Bible Dictionary,* "Alphabet."

Seven English Pages

II Nephi 11:4-16:9; Hebrew Text; Phönician Letters.

Hebrew translation II Nephi, Chapter 11:4 to 16:9 inclusive.
(Phönician or Old Israelitic characters. Seven English pages.)

by the scholars of the Old World, as their literary taste and requirements developed.

Some time in the dim past, perhaps two thousand years before
our era, Semitic scholars, probably Phöenicians, feeling the need
of simpler and more practical signs than those in use in Egypt, picked
out twenty-one of the old Hieratic characters, modified them, and
renamed them. This according to the famed French Egyptologist,
Emmanuel de Rouge, was the origin of the oldest Semitic alphabet.
It has been called the *Phöenician* or *Old Israelitic* alphabet. As a
matter of fact, it was the *Egyptian Reformed*, and was adapted to
Semitic speech. The *Law*, and most of the *Prophets*, were at one
time written in these characters.

Lehi, the scholarly ancestor of the Nephites and the Lamanites,
undoubtedly was familiar with it. It was the alphabet, we have no

doubt, on the Brass Plates of Laban, referred to as "the language of the Egyptians,"[5] (Mosiah 1:4) meaning, as explained, "the characters which are called among us the reformed Egyptian." (Mormon 9:32) Nephi knew this system of writing, for he had been "taught somewhat in all the learning of my father." (I Nephi 1:1) It would, therefore, be natural for him to make use of this Old Semitic alphabet as a foundation for the signs he needed for his record, modified so as to require but little space of the ponderous material on which they were engraved.

Here it should be recalled, perhaps, that we are not in possession of all that the Prophet translated from the record. Martin Harris lost, as is well known, one hundred-sixteen written pages of completed manuscript, which were not retranslated. Just how much printed space they would have occupied, we know not; but fifty pages we consider a very generous allowance for that space. Fifty printed pages would be equal to a little more than seven pages—four plates—if the Phöenician characters were used. Four plates, then, should be added to the forty-one already mentioned, making a total number of plates needed for the entire book that was translated, forty-five.

Hebrew Writing Requires Small Space. This may sound incredible to some, but it is easily explained. The Hebrews of old did not write vowels. They wrote only consonants, and they did not leave much space between words and lines as we do. Nor did they need so many small words as we do to complete a sentence. Frequently their auxiliary words consisted of a single letter attached to the main word, either as a prefix or suffix. And, finally, they used many abbreviations. All this meant a great saving of space.[6]

The entire volume was four inches thick (Martin Harris), or about six inches (Orson Pratt). Let us take the smaller number as the most probable. Mr. Lamb has allowed fifty plates to an inch, or two hundred plates to the four inches. One-third only was translated; that is, sixty-six and a fraction plates. But we have demonstrated that the entire book including the lost pages, could have been written on forty-five plates. If we allow sixty-six, or even fifty, we have ample space for a text engraved in large, legible characters.[7]

---

[5]"This little colony brought with them from Jerusalem their ancient scriptures engraved in Egyptian characters, on brass plates." Orson Pratt, in an article on the Book of Mormon, written in 1874 for the *Universal Cyclopedia*. *Millennial Star*, Vol. 38, p. 692.

[6]It is well known that the subdivision of the Hebrew text of the Bible was not begun before the Thirteenth Century of our era. The Masoretic punctuation, including most of the vowels now in use to aid the student in pronouncing the words, was not introduced until some time between the Sixth and Ninth Centuries. The separation of the text into words is not found in the oldest manuscripts. The square letters of the consonants were not employed before the Third Century of our era.

[7]The first edition of the Book of Mormon, printed in Palmyra, New York, 1830 has 590 pages, 12:mo. The first European edition, Liverpool, 1841, reprinted from the second American edition, has 634 pages. The third American edition, Nauvoo, has 571 pages. The second edition, Liverpool, 1849, has 563 pages. The American edition, 1920, has 522 pages.

Regarding the Weight. Thirty-five twenty-dollar gold pieces would cover a surface of about seven by eight inches. To make a column four inches high, forty-eight such pieces would be needed. Consequently, thirty-five times forty-eight twenty dollar gold pieces, or 1,680 in all, would make up the dimensions of the plates, seven by eight by four inches. A twenty-dollar gold piece weighs twenty-one and one-half penny-weights. That would make a total of 123 pounds.[8]

From this estimate liberal deductions must be made. The plates were not pure gold. The Plates of Nephi were made of *ore*, and Moroni also mentions *ore* as the material of which his plates were made. (Mormon 8:5) The *ore*, possibly a copper alloy, must have been considerably lighter in weight than the twenty-three karat gold of which a twenty-dollar piece is made. We cannot suppose that the plates fitted as closely together as gold coins do when stacked up in a column. There must have been some space between each pair, especially if, as is probable, they were hammered[9] and not cast. Then again, allowance must be made for the metal cut away by the engraver, from each plate. Everything considered, the volume must have weighed considerably less than a hundred pounds, even on the supposition that the dimensions given are strictly accurate and not mere approximations.

Another Calculation. The subject of weight may also be approached from another premise. Let us suppose that the entire text was engraved on forty-five plates, as has been shown to be possible. Forty-five would then be the number of the unsealed one-third and there would be ninety in the sealed two-thirds; that is a total of 135 plates. But if two-hundred weigh 123 pounds, 135 would weigh a small fraction over eighty-three pounds. When the necessary deductions, pointed out in the previous paragraph, are made, the entire volume could not have weighed fifty pounds. The plates that the Prophet had in his possession were not heavier than that he, who was an unusually strong man, could lift them and handle them.[10] That is the testimony of eye witnesses, and that testimony stands.

Similar Objections to Bible Statements. Curiously enough, at one time certain critics of the Bible used to raise objections to the Old Testament description of the Tabernacle furniture on the ground that gold was too heavy to handle. We are told that Bezaleel made an ark or box of wood, in which the Law was deposited. It was over-

---

[8]A solid brick of twenty-four karat gold, 7 x 8 x 4 inches in measurement, would weigh approximately 156 pounds, avoirdupois.
[9]*See,* Exodus 39:3. "And they did beat the gold into thin plates."
[10]*History of the Prophet Joseph by His Mother, Lucy Smith,* pp. 85 and 105. The incident told must have been related by the Prophet, himself.

aid with pure gold "within and without." The cover of this box was a lid made of pure gold (Exodus 25:17); two and one-half cubits long and one and one-half cubits wide. That is, it was an immense gold plaque four feet three inches by two feet seven inches, or about eleven square feet in size. On this lid two cherubs were placed, one at each end. These figures were hammered of pure gold. Their wings covered the lid, and they must have been of considerable size. This box, we are told, was carried by the priests before the Camp of Israel during the wanderings of the Children of Israel, but the critics referred to, used to tell us that was impossible. The box, with its solid gold lid, and immense solid gold statues, its stone tablets, its gold rings and staves, was too heavy to handle, except with machinery. But that kind of "criticism" is old and obsolete, whether applied to the Bible or Book of Mormon.

Metal Plates not Unknown. We have also been told the ancient scribes never used metal plates for their records, and that, therefore, Laban could not have had any brass plates.

Ivory tablets were used by the ancient Romans. They also used wooden tablets, beech and fir. Sometimes these were coated with wax, and the record was made with a *stylus.* Two or more of such tablets might be joined together by means of wire rings, similar to the Book of Mormon Plates. Parchment made of animal skins was a favorite material for important records, and vellum, or calf skin, was commonly used in early days for this purpose. But we also read that the High Priest wore a gold plate on his crown, on which words were engraved (Exodus 39:30), and Jeremiah exclaims: "The sin of Judah is written with a pen of iron, and with the point of a diamond: it is graven upon the table of their heart. . . ." (Jeremiah 17:1) This proves beyond question that the Israelites were familiar with engraved tables, for otherwise the words of the prophets would have been unintelligible to them.

See statement by Padre Gay, p. xi, Volume I, COMMENTARY ON THE BOOK OF MORMON.

Book of Mormon Names in American Geography

"There is a continuity in language which nothing equals; and there is an historical genuineness in ancient words, if but rigidly interpreted, which cannot be rivalled by manuscripts, or coins, or monumental inscriptions."

Max Muller, *The Beginning.*

In Palestine and other Bible lands the wanderer frequently finds himself in localities, cities, towns, or villages, the names of which are familiar to him from the Sacred Scriptures. He enters, perhaps, the sun-kissed city of Nazareth by the blue waters of the Sea of Galilee, where Joseph and Mary had their permanent home and where Jesus grew up, played, and labored and studied; or he ascends the Mount of Transfiguration, where he may enjoy an unexcelled view of the Holy Land; or he passes through one of the famous gates of Jerusalem, the Holy City, with its sacred temple grounds and the ever-memorable environs.

He takes, perhaps, a walk to Bethlehem, where, on the nearby fields, angels sang of peace and good will, and reverently he bows at the manger and lifts his heart in prayer to God; he may bathe in the crystal brine of the Dead Sea, or the turbulent waters of the Jordan; he may ascend to the roof of the house of Simon, the tanner, at Jaffa, where Peter, the Apostle, by revelation learned one of the most vital principles of the Gospel; he will travel over the Plains of Sharon, where the glory of the lilies surpasses even the splendor of the gold and purple of the famous King Solomon; he may climb to the top of Carmel, the mountain of Mighty Elijah.

On such a pilgrimage, his heart will be filled with awe, joy, peace, wonder, love, gratitude, humility, ecstacy—all blending into one and inspiring the immortal spirit with a vision of the gates of its eternal home.

Such a pilgrimage has more than just emotional value. It is an experience that is sure to lend strength to the faith of the believer, for such names as those mentioned, and many others, furnish irrefutable evidence for the authenticity of the books of the Bible, and especially for their historic accuracy.

This observation renews in the minds of thoughtful students of the Book of Mormon, at least two closely-related questions.

First: Of about 200 proper names appended to the latest editions of the Sacred Record, are any of them found among Indian names that have become known since the discovery of the Western Continents?

Second: Since it is claimed that a considerable part of the aborigines of America are of Semitic descent and that the Book of Mormon is the record of peoples of Hebrew origin, it is pertinent to ask, "Are there Hebrew words in the Book of Mormon? Have the Indians retained any Semitic names in their vocabularies? Is there, in other words, any linguistic evidence for the asserted relationship of the Indians with Semitic, especially Hebrew ancestry?" That class of evidence is as important to the student of the Book of Mormon as it is to the reader of the Bible.

But in considering these questions, we must first bear in mind that we cannot expect to find the same abundance of linguistic evidence for the Book of Mormon, in America, as has been found for the Bible in Palestine, Syria, Chaldea, and Egypt.

America was for centuries practically cut off from the rest of the world. During this time of isolation, peoples and individuals were so entirely occupied with strife, war, migrations to and from different parts of the country, and the unavoidable struggle for existence, that the preservation of their language, or languages, in the original form was out of the question. During this time their speech naturally suffered changes. Tribal dialects multiplied. Each developed within its own limited sphere, and, in the process lost original words and grammatical forms. History, as far as it was passed from tribe to tribe, from generation to generation, became myths and saga, and in this loose sand the traces of words were too often eliminated. Thus the facilities for a comparison of proper names and common nouns from the American languages with those of other tongues, and consequently also with the vocabulary of the Book of Mormon, are rather limited. That is one reason we may not expect too much from this otherwise valuable class of evidence.

But the Book of Mormon is written in a language which Nephi tersely describes as "the learning of the Jews and the language of the Egyptians." That can only mean that the language which Lehi brought to this continent was not that of the golden age of Hebrew literature, represented by David, Solomon, Isaiah, and some of the other early prophets, but a vernacular influenced by foreign, and especially Egyptian, elements. It is traces of this idiom that we may expect to find in the American languages.

However, the student who may be interested in this particular branch of inquiry must proceed carefully. The field is beset with difficulties. Hasty conclusions do not, as a rule, lead to truth. Words written may look alike, or when spoken may sound alike, or very nearly so, without being even distantly related. Take as an illustration the two words *desert* (an uncultivated region) and *desert* (that which is deserved). They look alike on paper, and, but for the accent, sound alike. And yet, the dictionaries tell us that one comes from *desero* (to forsake) and the other from *deservio* (to do service). On the other hand, consider the name of the famous explorer Americus Vespucius. *Americus* or, as it is also written, *Merigo*, does not look like, and does not sound like *Amalrich*. But that is said to be the German ancestor of that name. "*Amerigo* is an Italianized form of the old German *Amalrich*, not *Emmerich*, which in medieval French became *Amury* and in Latin, *Americus*." (John Fiske, *Myths and Myth Makers*)

One entirely unacquainted with the mysteries of etymology would hardly suspect *Merigo* and *Amury* of being the same word or name.

One rule that it is well to keep in mind is that phonetic changes nearly always tend toward simplification. Longer words are made shorter, and harsh sounds are softened. Many illustrations of this rule could be given. The great name *Lincoln* is said to be an abbreviation of *Lindum Colonia*. The old Greek *Melitia* is now *Malta*. *Macoraba* has become *Mekka*. *Chumley* was originally *Cholmondely*. *Sissiter* was *Cirencester*. *Affleck* was *Auchinleck*.

As an illustration of the changes names undergo, the Hebrew *peleshet*, from palash, "to go," "to rove," "to wander," may be mentioned. It has become *Philistia* and then *Palestine*. The Arabian *Djebel-al Tarik*, "the mountain on the road," has become *Gibraltar*. According to Fiske in *Myths and Myth-makers*, the name Odin, the chief god of the Teutonic races, which name was originally *Guodan*, has become *God* in English, the same as *Gott* in German and *Gut* in the Scandinavian languages. Fiske also shows that the English words *Divinity* and *Devil* may be traced from the same origin, the Zend *dev*, and the Sanskrit *deva*. In some languages this became *devil, teufel, djevul, djofull*. In others it became *Deus, Theos, Diewas, Dieu, Dios*, and our *divinity, divine*.

If we keep such transformations in mind, those of known words, the suggestions and arguments in the following paragraphs will not appear far-fetched. There will be little difficulty in accepting the conclusions, and their importance as evidence for the Book of Mormon will be apparent.

For the sake of emphasis we want to repeat that the Bible student knows the value of proper names as evidence of the truth of a sacred record. He knows that, while Bible names have been lost, some possibly forever, others, such as *Carmel, Jordan, Bethlehem, Ephesus,*

Syria, Egypt, Palestine, Persia, are still familiar to travelers and students, and they are unimpeachable witnesses to the authenticity of Scripture history.

The same may be said of Book of Mormon names. Many of them may be lost, or distorted beyond recognition, but others are still found in easily recognized forms.

The following list of Book of Mormon names is submitted, not as an infallible product of scientific research, but rather as a suggestion indicating what such research may be expected to yield.

YUCATAN. This is a peninsula which divides the Gulf of Mexico from the Caribbean Sea, and borders on British Honduras and Guatemala on the south. It was at one time part of the Maya Empire, and the ruins of Uxmal, Chichen Itza, Izamal, Mayapan, and others, bear witness to its former glory. It is now part of Mexico, and has a population in excess of 350,000, mostly Maya Indians.

Many attempts have been made to derive that name from different sources, but a satisfactory solution of its etymology has not been found. Our suggestion is that Yucatan was so named by the original settlers in memory of Joktan, the younger son of Eber.

We are told that Eber, who was the son of Shem, had two sons, Peleg and Joktan. (Gen. 10:25-30) Further, that Peleg (which means "division") was so named, "for in his days was the earth divided," which evidently refers to the allotment of the habitable portions of the earth to various families, tongues and nations after the flood, under patriarchal inspiration. (*See* Gen. 10:32; 11:8) Concerning this division of the land we are also informed (Deut. 32:8) that the Lord, in his allotment, had special reference to the number of the Children of Israel. The text referred to is, "When the Most High divided to the nations their inheritance, when he separated the sons of Adam, he set the bounds of the people according to the number of the children of Israel." In other words, he planned to reserve adequate place for the chosen race.

Now, the descendants of Shem through Eber, generally located in Chaldea, Armenia, and Syria. His descendants through Joktan went eastward to Jemen, and from there toward India, and perhaps to China. The Jemen Arabs still have preserved the tradition that they are the descendants of Joktan, whom, in their language, they call *Kachtan.* They consider themselves as "genuine" Arabs, different from the descendants of Ishmael.

It is not improbable that Jared and his wonderful brother, along with their companions in their miraculous voyage, came from this branch of the sons of Shem. They were, in other words, Joktanites.

The promise of the Lord to Jared and his brother was that He would go before them into a land "which is choice above all the lands of the earth." That is the entire America. "And there will I bless thee and thy seed," the Lord said, "and raise up unto me of thy seed, and of the seed of thy brother, and they who shall go with thee, a great nation. And there shall be none greater than the nation which I will raise up unto me of thy seed, upon all the face of the earth." (Ether 1:43) Accordingly, we may suppose that some of the Jaredites, in the course of time, came to Yucatan and perpetuated the name of their ancestor, by naming the country after him, in his honor.

TALE. It has been stated that according to the famous chronicler Bernal Diaz, the word *tale,* presumably in the Maya language means such little hills as those in which the Yucca plant grew. That seems to be a word of pure Semitic origin. For *tel* both in Hebrew and Arabic means a "hill," particularly a heap of stones. It was a place name in Babylon, (*Tel-melah, Tel-harsa, Tel-abib*) and also in Egypt (*Tel-el-Amarna*). There is a modern Tel-abib in Palestine, a very flourishing city.

The word *tale,* which we take to be identical with the Semitic *tel,* certainly points to a Semitic ancestry of the first settlers of this part of America. It was part of their language, even if it was not part of the name of their country, Yucatan.

ANGOLA. Angola was the name of a city which the Nephites occupied and fortified, under the leadership of Mormon, about A.D. 326 when the Lamanites drove them out into the north. (Mormon 2:4) The word occurs in the Lenape annals on the creation, and is a genuine Indian word. Rafinesque[1] observes: "This account of the creation is strikingly similar to the Mosaic and oriental accounts." He is also of the opinion that the *angel-atawiwak* of this story are the *Elohim* of the Hebrews, the *angelos* of the Pelasgians and the *h'ello* (old men) of the Egyptians.

ANTI. There are several words in the Book of Mormon in which *anti* is one of the component parts, as for instance, *Ani-Anti,* the name of an Amalekite village in which Aaron, Muloki, and Ammah preached the Gospel. (Alma 21:11) *Anti-Nephi-Lehi,* the name of a king and also of a people. (Alma 24:1-5) *Antion,* a piece of gold used as money. (Alma 11:19) *Antipas,* the name of a mountain. (Alma 47:7) All are instances, with others, that denote that the word was in common use among the people of Nephi.

The Indian word *Quichua* corresponding to *anti* is, we are assured, *anta,* which Garcilasso de la Vega[2] tells us means *copper.*

From *anta* the magnificent mountain chain that forms the backbone of South America was called the *Andes,* possibly because of the abundance of metal, especially copper, found in these mountains.

In the Book of Mormon, *anti* means a "mountain" or a "hill." When it is used to denote a country, it probably means a hilly or mountain country, and when the name is applied to a city, it may indicate its location in a mountain region. In the same way *Anti-Nephi-Lehies* may mean that they were located in a hilly or mountainous country. As applied to a piece of money, the word would indicate that they were made of an alloy in which copper formed a considerable part.

Anti appears in *Antisuyu,* the name given by the Peruvians to the eastern part of their vast domain; that is, to the part that was traversed by the loftiest ridges of the Andes Mountains. That proves, beyond question, that the Peruvians used the word exactly as we find it used in the Book of Mormon.

ANTIPAS. This is a name of a mount or hill on the summit of which Lamanite armies on one occasion had gathered themselves for battle. (Alma 47:7)

This is a genuine Indian word. On the mountain slopes of the Cordilleras, in the upper Amazon Basin, there is, according to Dr. Brinton,[3] a tribe of Indians, of the Jivaro linguistic stock, known as the *Antipas.* They are described as "rather tall, of light color, with thin lips, aquiline noses, straight eyes, prognathic jaws, hair black or with reddish tint."

HAGOTH. In the Book of Mormon, Hagoth, we are told, built an exceedingly large ship on the borders of the Land Bountiful, by the Land Desolation, and launched it forth into the West Sea, by the narrow neck of land which led into the land northward. Afterwards other expeditions were undertaken. This was about 55 B.C.

[1]*The American Nations,* Part 1, pp. 86, 87, 149.
[2]*Royal Commentaries,* Book 5, Chap. 14.
[3]*The American Race,* p. 284.

California Indians attribute a large artificial mound of mussel shells and bones of animals, on Point St. George, near San Francisco, to a prehistoric people which they call *Hohgates*. Whether this name is the Book of Mormon *Hagoth* is a question that seems pertinent.

According to the traditions, the Hohgates were seven strangers, who arrived from the sea and who were the first to build houses in which to live in that part of the country.[4] They hunted deer, sea lions, and seals. They gathered mussels on the nearby rocks, and the refuse from their meals was piled up around their dwellings. One day—so the tradition runs—they saw a gigantic seal into which they managed to drive a harpoon. The wounded animal fled seaward, dragging the boat with it toward the unknown world. At the moment the mariners were about to be engulfed, the seal disappeared and the boat was flung up into the air. Since then, the Hohgates, changed into stars, to return no more.

It is more than probable that there is an historic basis for this beautiful legend.

That sea voyages were not entirely unheard of in prehistoric America is evident from the many traditions still told by the inhabitants of the islands of the Pacific Ocean.

JACOBUGATH was the name of a great city mentioned in 3 Nephi 9:9. It was inhabited by the people of King Jacob, and, as *gath* means a wine press, it may have received its name from the fact that wine was made there, causing the wickedness for which it was finally destroyed.

The word should be compared with *Intibucat*, the name of an Indian dialect of the Lenca stock, spoken in Central Honduras in and about the pueblo of the same name,[5] not because the two are identical, but because their construction is the same.

LABAN was the name of a prominent resident of Jerusalem, a contemporary of Lehi, and the owner of certain brass plates containing historical and genealogical data of the greatest importance. (1 Ne. 3:5.)

Laman, the name of the eldest son of Lehi (1 Ne. 2:5), and also of a king mentioned in Mosiah 7:21, is the same name as Laban. *Lamoni* is formed from this word by the addition of the suffix "i."

The word is Hebrew and means "white." Several forms of it are found in the Old Testament, such as "Laban," the father-in-law of Jacob; "lebanah," the "moon," because of its whiteness; "Libnah," a place name (Num. 33:20); "Libni," the name of a person (Ex. 6:17); "Lebanon," the well-known name of a mountain, and "Libnites," as the descendants of Libni were called (Num. 3:21.)

Nor is the word confined to the Semitic group of languages. Compare the Greek "alphos" and "Olympos"; also the Latin "albus," from which we have a number of words, such as "albino," "Albion," "Albany," "album," the latter being originally white tablets for writing. Some derive even "Alps" from the same root, while others claim that this name is from a Gaelic source meaning "height."

It would, indeed, be a surprise if we should not find that word, so common in the Old World anciently, in use among the prehistoric Indians. But it seems to have been just as common on this side of the world.

Dr. Brinton tells us that the Yameos Indians on the Maranon are also called Llameos, Lamas, and Lamistas. In the Lama linguistic stock he places the *Alabonos*, the *Nahuapos*, and the *Napeanos*.[7] In *A-labono* we can easily recognize *Labon*, and in *Nahuapos* and *Napeanos* we seem to have the name of Nephi preserved, just as we

---

[4]Bancroft, *Native Races*, Vol. 3, p. 177.
[5]*The Incas of Peru*, p. 184-5.
[6]Dr. Cyrus Thomas, *Indian Languages of Mexico and Central America*, Bur. of Amer. Ethn., Bul. 44, Wash., 1911, p. 74.
[7]*The American Race*, p. 285.

have the name of *Laban*, or *Laman*, preserved in *Lamas* and *Lamistas*. Near Truxillo, in South America, there are also the *Lamanos* or *Lamistas*, of the Quichua linguistic stock.[8]

According to Reclus, quoted by Dr. Cyrus Thomas[9] there is, or was, a tribe of Indians, of the Ulva stock, near Blewfields, called *Lamans*. The Blewfields River was also called the *Lama* River. Dr. Brinton does not classify the Lamans, but he mentions the *Ramas* as living on a small island in the Blewfield Lagoon, and the Lamans and the Ramas may be the same name, since "l" and "r" interchange in all languages.[10]

In Yucatan we have the ancient city of *Labna*, which name certainly seems to be the same as *Laban*.

We are aware of the fact that *Lab-na* is said to mean "old house." But that does not say that the root of the word is not the same as the Hebrew "white." For white is often a sign of old age.

The word *Laban* means the same in the Indian, as in the Old World languages. In the Lenape, Rafinesque says, *Lapan-ibi* means "white water."[11] *Lumonaki*, according to the same authority, "white land." This word is also spelled *abnaki*, with the initial "l" dropped. Dr. Brinton[12] says the Algonquins used to call their eastern kindred *Abnakis*, "our white ancestors," an expression which, since [l]*abn* means "white," would be the same as "our Lamanite ancestors"; *aki*, however, means "land," and "white land" is, therefore, a better translation.[13]

Charles Christian Ravn, the Danish scholar, is authority for the statement that the Indians whom the Icelanders met when exploring the North American coast in the early part of the Eleventh Century, had a tradition concerning a country called, in Icelandic, *Hvitramannaland*, "White-men's-land." That would be identically the same name as *Lumon-aki*, or the land of Laman. Conjecture has located *Hvitramannaland* along the Chesapeake Bay, extending down into the Carolinas, and peopled it with "white" colonists, but it is more probable that it is the *Lumonaki* of the Algonquins and the *Lamoni* of the Book of Mormon.

LEHI. In the Hebrew this word is *Lechi*, the "ch" being practically the same as our "h." In Palestine a hilly district in Judea, near Jerusalem, was known as *Lehi*. (Judges 15:19) Samson, after his battle with the Philistines, threw away his unique weapon, the jawbone of an ass, and called the place of combat *Ramath-Lehi*, "the Hill of Lehi." Then he was thirsty, and the Lord, in answer to his prayer, opened a crevice in the hill,[14] and "there came water thereout." So he called the spring, *En-hakkore*, "the spring of him that called" (in answer to prayer), "which," we read, "is in Lehi unto this day." This incident is recalled by the name of the father of Nephi.

In the Lenape language the word is *lechau*, which is identical with the Hebrew *lechi*. In the Indian tongue it means a "fork of a river," and that may well have been suggested by the form of a jawbone of a donkey.

---

[8]Brinton, *The American Race*, p. 216. According to the Ethnological Appendix in Mr. H. W. Bates' *Central America*, London 1878, there were *Lamas* in Central California; *Laymons*, a tribe of Chochimis, in Lower California, and *Lemanos*, *also called Chimus*, on the coast south of Lima, Peru, where they had a civilization older than that of the Incas. So that, from the ethnological data available, it appears that the Lamanites were actually sprinkled all over the American continents.

[9]*Indian Languages of Mexico and Central America*, Bureau of Amer. Eth. Bul. 44, p. 79.

[10]*The American Race*, p. 163.

[11]*The American Nations*, Part 1, p. 144.

[12]*Myths of The New World*, p. 207.

[13]*Aki* is the same as our acre.

[14]Not in the jawbone, which he had thrown away, but in the hill which he had named after the jawbone Lehi.

T. A. Joyce[15] mentions an Indian tribe in Colombia, located to the north of the Chibchas, which he calls the *Laches*, a name which seems to be identical with the Hebrew *Lechi* and the Book of Mormon *Lehi*.

In North America there are several places named *Lehigh*. The Lehigh River in Pennsylvania, which flows into the Delaware at Easton, Northampton Co., is well known. The one-hundred mile channel through which it winds its way is called Lehigh Valley, and there is a good sized county having the same name.

We have noticed that the name is known far away in the Hawaiian Islands. In the November number, 1921, of *The Paradise of the Pacific*, a magazine published in Honolulu, the statement occurs that the ancient name for *Diamond Head*, a prominent volcanic mountain, was *Leahi*. This is but a very slight variation in spelling, from the name, as it is given in the Book of Mormon.

LIAHONA. This interesting word is Hebrew with an Egyptian ending. It is the name which Lehi gave to the ball or director he found outside his tent the very day he began his long journey through the "wilderness," after his little company had rested for some time in the Valley of Lemuel. (Ne. 16:10; Alma 37:88)

L is a Hebrew preposition meaning "to," and sometimes used to express the possessive case. *Iah* is a Hebrew abbreviated form of "Jehovah," common in Hebrew names. *On* is the Hebrew name of the Egyptian "City of the Sun," also known as Memphis and Heliopolis. *L-iah-on* means, therefore, literally, "To God is Light"; or, "of God is Light." That is to say, God gives light, as does the Sun. The final *a* reminds us that the Egyptian form of the Hebrew name *On* is *Annu*,[16] and that seems to be the form Lehi used.

Lehi had just received the divine command to begin his perilous journey. The question uppermost in his mind, after having received that call, must have been how to find the way. That must have been quite a problem. But he arose early in the morning, determined to carry out the command given. Undoubtedly he had prayed all night for light and guidance. And now, standing in the opening of the tent, perhaps as the first rays of the sun broke through the morning mists, his attention is attracted by a metal ball "of curious workmanship." He picks it up and examines it. And then, as he realizes that it is the guide for which he had been praying, he exclaims in ecstacy, *L-iah-on-a!* Which is as much as to say, This is God's light; it has come from him! And that became the name of the curious instrument. This was not a compass. It was a miraculously formed instrument which served both as compass and octant.

Now, the fact is that this manner of giving names was an ancient Semitic custom. Hagar, when her son was perishing in the wilderness and she beheld the angel by the life-giving spring, exclaimed, *Beer-lachai-roi!* which means, literally, "Well, to live, to see." That is to say, "the well of him that liveth and seeth me," for that was the thought that came to her mind. (Gen. 16:13, 14.) And that became the name of the well. In the same way, Abraham called the place where he had offered Isaac on the altar, *Jehovah-jireh*, "the Lord will provide"; because the Lord did provide for himself a ram instead of Isaac, as Abraham had assured his son the Lord would do. (Gen. 27:7-14.) And that became the name of the Mount "to this day."

Lehi gave the metal ball a name commemorative of one of the great experiences of his life, just as these Old Testament worthies had done. And, furthermore, he gave it a name that no one but a devout Hebrew influenced by Egyptian culture would have thought of. Is that not the strongest possible evidence of the truth of the historic part of the Book of Mormon?

---

[15]*South American Archeology*, p. 28.
[16]Dr. E. A. Wallis Budge, *Gods of the Egyptians*, Vol. 1, p. 100.

MANTI. In the Book of Mormon this word occurs as the name of the hill upon which Nehor, the murderer, was executed. (Alma 1:15.) It was also the name of a Nephite soldier (Alma 2:22), and there was a Land of Manti, on the head waters of the river Sidon (Alma 16:6, 7) and a city of the same name (Alma 57:22).

The name is very ancient. It is mentioned in the earliest Egyptian inscriptions as the name of an Asiatic people, probably the same as the Hyksos, or Shepherds,[17] or, perhaps, rather a tribe of that people.

In this country there was at one time, in South America, the Manta Indians, on the coast north of the Gulf of Guayaquil. In Stanford's *Compendium of Geography and Travel*, the Mantas are referred to as an extinct Quito race of ten tribes.[18] There was also a city of Manti and a district of the same name, as in the Book of Mormon.

ANOTHER MANTI. In 1836, the Prophet Joseph Smith, Brigham Young, and others, found it best, on account of apostasy and bitterness, to leave Kirtland and go to Far West, Mo., where the Saints were endeavoring to establish themselves. On September 25, they passed through Huntsville, Randolph Co., and the Prophet is said to have told the brethren that that place, where a stake of Zion had been established, was "the ancient site of the city of Manti." (Andrew Jenson, *Hist. Rec.*, p. 601.)

Whether "the ancient site of Manti" refers to the Manti in the Book of Mormon is a question that has been debated. Some prefer to regard it as a reference to a later City of Manti, built by descendants of Nephi in Missouri.[19] In either case, the information is both important and interesting.

According to Garcilasso de la Vega, the Mantas worshiped the ocean, fishes, lions, tigers, serpents, etc., but special veneration was paid to an emerald which was larger than an ostrich egg. At their principal festival they exhibited this jewel, and people from near and far came to see it and to offer presents, especially emeralds, which the Indians regarded as the children of the big stone. An incredible number of emeralds were thus accumulated in the sanctuary in the Manta Valley. Many of these gems fell into the hands of the Spaniards, and some were destroyed because the conquerors did not know their value, but the large stone was hidden, and has never been found.

The word is found all over America. It is the familiar word *manito*. In the Lenape annals on the creation we read:[20]

"It was then when the God-Creator made the makers or spirits—*Manito—Manitoak;* and also the angels, *Angelatawiwak*. And afterwards he made the man-being, Jinwis, ancestor of the men. He gave him the first mother, *Netamigaho*, mother of the first beings."

The *manitos* in this legend were spirits who had an existence before the first man appeared on earth.

In the Algonquin language the word is said to express divinity in its broadest sense. Schoolcraft[21] spells it *monedo*, and translates it "spirit," or whatever is mysterious. A *monedo*, or *manitou*, may be the Great Spirit, a witch or a wizard, a glass bead, a jewel, an insect, a reptile, or a place haunted by a spirit. It has frequently been translated "medicine," which may seem absurd, until we recall the fact that in early days all medicine was supposed to be "charms" and pharmacists were considered wizards. In Gal. 5:20 the word *Pharmakei* is translated *witchcraft,* showing how the Bible translators regarded pharmacy.

In the Haytian language, Rafinesque tells us, the word *manati*, evidently the same as *manta* and *manito*, means a great and eminent thing, and this would account for the naming of a hill Manti, as in the Book of Mormon.[22]

---

[17]Paul Pierret, *Dictionnaire D'Archeologie Egyptienne*, p. 337.
[18]*Central America, West Indies, and South America*, p. 520.
[19]That many of the descendants of Lehi, both Nephites and Lamanites, found their way to North America is beyond doubt.
[20]Rafinesque, *The American Nations*, Vol. 2, p. 152.

In Hebrew we have the word *man*, which means something mysterious, for the Children of Israel gave that name to the mysterious bread that came from heaven; for, they said, We "wist not what it was." That word Gesenius connects with *mannah*, to "divide," to "portion out," to "count." There is where we have obtained our word "money." If it is thought that *manti* and *manito* cannot be related to *manah* and *money*, because these words lack the "t," it should be remembered that the "t" re-appears in "mint," which also has something to do with "money." *Manti* should be compared with the English *mantic*, and the Greek *mantikos*.

MORMON. The Prophet Joseph, in a letter published in the *Times and Seasons*, Nauvoo, May 15, 1843,[23] furnished the following explanation concerning the meaning of the word:

"It has been stated that this word was derived from the Greek word *mormo*. This is not the case. There was no Greek or Latin upon the plates from which I, through the grace of the Lord, translated the Book of Mormon."

Then he quotes from the Book of Mormon (Morm. 9:32-34), where we are told that the characters used were the "reformed Egyptians." He continues:

"Here, then the subject is put to silence, for 'none other people knoweth our language'; therefore, the Lord, and not man, had to interpret, after the people were all dead. And as Paul said, 'The world by wisdom knew not God'; so the world by speculation are destitute of revelation; and as God, in his superior wisdom, has always given his Saints, whenever he had any on the earth, the same spirit, and that spirit, as John says, is the true spirit of prophecy, which is the testimony of Jesus, I may safely say that the word *Mormon* stands independent of the learning and wisdom of this generation.

"Before I give a definition, however, of the word, let me say that the Bible, in its widest sense, means *good;* for the Savior says, according to the Gospel of John, 'I am the Good Shepherd'; and it will not be beyond the common use of terms to say that *Good* is among the most important in use, and though known by the various names in different languages, still its meaning is the same, and is ever in opposition to *bad*."

The Prophet further says:

"We say, from the Saxon, *good;* from the Dane, *god;* the Goth, *goda;* the German, *gut;* the Dutch, *goed;* the Latin, *bonus;* the Greek, *kalos;* the Hebrew, *tob*, and the Egyptian, *mon*. Hence, with the addition of *more*, or the contraction, *mor*, we have the word *Mormon*, which means literally, *more good*."

Here we have the interesting information that the first part of the word is an abbreviation of the English adverb "more," and that the second part is the Egyptian adjective "mon." In other words, the Prophet found, on the plates, as a proper noun, a compound word meaning, literally, "better," and, under the influence of the Holy Spirit, he solved the problem of transliterating it, by translating the first part into English and copying the second part, and making of the two, one word, half English and half Egyptian. This, we admit, is an unusual literary procedure, but we have an instance of it in our Bible, where a place called Maaleh-acrabbim (Josh. 15:3) is also called "The Ascent of Akrabbim," (Num. 34:4.) Here half of the name is translated into English and the other half is a foreign word. *See also* Gen. 23:2 and 35:27, where Hebron is called, in the first passage, Kirjath-Arba, and in the second, "The

---

[21]*Indian Tribes of the United States*, Vol. 4, p. 375.

[22]In the Algonquin (Fox) *Mantetowa* is said to mean "mysterious being." *Manetowi aki* is "a mysterious country,"—William Jones, *Handbook Am. Lang.*, Smith. Inst., Bul. 40, Vol. 1, p. 850.

[23]The letter was revised by the Prophet, May 20, 1843. See the *Documentary History of the Church*, under that date.

City of Arbah," the first half of the name being translated into English and the second being left untranslated.[24] This, then, is how the word *Mormon* originated. And it means "more good"; that is "better."

The reference of the Prophet, in this connection, to the Bible would indicate that the *good* expressed in the word is the same as that which we call "good news," or "gospel," and that *Mormon,* therefore, means one who is the bearer of "good tidings."

It is probable that the *mon* in "Mormon" is akin to the *mon* or *men* in the Egyptian *Amon* or *Amen.* Dr. E. A. Wallis Budge, (*The Gods of the Egyptians,* Vol. 2, p. 2) says that *Amen* is from a root *men* "to abide, to be permanent, eternal." *Mon* or *men* (the vowel is indifferent) would, then, mean "good" in the sense of permanency, just as *nefer* means "good" in the sense of physical beauty. We gather this from what Champollion (*Precis du Systeme Hieroglyphique des Anciens Egyptiens,* p. 91) on the authority of Eusebius says, viz., that the divinity which takes the name *Amen* and *Kneph* or *Noub,* alternatively, was by the Greeks called *Agathodaimon,* and that Nero, when assuming a divine title, called himself *Neo-agathodaimon. Agathos* is, of course, the Greek word for "good," and it must have been suggested by the Egyptian *men* or *mon.*

It is a very interesting fact that many American languages, perhaps most of them, form their comparatives and superlatives by the use of the adverbs "more" and "most." In the Aztec, "better" is *ocahiqualli,* which means, literally, "more good." In the Otomi language "better" is *nra nho,* which means "more good." In the Maya, the comparative is formed by affixing the last vowel of the adjective with an "l" added or by simply affixing the particle *il.* For instance, from *Tibil,* a "good thing," *u tibil-il,* a "better thing" is formed.[25]

May we not ask, "What is the explanation of the singular fact that the Prophet Joseph seems to have had knowledge of how comparatives are formed in some of the principal American languages?"

MORONI. This is, as is well known, the name of the last of the Book of Mormon prophets, who finished the records of his father, Mormon, added his own abridgment of the plates of the Jaredites, and deposited the completed volume in the Hill, Cumorah, about A.D. 421 (Morm. 8:14; Moroni 10:2), in the same hill, where Mormon had deposited the original plates entrusted to his care, from which he had compiled his briefer history. (Morm. 6:6.)

Moroni was also the name of the great Nephite general who was the first to proclaim the American continents the *Land of Liberty,* or, as we should say, "The Land of the Free." (Alma 46:11-17.)

There was a City of Moroni on the East Sea, "on the south by the line of the possessions of the Lamanites" (Alma 50:13); and a Land of Moroni, "on the borders by the sea shore." (Alma 51:22; 62:25.)

---

[24]The familiar word *Iroquois* may possibly be another instance of this kind of word-building. The orators of that stock of Indians used to close their speeches by saying, *Hiro,* "I have spoken," very much as the Romans said, *Dixi.* Their sentinels had a cry of warning which sounded to the French something like *quai.* Out of these two words and a French ending, *ois,* the name Iroquois was composed.

[25]See Bancroft, *Native Races,* Vol. 3 pp. 733, 739. In the Egyptian, it seems, adjectives were without degrees of comparison, but the particle *er* meaning "to," "with," "between," etc., in various combinations, was used to express degrees of superiority, very much as the Hebrew "min." For instance: "She was fair (good) in her body, more than (*er*) other women," means, of course, that she was fairer—more good—than the rest. "Good is hearkening, more than anything," or hearkening is more good, means, "To obey is best of all." *Good* in these sentences is the word *nefer* but there is a verb, *mench,* "to do good," "to abide," and that may be akin to the "mon" in the name *Mormon.*

The word is Semitic. At the beginning of our era it had found its way into the Syriac spoken in Palestine, and was so generally understood that Paul used it in his first letter to the Corinthians (16:22), although that document was written in Greek, when he says: "If any man love not the Lord Jesus Christ, let him be Anathema Maranatha."

These words, *Maranatha*, have puzzled commentators, and various interpretations have been suggested, such as "In the coming of our Lord"; or, "Our Lord has come"; or, "Our Lord will come." Some read the word as two words, Marana tha, which would mean, "Come, Lord," and which is the very prayer that closes the Revelation by John, *erchou, Kyvie Iesou.* (Rev. 22:20.) It was, in all probability, a conventionalized expression of pious sentiment, something similar to the old, "Peace be with thee," or our own "adieu," or "goodbye," which, if spelled out, would, of course, be, "God be with you." But all agree that *Marana,* or as the word is transliterated in the Book of Mormon *Moroni* means "Our Lord." We have also, in the Book of Mormon, a longer form of the same word, *Moronihah,* which I take to mean, "Jehovah is my Lord," which gives us a meaning almost identical with that of the name *El-i-jah,* "Jehovah is my God."

This name, *Marana,* or *Moroni,* has been preserved in the name *Maranon,* which is the name by which the mighty Amazon River is known when it first begins its course towards the ocean.[26] In the valley of the Maranon remains of cyclopean buildings have been found, proving that the region was inhabited in prehistoric times. In 1840 a remarkable sculptured stone was found there, now known as the Chavin Stone, from the locality where it was discovered. It is 25 feet long by 2 feet 4 inches, and represents either some mighty ruler or some divine personage, standing under a number of rays, each ending in a serpent head, reminding one of an Egyptian pharaoh under the so-called Aten rays.

Dr. Brinton gives the name of a *Morona* tribe of Indians among the Zaparo linguistic stock, in the upper Amazon Valley.[27]

On the east coast there is also a river named after the great prophet. The *Maroni* River[28] flows from the Tumakurak range and forms the frontier line between French and Dutch Guiana, and, after a course of about 380 miles, reaches the Atlantic.

The name Moroni is found even in Peruvian literature. The Peruvians had a drama, called *Apu Ollantay,* composed about the year 1470, long before the arrival of the Spaniards,[29] and first committed to writing in 1770. Sir Clements Markham has published an elegant translation of it. Von Tschudi, in his work on the Quicha language, also gives it in full.

The first act is supposed to depict something that happened at the end of the 14th century of our era. The other two acts cover the first ten or twelve years of the 15th century. The hero is the great chief Ollanta, and the story is about his love for Cusi Coyllur, a daughter of the proud Inca Pachacutec at a time when such a

---

[26]The chain of the eastern Andes is penetrated by five great rivers, which unite to form the mighty Orellana. The first is Maranon, and, being the most western and distant in its source in the Andean lake of Lauricocha, is considered to be the source of the Amazon.—Sir Clements Markham, *The Incas of Peru,* p. 193.

"The least known and the least frequented district of Ecuador," another author says, "is the territory called *Del Oriente,* on the eastern side of the Cordilleras. This region, lying between Quito and the Amazons, is watered by the great rivers *Napo, Pastaza,* and *Morona,* and their numerous tributaries." So that the names of the two great Book of Mormon characters, Nephi and Moroni, have been immortalized in the names of two great rivers in South America.

[27]*The American Race,* p. 282.

[28]See, for instance, Joyce's *South American Archeology.*

[29]The Pizarros entered Caxamarca in the year 1532.

venture might have cost the lives of both. The first scene of the third act of this drama is laid in a street in Cuzo called *Pampa Moroni.*[30]

We know not how far back this name as a street name in Cuzco goes. Montesinos[31] says the fifth king, Inti Capac Yupanqui, divided Cuzco into two districts, Upper and Lower, and divided the first into streets to which he gave names. If it was this Inca who gave the street or square referred to, the name of Moroni, that name must have been so well known in Indian tradition, in the first half of the fifth century A.D., as to suggest the propriety of naming a public place in the "holy city" of the Peruvians in his honor.

MULEK is one of the very interesting words in the Book of Mormon. It was the name, or the title, of the young son of Zedekiah, who, with his attendants, escaped from the Babylonians, when Nebuchadnezzar had captured Jerusalem, about 599 B.C., and came to the Western Hemisphere, part of which became the "land north" (Hel. 6:10), "for the Lord did bring Mulek into the land north and Lehi into the land south." It was also the name of a city on "the east borders by the seashore" (Alma 51:26.) There was a land called *Melek* "on the west of the river Sidon" (Alma 8:3), which name is, clearly, but a variant of *Mulek.* From these words others are formed, such as *Muloki* (Alma 20:2), *Amulek* (Alma 8:21), and *Amaleki* and *Amalickiah* (Omni 30, Alma 46:3.)

There is, according to Mr. T. S. Denison[32] an Aryan root *mol*, Sanskrit *mr*, which means "to crush," "to grind," as in a mill. There is another root *inkh*, which means "to move." *Molinkh,* or *molik* with a slight variation, would, therefore, be one who makes the mill go; one who provides food, or who directs the work of preparing it.

In the Egyptian the "mill mover" became the "king," and so we have the Valley of the Kings, the *Biban el Molouk,* where royal bodies were interred, perhaps as far back as before the days of Moses.

There is a very interesting inscription in which the word has been discovered. In the fifth year of the reign of Rehoboam, king of Judah, about 933 B.C., Shishak, the Egyptian pharaoh, invaded Judea (1 Kings 14). Dr. W. M. Flinders Petri[33] suggests that, as Solomon had married a near relative of Shishak but not recognized her son as heir to the throne, he undertook that expedition to avenge a supposed insult and at the same time to strengthen the relations beween Egypt and the apostate kingdom of Israel. So he went through the land, plundered the temple and the royal palace, and carried off whatever valuables he could find, including, probably, the three hundred shields of gold made by Solomon and valued at over a million dollars in our money.[34] A record of this exploit was made upon one of the temple walls at Karnak, Egypt, and in this record there is a list of 156 names of places captured by the pharaoh. One of these places is called, as transcribed in Hebrew characters, *Judah-Malech,* but in English letters, *Yuteh-Mark.*[35] There is no real discrepancy in this, because the glyph representing an "l" could also represent an "r."[36] Champollion translates the

[30]Markham, *The Incas of Peru,* p. 379. The spelling on this page is, letter for letter, as in the Book of Mormon. On page 337 the spelling is *Maroni.* But even so, the word cannot be mistaken.

[31]*Antiquas Historiales del Peru, Trans.* published by the Hakluyt Soc., London, 1920, p. 29.

[32]*Primitive Aryans in America,* p. 29.

[33]*Egypt and Israel,* p. 72.

[34]*See* I Kings 10:17, Dr. Clarke's *Commentary.*

[35]Smith, *Bible Dictionary,* under Shishak.

[36]Le *lion couche* est l'equivalent hieroglyphique du *lamed* hebreu; mais il import de rapeller que, dans les noms propres grecs et latins, cet hieroglyphe represent souvent la consonne R, et qu'il existe en effet, dans la langue egyptienne, un dialect dont le trait distinctive etai de change indifferment les R en L.—Champollion, *Precis du Systeme Hieroglyphique des Anciens Egyptiens,* Paris, 1824, pp. 59 and 63.

name, "Kingdom of Judah," but Dr. Bird, more correctly, identifies it with the "City of the King of Judah," that is, Jerusalem.[37]

Here we have some very important information. We learn that the kingdom of Judah, or the capital of the kingdom, was known by a name in which *malech* formed an essential part. But *Malech* in this Egyptian inscription is, undoubtedly, the *Mulek* of the Book of Mormon. The Mulekites, therefore, in naming the land of their first settlement, gave it a name by which Judah, or Jerusalem, was known in the Old World. We also learn that the Egyptian character for "l" in this word sometimes represents an "r," and this is of importance in studying the derivatives of the word.

In the Hebrew the *molik* of the Sanskrit has become *malach*, "to possess," "to rule," the same as the Arabian *malaka*. From *malach* we have *melech* "king," *Malkoth*, "kingdom," and such names as *Malcham, Malchiel, Milcom, Moloch, Malchiah, Melchizedek, Meleketh,* and with the definite article, *Hammelech,* and *Hammoleketh,* and also such names as *Marcus* and *Mark,* where the "l" has become "r."

In the American languages there are a great many derivatives from the original *molik.* The Mexican word *molic-tli,* says Mr. Denison,[38] is the "mill mover," and its derivation seems clear. The ninth day of the Maya calendar is *Muluc,* and the eighth month is called *Mol.* Both names may be from the same root. Dr. Augustus le Plongeon in *Queen Moo,*[39] says that the Maya word *mol* means "to gather," and that *och* or *ooch* means "food," "provisions," "provender." The Maya *moloch* would, then, be the same as the original *molik* and the Mexican *molictli*—the mill-mover, the provider, the king.

The Peruvians had a word *malqui,* which signified the preserved body of the ancestors. But to them the ancestor of the tribe, or "lineage," was always the head, the king, and reverence was paid to him after death, as if he had been alive. The *malqui* was their *melech.*

From Rivero and Tschudi we gather that the *malqui* was sometimes called *marca,* changing the "l" into "r," as was noted in the consideration of the Egyptian inscription at Karnak. We read:[40]

"The Llacuaces, as foreigners, have many huacas and much worship, and venerate their malquis, which, as we have said, are the bodies of their dead ancestors."

Again:

"What they call marcayoc (malquis) . . . is sometimes of stone, sometimes the body of some of their dead progenitors."

This makes it beyond question that the word *malqui* has the same meaning as *melech* and *mulek,* and also that *marca* is the same as *Malqui.*

The *malqui* or *marca* of the great Inca Tupac Yupanqui was shamefully desecrated by the Spaniards, and the priest guarding it, the *malqui-villac,* and his assistants, were put to death.[41]

Now, the word *marca,* which, as we have seen, is the same as *mulek* and its relatives, is found all over America. We find it in *Maracaibo,* the name of the beautiful sheet of water in Venezuela; in *Maracay* and *Maraca,* names of two cities in that country; in *Cundinamarca,* the name of the highland plateau in Columbia; in *Cunturmarca* and *Papamarca,* places mentioned by Garcilasso de la Vega; in *Caxamarca,*[42]

---

[37]*See* a paper by Dr. George Frederick Wright, of the Oberlin College, in *Fundamentals,* Vol. 2, p. 11.

[38]*The Primitive Aryans of America,* p. 29.

[39]P. 61.

[40]Rivero and Tshudi, *Peruvian Antiquities,* pp. 174, 175.

[41]Clements Markham, *Incas of Peru,* p. 250.

[42]There are many modes of spelling this name. Garcilasso writes *Cassamarca.* Prescott spells it *Caxamalca* (Conquest of Peru, Vol. 1, p. 375), no doubt, following his excellent au-

the name of the Peruvian city in which Inca Atahualpa was murdered by Pizarro. It is, further, found in *Antamarca*, the name of the Peruvian city in which Inca Huascar, the brother of Atahualpa, was slain by his brother who was his rival in the struggle for the Incariat. In the Valley of Yucay—the Biban el Molouk of Peru—the places of interment on the steep mountain sides are called to this day, *Tantamamarca*.[43] In Argentina there is the province of *Catamarca*, and Joyce[44] mentions a river *Maraca* and an island, off the Amazon delta, having the same name. In the western division (the Chincasuyu) of the domain of the Incas there was a place called *Uramarca*, and the three towers of the fortress overlooking Cuzco, the Sacsahuaman, were called, respectively, *Mayocmarca*, *Paucarmarca*, and *Saclacmarca*,[45] not only because of their height but because they were royal towers, manned by the Incas and troops of the royal blood. One of them had a chamber profusely decorated with gold and silver ornaments, and the entire fort was dedicated to the sun, that is to say, to the omnipotent King and Ruler of the universe, of whom the sun was the most glorious, visible emblem.

The word *Marca* is, further, found in *Maracana*, the name of an Indian tribe which Fathers Cataldino and Moceta met in Paragua,[46] and perhaps in *Mariche*,[47] the name of some Indians in the highlands near Caracas, in the valley of Valencia, now extinct.

To this list should be added, we believe, the word *maraka*, the name given to a sacred instrument used by so-called medicine-men when engaged in miraculous healings. It is an Arawak word translated "rattle," and it denoted the authority wielded by an Indian clothed with the power and authority of some kind of priesthood among his people. It might better be called a scepter than a "rattle." It was an emblem of authority. It may be compared with the rod of Aaron (Ex. 7:10), or that of Moses (Ex. 9:23.) According to tradition the *maraka* was a gift of the spirits to man.[48]

In Central America the word *Marca* is also found in proper nouns. I make this statement on the authority of Prof. Marcou, who, in a remarkable article on the name America published in the *Atlantic Monthly* for March, 1875, says, in part:

"*Americ*, *Amerrique*, or *Amerique* is the name in Nicaragua for the high land or mountain range that lies between Juigalpa and Libertad, in the province of Chontales, and which reaches on the one side into the country of the Carcas Indians, and on the other into that of the Ramas Indians. The rios Mico, Artigua, and Carca that form the rio Bluefields; the rio Grande Matagalpa, and the rios Rama and Indio, that flow directly into the Atlantic; as well as the rios Comoapa, Mayales, Acoyapa, Ajoquapa, Oyale, and Teopenaguatapa, flowing into the Lake of Nicaragua, all have their sources in the Americ range. (See public documents of the Nicaragua government; and *The Naturalist in Nicaragua*, by Thomas Belt, 8vo, London, 1873.)

"The name of places, in the Indian dialects of Central America, often terminate in *ique* or *ic*, which seems to mean "great," "elevated," "prominent," and is always applied to dividing ridges, or to elevated, mountainous countries, but not to volcanic regions; as for instance, *Nique* and *Aglasinique* in the Isthmus of Darien."

The meaning of the Central American *ic* or *ique* identifies it with the mar-ca of

---

thorities. Nadaillac (*Preshist. Amer.*, edited by Dall, London, 1885, p. 381) has *Caxalmalca*, and *Cajamarca* is the spelling of Rivero and Tschudi (*Peruvian Antiquities*, p. 50), but the accepted spelling seems to be Caxamarca.

[43] Nadaillac, *Prehistoric America*, p. 435.
[44] *South American Archaeology*, p. 266.
[45] Garcilasso, *Com. Real.*, Book 8, Chap. 29.
[46] P. DeRoo, *America before Columbus*, p. 222.
[47] Brinton, *The American Race*, p. 180.
[48] Walter E. Roth, *An Inquiry into the Animism and Folk Lore of the Guiana Indians*, 30th *Annual Report of the Bureau of Am. Ethn.*, pp. 330-1.

the South American languages. For, according to Sir Clements Markham,[49] *marca*, in the Quichua means a "hill," or a terrace or a village on a hill.[50] The idea of elevation or prominence seems to be its fundamental meaning when used in names of places, and possessions, leadership, excellence, such as is supposed to belong to royalty, when applied to persons. That is, it means "head," "chief," "king," the same as *melech, malqui, mulek,* and the original *mol-ic.*

Sir Clements Markham also furnishes a clue to the meaning of the word. He tells the story[51] of a certain Peruvian, Martin Huaman, who, having saved the life of a Spaniard named Ayala, at the battle of Huarina, adopted the Spanish name and called himself, Martin Huaman Malqui de Ayala, where Malqui seems to be equivalent to "lord" or "king" of the man whose life he had saved.

Prof. Marcou was of the opinion that *America* is the accepted form of the old Indian *Americ* or *Amerique,* and not, as generally held, a name coined in glorification of Amerigo Vespucci.[52] If this view is correct, *America* is, both in form and meaning, identical with the Book of Mormon names, *Amaleki* and *Amalickiah,* the meaning of which is, "The King of Jehovah," and, as applied to the country, "The Land of the King of Jehovah"; that is to say, in other words, *The Land of Zion.*

NEPHI. Elder George Reynolds traces this celebrated name to an Egyptian root. He says:[53]

"Its roots are Egyptian; its meaning, good excellent, benevolent. . . . One of the names given to this god [Osiris], expressive of his attributes, was Nephi, or Dnephi, . . . and the chief city dedicated to him was called N-ph, translated into Hebrew as Noph, in which form it appears in Hosea, Isaiah, and Jeremiah. Its modern English name is Memphis."

This agrees with a statement credited to Eusebius, to the effect that the Egyptians called the Creator *Kneph,* and they pictured him as a man with a coiffure adorned with feathers; or as a serpent; and sometimes as a man with a solar disk on his head. *Noub,* or *Nouv,* according to Champollion, was the *Knouphis* of Strabo, and the same as the *Kneph* of Plutarch and Eusebius.

It is necessary to note that all these forms, Nephi, Dnephi, Kneph, Noub, Nouv, and Knouphis, are variants of the same name.

Wm. Osburn[54] connects the name also with Noah, thus:

"*Kneph, Nu* or *Noah* was a local god of some city of the Mendesian nome in the northeast of the delta. . . . A shrine dedicated to Kneph was found there by Mr. Burton. As we have explained, he was the god of the yearly overflow. His name was sometimes written (with hieroglyphics) which seem to mean, 'Nu (Noah) of the waters."

Isaiah calls the flood "The Waters of Noah."[55]

There is also a word *nebhu,* which Churchyard[56] says is a divine title meaning, the Everlasting, the Self-existent, the Eternal One.

Some Egyptian words have close relatives in the Hebrew, easily recognized. We believe this is one of them. *Nebi,* from Naba, is, evidently, the Nephi of the Book

---

[49]Introduction to *Memorias Antiguas Historiales del Peru,* by Montesinos, Hakluyt Society, London, 1920, p. 10.

[50]*The Incas of Peru,* p. 69.

[51]*The Incas of Peru,* p. 17.

[52]The name Amerigo is also spelled Amerrigo, Merigo, Almerico, Alberico, and Alberigo as well as Americus, and it is a question whether the last form was not coined as an explanation of the origin of *America,* by scholars who knew not the Indian word, Amerique.

[53]*The Story of the Book of Mormon,* p. 377 (1st Edition).

[54]*Monumental History of Egypt,* Vol. 1, p. 340.

[55]Isaiah 54:9.

[56]*Signs and Symbols of Primordial Man,* p. 365.

of Mormon, and the Kneph of the Egyptians. *Naba*, according to Gesenius,[57] in Niphil means "to speak under divine influence," as a prophet. One of the derivatives from this root is *Nebo*, a name given to the planet Mercury, by the Chaldeans, because they regarded that star as the celestial scribe.

How expressive the name Nephi is, when we understand its meaning! How well it corresponds with the character and mission of the great son of Lehi!

There are several names among American proper nouns, which seem to be derived from the same root as *Nephi*. In the northern part of Colombia, S.A., is a river and a city named Nechi. Compare the Hebrew spelling of Lehi (Lechi) with this and it is not too difficult, even for a novice, to see it is Nephi. And when we consider that the original inhabitants of America were a people who were versed "in the learning of the Jews and the language of the Egyptians" it is not surprising to find the name "Nephi" in its Egyptian form Necho (Pharaoh). One of the affluents of the Amazon is *Napo*, and in the upper Amazon Valley there is a tribe of Indians, of the Zaparo linguistic stock, known as the *Nepa* Indians. The *Nahuapos*, the *Napeanos*, the *Napos*, and the *Napotoas* are among the tribes enumerated by Dr. Brinton.[58] And then there are the *Nahuas*, of the great Uto-Aztecan stock of which tribes have been found all the way from the Isthmus to the banks of the Columbia River.

This word should be given special attention.

The Nahuas had lost all the labial sounds except "p" and "u." The sound of "b" or "f" or "ph" they would represent by a "u." "The change of *b, p,* to *u*," says Mr. Denison,[59] "is of very wide geographical reach, as Mexican *kauh*, 'ape,' Sansk. *kapi*." He also points out that the pseudo-labial "u" may represent a labial, such as "b," "p," "f," "v," or "w"; or even a lost "g" or "r." The word *Nahua* may, therefore, as far as the pronunciation indicates, be considered identical with *Nephi*.

The meaning of the word is variously given. Sahagun says that all who spoke the Mexican language *clearly* were called *Nahoas*. Molina traces the name through a verb meaning "to instruct," and especially in an occult sense. Brasseur de Bourbourg is more definite. He considers it a word of the Quiche language, meaning "to know," "to think," and, as a noun, "wisdom," "knowledge." It is, in fact, the Abbe suggests, identical with our "know-all," but it is frequently used to denote something mysterious, extraordinary, or marvelous.[60] According to these definitions, *Nao* is identical in meaning with the Hebrew *naba*, "to speak under divine influence," to "prophesy," and the Indian *Nahua* is the same as the Book of Mormon *Nephi*, and the Hebrew *Nabi*, a prophet.

The word *nepohualtzitzin* should be mentioned here. That, we are told, is an Aztec word.

Boturini makes the statement that the Nahuas used knotted cords, similar to the quipus of the Peruvians, to record events, but that their use had been discontinued before Aztec supremacy. Those knotted cords were called nepohualtzitzin. The Italian traveler even claims to have seen one of them in a very dilapidated condition at Tlascala, but Bancroft[61] rather doubts this. Be that as it may, the word itself is very instructive.

---

[57]*Naba*, in Kal, means "to boil up," as a fountain; hence to pour forth words, as those who speak under divine influence.

[58]*The American Race*, pp. 118, 282, 285.

[59]*The Primitive Aryans in America*, p. 94.

[60]Bancroft, *Native Races*, Vol. 2, p. 129. "On n'en trouve pas, Toutefois, la racine dans le mexicain. La langue quichee en donne une explication parfaite; il vient du verbe *nao ou naw*, connaitre, sentir, savoir, penser. *Tin nao*, je sais; *naoh*, sagesse, intelligence. Il y a encore le verbe radical *na*, sentir supconner. Le mot *nahual* dans son sens primitif et veritable, signifie, donc litteralment 'qui sait tout', c'est la meme chose absolutment que le mot anglais *know all*, avec lequel il at tant d'identite. Le Quiche et le Cakchiquel l' emploient frequement aussi dans le sens de mysterieux, extraordinaire, merveilleux."

[61]*Native Races*, p. 551.

To begin with the last part of it, *tzintzin*, seems to be the Hebrew *tsits* which means "a shining forth," "brightness." It was the name for the shining plate of gold worn by the high priest, and upon which "holiness to the Lord" was engraved.[62] *Tsitsith* was also the word by which the tassels or fringes prescribed in the Mosaic law[63] were designated. The Nahua word *tzitzin* may, if of Hebrew origin, therefore, be understood to refer to either engraved plates, or to knotted cords, or fringes.

If *Nepo*, as I believe, is Nephi, and *ual* gives the word to which it is attached the value of an adjective, as, for instance, *Nezahualcoyotl*, "The fasting coyote"; *Nezahualpilli*, "The Faster-for prince";[64]*Quetzalcoatl*, "feathered serpent," then, analogous with such construction, *Nepohual* would be "Nephite."

Nepohualtzitzin would, then, mean, "Nephite plates," or "Nephite cords." It is easily understood how knotted cords used as "records" could be called *tzitzin*, "plates," figuratively speaking, if we remember that our records are still "books" from the time when "beech" staves were used as we use paper.

The word *Anahuac*, as the country of the Nahuas was called, the authorities tell us, has no relationship to *Nahua;* it means the country, or any country, near the water. But, notwithstanding the authorities, it is not impossible that it is very closely related to *Nahua*, and that its true meaning is, "The Land of Nephi, by the Water."

Napa was, further, the name by which a sacred figure of the llama was known by the Peruvians.[65] At a certain festival a number of those animals were sacrificed. The shepherds came with a special llama, draped in red cloth and wearing golden earrings. This llama was the *napa*. The insignia of the Inca was brought out in honor of that animal, and dancing was performed as part of the sacred ceremonies.

This, I think, shows clearly that the word stands for something sacred, something in a special manner connected with the divine service.

ONIDAH. This is the name of a hill on which Alma preached the gospel to the Zoramites (Alma 32:4), and the place where Lamanites, later, gathered themselves when they expected to be attacked by Amalickiah. (Alma 47:5.)

It is a genuine Indian word. According to Schoolcraft,[66] its Indian form is, *oneotaug*, which means "stone people." That would, reasonably, be "hill people," and that would confirm the use of the word in the Book of Mormon as the name of a hill. The proper analysis of the word is *Onia*, "stone," *oda*, "people," and *aug*, a plural ending.

The *Oneida* Indians formed one of the five tribes (the Onondagas, the Mohawks, the Senecas, and the Cayugas were the others) who united into a federation under the leadership of Hiawatha, for the purpose of abolishing war in the world.

There is an *Oneida* valley in the state of New York, and a number of other places in America are known by this Book of Mormon name.

PACHUS was the name of a king who ruled the "dissenters" that had driven the "Freemen" out of Zarahemla and taken possession of the land. (Alma 62:6.)

This word is found in the Peruvian *Pacha-camac*, which means *world-creator*, and was the name given to the Deity." The Chibchas, in what is now Colombia, had the same name for God, in the shorter form, *Bochi-ca*.[67] It is also found in such royal titles as *Pacha*-cutec Inca Yupanqui, where it seems to be equivalent to "lord." In that

[62]Ex. 28:36-38.
[63]Num. 15:38.
[64]Comp. Bancroft, *Native Races*, Vol. 5, p. 372. Prescott, *Conq. of Mex.*, Vol. 1 pp. 86 and 151.
[65]Sir Clements Markham, *The Incas of Peru*, p. 51.
[66]*Indian Tribes in the United States*, Vol. 4, p. 384.
[67]John Fiske, *The Discovery of America*, Vol. 2, p. 338.

case it is identical in meaning with the Pachus of the Book of Mormon, the title assumed by the dissenting king.

Pacha means both "world" and "time," or perhaps an "eternity." That connects it in meaning, though not in form, with the Hebrew *olam*, which also means both *world* and *eternity*.

SIDON. This was the name of the river that is so often mentioned in the Book of Mormon. (Alma 2:15.) *Sidon* means "fishing," and the *River Sidon* means, therefore, the same as "Fishing River." It is the same name as that which was given to the river, on the banks of which Zion's Camp was located, in Missouri, June 19, 1834, where the important revelation, Doctrine and Covenants Sec. 105, was given, June 22, the same year.

The name "Sidon" may not have been retained in the languages of the descendants of the people of Zarahemla, but the Lenni Lenape Indians have preserved a tradition in which the name "Fishing River" is mentioned. According to their tradition, the Lenni Lenape, many centuries ago, lived somewhere in the western part of the American continent. For some reason or other they decided to migrate. After a very long journey they arrived on the *Namesi Sipu*,[68] which in their language means "Fish River," the same as "Sidon." Here they met another tribe, which they called Mengwe. By their scouts they had been informed that the Talligewi, or Alligewi who lived east of the Mississippi, were a powerful nation which had built many cities and regular fortifications. The Lenape and Mengwe united and made war upon the Alligewi, though these were a people of gigantic stature.[69] They do not claim that the entire nation crossed the Namesi Sipu. Many, they say, remained in order to assist those who had not crossed over but who had "retreated into the interior of the country on the other side." Those who did emigrate finally settled on the four rivers, Delaware, Hudson, Susquehannah, and Potomac.

TIMOTHY is the name of one of the Twelve appointed by our Savior in this country, to carry the gospel message to the people here. On the face of it it appears to be a Greek word, meaning "Honoring God."

But it is also Indian. Dr. Brinton[70] tells us that in the mountain district south of the plains near Maracaibo, in South America, there are some Indian bands, or what remains of them, known as the *Timotes*.

ZARAHEMLA. Elder George Reynolds[71] suggests that this word means either, "A rising of Light," or, "Whom God Will Fill Up." The latter I consider the better rendering of the two. The word *zara* is Peruvian for "corn," or "maize." It is also Hebrew for "seed," especially in the sense of offspring. "Hemla" is, probably, the Hebrew *hamulah* "abundance," and *Zarahemla* would then mean, applied to the country, "a place where there is a seed abundance"; that is, Bountiful; applied to a person, it would mean one "who has a numerous offspring."

That *Bountiful* and *Zarahemla* refer to the same country seems to be clear from these passages: "Thus the land on the northward was called Desolation, and the land on the southward was called Bountiful." (Alma 22:31.) "The land southward which was called by the Nephites Zarahemla." (Ether 9:31.) That the two countries were identical only in part, however, may be inferred from this reference to the two

---

[68] From *names*, "fish," and *sipi*, "river"; see Brinton, *Library of Aboriginal American Literature*, Vocabulary, Vol. 5.

[69] Brinton, *Libr. of Abor. Amer. Liter.*, Vol. 5, p. 141. The Delawares, says Dr. Brinton, applied the name "Fish River" to several streams, but not to the Mississippi.

[70] *The American Race*, p. 179.

[71] *The Story of the Book of Mormon.*

countries: "And the land which was appointed was the land of Zarahemla and the land Bountiful, yea, to the line which was between the land Bountiful and the land of Desolation." (3 Ne. 3:23.) From which it appears that the two countries were adjacent, but that Zarahemla did not extend as far as the boundary line between Desolation and the land on the southward, but that Bountiful did.

THE SCATTERED OF ISRAEL

A Help to the Study of the Parable of the "Tame Olive Tree"
Given by the Prophet Zenos
Recorded in the Book of Jacob, Chapter 5

"Israel shall blossom and bud and fill the world with fruit."—Isaiah

PART 1

Introductory—The Promises of God to Abraham and His Posterity—The Seed of Joseph in America—The Journey of the Ten Tribes Northward—Ephraim Mixed With All Nations—The Testimony of President Brigham Young.

The belief of the Latter-day Saints that the majority of their numbers are of the House of Israel, and heirs to the promises made to Abraham, to Isaac, and to Jacob, like many other portions of their faith, has received the ridicule of the ungodly, and the contempt of the unthinking. However, it is not our present intention to answer this criticism, but to seek to adduce evidence outside of the sure word of modern revelation, to prove that Latter-day Saints have good reasons, drawn from history and analogy, for believing the words of their patriarchs who, in blessing them, pronounce them to be of the House of Abraham, and of the Seed of Jacob.

It is unnecessary to quote all of the many gracious promises made by the Great Father of us all, to his friend, Abraham, and to that Patriarch's immediate posterity, yet, as the promises are cherished by the Saints as of more than earthly value, as pearls beyond all price, as sweet comforters in the day of trial, and as strong towers of defense in the hour of temptation, it may not be out of place to refresh our minds by the recital of a few of the most prominent, that we may better comprehend the ideas and the statements that follow after.

It is recorded that the Lord covenanted with Abraham, saying:

As for me, behold, my covenant is with thee, and thou shalt be a father of many nations. Neither shall thy name any more be called Abram, but thy name shall be Abraham; for a father of many nations have I made thee. And I will make thee exceeding fruitful, and I will make nations of thee, and kings shall come out of thee. And I will establish my covenant between me and thee and thy seed after thee in their generations, for an everlasting covenant, to be a God, unto thee, and to thy seed after thee. (Genesis 17:4-7)

Again, Jehovah declares:

By myself have I sworn, saith the Lord, for because thou hast done this thing, and has not withheld thy son, thine only son: That in blessing I will bless thee, and in multiplying I will multiply thy seed as the stars of the heaven, and as the sand which is upon the sea shore; and thy seed shall possess the gate of his enemies; and in thy seed shall all the nations of the earth be blessed. (Genesis 22:16-18)

To Isaac and to Jacob were these glorious promises confirmed, if possible, in yet stronger wording. To the latter, it was said:

And thy seed shall be as the dust of the earth, and thou shalt spread abroad to the west, and to the east, and to the north, and to the south; and in thee and in thy seed shall all the families of the earth be blessed. (Genesis 28:14; See also Genesis 26:4-10)

The blessing of Jacob upon his son, Joseph, is doubtless so familiar to the majority of our readers, that we shall simply quote the latter portion:

The blessings of thy father have prevailed above the blessings of my progenitors unto the utmost bound of the everlasting hills: they shall be on the head of Joseph, and on the crown of the head of him that was separate from his brethren. (Genesis 49:26)

We will take but one step farther in this direction. Jacob, in blessing Ephraim and Manasseh, the sons of Joseph, said:

. . . let my name be named on them, and the name of my fathers Abraham and Isaac; and let them grow into a multitude in the midst of the earth." (Genesis 48:16)

When Joseph reminded the aged Patriarch that his right hand was placed on the head of the younger boy, he declared:

I know it, my son, I know it; he also shall become a people and he shall become great: but truly his younger brother shall be greater than he, and his seed shall become a multitude of nations. (Genesis 48:19)

There are two points in these blessings that are very important, or noteworthy. The first, that the seed of these Patriarchs should become innumerable, and grow to be a multitude of nations in the midst of the earth. The second, that in or through their seed, all the nations and families of the earth should be blessed. A covenant was made by the Most High with Abraham, that he should become the father of many nations, and when we have laid aside the descendants of Ishmael — the Arabians and their fellows, who have grown into mighty multitudes, and not even counted the posterity of the sons of Keturah and of Abraham's other wives — yet in the one son, Isaac, the promise is renewed; his seed is to multiply "as the stars of heaven." Once again, we will divide the posterity, and leave unnoticed the dukes of Edom and the other descendants of Isaac's favorite son.

We will speak alone of Jacob. To him was repeated the divine promise: "Thy seed shall be as the dust of the earth"; and again, "A nation and a company of nations shall be of thee." Here, let us pause for a moment and ask, "Are they whom the world regard as the only representatives of Jacob today — the dispersed of Judah — all that that holy man has to show as the fulfillment of so great a promise as the last one quoted?" We think not, but believe that future research will vindicate prophecy, and prove that the promises of the Eternal Father are not cut short in their complete fulfillment.

We are well aware, so great is the tendency of the races of the earth to mix and intermingle, that the Jews, as well as the Christians, point to their continued existence as a distinct people, as an unanswerable argument in favor of the divinity of their Scriptures and the inspiration of their prophets. But their history, their exclusiveness, and their dispersion, do not fulfill a vast number of the prophecies uttered with regard to Israel. Yet, when the history of all Israel is written, of Ephraim as well as Judah, we are satisfied that no portion of God's holy word will be found to have returned to His mouth unfulfilled, and He will be as much glorified in the hiding up of the Ten Tribes and the mixing of Ephraim among the nations, as in the scattering of the sons and the daughters of Judah.

Jacob had one son, and he was not the ancestor of the Jews, to whom these blessings were not only renewed, but also extended. To Joseph it was said that his blessings have prevailed above the blessings of his ancestors, or his progenitors, unto the bounds of the everlasting hills, while of Joseph's younger son it was declared, "His seed shall be a multitude of nations." Thus we observe that with each succeeding heir to these choice blessings, the promises seem to have grown, extended, and spread out. To Abraham, it was promised that he should be the father of many nations; to Ephraim, his grandson's grandson, it was said of his seed, and his seed alone, that it should become a multitude of nations. Where is that multitude of nations today? That seems a pertinent question, for God has promised it and they must exist.

The average student of history cannot answer this question. He knows nothing of the posterity of Ephraim; they are hidden from his sight. But the believer in the Book of Mormon will point to the record and declare that in the aborigines of both North and South America, and of many of the Pacific Islands, we find the seed of Joseph grown into a multitude of tribes, peoples and nations. We thankfully admit this truth; we cannot contradict it, even if it served our purpose to do so. God has so revealed it, and the external confirmatory evidences are growing stronger and more convincing every year. Yet, another pertinent question presents itself here. We understand, from the Book of Mormon, that the Lamanites are of the house of Manasseh; that is, their great father, Lehi, and his sons, were of that tribe. If so, his greatness does not fulfill the promises made to Ephraim, who was to be greater than was Manasseh. Surely, the Lord, having so abundantly fulfilled His promise to the one brother, has not forgotten His covenant with the "first born." But shall we be deemed inconsistent if we say that we do not think that the whole of that multitude of nations is found in the descendants of Lehi, of Mulek, and their companions. Is it supposable that the Lord has confined the fulfillment of the promises to Joseph, whose blessings were to prevail above those of his progenitors, to tribes who are today and the majority of which have for fifteen hundred years, or one-quarter of this world's existence since mortals dwelt on it, been among the wildest and the most degraded of mankind? If so, the descendants of those to whom no promises were made have enjoyed the greater blessings.

We contend that where Israel is not under the ban of God's displeasure through his sins and follies, Israel leads the world. His sons are princes among men, and the ministers of God's law to all people. Indeed, in him, according to the oft repeated promise, all the families of the earth will be blessed. Here we may be interrupted by our readers, for it is the Latter-day Saints we are addressing, with the question, "Have we forgotten the Ten Tribes hidden by Divine Providence in the far off regions of the north, and who are environed by a belt of snow and ice so impenetrable that no man in modern days has reached them?" No, we have not forgotten them, and through them, we believe, as we believe that through Lehi and others, the promises of God to Jacob, and to Joseph have been, and are being fulfilled. But we ask further, "Is it altogether improbable that in that long journey of one and one-half years, as Esdras states it, from Media, the land of their captivity to the north-lands, that some of the back-sliding Israelites rebelled, turned aside from the main body, forgot their God, by and by mingled with the Gentiles and became the leaven, which leavened all the nations with the promised seed of Jacob?"

The account given in the Book of Mormon, of a single family of this same House, its waywardness, its stiffneckedness before God, its internal quarrels and family feuds are, we fear, an example on a small scale of what most probably happened in the vast bodies of Israelites, who for so many months wended their way northward. Laman and Lemuel had, no doubt, many counterparts in the journeying of the Ten Tribes. And who is so likely to rebel than stubborn, impetuous, proud, and warlike Ephraim? Rebellion and backsliding have been so characteristically the story of Ephraim's career that we can scarcely conceive that it could be otherwise, and yet preserve the unities of that people's history. Can it be any wonder, then, that so much of the blood of Ephraim has been found hidden and unknown in the midst of the nations of Northern

Europe and in other parts, until the spirit of prophecy revealed its existence? But before proceeding further in our research, it may be well to insert the words of one having authority, to the effect that the Latter-day Saints are of Ephraim; to adduce ideas and reasons to substantiate this statement will be our pleasure as we proceed.

President Brigham Young delivered a discourse in the Tabernacle, Salt Lake City, April 8, 1855, from which the following are extracts:

> The set time has come for God to gather Israel, and for his work to commence upon the face of the whole earth, and the Elders who have arisen in this Church and kingdom are actually of Israel. Take the Elders who are now in this house, and you can scarcely find one out of a hundred but what he is of the House of Israel. It has been remarked that the Gentiles have been cut off, and I doubt whether another Gentile ever comes into this Church.

> Will we go to the Gentile nations to preach the Gospel? Yes, and gather out the Israelites wherever they are mixed among the nations of the earth. What part or portion of them? The same part or portion that redeemed the House of Jacob, and saved them from perishing with famine in Egypt. When Jacob blessed the two sons of Joseph, "guiding his hands wittingly," he placed his right hand upon Ephraim, "and he blessed Joseph, and said, God, before whom my fathers Abraham and Isaac did walk, the God which fed me all my life long unto this day, the angel which redeemed me from all evil, bless the lads," etc. Joseph was about to remove the old man's hands, and bringing his right hand upon the head of the oldest boy, saying, "Not so, my father; for this is the first born; put thy right hand upon his head." And his father refused, and said, I know it, my son, I know it: he also shall become a people, and he also shall be great; but truly his younger brother shall be greater than he, and his seed shall become a multitude of nations."

> Ephraim has become mixed with all the nations of the earth, and it is Ephraim that is gathering together.

> It is Ephraim that I have been searching for all the days of my preaching, and that is the blood which ran in my veins when I embraced the Gospel. If there are any of the other tribes of Israel mixed with the Gentiles, we are searching for them. Though the Gentiles are cut off, do not suppose that we are not going to preach the Gospel among the Gentile nations, for they are mingled with the House of Israel, and when we send to the nations we do not seek for the Gentiles, because they are rebellious and disobedient. We want the blood of Jacob, and that of his father, Isaac, and Abraham, which runs in the veins of the people. There is a particle of it here, and another there, blessing the nations as predicted.

> Take a family of ten children, for instance, and you may find nine of them purely of the Gentile stock, and one son, or one daughter in that family who is purely of the blood of Ephraim. It was in the veins of the father or the mother, and was produced in the son or daughter, while all the rest of the family are Gentiles. You may think that it is singular, but it is true. It is the House of Israel we are after, and we care not whether they come from the east, the west, the north, or the south; from China, Russia, England, California, North or South America, or some other locality; and it is the very lad on whom father Jacob laid his hands, that will save the House of Israel. The Book of Mormon came to Ephraim, for Joseph Smith was a pure Ephraimite, and the Book of Mormon was revealed to him, and while he lived he made it his business to search for those who believed the Gospel. . . . You understand who we are; we are of the House of Israel, of the royal seed, of the royal blood."

PART 2

Israel a Maritime Nation—Tyre and Sidon—The Lacedemonians Claim Relationship with Israel—The Ionians, Etrurians, Danes, Jutes, etc.—The Various Captives of Israel and Judah—Media.

The idea, though not until lately, widely diffused, that many of the races inhabiting Europe are impregnated with the blood of Israel, is by no means a new one. Many writers, in their researches into the early history of that continent, have been forcibly struck with the similarity that existed between the laws, manners, and customs, of the ancient inhabitants of its northern and north-western portions and those of ancient Israel. These writers have endeavored to account for this peculiarity in two ways. First, by the supposition that Israelitish colonies, for various causes, left the land of their inheritance and gradually worked themselves north and north-west-ward over Europe; and second, by the argument that remnants or branches of the lost Ten Tribes had emigrated from Media into Europe, and through the ignorance of historians, disguised under other names, they had remained unknown until the present; their habits, customs, and traditions, having in the meanwhile become so greatly changed by time and circumstances, as to render them unrecognizable at this late day.

We will take up the first of these ideas, and present a few of the arguments advanced by those who support it. It is asserted by them that Israel early became a maritime nation, that its location on the Mediterranean Sea, admirably adapted its people for such a pursuit. By means of the Red Sea at its back, it also had undisturbed access to Africa, India, and the isles beyond. As early as the days of the Judges, about 1300 B.C., we find that Deborah and Barak, in their song of triumph, complain that Dan did not come up to the aid of Israel in the hour of need, but remained in his ships while his fellows were contending with Sisera and his hosts. "Why did Dan remain in his ships?" (Judges verse 17) is the exact question asked. This shows that early in Israel's history it had commenced to hold commercial relations with its neighbors.* The tribes whose inheritances bordered on the Mediterranean, commencing at the north, were Asher, Manasseh, Ephraim, Dan, and Simeon. Asher's inheritance lay contiguous to the great ports of Tyre and Sidon, while Simeon's bordered on Egypt, and contained within its confines other seaports of the Philistines or Phoenicians, to whom, we think,

---

*We have seen a translation of an ancient Danish history, in which it is asserted that Angul of Issacher, a brother of Tola, who judged Israel about 1225 years B.C., invaded England, and was assisted by Tola in so doing. In the name of *Angul* we find another derivation of the proper noun *Angleland*, England.

profane writers have given credit for many of the commercial ventures undertaken by the Israelites.

It must not be supposed that these maritime tribes were the only ones that would be found spreading abroad. The members of the various tribes did not strictly confine themselves to the boundaries assigned their tribes by Joshua, but they intermingled for trade, and many men of other tribes resided within the borders of Judah's inheritance, and vice versa.

We have a notable example of this in the case of Lehi and Laban (600 B.C.), who were the seed of Joseph, yet they were residents of Jerusalem, and Nephi incidentally remarks that his father, Lehi, had dwelt in that city "all his days." The children of Ephraim, from their great enterprise and force of character, seem to have early spread, not only among other tribes, but also into foreign nations, notably to Egypt; and the anger of the Lord is repeatedly expressed through His prophets at His people's disregard of His law in mixing with the heathen. In Isaiah's time, Ephraim had, like a "silly dove," mingled himself among the people to the displeasure of God.

But it was not only for trade and commerce that Israel spread abroad; but also her children were sometimes forced to foreign lands against their will. Two hundred years before Lehi left Jerusalem, the Lord upbraided Tyre and Sidon, through Joel, his servant, telling them, among other things, "The children also of Judah, and the children of Jerusalem have ye sold unto the Grecians," (or Gentiles), "that ye might remove them far from their border." (Joel 3:6) Here we obtain a glimpse of the policy of these two cities; they sought to weaken Israel by deporting her children as captives to other nations afar off, and with true commercial instincts, endeavored to make the transaction a profitable one. And if Judah, with Jerusalem at the other end of the land, thus suffered at the hands of Tyre and her sister city, is it not a certainty that the other tribes, living nearer, would suffer from this same cause, and probably more severely?

We are of the opinion that this wholesale slave trade of the Phoenicians is greatly underestimated as a factor in the diffusion of Israelitish blood throughout the world. So great was the number of slaves held by these people, that at one time in their chief city, the slaves exceeded the freemen in number, and their maritime enterprise was such that they established colonies or depots on all the islands of the Mediterranean Sea, in France, Spain, Italy, Britain, and probably Germany. The whole coast of northern Africa was studded with their colonies, which they carried south as far as Timbuctoo and the Niger, while by way of the Red Sea, they reached eastern Africa, Persia, India, and some suppose China. In fact, they traded with, and established colonies all over the then known world.*

It is also a remarkable fact that a few hundred years after Joel had delivered his message of condemnation to Tyre and Sidon, the people of one of these Grecian States, the Lacedemonians, or Spartans, claimed relationship with Israel as children of Abraham, and had their claim allowed. Still more remarkable is that these Lacedemonians were the ones used by Alexander the Great in the destruction of Tyre, and in fulfillment of the words of the Lord through Joel: "Behold I will raise them out of the place whither ye have sold them, and I will return your recompense upon your own head." (Joel 3:7) It would appear that the sons destroyed the cities that had sold their fathers into captivity.

The fact that these Lacedemonians did claim kindred with Israel, is narrated both by Josephus and the author of the First Book of Maccabees. The writers of both histories gave a synopsis of the letter sent by Oresus, king of the Lacedemonians, to Onias, the High Priest of Israel. The two accounts agree very closely.

Josephus gives the opening clause of the king's letter in these terms: "We have met with a certain writing whereby we have discovered that both Jews and Lacedemonians are of one stock, and are derived from the kindred of Abraham."

In the Book of Maccabees it runs as follows: "It is found in writing that the Spartans and Jews are brethren, and come out of the generation of Abraham." (I Mac. 12)

---

*Although the ancient Jews were principally an agricultural nation, the geographical position of Palestine and the contiguity of some of the tribes of Israel to the Mediterranean Sea, induced the Jewish people to make common cause of their friendly neighbors, the sea-faring Phoenicians. There were two causes which conduced to render the Jews well acquainted with navigation on high-seas. Many of them were carried away as captives in their frequent, and often unsuccessful, warfare with more powerful nations. The prisoners of war were forced to serve on land and sea. Allusions to redeemed prisoners, returning from the Islands of the Sea and from the "four corners of the earth," occur in many parts of the Hebrew Scripture and the experiences of the Jews in sea voyages are graphically depicted in the Bible (Psalm 107). Then there were missionary voyages of the Jews for the inculcation of monotheistic teachings. The Jewish missionaries visited many lands across the seas, as is attested in many parts of the prophetic writings. Allusions to a life on the ocean and to the unpleasant experiences of sea-sickness occur in several places in the scriptures together with magnificent representations of the wondrous sights of mid-ocean. Such descriptions were not borrowed from alien and pagan nations for the simple reason that the admirers of God's marvelous work on the sea are mentioned as coming home from the perilous expeditions of their expeditions abroad, and praising God's glory in the midst of their own people. The distribution of the Jews in many sea-girt places of the Gentiles is often mentioned in the Hebrew Bible and bears evidence to the sea-going habits of many Jewish families; David's conquest of Ezeon-Gaber: the greatest seaport in Southern Arabia, was followed by other kings, Jewish and non-Jewish, who coveted the possession of that harbor. The history of King Solomon's alliance with the Phoenician King Hiram is given in the Book of Kings. The building of merchant-men in Ezeon-Gaber and the voyages undertaken by the Jewish mariners could not be merely legendary seeing that even in the latter days when the Romans attacked the Jews, the latter had numerous ships and seamen on the inland seas. On this subject we find many notices in the works of Josephus and in parts of the New Testament."—Dr. Lowry.

The Jews admitted the relationship in a letter full of sentiments of friendship and brotherhood, sent by a special embassy to the Spartan Court. This letter is given in full in I Maccabees, Chapter 12. In neither history is any hint given as to which branch of Abraham's family the records showed that the Lacedemonians belonged, but from their rigid virtue and honesty, and their near approach to the United Order in their daily lives, it is presumable that they had not long been separate from people in whose midst the law of the true God was known and observed.

It being thus admitted that the people of one Grecian state were of the family of Abraham, students of history have endeavored to trace Israel to other parts. The inhabitants of the Commonwealth of Ionia, one of the most enterprising communities of ancient Greece, are claimed to have been of Israelitish stock. The most weighty arguments used in advocacy of this idea is the similarity that existed between their laws and customs, and those of the Jews. Attention is especially drawn to the fact that the Ionians were divided from choice, and not from the force of circumstances or geographical position, into twelve communities, corresponding with the Twelve Tribes of Israel. The same argument is advanced regarding the Etrurians, who were among the earliest settlers in Italy, and who, tradition says, emigrated from Tyre or its neighborhood. They also were divided into twelve communities or states, but all were under one king. Admitting that these two nationalities were of the outcast of Israel, there is no difficulty in understanding how the children of Jacob spread abroad over all the coasts of Europe and northern Africa, as they were (especially the Ionians) renowned for enterprise at sea. The Ionians were the first people among the Greeks to undertake long voyages.

More than one author has advanced the idea that the Welsh are of the tribe of Manasseh. There are some vague traditions that point in that direction. It has also been asserted that the Irish are of that tribe. From this idea, we differ. With greater show of reason it has been claimed that Denmark was colonized by the tribe of Dan (in Danish, it is Danmark, or Dan's land) so, according to this, a Dane is simply a Danite. Jutland, adjoining, is regarded as Judah's land, Jute being considered merely another form of the word, *Jew*. A little further northward is found Gottland, Gothland, or God's land, as some writers believe. Thus, we have in their immediate proximity, the homes of three prominent Tribes of Israel through the names given to the regions they settled in.

Some who, of late years, have made the subject of Israel's *identification* their study, have gone almost to the verge of the ridiculous in the minuteness with which they have endeavored to fix the boundaries of the lands which, they assert, were occupied by descendants of the different tribes. Our position is the Biblical, or the prophetical one, that Ephraim has mixed himself with the nations; theirs, that remnants of all the tribes can be localized and their descendants determined with the same certainty as the posterity of those races who have never in God's providences, and for the accomplishments of His purposes, been *lost*. One set of these inquirers claim to have made the following discoveries. They have traced the Tribe of Dan to the north of Ireland and of Scotland; Simeon to Wales, Naphtali, as Jutes, to Kent; Gad and Asher, as Angles and South Angles, to Mercia and East Anglia in England; Ephraim to Northumberland and as far north as Edinburgh; Manasseh to the north of England; Reuben as East Saxons, to Essex; Zebulon, as West Saxons, to Wessex; Issacher, as South Saxons, to Sussex; all these last named places being in England.

There is another cause that led to the migration of certain families of Israel and Judah. Before the final captivity of either kingdom was brought about, there were several partial deportations of the people to Assyria and Babylon, or local captivities. Assyria commenced by carrying off the inhabitants nearest her dominions and gradually extended her incursions. The captivity of Judah was still later. In the interval, it is argued, many Israelites, believing in the words of the prophets and seeing the evils that were coming upon them, migrated to Egypt, Greece, or other convenient lands. Some, no doubt, were led, as was Lehi, and as was the son of Zedekiah, by revelation and the commandment of God. Others simply followed the inclinations of their own feelings.

As abundant proof that many were led by the Lord from the Land of Promise before the days of the captivity, we have the words of Nephi:

> For it appears that the house of Israel, sooner or later, will be scattered upon all the face of the earth, and also among all nations. And behold, there are many who are already lost from the knowledge of those who are at Jerusalem. Yea, the more part of all the tribes have been led away; and they are scattered to and fro upon the isles of the sea; and whither they are, none of us knoweth, save that we know that they have been led away. And since they have been led away, these things have been prophesied concerning them, and also concerning all those who shall hereafter be scattered and be confounded. (1 Nephi 22:3-5)

Also the testimony of Nephi's brother, Jacob:

> And now, my beloved brethren, seeing that our merciful God has given us so great knowledge concerning these things, let us remember him, and lay aside our sins, and not hang down our heads, for we are not cast off; nevertheless, we have been driven out of the land of our inheritance; but we have been led to a better land, for the Lord has made the sea our path, and we are upon an isle of the sea. But great are the promises of the Lord unto them who are upon the isles of the sea; wherefore as it says isles, there must needs be more than this, and they are inhabited also by our brethren. For behold, the Lord God has led away from time

to time from the house of Israel, according to his will and pleasure. And now behold, the Lord remembereth all them who have been broken off, wherefore he remembereth us also. (2 Nephi 10:20-22)

That we may better understand the various partial and subsequent general captivities of Israel and Judah, the following short statement thereof is here inserted. The dates given are those commonly accepted in the study of chronology:

Pul, or Sardanapalus, imposed a tribute on Menahen, King of Israel, about 770 B.C.

Tiglath Pileser carried away the tribes living east of the Jordan and in Galilee, 740 B.C.

Shalamaneser twice invaded the kingdom of Israel, took Samaria after three years' siege, and carried the people captive to Assyria, 721 B.C.

Cennacherib is stated to have carried 200,000 captives into Assyria from the Jewish cities that he captured, 713 B.C.

Nebuchadnezzar, in the first half of his reign, repeatedly invaded Judea, besieged Jerusalem, and carried its inhabitants to Babylon, 605-562 B.C.

The next question that presents itself is, "To what portion of the land of Assyria were the Israelitish captives taken?" Scripture has not left us in the dark on this point. Both the Book of Chronicles (I Chron. v. 26), and the Book of Kings (II Kings 27:6) give us the needed information. In the latter book it is stated, and the statement made in the Book of Chronicles is almost identical therewith, that the king of Assyria "carried Israel away captive into Assyria, and placed them in Halah, and in Harbor, by the river Gozan, and in the cities of the Medes."

Media, the land of the Medes, lay to the north of Assyria proper, embracing the country lying on the southern border of the Caspian Sea, as far west as the River Araxes. The exact location of Halah and Harbor has long since been lost sight of, and the only river that today, in name, bears any affinity to the Gozan, is the Kuzal Ozan, which empties into the Caspian Sea to the southeast of the Araxes.

PART 3

The Land of the North—Jeremiah, Esther's and Esdra's Testimonies—The Course of the Israelites Northward—The Jordan, the Don, the Danube, etc.—The Land of Moesia and Dacia—The Getae—Zalmoxes.

Having traced the Ten Tribes to Media, the next question is, "What has become of them for they are not to be found in that land today?" Many attempts have, at various times, been made to discover the Ten Tribes of Israel as a distinct community, but all such efforts have failed. Josephus (*Antiquities II*) believed that in his day they dwelt in large multitudes somewhere beyond the Euphrates, in Asareth, but Asareth was an unknown land to him. Rabbinical traditions and fables, committed to writing in the Middle Ages, assert same fact, with many wonderful amplifications. The imaginations of certain Christian writers have sought them in the neighborhood of their last recorded habitation. Jewish features have been traced in the Afghan tribes; statements are made occasionally of Jewish colonies in China, Tibet, and Hindustan (the Beni-Israel), while the Black Jews of Malabar, claim affinity with Israel. But none of these people would, in any degree, but the slightest, fill the place accorded in the prophecies to Ephraim and his fellows.

The fact that James, the Apostle, opens his Epistle with the following words, has been adduced as an argument that the condition of the Ten Tribes was known to the early Christians: "James, a servant of God and of the Lord Jesus Christ, to the twelve tribes who are scattered abroad, greeting." But it would rather convey the idea to our minds that the Epistle was addressed to those of the Houses of Israel and Judah, who, for the various reasons before cited, and which by that time had multiplied, had wandered into Egypt, Greece, Rome, and other parts of the earth, and not to those whom God had hidden to fulfill more completely His promise to the patriarchs.

We have before stated that Latter-day Saints believe that the Ten Tribes still exist, and that their home is in the far north. That they still exist is absolutely necessary to fulfill the unfailing promises of Jehovah to Israel, and to all mankind. The presence of the remnants of Judah, in every land today, is an uncontrovertible testimony that the covenant God made with Abraham has not been abrogated or annulled. The vitality of the Jewish race is proverbial, and can we reasonably expect that when one branch of a tree shows such native strength, that all the other branches will not be proportionately vital? Is it not more consistent to believe that, as the Jewish race under the curse of the Almighty, and suffering centuries of persecution, still survives? So is it with the rest of Jacob's seed, rather than that they, ages ago, were blotted out of earthly existence.

The belief that Latter-day Saints hold that these tribes are residents of the northern regions of the earth, is sustained by a cloud of scriptural witnesses of *ancient* and *modern* days, to whom we now appeal. Our first witness shall be the Prophet Jeremiah. In his prophecies, we find the Lord rebuking both Israel and Judah for their treachery and backsliding, yet still proclaiming His long suffering and mercy to His covenant people. He then gives command to the Prophet, saying:

Go and proclaim these words toward the *north*, and say, Return, thou backsliding Israel, said the Lord; and I will not cause mine anger to fall upon you: for I am merciful, saith the Lord, and I will not keep anger for ever. . . . In those days (the latter days) the house of Judah shall walk with the house of Israel, and they shall come together *out of the land of the north* to the land that I have given for an inheritance to your fathers. (Jeremiah 3:12, 18)

Again, in speaking of the mighty works accompanying the final glorious restoration of the House of Jacob, the same prophet declares:

Therefore, behold, the days come, saith the Lord, that they shall no more say, the Lord liveth which brought up the children of Israel out of the land of Egypt, but the Lord liveth which brought up and which led the seed of the house of Israel out of the *north country* and from all countries whither I have driven them, and they shall dwell in their own land. (Jeremiah 23:7, 8)

Again it is written, (Jeremiah 31:7-9)

For thus saith the Lord; Sing with gladness for Jacob, and shout among the chief of the nations; publish ye, praise ye, and say, O Lord save thy people, the remnant of Israel. Behold I will bring them from the *north country* and gather them from the coasts of the earth. . . . I am a father to Israel, and Ephraim is my first born."

We will turn for a moment from the Asiatic to the American Continent. There we find Ether, the Jaredite, about 600 years B.C., prophesying of the latter days:

And then also cometh the Jerusalem of old; and the inhabitants thereof, blessed are they, for they have been washed in the blood of the lamb; and they are they who were scattered and gathered in from the four quarters of the earth, and from the *north countries* and are partakers of the fulfilling of the covenants which God made with their father Abraham. (Ether 13:11)

But the most definite word on this subject given by any of the ancient writers of the Asiatic Continent is contained in Esdras, a book of the Apocrypha (II Esdras 13). Therein is given a dream and its interpretation showing forth the works and the power of the Son of God. It is to Him and His gathering of the people together that the prophet refers. The verses more particularly bearing on our subject read as follows:

And whereas thou sawest that he gathered another peaceable people unto him.

Those are the ten tribes which were carried away captives out of their own land in the time of Oseas the king who Shalmaneser the king of the Assyrians took captive, and crossed them beyond the river; so were they brought into another land.

But they took this counsel to themselves, that they would leave the multitude of the heathen, and go forth unto a further country where man never dwelt.

That they might there keep their statutes, which they never kept in their own land.

And they entered in at the narrow passages of the River Euphrates.

For the Most High then showed them signs, and stayed the springs of the flood till they were passed over.

For through the country there was great journey, even of a year and a half, and the same region is called Arsareth.

Then dwelt they there until the latter time, and when they came forth again.

The Most High shall hold still the springs of the river again that they may go through; therefore sawest thou the multitude peaceable. (II Esdras 13:39-47)

The statements of Esdras throw considerable light upon the reasons why the captives in Media preferred not to return to their ancient home in Canaan supposing always the privilege had been accorded to them as well as to the captives of the House of Judah. In their home in the Promised Land, they had seldom kept the counsels and commandments of God, and if they returned it is probable they would do no better, especially as the Assyrians had filled their land with heathen colonists whose influence would not assist them to carry out their new resolutions.

Hence they determined to go to a land "where never men dwelt," that they might be free from all contaminating influences. That country could only be found in the north. Southern Asia was already the seat of a comparatively ancient civilization. Egypt flourished in Northern Africa, and Southern Europe was rapidly filling up with the future rulers of the world. They had, therefore, no choice but to turn their faces northward. The first portion of their journey was not however north. According to the account of Esdras, they appear to have at first moved in the direction of their old homes. It is possible that they originally started with the intention of returning thereto, or probably in order to deceive the Assyrians, they started as if to return to Canaan, and when they had crossed the Euphrates, and were out of danger from the hosts of the Medes and Persians, then they returned their journeying feet toward the Polar Star. Esdras states that they entered in at the narrow passage of the River Euphrates, the Lord staying the "springs of the flood until they were passed over." The point on the River Euphrates at which they crossed would necessarily be in the upper portion, as lower down would be too far south for their purpose.

The upper course of the Euphrates lies among lofty mountains, and near the village of Pastash it plunges through a gorge formed by precipices more than a thousand feet in height, and is so narrow that it is bridged at the top; shortly afterwards, it enters the plains of Mesopotamia. How accurately this portion of the River answers the description given by Esdras of the *Narrows* where the Israelites crossed!

From the Euphrates the wandering host could take but one course in their journey northward, and that was along the back or eastern short of the Black Sea. All other roads were impassable to them, as the Caucassian Mountains, with only two or three passes throughout its whole extent, ran as a lofty barrier from the Black

Sea to the Caspian. To go east would take them back to Media, and a westward journey would carry them through Asia Minor to the coasts of the Mediterranean. Skirting along the Black Sea, they would pass the Caucassian range, cross the Kuban River, be prevented by the Sea of Azof from turning westward and then would reach the present home of the Don Cossacks. It is asserted, on goodly authority, that along this route and for "an immense distance" northward, the country is full of tombs of great antiquity, the construction of which, the way in which the dead are buried therein, and the jewelry and curiosities found on opening them, prove that they were built by a people of similar habits to the Israelites. Dr. Clark, a well known traveler, states that he counted more than ninety such mounds at one view near the Kuban River.

We will here digress and give some of the ideas written on the Israelitish origin of the nations of modern Europe (Mr. J. Wilson), though in our own words. He endeavors to prove that Israel traveled northwestward from the neighborhood last spoken of, and claims that the names of all of the principal rivers, in the regions round about, show that colonists from the Holy Land gave them. The Jordan was distinctly the River of Canaan, as the Nile was of Egypt. The word *Jordan* is by some claimed to mean, "flowing," by others, the *River of Eden*. There was also the *Dedan*, or *Dan* (*el Leddan*) flowing into it, which would lead to the supposition that the word Dan had some connection with Israelitish rivers, not now understood.

Suffice it, the exiles doubtless carried with them many hallowed recollections of their ancient river, which it was but natural that they should seek to perpetuate as they journeyed farther and farther from its waters, and far from their long cherished home. As a result we find in southwestern Europe the Don, the Daniz or *Donitz*, the *Danieper* and *Daniester*, now contracted to *Dnieper* and *Dniester*, and the *Danube*. The conclusions of the writer already referred to are that Israel gradually drifted westward to the region known to secular history as *Moesia* and *Dacia,* the one north and the other south of the Danube, and called by modern English speaking people, Roumania and Bulgaria.

To strengthen further his theory, he claims that *Moesia* means the "land of Moses," and *Dacia,* the "land of David," after Israel's Shepherd King, and that the people of the latter kingdoms were called the *Davi.* In this country dwelt also the *Getae,* a Latinized form of *God,* who, some historians assert, were the forefathers of the Goths, of whom we shall speak again, hereafter. The historian, Herodotus, in recounting the conquest of his people by Darius, states, that the Getae "believed themselves to be immortal; and whenever one dies, they believe that he is removed to the presence of their god

Zamoxis (Zalmoxis), . . . and they sincerely believe that there is no other deity."

He also states that this god left them the institutions of their religion in books. Wilson directs attention to this idea of only one God, so different to the Pantheism of the surrounding peoples, and that of man's immortality as tending to prove the Israelitish origin of the Gatae, particularly as in analyzing the word *Zalmoxis* he finds it to be composed of *Za, el,* "Moses." If his facts are correct, his conclusions are warranted, but of his facts we express no opinion.

PART 4

Israel's Journey Northward—Esdras and Modern Revelation Compared—The Testimony of Jesus to the Nephites—Ephraim to be Gathered from all Countries—The Coasts of the Earth—The Ancestors of the Latter-day Saints.

Having considered the causes that led the outcasts of Israel to determine to seek a home in a new and uninhabited land, we now may be excused if we endeavor to follow them in fancy in their journey northward. We have no way of accurately estimating their numbers, but if the posterity of all those who were carried into captivity started on this perilous journey, they must have formed a mighty host. Necessarily they moved slowly. They were encumbered with the aged and infirm, the young and the helpless, with flocks and herds, and weighed down with the provisions and the utensils of the household. Roads had to be made, bridges built, and the course marked out, and decided upon by their leaders.*

Inasmuch as they had turned to the Lord and were seeking a new home wherein they could better serve Him, they were doubtless guided by inspired leaders, who, by Urim and Thummim, or through dreams and visions, pointed out the paths ahead. Perhaps, as in the days of the deliverance from Egypt, a pillar of cloud by day and of fire by night, guided their footsteps. No matter the means, the end was accomplished, and slowly and gradually they crossed the plains, whence they neared the frozen regions of the Arctic zone. The distance in a direct line from the conjectured crossing of the Euphrates to the coasts of the Arctic Ocean, would be about 2,800 miles, or a seven months' journey, averaging fifteen miles a day. But according to Esdras, one year and a half was consumed in the journey, which is an evidence that they were encumbered with families and cattle, who could only travel slowly and for whom many resting places had to be found where they could recuperate. It is highly probable that, like modern Israel in its journey westward

---

*Jesus distinctly states to the Nephites, that these tribes were led "by the Father out of the land."

to the valleys of the Rockies, they established temporary colonies by the way, where the weary rested and crops were raised for future use.

The length of the journey had its advantages as well as its drawbacks. The slow rate at which they traveled enabled them to become acclimatized to the regions where the rigors of the frigid zone were to be met. We must recollect that we are dealing with a people cradled in the burning sands of Egypt, and who, for many generations, had dwelt in one of the most balmy and genial climates on this globe. Their temporary sojourn in the bleaker regions near the Caspian Sea, had partially prepared them for that which was to come, but it required time to give them the capability to endure the rigors of a northern climate, as they were, by ancestry and location, distinctly children of the sunny south.

No doubt, as the hosts of Israel advanced, the change in the climate, the difference in the length of the days and nights, the altered appearance of the face of the country and the newness, to them, of many of its animals and vegetable productions, struck them with amazement, perhaps with terror, causing some of the weak-kneed to falter and tarry by the way. These defections probably increased as the changes became more apparent and the toils of the journey grew more severe. But what must have been their sensations when they came into view of the limitless expanse of the Arctic Ocean, which lay before them, if the climate conditions were the same as those which exist today; of which, however, there is perhaps some reason to doubt.

No matter whether they drew nigh unto it in winter or in summer, the prospect must have been appalling to the bravest heart not sustained by the strongest and most undeviating faith in the promises of Jehovah. Supposing they reached the northern confines of the European continent in summer, they were in a land where the snow is almost perpetual, and scarcely else but mosses grow. Before them, was a troubled ocean of unknown width; every step they advanced took them farther north into greater extremes of cold. Well might they question, if so little is here produced for the food of man and beast, how will it be yet farther northward? Must we perish of hunger? If, on the other hand, they approached the frozen shores of this unexplored waste of waters in the gloom of the long night of an Arctic winter, with the intense cold freezing their very blood, their feelings of dread must have yet been more intense. No wonder if some turned aside, declared they would go no farther and gradually wandered back through northern Europe to more congenial climes.

Again, it may be asked, "How did this unnumbered host cross

this frigid ocean to their present hiding place?" On this point history and revelation are silent. The Arctic Ocean was no narrow neck of the waters like the Red Sea, with the mountains of the opposite shore full in view. No, it spread out before them eternally—north, east, and west, with no inviting shore in sight beyond. Yet, despite all this, they did cross it, but how, we know not—perhaps on the ice of winter, perhaps the Lord threw up a highway, or divided the waters as He did before time, that they passed through dry shod. But we must abide His time, when this and other secrets of their history shall be revealed.

Since penning the foregoing ideas, we have been informed that certain ancient Scandinavian legends entirely agree with our theory. We understand that these legends state that the Ten Tribes, in their journey northward, erected at various points, on prominent mountain heights and such, monuments or heaps of stones, so that if they determined to return, they might have some guides on the road back to the Euphrates. These same traditions state that colonies of the very young and the infirm, as well as the wayward and rebellious, were left by the wayside, and from these colonies the fathers of the Norsemen sprang. These legends in time became crystalized and made their appearance as verities in the traditional histories of the nations of northern Europe.

Esdras says that he was shown that they abide in this north country until the latter time, when they were to come forth again, a great multitude, to add to the glory of Messiah's Kingdom. This statement agrees with the word of modern revelation to which we now draw attention.

More than half a century ago the Lord, through Joseph Smith, in speaking of the lost Ten Tribes, said:

> They who are in the North countries shall come in remembrance before the Lord, and their prophets shall hear His voice, and shall no longer stay themselves, and they shall smite the rocks and the ice shall flow down at their presence. And an highway shall be cast up in the midst of the great deep.* Their enemies shall become a prey unto them, and in the barren deserts there shall come forth pools of living water; and the parched ground shall no longer be thirsty land. And they shall bring forth their rich treasures unto the children of Ephraim, My servants. And the boundaries of the everlasting hills shall tremble at their presence. And they shall fall down and be crowned with glory, even in Zion, by the hands of the servants of the Lord, even the children of Ephraim. (D. and C., Revelation called the *Appendix*.)

It is very evident from the foregoing quotation that Ephraim or at least a large portion of that tribe, had at some period of its history, separated from the rest of the Tribes of Israel, and at the time of this restitution it was to dwell in a land far from the north country in which the residue were hidden. These tribes are to have the frozen barriers of the north melted, so that the ice shall flow down, then a highway is to be cast up for them, in the midst of the great deep; next, they cross barren deserts, and a thirsty land and eventually arrive with their rich treasures at the home of Ephraim, the first born of God of the House of Israel, to be crowned with glory at his hands.

We must now draw the attention of our readers to certain extracts from the Book of Mormon, which show that at the time of our Savior's visit to this continent, Ephraim and the Ten Tribes dwelt neither on this land nor on the Land of Jerusalem. Jesus says:

> Verily, verily, I say unto you that I have other sheep which are not of this land, neither of the land of Jerusalem, neither in any parts of that land round about whither I have been to minister. For they of whom I speak have not as yet heard my voice; neither have I at any time manifested myself unto them. But I have received a commandment of the Father that I should go unto them, and they shall be numbered among my sheep, that there shall be one fold and one shepherd; therefore I go to show myself unto them. And I command you that ye shall write these sayings, after I am gone, that if it so be that my people at Jerusalem, they who have seen me, and been with me in my ministry, do not ask the Father in my name that they may receive a knowledge of you by the Holy Ghost, and also of the other tribes whom they know not of, that these sayings which ye shall write shall be kept and shall be manifested unto the Gentiles, that through the fullness of the Gentiles, the remnant of their seed, who shall be scattered forth upon the face of the earth because of their unbelief, may be brought . . . to a knowledge of me, their Redeemer. And then will I gather them in from the four quarters of the earth; and then will I fulfill the covenant which the Father hath made unto all the people of the house of Israel. (3 Nephi 16:1-5)

This statement of Jesus, that the Ten Tribes did not dwell in the land of Jerusalem, *neither in any parts of that land round about,* effectually disposes of the theory of Josephus and others, that they dwelt near the River Euphrates. The reason why the Jews had lost sight of their brethren of the House of Israel is explained by Jesus in the same chapter of the Book of Mormon. "The other tribes hath the Father separated from them [the Jews]; and it is because of their iniquity that they knew not of them." (*Ibid.*)

Some have imagined that it is not scriptural to look for Israel except in three places: The scattered Jews in all the world, the Lamanites on this continent, and the Ten Tribes in Azareth. But we claim that there are abundant reasons from Scripture to expect to find the seed of Joseph as well as that of Judah in every nation under heaven. The prophecies recorded in the Old Testament expressly state that Israel, especially Ephraim, was to be scattered among all people.

How completely they were to be scattered is shown by the following prophecies:

Hosea, in rebuking Ephraim's idolatry in the name of the Lord, says,

---

*Query—The Arctic and North Atlantic Oceans.

Therefore they shall be as the morning cloud, and as the early dew that passeth away, as the chaff that is driven with the whirlwind out of the floor, and as the smoke out of the chimney. (Hosea 13:3)

Amos states:

Behold the eyes of the Lord God are upon the sinful kingdom [of Israel], and I will destroy it from off the face of the earth; saving that I will not utterly destroy the house of Jacob, saith the Lord. For, lo I will command, and I will sift the house of Israel among all nations, like as corn is sifted in a sieve, yet shall not the least grain fall upon the earth. (Amos 9:8-9)

Could any scattering be more complete?

We are directly told that the Lord will bring His sons (Ephraim still being His first born) from afar and His daughters from the ends of the earth. It is further said that He will gather His Israel — not from the north alone—but from the north and the south, from the east and the west, and bring them to Zion; and that He will gather them from all countries (not America nor the polar regions only, but *all* countries) in which He has scattered them; among other places from the coasts of the earth. How apt a description is the last sentence of the lands from which the great bulk of modern Israel have been gathered. From the coasts of the Atlantic Ocean, from the coasts of the North and the Baltic Seas, they have come to Zion by tens of thousands.

President Brigham Young states in the discourse quoted previously, that ninety-nine out of every hundred elders of the Church of Jesus Christ were of the blood of Israel. The people whom he was addressing were men of various nationalities, but by far the greater portion of them were descendants of those races that in the fourth and succeeding centuries of the Christian era swarmed in myriads out of that mother of nations, Scandinavia, and filled central and western Europe with a new civilization, the people, in fact, who overthrew the great Roman Empire and laid the foundation of the majority of the nations of modern Europe.

It was to the descendants of the Goths, the Danes, the Jutes, the Angles, the Saxons, the Normans, the Franks, that he was talking, and in our next part of this writing we will bring forward some of the historical arguments used by Gentile writers to prove the Israelitish descent of these races, more particularly of that dominant one, known as the Anglo-Saxon. We do not do this because we think the work of God's servants required proving by Gentile evidence, but because it is a satisfaction to many minds, not only to know that a thing is so, but also to be able to give a reason, or advance an argument to demonstrate *why* it is so.

PART 5

The Origin of the Anglo-Saxons—Derivation of the Word Saxon—The Goths and Vandals—Overthrow of the Roman Empire—The Mythology of the Ancient Scandinavians—Baldur—Their Early Literature.

Even as the question, "What became of the Ten Tribes?" still remains to the world an unanswered enigma, so also is the question unanswered, "Whence originated the vast hosts of so-called barbarians who, descending from the frigid regions of Scandinavia, filled Europe with new races, new laws, new ideas, new languages, and new institutions?"

Some have traced a connection between the loss of one people and the advent of the other, and one author of repute, Sharon Turner, extensively quoted in this connection, claims that the original home of the Anglo-Saxons was in the very country where Israel is lost, and further states that these people commenced their migration therefrom about the same time as the tribes of Jacob must have taken their journey northward.

Turner, in his valuable history of the Anglo-Saxons, while discussing the Teutonic descent of many of the nations of modern Europe, says:

It is peculiarly interesting to us, because, from its branches, not only our own immediate ancestors, but also those of the most celebrated nations of modern Europe have unquestionably descended. The Anglo-Saxons, Lowland Scotch, Normans, Danes, Norwegians, Swedes, Germans, Dutch, Belgians, Lombards, and Franks, have all sprung from that great fountain of the human race, which we have distinguished by the terms, Scythian, German, or Gothic. The first appearance of the Scythian tribes in Europe, may be placed, according to Strabo and Homer, about the eighth, or according to Herodotus, in the seventh century before Christ, or the Christian era. The first scenes of their civil existence, and of their progressive power were in Asia, to the east of the Araxes. Here they multiplied and extended their territorial limits for some centuries, unknown to Europe." With regard to the Saxons, Mr. Turner writes: "They were a German or Teutonic, that is a Gothic or Scythian tribe: and of the various Scythian nations which have been recorded, the Sakai or Sacae are the people from whom the descent of the Saxons may be inferred, with the least violation of probability. They were so celebrated that the Persians called all the Scythians by the name of Sacre . . . That some of the divisions of this people were really called Saka-suna, spelt by a person who was unacquainted with the meaning of the combined for, he says, that the Sakai who settled in Armenia were named Sacassani, which is Saka-suna, spelt by a person who was unacquainted with the meaning of the combined words; and the name Sacasina, which they gave to that part of Armenia they occupied, is nearly the same sound as Saxonia. It is also important to remark, that Ptolemy mentions a Scythian people from the Sakai, who resided near the Baltic Sea, by the name of Saxones.

Mr. Turner was not advocating the Israelitish ancestry of the Saxons, hence those who believe in that theory put the greater stress on his two most important statements, *viz.*, that the forefathers of this race dwelt in the region east of the Araxes, the exact spot to which Israel was carried captive, and that they began to spread out therefrom some six or seven hundred years before Christ, answering to the very period that the children of Jacob dwelt captives in that country. One author has assumed a very unique derivation for the word Saxon. He says:

> We suppose it is derived from Isaac, by which we find from Amos, this House of Israel had begun to denominate itself, just before the captivity. It was usual to contract the commencement of the name, especially when they combined it with any other word, or when it came to be familiarly applied. Saxon is, literally or fully expressed, the son of Isaac.

Dickson in modern English is similarly abbreviated to Dixon. Such abbreviations, we may remark in passing, are familiar in our name of the Indian tribe, the *Shoshones,* also a remnant of the seed of Jacob. It is also claimed that the word *Brahmin* is an abbreviation of *Abraham;* in fact, that god *Brahma* is the patriarch, himself, deified. One writer on this portion of the subject sees in this explanation of the word *Saxon,* a fulfillment of the promise made to our father Abraham, "In Isaac shall thy seed be called," and goes as far as to advance the argument that *Cossac* is another expression of this same idea, or that a *Don Cossack* is literally and truly a son of Isaac, of the Tribe of Dan.

The ferocity of the northern races, who overthrew the Roman Empire, is thought by some to argue against their Israelitish origin. But we must recollect that the pictures of the Goths and Vandals, which have been handed down to us, were painted by their enemies. Nor would the argument, however true, have any weight with us were the rest proven. If they were of Israel, they had been wandering, fighting, and colonizing for a thousand years since they left Palestine before they overwhelmed Rome.

And as far as ferocity is concerned, they cannot equal the seed of Joseph on this continent, who but three hundred years after the fullness of the Gospel was proclaimed to their fathers by the Resurrected Redeemer, committed atrocities that no Goth or Vandal ever executed. A very pretty theory has been advocated in connection with this portion of their history, to the effect that as the Roman Empire was used by the Lord to destroy the House of Judah and slay millions of that devoted race, so the Lord chose a portion of the House of Israel (unknown to both themselves and their enemies) to destroy the Gentile rulers of the world who had slain and scattered their brother's house.

The mythology of the northern race of Europe may also be noticed in connection with these inquiries. Those who are learned in the mythologies of ancient Rome and Greece, say that it bears no likeness to them; its peculiarities would rather tend to the idea that it was of Persian origin (*British Encyclopedia*). Some of the early Christian fathers fancied they discovered a great resemblance between one of their deities, named *Baldur* or *Balder*, and our Savior.* This god is represented as the son of Odin and Frigga; he was said to be youthful, beautiful and benignant, the dispenser of kindness, the bringer of joy and blessings, who loves to dwell with men, and whom all men love. But he was killed by the wicked. The manner of his death is surrounded with mythological nonsense. All men mourn the loss of their friend, and search through the world for some remedy to bring him to life, but in vain; stern death has taken him away to the realms of the dead, and he cannot return. His wife Nanna, that she may not be separated from him, has gone to dwell with him there. At last Frigga, his mother, sends a messenger to obtain his release. He leaps the gate of the gloomy world, sees Baldur, and speaks with him, but no, Baldur cannot be released, here he must remain, and his wife, Nanna, must dwell with him forever.

From some of the details not here inserted, we incline somewhat to the opinion that the above narration is a confused tradition of the way death was brought into the world through the transgression of Adam and Eve, rather than that it bears relation to the life of the Savior. We draw attention to the way Baldur's death was brought about. The tradition runs (*American Cyclopedia*), that because Baldur having long been troubled by dreams and evil omens, indicating danger to his life, his mother traveled through the whole universe, eliciting from every created thing a promise not to injure the god. But she neglected to ask it from the apparently harmless mistletoe. Loki, the most deceitful of the gods, an enemy of Baldur, noticed the omission, and cut from the mistletoe a piece for the point of a dart. The other gods, surrounding Baldur, made proof of his invulnerability in sport, by casting at him their weapons, with stones, but nothing injured him. Loki approached and induced the blind god, Hodur, to throw the dart he had made from the forgotten mistletoe. Baldur was pierced by it and killed. In this tradition Loki took the place of Satan; Hodur typified the serpent, and the mistletoe the tree of knowledge of good and evil. It is also noticeable that they represent, in this tradition, that man could do nothing of himself, to overcome the power of death.

The very earliest literature of the Scandinavian people, preserved on the Island of Iceland, adds many testimonies to the Scandinavians' Israelitish origin. On this point, *Encyclopedia Britannica* says:

> On entering on these ancient books, we are immediately struck with the corroborative evidence which they furnish of the eastern origin of the Goths, the fathers

---

*From *The Early Saxons*. American S. S. Union, Philadelphia.

of the Scandinavians. As all languages, so all mythologies run in lines, which converge in a common center . . . Central Asia. And little as we might expect it, no sooner do we open the ancient religious books of Scandinavia that we are carried back thither. Our northern people are a people of eastern origin. Odin* and his Asar, are Asiatics, declare themselves to be from the great Svithiod, a country which appears to have been the present Circassia, lying between the Black and Caspian Seas. The whole of their memoirs abounded with the proofs of it. They brought with them abundant eastern customs, those of burning the dead, and burying under mounds. They practiced polygamy, looked back with imperishable affection to the great Svithiod, to the primitive district of Asgord and the city of Gudahem, or the homes of the gods. They transferred a religion bearing the primal features of those of Persia, India, and Greece, to the snowy mountains of Scandinavia.

In reading the above we are impressed with the geographical idea there expressed. Without any stretch of the imagination we could easily consider the traditions regarding the great Svithiod, to refer to Media, the primitive district of Asgord, to be the dim remembrance of their first home in the Land of Promise, and Gudahem, the home of the gods to be Jerusalem, the city of the great King. The parallel we consider to be very significant.

PART 6

The Numerous Identifications Considered—Religion and Laws of the Ancient Northern Races—Free Masonry—Language.

It would be almost impossible to enumerate the multitude of likenesses that have been found by authors, predisposed in that direction, between the habits, manners, customs, and personal appearances of the Israelites and the Anglo-Saxons. To give even a cursory glance at these "identifications" would occupy more space than we feel would be desirable. We will simply mention a few that have been advanced by various writers, and then proceed to a short consideration of their laws; it may be observed, however, that some of their identifications are very remarkable, while others, in our opinion, are purile, and would be advanced by none but zealots.

Great similarities have been claimed between the form of the Jewish and Saxon heads, and the great beauty of both races has been advanced as a proof of common ancestry. The style of dress of the early northern European nations has also been claimed to be distinctly Israelitish. The care with which both people kept their records of chronicles has been largely commented upon. One author claims connection between the two in the manner that they mustered their forces in battle, and their love of distinctive or tribal banners, giving rise in Europe to the system of heraldry and the development of chivalry. Their division of the people into tithings, hundreds,

---

*Rev. A. B. Grimaldi, A. M., states: "The Saxon kings traced themselves back to Odin, who was traced back in his descent from David, as may be seen in a very ancient MSS. in the Herald's College, London, England, and in Sharon Turner."

and thousands, has been a strong argument in favor of the Saxon's Jewish descent.

The three great yearly convocations of the people are also said to have taken place on the same dates as the three great feasts of the Jews. The Saxons' marriage ceremonies, their respect for women, and the great misfortune which the latter esteemed it, to be without children, are also adverted to as links in the chain of evidence.

Another author, Ed. Hine, pursues a different line of argument and makes the history of the English nation, its constitution, laws, and insular position fulfill the varied prophecies of the ancient servants of God with regard to the Ten Tribes. To our minds, however, these fulfillments of ancient prophecy are often strained and frequently untenable.

In the religion of the ancient Scandinavians, terrible and bloodthirsty as were many of its rites, students have found striking analogies to the religion of ancient Israel; so much so, that it seems and is one of the strongest proofs to be considered of the ancestry of this people in Jacob. And it is claimed that the further we trace the matter back through the centuries, the greater does the likeness become. Lest we shall be considered as straining this point we will quote the language of another:

They (the Anglo-Saxons and their brethren of the north of Europe) are described as having been acquainted with that great doctrine, of one supreme Deity, the Author of everything that existeth; the eternal, the living, the ancient, the searcher into concealed things; the Being that never changeth; who liveth and governeth during the ages; directeth everything that is high, and everything that is low; of his glorious Being they had anciently esteemed it impious to make any visible representation, or to imagine it possible that he could be confined within the walls of the temple.

These great truths, the same as we know were taught to Israel, had in a greater measure become lost or obscured before the people's coming to Britain. But this very obscuration itself, speaks of their origin; it having chiefly taken place, it is said, in consequence of their receiving a mighty conqueror from the east as their god in human form or nature, corresponding to the expectation of Israel with regard to the Messiah. This supposed god incarnate is thought to have presented himself among these people about the same time as the true Messiah appeared among the Jews.

Is it probable that tidings of Jesus' visit to the Ten Tribes could have been conveyed to them or have reached them in a vague or adulterated form?

The name of this pretender was Odin, or Wodin, and he was esteemed the great dispenser of happiness to his followers, as well as fury to his enemies. When Wodin was removed from them they placed his image in their most holy place, where there was a kind of raised place or ark, as if in imitation of that at Jerusalem, where, between the Cherubim, the divine presence was supposed to abide. . . . Before this elevation or Ark, in the most holy place on which the symbols of their worship were placed, they had an altar, on which the holy fire burned continually; and near it was a vase for receiving the blood of the victims, and a brush for sprinkling the blood upon the people; reminding us again of what was done in ancient Israel. They had, generally, one great temple for the whole nation, and in one of these, it is particularly noticed, they had twelve priests who were presided over by a high priest, and having under their charge the religious concerns of the whole people. This temple is said to have been of the most splendid description, of incredible grandeur and magnificence. It was at Upsala, Sweden.

As closely related to this branch of our subject, it has been remarked that Free Masonry was first known in Europe among these people, a fact that will have its weight among Latter-day Saints. In the Middle Ages these lodges of Free Masons built the cathedrals of Europe, and it is asserted that "the English cathedrals appear to have been built after the fashion of the temples that they frequented previous to their conversion to Christianity. And these cathedrals, it has been observed, seem evidently to be built after the design of the temple at Jerusalem. Like this, they have their most holy place, the altar, choir, and the court outward from thence for the body of the people."

It is somewhat remarkable that the only Gentile people of old, among whom anything like Free Masonry was found, were the Ionians, for whom we stated in a previous chapter some claim an Israelitish ancestry. Their temples dedicated to Bacchus and other heathen gods, were built by lodges, who had secret signs, etc., and conducted their affairs much after the manner of the masons of the Middle Ages.

But the strongest of all the supposed identifications of the two races, stronger even than the religious phases of the subject, is the peculiar Masonic tendency of the ancient Norseman's laws. So great is the similarity that most writers on this subject have been greatly puzzled to account therefore. It is written:

> To those who have attentively studied the institutions of Moses, and compared them with the Saxon, there must appear a similarity as will be apt to lead to the conclusion that the Saxon commonwealth was thus framed, after their becoming acquainted with Christianity. This, however, does not appear to have been the case. They brought these institutions with them into England, and left similar institutions among the people in the north of Europe, with whom they had been from time immemorial. Limited monarchy, constitutional law, and representative government, an efficient civil police, and trial by jury, are among the most important legacies left the English nation by their Anglo-Saxon forefathers, and these may all be easily traced to an Israelitish origin. And to this origin they have been traced . . . even by those who were obliged, in rather an unphilosophical way, to account for the connection.

Among the Anglo-Saxons the theory of their constitution seems to have been, that every ten men or heads of families, should choose one from among them to act for them in council of their little community, consisting generally of ten such compartments, or wards. Ten of these wards formed a tithing, or parish. And ten of these tithings formed a hundred, the elders of which, thus chosen, were supposed to meet for the management of matters belonging to the ten tithings in general; while each tithing took charge of the affairs that especially belonged to itself. The county which was still more extensive corresponded to the tribe in Israel. The word *county* or *compte* seems to be derived from the Hebrew word signifying *to rise up,* to *stand,* and refers to the rod or ensign of the tribe to which they congregated themselves in the large assemblies of the people. . . . The nation of Israel, we have seen, were at times at an earlier period of their history given proper rules for their association, such as were equally adapted for a small society or for a large one. The people were given to have a mutual oversight of each other in tens; each ten had one who represented and acted for them. *See* Deuteronomy Chapter 1.

So I [Moses] took the chiefs of your tribes, wise men and known, and made them heads over you, captains over thousands, and captains over hundreds and captains over fifties, and captains over tens, and officers among your tribes.

The law of primogeniture, so prevalent in different degrees among the nations overrun by the Goths and Vandals, and their kinsmen, strikes us as being a relic of Mosaic law. According to Hebrew law, the first-born son received a double portion of his father's estate. The English law greatly resembles this.

It would almost appear that this double portion was conferred, among the Hebrews, on the oldest male child, to compensate in some degree for the loss of the Priesthood held by him of right in patriarchal days, but under the Mosaic dispensation was vested in the House of Aaron, so far as the Lesser Priesthood called after his name is concerned, while the Higher, or Melchizedek Priesthood appears, after the days of Moses until the coming of Christ, only to have been held by a certain favored few, who, because of their righteousness, were endowed with this special measure of Divine favor.

With a certain class of scientists, the language of a people has great weight in determining its origin. This test has been applied to the language of the Anglo-Saxons, and it has been found that a number of Hebrew words exist almost unaltered in our modern English tongue. On this point, one author writes:

As to language, it is granted, that this, of itself, could not identify a people, or distinguish Israel, for example, from the Canaanites. . . . Still it may be expected that a sufficiency would remain of the Hebrew to tell of this people's (the Saxon's) acquaintance therewith; and such is the case. It has been observed by linguists, that a very great deal of the ancient language of Israel exists in the modern languages of Europe, and that it is through a Gothic medium that this plentiful supply of Hebrew has come. So much have these languages been thrown into a Hebrew mould, that a French Abbe has lately proposed to make use of the Hebrew as a key to these languages. (Wilson, *Our Israelitish Origin.*)

Another writer, referring to Wilson's statements, remarks:

There is no reason to doubt that in common with the wave of nations speaking the Indo-Germanic dialects, which overflowed Europe on the breaking up of the Roman Empire, the Anglo-Saxons came from the Zend-speaking districts of Asia. And while Mr. Wilson adduces reasons from the language of the Anglo-Saxons and Danes, for believing that a long and intimate association had existed between these people and the Persians before the former moved westward, he also proves the existence of a large admixture of Hebrew words in the language of the Anglo-Saxons, and not the least in the Scottish branch of that people. In this he sets a proof of the descent of these people from the Israelitish tribes that were removed by the kings of Ninevah, from their native land, and planted in the cities of Media and Persia. They had retained, in their new abode, much of their Hebrew mother-tongue, while gradually adopting the Zend as the body of their new language. An additional and most important confirmation of Mr. Wilson's idea has been supplied by Prof. C. P. Smyth. This is seen in the circumstance that the Anglo-Saxons possessed a metrology** corresponding exactly, as far as it extended, with the metrology common to the temple of Jerusalem and the Great Pyramid.

PART 7

Salvation a Gift for All—God's Covenant with Abraham—Proselytes—The Dispersion —Conclusions.

Before proceeding farther we wish to remark that we trust no one will imagine, from these comments that we believe that the literal descendants of Abraham will be the only ones saved in the Kingdom of God. To the contrary, we are fully aware that God has made of one blood all the nations of the earth, and realize that all men of every clime and age, may be partakers of the priceless blessings resulting to fallen humanity from the Infinite Sacrifice on Calvary. We are firmly of the belief that within the scope of the Gospel Covenant are provisions, and ways and means, by which the obedient of all races become the recognized children of Abraham, and heirs, by adoption, to all the God given promises to that Patriarch. John the Baptist told the degenerate Jews of his day who were boasting their Abrahamic descent, that of the very stones in the roadway, if it so pleased Him, God coud raise up children unto Abraham. All we claim for Israel, no more, no less, is the fulfillment of God's covenant with the father of the faithful, which covenant modern revelation lays before us in the following language:

My name is Jehovah, and I know the end from the beginning; therefore my hand shall be over thee [Abraham] and I will make of thee a great nation, and I will bless thee above measure, and make thy name great among all nations, and thou shalt be blessed unto thy seed after thee, that in their hands they shall bear this ministry and Priesthood unto all nations, and I will bless them through thy name; for as many as receive this Gospel, shall be called after thy name, and shall be accounted thy seed, and shall rise up and bless thee, as their father; and I will bless them that bless thee, and curse them that curse thee, and in thee [that is in thy Priesthood] and in thy seed [that is thy Priesthood], for I give unto thee a promise that this right shall continue in thee, and in thy seed after thee (that is to say, the literal seed, or the seed of thy body) shall all the families of the earth be blessed, even

---

*"Ethnic Inspiration" by Rev. J. T. Goodsir.
*Metrology—the science of measure.

with the blessings of the Gospel, which are the blessings of salvation, even of Life Eternal.—*Book of Abraham.*

From this we learn that it has been covenanted by the Eternal One, that Abraham's seed shall bear the message and minister God's grace to all nations, and that through him and his seed all the families of the earth shall be blessed with the blessings of the Gospel which through obedience, brings salvation and eternal lives; also as many as receive the Gospel shall be called after his (Abraham's) name, shall be accounted his seed, and shall rise up and bless him as their father.

The last mentioned portion of the covenant was well understood by the Jews and acted upon by them, even though they cringed from obedience to the fullness of the Gospel, and were living under a lesser law of bondage and carnal commandments. The manner in which the Israelites received and treated proselytes is certainly not one of the least interesting features of their policy and history, and may here be glanced at, without wandering far from the question under consideration.

There appears to have been two classes of proselytes recognized among the ancient Jews. The first, known as *Proselytes of Righteousness,* or *Proselytes of the Covenant,* became perfect Israelites, and, according to the *Talmud,* were admitted to the Household of Abraham by circumcision and baptism. The other class were termed *Proselytes of the Gate* ("the stranger that is within thy gate"). It is said converts of this class were not bound by circumcision and other special laws of the Mosiac Code. It was enough for such to observe the precepts against idolatry, blasphemy, bloodshed, uncleanness, and theft, and of obedience, also, to that precept against eating "flesh with the blood thereof." Of this latter class there were converts who embraced Judahism for other than the purest motives — for the sake of a lover, a husband or a wife, to court favor and promotion, or in dread of some calamity or threatened judgment. Such converts were regarded by the ancient Jews much in the same manner as their counterparts are regarded among the Latter-day Saints.

Again, the Jews sometimes spread their faith with the same weapons as those with which they had defended it. The Idumeans, after their conquest by John Hyrcanus, had the alternative of death, exile, or circumcision offered to them. They chose the latter. The Iturians were converted (?) in the same way by Aristobolus.

In the days of Jesus, when the light of truth shone but dimly in the Jewish creed, and the vices of the degenerate Jews had been engrafted on those of the profligate heathen, the Savior cried:

Woe unto you, scribes and Pharisees, hypocrites! for ye compass sea and land to make one proselyte, and when he is made, ye make him twofold more the child of hell than yourselves. (Matthew 23:15)

There is one factor that tended greatly to the diffusion of Israelitish blood, one that we have scarcely noticed, as it relates far more largely to Judah than to Ephraim. We refer to those who remained settled in foreign countries after the return of the Jews from Babylonian captivity, and during the period of the second temple. At the beginning of the Christian era, the dispersed were divided into three great sections, the Babylonian, the Syrian, and the Egyptian. From Babylon the Jews spread through Persia, Media, and Parthia. The Greek conquests in Asia extended the limits of this dispersion. Large settlements of the children of Judah were established in Cyprus, and on the western coast of Asia Minor. These latter, to a larger and very unfortunate extent, adopted the Greek language, and Greek ideas. In Africa, Alexander the Great and Ptolemy I, established large colonies of Jews at Alexandria, not far from which place a temple was erected to Jehovah after the order of that at Jerusalem. From Alexandria the Jews spread out over the coasts of northern and eastern Africa.

How greatly the Jews had become scattered in the time of Christ, may be judged from the devout men who came up to worship and keep the passover at Jerusalem, and who listened to the preaching of the Apostle Peter, and others, on the Day of Pentecost. They are stated to have been Parthians, Medes, Elamites (Persians), dwellers in Mesopotamia, Judea, Cappadocia, Pontus, Asia, Phrygia, Pamphillia, Egypt, Cyrene (Tripoli), Cretes, Arabians, Romans, Jews and proselytes. (Acts Chapter 2)

There is also another view of the subject, which we are not prepared to enlarge upon here, but which bears the weight of abundant proof. It is that the Latter-day Saints have been, and are today, fulfilling the work that it has oft been foretold Ephraim and his fellows should do. Then, if we are doing the work and claim that we are they who should do it, and it being impossible to invalidate our assumption, is not our claim worthy of thoughtful consideration and average respect? God has declared that he will make of His Latter-day Israel a nation of kings and priests. In former dispensations (except that lesser authority among the Jews given to the House of Aaron) the Priesthood was conferred upon a few. It was an honor of the highest kind; but in the dispensation of the fullness of times, the whole people are to be a race of kings and priests, and not less honorable because of the multitude. To our minds, this is a great proof that that people will be of Ephraim. There is a cause for all God's promises—there is none for this. In the order of the

Higher Law, the Priesthood belongs to the first-born in all the races of mankind, therefore, by right of adoption, they are a nation of priests—priests of God after the Order of Melchizedek, under Jesus our Redeemer.

To conclude: We believe that there is scarcely a people or nation under heaven in which is not found some of the blood of Abraham, leavening with this promised seed all the families of the earth. And this chosen generation will, by right of kindred, minister to all people, the Word of God, and as saviors will stand upon Mount Zion, drawing all men unto the great Savior of our race, who will stand in their midst, on the right hand of the Father, crowned and exalted as King of kings, and Lord of lords, the great Apostle and High Priest of our salvation.   Truly, the Lord is fulfilling His promises, Israel has blossomed and budded and filled the earth with fruit, and in the great future He will do it even more abundantly and gloriously.

THE FINE ARTS IN ANCIENT AMERICA

WHAT THE SPANIARDS FOUND

The following article is based upon statements made in a small brochure published by the Museum of the American Indian, Heye Foundation, New York City, 1920, and entitled "Goldsmith's Art in Ancient Mexico," by Marshall H. Saville. Mr. Saville is an authority on American antiquities and a student of the cultures found therein. The statements made bear the mark of genuineness, and our use of them attest the reliability we place on his accurate reporting.

"Peter Martyr, the first chronicler of events in the New World, commenting on conditions therein, and especially in the larger islands of the West Indies, writes that, 'Our men's insatiable desire for gold so oppressed these poor wretches with extreme labor and toil, whereas before they lived pleasantly and at liberty, given only to plays and pastimes as dancing, fishing, fowling, and hunting for little conies, that many of them perished even for the very anguish of mind, the which (their unaccustomed labor) are things of themselves sufficient to engender new diseases. . . . But it shall suffice to have said this much of the pestiferous hunger for gold. . . . The ravenous hunger hath hitherto greatly hindered our men from tillage of the soil.' "

The Spaniards first learned of the gold in New Spain when the expedition of Cordoba (Cuba, 1517) reached Santiago (De Cuba) after exploring the coast of the mainland. On this expedition Yucatan was discovered. On his arrival at Santiago, Cordoba presented the governor with golden diadems and others objects of great value. Valasquez, the governor, on seeing their worth and fine workmanship, decided to send his nephew, Juan de Grijalva, to carry on the findings of Cordoba. "Peter Martyr, in the Fourth Decade of his *De Orbo Novo*, first printed in 1521, in describing the voyage of Grijalva, writes: 'Off the coast of Yucatan and well on the way from the island of Cozumel, the Spaniards encountered a canoe filled with fishermen. There were nine of them, and they fished with golden hooks.' "

When it became necessary that the expedition of Grijalva return to Cuba, the Spaniards there became extremely excited over the gold the expedition had been able to obtain.

"Valasquez now decided to send another expedition to estab-

"When all this treasure thus brought together was ready to be forth from Cuba under command of Hernan Cortes. After the arrival of the Spaniards on the coast of Vera Cruz, the Indians were not long in ignorance of the consuming thirst of the conquerors for gold. In order to placate the formidable strangers and with childlike confidence that by giving them their wish the invasion of his dominions would be averted, Montezuma sent rich presents to Cortes through Tendile (Teuhtlile), governor of Cuetlaxtla (the modern Cotastla), which was then under (subject to) the Aztecs.

"When all this treasure thus brought together was ready to be sent to Spain, with the report of the voyage, an inventory or list of the objects was drawn up and dispatched with two special messengers, Alonzo Portocarrero and Francisco de Montejo, who were charged to deliver the treasure to the King. These valuable gifts have been briefly described by several members of the expedition who saw them before they left Mexico, and on their receipt in Spain they were described by various chroniclers."

A good and complete translation of this important inventory is made part of this writing.

"This inventory was published by Navarrete in 1842, at the end of the 'Relacion del descubrimiento y conquista de Nueva Espana, hecha por la Justicia y Regimiento de la nueva ciuad de Villa de Vera Cruz, a julio de 1519,' in *Coleccion de Documentos Ineditos para la Historia de Espana,* pp. 461-472. It was utilized by Prescott in his *Conquest of Mexico* appearing in 1843; he gives very free translation of a few of the items. It was reprinted by Mora in Mexico in 1844, as an appendix to his Spanish translation of Clavigero's *Historia Antigua de Mexico y de su Conquista.* Finally, it was included by Cayangos in his edition of the *Cartas y Relaciones de Hernan Cortes,* published in Paris in 1866."

INVENTORY

"Report of the Jewels, Shields, and Clothing sent to the Emperor Charles the Fifth by Don Fernando Cortes and the town Council of Vera Cruz with their proctors Francisco de Montejo and Alanzo Hernanez Puertocarrero.

"That which is contained in this report is of the greatest interest, because it manifests what was the state of the fine arts of the Mexicans before they had any communications with the Europeans. D. Juan Munoz collated, on March 30, 1784, the report which follows of the presents sent from New Spain, with another which he found in a book called '*Manual del Tesorero*' of the Casa de la Contratacion of Seville.

"The gold and jewels and stones and featherwork which they had in these newly discovered places, after we arrived here, which you, Alonzo Fernandez Puertocarrero and Francisco de Montejo who go as proctors of this rich town of Vera Cruz, carry to the very excellent princes and very Catholic and very great princes and lords, the Queen Dona Juanna and Don Carlos her son, our Lords, are the following:

council of this town place at the service of their Highnesses, with all the rest that is contained in this report, which belongs to those of this town.

"Item: two collars of gold and stone mosaic-work (precious stones), one of which has eight strings, and in them two hundred and thirty-two red stones, and one hundred sixty-three green stones; and hanging from the said collar from the border of it twenty-seven gold bells, and in the center of them there are four figures of large stones set in gold, and from each one of the two in the center hang simple pendants, and of those at the ends each (has) four doubled pendants. And the other collar has four strings that have one hundred and seventy-two stones that appear to have a green color, and around the said stones twenty-six gold bells, and in the said collar ten large stones set in gold, from which hang one-hundred and forty-two pendants of gold.

"Four pairs of antiparras (leggings), two pairs being of delicate gold leaf, and a trimming of yellow deerskin, and the other two (pairs), of thin silver leaf, with a trimming of white deerskin, and the others of feather-work of divers colors, and very well made, from each one of which hang sixteen gold bells, and all trimmed with red deerskin.

"Another item: a hundred ounces of gold for casting, so that their Highnesses might see how they get gold here from the mines.

"Another item: a box of a large piece of feather-work lined with leather, the colors seeming like martens, and fastened and placed in the said piece, and in the center a large disc of gold, which weighed sixty ounces of gold, and a piece of blue stone mosaic-work a little reddish, and at the end of the piece another piece of feather-work that hangs from it.

"A fan of colored feather-work with thirty-seven small rods covered with gold.

"Another item: a large piece of colored leather-work which is to be worn on the head, which is surrounded by sixty-eight small pieces of gold, each one is as large as a half copper coin, and below them are twenty little turrets of gold.

"Item: a mitre of blue stone mosaic-work with the figure of monsters in the center of it, and lined with leather which seems to be in its colors to be that of martens, with a small (piece) of leather-work which is, as the one mentioned above, of this same mitre.

"Item: four harpoons of feather-work with their points of flint fastened with a gold thread, and a scepter of stone mosaic-work with two rings of gold, and the rest of feather-work.

"Item: an armlet of stone mosaic-work, and furthermore, a piece of small black feather-work with other colors.

"Item: a pair of large sandals of colored leather that appears like martens, the soles white, sewed with threads of gold.

"Furthermore: a mirror placed in a piece of blue and red stone mosaic-work with feather-work stuck to it, and another skin that seems like those martens.

"Three colored (pieces) of feather-work, which are (pertain to) a large gold head like a crocodile.

"Item: some leggings of blue mosaic-work, lined with leather, of which the colors seem like martens; on each one of them (there are) fifteen gold bells.

"Item: two pieces of head armor.

"More, two other (pieces of) colored feather-work which are for two pieces of gold which they wear on the head, made like great shells.

"More, two birds of green feathers with their feet, beaks and eyes (made) of gold, which are put in a piece of one of those shell-like pieces of gold.

"More, two guariques[1] (ear ornaments) of blue stone mosaic-work which are to be put in the big head of the crocodile.

"In another square box of a large crocodile of gold, which is the one spoken of above, where the said pieces are placed.

"More, another head armor of blue stone mosaic-work with twenty gold bells which hang pendant to the border, with two strings of beads which are above each bell, and two guariques of wood with two plates of gold.

"More, a bird of green feathers and the feet, beak and eyes of gold.

"Item, another head armor of blue stone mosaic-work with twenty-five gold bells, and two beads of gold above each bell, that hang around it with some guariques of wood with plates of gold, and a bird of green plumage with the feet, beak and eyes of gold.

"Item: in an haba of reed two large pieces of gold which they put on the head, which are made like a gold shell with their guariques of wood and plates of gold, and besides, two birds of green plumage, with their feet, beaks and eyes of gold.

"Moreover, sixteen shields of stone mosaic-work, with their colored feather-work hanging from the edge of them, and a wide angled slab with stone mosaic-work with its colored feather-work, and in the center of said slab, made of the said stone mosaic-work, a cross of a wheel which is lined with leather, which has the color of martens.

"Again, a scepter of red stone mosaic-work, made like a snake, with its head, teeth and eyes from what appears to be mother-of-pearl, and the hilt is adorned with a skin of a spotted animal, and below the said hilt hang six small pieces of feather-work.

"Another item: a fan of feather-work, placed in a reed adorned with a skin of a spotted animal, after the manner of a weather-cock, and above it has a crown of feather-work, and finally has all over it long green feathers.

"Item: two birds made of thread and feather-work, having the quills of their wings, tails and the claws of their feet, and the ends of their beaks made of gold, placed in respective reeds, covered with gold, and below some feather down, one white, the other yellow, with certain gold embroidery between the feathers, and from each one hang seven strands of feathers.

"Item: four feet made after the manner of skates placed in respective canes covered with gold, having the tails and the organs of respiration, and the eyes and mouths of gold; below in the tails some green leather-work, and having toward the mouths of said skates respective crowns of colored feather-work, and on some of the white feathers are hanging certain gold embroidery, and below each hand six strands of colored feather-work.

"Item: a small copper rod with a skin in which is placed a piece of gold after the manner of feather-work, which above and below has certain colored feather-work.

"Another item: five fans of colored feather-work, four of them have ten small quills covered with gold, and the other has thirteen.

"Item: four harpoons of white flint, placed in four rods of feather-work.

"Item: a large shield of feather-work lined on the back with the skin of a spotted animal; in the center of the field of the said shield is a plate of gold with a figure, like those that the Indians make, with four other half plates of gold on the edge, which altogether form a cross.

"Another item: a piece of feather-work of divers colors, made like a half chasuble, lined with the skin of a spotted animal, which the lords of these parts whom we have

---

[1]"The word *guarique*, unintelligible to Mora, was thought by Gaganos 'to be the Arabic *waric*, which signifies, work of leaves.' "

seen up to now, place hanging over the neck, and over the chest they have thirteen pieces of gold well fitted to-gether.

"Item: a piece of feather-work which the lords of this land are wont to put on their heads, and from it hang two ear-ornaments of stone mosaic-work with two bells and two beads of gold, and above a feather-work of wide green feathers, and below hang some white, long hairs.

"Again, four heads of animals: two seem to be wolves, and the other two tigers, with some spotted skins, and from it hang metal bells.

"Item: two skins of spotted animals, lined on some mantles of cotton, and the skins seem like that of the gato cerval (wildcat).

"Item: a reddish and grayish skin of another animal, and two skins that seem like deer.

"Item: four skins of small deer from which they make a small prepared glove.

"Moreover, two books of those which the Indians have here.

"Moreover, a half dozen fans of colored feather-work.

"Moreover, a perfume censer of colored feathers, with certain embroidery on it.

"Again: a large wheel of silver which weighed forty-eight marks of silver; moreover, some armlets and some beaten silver leaves, weighing a mark and five ounces, and forty adarmes of silver. And a large shield and another small one of silver which weighed four marks and two ounces; and two others that appear to be silver, weighing six marks, two ounces. And another shield which appears to be also of silver weighing one mark, seven ounces: which (shields) altogether weigh sixty-two marks of silver.

COTTON CLOTHING[1]

"Another item: two large pieces of cotton woven in patterns of white and black, very rich.

"Item: two pieces woven with feathers and another piece woven in various colors; another piece woven in red, black, and white patterns, and on the back the patterns do not appear.

"Item: another piece woven in patterns, and in the center are some black wheels of feathers.

"Item: two white cotton clothes with some feather-work woven in.

"Item: another cloth with some colored cords attached to it.

"A loose garment of the men of the land.

"A white piece with a great wheel of white feathers in the center.

"Two pieces of grayish guascasa with some wheels of feathers, and two others of tawny guascasa.

"Six painted pieces, another red piece with some wheels, and two other blue painted pieces, and two women's shirts.

"Eleven veils.

"Six shields, each one having a plate of gold, that covers the shield, and a half miter of gold.

"Which things, each one of them, as set forth in these chapters that declare and settle it, we, Alonzo Fernandez Puerto carrero and Francisco de Montejo, the said proctors, (certify) it is true that we have received them, and they were delivered to us to carry to their Highnesses in these parts, and from you, Alonzo de Avila and Alonzo de Grado, treasurer and over-seer of their Highnesses over here. And because it is true, we sign it with our names. Dated, the Sixth of July of the year 1519.

Puertocarrero.

Francisco de Montejo.

---

[1]"This title is lacking in the manuscript of Vienna."

"The things above enumerated in the said memorial, with the aforesaid letter and report sent by the Council of Vera Cruz, were received by our Lord, the King, Charles the Fifth, as has been beforesaid, in Valladolid during Holy Week, at the beginning of April, of the year of our Lord, 1520." (At end of inventory.)

Note by Mora

"The antiparras or antiparas are described in this manner in the first dictionary of the Spanish language, published by the Academy of Languages in 1726, that gives the origin and authorities in which the meaning is founded: 'certain kind of stockings reaching to the knees or leggings that cover the legs and the feet only, for the front part.'"

ANTIPARAH, is a name of a city mentioned in the Book of Mormon.

"The woven pieces of cotton with designs that do not appear on the reverse side, prove the advancement that they had made, for they knew how to weave with double woof, for that is what this artifice consisted of." (Mora, in his edition of the work of Clavigero.)

"The two great discs of gold and silver, likened to cartwheels in size, which figure as the most imposing of the presents given to Cortes at this time, are described by a number of persons who examined the treasure. These notable pieces were seen and commented upon by Bernal Diaz, Andres de Tapia, Francisco de Aguilar, and a serving man, before they left Mexico. It is strange that they are not mentioned in a letter sent to the Queen and Emperor of Spain by the judiciary and municipal authorities of the newly-founded city of Villa Rica de la Vera Cruz, which is dated July 10.

"After their receipt in Spain, these wheels, with the rest of the objects, were examined in Seville by Oviedo y Valdes, one Diego Dienz and an anonymous writer, and in Valladolid by Peter Martyr and Las Casas. Descriptions more or less brief of all these persons have been published, and they all agree in the main. Measurements are at hand to establish the immense size of these discs. The gold wheel, according to Peter Martyr, was 28 palms in circumference; Oviedo and Gomero make it 30. In diameter, Oviedo gives it as 9½ palms wide, Gomero makes it 10, while the servant makes it 7. All the writers say it was the size of a cart-wheel, except Martyr, who likens it to the size of a mill-stone. The palm is about 8½ inches, hence, from the estimates of the diameter, it is safe to say that it measured between five to a little less than seven feet in width and height. The estimates of the circumference would make it fully 6½ feet in diameter. The weight in gold is given in the *Inventory* as 3800 pesos. Peter Martyr writes 3800 castellanos, while Oviedo makes it 4800 pesos, and Las Casas simply thinks that it weighed more than 100 marks, and other writers have different estimates. We are safe in following the 3800 pesos of the *Inventory*. Only one estimate is given of its thickness, that of Las Casas, who says it was the thickness of a four-real coin, but both Las Casas and Peter Martyr agree in saying that it was massive, hence probably not very flexible.

"There can be no doubt that the Mexican calendar was represented on this golden disc, for we have the specific statement that the sun was depicted, by Bernal Diaz, Andres de Tapia, and Francisco de Aguilar, Oviedo, and Las Casas."

All say it had on it various kinds of pictures: animals, human beings, figures and nocturnal goblins. In the *Inventory* we find the statement that it had on it the figures of monsters.

"The silver disc is generally described as being about the same size as the one of gold, one statement being that it was a little finger smaller. All agree that it represented the moon. Clavigero writes that according to what Gomara says, the gold disc represents the figure of their century, and the silver wheel, the figure of the year. That these extra ordinary objects were not preserved is a matter of lasting regret."

While Cortes was on his famous journey from the coast to the valley of Mexico, he received from Montezuma, both by courtier and in person, valuable gifts made of gold. This made Cortes more greedy and covetous than ever and instead of quieting his desire for plunder and conquest had exactly the opposite effect. The treasures that he had obtained were little compared to the vast loot he obtained after the invasion of the Aztec capital.

"Cortez does not expatiate in his letter about this hoard of gold and other precious objects which had been accumulated and augmented by the different kings of the Aztecs and handed from monarch to monarch as the property of the people. He mentions in his report to the King of Spain that Montezuma, in refuting the 'fabulous stories' about the vast wealth he possessed, such as 'houses with walls of gold' and furniture and other things of the same material, stated, 'It is true, indeed, that I have some things of gold, which have been left to me by my forefathers. All that I possess you may have whenever you wish.' "

This did not appease Cortes, and what followed forms one of the blackest pages of history. At least five accounts of the conquest were made by eyewitnesses. All attest the brutality and trickery of the Spaniards, and all agree to the stories of pillage and plunder. Detailed accounts are given by them about the great wealth Montezuma had stored in a secret chamber. Bernal Diaz, says that while erecting an altar in their quarters where they were established: "Two of our soldiers, one of whom was a carpenter, named Alonzo Yanes, noticed on one of the walls marks showing that there had been a door there, and it had been closed up and plastered over and burnished. Now, as there was a rumor and we had heard the story that Montezuma kept the treasure of his father Axayaca in that building, it was suspected that it might be this chamber which had been closed up and cemented only a few days before. Yanes spoke about it to Juan Velasquez de Leon and Francisco de Lugo, who were captains and relations of mine, and Alonzo Yanes had attached himself to their company as a servant, and those captains told the story to Cortes, and the door was secretly opened. When it was open Cortes and some of his captains went in first, and they saw such a number of jewels and *slabs* and *plates* of gold and *chalchihuites* and other great riches, that they were quite carried away and did not know what to say about such riches.

"None of the gold specimens of this great loot are now known to exist, and none, undoubtedly, escaped the melting pot."

Continuing the account of Bernal Diaz, who subsequently indicated that Montezuma knew all about the discovery of the secret chamber and its hoard of gold, despite the Spaniards' efforts to conceal the fact of their finding it, he wrote:

"After some more polite conversation, Montezuma at once sent his majordomo to hand over all this treasure and gold and wealth that were in the plastered chamber, and in looking it over and taking off the embroidery with which it was set, we were occupied for three days, and to assist us in undoing it and taking it to pieces, there came Montezuma's goldsmiths from the town named *Azcapotzalco*, and I say there was so much, that after it was taken to pieces there were three heaps of gold, and they weighed over six hundred thousand pesos, as I shall tell further on, without the silver and many other rich things, and not counting the ingots and slabs of gold, and the grains from the mines.

"We began to melt it down with the help of the natives of *Azcapotzalco*, and they made large bars of it, each bar measuring three fingers of the hand across. When it was already melted and made into bars, they brought another present separately, which the grand Montezuma said he would give, and it was a wonderful thing to behold, for some of the *chalchihuites* were so fine that among these *caciques* they were worth a vast quantity of gold.

"After the weight was taken, the officers of the king said that was of gold, both of which was cast in bars as well as grains from the mines, and in ingots and jewels, more than six hundred thousand pesos, and this was without counting the silver and other jewels which were not yet valued."

Before ending this remarkable story, here is what the leader, himself, said about this spoil.

"This decision and offer of the said lords, for the royal service of Your Majesty having been completed, I spoke to Montezuma one day, and told him Your Highness was in need of gold, on account of certain works ordered to be made, and I besought him to send some of his people, and I would also send some Spaniards, to the provinces and houses of the lords who had submitted themselves, to pray them to assist Your Majesty with some part of what they had. Besides Your Majesty's need, this would testify that they began to render service, and Your Highness would esteem it more as their good will toward your service; and I told him that he should also give me from his treasures, as I wished to send them to Your Majesty, as I had done with the other things.

"He asked me afterward to choose the Spaniards whom I wished to send, and two by two, and five by five, he distributed them through many provinces and cities, whose names I do not remember, as the papers have been lost and also because they were many and divers; and moreover some of them were at eighty and one hundred leagues from the said city of *Temixtitan*. He sent some of his people with them, ordering them to go to the lords of these cities and provinces, and tell them that I have commanded each one of them to contribute a certain measure of gold which he gave them.

"Thus it was done, and all these lords to whom he sent gave very compliantly, as had been asked, not only in valuables, but also in *bars* and *sheets of gold*, besides all the jewels of gold, and silver, and the feather-work, and the stones, and the many other things of value which I assigned and alloted to Your Sacred Majesty, amounting to one hundred ducats and more.

"These, beside their value, are such, and so marvelous, that for their novelty and strangeness they have no price, nor is it probable that all the princes ever heard of in the world such treasures. Let not what I say appear fabulous to Your Majesty, because, in truth, all the things created on land, as well as in the sea, of which Montezuma had ever heard were imitated in gold, most naturally, as well as in silver, and in precious stones, and feather-work, with such perfection that they seemed almost real. He gave me a large number of them for Your Highness, besides others he ordered to be made in gold, for which I furnished him the designs, such images, crucifixes, medals, jewelry of small value, and many other things which I made them copy. In the same manner Your Highness obtained, as the one-fifth of the silver which was received, one hundred and odd marks, which I made the natives cast in large and small plates, porringers, cups, and spoons, which they executed as perfectly as we could make them comprehend.

"Besides these Montezuma gave me a large quantity of stuff, which, considering it was cotton and not silk, was such that it could not be woven anything similar in the whole world for texture, colors, and handiwork. Amongst these, were many marvelous dresses for men and women, bed clothing with which that made of silk could not be compared, and other stuffs, such as tapestry, suitable for drawing-rooms and churches. There were also blankets and rugs, for beds, both made of feather-work and of cotton in divers colors, also very marvelous, and many other things so curious and numerous I do not know how to specify them to Your Majesty.

"He also gave me a dozen *cerbatanas* (blow guns) with which he shoots, and of their perfection I likewise know not what to say to Your Highness; for they were decorated with very excellent paintings of perfect hues, in which there were many different kinds of birds, animals, trees, flowers, and divers other objects, and the mouthpieces and extremeties were bordered with gold, a span deep, as was also the middle, all beautifully worked. He gave me a pouch of gold network for a ball, which he told me he would also give me of gold. He gave me also some turquoises of gold (set in), and many other things, whose number is almost infinite." (From *The Letters of Cortes*, edition of Francis A. MacNutt, Vol. 1, Second letter, pp 253-255, New York, 1908.)

Finally,

"It is a well established fact that the arts and industries of ancient Mexico had come to a high degree of perfection. The historians of the Conquest are full of admiration for the works that Mexican gold-workers executed, as well as the stone workers, the jewelers and the artisans of feather-work." (Professor Eduard Seler, Paris 1890, in a paper read at the Eighth Session of the Congress—International des Americanistes.) "The paper in which this statement is made and with slight changes that have been made in the French translation of the *Natuahl* text, and some revision is included in his *Gesammelte Abhandlungen zur Amerikanischen Sprach- und Altertumskunde*, Zweiter Band, Berlin, 1904, pp. 620-634.

THE LANDS OF THE NEPHITES

The Lands of the Nephites—Mulek and Lehi—Zarahemla and Nephi—The Wilderness—The Land of First Inheritance—The Journeys Northward—The Waters of Mormon—Lehi-Nephi.

To the ancient Nephites the whole of North America was known as the Land of Mulek, and South America as the Land of Lehi; or, to use the exact language of the Book of Mormon, "the land south was called Lehi and the land north was called Mulek."

The reason why these names were so given was because the Lord brought Mulek into the land north, and Lehi into the land south, when he led them from Judea to this greater land of promise.

From the days of the first Mosiah to the era of Christ's advent, South America was divided into two grand divisions. These were the Land of Zarahemla and the Land of Nephi. During this period, except in times of war, the Lamanites occupied the Land of Nephi, and the Nephites inhabited the Land of Zarahemla.

That these two lands occupied the whole of the southern continent is shown by the statement of the sacred writer: "Thus the land of Nephi and the land of Zarahemla were nearly surrounded by water, there being a small neck of land between the land north ward and the land southward." The width of this narrow neck of land that connected the two continents is in one place said to have been *the distance of a day and a half's journey for a Nephite.* In another place it is called a *day's journey.* Perhaps the places spoken of are not identical, but one may have been slightly to the north of the other along the line of the Isthmus of Panama.

Both the Lands of Nephi and Zarahemla were subdivided, for governmental purposes, into smaller lands, states or districts. Among the Nephites, these lands, in the days of the Republic, were ruled by a local chief judge, subject to the Chief Judge of the whole nation; and among the Lamanites by kings, who were tributary to the head king, whose seat of government was at the City of Lehi-Nephi or Nephi.

The Land of Nephi covered a much larger area of country than did the Land of Zarahemla. The two countries were separated by the wilderness which extended entirely across the continent from the shores of the Atlantic Ocean to the Pacific. The northern edge of this wilderness ran in a line almost due east and west, and passed near the head of the river Sidon. The Sidon is generally understood to be the river in these days called the Magdalena.

All north of this belt of wilderness was considered the Land of Zarahemla; all south of it was included in the Land of Nephi. We are nowhere told its exact breadth, and can only judge thereof from casual references in the narrative of the Book of Mormon.

The River Sidon flowed through the center of the Nephite civilization of the days of the Republic. After the convulsions that attended the Crucifixion of the Holy Messiah, the physical and political geography of the continent was greatly changed, and the new conditions are very vaguely defined by the inspired historians.

On the western bank of the River Sidon was built the City of Zarahemla. From the time of its first occupancy by the Nephites, to the date of its destruction by fire at the Crucifixion, it was the capital or chief city of the nation, the center of commercial activities, and the seat of government. It was the largest and oldest city within their borders, having been founded by the people of Zarahemla before the exodus of the Nephites, under the first Mosiah, from the Land of Nephi.

When the Nephites, by reason of increasing numbers, the exigencies of war, or for other causes founded new cities, the cities so built were generally called after the name of the leader of the colony or some illustrious citizen, and the land immediately surrounding, contiguous or tributary to the new city was called by the same name. As an example we will take the City or Land of Ammonihah, regarding which it is written: "Now it was the custom of the people of Nephi to call their lands, and their cities, and their villages, yea, even all their small villages, after the name of him who first possessed them; and thus it was with the land of Ammonihah." (Alma 8:7)

Some of these lands appear to have been relatively small, more resembling a county, or possibly a township, than any other division at present prevailing in this country. Such we suppose to have been the Lands of Helam and Morianton. Others, such as the Lands of Bountiful and Desolation, embraced wide, extended tracts of country.

The exact place where Lehi and his little colony first landed on this continent is not stated in the Book of Mormon: but it is generally believed among the Latter-day Saints to have been on the coast of Chili in thirty degrees south latitude.

We do not think it possible, without divine revelation, to determine with accuracy the identical spot where Lehi and his colony landed. We believe that the coast line of that region has entirely changed since those days. Even if we do not take into consideration the overwhelming convulsions that took place at the Crucifixion of our Lord, which changed the entire face of nature, there remains the general elevation or subsistence of the land which is continually taking place the world over. Some coasts are rising, some are falling. The land in South America, on its western or Pacific shores, has long been rising, some think for ages.

If this be so, the rise of an inch a year would entirely change the configuration of the seashore, and give this generation shallows and dry land, where but a few centuries ago there were deep waters. But so far as the results growing out of the terrible earthquakes that occurred at the death of the Savior are concerned, we can form no conclusions, for they were variable. In some regions the waters usurped the place of the land, in others the land encroached upon the waters. Which way it happened near the place where Lehi landed we have no record, and consequently can say nothing. For all we know a huge mountain may now cover the spot, or it may be hidden beneath the blue waters of the Pacific, scores of miles away from any present landing place.

In the region that Lehi landed there he also died. Soon after his death, Nephi, and those of the colony who wished to serve the Lord, departed for another country. They did so by direct command of heaven. The reason for this command was the murderous hatred shown by Laman and Lemuel towards Nephi and his friends. These vicious men determined to kill Nephi, that he might not be a king and a ruler over them. Their hearts were wicked; they loved sin and were resolved that they would not be governed by their virtuous and heaven-favored brother.

Nephi and his company journeyed in the wilderness for many days. By the expression "the wilderness," we understand the inspired writer to mean the uncultivated and uninhabited portion of the land. This word appears to be frequently used in after years, with this signification. At other times it is applied to the desert and uninhabitable regions, the tropical forests, and jungles infested with wild beasts. The journey of the Nephites was northward, as is shown by their later history; but Nephi, in his very brief account of this migration, says nothing with regard to the direction in which they traveled.

At the end of many days a land was found which was deemed suitable for settlement. There the company pitched their tents, and commenced the tillage of the soil. In honor of their leader, it was called the Land of Nephi; or to use the modest language of Nephi, "My people would that we should call the name of the place Nephi; wherefore we did call it Nephi."

No doubt the choice of location was made by divine inspiration.

It was a highly-favored land, rich in mineral and vegetable productions, and yielded abundant crops to the labors of the husbandman.

In this happy country the Nephites dwelt, prospered and increased until they again moved northward. Perhaps not once nor twice they migrated, but several times; for we hold it to be inconsistent with the story of the record and with good judgment to believe that in their first journey they traveled as far north as they were found four hundred years afterwards, when they again took up their line of march, and finally settled in the Land of Zarahemla.

In the first place there was no necessity for Nephi and his people taking such a lengthy, tedious and hazardous journey; in the second place, in their weak condition, it was nigh unto an impossibility. To have taken a journey of a few hundred miles would have placed them out of the reach of the Lamanites; there was no need for them to travel thousands. Again, in a few years the Lamanites had followed and come up to them; it is altogether inconsistent to think that that people, with its racial characteristics, would in so short a time have accomplished so marvelous a triumph as to follow, hunt up and attack their late brethren if the latter had placed all the distance from Chili to Ecuador between them and their pursuers. When we consider the difficulties of travel through the trackless wilderness, the obstacles interposed by nature, the lack of all roads or other guides to indicate where the Nephites had gone, it seems out of the question to imagine that in twenty years or so, the shiftless, unenterprising Lamanites had accomplished such a feat. To the contrary, we believe that Nephi and those with him traveled until they considered themselves safe, then settled down in a spot which they deemed desirable. By and by the Lamanites came upon them; the Nephites defended themselves as long as they could, and when they could do so no longer they again moved to the northward. Their early history was one of frequent wars; and as the Lord used the Lamanites as thorns in their sides when they turned from Him, we judge for this reason, and that they were found so far north in the days of Amaleki and Mosiah, that the savage descendants of Laman had frequently defeated them and driven them farther and farther away from the land of their first possession.

The inquiry will naturally arise, as a result of these suggestions: "In what portion of the South American continent lay the home of the Nephites in the days of Mosiah?" This cannot be answered authoritatively. We are nowhere told its exact situation. Still, there are many references in the Book of Mormon from which we can judge, to some extent, of its location. Elder Orson Pratt suggests that it was in the country we now call Ecuador. These writers entirely agree with Elder Pratt's suggestion. Other brethren have placed it considerably farther south; but in our reading of the Book of Mormon we have found no evidence to confirm their suppositions, but much to contradict them.

We believe that the lands occupied by the Nephites before they went down into the Land of Zarahemla were situated among the table lands or high valleys of the Andes, much as Utah is located in the bosom of the Rocky Mountains and parallel chains. For these reasons:

First—They were lands rich in minerals, which all through the American continents are found most abundantly in mountain regions. We may (so far as mineral proximity is concerned) compare the country east of this portion of the Andes—the unexplored, alluvial silvas of the Amazon—to the great plains or prairies east of the Rocky Mountains. These silvas, stretching from the Andes to the Atlantic, we regard as the great wilderness south of Zarahemla so often spoken of in the annals of the Judges.

Secondly, the climate of the torrid low lands, almost directly under the equator, would be intolerable for its heat, and deadly in its humidity; while the country in the high valleys and table lands would be excellently adapted to human life, especially (we may presume) before the great upheavals and convulsions that marked the death of the Redeemer. As the Nephites spread over the country they shunned regions where fevers were common, possibly in those parts rendered unhealthy by the overflowing of the rivers, which, when they receded, left large bodies of stagnant water covering the surface of the ground for the greater portion of the year.

It is probable that in their journeys the Nephites would follow the most available route, rather than plunge into the dense, untrodden, primeval forests of the wilderness; the home of all manner of savage animals, venomous snakes and poisonous reptiles; where a road would have to be cut every foot of the way through the most luxuriant and gigantic tropical vegetation to be found on the face of the globe. Therefore we regard its accessibility as another reason for believing that the Nephites did not leave the great backbone of the continent to descend into the unexplored depths of the region whose character they aptly sum up in one word, *wilderness*.

Our readers must not forget that there were two Lands called by the name of Nephi. The one was a limited district immediately surrounding the City of Lehi-Nephi or Nephi. There Mosiah and the Nephites dwelt, about two hundred years before Christ. The other Land of Nephi occupied the whole of the continent south of the great wilderness. This wilderness formed its northern boundary, and its frontier thereon ran in a straight course from the east to the west sea, or, to use our modern geographical names, in a straight line from the Atlantic to the Pacific Ocean.

As this wilderness, though of great length east and west, was but a narrow strip north and south, and its northern edge ran close to the head waters of the River Sidon (or Magdalena), it is evident that the Land of Nephi covered by far the greater portion of South America. Within its wide boundaries was situated the original Land of Nephi; as well as many other lands called by various local names, just in the same way as there are many states in these United States, all together forming one great nation.

It is very obvious how there grew to be these two Lands of Nephi. At first, the small district around the capital city comprised all the territory occupied by the Nephites. As they spread out, whatever valley, plain, etc., they reclaimed from the wilderness was considered a part of that land; and thus, year by year, its borders grew wider and wider, while for convenience sake or governmental purposes, the newly built cities and the land surrounding were called by varied names, according to the wishes of the people, most frequently after the leader of the out-going colony or founder of the city. Thus we have a Land of Nephi within the Land of Nephi; just as we have now-a-days Utah County within Utah State; and the City of New York and the County of New York within the State of New York. To distinguish the smaller Land of Nephi from the whole country, it is sometimes called the Land of Lehi-Nephi.

We have stated that the small Land of Nephi was a very limited district. We think this is easily proven. It was so limited in extent that we are told King Noah built a tower near the temple so high that he could stand upon the top thereof and overlook not only the Land of Lehi-Nephi where it was built, but also the Land of Shilom and the Land of Shemlon, which last named land was possessed by the Lamanites. No matter how high the tower, these lands must have been comparatively small (or at any rate the Land of Lehi-Nephi was) to have enabled a man to overlook the whole three from the top of one building.

It was on the borders of this land, at the outer edge of its cultivated grounds, in the forest (or thicket) of Mormon, that Alma used to hide himself in the daytime, from the searches of the king, while he ministered among the people when the shades of evening gave him security. It was there he gathered the believers in his teachings, baptized them in the waters of Mormon, and organized the Church of Jesus Christ. From the waters of Mormon to Zarahemla it was twenty-two days' actual travel for an emigrant train.

Alma having been warned of the Lord that the armies of King Noah would come upon his people, the latter gathered together their flocks, and took of their grain and departed into the wilderness which divided the Lands of Nephi and Zarahemla. They fled eight days' journey into the wilderness when they rested and commenced to build a city, which they called Helam. Being afterwards compelled to leave this city, on account of the persecutions of the Lamanites and Amulonites, they again took their journey northward, and reached the homes of the main body of the Nephites in Zarahemla in about fourteen days.

Here we have a people encumbered and delayed by flocks and herds, heavily laden with grain, etc., making the journey (in two separate stages) in twenty-two days. It is scarcely supposable that they traveled in a direct line; mountains, rivers and swamps would render the journey somewhat circuitous or winding. But even supposing that they did advance in an almost direct line from point to point, it would only make the distance between Nephi and Zarahemla 220 miles if they traveled ten miles a day; 330, if they traveled fifteen miles; and 440 if they journeyed twenty miles a day.

Our readers must decide for themselves which distance per day is the most likely that a company, driving their flocks and herds before them, would advance through an unexplored wilderness, full of natural hindrances, and without roads, bridges, ferries and other helps to the traveler.

Zarahemla was situated on the Sidon, certainly a considerable distance from its head waters, as other lands and cities (such as Minon and Manti) are mentioned as lying far above it. If we measure the distance from such a point southward, either 200, 300 or 400 miles, all these measurements will bring us into the country now called Ecuador.

We are of the opinion that the Land of Lehi-Nephi was situated in one of the higher valleys, or extensive plateaus of the Andes. In the first place, admitting it was in Ecuador, it would lie almost immediately under the equator, and the lowlands, as before suggested, would be unbearable for an industrious population on account of the great heat, as well as exceedingly unhealthy by reason of chills, fever, and like complaints.

Again, the crops of which the Nephites raised most abundantly —barley and wheat—are not those that flourish in a tropical climate, but can be grown most advantageously in a temperate region such as could be found in these higher valleys.

It was also a land rich in mineral wealth which is not probable would have been the case if it had been situated among the wide-spreading alluvial plains east of the Andes.

It is likewise spoken of as a hilly or mountainous country. The hill north of the land of Shilom is frequently mentioned in the historical narrative. For instance:

Ammon came to a hill, which is north of the land of Shilom (Mosiah 7:5).

King Limhi caused his guards to go to the hill which was north of Shilom (Mosiah 7:16).

King Noah erected a great tower on the hill north of the land of Shilom (Mosiah 11:13).

For another reason, the expression "up" is almost always used when reference is made to persons going towards the Land of Nephi. Not only did they travel from Zarahemla up the Sidon and across the wilderness to Nephi, but also *up* from the Land of Ishmael and other portions of the Land of Nephi to the City of Nephi and its surroundings. In contradistinction to this, persons leaving Nephi went down to the Land of Zarahemla and other places.

The only time in which the word down is used, when referring to persons going towards Nephi, is when certain persons came down to the city from off the hill mentioned above.

Some of our readers may object to the statement that the City of Nephi and the City of Lehi-Nephi were one and the same place; and that the land round about was sometimes called the Land of Lehi-Nephi, and sometimes the Land of Nephi only. But we think that a careful perusal of the record of Zeniff, in the Book of Mormon, will convince them of the fact; especially if they will compare it with the last few verses of the book of Omni. Zeniff in one place speaks of possessing, by treaty with the Lamanites, the Land of Lehi-Nephi (Mosiah 9:6), and a few verses later on (verse 14), he talks of the thirteenth year of his reign in the Land of Nephi.

If we mistake not, the name of Lehi-Nephi occurs only seven times in the Book of Mormon; everywhere else the name of Nephi is used when referring to this land.

In the second generation the Nephites began to grow numerous, and iniquity made its appearance among them. It was then that Jacob their priest (the younger brother of Nephi), prophesied: "The time speedily cometh, that except ye repent, they [the Lamanites] shall possess the land of your inheritance, and the Lord God will lead away the righteous out from among you." This prophesy was completely fulfilled, if not on previous occasions, about 300 years or so afterwards, when Mosiah, by the command of God, led the righteous Nephites out of the land of their inheritance—the Land of Nephi—down into the Land of Zarahemla.

From that time the Land of Nephi was possessed and ruled by the posterity of Laman, Lemuel and Ishmael; or by Nephite apostates, who, with superior cunning, worked themselves on to the Lamanitish throne.

During the era that the Nephites dwelt in the Land of Nephi they built several cities. These the Lamanites eagerly took possession of when Mosiah and his people vacated them. We are not told when and by whom these cities were founded; such particulars, doubtless, appear on the plates of the kings. It is only incidentally that we learn anything regarding them; reference to them is found in the record of Zeniff's return from Zarahemla, and re-occupancy, by treaty with the Lamanites, of a portion of the old Nephite home.

The Lamanites of that age were a wild, ferocious, bloodthirsty and nomadic race, who did not build cities, for the simple reason that they had neither the inclination nor the skill. But when they found the Nephite cities deserted by their inhabitants they immediately occupied them. Even then, they did not enlarge or repair them, but let them fall into gradual decay.

No sooner had the Lamanites surrendered the Cities of Lehi-Nephi and Shilom to Zeniff than his people set to work to build buildings and to repair their walls. In the next generation King Noah caused many fine buildings and towers to be built in both the Lands of Lehi-Nephi and Shilom.

The two cities above mentioned are the only ones directly spoken of in the Book of Mormon up to this time. There was most probably a city built in the contiguous Land of Shemlon, which was held by the Lamanites, but it is never mentioned by name.

We judge Shilom lay to the northward of Lehi-Nephi, and in the same valley or plateau; otherwise it could not have been so completely viewed from King Noah's tower, mentioned in our last chapter. Its relative position to Lehi-Nephi appears from the fact that those who went to or from the Land of Zarahemla, generally did so by way of Shilom; it seems to have lain in the direct route between the two capital cities. Ammon, the Zarahemlite, and his company entered in that way, and Limhi and his people escaped in the same direction.

The next city that we read of is called Helam. It was located eight days' journey from Nephi towards Zarahemla, and was founded by Alma, the elder, and his followers, when they fled from the murderous persecutions of King Noah. This city and the surrounding country were called after the first man baptized by Alma in the waters of Mormon. His name was Helam, and he was doubtless a leader among that people.

In the same direction from Nephi as Helam, and apparently adjoining thereto, lay the land of Amulon. It was first peopled by the fugitive priests of Noah, when they fled from the vengeance of the justly incensed Nephites. The leader of this band of wicked men was named Amulon, and in his honor the land was so called. The king of the Lamanites afterwards made Amulon the tributary king or chief local ruler over the Lands of Helam and Amulon. From this we judge that they lay side by side, their boundaries extending indefinitely into the great wilderness.

Our next information regarding the condition of the Land of Nephi is gleaned from the history of the mission of the sons of King Mosiah to the Lamanites in that region. This mission commenced 91 B.C., and lasted fourteen years.

We find the Lamanites of that age considerably advanced in civilization, many of them inhabiting populous cities. The country was divided into several distinct kingdoms, each ruled by its own king, but all subject to the head monarch whose court was at Nephi.

The lands specially mentioned in connection with this mission are those of Nephi, Middoni, Ishmael, Shilom, Shemlon, Helam, Amulon and Jerusalem.

Shilom and Shemlom we have already shown to be in the neighborhood of Lehi-Nephi; Helam, eight days' journey for loaded teams to the north, and Amulon not far distant therefrom. We may next inquire what can be learned of the Lands of Jerusalem, Ishmael and Middoni.

The location of the Land of Jerusalem is clearly stated. It was away joining the borders of Mormon, that is, on the other side, probably east or north from Nephi. There, somewhere about 100 B.C., the Lamanites, with Amulonites and other apostate Nephites, built a great and thriving city, which they called Jerusalem, after their father's ancient home in Judea.

There Aaron, the son of Mosiah, unsuccessfully preached the Gospel. Its apostate citizens were too sin-hardened to accept the message he bore. This city was afterwards destroyed on account of its great wickedness and persecution of the Saints, in the terrors that attended the crucifixion of the Savior, and waters came up in the place thereof. A stagnant sea, akin to that which covers Sodom and Gomorrah, occupies the place where once its proud places and rich synagogues stood.

The first land visited by the missionary prince, Ammon, was Ishmael; its situation is not clearly stated. It was *down* from Nephi.

This leads to the thought that it lay in the alluvial plains considerably east of the Andes. It does not seem compatible with the narrative of Ammon's mission to believe it was situated in the narrow strip of wilderness that lay between the mountains and the Pacific Ocean. Its relative position to other lands precludes this idea.

Near the highway that connected Ishmael and Nephi lay the Land of Middoni. This is shown by the fact that when Ammon and King Lamoni were traveling from Ishmael towards Middoni they met Lamoni's father, the head king of all the land, coming from Nephi. This leads to the conclusion that the same road from Ishmael led to both Nephi and Middoni.

Nephi is called *up* from both these lands; we, therefore, suggest that, like Ishmael, Middoni occupied a portion of the lower lands on the eastern borders of the Andes, but somewhat nearer the capital city.

INDEX

— A

Aaron, 299; son of Mosiah, 385

Abinadi, prophecy of, 95; denounces King Noah, 120; biography of, 122; cast into prison, 124ff; divinely protected, 137ff; quotes Isaiah, 152; continues to prophesy, 177; martyrdom of, 188ff; prophecies of, 253

Aborigines, 338

Abraham, vision of, 105; father of many nations, 337; God's covenant with, 336, 363; promises made to, 336, 338

Abridgment, Mormon's, 19ff

Adam, concordance of word, 74

Adultery, 145, 296

Alma the Elder, cried repentance, 60; pleads for Abinadi, 126; begins ministry, 193ff; ordained priests, 197; biography of, 216ff; refuses to be king, 242; teaches Nephites, 244ff; pursued by Lamanites, 255; authorized to establish church, 260; instructed by the Lord, 261ff; judged the wicked, 262; blessed by the Lord, 265; gives instructions about sinners, 271; confers with priests, 272; death of, 291

Alma the Younger, is unbeliever, 273; conversion of, 274ff; becomes preacher of righteousness, 279ff; appointed custodian of plates, 286, 298, 307, 381; appearance of angel to, 298; conversion of, 299; custodian of plates, 299; directed by angel, 302; freed by earthquake, 304; imprisoned with Amulek, 303; labors in vain, 302; ministerial labors at Zarahemla, 301; mission to Zoramites, 306; mouthpiece of God, 305; presiding high priest and chief judge, 299; prophesies the coming of Messiah, 302; repentance of, 298; resigned judgeship, 301

Alphabet, Aramean, 311; Phoenician or Old Israelitic, 312; Semitic, 311-12

Amazon River, 380

Amlici, joins Lamanites, 300; slain by Alma, 301

Ammon, expedition of, 88; genealogy of, 90; biography, 96; discovers 24 Gold Plates, 99ff, 234; leads people to Zarahemla, 240, 305; visits land of Ishmael, 385

Ammonihah, destroyed, 304; Saints cast out of, 304; warned of approaching desolation, 303

Amnihu, 300

Amnor, 300

Amulon, governs priests, 249; biography of, 250-51; persecutes Alma, 252

Amulon, Children of, 258

Amulon, land of, 284

Amulek, freed by earthquake, 304; imprisoned with Alma, 303; mission to Zarahemla, 306

Ancestors of Latter-day Saints, 355

Andes Mountains, 380, 382

Anglo-Saxon language, 362

Angola, city of, 320

"Anti," use of word in Book of Mormon, 320

Antipas, 320

Apostates, 306

Arctic Ocean, 351-53

"Arm, His Holy," 130

Arts in ancient Mexico, 364-75

Asher, 341; tribe of, 345

Assyria, deportation of people to, 345-46

Assyrians, 349

Atheism, 69

"Atone," concordance of word, 74

"Atonement," 56ff; concordance of word, 74

— B —

Babylon, deportation of people to, 345

Baldur, 358

Baptism, 193ff; notes on, 199ff; concordance of word, 207ff; King Limhi requests, 259ff

Beggars, Are we not all?, 71

Behavior, righteous, 11

Benjamin, King, biography of, 25, 28, 31; waxed old, 33; biography of 36ff; great discourse of, 41ff; concludes discourse, 65ff; effect of his discourse, 78ff; death of, 86

Bethlehem, 316

Bezaleel, made ark or box, 314

Black Sea, 349

Blessings, made to Abraham and his seed, 336-39

Blood of Abraham, scarcely nation without, 366

Book of Mormon, see Plates

Book of Mormon, editions of, 313; language of, 317; names in American geography, 316-34

Borrowing, from neighbor, 73

Bountiful, land of, 305

Brass, Plates of, 31

Breastplate, 105
Bryan, William Jennings, 77

— C —

Canaan, 349
Captivities of Israel and Judah, 346
Carmel, mountain of Elijah, 316
Caspian Sea, 350
Caucassian Mountains, 349
Children, Book of Mormon passages about 62, 79; salvation of, 175
Children of Christ, 81
"Christ," concordance of word, 63ff, 81
Christs, false, 28
Christ, Jesus, prophecy concerning, 54ff; atonement of, 56ff; Nephites covenant with, 78ff, 155ff; called the "Father," 164ff; the only Redeemer, 179; Church of, 266; home of, 316; to atone for sins, 299
Chronology, Book of Mormon, 6ff
Chronology, Book of Mormon historians, 27
"Church," concordance of word, 210ff
Church discipline, 270
Church of Christ, Alma established, 260
Church of God, 196; membership in, 266, 298
Church of Jesus Christ of Latter-day Saints, 84
Civilization, Roman and Nephite, 292
Clothing of ancient Mexico, 368-75
Commandments, First, 135; Second, 141ff; Third, 143; Fourth, 143-44; Fifth, 145; Sixth, 145; Seventh, 145; Eighth, 145; Ninth, 145; Tenth, 146
Commandments, King Benjamin's discourse on, 48ff
Commentary on the Book of Mormon, Volume II, 6ff; Volume I, 15
Cortes, 373
Covenant, Nephite, 78ff, 85
Covetness, 146
Cuba, 364

— D —

Dacia, land of, 350
Dan, 341; tribe of, 345
Daughters of Lamanites captured, 226
Day of the Lord, 136
Day, Sabbath, 143
Decalogue, meaning of, 151
Demotic Script, 311
Denmark, colonized by tribe of Dan, 344

Derivation of word "Saxon," 357
Diffusion of Israelitish blood, 365
Diligence enjoined, 73
Discipline, church, 270-71
Doctrine and Covenants, Section 10, 23ff
"Down by the River's Verdant Side," (hymn), 131

— E —

Ecuador, 379, 382
Egyptian idolatry, 142
Eighth Commandment, 145
Enchorian script, 311
Enoch, vision of, 105
Equality enjoined, 272
Ephraim, mixing of among nations, 338-39, 341, 345; to be scattered among all people, 354; to be gathered from all countries, 355; tribe of, 353
Ertrurians, 344
Esdras, prophecy of on Ten Tribes, 348-49
"Establish," concordance of word, 264ff
Ether, prophecy of on Ten Tribes, 348
Euphrates, 349, 351, 353
Everlasting Gospel, principles of, 305
Evil doers, treatment for, 261
Expedition to Land of Lehi-Nephi, 88
"Eye," concordance of word, 177

— F —

False witness, 145
Father, honor thy, 145
"Feet upon the Mountain," 128
Fifth Commandment, 145
Fine arts in ancient America, 364-75
First Commandment, 135
Free Masonry, 361
Forgiveness required, 268
Fourth Commandment, 143-44

— G —

Gad, tribe of, 345
"Gemara," definition of, 161
Gideon, insurrection of, 220; biography of, 224ff; proposes Nephites' escape, 238-39
Gideon, city of, 302
God, no other before me, 135; a jealous, 143; bar of, 298; power, 304; servants of, 305; sitting upon his throne, 299
God, Church of, 196

Godhead, Latter-day Saint doctrine of, 84, 164ff

God, Temple of, 128

God's covenant with Abraham, 363

Goldsmith's art in ancient America, 364-75

Gospel laws, forbids appearance of sin, 306

Goths, 357

Government, representative, recommended, 290

Grant, Heber J., 47

— H —

Hagoth, 320

"Hand, right," concordance of, 80

Handel, George Frederick, 157

"Hands, Own," concordance of, 197

Harris, Martin, 21ff; description of plates of Book of Mormon, 309

Hebrew writing, 313

Helam, city of, 245-46, 384; land of, 277, 298, 385

Helaman, given custody of sacred plates, 306; son of Alma the Younger, 299, 306

Helam, biography of, 96; baptized, 194, 217; biography of, 219

Hermounts, 301

Herodotus, 311

Historians, Book of Mormon, 27

Holy Ghost, 167ff; Alma and Amulek filled with, 302, 306

Holy Spirit, 168

House of Israel, majority of Latter-day Saints belong to, 336, 340, 357

House of Judah, 357

Hymns, "Down by the River's Verdant Side," 131; "A Poor Wayfaring Man of Grief," 157

— I —

Identification of races, 359-63

Illustrations of Hebrew translations, 311-12; of name changes, 318

Images, graven, 135-36, 141ff

Immortality, 180

Indians, 364

Industries in ancient Mexico, 364-75

Interpreters (Urim and Thummim), 105, 285

Inventory of gifts sent to Spain from ancient Mexico, 368-75

Ionians, 344; Free Masonry found among, 361

Irish, 344

Isaac, promises made to, 336-37

Isaiah, writings of, 127ff; quoted by Abinadi, 152

Ishmael, land of, 385

Israel, a maritime nation, 341; Twelve Tribes of, 344

Israelites, journey northward, 349, 351-53; migration of to Egypt and Greece, 345

Israelitish origin of European nations, 350

Ivins, Anthony W., 84

— J —

Jacob, blessing given by to Ephraim, 337-38; blessing given by to Joseph, 337; promises made to, 336-37; prophecy, 383

Jacobugath, 320

Jaffa, 316

Jared, 319

Jared, Brother of, visions of, 283

Jehovah, power of, 304

Jaredite record, 284

Jeremiah, prophecy of on Ten Tribes, 348

Jershon, land of, 305

Jerusalem, 316, 385

Jesus, see Christ, Jesus

Jewels of ancient Mexico, 368-75

Jewish race, vitality of, 347

Jews, distribution of, 343, 347

Joel, 342

Joktanites, 319

Jordan River, 350

Joshua, 299, 341

Judah, remnants of, 347

Judges, people chose, 290

Judgment Day, concordance of word, 181

Justin Martyr, 198

— K —

Kill, thou shalt not, 145

King, Alma refused to be crowned, 242

"Kingcraft," 287

Korihor, anti-Christ, 305-06

Kuban River, 350

— L —

Laban, 320, 342

Lacedemonians, 343

Laman, King, deceived Zeniff, 92ff; biography of, 96ff; craftiness of, 108; death of, 113; makes appointments, 252-53, 320, 339, 378

Lamanites, should not be destroyed, 107; a ferocious people, 115; attack King Noah, 119; army of, 249; pursue Alma, 255; invade Nephite land, 305

Lamb, Reverend Mr. M. T., objections to Book of Mormon, 308

Lamoni, King, 385

Land of Promise, people led from, 345

Language, of ancient northern races, 360; of Book of Mormon, 316

"Last Days," Alma's teachings about the, 247

Latter-day Saints, ancestors of, 355

Laws of ancient northern races, 361

Lehi, used as name for geographical places, 323; descendants of, 339, 342; land of, 376; where he landed not known, 377

Lehi-Nephi, repairing city of, 109; city surrendered to Zeniff, 384; land of, 381-83

Lemuel, 339, 378

Lesser Priesthood, 362

"Liahona," origin of name, 323

Liberality enjoined, 73

Limher, 300

Limhi, King, expedition to, 88; biography of, 98; with Ammon, 99ff; succeeded father, 223; attacked by Lamanites, 226ff; requests baptism, 259, 382.

— M —

Maccabees, Book of, 343-44

Manasseh, 336, 338, 341

Man, existence of on earth, 76

"Man of Grief, A Poor Wayfaring," (hymn), 157

Man's dependence upon God, 71

Manti, 300, 305, 324

Manti Temple, 47

Manuscript, 116 pages of lost, 21

Martyrs, burned to death, 303

Mary, mother of Jesus, 55

Materials used for records, 315

Media, 346

Melchizedek Priesthood, 362

Melek, land of, 302, 307, 376

Men, old, 51

Mesopotamia, plains of, 349

"Messiah, The," by Handel, 157

Middoni, land of, 385-86

Mishna, definition of, 161

Missionaries to Zoramites, 306

Moesia, land of, 350

Montezuma, 364, 373-74

Morianton, land of, 377

Mormon, who was?, 18; instructed concerning plates, 285

Mormon, Waters of, 193, 381; land of, 298; origin and use of word, 325; forest of, 381

Mormon, words of, 17

Mormon's abridgement, 19

Moroni, comments of on Gold Plates, 103, 105; in charge of Nephite armies, 307

Moses, Book of, 33

Moses, Laws of, 132ff, 147ff, 150

Mosiah, 26; succeeds King Benjamin, 34ff, 87; biography of, 38; translates Gold Plates, 102; called people together, 256ff; grants Alma permission to organize church, 260; confers with priests, 272; makes proclamation, 273; sons of, 273; permits sons to preach to Lamanites, 281; translates Gold Plates, 283; completes translation, 286; discourse of on "kingcraft," 287; death of, 291, 299, 380, 383

Mosiah, Sons of, conversion of, 275ff

Mother, honor thy, 145

"Mountains, How Beautiful Upon the," 128

Mount of Transfiguration, 316

Mulek, ancestor of Zarahemla, 256; use of word in Book of Mormon, 328-31

Murder, 145, 296

Mythology of ancient Scandinavians, 357-59

— N —

Names, Book of Mormon in American geography, 316

Nazareth, 316

Nehor, apostasy of, 300; order of, 303

Neighbor, 145

Nephi, origin, meaning, and use of name, 88, 331-333

Nephi, Plates of, 33

Nephi, teachings of, 79ff

Nephi, 342; city of, 383; land of, 376, 383-84; two lands called, 380

Nephihah, chief judge of Nephites, 301

Nephite cities, 377; named for leaders, 377

Nephite constitution, 305

Nephites, ruled by King Benjamin, 43ff; enjoy peace, 113; in bondage, 230ff; seek freedom, 238; escape to Zarahemla, 242; seek deliverance, 253 laws of, 292; political history of, 294; journey of, 378-79; lands of, 376-86; loss in war, 301; ruled by kings, 299

Ninevehites, 302

Ninth Commandment, 145

Noah, King, 92, 95; with wicked priests, 117; seeks Abinadi's life, 121; biography of, 122ff; judges Abinadi, 126; condemns Abinadi, 189; death of, 222, 253, 381, 383

— O —

"Onidah," use of word, 333
Origin of Anglo-Saxons, 356
"Own hands," concordance of word, 197

— P —

"Pachus," use of word, 333
Paul, Apostle, 83
Pentateuch, The, 134
Persecution forbidden, 272
Peter, 316
Philistines, 341
Phoenicians, 341; slave trade of, 342
Plates, Brass, 31
Plates, Gold, translated, 106, 283; Ammon discovers, 99
Plates, Large, 17, 25ff
Plates of Nephi, 33
Plates, Small, 15, 17, 25ff
Plates, Twenty-Four, discovered by King Limhi's men, 234; translated, 282
Plates, What became of the?, 29ff
Plates of Book of Mormon, 308-15; description of by Martin Harris, David Whitmer, Joseph Smith, Orson Pratt, 310; size of 308, 310, 313; weight of, 308, 314
Poems, servant, 152
Pratt, Orson, 170, 279, 309
Priestcraft, established by Nehor, 300
Priesthood, 236, 362
Priests, appointed, 85ff; to labor with hands, 197; wicked carry off daughters of Lamanites, 226
Primogeniture, law of, 362
Prodigal Son, parable of, 276
Profanity, 143
Promised Land, 349
Prophecy, Alma's to be recorded by Helaman, 307
Proselytes, 364

— R —

"Redeem," concordance of word, 183
"Redeemer," concordance of word, 184

"Redeemeth," concordance of word, 185
"Redemption," 172; concordance of word, 185
Religion of ancient northern races, 359-60
Resurrection, 171ff; 179ff; concordance of word, 185, 267; Second, 267
Reynolds, George, 5, 88
Reynolds, Philip C., 10
"Right Hand," concordance of word, 80
River of Canaan, 350
River Sidon, 377, 380
Robbery, 296
Rod and thy staff, thy, 183
Roman civilization, 292
Roman Empire, overthrow of, 357

— S —

Sabbath Day, 143-44, 197
Salvation, 177, 204; conditions of, 67ff; of children, 175
Sanhedrin, 161
Saul of Tarsus, 299
"Saxon," derivation of word, 357
Scattered of Israel, The, 336
Scattering of Jews at time of Jesus, 365
Sea of Galilee, 316
Second Commandment, 141ff
Second Resurrection, 267
Seed of Joseph, found in aborigines, 338, 357
Septuagint, definition of, 162
Servant Poems, 152
Servants, unprofitable, 45
Service, King Benjamin's discourse on, 44
Seventh Commandment, 145
"Shabbath," Hebrew word, 144
Shemlon, land of, 385
Shilom, 384-85
Shimlon, repairs to city of, 109
Sidon, River, 300-01; use of water, 334
Simeon, 341
Similarities of races, 359-63
Sixth Commandment, 145
Size of Book of Mormon plates, 308-13
Sjodahl, Janne M., 5, 47
Smith, Joseph, 21ff; and Urim and Thummim, 105; defines Holy Ghost, 169, 308
Sons of King Mosiah, 273, 298, 305, 306
South America, preponderantly Lamanite, 256
Spaniards, What they found in ancient America, 364
Spirit, immortal, 47

Spirit of the Lord, 168
Steal, thou shalt not, 145
"Stiffnecked," concordance of word, 149-50
Stones, The Two, 105

— T —

Tale, 319
Talmage, James E., 169, 170
Talmud, description of, 161
Taylor, John, 47
Temple, Manti, 47
Ten Commandments, 146, 151
Ten Tribes, did not dwell in Jerusalem, 354; hiding of, 338-39; in Azareth, 354; residents of the land of the North, 347; revelation about through Joseph Smith, 353; still in existence, 347; traced to Media, 346
Theft, 296
Theory of Anglo-Saxon constitution, 361
Third Commandment, 143
"Timothy," use of word, 334
Tyre and Sidon, 342

— U —

Unbelievers, treatment for, 261
United Order, 344
Urim and Thummim, 105, 285; concordance of the word in the Bible, 285, 309, 351

— V —

Valley of Gideon, 300
Vandals, 357
Velasquez, 364

— W —

Watchmen, 129, 176
Waters of Mormon, 193
Weight of Book of Mormon plates, 314
Welsh, 344
Whitmer, David, description of Book of Mormon plates, 309
Wisdom enjoined, 73; meaning of, 103
Witness, false, 145
"Wo," concordance of word, 58ff
"Works," concordance of word, 180

— Y —

Yucatan, 319
Young, Brigham, 29ff; testimony of, 340

— Z —

Zalmoxis, 351
Zara, meaning of word, 155
Zarahemla, descendant of Mulek, 256
Zarahemla, Nephites escape to, 240, 255; chief city of, 301, 304-05, 377; land of, 31, 298, 300, 307, 376, 379, 383; located on Sidon, 382; use of word, 334
Zeezrom, 303-04, 306
Zeniff, deceived by King Laman, 92; possesses land, 107; record of, 10; biography of, 111; end of record, 240, 244, 257; cities surrendered to, 384; return from Zarahemla, 384
Zerom, 300
Ziff, a metal, 118
Zoram, commander of Nephite army, 305
Zoramites, 305-06